T0330328

DERIVATIVES MARKETS AND ANALYSIS

The Bloomberg Financial Series provides both core reference knowledge and actionable information for financial professionals. The books are written by experts familiar with the work flows, challenges, and demands of investment professionals who trade the markets, manage money, and analyze investments in their capacity of growing and protecting wealth, hedging risk, and generating revenue.

Since 1996, Bloomberg Press has published books for financial professionals on investing, economics, and policy affecting investors. Titles are written by leading practitioners and authorities, and have been translated into more than 20 languages.

For a list of available titles, please visit our website at www.wiley.com/go/bloombergpress.

DERIVATIVES MARKETS AND ANALYSIS

R. Stafford Johnson

WILEY

Published by John Wiley & Sons, Inc., Hoboken, New Jersey.

Published simultaneously in Canada.

For general information on our other products and services or for technical support, please contact our Customer Care Department within the United States at (800) 762-2974, outside the United States at (317) 572-3993 or fax (317) 572-4002.

Wiley publishes in a variety of print and electronic formats and by print-on-demand. Some material included with standard print versions of this book may not be included in e-books or in print-on-demand. If this book refers to media such as a CD or DVD that is not included in the version you purchased, you may download this material at http://booksupport.wiley.com. For more information about Wiley products, visit www.wiley.com.

Library of Congress Cataloging-in-Publication Data is Available

ISBN 978-1-118-20269-2 (Hardcover)
ISBN 978-1-118-22828-9 (ePDF)
ISBN 978-1-118-24072-4 (ePub)

Cover Design: C. Wallace
Cover Images: Abstract Background
© iStockphoto / jcarroll-images;
Chart Courtesy of R. Stafford Johnson

Printed in the United States of America

10 9 8 7 6 5 4 3 2 1

MIX
Paper from responsible sources
FSC® C132124
www.fsc.org

This book is dedicated to Nancy Shiels—My beacon

Contents

Preface

In 1973, the Chicago Board of Trade formed the Chicago Board Options Exchange (CBOE). The CBOE was the first organized option exchange for the trading of options. Just as the Chicago Board of Trade had served to increase the popularity of futures, the CBOE helped to increase the trading of options by making the contracts more marketable. Since the creation of the CBOE, organized stock exchanges in the United States, most of the organized futures exchanges, and many security exchanges outside the United States also began offering markets for the trading of options. As the number of exchanges offering options increased, so did the number of securities and instruments with options written on them. Today, option contracts exist not only on stocks but also on currencies, indexes, futures contracts, and debt and interest rate-sensitive securities. There is also a large over-the-counter option market in currency, debt, and interest-sensitive securities and products in the United States and a growing over-the-counter option market outside the United States. Just as impressive as the growth in options trading has been the growth in the futures market. Today, there are futures contracts on commodities, equity indexes, currencies, bonds, and interest rates, as well as such hybrid contracts as swaps. Options, futures, and swaps are derivatives—securities that derive their values from the underlying asset. Derivatives are used by institutional investors, portfolio managers, and corporations for speculation and hedging, as well as financial engineering in creating structured currency, equity, and debt positions.

Over the past 50 years, the investment industry has seen not only the proliferation of derivative securities and markets, but also academic contributions to the study of derivatives: The Black-Scholes Option Pricing Model, index arbitrage, financial engineering, and dynamic portfolio insurance. The growth in the derivative markets and the academic contributions together point out the challenges in mastering an understanding and developing a knowledge of derivatives. The purpose of this text is to provide professionals and finance students with an exposition on derivatives that will take them from the basic concepts, strategies, and fundamentals to a more detailed understanding of the markets, advanced strategies, and models.

Derivative Markets and Analysis is the last in a three-part series on securities from Bloomberg Press's Financial Series. The first, *Debt Markets and Analysis,* covered fixed-income securities, and the second, *Equity Markets and Analysis,* focused on stock and stock portfolios. This book covers subjects presented in many derivative texts: futures and forward markets, the carrying-cost model for pricing futures, option strategies, the Black-Scholes and Binomial Option Pricing models, futures options, and swaps.

Today, many practitioners manage their securities and portfolios using a Bloomberg terminal. Bloomberg is a computer information and retrieval system providing access to financial and economic data, news, and analytics. Bloomberg terminals are common on most trading floors and are becoming more common in universities where they are used for research, teaching, and managing student investment funds. Given this widespread use of the Bloomberg system, the text also provides guides for using Bloomberg data and analytical functions for the topics covered in each chapter. There are also supplemental appendices with detailed descriptions of the Bloomberg system and a listing of many of the analytical functions that can be applied to investment analysis.

It is my hope that the synthesis of fundamental and advanced topics with Bloomberg information and analytics will provide professionals and students of finance not only with a better foundation in understanding the complexities and subtleties of derivatives, but also with the ability to apply that understanding to real-world investment decisions—to grasp how "it is done on the street." It is also my hope that the integration of Bloomberg with derivative concepts and theories enhances the readers' intellectual depth and understanding of finance. Finance and economics professors frequently require that students explain a theory, strategy, or idea mathematically, graphically, and intuitively. By so doing, students' depth of understanding, as well as retention, of the theory and idea is often enhanced. It has been my experience in using Bloomberg in my derivatives classes that it too enhances a student's depth and knowledge of derivatives.

The book is designed for professors offering a one-semester derivatives course. The Bloomberg material is presented at the end of each chapter, allowing the material to be presented separately. The book is also written for professionals in the investment industry. For professionals, the text can be used as an instructional source and as a guide on how to apply Bloomberg to derivative markets and analysis, as well as a review of fundamental derivative concepts and theories.

Content

The book is comprehensive, covering derivative securities and markets, the major theories and models, and the practical applications of the models. The book is divided into five parts: Part 1 deals with the markets and strategies associated with futures and forward contracts; Part 2 examines options markets and strategies; Part 3 examines the pricing of options; Part 4 examines financial swaps; and Part 5 provides supplemental appendices.

Part 1 consists of four chapters. Chapter 1 examines the markets, uses, and pricing of commodity futures contracts. Chapter 2 covers futures and forward contracts on currency. Chapter 3 focuses on equity index contracts, and Chapter 4 covers interest rate and bond contracts.

Part 2 consists of four chapters. Stock options are examined in Chapter 5 in terms of fundamental option strategies and the functions and operations of the option exchange. The markets and uses of non-stock options are explored in Chapter 6: equity-index options, futures options, over-the-counter options, convertible securities, and embedded options. In Chapter 7, option analysis is expanded with a more detailed examination of the fundamental strategies and an analysis of other strategies. Finally, in Chapter 8, the hedging uses of options are explored.

Part 3 consists of five chapters. In Chapter 9, the fundamental option pricing relationships and option boundary conditions are presented. The Binomial Option Pricing model is derived in Chapter 10, and the seminal Black-Scholes option pricing model is presented in Chapter 11. In Chapter 12, the pricing of non-stock options is examined: spot indexes, currency options, futures options, and convertibles. The pricing of bond and interest rate options is examined using the binomial interest rate model in Chapter 13.

Part 4 consists of two chapters on financial swaps. The markets, uses, and pricing of generic interest rate swaps, forward swaps, and swaptions are presented in Chapter 14, and the markets, uses, and pricing of credit default swaps and currency swaps are the focus of Chapter 15.

The text stresses concepts, model construction, numerical examples, and Bloomberg applications and information sources. The text also includes end-of-the-chapter problems and Bloomberg exercises. The Bloomberg exercises are designed for practitioners who have access to such terminals at their jobs, for professors and students who have access to Bloomberg terminals at their universities, and for students who have access to Bloomberg either at their university or possibly through internships they may have at financial companies. As I noted previously, it is my hope that the Bloomberg exercises will add depth to one's understanding of derivatives, as well as an appreciation of the breadth of financial information and analytics provided by the Bloomberg system. Students are invited to visit www.wiley.com for additional materials, such as Excel spreadsheet programs that can be used to solve a number of the problems at the end of the chapters and videos that explain how to work some Bloomberg exercises. Also located at the Wiley website is an instructor site that includes chapter PowerPoint slides and an instructor's manual with solutions to end-of-the-chapter problems.

The book draws some material from some of my earlier texts: *Debt Markets and Analysis, Equity Markets and Analysis,* and *Introduction to Derivatives.* The Bloomberg material presented here comes from knowledge gained from using the terminal (or learned from my students who used Bloomberg) when I was the fund professor for the student equity investment fund and bond investment fund at Xavier University.

Acknowledgments

Many people have contributed to this text. First, I wish to personally thank Stephen Smith, Brandywine Global Investment Management, and the Smith Center for the Study of Capitalism and Society for their backing and support. I also thank my colleagues and students at Xavier University for their many years of support and encouragement. My appreciation is extended to the editors and staff at John Wiley & Sons, Inc., particularly Bill Falloon, executive editor; Jeremy Chia, project editor; Sharmila Srinivasan, production editor; and Cheryl Ferguson, copy editor. My appreciation is also extended to Stephen Isaacs, Bloomberg Press, for his support, help, and encouragement on this project.

I also wish to thank my children and their spouses, Wendi, Jamey, Matt, Shayna, and Scott, and my grandchildren, Bryce, Kendall, Malin, Kylee, and Ryan, and Mary Frances Johnson and Marlyn Erhart for their support, encouragement, and understanding. I also would like to recognize the pioneers in the academic study of derivatives: Fischer Black, Myron Scholes, Robert Merton, Stephen Ross, Mark Rubinstein, and others cited in the pages that follow. Without their contributions, this text could not have been written. Finally, I extend my gratitude to the many people who make up the soul of the Bloomberg system—analysts, programmers, systems experts, reps, and journalists. It is truly a remarkable system.

I encourage you to send your comments and suggestions to me: johnsons@xavier.edu.

R. Stafford Johnson
Xavier University

About the Author

R. Stafford Johnson is Professor of Finance and Director of the Smith Center for the Study of Capitalism and Society at the Williams College of Business, Xavier University. He is the author of six books: *Options and Futures*; *Introduction to Derivatives*; two editions of *Bond Evaluation, Selection, and Management*; *Debt Markets and Analysis*; and *Equity Markets and Portfolio Analysis*. He has also authored or co-authored over 50 academic articles. His *Equity Markets and Portfolio Analysis* and *Debt Markets and Analysis* texts are core equity and fixed-income investment books that cover extensively the functionality of Bloomberg terminals and its applicability to investments.

PART 1

Futures and Forward Contracts

CHAPTER 1

Futures Markets

In the mid-1800s, Chicago was the transportation and distribution center for agriculture products. Farmers in the Midwest transported and sold their products to wholesalers and merchants in Chicago, who often would store and later transport the products by either rail or the Great Lakes to population centers in the East. Because of the seasonal nature of grains and other agriculture products and the lack of adequate storage facilities, farmers and merchants began to use *forward contracts* as a way of avoiding storage costs and pricing risk. These contracts were agreements in which two parties agreed to exchange commodities for cash at a future date, but with the terms and the price agreed upon in the present. An Ohio farmer in June might agree to sell his expected wheat harvest to a Chicago grain dealer in September at an agreed-upon price. This forward contract enabled both the farmer and the dealer to lock in the September wheat price in June. In 1848, the Chicago Board of Trade (CBT) was formed by a group of Chicago merchants to facilitate the trading of grain. This organization subsequently introduced the first standardized forward contract, called a "to-arrive" contract. Later, it established rules for trading the contracts and developed a system in which traders ensured their performance by depositing good-faith money to a third party. These actions made it possible for speculators as well as farmers and dealers who were hedging their positions to trade their forward contracts. By definition, *futures* are marketable forward contracts. Thus, the CBT evolved from a board offering forward contracts to the United States' first organized exchange listing futures contracts—a futures exchange.

Introduction to Futures and Options Markets

Futures and options contracts on stock, debt, and currency, as well as such hybrid derivatives as swaps, interest rate options, caps, and floors, are an important risk-management tool. Farmers, portfolio managers, multinational businesses, and financial institutions often buy and sell derivatives to hedge positions they have in the derivative's underlying asset against adverse price changes. Derivatives also are used for speculation. Many investors find buying or selling options or taking futures positions an attractive alternative to buying or selling the derivative's underlying security. Finally, many institutional investors, portfolio managers, and corporations use derivatives for *financial engineering*, combining their debt, equity, or currency positions with different derivatives to create a structured investment or debt position with certain desired risk-return features.

This book is an exposition on derivatives, describing the markets in which derivatives are traded, how they are used for speculating, hedging, and financial engineering, and how their prices are determined. Part 1 examines the markets, strategies, and pricing of futures and forward contracts, while Parts 2 and 3 focus on options contracts and pricing. Part 4, in turn, examines the swap market.

Overview of Futures Markets

As new exchanges were formed in New York, London, Singapore, and other large cities throughout the world, the types of futures contracts grew from grains and agricultural products to commodities and metals and finally to financial futures: futures on foreign currency, debt securities, and security indexes. Because of their use as a hedging tool by financial managers and investment bankers, the introduction of financial futures in the early 1970s led to a dramatic growth in futures trading. The financial futures market formally began in 1972 when the Chicago Mercantile Exchange (CME) created the International Monetary Market (IMM) division to trade futures contracts on foreign currency. In 1976, the CME extended its listings to include a futures contract on a Treasury bill. The CBT introduced its first futures contract in October 1975 with a contract on the Government National Mortgage Association (GNMA) pass-through, and in 1977, it introduced the Treasury bond futures contract. The Kansas City Board of Trade was the first exchange to offer trading on a futures contract on an equity index, when it introduced the Value Line Composite Index (VLCI) contract in 1983. This was followed by the introduction of the Standard & Poor's (S&P) 500 futures contract by the CME and the New York Stock Exchange (NYSE) index futures contract by the New York Futures Exchange (NYFE).

Whereas the 1970s marked the advent of financial futures, the 1980s saw the globalization of futures markets with the openings of the London International Financial Futures Exchange (LIFFE) in 1982, Singapore International Monetary Market in 1986, and the Toronto Futures Exchange in 1984. The increase in the number of futures exchanges internationally led to a number of trading innovations: electronic trading systems, 24-hour worldwide trading, and alliances between exchanges. Concomitant with the growth in future trading on organized exchanges has been the growth in futures contracts offered and traded on the over-the-counter (OTC) market.

In this market, dealers offer and make markets in more tailor-made forward contracts in currencies, indexes, and various interest rate products. The combined growth in the futures and forward contracts has also created a need for more governmental oversight to ensure market efficiency and to guard against abuses. In 1974, Congress created the Commodity Futures Trading Commission (CFTC) to monitor and regulate futures trading. In that legislation, Congress also allowed the creation of self-regulatory organizations, and in 1982, the National Futures Association (NFA), an organization of futures market participants, was established to oversee futures trading. Finally, the growth in futures markets led to the consolidation of exchanges. In 2006, the CME and the CBT approved a deal in which the CME acquired the CBT, forming the CME Group, Inc. With this and other consolidations, the major exchanges today offering derivatives include CBT/CME, Eurex, ICE, Hong Kong Futures Exchange, Singapore Exchange, Dubai Mercantile Exchange, Bolsa De Mercadorias & Futuros, and the Australian Stock Exchange. Exhibit 1.1 shows the Bloomberg CTM screen that lists the major exchanges trading futures and derivatives today.

EXHIBIT 1.1   Major Futures and Derivative Exchanges

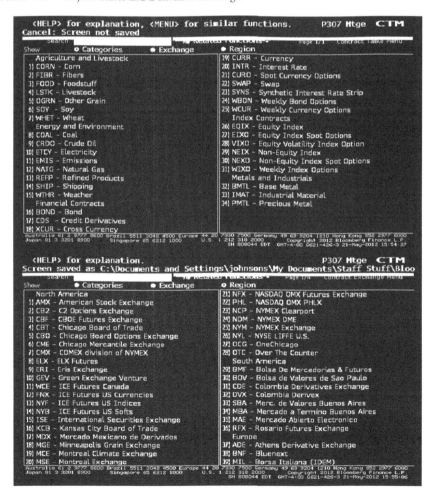

EXHIBIT 1.1 (*Continued*)

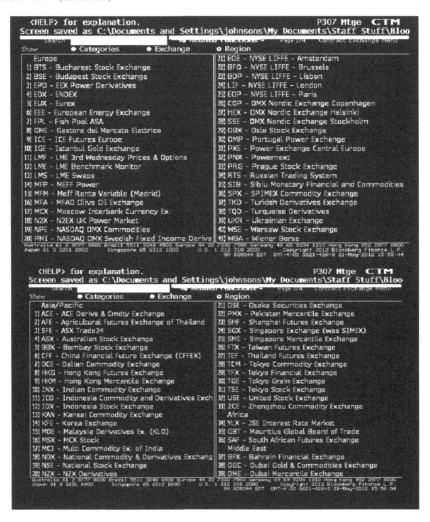

Formally, a forward contract is an agreement between two parties to trade a specific asset at a future date with the terms and price agreed upon today. A futures contract, in turn, is a "marketable" forward contract, with marketability (the ease or speed in trading a security) provided through futures exchanges that not only list hundreds of contracts that can be traded but provide the mechanisms for facilitating the trades. Futures and forward contracts are known as *derivative securities*. A derivative security is one whose value depends on the values of another asset (e.g., the price of the underlying commodity or security). Another important derivative is an option. An option is a security that gives the holder the right, but not the obligation, to buy or sell a particular asset at a specified price on, or possibly before, a specific date.

Overview of Options Markets

Like the futures market, the US options market can be traced back to the 1840s when options on agriculture commodities were traded in New York. These option contracts gave the holders the right, but not the obligation, to purchase or to sell a commodity at a specific price on or possibly before a specified date. Like forward contracts, options made it possible for farmers or agriculture dealers to lock in future prices. In contrast to commodity futures trading, however, the early market for commodity options trading was relatively thin. The market did grow marginally when options on stocks began trading on the over-the-counter (OTC) market in the early 1900s. This market began when a group of investment firms formed the Put and Call Brokers and Dealers Association. Through this association, an investor who wanted to buy an option could do so through a member who either would find a seller through other members or would sell (write) the option himself.

The OTC option market was functional, but suffered because it failed to provide an adequate secondary market. In 1973, the CBT formed the Chicago Board Options Exchange (CBOE). The CBOE was the first organized option exchange for the trading of options. Just as the CBT had served to increase the popularity of futures, the CBOE helped to increase the trading of options by making the contracts more marketable. Since the creation of the CBOE, organized stock exchanges in the United States, most of the organized futures exchanges, and many security exchanges outside the United States also began offering markets for the trading of options. As the number of exchanges offering options increased, so did the number of securities and instruments with options written on them. Today, option contracts exist not only on stocks but also on foreign currencies, indexes, futures contracts, and debt and interest rate-sensitive securities.

In addition to options listed on organized exchanges, there is also a large OTC market in currency, debt, and interest-sensitive securities and products in the United States and a growing OTC market outside the United States. OTC debt derivatives are primarily used by financial institutions and nonfinancial corporations to manage their interest rate positions. The derivative contracts offered in the OTC market include spot options and forward contracts on Treasury securities, London Interbank Offered Rate–related (LIBOR-related) securities, and special types of interest rate products, such as interest rate calls and puts, caps, floors, and collars. OTC interest rate derivatives products are typically private, customized contracts between two financial institutions or between a financial institution and one of its clients.

The Nature of Futures Trading and the Role of the Clearinghouse

Futures Positions

A speculator or hedger can take one of two positions on a futures (or forward) contract: a long position (or futures purchase) or a short position (futures sale). In a long futures position, one agrees to buy the contract's underlying asset at a specified price, with the payment and delivery to occur on the expiration date (also referred to as the delivery date). In a short position, one agrees to sell an asset at a specific price, with delivery and payment occurring at expiration.

To illustrate how positions are taken, suppose in December, Speculator X believes that summer will be unusually dry in the Midwest, resulting in increases in the price of corn. With hopes of profiting from this expectation, suppose on 12/14/15 Speculator X decides to take a long position in a July corn futures contract and instructs her broker to buy one July corn futures contract listed on the CBT (one contract is for 5,000 bushels, see Exhibit 1.2). To fulfill this order, suppose X's broker finds a broker representing Speculator Y, who believes that the summer corn harvest will be above normal and therefore hopes to profit by taking a short position in the July corn contract. After negotiating with each other, suppose the brokers agree to a price of $3.89/bu. on the July contract for their clients. In terms of futures positions, Speculator X would have a long position in which she agrees to buy 5,000 bushels of corn at $3.89/bu. from Speculator Y at the delivery date in July, and Speculator Y would have a short position in which he agrees to sell 5,000 bushels of corn at $3.89/bu. at the delivery date in September.

If both parties hold their contracts to delivery, their profits or losses would be determined by the price of corn on the spot market (also called cash, physical, or actual market). For example, suppose the summer turns out to be mild, causing the spot price of corn to trade at $3.32/bu. at the grain elevators in the Midwest at or near the delivery date on the July corn futures contract. Accordingly, Speculator Y with his short position would buy the corn on the spot market for $3.32/bu, and then sell it on the futures contract to Speculator X for $3.89/bu., resulting in a $2,850 profit minus commission and transportation costs. Speculator X with her long position, in turn, would have to buy 5,000 bushels of corn on her corn futures contract at $3.89/bu. from Speculator Y, and then sell the corn for $3.32/bu. on the spot market, losing $2,850 plus commission and transportation costs.

Clearinghouse

To provide contracts with marketability, futures exchanges use clearinghouses. The clearinghouses associated with futures exchanges guarantee each contract and act as intermediaries by breaking up each contract after the trade has taken place. Thus, in the previous example, the clearinghouse (CH) would come in after Speculators X and Y have reached an agreement on the price of the July corn, becoming the effective seller on X's long position and the effective buyer on Y's short position. Once the clearinghouse has broken up the contracts, then X's and Y's contracts would be with the clearinghouse. The clearinghouse, in turn, would record the following entries in its computers:

	Clearinghouse Record:
1.	Speculator X agrees to buy July corn at $3.89/bu. from the clearinghouse.
2.	Speculator Y agrees to sell July corn at $3.89/bu. to the clearinghouse.

This intermediary role of the clearinghouse makes it easier for futures traders to close their positions before expiration. Returning to our example, suppose that early summer is dry in the Midwest, leading a third speculator, Speculator Z, to want to take a long position in the listed July corn futures contract. Seeing a profit opportunity from the greater demand for long positions in the July contract, suppose in June Speculator X agrees to sell a July corn futures contract to Speculator Z for $4.14/bu. Upon doing this, Speculator X now would be short in the new July contract, with Speculator Z having a long position, and there now would be two contracts on July corn. After the new contract between X and Z has been established, the clearinghouse would step in and break it up. For Speculator X, the clearinghouse's record would now show the following:

	Clearinghouse Record for X:
1.	Speculator X agrees to buy July corn at $3.89/bu. from the clearinghouse.
2.	Speculator X agrees to sell July corn at $4.14/bu. to the clearinghouse.
Close	Thus, to close, the Clearinghouse owes X $0.25 per contract to be paid at expiration: ($0.25/bu.)(5,000 bu.) = $1,250.

The clearinghouse accordingly would close Speculator X's positions by paying her $0.25/bu. ($4.14/bu. − $3.89/bu.), a total of $1,250 on the contract [(5,000 bu.)($0.25/bu.)]. Since Speculator X's short position effectively closes her long position, it is variously referred to as a *closing, reversing out*, or *offsetting position* or simply as an *offset*. Thus, the clearinghouse makes it easier for futures contracts to be closed prior to expiration.

Commission costs and the costs of transporting commodities cause most futures traders to close their positions instead of taking delivery. As the delivery date approaches the number of outstanding contracts, known as *open interest*, declines, with only a relatively few contracts still outstanding at delivery. Moreover, at expiration, the contract prices on futures contracts established on that date (f_T) should be equal (or approximately equal) to the prevailing spot price on the underlying asset (S_T). That is, at expiration: $f_T = S_T$. If f_T does not equal S_T at expiration, an arbitrage opportunity would exist. Arbitrageurs could take a position in the futures contract and an opposite position in the spot market. For example, if the July corn futures contract were available at $3.25 on the delivery date in July and the spot price for corn were $3.32 at a grain elevator near the delivery place specified on the contract (resulting in no hauling cost), then arbitrageurs could go long in the July contract, take delivery by buying the corn at $3.25 on the futures contract, and then sell the corn on the spot at $3.32 to earn a riskless profit of $0.07/bu. Arbitrageurs' efforts to take long positions, however, would drive the contract price up to $3.32. On the other hand, if f_T exceeds $3.32, then arbitrageurs would reverse their strategy, pushing f_T to $3.32/bu. Thus, at delivery, arbitrageurs will ensure that the prices on expiring contracts are equal to the spot price or the spot prices plus the hauling cost. As a result, closing a futures contract with an offsetting position at expiration will yield the same profits or losses as closing futures positions on the spot by purchasing (selling) the asset on the spot and selling (buying) it on the futures contract.

Returning to our example, suppose that near the delivery date on the July contract, the spot price of corn and the price on the expiring corn futures contracts are $3.63/bu. To close his existing short contract, Speculator Y would need to take a long position in the July contract, while to offset her long contract, Speculator Z would need to take a short position. Suppose Speculators Y and Z take their offsetting positions with each other on the expiring July corn contract priced at $f_T = S_T = $3.63/bu. After the clearinghouse breaks up the new contract, Speculator Y would receive $0.26/bu. from the clearinghouse and Speculator Z would pay $0.51/bu. to the clearinghouse:

	Clearinghouse Records for Speculator Y:
1.	Speculator Y agrees to *sell* July corn to CH for $3.89/bu.
2.	Speculator Y agrees to *buy* September wheat from CH at $3.63/bu.
Close	Thus, to close Speculator Y owes the Clearinghouse $0.26/bu.
	($0.26/bu.)(5,000 bu.) = $1,300.

	Clearinghouse Records or Speculator Z:
1.	Speculator Z agrees to *buy* September wheat at $4.14/bu.
2.	Speculator Z agrees to *sell* September wheat for $3.63/bu.
Close	Thus, to close the Speculator Z owes Clearinghouse $0.51/bu.
	(–$0.51/bu.)(5,000 bu.) = –$2,550.

To recapitulate, in this example, the contract prices on July corn contracts went from $3.89/bu. on the X and Y contract, to $4.14/bu. on the X and Z contract, to $3.32/bu. on the Y and Z contract at expiration. Speculator X received $0.25 and Speculator Y received $0.26/bu. from clearinghouse, while Speculator Z paid $0.51/bu. to the clearinghouse. The clearinghouse with a perfect hedge on each contract received nothing (other than clearinghouse fees attached to the commission charges), and no corn was purchased or delivered.

Note: This example is based on a July 2016 corn futures prices and spot prices. As shown in the Bloomberg Description screen in Exhibit 1.2, the July contract calls for purchase or delivery of 5,000 bushels of No. 2 yellow corn. The futures and spot price graphs (GP) in Exhibit 1.3 show the futures price was ¢389 (cents per bushel) on 12/14/15, ¢414 on 6/1/16, and ¢363 ½ on 7/15/16 (expiration date) when the spot corn price was $3.32 ½ and the implied hauling cost was $0.31/bu.

EXHIBIT 1.2   Bloomberg Spot and Futures Corn Prices

July 2016 CBT Corn Futures Contract on 7/15/16 (C N6 <Comdty>)

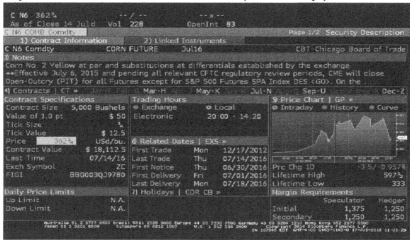

Yellow Corn Spot Prices, 7/15/16 (CORNILNC <Index>)

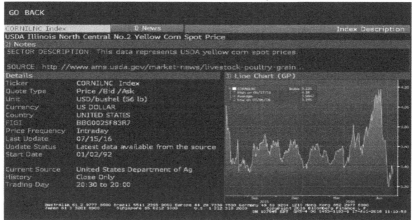

Types of Futures Contracts

Various types of futures contracts are traded on the CBT, CME, Eurex, Singapore, and other exchanges. There are also a number of competing contracts offered by dealers on the OTC market. Futures and forward contracts can be classified either as a physical commodity, energy, equity index, foreign currency, bond, and interest rate.

Physical Commodities

Physical commodities include both agriculture and metallurgical. Agriculture commodities consist of grains (e.g., wheat, corn, and oats), oil and meal (e.g., soybeans and sunflower), livestock (e.g., cattle, pork bellies, and live hogs), forest products

EXHIBIT 1.3   Prices on July 2016 CBT Corn Futures Contracts and Yellow Corn Spot Prices, 7/1/15 to 7/15/16

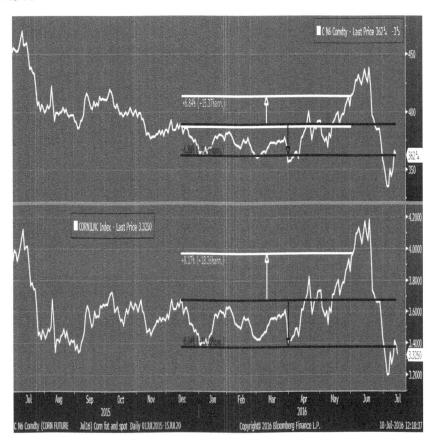

(e.g., plywood), foodstuffs (e.g., orange juice, coffee, and sugar) and textile (e.g., cotton). Many of the agricultural commodities have different contracts for different grades and expiration months, with the expiration months on crops typically set up to conform to their harvest patterns. Metallurgical contracts include metal (e.g., gold, silver, platinum, and copper) and petroleum products (e.g., heating oil, crude oil, gasoline, and propane).

The New York Mercantile Exchange (NYMEX), ICE, Dubai Exchange, and other exchanges offer a number of futures contracts on crude oil, gasoline, and heating oil. Some of these contracts require a cash settlement, while others require physical delivery. Exhibit 1.4 shows the Bloomberg Description screen for the NYMEX's July 2016 crude oil futures contract and a spot contract on West Texas crude. The NYMEX also offers contracts on natural gas. One of the NYMEX contracts calls for the physical delivery of 10,000 million British thermal units (Btu) of natural gas to be made during the delivery month at a uniform rate. Finally, the NYMEX offer contracts on electricity. A typical contract calls for receiving (delivering) a specified number of megawatt-hours for a specified price at a specified location during a particular month. The contracts can vary from a 5 × 8 contract in which power is received five days a week during the

EXHIBIT 1.4 NYMEX August 2016 Crude Oil Futures Contract and Spot Index, 7/15/16 Bloomberg Description Screen (CLQ6 <Comdty>, USCRWTIC <Index>)

August Crude Oil Contract

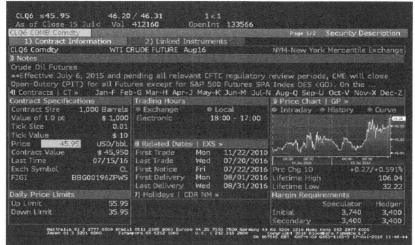

Bloomberg West Texas Intermediate (WTI) Crushing Crude Oil Spot Price Index

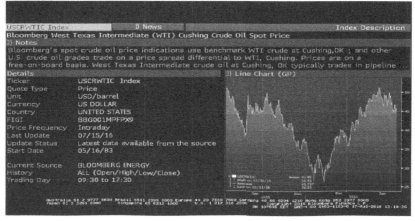

off-peak hours for a specified month to a 7 × 24 contract that calls for receiving power every day and hour during the month.

A somewhat-related contract is a weather derivative. In 1999, the CME offered contracts on cumulative heating degree days (*HDD*) and cooling degree days (*CDD*). A day's *HDD* is a measure of the volume of energy needed for heating during a day, and a *CDD* is measure of the volume of energy required for cooling during a day. Each can be measure as

$$HDD = \text{Max} \, [65° - A, \, 0]$$

$$CDD = \text{Max} \, [A - 65°, \, 0]$$

where:

A = average high and low temperature during a day.

The CME contracts are measured in terms of cumulative *HDD* or *CDD* for a specified month at a specified weather station (e.g., Atlanta, New York, or Cincinnati). These contracts call for a cash settlement. Exhibit 1.5 shows the Bloomberg Description screen for the CME's October 2016 Cincinnati *HDD* futures contract.

In addition to exchange-traded energy and weather futures contracts, the exchanges also offer spot options and futures option contracts on energy and weather products. There is also an extensive OTC market for energy derivatives, as well as other commodity contract. For example, OTC dealers have offered for a number of years a long-term swap arrangement on crude oil in which one party agrees to exchange a fixed price on oil to another party who agrees to exchange a floating price. Weather derivatives have been offered since the 1970s by OTC dealers.

Currency Futures and Forward Contracts

As noted in the introduction, foreign currency futures contracts were introduced in May of 1972 by the CME. Today, currency futures are listed on various futures exchanges (see Exhibit 2.1 in Chapter 2). The CME is the largest currency futures exchange. The contracts on the CME call for the delivery (or purchase) of a specified amount of foreign currency at the delivery date. The contract prices are quoted in terms of dollars per unit of foreign currency.

Forward contracts on foreign currencies are provided in the Interbank Foreign Exchange Market. This OTC market is larger than the currency futures market,

EXHIBIT 1.5   CME October 2016 Cincinnati HDD Oil Futures Contract, 7/15/16 Bloomberg Description Screen (CJV6 <Index>)

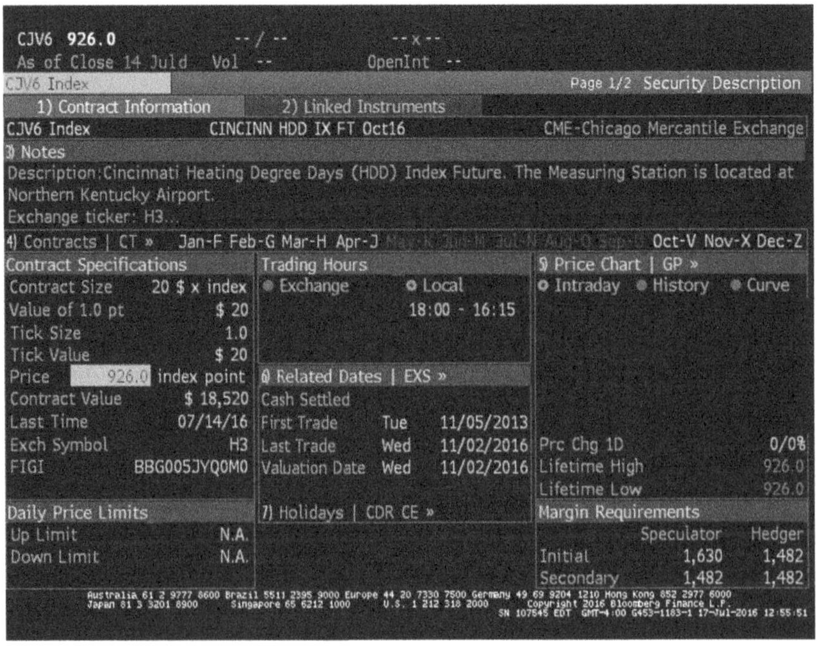

consisting primarily of major banks that provide forward contracts to their clients, which often are large multinational corporations and institutions. In the interbank market, banks provide tailor-made contracts to their customers. Typically, the minimum size of an interbank forward contract is $1 million, with expirations ranging from one to 12 months, although longer-term maturities can be arranged. Currency futures and forward contracts are examined in Chapter 2.

Equity Indexes

There are a number of index futures contracts available on various US and non-US derivative exchanges. Many of the contracts are on equity indexes, but there are also non-equity indexes on bond, commodity, currency, volatility, and spread indexes. The size of index futures contracts is equal to a multiple of the index value, and the futures contracts are cash-settled contracts. Equity index futures contracts are examined in Chapter 3.

Bond and Interest Rate Futures

The most popular bond and interest rate futures contracts are the Eurodollar deposit, T-bonds, and T-notes contracts. T-bills offered on the CME were at one time popular, but due to the popularity of Eurodollar futures contracts, they were delisted. The features of bond and interest rate contracts and their uses are examined in Chapter 4.

The Organized Markets and Characteristics of Futures Trading

The purpose of organized exchanges is to provide marketability: the ease and speed of trading securities. As we examined earlier, one important way that futures exchanges provided marketability is by setting up a clearinghouse for guaranteeing and inter-mediating contracts. The exchanges also provide marketability by providing physical or electronic platforms for brokers and dealers to trade, standardizing contracts, and establishing trading rules.

For many years, the mode of trading on futures exchanges was that of brokers and dealers going to a pit and using the *open-outcry* method to trade. In this system, orders were relayed to the floor by runners or by hand signals to a specified trading pit. An order was then offered in open outcry to all participants (e.g., commission brokers or locals [those trading for their own accounts]) in the pit, with the trade being done with the first person to respond.

Although the open-outcry system is still used, electronic trading systems are today the primary mode used by the organized exchanges to trade derivatives. The CME and CBT developed with Reuters (the electronic information service company) the *GLOBEX* trading system. This is a computerized order-matching system with an inter-national network linking member traders. Since 1985, all new derivative exchanges have been organized as electronic exchanges. Most of these electronic trading systems are order-driven systems in which customer orders (bid and ask prices and size) are collected and matched by a computerized matching system. In addition to linking futures traders, the futures exchanges also make contracts more marketable by standardizing contracts, providing continuous trading, establishing delivery procedures, and providing 24-hour trading through exchange alliances.

Standardization

The futures exchanges provide standardization by specifying the grade or type of each asset and the size of the underlying asset. Exchanges also specify how contract prices are quoted. For example, the contract sizes on most wheat and corn contracts on the Chicago Board of Trade are 5,000 bushels, the size of the crude oil contracts on the New York Mercantile Exchange are 1,000 barrels, gold contracts listed on the CMX Commodity Exchange are 100 troy ounces, and euro contracts on the Chicago Mercantile Exchange are for 125,000 euros.

Continuous Trading

On many futures exchanges, continuous trading is through locals who are dealers that are willing to take temporary positions in one or more futures. These dealers fall into one of three categories: *scalpers,* who offer to buy and sell simultaneously, holding their positions for only a few minutes and profiting from a bid-ask spread; *day traders,* who hold positions for less than a day; and *position traders,* who hold positions for as long as a week before they close. Collectively, these dealers make it possible for the futures markets to provide frequent, if not continuous, trading.

Price and Positions Limits

Futures exchanges often impose price limits as a tool to stop possible destabilizing price trends from occurring. When done, the exchanges specify the maximum price change that can occur from the previous day's settlement price. The price of a contract must be within its daily price limits, unless the exchange intervenes and changes the limit. For example, the crude oil futures contract shown in Exhibit 1.4, in turn, is shown trading at $45.90 per barrel on 7/15/16, with an up limit of $55.95 and down limit of $35.95. When the contract price hits its maximum or minimum limit, it is referred to as being limited up or limited down. In addition to price limits, futures exchanges also can set position limits on many of their futures contracts. This is done as a safety measure both to ensure sufficient liquidity and to minimize the chances of a trader trying to corner a particular asset.

Delivery Procedure

Only a small number of futures contracts are actually delivered. Nevertheless, detailed delivery procedures are important to ensure that the contract price on a futures contract is determined by the spot price on the underlying asset and that the futures price converges to the spot price at expiration. The exchanges have various rules and procedures governing the deliveries of contracts and delivery dates. The date or period in which delivery can take place is determined by the exchange. When there is a delivery period, the party agreeing to sell has the right to determine when the asset will be delivered during that period. For example, the first delivery date on the July 2016 corn futures contract shown in Exhibit 1.2 is 7/1/16, the last delivery date is 7/18/16, and the first notification date is 6/30/16.

Alliances and 24-Hour Trading

In addition to providing off-hour trading via electronic trading systems, 24-hour trading is also possible by using futures exchanges that offer trading on the same contract. A number of exchanges offer identical contracts. This makes it possible to trade the contract in the United States, Europe, and the Far East. Moreover, these exchanges have alliance agreements making it possible for traders to open a position in one market and close it in another.

Margin Requirements

Since a futures contract is an agreement, it has no initial value. Futures traders, however, are required to post some security or good faith money—margin—with their brokers. Depending on the brokerage firm, the customer's margin requirement can be satisfied either in the form of cash or cash equivalents. The margins differ depending on whether the trader is a hedger or speculator. The dollar margin requirements are shown in the lower right corner of the Bloomberg Description screens (Exhibits 1.2, 1.4, 1.5, 1.11, 1.13, and 1.16). As a proportion of their contract values, the margins are approximately 5% for speculator and slightly less for hedgers.

Futures contracts have both initial and maintenance margin requirements. The *initial* (or *performance*) *margin* is the amount of cash or cash equivalents that must be deposited by the investor on the day the futures position is established. The futures trader does this by setting up a margin (or commodity) account with the broker and depositing the required cash or cash equivalents. The amount of the margin is determined by the margin requirement, defined as a proportion (m) of the contract value (e.g., 5%). For example, if the initial margin requirement is 5%, then corn Speculators X and Y in our first example would be required to deposit $972.50 in cash or cash equivalents in their commodity accounts as good faith money on their $3.89 July wheat futures contracts:

$$m[\text{Contract Value}] = 0.05[(\$3.89/\text{bu.})(5{,}000 \text{ bu.})] = \$972.50$$

At the end of each trading day, the futures trader's account is adjusted to reflect any gains or losses based on the settlement price on new contracts. In our example, suppose the day after Speculators X and Y established their respective long and short positions, the settlement price on the July corn contact were $f_T = \$3.85/bu$. The value of X's and Y's margin accounts would therefore be:

X : Account Value $= \$972.50 + (\$3.85/bu. - \$3.89/bu.)(5,000\ bu.) = \$772.50$

Y : Account Value $= \$972.50 + (\$3.89/bu. - \$3.85/bu.)(5,000\ bu.) = \$1,172.50$

With the lower futures price, X's long position decreased in value by $200 and Y's short position increased by $200. When there is a decrease in the account value, the futures trader's broker has to exchange money through the clearing firm equal to the loss on the position to the broker and clearinghouse with the gain. This process is known as *marking to market*. Thus, in our case, X's broker and clearing firm would pass on $200 to Y's broker and clearing firm.

To ensure that the balance in the trader's account does not become negative, the brokerage firm requires a *maintenance margin* (or *variation margin*) be maintained by the futures traders. The maintenance margin is the amount of additional cash or cash equivalents that futures traders must deposit to keep the equity in their commodity account equal to a certain percentage (e.g., 75%) of the initial margin value. If the maintenance margin requirement were set at 100% of the initial margin, then the equity value of X's and Y's accounts would each have to be at least $972.50. If Speculator X did not deposit the $200 required margin, then she would receive a *margin call* from the broker instructing her to post the required amount of funds. If Speculator X did not comply with the margin call, the broker would close the position.

It should be noted that the margin requirements and clearinghouse mechanism that characterize futures exchanges also serve to differentiate them from customized forward contract positions written by banks and investment companies. Forward contacts are more tailor-made contracts, usually do not require margins, and the underlying asset is typically delivered at maturity instead of closed; they are, however, less marketable than exchange-traded futures.

Transaction Costs

Maintaining margin accounts can be viewed as part of the cost of trading futures. In addition to margin requirements, transaction costs are also involved in establishing futures positions. Such costs include broker commissions, clearinghouse fees, and the bid-ask spread. On futures contracts, commission fees usually are charged on a per contract basis and for a round lot, and the fees are negotiable. The clearinghouse fee is relatively small and is collected along with the commission fee by the broker. The bid-ask spreads are set by dealers and represent an indirect cost of trading.

A Note on Taxes

In the United States, futures positions are treated as capital gains and losses for tax purposes. For speculators, a marked-to-market rule applies in which the profits on a futures position are taxed in the year the contract is established. That is, at the end of the year, all futures contracts are marked to the market to determine any unrealized gain or loss for tax purposes. For example, suppose in September a futures speculator takes a long position on a March contract at a contract price of $1,000. If the position were still open at the end of the year, the speculator's taxes on the position would be based on the settlement price at year's end. If the contract were marked to market at $1,200 at the end of the year, then a $200 capital gain would need to be added to the speculator's net capital gains to determine her tax liability. If the speculator's position were later closed in March of the following year at a contract price of $1,100, then she would realize an actual capital gain of $100. For tax purposes, though, the speculator would report a loss equal to the difference in the settlement price at the end of the year ($1,200) and the position's closing price ($1,100): that is, a $100 loss. Both realized and unrealized capital losses, in turn, are deductibles that are subtracted from the investor's capital gains.

Note: The end-of-the-year marked-to-market rule on futures applies only to speculative positions and not to hedging positions. Gains or losses from hedges are treated as ordinary income with the time of the recognition occurring at the time of the gain or loss of income from the hedged item. Also note that when delivery on a futures contract takes place, taxes are applied when the asset actually is sold.

Commodity Futures Hedging

Exchange futures and OTC forward contracts provide investors, businesses, and other economic entities a means for hedging their particular spot positions against adverse price movements. Two hedging positions exist: long hedge and short hedge. In a *long hedge* (or hedge purchase), a hedger takes a long position in a futures contract to protect against an increase in the price of the underlying asset or commodity. Long hedge positions are used, for example, by manufacturers to lock in their future costs of purchasing raw materials, by portfolio managers to fix the price they will pay for securities in the future, or by US multinational corporations that want to lock in the dollar costs of buying foreign currency at some future date. In a *short hedge*, the hedger takes a short futures position to protect against a decrease in the price of the underlying asset. In contrast to long hedging, short hedge positions are used, for example, by farmers who want to lock in the price they will sell their crops for at harvest, by portfolio managers and investment bankers who are planning to sell securities in the future and want to minimize price risk, or by US multinational corporations who have to convert future foreign currency cash flows into dollars and want to immunize the future exchange against adverse changes in exchange rates.

Long Commodity Hedge Example

To illustrate a long hedge position, consider the case of an oil refinery that, in January, anticipates purchasing 100,000 barrels of crude oil in July. Suppose the refinery wants to avoid the price risk associated with buying crude oil on the spot market in July.

In the absence of a forward contract or futures markets for crude oil, the only way the refining company could avoid price risk would be to buy the crude oil in January and store it until July. With crude oil futures contracts listed on the NYMEX, however, the refinery alternatively can minimize price risk by taking a long position in the July crude oil contract (see Exhibit 1.6). With the standard size on crude oil futures of 1,000 barrels, the company would need to go long in 100 July crude oil contracts to hedge its July spot purchase. To this end, suppose the refinery goes long in 100 July contracts at $f_T = \$32.54$/barrel; that is, agrees to buy 100,000 barrels of crude oil (100 contracts with each contract 1,000 barrels) at \$32.54/barrel at the expiration date on the July contract). At expiration, the company would probably find it advantageous (lower transportation costs) to purchase its 100,000 barrels of crude oil on the spot market at the spot price, then close its futures position by going short in the expiring July crude oil futures contract. Given that the spot and expiring futures prices must be equal (or approximately equal), the refinery will find that any additional costs of buying crude oil above the \$32.54/barrel price on the spot market will be offset by a profit from its futures position; while on the other hand, any benefits from the costs of crude oil being less than the \$32.54/barrel price would be negated by losses on the refinery's futures position. As a result, the refining company's costs of buying crude oil on the spot and closing its futures position would be \$32.54/barrel, which is the initial July crude oil contract price they obtained in January.

EXHIBIT 1.6   Prices on NYMEX July 2016 Crude Oil Futures Contract and West Texas Spot Index, 7/17/15 to 7/1/16 Bloomberg GP Screens (CLQ6 <Comdty>, USCRWTIC <Index>)

EXHIBIT 1.7   Long Hedge Example

Initial Position:

Long in July crude oil futures contracts at $32.54/barrel to hedge crude oil purchases in July.

At Delivery:

Close July crude oil contract at $f_T = S_T$ and purchase crude oil on the spot market at S_T.

Positions	Costs		
(1) July Spot Price	$25.00	$32.54	$50.00
(2) Cost of 100,000 Barrels	$2,500,000	$3,254,000	$5,000,000
(3) Profit on Futures	−$754,000	0	$1,746,000
(4) Net Costs: Row (2) − Row (3)	$3,254,000	$3,254,000	$3,254,000

(Profit on futures)/barrel = 100 $(f_T − \$32.54)$/barrel)(1,000 barrels)

The refining company's long hedge position is shown in Exhibit 1.7. In the exhibit, the first row shows three possible spot prices at the July delivery date of $25.00, $32.54, and $50.00. The second row shows the cost of buying 100,000 barrels of crude oil on the spot markets, and the third row shows the profits and losses from the long futures position, in which the offset position has a contract price (f_T) equal to the spot price (S_T). The last row shows the net costs of buying 100,000 barrels of $3,254,000 resulting from purchasing the crude and closing the futures position. Thus, if the price of crude oil on the spot market were $25.00 at the July delivery date, the refinery would pay $2,500,000 for 100,000 barrels of crude oil and $754,000 to the clearinghouse to close its futures positions (i.e., the agreement to buy 100,000 barrels at $32.54 and the offsetting agreement to sell 100,000 barrels at $25.00 means the refining company must pay the clearinghouse $754,000). By contrast, if the spot crude oil price were $50.00, the company would have to pay $5,000,000 for 100,000 barrels of crude oil, but could finance part of that expenditure with the $1,746,000 receipt from the clearinghouse from closing (i.e., agreement to buy at 100,000 barrels at $32.54 and the offsetting agreement to sell 100,000 barrels at $50.00, means the clearinghouse will pay the refining company $1,746,000).

Note: As shown in Exhibit 1.6, the July 2016 futures price of crude oil contracts trading on the MYMEX was $32.54/barrel on 1/20/16. A long hedger with 100 contracts on the July contract would agree to buy 100,000 barrels of light crude oil at $32.54/barrel ($3,254,000 cost). From January to July 2016, the price of crude oil increased. On 6/20/16, the spot price of West Texas crude oil was $49.37 and the July 2016 futures price was $48.85. If the hedger bought 100,000 barrels of crude oil on the spot, the cost would be $4,937,000. However, the hedger would receive $1,631,000 from closing the 100 futures contracts. That is, to close on July 20, 2016, the hedger would have had to go short in 100 July 2016 futures contracts at $48.85 per barrel (i.e., agree to sell 100,000 barrels at $48.85) in order to close the 100 long July contracts at $32.54/barrel that was set up in January (i.e., the agreement to buy 100,000 barrels at $32.54); thus, the hedger would receive $1,631,000 from the clearinghouse.

EXHIBIT 1.8   Long Crude Oil Hedge of July 2016 Crude Oil Purchase

	Clearinghouse Records for Long Crude Oil Hedger:
1/20/16	Hedger agrees to *buy* July crude oil at $32.54/barrel; 100 contracts; 1,000 barrels per contract.
6/20/16	Hedger agrees to *sell* July crude oil at $48.85/barrel; 100 contracts; 1,000 barrels per contract.
Close	Clearinghouse pays the hedger $16.31/barrel Total Receipt: (100)($16.31/barrel)(1,000 barrels) = $1,631,000
6/20/16	Cost of Crude Oil: $4,937,000 = (100,000 barrels) ($49.37/barrel) Hedged Cost = Cost of Crude − Futures Profit Hedged Cost = $4,937,000 − $1,631,000 = $3,306,000

In this case, the hedger's hedged cost on July 20, 2016, of buying crude oil on the spot at $4,937,000 and receiving $1,631,000 from the clearinghouse would have been $3,306,000 (see Exhibit 1.8). In retrospect, the hedger would have been pleased by having set up the hedge.

Short Commodity Hedge Example

To illustrate how a short hedge works, consider the case of a corn farmer who, in December, wants to lock in the price he will receive for his estimated 100,000 bushels of corn expected to be harvested in July. If the farmer goes short in 20 July corn futures contracts (contract size is 5,000 bushels) priced at $3.90/bu. on 12/14/16, he would be able to receive approximately $3.89/bu. in revenue at the delivery date in July from selling the corn on the spot market and closing the futures contracts by going long in the expiring July contracts trading at the spot price. This can be seen in Exhibit 1.9. In the exhibit, the first row shows three possible spot prices of $4.10, $3.90, and $3.70, the second row shows revenues from selling 100,000 bushels on the spot market, the third row shows the profits and losses from the futures position, and the fourth row shows the constant hedged revenue $390,000 from aggregating both positions. If the farmer receives $3.70 per bushel for his corn and therefore only $370,000 from selling his 100,000 bushels, he also realizes a $20,000 profit from futures position (the agreement to sell 100,000 bushels of July corn for $3.90 is closed with an agreement to buy 100,000 bushels of July corn for $3.70, resulting in a $20,000 receipt from the clearinghouse). On the other hand, if the farmer is able to sell his corn for $4.10 per bushel and therefore $410,000, he also will have to pay the clearinghouse $20,000 (the agreement to sell 100,000 bushels of July corn for $3.90 is closed with an agreement to buy 100,000 bushels of July corn for $4.10), resulting in a $20,000 receipt from the clearinghouse Thus, regardless of the spot price, the farmer receives $390,000.

Exhibit 1.3 shows the prices on the July 2016 corn futures contract listed on the CBT from 7/1/15 to 7/14/16 and the spot prices on yellow corn. On 12/14/15, a

EXHIBIT 1.9   Short Corn Hedge Example

Initial Position:

Short in 20 July corn futures contracts at $3.90/bu. to hedge corn sale in July.

At Delivery:

Close corn futures contracts at $f_T = S_T$ and sell the harvested corn on the spot market at S_T.

Positions	Revenue per Bushel		
(1) Spot Corn Price	$4.10	$3.90	$3.70
(2) Revenue: S_T (5,000 bu)	$410,00	$390,000	$370,000
(3) Profit from Futures	−$20,000	0	$20,000
(4) Net Revenue = Row (2) + (3)	$390,000	$390,000	$390,000

(Profit from Futures) = (5,000 bu.)(($3.90 − f_T)/bu.)

farmer wanting to hedge 100,000 bushels of corn to be harvested and sold on 7/15/16 would have been able to go short in 20 July 2016 corn futures contracts at $3.89 per bushel; a contract value of $389,000 (= (20)(5,000 bushes)($3.89/bu.)). From 12/14/15 to 7/14/16, the spot price of corn decreased approximately 8.00% from $3.67 to $3.375. On 7/15/16, the spot price of yellow corn was $3.375/bu. and the July 2016 corn futures price was $3.6225. If the farmer sold his 100,000 bushels on the spot on 7/14/16, he would have received $337,500 for his corn. However, he would also have received $26,750 when he closed his 20 corn futures contracts. That is, to close on 7/15/16, the hedger would have had to go long in 20 July 2016 futures contracts at $3.6225 (i.e., agree to buy 100,000 bushels at $3.6225) in order to close the 20 short July contracts at $3.89/bu. that was set up on 12/14/16 (i.e., the agreement to sell 100,000 bushels at $3.89); thus, the farmer would receive $26,750 from the clearinghouse. In this case, the farmer's hedged revenue on July 15, 2016, of selling corn on the spot for $337,500 and receiving $26,750 from the clearinghouse would have been $364,250 (see Exhibit 1.10). In retrospect, the farmer would have been pleased by having set up the short hedge.

EXHIBIT 1.10   Short Corn Hedge of July 2016 Corn

	Clearinghouse Records for Short Corn Futures Hedger:
12/14/16	Hedger agrees to *sell* July corn at $3.89/bu.; 20 contracts; 5,000 bushels per contract.
7/14/16	Hedger agrees to *buy* July corn at $3.6225/bu.; 20 contracts; 5,000 bushels per contract.
Close	Clearinghouse pays the hedger $0.2675 Total Receipt: (20)($0.2675/barrel)(5,000 bushels) = $26,750
7/14/16	Sale of Corn on the spot at $3.375: $337,500 = (100,000 bushels) ($3.375/bu.)
	Hedged Revenue = Corn Sale + Futures Profit Hedged Revenue = $337,500 + $26,750 = $364,250

Hedging Risk

These examples in which the hedger closed the futures position at an expiring futures price equal to the spot represent perfect hedging cases in which certain revenues or costs can be locked in at a future date. In practice, perfect hedges are the exception and not the rule. This was seen in the case in which the farmer sold his corn at $3.375 on the spot and closed his futures at $3.6225. There are three types of hedging risk that preclude one from obtaining a zero risk position: *quality risk, timing risk*, and *quantity risk*.

Quality risk exists when the commodity or asset being hedged is not identical to the one underlying the futures contract. The oil refinery in our first hedging example, for instance, may need to purchase a different grade or quality of crude oil than the one specified in the futures contract. In our corn example, the price difference between the spot and futures can be explained in the differences in types of corn on the spot and futures and the hauling cost. In certain hedging cases, futures contracts written on a different underlying asset are used to hedge the spot asset. For example, a portfolio manager planning to buy corporate bonds in the future might hedge the acquisition by going long in T-bond futures. This type of hedge is known as a *cross hedge*. Different from *direct hedges* in which the futures' underlying assets is the same as the asset being hedged, cross-hedging cannot eliminate risk, but can minimize it.

Timing risk occurs when the delivery date on the futures contract does not coincide with the date the hedged assets or liabilities need to be purchased or sold. For example, timing risk would exist in our second hedging example if the corn farmer expected to harvest his corn in late June instead of mid-July. If the spot asset or commodity is purchased or sold at a date t that differs from the expiration date on the futures contract, then the price on the futures (f_t) and the spot price (S_t) will not necessarily be equal. The difference between the futures and spot price is called the *basis* (B_t). The basis tends to narrow as expiration nears, converging to zero at expiration ($B_T = 0$). Prior to expiration, the basis can vary, with greater variability usually observed the longer the time is to expiration. Given this *basis risk*, the greater the time difference between buying or selling the hedged asset and the futures' expiration date, the less perfect the hedge. To minimize timing risk or basis risk, hedgers often select futures contracts that mature before the hedged asset is to be bought or sold but as close as possible to that date. For very distant horizon dates, though, hedgers sometimes follow a strategy known as *rolling the hedge forward*. This hedging strategy involves taking a futures position, then at expiration closing the position and taking a new one.

Finally, because of the standardization of futures contracts, futures hedging also is subject to quantity risk. Quantity risk would have been present in our second hedging example if the farmer had expected a harvest of 102,000 bushels instead of 100,000 bushels. With the contract size on the corn futures contract being 5,000 bushels, 100,000 bushels of the farmer's harvest could be hedged, but 2,000 would be subject to price risk.

Hedging Models

The presence of quality, timing, and quantity risk means that pricing risk cannot be eliminated totally by hedging with futures contracts. As a result, the objective in hedging is to try to minimize risk. Several hedging models try to achieve this objective: price-sensitivity model, minimum variance model, naive-hedge model, and utility-based hedging model. These models have as their common objective the determination of a *hedge ratio*: the optimal number of futures contracts needed to hedge a position. In later chapters, we will define and examine how some of these models can be used to hedge stock portfolios, debt securities, and foreign currency positions.

Commodity Speculating with Futures

Although futures are used quite extensively for hedging, they are also used to speculate on expected price changes. A long futures position is taken when the price of the underlying asset is expected to rise and a short position is taken when the price is expected to fall. Such positions are referred to as *outright futures positions*. For example, consider coffee speculators tracking the July 2016 coffee futures prices shown in Exhibit 1.11. On 1/22/16, financial news reported coffee crop declines in Brazil and expectant doubling of Starbucks in China. Based on these reports, suppose a bullish coffee speculator took a long position on 1/22/16 in one July 2016 coffee contract at 120.15 cents ($1.2015). The contract would require the speculator to buy 37,500 pounds of coffee at $1.2015 in July with the first delivery date being July 1, 2016 (see Bloomberg Description page in Exhibit 1.11). As shown in the graph in Exhibit 1.11, if the long speculator closed her position on 7/1/16 when the July futures contract was trading at $1.4485, she would have realized a profit of $9,262.50. By contrast, a bearish speculator who took a short position in the July coffee futures on 1/22/16, perhaps after observing recent price decline, would have lost $9,262.50 by taking a short position on 1/22/16 at $1.2015 and closing it at $1.4485 on 7/1/16 (see Exhibit 1.12).

Speculating on a change in the price of an asset or commodity by taking such outright or naked futures positions represents an alternative to buying or short selling an asset or commodity on the spot market. Because of the risk inherent in such outright futures positions, some speculators form spreads instead of taking a naked position. A futures spread is formed by taking long and short positions on different futures contracts simultaneously. There are two general types of spreads: intracommodity and intercommodity. An *intracommodity spread* is formed with futures contracts on the same asset but with different expiration dates; an *intercommodity spread* is formed with two futures contracts with the same expiration but on different assets.

EXHIBIT 1.11   2016 July Coffee Futures Contract Bloomberg Description Screen

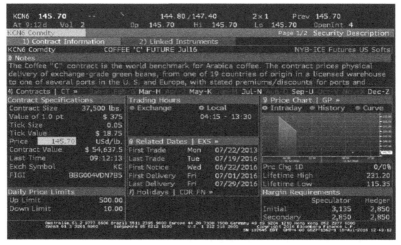

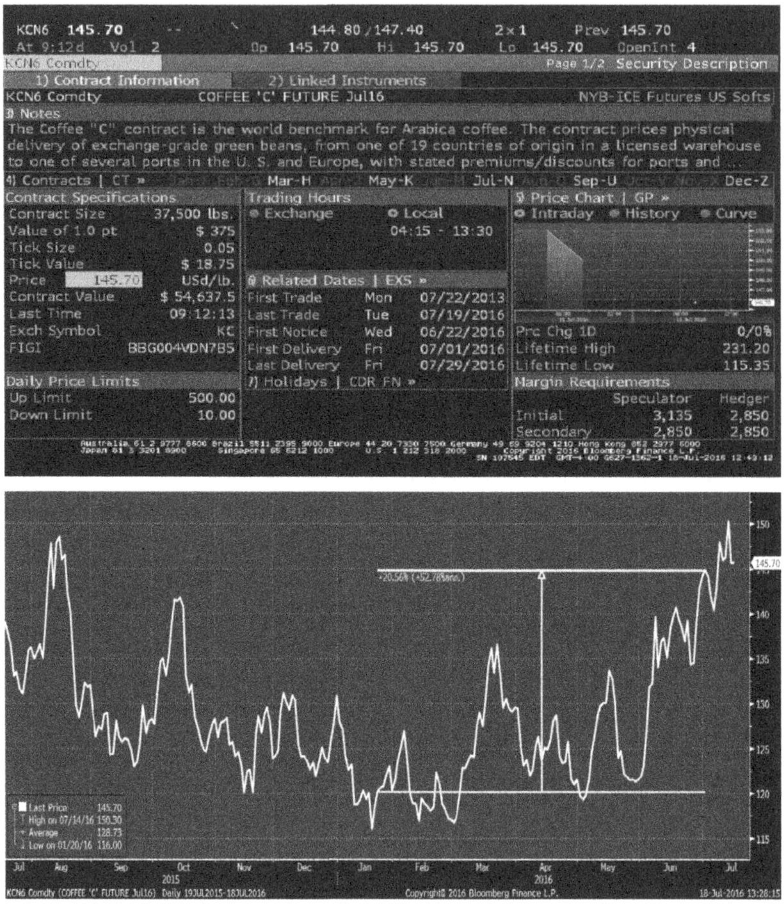

EXHIBIT 1.12   Outright Positions in July 2016 Coffee Futures Positions

	Clearinghouse Records for Long Coffee Speculator:
1/22/16	Speculator agrees to buy 37,500 pounds of coffee in July for $1.2015 per lb.
7/1/16	Speculator agrees to sell 37,500 pounds of coffee in July at $1.4485 per lb.
Close	Clearinghouse pays Speculator $9,262.50 Closing receipt from clearinghouse: 37,500 lbs. ($1.4485/lb. − $1.2015/lb.) = $9,262.50

	Clearinghouse Records for Short Coffee Speculator:
1/22/16	Speculator agrees to sell 37,500 pounds of coffee in July for $1.2015 per lb.
7/1/16	Speculator agrees to buy 37,500 pounds of coffee in July at $1.4485 per lb.
Close	Speculator pays clearinghouse Speculator $9,262.50 Closing payment to clearinghouse: 37,500 lbs. ($1.2015 − $1.4485/lb.) = −$9,262.50

Intracommodity Spread

An intracommodity spread is often used to reduce the risk associated with a pure outright position. More distant futures contracts (T_2) are sometimes more price sensitive to changes in the spot price, S, than near-term futures contracts (T_1):

$$\frac{\%\Delta f_{T_2}}{\%\Delta S} > \frac{\%\Delta f_{T_1}}{\%\Delta S}$$

Thus, a speculator who expects the price of a commodity or asset to increase in the future could form an intracommodity spread by going long in the asset's or commodity's longer-term futures contract and short in a shorter-term one. This type of intracommodity spread will be profitable if the expectation of the price increasing occurs. That is, the increase in the commodity or asset price will cause the price on the longer-term futures to increase more than the shorter-term one. As a result, a speculator's gains from his long position in the longer-term futures will exceed his losses from his short position. If the spot price falls, though, losses will occur on the long position; these losses will be partially offset by profits realized from the short position on the shorter-term contract. On the other hand, if a speculator believes the spot price will decrease but did not want to assume the risk inherent in an outright short position, he could form a spread with a short position in a longer-term contract and a long position in the shorter-term one. Note that in forming a spread, the speculator does not have to keep the ratio of long-to-short positions one-to-one, but instead could use any ratio (2-to-1, 3-to-2, etc.) to obtain her desired return-risk combination.

Exhibit 1.13 shows the prices from 1/10/2014 to 2/25/15 for a COMEX October 2015 gold futures contract (GCV5) and a December 2017 gold futures contract (GCZ7), along with gold spot prices (XAU) (COMEXC is a division of the NYMEX). Suppose a speculator bullish on gold formed an intracommodity spread on 1/16/14 by going long in one COMEX December 2017 gold contract (100 troy ounces) at $1,305.00/oz. and short in one October 2015 gold contract at $1,250.20. From 1/16/2014 to 2/25/2015, spot gold prices decreased 3.37% from $1,242.39 to $1,200.53, the longer-term December 2017 contract decreased 6.16% to $1,224.66, and the shorter-term October 2015 contract decreased 3.74% to $1,203.56. If the bullish spreader closed his position on 2/25/2015, he would have realized a loss of $8,034 on the December 2017 contract and a gain of $4,670 on the October 2015 contract, for a net loss of $3,364 (see Exhibit 1.14).

In retrospect, the spreader would have wished he had taken an outright short position in the longer-term December 2017 contract where he would have realized a profit of $8,034. The bullish spreader's short position, however, was used to give him protection if gold prices decreased, which was the case for this time period. In contrast, a bearish speculator who took a bearish intracommodity spread on 1/16/14 by going short in the December 2017 contract and long in the October 2015 contract would have gained $3,364 if she closed the positions on 1/23/2015. Thus, the intracommodity spread provides the speculator with a lower return opportunity but also lower risk than the outright position.

EXHIBIT 1.13 Bloomberg Description Screen for December 2017 Gold Futures Contract and Prices on October 2015 Gold Futures, December 2017 Gold Futures, and Gold Spot 1/10/2014 to 2/16/2105

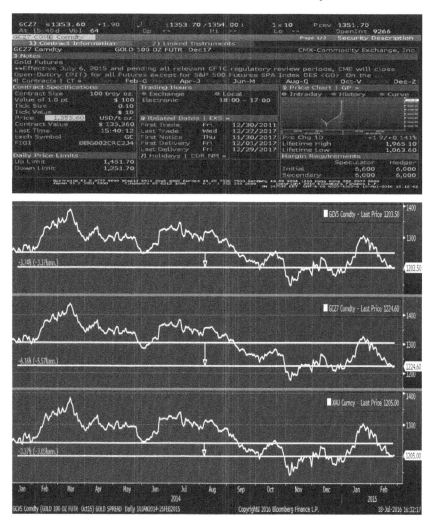

It should be noted that differences in futures price with different expiations depend, in part, on interest rates and difference in the expiration period. When interest rates are low, the price differences with contracts with different expiration may be small, and as a result, the applicability of using intracommodity spreads to provide different return-risk may be only minimal.

Intercommodity Spread

An intercommodity spread is formed with two futures contracts with the same expiration dates but on different commodities (e.g., opposite positions on a July gold futures contract and a July silver contract). In constructing intercommodity spreads, a spreader

EXHIBIT 1.14 Intracommodity Spread: Long in One December 2017 Gold Futures Contract and Short in One October 2015 Futures Contracts

1/16/14 to 2/25/15	Clearinghouse Records for Long December 2017 Position
1/16/14	Speculator agrees to buy 100 troy ounces of gold in December 2017 for $1,305.00/oz.
2/25/15	Speculator agrees to sell 100 troy ounces of gold in December 2017 for $1,224.66/oz.
Close	Speculators pays $8,034 to the clearinghouse: 100 oz. ($1,224.66/oz. − $1,305.00/oz.) = −$8,034
	Clearinghouse Records for Short October 2015 Position
1/16/14	Speculator agrees to sell 100 troy ounces of gold in October of 2015 for $1,250.20/oz.
2/25/15	Speculator agrees to buy 100 troy ounces gold in October 2015 for $1,203.50/oz.
Close	Speculators receives $4,670 from the clearinghouse: 100 oz. ($1,250.20/oz. − $1,203.50/oz.) = $4,670
	Net Position
2/25/15	$4,670 − $8,034 = −$3,364

often makes use of the correlation between the underlying assets. Exhibit 1.15 shows an estimated regression relation between the percent change in the spot price of silver per troy ounce and the percent change in the spot price of gold per troy ounce.

EXHIBIT 1.15 Regression Relation between Percentage Change in Gold Prices (XAU) and Silver Prices (XAG), 7/19/2014 to 7/18/16

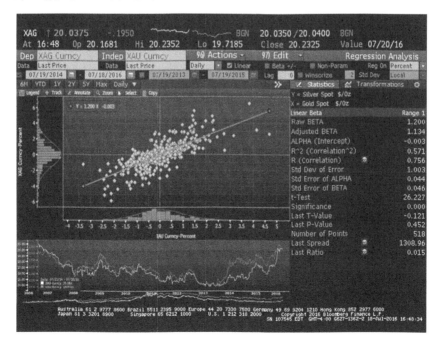

The slope of the regression line is % Change Silver/% Change Gold = 1.134. A mildly bullish precious metals speculator who wanted a lower return-risk combination than implied by either metal could form an intercommodity spread by going long in one COMEX silver futures contract and short in one gold futures contract. Based on the regression relationship, there would be an 11.34% increase (decrease) in silver prices for a 10% increase (decrease) in gold prices. Thus, for a 10% increase in gold prices, the bullish spreader would, in turn, realize a 1.34% gain, and for a 10% decrease in gold price, the spreader would lose 1.34%.

EXHIBIT 1.16   Bloomberg Description Screen for Prices on July 2016 Silver Futures and July 2016 Gold Futures, 5/2/16 to 7/18/16

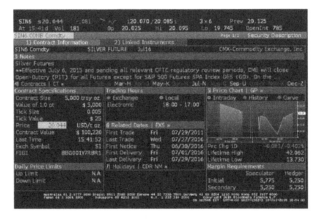

July 2016 Silver Futures Contract Prices

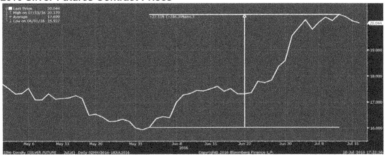

July 2016 Gold Futures Contract Prices

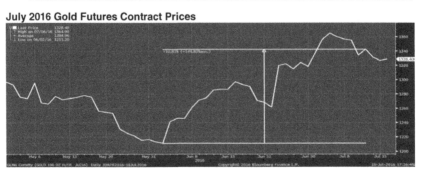

Exhibit 1.16 shows the prices for a July 2016 silver futures contract and a July 2016 gold contract. As shown in the Bloomberg Description screen in the exhibit, the contract on silver calls for the delivery or purchase of 5,000 troy ounces of silver in July. The gold contract (see Exhibit 1.13), in turn, calls for the delivery or purchase of 100 troy ounces of gold in July. Suppose a speculator, expecting the price of precious metal to increase in the near future, formed an intercommodity spread on 5/2/16 by going long in one July silver contract at $16.025 and short in one July gold contract at $1,211.20. From 5/2/16 to 6/2/16, precious metal prices did increase, resulting in a 27.11% increase in July silver futures to $20.37 and a 10.83% increase in July gold futures prices to $1,342.40. If the spreader closed her intercommodity spread on 6/2/16, she would have realized a profit of $21,725 on her long July silver futures contract and a loss of $13,120 on her short July gold futures contract, resulting in a net gain of $8,605 (see Exhibit 1.17).

The spreader probably regretted that she did not take an outright long position in the silver contract where she would have realized a $21,725 gain. Her short position in gold, however, was taken to give her some protection in case the price of precious metals decreased.

EXHIBIT 1.17   Intercommodity Spread: Long in July 2016 Silver Futures Contract and Short in July 2016 Gold Futures Contract

5/2/16 to 6//2/16	Clearinghouse Records for Long July 2016 Silver Futures Position
5/2/16	Opening Position: Long in one July silver futures contract (contract size = 5,000 oz.):
	Speculator agrees to buy 5,000 troy ounces of silver in July for $16.025/oz.
6/2/16	Closing Position: Short in one July silver futures contract:
	Speculator agrees to sell 5,000 troy ounces in July for $20.37/oz.
Close	Speculator receives $21,725 from the clearinghouse:
	($20.37/oz. − $16.025/oz.)(5,000 oz.) = $21,725
	Clearinghouse Records for Short July 2016 Gold Futures Position
5/2/16	Opening Position: Short in one July gold futures contract (contract size = 100 troy ounces):
	Speculator agrees to sell 100 troy ounces in July for $1,211.20
6/2/16	Closing Position: Long in one July gold futures contract:
	Speculator agrees to buy 100 troy ounces in July for $1,342.40
	Speculators pays clearinghouse $13,120:
Close	($1,211.20/oz. − $1,342.40/oz.)(100 oz.) = −$13,120
	Net Position
6/2/16	$21,725 − $13,120 = $8,605

Pricing Futures and Forward Contracts: Carrying-Cost Model

Basis

As a derivative security, the price on a futures contract depends on the price of the underlying asset. The difference between the futures price and the spot price is called the basis (B_t):

$$\text{Basis} = B_t = f_t - S_t$$

(The basis also can be expressed as $S_t - f_t$.) For most futures contracts, the futures price exceeds the spot price before expiration and approaches the spot price as expiration nears. Thus, the basis usually is positive and decreasing over time, equaling zero at expiration ($B_T = 0$). Futures and spot prices also tend to be highly correlated with each other, increasing and decreasing together. Their correlation, though, is not perfect. As a result, the basis tends to be relatively stable along its declining trend, even when futures and spot prices vacillate.

By definition, a normal market is one in which the futures price exceeds the spot price and is referred to as a *contango*. In contrast, if the market is inverted with the futures price less than the spot price (a negative basis), the costs of carrying the asset is said to have a *convenience yield* in which the benefits from holding the asset exceed the costs. An inverted market in which the basis is negative is referred to as *backwardation*.

Carrying-Cost Model for a Commodity

The relation between the futures (or forward) price and the spot price is governed by an arbitrage relation that is explained by the *carrying-cost model* (or *cost-of-carry model*). This model determines the equilibrium futures price by solving for that price that is equal to the cost of carrying the underlying asset for the time period from the present to the expiration on the contract (i.e., the net cost of buying the underlying asset and holding it for the period). If the futures price does not equal the cost of carrying the underlying asset, then an arbitrage opportunity exists by taking a position in futures and an opposite position in the underlying asset. Thus, in the absence of arbitrage, the price on the futures contract is equal to the cost of carrying the asset. The model is used to explain what determines the equilibrium price on a forward contract. If short-term interest rates are relatively constant, futures and forward prices will be equal, and thus the carrying-cost model can be extended to price futures contracts as well.

For financial futures, the carrying costs include the financing costs of holding the underlying asset to expiration minus the benefits from coupon interest or dividends earned from holding the asset. For commodities, the carrying costs include not only financing costs but also storage and transportation costs, and generally there are no benefits. The carrying-cost model for a typical commodity forward contract is:

$$f_0^* = S_0 \left(1 + R_f\right)^T + (K)(T) + TRC$$

where:

K = storage costs per unit of the commodity per period
TRC = transportation costs
T = time to delivery as a proportion of a year

To illustrate, suppose on April 15 the spot price of a bushel of corn is $3.66 (see Exhibit 1.3), the annual storage costs is $0.35 per/bushel, the risk-free rate is 3%, and the costs of hauling corn from the destination point specified on the futures contract to a local grain elevator, or vice versa, is $0.035/bu. By the cost of carry model, the equilibrium price of a futures contract on the July corn (expiration of $T = 0.25$) would be $3.81/bu.:

$$f_0^* = (\$3.66/\text{bu.})(1.03)^{0.25} + (0.35/\text{bu.})(0.25) + \$0.035/\text{bu.} = \$3.81/\text{bu.}$$

If the futures price in the market, f^M, was $3.85/bu. (above the equilibrium price), an arbitrageur could:

1. Take a short position in the futures contract: agree to sell a July bushel of corn for $3.85.
2. Borrow $3.66 at 3% interest.
3. Use the loan proceeds to buy a bushel of corn for $3.66, and then store it for three months.
4. At expiration: (1) pay the financing costs of $3.687/bu. (= $3.66(1.03)^{0.25}$), (2) pay the storage costs of ($0.35/bu.)(0.25) = $0.0875/bu., (3) transport the corn from the grain elevator to the specified destination point on the futures contract for $0.035/bu., and (4) sell the bushel of corn on the futures contract at $3.85/bu.

From this cash-and-carry strategy, the arbitrageur would earn a riskless return of $0.04/bu.

$$f_0^M - f_0^* = \$3.85 - [\$3.66(1.03)^{0.25} + (0.35)(0.25) + \$0.035] = \$0.04$$

If the futures price on a commodity is below the equilibrium price, the strategy would need to be reversed. This would entail taking a short position in the spot commodity and a long position in the futures contract. In our corn example, such an opportunity might be available, for example, to a mill company maintaining an inventory of corn. Instead of holding all of its corn, the company might sell some of it on the spot market and invest the proceeds in a risk-free security for the period, then go long in a futures contract to buy the corn back. For many commodities, though, this reverse strategy may not be practical. For those commodities in which the reverse cash-and-carry arbitrage strategy does not apply, the equilibrium condition for the futures contract needs to be specified as an inequality:

$$f_0^* \leq S_0 (1 + R_f)^T + (K)(T) + TRC$$

For commodity futures, an inverted market in which the spot price exceeds the futures price often exists for unstorable commodities (e.g., eggs) or can occur in certain situations in which the existing supplies of a commodity (e.g., corn) are limited, but future supplies (e.g., the next corn harvest) are expected to be abundant.

Pricing the CBT September 2016 Corn Futures Contract

Exhibit 1.18 shows the futures price on the CBT September 2016 contract, the spot prices on yellow corn, and Bloomberg's GRCC screen (grain cash and carry analysis). On 7/14/16, the spot price of yellow corn was $3.3759/bu., short-term interest rates were approximately 1%, the storage cost for Iowa yellow corn for three months was 0.03/bu, the cost of hauling corn 60 miles from River Gulf Grain Elevator in Bettendorf, Iowa, was $0.15/bu, and the time to the September contract was $T = 0.25$ per year. Using these numbers, the carrying-cost price on the September CBT corn futures on 7/14/16 would have been $3.5643/bu.

$$f_0^* = S_0(1 + R_f)^T + (K)(T) + TRC$$

$$f_0^* = (\$3.3759/\text{bu.})(1.01)^{0.25} + (0.03/\text{bu.}) + \$0.15/\text{bu.}] = \$3.5643/\text{bu.}$$

EXHIBIT 1.18   Bloomberg Grain and Cash and Carry Analysis Screen (GRCC) for Yellow Corn on 7/15/16 and Prices on September 2016 CBT Corn Futures Contracts and Yellow Corn Spot Prices, 7/20/15 to 7/14/16

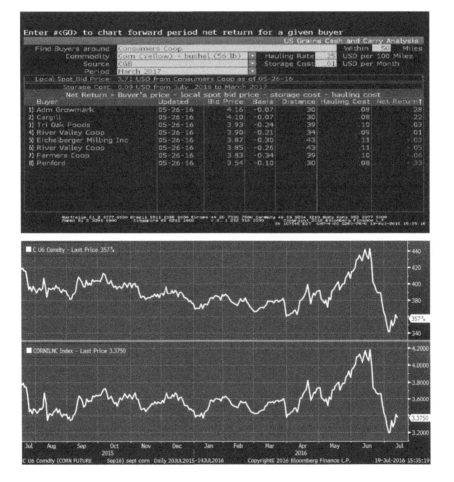

This price, in turn, is close to the actual futures price on the September contract on 7/14/16 where the September corn's last price was \$3.5775, the bid was \$3.5675, and the ask was \$3.56.

Price Relationship Between Futures Contracts with Different Expirations

The same arbitrage arguments governing the futures and spot price relation also can be extended to establish the equilibrium relationship between futures prices with different expirations. Specifically, given a distant futures contract expiring in T_2 and a nearby contract on the same asset expiring in T_1, the equilibrium relationship between the futures prices on the two contracts (f_{T2} and f_{T1}) is:

$$f_{T2}^* = f_{T1}(1 + R_{T1})^{T2-T1} + (K)(T_2 - T_1) + TRC$$

where:

R_{T1} = risk-free rate or repo rate at time T_1. This rate can be locked in with a forward contract to borrow funds at R_{T1} (see Chapter 4).

If the market price of the forward contract with T_2 expiration (f^M_{T2}) exceeded the equilibrium price, an arbitrageur could profit by forming an intracommodity spread by:

1. Taking a long position in the T_1 futures contract
2. Taking a short position in the T_2 futures contract
3. Entering a forward contract to borrow at time T_1, f_{T1} dollars at rate R_{T1} for the period from T_1 to T_2

At T_1 expiration, the arbitrageur would:

1. Borrow f_{T1} dollars at a rate of R_{T1} on the forward contract.
2. Buy the commodity on the T_1 futures contract for f_{T1}.
3. Transport and store the commodity for the period at a costs of $K(T_2 - T_1) + TRC$.

At the T_2 expiration, the arbitrageur would:

1. Sell the asset on the T_2 futures contract for f_{T2}.
2. Repay the loan of $f_{T1}(1 + R_{T1})^{T2-T1}$.
3. Pay the transportation and storage costs of $K(T_2 - T_1) + TRC$.
4. Transport the commodity to the specified destination point on the futures contract.

The arbitrageur's actions would result in a riskless *CF* of

$$CF = f_{T2}^M - [f_{T1}(1 + R_{T1})^{T2-T1} + (K)(T_2 - T_1) + TRC]$$

Such actions, in turn, would continue until the equilibrium condition is satisfied.

To illustrate, consider the forward price relationship for October and July corn contracts. Suppose the following conditions are present:

1. The future price on the July corn contract is $f_{T1} = \$3.81/\text{bu.}$
2. The July forward interest rate on a three-month loan is 3% (annual).
3. The storage costs for corn is $0.35/bu. per year.
4. The costs of transporting are $0.035/bu.

If the time period between the expiration on the July corn contract and the October contract is $T_2 - T_1 = 0.25/\text{year}$, then the equilibrium price on the October contract would be $3.96/bu.

$$f_{T2}^* = \$3.81(1.03)^{0.50-0.25} + (\$0.35)(0.50 - 0.25) + \$0.035/\text{bu.} = \$3.96/\text{bu.}$$

If the October corn futures contract is $4.00, then an arbitrageur could earn a $0.04/bu. profit by:

1. Entering a July forward contract to borrow $3.81 at $R_{T1} = 3\%$
2. Going long in the July corn contract at $f_{T1} = \$3.81/\text{bu.}$
3. Taking a short position on the October corn contract at $f_{T2} = \$4.00$

In July, the arbitrageur would:

1. Borrow $3.81 at 3% interest on the forward contract.
2. Purchase the corn on the July contract at $3.81.
3. Store the corn at an annual rate of $0.35/bu. for 0.25 of a year.

At the October expiration the arbitrageur would realize a $0.04/bu. profit. by:

1. Selling the corn on the October contract for $4.00/bu.
2. Repaying the loan of $3.838 (= $3.81(1.03)^{0.25}$)
3. Paying the storage costs of $0.0875 (= ($0.35/bu.)(0.25))
4. Transporting the corn from the grain elevator to the specified destination point on the futures contract for $0.035/bu.

$$CF = f_{T2}^M - f_{T2}^*$$
$$CF = \$4.00 - [\$3.81(1.03)^{0.50-0.25} + (0.35)(0.50 - 0.25) + \$0.035]$$
$$CF = \$0.04$$

If the October corn contract is less than the equilibrium price, the above intracommodity spread strategy would need to be reversed. This would require taking a short position in the July contract, a long position in the October contract, and entering a forward contract to invest f_{T1} funds at rate R_{T1} for $T_2 - T_1$. The implementation of this reverse strategy may or may not be practical. For financial futures, for example, this reverse strategy generally can be applied. However, as noted for some commodity futures contracts, the reverse strategy does not hold. For such commodity futures, the carry-cost, in turn, needs to be expressed as an inequality.

The Value of Futures and Forward Contracts

The carrying-cost model determines the forward or futures price. A separate question is whether there is any value to the futures or forward contract. A futures or forward contract is simply an agreement that has no inherent value when it is introduced. In the case of forward contracts, there is a value to an existing contract. After its introduction, the value of a forward contract at time t should be equal to the present value of the difference between its initial contract price (F_0) and the contract price on a new forward contract with the same expiration date and underlying asset (F_t). That is, the value of a long position on the initial forward contract at time t (V_t) is:

$$V_t = \frac{F_t - F_0}{(1 + R)^t}$$

For example, if the forward contract price on September corn is \$3.83 (F_t) when there is one month to expiration ($t = 1/12$ of a year) and the annual risk-free rate is 3%, then the value of a long position on a September wheat forward contract initiated earlier at \$3.81 would be \$0.01995:

$$V_t = \frac{F_t - F_0}{(1 + R)^t} = \frac{\$3.83 - \$3.81}{(1.03)^{1/12}} = \$0.01995$$

With one month to delivery, the \$0.01995 value of the earlier contract reflects the \$0.02 riskless return that can be realized at the end of one month by the holder of the earlier contract forming an intracommodity spread by taking a short position in the new contract. At the expiration, the spreader would be able to buy the corn at \$3.81 and sell it at \$3.83.

Like forward contracts, futures contracts also can have values after their inceptions, but only until they are marked to market. Once a futures contract is marked to market, its value reverts to zero.

The Relation between Futures and Forward Prices

The price relationships we've described thus far hold strictly for forward contracts that have no initial or maintenance margin requirements. As noted, if short-term interest rates are relatively constant over time, it can be shown that the prices of futures and forward contracts on the same underlying asset are the same. The proof of this relation, as well as the relation between futures prices and expected spot prices, is presented in many derivative texts.

Conclusion

In this chapter, we have provided an overview of futures and forward contracts. These derivatives can be used as speculative tools to profit from changes in asset prices and as hedging tools to minimize price risk. Futures contracts are traded on organized exchanges that establish trading rules and procedures for buying and selling contracts. In this chapter, we examined the speculative and hedging uses of physical commodities. In the next chapter, we examine the hedging and speculative uses of currency futures and forward contracts. In Chapters 3 and 4, we respectively examine equity index and interest rate contracts.

BLOOMBERG: COMMODITY FUTURES AND RELATED SCREENS

Appendix A at the end of this book presents an overview and guide to the Bloomberg system. In this section, we identify screens and functions related to commodity futures. In subsequent chapters, we identify Bloomberg screens and functions applicable to that chapter's subject.

BLOOMBERG CTM SCREEN AND UPLOADING

Bloomberg Commodity Screens, CTM
Exchange-listed commodity futures contracts can be found by accessing the CTM screen shown in Exhibit 1.1: CTM <Enter>. Contracts can be found by category, exchange, and region. For example, to find the corn contract offered by the CBT, use the CBT Exchange screen and click "Corn" from the dropdown menu in the "Category" column. Alternatively, click "Categories" and "Commodities" and then type the name of the exchange (e.g., CBT) in the amber Exchange box and find the contract of interest.

Uploading a Futures Contract
To upload a futures contract's menu screen enter: Ticker <Comdty> (e.g., C A <Comdty> for the CBT's corn futures contract menu), and then use the Expiration screen (EXS) on the contract's menu page to find the ticker for the contract with the expiration month you want to analyze: Ticker <Comdty> (e.g., C H7 <Comdty> for the March 2017 contract). View screens to examine:

- CT: Contract Table
- EXS: Expiration Schedule
- GP: Price Graph
- GIP: Intraday Graph
- COSY: Commodity Studies

SECF for Finding and Uploading Futures, Forward, and Spot Contracts
The SECF screen can be used to find the tickers for a select commodity's futures, forward, and spot contracts: SECF <Enter>; select "Commodities" from the Category dropdown, select type from the tabs (e.g., Agriculture), select subtype from "Category" dropdown (e.g., corn), select type of contract from the "Instrument" dropdown (e.g., futures, forward, and spot. To upload the menu screens, enter: Ticker <Comdty> or <Index> (e.g., CORNILNC <Index> for North Central Illinois No. 2 Corn Spot Prices.
    The menu includes:

- Des: Description
- GP: Price Graph

- GIP: Intraday Graph
- COSY: Commodity Studies

COST OF CARRY

Grain Cash and Carry Analysis (GRCC)

The GRCC screen can be used to search for the best grain prices. The screen monitors real-time prices from over 10,000 US grain elevators (combined with road networks and trucking rates) to pinpoint cheapest-to-deliver grain prices within a certain radius. You can also compare spot and forward delivery prices when buying from a specific grain elevator. See Exhibit 1.18.

Commodity Price Forecast (CPFC)

CPFC allows you to compare price forecasts for major commodity products, such as crude oil, natural gas, and metals. The screen displays analysts' estimates. CPFC also allows you to compare forecasts against the current forwards.

BLOOMBERG CHARTS AND ANNOTATIONS TOOLS

Charts Homepage: Chart <Enter>

The chart homepage has five box areas: Custom charts, sample charts, new charting analytics, chart resources, and chart of the day newswire (See Exhibit 1.19).

EXHIBIT 1.19 Bloomberg Custom Chart Screen

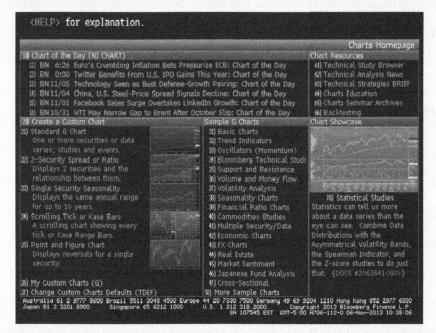

(Continued)

Custom Chart (G <Enter>)

On the Custom Chart screen, you can create and customize charts representing different relationships, showing various technical studies. Charts created on other screens, such as GP, can also be saved to the Custom Chart screen by clicking the "Save as" tab on that screen. To create a new chart, click "Create Chart" tab and then select type. On the graph screens, you can edit the graph by going to the "Edit" dropdown tab. From the "Edit" dropdown, you can place graphs in separate panels (Securities and Data) and change colors and lines (Chart Colors and Lines).

Annotations

Lines, regression lines, bands, and other drawings can be included on a graph by clicking the "Annotate" button on the gray toolbar at the top of the price chart. Clicking the button will bring up an annotations palette showing all of the tools for drawing on the chart, editing, and deleting.

News: Also on the gray toolbar is the "News" button. Clicking this button will bring up an orange vertical bar. You can move the bar to a date of interest and then click to bring up a news box of stories related to your loaded security or index.

Selected References

Arrow, K. "Futures Markets: Some Theoretical Perspectives." *Journal of Futures Markets* 1 (Summer 1981): 107–116.

Cao, M., and Wei, J. "Weather Derivatives: Valuation and the Market Price on Weather Derivatives." *Journal of Futures Markets* 21, 11 (November 2004): 1065–1089.

Carlton, D. "Futures Markets: Their Purpose, Their History, Their Growth, Their Successes and Failures." *Journal of Futures Markets* 4 (1984): 237–271.

Hardy, C. *Risk and Risk Bearing*. Chicago: University of Chicago Press, 1940, 67–69.

Hardy, C., and Lyon, L. "The Theory of Hedging." *Journal of Political Economy*, 31 (1923): 271–287.

Johnson, R. S. *Introduction to Derivatives: Options, Futures, and Swaps*. New York: Oxford University Press, 2009, Chapter 10.

Problems and Questions

1. Explain the differences between forward, futures, and options contracts.
2. Define and explain the functions provided by futures exchanges.
3. Explain how the clearinghouse would record the following:
   a. Mr. A buys a September wheat futures contract from Ms. B for $4.00/bu. on July 20.
   b. Mr. D buys a September wheat futures contract from Mr. E for $3.95 on July 25.
   c. Ms. B buys a September wheat futures contract from Mr. D for $4.01 on July 30.
   d. Mr. E buys a September wheat futures contract from Mr. A for $4.06 on August 3.

   Show the clearinghouse's payments and receipts needed to close each position.
4. Explain why the price on an expiring futures contract must be equal or approximately equal to the spot price on the contract's underlying asset.

5. Suppose on March 1 you take a long position in a June crude oil futures contract at $50/barrel (contract size = 1,000 barrels).

   a. How much cash or risk-free securities would you have to deposit to satisfy an initial margin requirement of 5%?

   b. Calculate the values of your commodity account on the following days, given the following settlement prices:

3/2	$50.50
3/3	50.75
3/4	50.25
3/5	49.50
3/8	49.00
3/9	50.00

   c. If the maintenance margin requirement specifies keeping the value of the commodity account equal to 100% of the initial margin requirement each day, how much cash would you need to deposit in your commodity account each day?

6. What is the major economic justification of the futures market?

7. Ms. Hunter is the chief financial officer for Atlanta Developers. In January, she estimates that the company will need to purchase 300,000 square feet of plywood in June to meet its material needs on one of its office construction jobs.

   a. Suppose there is a June plywood contract trading at $f_0 = \$0.20$/sq. ft. (contract size is 5,000 square feet). Explain how Ms. Hunter could hedge the company's June plywood costs with a position in the June plywood contract.

   b. Show in a table Ms. Hunter's net costs at the futures' expiration date of buying plywood on the spot market at possible spot prices of 0.18/sq. ft., 0.20/sq. ft., 0.22/sq. ft., and 0.24/sq. ft. and closing the futures position. Assume no quality, quantity, and timing risk.

   c. Define the three types of hedging risk and give an example of each in the context of this problem.

   d. How much cash or risk-free securities would Ms. Hunter have to deposit to satisfy an initial margin requirement of 5%?

8. In May, Mr. Smith planted a wheat crop, which he expects to harvest in September. He anticipates the September harvest to be 10,000 bushels and would like to hedge the price he can get for his wheat by taking a position in a September wheat futures contract.

   a. Explain how Mr. Smith could lock in the price he sells his wheat with a September wheat futures contract trading in May at $f_0 = \$4.50$/bu. (contract size of 5,000 bushels).

   b. Show in a table Mr. Smith's revenue at the futures' expiration date from closing the futures position and selling 10,000 bushels of wheat on the spot market at possible spot prices of $4.00/bu., $4.50/bu., and $5.00/bu. Assume no quality, quantity, or timing risk.

   c. Give examples of the three types of hedging risk in the context of problem b.

   d. How much cash or risk-free securities would Mr. Smith have to deposit to satisfy an initial margin requirement of 5%?

9. What spread positions would you form in the following cases:

   a. In July, you expect the spot price of wheat to increase, and September and October wheat futures contracts are available.

   b. The estimated relationship between the price of copper (P_c) and the price of lead (P_L) is $\%\Delta P_c = 0.9(\%\Delta P_L)$. You expect a decrease in the price of metals and futures contracts are available on both metals.

10. Define the basis and its relationship to the time to expiration.

11. Suppose the spot price of a bushel of wheat is $2.00, the annual storage cost is $0.30 per/bushel, the risk-free rate is 8%, and the costs of transporting wheat from the destination point specified on the futures contract to a local grain elevator, or vice versa, is $0.01/bu.

    a. Use the cost-of-carry model to determine the equilibrium price of a September wheat futures contract (expiration of $T = 0.25$).

    b. Explain the arbitrage strategy an arbitrageur would pursue if the September wheat contract is trading at $2.16/bu.

12. Suppose the following conditions are present:

    • The forward price on the March lumber contract is $f_{T1} = \$0.24$/sq. ft.
    • The March forward interest rate on a three-month loan is 8% (annual).
    • The storage costs for lumber is $0.06/sq. ft. per year.
    • The carrying-costs benefits and the costs of transporting lumber are zero (assume there is a storage facility at the location point specified on the lumber forward contract).
    • The time period between the expiration on a June lumber contract and the March contract is $T_2 - T_1 = 0.25$/year.

    a. Using the carrying-cost model, determine the equilibrium price on the June contract.

    b. Explain the arbitrage strategy an arbitrageur would pursue if the June contract were trading at $0.30/sq. ft.

13. What would be the July 1 value of a September forward contract initiated on June 1 to purchase crude oil for $50/barrel on September 1, if the same contract were available on July 1, but with a contract price of $55/barrel? Assume on July 1 there are exactly two months to expiration, the risk-free rate is 6% (annual), and the forward contracts are not marked to market. What arbitrage strategy could the June 1 holder of the September contract employ if the contract price in July is not correctly priced?

14. Briefly comment on the following:

    a. The importance of the delivery procedure on futures contracts, even though most futures contracts are closed by offsetting positions.

    b. The advantages and disadvantages of price limits.

    c. The marked-to-market tax rule on speculative futures positions.

    d. Rolling the hedge.

15. Short-answer questions:

    a. What was the primary factor that contributed to the dramatic growth in the futures trading over the last 30 years?
    b. What is a hedge called in which the asset underlying the futures contract is not the same as the asset being hedged?
    c. A farmer who hedged his expected sale of 7,000 bushels in early September with CBT wheat futures contracts would be subject to what types of hedging risks?
    d. Who ensures that the price on an expiring futures contract is equal or approximately equal to its spot price?
    e. What is the number of futures contracts outstanding at a given point in time called?
    f. How does a futures market provide continuous trading without market makers or specialists?

Bloomberg Exercises

1. Access Bloomberg information on a CBT futures contract on an agriculture commodity such as wheat or corn contracts using the CTM screen: Type CTM to bring up the "Contract Table Menu," click "Categories," select the commodity (such as "Corn," search for CBT on the Menu (type CBT in the amber Exchange box), find the CBT contract of interest, and bring up the contract's menu screen (Ticker <Comdty>; e.g., C A <Comdty> for corn). Then use the Expiration screen (EXS) on the contract's menu page to find the ticker for the contract with the expiation month you want to analyze (Ticker <Comdty>; e.g., C H7 <Comdty> for the March 2017 contract). View screens to examine: DES, GP, and COSY.

2. Access Bloomberg information on a futures contract on energy, such as crude oil, coal, or natural gas contracts, using the CTM screen: Type CTM to bring up the "Contract Table Menu," click "Categories," select the commodity (such as "Crude Oil," search for Exchange (e.g., NYMEX) on the Menu (type NYMEX in the amber Exchange box), find the NYMEX contract of interest, bring up the contract's menu screen (Ticker <Comdty>; e.g., CLA <Comdty> for crude oil), and then use the Expiration screen (EXS) on the contract's menu page to find the ticker for the contract with the expiation month you want to analyze (Ticker <Comdty>; e.g., CLH7 <Comdty> for the March 2017 contract). View screens to examine: DES, GP, and COSY.

3. Use the SECF screen to find the tickers for a select futures contracts and the spot prices related to the contract: SECF <Enter>; select "Commodities" from the "Category" dropdown, select the type of contract from the tabs (e.g., Agriculture), select subtype from "Category" dropdown (e.g., corn), and select type of contract from the "Instrument" dropdown (e.g., futures or spot). To upload the menu screens, enter: Ticker <Comdty> or Ticker <Index> (e.g., C A <Comdty> for corn futures and CORNILNC <Index> for North Central Illinois No. 2 Corn

Spot Prices). On each of the menu screens, analyze some of its screens (e.g., DES and GP).

4. Following the steps similar to the ones identified in Exercises 1 and 3, access Bloomberg information from the CTM or SECF screens and the menu screens for the following types of futures contract:

   a. Precious Metals
   b. Foodstuff
   c. Livestock
   d. Base Metals

5. Using the GP screen, examine the historical prices of the agriculture futures contract you selected in Exercise 1. Select a time period that the contract was active.

   a. Select a period in which you would have taken a long position and calculate the profit from opening and closing at the futures price at the beginning and ending dates for your selected period. Calculate the losses if you had taken a short position.
   b. Select a period in which you would have taken a short position and calculate the profits from opening and closing at the futures price at the beginning and ending dates for your selected period. Calculate the losses if you had taken a long position.
   c. Using the annotation bar, apply the "% Change" tool to calculate the percentage change for your select periods, and then click the "News" icon on the annotation bar to find relevant news events on or preceding the opening date.
   d. Examine the spot index for the period that your futures contract was active. The ticker for the index can be found using SECF. Use the "Chart" screen (Chart <Enter>) to create multigraphs for the prices on the futures contract and the spot price. On the Chart Menu screen, select Standard G chart; once you have loaded your securities, go to "Edit" to put your graphs in separate panels.

6. Using the GP screen, examine the historical prices of the energy futures contract you selected in Exercise 2. Select a time period that the contract was active.

   a. Select a period in which you would have taken a long position and calculate the profit from opening and closing at the futures price at the beginning and ending dates for your selected period. Calculate the losses if you had taken a short position.
   b. Select a period in which you would have taken a short position and calculate the profits from opening and closing at the futures price at the beginning and ending dates for your selected period. Calculate the losses if you had taken a long position.
   c. Using the annotation bar, apply the "% Change" tool to calculate the percentage change for your select periods, and then click the "News" icon on the annotation bar to find relevant news events on or preceding the opening date.
   d. Examine the spot price for the period that your futures contract was active. The ticker for spot prices can be found using SECF. Use the "Chart" screen (Chart <Enter>) to create multigraphs for the prices on the futures contract

and the spot price. On the Chart Menu screen, select Standard G chart; once you have loaded your securities, go to "Edit" to put your graphs in separate panels.

7. Using the GP screen, examine the historical prices of one or more of the contracts you selected in Exercise 4. Select a time period that the contract was active.

   a. Select a period in which you would have taken a long position and calculate the profit from opening and closing at the futures price at the beginning and ending dates for your selected period. Calculate the losses if you had taken a short position.

   b. Select a period in which you would have taken a short position and calculate the profits from opening and closing at the futures price at the beginning and ending dates for your selected period. Calculate the losses if you had taken a long position.

   c. Using the annotation bar, apply the "% Change" tool to calculate the percentage change for your select periods, and then click the "News" icon on the annotation bar to find relevant news events on or preceding the opening date.

   d. Examine the spot price for the period that your futures contract was active. The ticker for spot prices can be found using SECF. Use the "Chart" screen (Chart <Enter>) to create multigraphs for the prices on the futures contract and the spot price. On the Chart Menu screen, select Standard G chart; once you have loaded your securities, go to "Edit" to put your graphs in separate panels.

8. Examine an ex-post long hedging position for a futures commodity purchase.

   a. Select a futures contract and use the expiration date on the futures contract as the date of your purchase.

   b. Use the "Chart" screen (Chart <Enter>) to create multigraphs for the prices on the futures and spot price (use SECF to find the spot prices on the commodity). On the Chart Menu screen, select Standard G chart; once you have loaded your futures and commodity, go to "Edit" to put your graphs in separate panels.

   c. Select a beginning date that you would have implemented your hedge and a closing date near the futures expiration as the date for purchasing the commodity and closing your hedge. Calculate the profit or loss on the futures position from opening and closing at the futures prices at the beginning and ending dates, the cost of purchasing the commodity on the closing date, and the hedged cost (commodity purchase minus futures profit). Compare your hedged cost to the unhedged cost. In retrospect, was the hedge a good strategy?

9. Examine an ex-post short hedging position for a future commodity sale.

   a. Select a futures contract and use the expiration date on the futures as the date of your sale.

   b. Use the "Chart" screen (Chart <Enter>) to create multigraphs for the prices on futures and spot (use SECF to find the spot prices on the commodity). On the Chart Menu screen, select Standard G chart; once you have loaded your futures and commodity, go to "Edit" to put your graphs in separate panels.

    c. Select a beginning date that you would have implemented your hedge and a closing date near the futures expiration as the date for the commodity sale and closing your hedge. Calculate the profit or loss on the futures position from opening and closing at the futures prices at the beginning and ending dates, the revenue from selling the commodity on the closing date, and the hedged revenue (sales revenue plus futures profit). Compare your hedged revenue to the unhedged revenue. In retrospect, was the hedge a good strategy?

10. Using the Bloomberg HRA Regression screen, estimate the relation between two commodities in the same category (e.g., precious metal). Load your selected spot prices (e.g., SLVR <Index> for the silver), and then go to the HRA screen for the regression. On the HRA screen, enter the other commodity as the independent variable in the amber box (e.g., XAU <Index> for gold) and select the time period and periodicity (e.g., daily).

    a. Comment on the regression results and the relation (beta).

    b. Explain how you would form a bullish and bearish intercommodity spreads with the futures contracts on the underlying commodities.

11. Using the Chart screen (Chart <Enter>), examine the intercommodity spread you identified in Exercise 10. Note than the contracts have to have the same expiration and may need to be adjusted for possible differences in the size of their contracts.

    a. Use the "Chart" screen (Chart <Enter>) to create multigraphs for the futures contracts. On the Chart Menu screen, select Standard G chart; once you have loaded your securities, go to "Edit" to put your graphs in separate panels.

    b. Select a period in which you would have taken a bullish spread position and calculate the profit you would have realized from opening and closing at the futures prices at the beginning and ending dates for your selected period. Calculate the losses if you had taken a bearish intercommodity position.

    c. Select a period in which you would have taken a bearish spread position and calculate the profit you would have realized from opening and closing at the futures prices at the beginning and ending dates for your selected period. Calculate the losses if you had taken a bullish position.

    d. Using the annotation bar, apply the "% Change" tool to calculate the percentage change for your select periods, and then click the "News" icon on the annotation bar to find relevant news events on or preceding the opening date.

12. Examine the cost of carrying corn or soybeans for different periods using Bloomberg's Grain Cash and Carry Analysis (GRCC) screen.

CHAPTER 2

Currency Futures and Forward Contracts

Foreign currency futures contracts were introduced in 1972 by the CME. Today, the CME is the largest foreign currency futures exchange. The contracts on the CME call for the delivery (or purchase) of a specified amount of foreign currency at the delivery date. Exhibit 2.1 lists many of the currency futures contracts traded on the CME and Exhibit 2.2 shows Bloomberg Description and Price screens for the CME's December 2016 British pound (BP) futures contract. The futures contract price on the British pound (BPA <Curncy>) is quoted in cents, and the size of the contract calls for the purchase or delivery of 62,500 BPs. The delivery date on the December contract is 12/21/16, and on 7/14/16 the futures prices was ¢133.70/BP.

Forward contracts on foreign currencies are provided in the Interbank Foreign Exchange Market. As noted in Chapter 1, this OTC market consists primarily of major banks that provide tailor-made forward contracts to their clients, which often are large multinational corporations and institutions. Exhibit 2.3 shows a three-month British pound forward rates description and price graphs (GBP3M <Curncy>) and Exhibit 2.4 shows the bid quotes as of 7/14/16 on three-month, six-month, and one-year forward contracts for 10 major currencies.

Currency futures and OTC forward contracts provide investors, businesses, and other economic entities a tool for hedging and speculating on currency positions. Long currency hedge positions are used to lock in the future costs of purchasing currency, while short hedges are used to lock in the price on the future sale of a currency.

EXHIBIT 2.1   Currency Futures Contracts Listed on the CME

Chicago Mercantile Exchange, CME: Currency Ticker	Description	Options	Volume 7/14/2016	Open Interest 7/14/2016
ADA Curncy	AUD/USD Future	Yes	94,129	88,594
BPA Curncy	GBP/USD Future	Yes	134,116	237,330
BRA Curncy	BRL/USD Future	Yes	517	26,871
CDA Curncy	CAD/USD Future	Yes	93,463	116,287
CRDA Curncy	E-Micro, AUD/USD	No	8,173	1,847
CREA Curncy	E-Micro, EUR/USD	No	14,466	4,062
CRPA Curncy	E-Micro, GBP/USD	No	5,096	2,575
DOA Curncy	CNY/USD Fut Chinese Yuan	Yes	3	358
ECA Curncy	EUR/USD Future	Yes	129,021	370,525
EEA Curncy	EUR/USD Emini Future	No	3,978	4,398
JEA Curncy	JPY/USD E-Mini Future	No	1,219	1,422
JYA Curncy	JPY/USD Future	Yes	144,023	160,831
MCDA Curncy	E-Micro, CAD/USD	No	1,416	845
MIRA Curncy	E-Micro, INR/USD	No	73	217
MJYA Curncy	E-Micro, JPY/USD	No	1,906	1,297
MSSA Curncy	E-Micro, CHF/USD	No	33	207
NOA Curncy	NOK/USD Future	No	25	820
NVA Curncy	NZD/USD Future	Yes	19,755	43,786
OSA Curncy	CHF/USD AON Future	Yes	18,271	39,946
PEA Curncy	MXN/USD Future	Yes	36,431	97,964
SFA Curncy	CHF/USD Future	Yes	18,271	39,946

Currency futures and forward contracts are also used to speculate on expected price changes. An outright long currency futures position is taken when the price of the currency is expected to rise and a short outright position is taken when the price is expected to fall. Speculators can also form intracommodity and intercommodity spreads to obtain different return-risk exposure for their speculative positions. Finally, like commodities, currency futures and forward prices are governed by the cost of carrying the underlying asset.

In Chapter 1, our hedging, speculation, and arbitrage examples were with commodity futures, such as crude oil, corn, coffee, and precious metals. In this chapter, we extend our analysis of hedging, speculation, and arbitrage to currency futures and forward contracts—the first financial futures contract.

Hedging with Foreign Currency Futures and Forward Contracts

With foreign currency futures and forward contracts, the domestic currency value of future cash flows or the future dollar value of assets and liabilities denominated in another currency can be hedged. Large multinational corporations usually hedge their currency positions in the interbank forward market, while smaller companies, some portfolio managers, and individuals typically use the organized futures markets.

EXHIBIT 2.2   CME December British Pound Futures Contract Bloomberg Description and Price Screens, BPZ6 <Curncy>

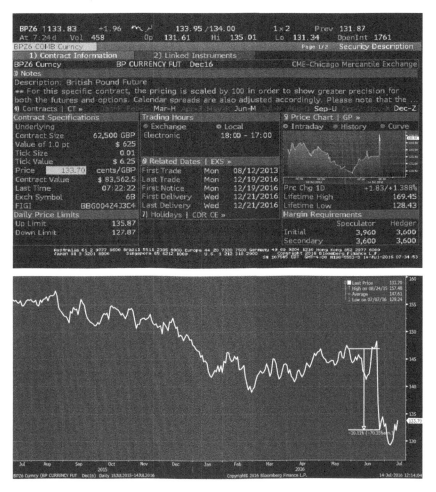

In either case, the currency position usually is hedged with a naive hedging model in which the number of futures and forward contracts is equal to the value of the foreign currency position to be hedged.

Short Hedge

To illustrate currency hedging, consider the case of a US investment fund expecting a payment of £10,000,000 in principal on its Eurobonds next September. Suppose the US fund is concerned about a \$/BP exchange rate (E_t) decrease and decides to hedge its September BP receipt with a BP forward contract. In this case, the fund would enter an agreement to sell £10,000,000 with a dealer (such as a bank) in the interbank dealer's market on a specified September delivery date at a forward price of, say, $f_0 = \$1.50/\text{BP}$. The fund would have a short position in which it agrees to sell and

EXHIBIT 2.3 Three-Month British Pound Forward Rates Bloomberg Description and Price Screens, GBP3M <Curncy>

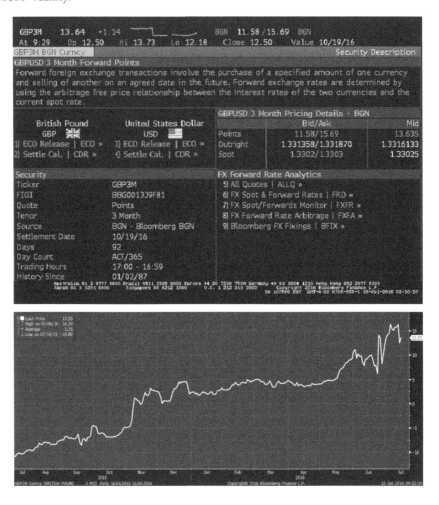

EXHIBIT 2.4 Forward Rates, 7/14/2016

Currency	Spot 7/14/2016	3-Month Forward 07/14/2016 10/18/2016	6-Month Forward 07/14/2016 01/18/2017	1-Year Forward 07/15/2016 07/18/2017
EURUSD	1.1112	1.115048	1.119592	1.12858
USDJPY	105.65	105.3086	104.8546	103.9465
AUDUSD	0.763	0.760698	0.75844	0.75457
GBPUSD	1.3295	1.330872	1.332743	1.336913
USDCAD	1.2933	1.293282	1.29311	1.29231
USDDKK	6.6943	6.67071	6.642758	6.583762
NZDUSD	0.7185	0.71549	0.712569	0.707507
USDNOK	8.3786	8.37893	8.377055	8.364083
USDSEK	8.4978	8.464869	8.427289	8.362952
USDCHF	0.9816	0.976974	0.971736	0.96137

the dealer would have a long position in which she agrees to buy. On the September delivery date, the fund would receive its £10,000,000 principal from its Eurobonds, which it would then sell on its forward contract to the dealer at $f_0 = \$1.50/BP$ for $15,000,000. If the spot exchange rate at the September delivery date were less than $f_0 = \$1.50/BP$, then the fund would be pleased that it used the forward contract to lock in its $15,000,000 receipt instead of converting on the spot. However, if the spot exchange rate at the September delivery date were greater than $f_0 = \$1.50/BP$, then the fund would be disappointed that it used the forward contract to lock in its $15,000,000 receipt instead of converting its £10,000,000 on the spot at a higher $/BP exchange rate.

Instead of a forward hedge, the fund could alternatively hedge with a futures contract. Suppose September BP futures on the CME are trading at $f_0 = \$1.50/BP$. Since the contract size on the BP futures contract is 62,500 BP, the fund would need to go short in 160 BP contracts: $n_f = £10,000,000/£62,500 = 160$ BP contracts. At expiration, the fund would find it easier and less expensive in terms of commission costs to sell its £10,000,000 on the spot market at the spot exchange rate, and then close its futures position by going long in an expiring September BP futures contract at an expiring future price equal (or approximately equal) to the spot exchange rate $(f_T = E_T)$. Given that the spot and expiring futures prices are equal (or approximately equal), the fund would find that any less dollar revenue resulting from the spot rate being less than $1.50/BP would be offset by a profit from its futures position. On the other hand, any greater dollar revenue from the spot exchange rate exceeding $1.50 would be negated by losses on the fund's futures position. As a result, the fund's dollar revenue of selling £10,000,000 on the spot and closing its 160 BP futures contracts would be $15,000,000.

This futures hedge can be seen in Exhibit 2.5. In the exhibit, the first row shows three possible spot exchange rates of $1.40, $1.50, and $1.60, the second row shows revenues from selling £10,000,000 on the spot exchange market, the third

EXHIBIT 2.5   Short Hedge Example

Initial Position:

Short in 160 September BP futures contracts (Size = 62,500 BP) at $1.50/BP to hedge conversion of £10,000,000 to dollars in September.

Delivery:

- Close BP futures contracts by going long in 160 expiring September futures at $f_T = E_T$.
- Sell £10,000,000 on the spot market at spot exchange rate E_T.

Positions	Hedged Revenue		
(1) $f_T = E_T$	$1.40/BP	$1.50/BP	$1.60/BP
(2) $ Revenue: E_T (£10,000,000)	$14,000,000	$15,000,000	$16,000,000
(3) Profit from Futures	$1,000,000	0	−$1,000,000
(4) Net Revenue = Row (2) + (3)	$15,000,000	$15,000,000	$15,000,000

Profit from Futures = $(160)(62{,}500 \text{ BP})(\$1.50/\text{BP} - f_T)$

row shows the profits and losses from the futures position, and the fourth row shows the constant hedged revenue of $15,000,000 from aggregating both positions. If $E_T = \$1.40/BP$, the fund receives $14,000,000 from selling £10,000,000 at $1.40/BP, but receives $1,000,000 profit from its futures position; that is, the agreement to sell £10,000,000 (= (160)(62,500 BP)) September BPs for $1.50 is closed with an agreement to buy £10,000,000 (= (160)(62,500 BP)) September BPs for $1.40/BP, resulting in a $1,000,000 receipt from the clearinghouse. On the other hand, if $E_T = \$1.60/BP$, the fund receives $16,000,000 from selling its £10,000,000 at the spot rate of $1.60/BP, but it has to pay the clearinghouse $1,000,000 to close the futures position; that is, the agreement to sell £10,000,000 (= (160)(62,500 BP)) September BPs for $1.50 is closed with an agreement to buy £10,000,000 (= (160)(62,500 BP)) September BP for $1.60/BP, resulting in a $1,000,000 payment to the clearinghouse. Thus, regardless of the spot exchange rate at the September expiration date, the fund receives $15,000,000.

Long Hedge

If a US economic entity has a future debt obligation or payment that it is required to pay in foreign currency, then it could hedge the dollar cost by taking a long currency futures or forward contract. To illustrate this hedge, consider a US company that owed £10,000,000, with the payment to be made in September. If the company believed that $/BP, exchange rate were more likely to increase, it could lock in the dollar cost of buying £10,000,000 by going long in a forward contract. In this case, the company would enter an agreement to buy £10,000,000 with a dealer in the interbank dealer's market on a specified September delivery date at a forward price of, say, $f_0 = \$1.50/BP$. The company would have a long position with an agreement to buy and the dealer would have a short position with an agreement to sell. On the September delivery date, the fund would buy £10,000,000 on its forward contract from the dealer at $f_0 = \$1.50/BP$ for $15,000,000 and then pay its £10,000,000 obligation. If the spot exchange rate at the September delivery date were greater than $f_0 = \$1.50/BP$, then the company would be pleased that it used the forward contract to lock in its $15,000,000 cost instead of buying BP on the spot. However, if the spot exchange rate at the September delivery date were less than $f_0 = \$1.50/BP$, then the company would be disappointed that it used the forward contract to lock in its $15,000,000 cost instead of buying the BP on the spot at the $/BP exchange rate.

Alternatively, the company could hedge the September dollar cost of buying £10,000,000 by going long in a September BP futures contract. Again, suppose September BP futures on the CME are trading at $f_0 = \$1.50/£$. To hedge its dollar cost, the company would need to go long in 160 BP contracts: $n_f = £10,000,000/62,500$ BP = 160 BP contracts. Doing this, the company would, in turn, ensure itself of a $15,000,000 cost at the futures September expiration when it purchased the £10,000,000 at the spot $/BP exchange rate and closed its long futures contracts at futures prices equal to the spot exchange rate. This futures hedge can be seen in Exhibit 2.6. In the exhibit, the first row shows three possible spot exchange rates of

EXHIBIT 2.6   Long Currency Hedge Example

Initial Position:

Long in 160 September BP futures contracts (size = 62,500 BP) at $1.50/BP to hedge dollar purchase of £10,000,000 in September.

At Delivery:

- Close BP futures contracts by going short in 160 expiring September BP futures at $f_T = E_T$.
- Buy £10,000,000 on the spot market at spot exchange rate E_T.

Positions		Hedged Cost	
(1) $f_T = E_T$	$1.40/BP	$1.50/BP	$1.60/BP
(2) $ Cost: E_T (£10,000,000)	$14,000,000	$15,000,000	$16,000,000
(3) Profit from Futures	− $1,000,000	0	$1,000,000
(4) Net Revenue = Row (2) − (3)	$15,000,000	$15,000,000	$15,000,000

Profit from Futures = (160)(62,500 BP)(f_T − $1.50)

$1.40, $1.50, and $1.60, the second row shows the dollar cost of buying £10,000,000 at the spot exchange rate of E_T, the third row shows the profits and losses from the futures position, and the fourth row shows the constant hedged cost of $15,000,000 from the positions. If $E_T = $1.40/BP, the company pays only $14,000,000 for £10,000,000, but would have to pay $1,000,000 on its futures position; that is, the agreement to buy £10,000,000 (= (160)(62,500 BP)) September BPs at $1.50 is closed with an agreement to sell £10,000,000 (= (160)(62,500 BP)) of September BPs for $1.40/BP, resulting in a $1,000,000 payment to the clearinghouse. On the other hand, if $E_T = $1.60/BP, the fund pays $16,000,000 for £10,000,000, but it would receive $1,000,000 on its futures position; that is, the agreement to buy £10,000,000 (= (160)(62,500 BP)) September BPs for $1.50 is closed with an agreement to sell £10,000,000 (= (160)(62,500 BP)) September BPs for $1.60/BP, resulting in $1,000,000 in receipts from the clearinghouse. Thus, regardless of the spot exchange rate at the September expiration date, the fund pays $15,000,000.

Hedging Risk

These examples represent perfect hedging cases in which certain revenues or costs can be locked in at a future date. In practice, perfect hedges are the exception and not the rule. As noted in Chapter 1, there are three types of hedging risk that preclude one from obtaining a zero risk position: *quality risk, timing risk,* and *quantity risk.*

Quality risk exists when the commodity or asset being hedged is not identical to the one underlying the futures contract. In hedging currency positions, there is usually no quality risk, but there can be timing and quantity risk. Timing risk would exist in our previous hedging cases if the manager or company needed to sell or buy BPs at a time different from the futures expiration. As noted in Chapter 1, the difference between the futures and spot price is called the basis (B_t). The basis tends to narrow as expiration nears, converging to zero at expiration ($B_T = 0$).

Hedging International Investments

Portfolio managers often use currency futures and forward contracts to immunize their international portfolios against exchange rate risk. For example, suppose a US institutional investment fund that owned 10,000 shares of a French stock currently worth 100 euros per share wanted to hedge the dollar value of its investment. Suppose the \$/€ spot and three-month CME futures exchange rates are both \$1.20/€ (or €0.8333/\$), making the current dollar value of the stock worth \$1,200,000 (= (\$1.20/€)(10,000)(€100)). If the fund wanted to hedge the dollar value of its stock at the end of three months against exchange rate risk, it would need to go short in eight euro futures contracts (contract size is 125,000 euros):

$$n_f = \frac{\$1,200,000}{(\$1.20/\text{euro})(125,000 \text{ euros})} = 8 \text{ short euros futures contracts}$$

If, at the end of three months, there is no change in the price of the French stock, then the futures-hedged dollar value of the stock would be \$1,200,000, irrespective of the spot \$/€ exchange rate. If the \$/€ decreased by 10% over the period from \$1.20/€ to \$1.08, then the dollar value of the stock also would decrease by 10% from \$1,200,000 to \$1,080,000; this decrease, though, would be offset by a \$120,000 profit from the futures position: 8[125,000 euros][\$1.20/€ − \$1.08/€] = \$120,000.

Hedging with currency futures or forward contracts allows international investors to focus on selecting stocks or portfolios, without having to worry about changes in the exchange rate. For instance, in the above example, if the price of the French stock increased by 5% from €100 to €105 at the same time the dollar appreciated by 10% against the euro, then an unhedged position would lose 5.5% in dollars:

$$\text{Rate} = \frac{(\$1.08/\text{euros})(105 \text{ euros})(10,000)}{\$1,200,000} - 1$$

$$\text{Rate} = -.055$$

If the position is hedged with eight euro futures contracts, though, the fund would receive a \$120,000 futures profit and the rate of return on the currency-hedged investment would be 4.5%:

$$\text{Rate} = \frac{(\$1.08/\text{euros})(105 \text{ euros})(10,000) + \$120,000}{\$1,200,000} - 1$$

$$\text{Rate} = .045$$

Thus, the futures hedge allows the investor to profit from good stock selection.

It should be noted that the rate of return in dollars earned from the currency-hedged stock in the previous example is less than the 5% increase in the stock price. This is because the hedge that was set up protects only the initial value; dividends and stock appreciation were not hedged against exchange rate risk. To also hedge stock price changes against exchange rate changes would require knowing the correlation between the changes in the exchange rate changes and the stock price.

Speculating with Foreign Currency Futures and Forward Contracts

Currency futures and forward contracts are used for speculating on expected changes in the spot exchange rate. In using currency futures or forward contracts, speculators can take either outright positions or intracommodity or intercommodity spreads with different currency futures.

Outright Positions

A speculator expecting an increase in the spot dollar price of a currency (\$/FC) could take a long currency futures or forward contract. For example a US dollar investor who in June believed that the \$/BP exchange rate would increase by September could go long in a September BP forward contract. Suppose the speculator entered an agreement to buy £10,000,000 from a dealer in the interbank market on a specified September delivery date at a forward price of, say, $f_0 = \$1.50/BP$. The speculator would have a long position with an agreement to buy and the dealer would have a short position with an agreement to sell. On the September delivery date, the speculator would buy £10,000,000 on her forward contract from the dealer at $f_0 = \$1.50/BP$ for \$15,000,000 and then sell the £10,000,000 on the spot market. If the speculator's expectations were correct and the spot \$/BP had increased to, say, \$1.60/BP, then the speculator would realize a profit of \$1,000,000 when she sold her £10,000,000 on the spot for \$16,000,000. On the other hand, if her expectations were wrong and the spot \$/BP had decreased to, say, \$1.40/BP, then the speculator would realize a loss of \$1,000,000 when she sold her £10,000,000 on the spot for \$14,000,000.

A speculator expecting a decrease in the spot dollar price of a currency (\$/FC) could take a short currency futures or forward contract. For example, if the US dollar investor in the preceding example believed in June that the \$/BP exchange rate would decrease by September, she would go short in the BP forward contract, entering an agreement to buy £10,000,000 from a dealer in the interbank market on a specified September delivery date at a forward price of, say, $f_0 = \$1.50/BP$. On the September delivery date, the speculator would buy £10,000,000 on the spot market and sell the British pound on her forward contract to the dealer (at $f_0 = \$1.50/BP$) for \$15,000,000. If the speculator's expectations were correct and the spot \$/BP had decreased to, say, \$1.40/BP, then the speculator would realize a profit of \$1,000,000 when she bought her £10,000,000 on the spot for \$14,000,000 and sold them on the futures for \$15,000,000. On the other hand, if her expectations were wrong and the spot \$/BP had increased to, say, \$1.60/BP, then the speculator would realize a loss of \$1,000,000 when she bought her £10,000,000 on the spot for \$16,000,000 and sold them on the forward for \$15,000,000.

Alternatively, the speculator could take a position in a September BP futures contract listed on the CME. If she were bullish, she would go long in 160 BP contracts: $n_f = £10,000,000/£62,500 = 160$ BP contracts at, say, at $f_0 = \$1.50/BP$. At the futures September expiration she would close her long futures contracts at a

EXHIBIT 2.7 Long Speculative Currency Position

Initial Position:

Long in 160 September BP futures contracts (size = 62,500 BP) at $1.50/BP

At Delivery:

Close BP futures contracts by going short in 160 expiring September BP futures at $f_T = E_T$.

Positions	Speculative Position		
(1) $f_T = E_T$	$1.40/BP	$1.50/BP	$1.60/BP
(2) Profit from Futures (160)(62,500 BP) (((f_T − $1.50))	− $1,000,000	0	$1,000,000

futures price equal (or approximately equal) to the spot exchange rate. This long speculative position is shown in Exhibit 2.7. In the exhibit, the first row shows three possible spot exchange rates of $1.40, $1.50, and $1.60 and the second row shows the profits and losses from the futures position. Thus, if the spot exchange rate equaled $E_T = \$1.40/BP$, our hedger would have to pay $1,000,000 to the clearinghouse; that is, the agreement to buy £10,000,000 (= (160)(62,500 BP)) September BPs at $1.50 is closed with an agreement to sell £10,000,000 (= (160)(62,500 BP)) September BPs for $1.40/BP, resulting in a $1,000,000 payment to the clearinghouse. On the other hand, if $E_T = \$1.60/BP$, our hedger would receive $1,000,000 on her futures position; that is, the agreement to buy £10,000,000 (= (160)(62,500 BP)) September BPs for $1.50 is closed with an agreement to sell £10,000,000 (= (160)(62,500 BP)) September BPs for $1.60/BP, resulting in a $1,000,000 receipt from the clearinghouse.

If the speculator were bearish, she would go short in 160 BP contracts: $n_f =$ £10,000,000/£62,500 = 160 BP contracts at, say, at $f_0 = \$1.50/BP$. At the futures September expiration, she would close her short futures contracts at a futures price equal (or approximately equal) to the spot exchange rate. This short speculative position is shown in Exhibit 2.8, which shows three possible spot exchange rates of

EXHIBIT 2.8 Short Speculative Position

Initial Position:

Short in 160 September BP futures contracts (size = 62,500 BP) at $1.50/BP

At Delivery:

Close BP futures contract by going long in 160 expiring September BP futures at $f_T = E_T$

Positions	Speculative Position		
(1) $f_T = E_T$	$1.40/BP	$1.50/BP	$1.60/BP
(2) Profit from Futures: (160) (62,500 BP)(($1.50 − f_T)	$1,000,000	0	−$1,000,000

$1.40, $1.50, and $1.60 and their corresponding profits and losses from the futures positions. In this case, if $E_T = \$1.40/BP$, the hedger would receive $1,000,000 from the clearinghouse; that is, the agreement to sell £10,000,000 September BPs at $1.50 is closed with an agreement to buy £10,000,000 September BPs for $1.40/BP, resulting in a $1,000,000 receipt from the clearinghouse. On the other hand, if $E_T = \$1.60/BP$, she would pay $1,000,000 on her futures position; that is, the agreement to sell £10,000,000 September BPs for $1.50/BP is closed with an agreement to buy £10,000,000 September BPs for $1.60/BP, resulting in a $1,000,000 payment to the clearinghouse.

Case: Speculating on the BP with Futures

Suppose on 5/26/2016, a dollar currency speculator expecting Britain to vote in favor of staying in the European Union took a long position in one December 2016 BP contract at $1.4688 (146.88 cents). The contract would require the speculator to buy 62,500 BP on 12/21/16 (see Bloomberg Description page and price graph in Exhibit 2.2). On the other hand, suppose another currency speculator expected Britain to vote to exit the EU and took a short position on 5/26/2016 in the December BP contract. The contract would require the speculator to deliver 62,500 BP for $1.4688 on 12/21/16. On 6/23/16, Britain voted to leave the EU and on 6/27/16 the December futures price had decreased to $1.3203/BP. If both the long and short speculators closed their outright position on 6/23/16, the long speculator would have incurred a loss of $9,281.25 from her long December British pound contract, while the short speculator would have realized a profit of $9,281.25 (see Exhibit 2.9).

EXHIBIT 2.9 Speculative Positions on December 2016 BP Futures, 5/26/16 to 6/27/16

	Clearinghouse Records for Long BP Speculator
5/26/16	Speculator agrees to buy 62,500 BP in December for $1.4688/BP
6/27/16	Speculator agrees to sell 62,500 BP in March at $1.3203
Close	Speculators pays clearinghouse $9,281.25
	Closing payment to clearinghouse:
	62,500 BP ($1.3203/BP − $1.4688/BP) = −$9,281.25
	Clearinghouse Records for Short BP Speculator
5/26/16	Speculator agrees to sell 62,500 BP in March for $1.4688/BP
6/27/16	Speculator agrees to buy 62,500 BP in March for $1.3203/BP
Close	Clearinghouse pays short speculator $9,281.25
	Closing Receipt from clearinghouse:
	62,500 BP ($1.4688/BP − $1.3201/BP) = $9,281.25

Currency Futures Spreads

Instead of assuming the risk inherent in an outright futures position, speculators could reduce their exchange rate risk by forming intracommodity or intercommodity currency spreads. A US speculator who expects the $/BP exchange rate to change, for example, could form an intracommodity spread by taking a position in a nearby BP currency futures or forward contract and an opposite position in more deferred BP currency futures or forward contract. A speculator also could form an intercommodity spread by going long and short in different currency futures or forward contracts. For example, if a speculator expects the dollar price of both the euro and British pound to increase, she could form an intercommodity spread by going long in the currency with the greater exchange rate elasticity and short in the other currency.

Intracommodity Spread

As noted in Chapter 1, more distant futures contracts (T_2) are generally more price sensitive to changes in the spot price, S, than near-term futures contracts (T_1):

$$\frac{\%\Delta f_{T_2}}{\%\Delta S} > \frac{\%\Delta f_{T_1}}{\%\Delta S}$$

Thus, a speculator who expects the price of a currency to increase in the future could form an intracommodity spread by going long in the longer-term currency futures and short in a shorter-term one. This type of intracommodity spread will be profitable if the expectation of the price increasing occurs. That is, the increase in the spot exchange causes the price on the longer-term currency futures to increase more than the shorter-term one. As a result, a speculator's gains from his long position in the longer-term futures will exceed his losses from his short position. If the spot price falls, though, losses will occur on the long position; these losses will be partially offset by profits realized from the short position on the shorter-term contract. On the other hand, if a speculator believes the spot exchange rate will decrease but did not want to assume the risk inherent in an outright short position, he could form a spread with a short position in a longer-term contract and a long position in the shorter-term one. As we noted in Chapter 1, the speculator does not have to keep the ratio of long-to-short positions 1-to-1, but instead could use any ratio (2-to-1, 3-to-2, etc.) to obtain his desired return-risk combination.

It should be noted that the difference in price sensitivity between shorter-term and longer-term futures prices may be minimal if the futures and spot prices are equal. This can be the case on currency futures when interest rates are equal in each country. Currency futures pricing is examined later in this chapter.

Intercommodity Spread

An intercommodity currency spread is formed with two futures contracts with the same expiration dates but on different currencies. In constructing intercommodity

EXHIBIT 2.10   Regression Relation between British Pound (BP) and Australian Dollar (AUD)

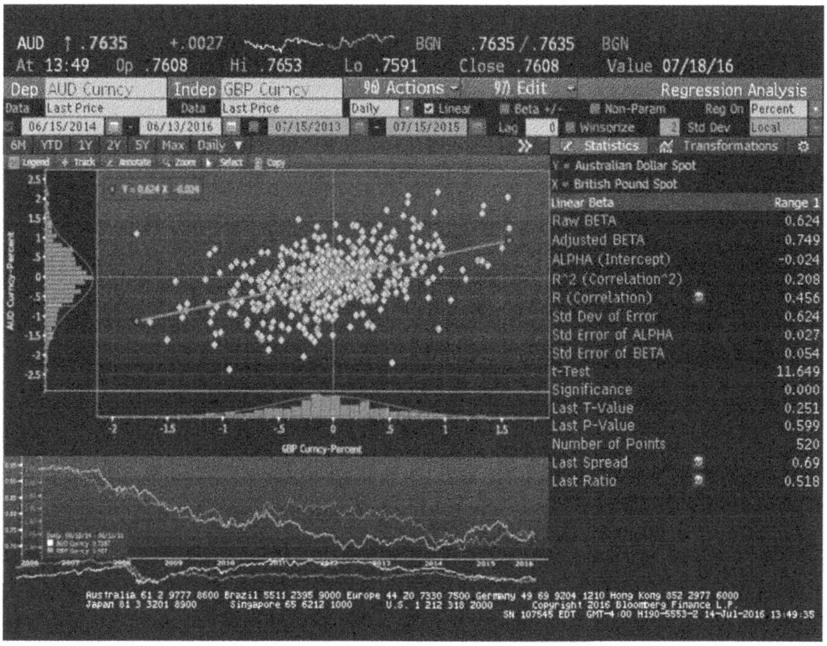

spreads, a spreader often makes use of the correlation between the underlying exchange rates. Exhibit 2.10 shows an estimated regression relation between the US dollar price of the Australian dollar (AUD) and the US dollar price of the British pound (BP). The slope of the regression line is $\Delta AUD/\Delta GBP = 0.749$. A currency speculator expecting the US dollar to depreciate (appreciate) with the US dollar price of the AUD and BP increasing (decreasing) could form an intercommodity spread by going long (short) in BP futures and short (long) in the AUD contract. Exhibit 2.11 shows the prices for a June 2016 AUD and BP futures contracts from 1/4/16 to 6/13/16. Suppose a speculator expecting the dollar to depreciate against some of the major currencies formed an intercommodity spread on 4/7/16 by going short in two June 2016 British pound contracts (contract size = 62,500 British pounds) at $1.4063 and long in one June 2016 AUD contract (contract size = 100,000 AUD) at $0.7485. From 4/7/16 to 4/26/16, the dollar did depreciate against a number of currencies, resulting in a 3.68% increase in the $/BP from $1.4063 to $1.458 and a 3.15% increase in the $/AUD from $0.7485 to $0.7721. If the spreader closed her intercommodity spread on 4/26/16, she would have realized a profit of $6,462.50 on her two long June British pound futures contract and a loss of $2,360 on her one short June AUD futures contract, resulting in a net gain of $4,102.50 (see Exhibit 2.12).

The spreader probably regretted that she did not take an outright long position in the British pound where she would have realized a $6,462.50 gain. Her long position in Australian dollars, however, was taken to give her some protection if the dollar price of the BP and AUD decreased. The spread provides the speculator a lower return opportunity but also lower risk than the outright position. Moreover, as noted in

EXHIBIT 2.11 Prices on June 2016 BP Futures Contracts and June 2016 AUD Futures Contracts, 1/4/16 to 6/13/16

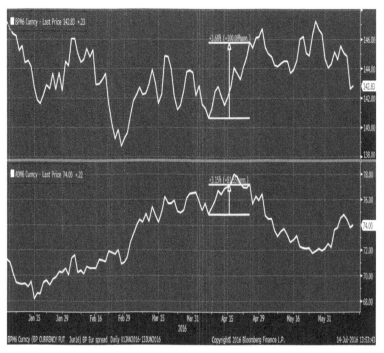

EXHIBIT 2.12 Intercommodity Spread: Long in Two June 2016 BP Futures Contracts and Short in One June AUD Futures Contracts

	Clearinghouse Records for Two Long June 2016 British Pound Futures Position
4/1/16	Opening Position: Long two BP June futures contracts (contract size = 62,500 BP):
	Speculator agrees to buy 125,000 BP on June 13, 2016 for $1.4063/BP.
4/26/16	Closing Position: Short two BP June futures contracts:
	Speculator agrees to sell 125,000 BP on June 13, 2016 for $1.458/BP.
Close	Speculator receives $6,462.50 from the clearinghouse:
	125,000 BP ($1.458/BP − $1.4063/BP) = $6,462.50
	Clearinghouse Records for One Short June 2016 AUD Futures Position
4/1/16	Opening Position: Short one June AUD futures contract (contract size = 100,000 AUD):
	Speculator agrees to sell 100,000 AUD on June 13, 2016, for $0.7485/AUD.
4/26/16	Closing Position: Long one June AUD futures contract:
	Speculator agrees to buy 100,000 AUD on June 13, 2016, for $0.7721/AUD.
	Speculator pays clearinghouse $2,360:
Close	100,000 AUD ($0.7485/AUD − $0.7721/AUD) = −$2,360
	Net Position
4/26/16	$6,462.50 − $2,360 = $4,102.50

Chapter 1, many different spreads, each with different return-risk combinations, can be formed by changing the ratio of long to short positions.

Hedging and Speculating with Equivalent Money Market Positions

Hedging Currency Positions Using the Money Market

Instead of forward or futures contracts, financial and nonfinancial companies can also hedge their positions by using a money market position. For example, the US company in our long hedging example with the September £10,000,000 liability could lock in an effective dollar cost of buying the BP by creating a BP asset worth £10,000,000 in September and a US dollar liability in September. To see this, suppose the company can borrow dollars at 3% and invest BP at 3%, the spot exchange rate is $1.50/£ or £0.6667/$ and the September payment date is one year from the present. To fix its dollar cost, the company would need to borrow $14,563,106.80 (the present value of $15,000,000 = PV($15,000,000) = PV[(£10,000,000)($1.50/BP)] = $15,000,000/1.03), convert at £0.6667/$ to £9,708,737.86, and invest at 3%. One year later, the company would have £10,000,000 (= £9,708,737.86 (1.03)) from its BP investment that it could use to cover its £10,000,000 debt, and it would owe $15,000,000 (=$14,563,106.80 (1.03))—the same dollar obligation it had by hedging with the long futures or forward contracts.

By contrast, the investment fund in our short hedge case with the £10,000,000 September principal receipt could hedge the dollar value of its receipt by creating a £10,000,000 liability and a dollar asset. For example, suppose the trust can invest dollars at 3% and borrow BP at 3%, the spot exchange rate is $1.50/£, and the September receipt date is one year from the present. To fix its dollar revenue, the company would need to borrow £9,708,737.86 (PV(£10,000,000) = (£10,000,000)/1.03), convert to $14,563,106.80 (= ($1.50/£) £9,708,737.86), and invest at 3%. One year later, the company would owe £10,000,000 (= £9,708,737.86 (1.03)) from its BP loan that it would pay with its £10,000,000 Eurobond principal revenue, and it would receive $15,000,000 (= $14,563,106.80 (1.03)) from its dollar investment—the same dollar revenue it had by hedging with the short future contracts.

Money market positions are useful for hedging currency position with long-term horizons that are not possible with futures contracts whose original maturities may only go out two years. For example, in the previous case, a short hedger who wanted to lock in dollar value of converting £10,000,000 in, say, five years, could hedge the currency position by borrowing the present value of £10,000,000 for five years (£10,000,000/$(1.03)^5$ = £8,626,087.84), converting to dollars (($1.50/BP)(£8,626,087.84) = $12,939,131.77), and then investing the dollars for five years. At the end of five years, the BP cash inflow (£10,000,000) would exactly cover the BP debt (£8,626,087.84)$(1.03)^5$ = £10,000,000 and the dollar investment would be worth $15,000,000 (= ($12,939,131.77)$(1.03)^5$). Such five-year hedging again would not be possible with BP futures contracts with maturities only going out two years. It is possible, however, that a hedger could find a dealer in the interbank forward market to offer a tailor-made five-year contract.

Speculating with Equivalent Money Market Positions

Instead of speculating on the spot exchange rate using futures or forward contracts, a speculator can alternatively use the money market. For example, suppose our currency speculator in our previous example expected the $/£ rate to increase in one year from its current $1.50/£ level (or £0.6667/$), and he could borrow dollars at 3% and invest BP at 3%. To speculate on a $/£ exchange rate increase, the speculator could borrow $14,563,106.80, the present value of $15,000,000 (PV($15,000,000) = $15,000,000/1.03), convert at 0.6667£/$ to £9,708,737.86 and invest the BPs at 3%. One year later, the speculator would have a £10,000,000 investment (= £9,708,737.86 (1.03)) and $15,000,000 debt (= $14,563,106.80 (1.03)). If the spot $/BP rate increased from $1.50 to, say, $1.60/BP, then the speculator would gain $1,000,000 when he converts his £10,000,000 at $1.60/£ to $16,000,000 and pays his $15,000,000 debt. However, if the spot rate decreased from $1.50 to, say, $1.40/BP, then the speculator would lose $1,000,000 when he converts his £10,000,000 at $1.40/£ to $14,000,000 and pays his $15,000,000 debt (see Exhibit 2.13). This is the same profits and loss scenarios that he would have realized by speculating with long positions in futures and forward contracts.

Suppose our currency speculator expected the $/£ rate to decrease in one year from its current $1.50/£ level (or £0.6667/$), and he could borrow BP at 3% and

EXHIBIT 2.13 Long Speculative Position Using Money Market

- Borrowing and Lending Rate on US dollars = 3%
- Borrowing and Lending Rate on BP = 3%
- Current spot exchange rate = $1.50/£ or 0.6667£/$

Initial Position:
- Borrow $14,563,106.80, present value of $15,000,000 (PV($15,000,000) = (£10,000,000) ($1.50/BP)/1.03)
- Convert at 0.6667£/$ to £9,708,737.86 and invest the BPs at 3%

Closing Position one year later:
- BP Investment: £10,000,000 (= £9,708,737.86 (1.03))
- Dollar Liability: $15,000,000 (=$14,563,106.80 (1.03))
- Convert £10,000,000 to dollars at spot E_T = $/BP and pay $15,000,000 debt

Positions	Speculative Position		
(1) $f_T = E_T$	$1.40/BP	$1.50/BP	$1.60/BP
(2) BP Investment	£10,000,000	£10,000,000	£10,000,000
(3) Conversion: (£10,000,00)(E_T)	$14,000,000	$15,000,000	$16,000,000
(4) $ Debt	$15,000,000	$15,000,000	$15,000,000
(5) Net Position: (3) − (4)	−$1,000,000	0	$1,000,000

invest dollars at 3%. To speculate on the \$/BP exchange rate decrease using the money market, the speculator would borrow £9,708,737.86 (PV(£10,000,000) = (£10,000,000)/1.03), convert to \$14,563,106.80 (= (\$1.50/£) £9,708,737.86) and invest the dollars at 3%. One year later, the speculator would have a \$15,000,000 investment (= \$14,563,106.80 (1.03)) and a £10,000,000 debt (= £9,708,737.86 (1.03)). If the spot \$/BP rate decreased from \$1.50 to, say, \$1.40/BP, then the speculator would profit by \$1,000,000 when he buys £10,000,000 at \$1.40/BP for \$14,000,000 and pays his £10,000,000 debt and collects \$15,000,000 from his dollar investment (\$15,000,000 = \$14,563,106.80(1.03)). However, if the spot rate increased from \$1.50 to, say, \$1.60/BP, then the speculator would lose \$1,000,000 when he buys £10,000,000 for \$16,000,000 at \$1.60/BP and receives only \$15,000,000 from his dollar investment (see Exhibit 2.14). This is the same profit-and-loss scenario that he would have realized by speculating with short positions in futures and forward contracts.

Money market positions are useful for speculating on change in exchange rate occurring over a long-term horizon that the maturity of futures contracts does not provide. For example, in the previous case, a speculator expecting the \$/BP to increase over the next five years could borrow dollars for five years, convert to pounds, and then invest the pounds for five years, hoping at the end of five years the \$/BP exchange was greater than \$1.50. Such five-year speculative positions would not be possible with BP futures contracts with maturities only going out two years. It is possible, however, that a speculator could find a dealer in the interbank forward market to offer a tailor-made five-year contract.

EXHIBIT 2.14 Short Speculative Position Using Money Market

- Borrowing and lending rate on US dollars = 3%
- Borrowing and lending rate on BP = 3%
- Current spot exchange rate = \$1.50/£ or 0.6667£/\$

Initial Position:
- Borrow £9,708,737.86 (PV(£10,000,000) = (£10,000,000)/1.03).
- Convert to \$14,563,106.80 (= (\$1.50/£) £9,708,737.86).
- Invest the \$14,563,106.80 at 3%.

Closing Position one year later:
- BP Liability: £10,000,000 (= £9,708,737.86 (1.03))
- Dollar Investment: \$15,000,000 (= \$14,563,106.80 (1.03))
- Buy £10,000,000 at spot E_T = \$/BP to pay £10,000,000 debt

Positions	Speculative Position		
(1) $f_T = E_T$	\$1.40/BP	\$1.50/BP	\$1.60/BP
(2) BP debt	£10,000,000	£10,000,000	£10,000,000
(3) Conversion: (£10,000,00)(E_T)	\$14,000,000	\$15,000,000	\$16,000,000
(4) \$ Investment	\$15,000,000	\$15,000,000	\$15,000,000
(5) Net Position: (4) − (3)	\$1,000,000	0	−\$1,000,000

Arbitrage Opportunities

It should be noted that in the above cases, speculating with the money market positon yielded the same possible cash flows as the forward or futures position taken with a futures price of $f_0 = \$1.50$. Note that in our example, if the futures price did not equal $f_0 = \$1.50$, then there would be an arbitrage opportunity by taking opposite positions in the futures and money market. For example, if $f_0 < \$1.50$, then an arbitrageur could earn a riskless profit by going long in the futures position at $f_0 < \$1.50$ and taking the short speculative money market position. As shown in Exhibit 2.15, if $f_0 = \$1.45/BP$, an arbitrageur would realize a cash flow of \$500,000 one year later, regardless of the exchange rate. On the other hand, if $f_0 > \$1.50$, then an arbitrageur could earn a riskless profit by going short in the futures position at $f_0 > \$1.50$ and taking the long speculative money market position. As shown in Exhibit 2.16, if $f_0 = \$1.55/BP$, an arbitrageur would realize a cash flow of \$500,000 one year later, regardless of the exchange rate. Moreover, arbitrageurs by exploiting these arbitrage opportunities when f_0 does not equal \$1.50 by their actions (going long when $f_0 < \$1.50$ and short when $f_0 > \$1.50$), will push the price of the BP currency futures to $f_0 = \$1.50$. At \$1.50, the arbitrage is zero. Thus, \$1.50 is the equilibrium futures price. As we will examine in more detail in the next section, the equilibrium price of futures and forward contracts is determined by arbitrage relations similar to this currency case.

EXHIBIT 2.15   Arbitrage when $f_0 < \$1.50$: Long Futures and Short Money Market Position

- Borrowing and lending rate on US dollars = 3%
- Borrowing and lending rate on BP = 3%
- Current spot exchange rate = \$1.50/£ or 0.6667£/\$

Initial Position:
- Long in 160 September BP futures contracts (size = 62,500 BP) at **\$1.45/BP**
- Borrow £9,708,737.86 (PV(£10,000,000) = (£10,000,000)/1.03)
- Convert to \$14,563,106.80 (= (\$1.50/£) £9,708,737.86)
- Invest the \$14,563,106.80 at 3%
- Initial Cash Flow = 0

Closing Position One Year Later:
- BP Liability: £10,000,000 (= £9,708,737.86 (1.03))
- Dollar Investment: \$15,000,000 (= \$14,563,106.80 (1.03))
- Buy £10,000,000 at spot $E_T = \$/BP$ to pay £10,000,000 debt
- Close BP futures contract by going short in 160 expiring September BP futures at $f_T = E_T$

Positions	Speculative Position		
(1) $f_T = E_T$	\$1.40/BP	\$1.50/BP	\$1.60/BP
(2) Profit from Futures: (160)(62,500 BP) $((f_T - \$1.45)$	−\$500,000	\$500,000	\$1,500,000
(3) BP Debt	£10,000,000	£10,000,000	£10,000,000
(4) Conversion: (£10,000,00)(E_T)	\$14,000,000	\$15,000,000	\$16,000,000
(5) \$ Investment	\$15,000,000	\$15,000,000	\$15,000,000
(6) Net Position: (2) + (5) − (4)	\$500,000	\$500,000	\$500,000

EXHIBIT 2.16   Arbitrage when $f_0 > \$1.50$: Short Futures and Long Money Market Position

- Borrowing and lending rate on US dollars = 3%
- Borrowing and lending rate on BP = 3%
- Current spot exchange rate = $1.50/£ or 0.6667£/$

Initial Position:
- Short in 160 September BP futures contracts (size = 62,500 BP) at **$1.55/BP.**
- Borrow $14,563,106.80, present value of $15,000,000 (PV($15,000,000) = (£10,000,000) ($1.50/BP)/1.03).
- Convert at 0.6667£/$ to £9,708,737.86 and invest the BPs at 3%.

Closing Position One Year Later:
- BP investment: £10,000,000 (= £9,708,737.86 (1.03))
- Dollar liability: $15,000,000 (= $14,563,106.80 (1.03))
- Convert £10,000,000 to dollars at spot $E_T = \$/BP$ and pay $15,000,000 debt
- Close BP futures contracts by going long in 160 expiring September BP futures at $f_T = E_T$

Positions	Speculative Position		
(1) $f_T = E_T$	$1.40/BP	$1.50/BP	$1.60/BP
(2) Profit from Futures: (160)(62,500 BP) (($1.55 − f_T))	$1,500,000	$500,000	−$500,000
(3) BP Investment	£10,000,000	£10,000,000	£10,000,000
(4) Conversion: (£10,000,00)(E_T)	$14,000,000	$15,000,000	$16,000,000
(5) $ Debt	$15,000,000	$15,000,000	$15,000,000
(6) Net Position: (2) + (4) − (5)	$500,000	$500,000	$500,000

Carrying-Cost Model for a Currency

In international finance, the carrying cost model governing the relationship between spot and forward or futures prices is referred to as the *interest rate parity theorem* (IRPT). In terms of IRPT, the forward price of a currency or forward exchange rate is equal to the cost of carrying the spot currency (priced at the spot exchange rate of E_0) for the contract's expiration period.

In terms of a US dollar position, carrying a foreign currency for the period (T) would require borrowing $E_0/(1+ R_F)^T$ dollars at the rate R_{US}, where R_F is the foreign risk-free rate (the rate paid on foreign currency), converting the dollars to $1/(1+ R_F)^T$ units of foreign currency (FC) at the spot exchange rate of E_0, and investing the currency in the foreign risk-free security yielding R_F. At the end of the period, this arbitrage would yield one unit of FC and a debt obligation of $[E_0/(1+ R_F)^T](1+R_{US})^T$. Thus, the forward or futures price of purchasing one unit of currency at T should not be different from the debt obligation or net financing cost of carrying the currency. Thus, the equilibrium forward or futures price or exchange rate is

$$f_0 = E_0 \frac{(1 + R_{US})^T}{(1 + R_F)^T}$$

or in terms of continuously compounded US and foreign annualized risk-free rates:

$$f_0 = E_0 \, e^{(R_{US}^A - R_F^A)T}$$

These equations define IRPT. The equation, in turn, shows that the relation between the forward or futures rate and the spot rate depends on the relative levels of domestic and foreign interest rates. If the interest rate parity condition does not hold, an arbitrage opportunity will exist. The arbitrage strategy to apply in such situations is known as *covered interest arbitrage* (CIA). Introduced by John Maynard Keynes, CIA involves taking long and short positions in the currency spot and forward or futures markets, as well as positions in the domestic and foreign money markets. To illustrate, suppose the annualized US and foreign currency interest rates are $R_{US} = 4\%$ and $R_F = 6\%$, respectively, and the spot exchange rate is $E_0 = \$0.40/FC$. By IRPT, a one-year future contract would be equal to $\$0.39245283/FC$:

$$f_0 = [\$0.40/FC] \left(\frac{1.04}{1.06} \right) = \$0.39245283/FC$$

If the actual (market) forward rate, f_0^M, exceeds $\$0.39245283/FC$, an arbitrage profit would exist by: (1) borrowing dollars at R_{US}, (2) converting the dollar to FC at E_0, (3) investing the FC in a foreign risk-free rate at the rate R_F, and (4) and entering a short futures contract to sell the FC at the end of the period at F_0^M. For example, if $F_0^M = \$0.40/FC$, an arbitrageur could:

1. Borrow \$40,000 at $R_{US} = 4\%$ [creating a loan obligation at the end of the period of \$41,600 = (\$40,000)(1.04)].
2. Convert the dollars at the spot exchange rate of $E_0 = \$0.40/FC$ to 100,000 FC (= (2.5FC/\$)(\$40,000)).
3. Invest the 100,000 FC in the foreign risk-free security at $R_F = 6\%$ [creating a return of principal and interest of 106,000 FC one year later].
4. Enter a futures contract to sell 106,000 FC at the end of the year at $F_0^M = \$0.40/FC$.

One year later, the arbitrageur would receive \$42,400 when she sells the 106,000 FC on the futures contract and would owe \$41,600 on her debt obligation, for an arbitrage return of \$800. Such risk-free profit opportunities, in turn, would lead arbitrageurs to try to implement the CIA strategy. This would cause the price on the futures contract to fall until the riskless opportunity disappears. The zero arbitrage profit would occur when the interest rate parity condition is satisfied.

If the futures rate is below the equilibrium value, then the CIA is reversed. In this example, if $F_0^M = \$0.38/FC$, an arbitrageur could:

1. Borrow 100,000 FC at $R_F = 6\%$ [creating a 106,000 FC debt].
2. Convert the 100,000 FC at the spot exchange rate to \$40,000.
3. Invest the \$40,000 in the US risk-free security at $R_{US} = 4\%$.
4. Enter a futures contract to buy 106,000 FC at the end of the year at $f_0^M = \$0.38/FC$.

At the end of the period, the arbitrageur's profit would be $1,320:

$$\$40,000(1.04) - (\$0.38/FC)(106,000) = \$1,320$$

As arbitrageurs attempt to implement this strategy, they will push up the price on the futures contract until the arbitrage profit is zero; this occurs when the interest rate parity condition is satisfied.

Hedging Interbank Forward Contracts

Banks that provide forward contracts to their customers typically use the IRPT to hedge their contracts by taking a position in the spot markets. For example, given $R_{US} = 4\%$, $R_F = 6\%$, and $E_0 = \$0.40/FC$, a bank could offer a one-year forward contract at $F_0 = \$0.39245283/FC$, then hedge the contract by using a CIA strategy. For example, if a bank's customer wanted to buy 10,000,000 FC one year from the present, then the bank could provide the customer with a forward contract in which the bank agrees to sell forward 10,000,000 FC to the customer at the end of one year for $3,924,528. To hedge this short forward position, the bank, in turn, could:

1. Borrow $3,773,585 (= (10,000,000 FC/1.04)($0.39245283)).
2. Convert the $3,773,585 to 9,433,962 FC (= $3,773,585(2.5FC/$)).
3. Invest the 9,433,962 FC for one year at $R_F = 6\%$.

One year later, the bank would have 10,000,000 FC (= 9,443,962(1.06)) and would owe $3,924,528 (= $3,773,585(1.04)), which would exactly offset the bank's forward position.

On the other hand, if a bank's customer wanted to sell 10,000,000 FC one year from the present, then the bank could provide the customer with a forward contract in which it agrees to buy forward 10,000,000 FC to the customer at the end of one year for $3,924,528. To hedge this long forward position, the bank would reverse the previous strategy: Borrow 9,433,962 FC at 6%, convert to $3,773,585, and invest in US security at 4%. At the end of one year, the bank would have $3,924,528 and would owe 10,000,000 FC, which would offset its long forward position.

In hedging their forward contracts, banks are in a position in which they can take care of any mispricing that occurs if the forward price does not satisfy the interest rate parity condition. By taking advantage of such opportunities, they would push the forward price to its equilibrium level.

Currency Futures Prices

Note that a sufficient condition for futures and forward prices to be equal is for short-term interest rates to be constant over time. In the case of currency futures and forward contracts, the requirement for equality is for both the foreign and domestic short-term rates to be constant. If this occurs, then, theoretically, the IRPT can be extended to determining the equilibrium futures exchange rate; if these rates are not stable, though, then the interest rate parity model would be only an estimate of the equilibrium futures price. Empirically, several studies comparing currency futures and forward exchange rates have found no significant differences between them. Thus, even with market imperfections such as taxes and transaction costs, the IRPT appears to be a good description of what determines both the forward and futures exchange rates.

Pricing a British Pound Futures Contract

Exhibit 2.11 shows the prices on the June 2016 British pound from 1/4/16 to 6/13/16 (expiration date on the contract). On 3/14/16 the three-month US dollar deposit rate (USDRC <Curncy>) was 0.5392% and the British pound three-month deposit rate (GBP3M <Curncy>) was 0.57%. Using a 30-day, 360-day day-count convention, the maturity on the June futures (6/13/16) would have been $T = 90/360 = 0.25$ on 3/14/16. The spot $/BP was $1.4302 on 3/14/16. Using the carrying-cost model, the equilibrium price of the June BP futures contract on 3/14/16 would have been $1.4301:

$$f_0^* = E_0 \frac{(1 + R_{US})^T}{(1 + R_F)^T}$$

$$f_0^* = \$1.4302 \frac{(1.005392)^{0.25}}{(1.005700)^{0.25}} = \$1.4301$$

The actual futures price on the June BP contract on 3/14/16 was also $1.4301.

It should be noted that when interest rates on the two currencies are equal, then the futures price will be equal to the spot. Thus, the only minimal difference between the spot and futures price, is due to the small difference between the rate paid on dollars and the rate paid on BP.

Investment Uses of Interest Rate Parity Theorem

In addition to determining the equilibrium currency futures or forward price, investors and borrowers can also use the IRPT to define the cutoff expected spot exchange rate for determining whether they should invest or borrow domestically or internationally. To illustrate, consider our earlier example where $R_{US} = 4\%$ and $R_F = 6\%$, $E_0 = \$0.40/FC$, and $f_0 = \$0.39245283/FC$. If an investor knew with certainty that the exchange rate one year later would be $f_0 = \$0.39245283/FC$, then she would be indifferent to an investment in a one-year US risk-free security yielding 4% and a one-year foreign risk-free security yielding 6%. If the US investor, however, were certain that the spot exchange one year later would exceed $0.39245283/FC, she would prefer to invest her dollars in the foreign security rather than the US one. For example, if a US investor knew the spot exchange rate one year later would be $E(E_T) = \$0.41/FC$, then she would prefer the foreign investment, in which a rate of 8.65% could be earned, instead of the US security, which earns only 4%. To attain 8.65%, the investor would have to convert each of her investment dollars to $1/E_0 = 1/\$0.40/FC = 2.5$ FC and invest the 2.5 FC at $R_F = 6\%$. One year later, the investor would have 2.65 FC ($= 2.5FC(1.06)$), which she would be able to convert to $1.0865 if the spot exchange rate were \$0.41/FC. Thus, the dollar investment in the foreign security would yield an expected dollar rate of 8.65%.

$$\text{Rate} = \frac{(\$0.41/\text{FC})[2.5\,\text{FC}(1.06)]}{\$1} - 1 = 0.0865$$

On the other hand, if a US investor expected the exchange rate would be less than \$0.39245283/FC, then she would prefer the US risk-free investment to the foreign one. For example, if $E(E_T) = \$0.39/\text{FC}$, then the US investor would earn only 3.35% from the foreign investment compared to 4% from the US investment:

$$\text{Rate} = \frac{(\$0.39/\text{FC})[2.5\,\text{FC}(1.06)]}{\$1} - 1 = 0.0335$$

The example suggests that in a world of certainty, the equilibrium forward rate as specified by the IRPT can be used to define the expected cutoff exchange rate, $E(E_T^c)$, needed to determine if one should invest in a domestic or risk-free security:

$$E(E_T^c) = f_0 = E_0\frac{(1 + R_{\text{US}})^T}{(1 + R_{\text{f}})^T}$$

In a real world of uncertainty in which futures spot exchange rates are unknown, however, the required cutoff rate depends on investors' attitudes toward risk. For example, if investors were risk-neutral, then they would require no risk premium and their required expected rate from the risky investment would be equal to the risk-free investment. In this case, the cutoff exchange rate for investors would be the equilibrium forward rate. However, if investors were risk-averse, as we would expect, then the required expected rate from the risky investment would have to exceed the risk-free rate. This would require that investors' cutoff exchange rate exceed the forward rate. For example, if risk-averse US investors required an annualized 2% risk premium (RP) in order to invest in a foreign security, then the expected cutoff exchange rate would be \$0.40/FC:

$$E(E_T^c) = E_0\frac{(1 + R_{\text{US}} + RP)^T}{(1 + R_{\text{f}})^T}$$

$$E(E_T^c) = (\$0.40/\text{FC})\frac{(1 + .04 + .02)^T}{(1.06)^T} = \$0.40/\text{FC}$$

Thus, if investors are risk averse, then $E(E_T)$ would have to be greater than f_0 for them to invest in the foreign security that is subject to exchange rate risk instead of the domestic investment.

Cross-Exchange Rate Relations

The cross exchange rate defines the relationship between different exchange rates. For example, on 7/14/16, the spot BP/dollar (BP/\$) exchange rate was 0.7499625 BP/\$ (US dollar/BP rate = \$1.3334/BP) and the Australian dollar/US dollar (AUD/\$) was

1.31027 AUD/$ ($/AUD = $0.7632). Given BP/$ and AUD/$ rates, the equilibrium BP/AUD exchange rate would have to be 0.572 BP/AUD and the AUD/BP rate would have to be 1.748 AUD/BP.

$$0.7499625 \text{ BP} = \$1 = 1.31027 \text{ AUD}$$

$$0.7499625 \text{ BP} = 1.31027 \text{ AUD}$$

$$\frac{0.7499625 \text{ BP}}{1.31027 \text{ AUD}} = \frac{0.572 \text{ BP}}{\text{AUD}}$$

$$\text{and}$$

$$\frac{1.31027 \text{ AUD}}{0.7499625 \text{ BP}} = \frac{1.748 \text{ AUD}}{\text{BP}}$$

This carry-cost price, in turn, equals the actual BP/AUD price on 7/14/16 of 1.748 AUD/BP and 0.572 BP/AUD.

If the actual BP/AUD exchange rate were not equal to 1.748 BP/AUD or 0.572 AUD/BP, then an arbitrage strategy, defined as *triangular arbitrage*, could have been exploited to earn riskless profit. For example, suppose the BP/AUD exchange rate were 0.60 BP/AUD on 7/14/16. An arbitrageur with a position in dollars could earn a riskless return of $0.048 for each dollar invested using this approach:

1. Buy 1.31027 AUD with $1.
2. Convert the 1.31027 AUD to 0.786162 BP: (1.31027 AUD)(0.60 BP/AUD) = 0.786162 BP.
3. Convert the 0.786162 BP to $1.048: (0.786162 BP)($1.3334/BP) = $1.048.

By executing this triangular arbitrage strategy, the arbitrageur would be buying BP with AUD, which would push the BP/AUD exchange rate toward 0.572. On the other hand, if the BP/ADU exchange rate were at 0.55 (or 1.8182 AUD/BP), an arbitrageur could earn a riskless return of $0.04 for each dollar invested using this approach:

1. Buy 0.7499625 BP for $1.
2. Convert the 0.7499625 BP to 1.36358 AUD: (0.7499625 BP)(1.8182 AUD/BP) = 1.36358 AUD.
3. Convert the 1.36358 AUD to $1.04: (1.36358 AUD)($0.7632/AUD) = $1.04.

These actions, in turn, would serve to push the BP/AUD exchange rate up toward 0.572.

Conclusion

The flexible exchange rate system makes it necessary for multinational corporations, international investors, and international organizations to deal with the problems of exchange-rate risk. To this end, forward contracts on the interbank market and futures contracts on the exchanges have provided these entities with a relatively effective exchange rate risk-reduction tool. In this chapter, we have examined the markets, the hedging and speculative uses, and the pricing of these contracts.

BLOOMBERG: CURRENCY FUTURES AND RELATED SCREENS

BLOOMBERG COMMODITY SCREENS, CTM

Exchange-listed currency contracts can be found by accessing the CTM screen: CTM <Enter>. Contracts can be found by category, exchange, and region. For example, to find a currency futures offered on the CME, use the CME Exchange screen and click "Currencies" from the dropdown menu in the "Category" column. Alternatively, click "Categories" and "Currencies" and then type the name of the exchange (e.g., CME) in the amber Exchange box to find the contract of interest.

UPLOADING A FUTURES CONTRACT

To upload a currency futures contract's menu screen, enter: Ticker <Curncy> (e.g., BPA <Curncy> for the British pound futures contract menu), and then use the Expiration screen (EXS) to find the ticker for the contract with the expiration month you want to analyze: Ticker <Curncy> (e.g., BPH7 <Curncy> for the March 2017 contract). The menu includes:

- CT: Contract Table
- EXS: Expiration Schedule
- GP: Price Graph
- GIP Intraday Graph

SECF AND UPLOADING SPOT, FORWARD, DEPOSIT RATES, AND FUTURES

The SECF screen can be used to find the tickers for a select currency's spot exchange rate, deposit rates, forward rates, and futures: Enter SECF <Enter>, select "Currencies" from the dropdown "Category" tab, type in currency name in the amber "Name" box, and select tabs: Spots, Depos, Fwds, and Futr. To upload the menu screens, enter: Ticker <Curncy> (e.g., GBP <Curncy> for BP/$ spot rate, BPDRC <Curncy> for BP three-month deposit rate, GBP3M <Curncy> for three-month British pound forward rate, and BPA <Curncy> for BP/$ active futures).

   Bloomberg Currency Screens

- FXFR: Spots/Forwards Monitor
- FXFA: FX-Interest Rate Arbitrage
- FRD: FX Forward Calculator
- FXIP: Foreign Exchange Information Portal
- FXC: Currency Rate Matrix
- WCR: World Currency Rates
- GMM Global Macro Movers
- BBC: Currency Deposit Rates
- PEG: Pegged Currencies

Selected References

Branson, W. "The Minimum Covered Interest Differential Needed for International Arbitrage Activity." *Journal of Political Economy* (December 1979): 1029–1034.

Cornell, B. "Spot Rates, Forward Rates, and Exchange Market Efficiency." *Journal of Financial Economics* (August 1977): 55–65.

Huang, R. "Some Alternative Tests of Forward Exchange Rates as Predictors of Future Spot Rates." *Journal of International Money and Finance* (August 1984): 153–178.

Johnson, R. Stafford. *Introduction to Derivatives: Options, Futures, and Swaps.* Oxford: Oxford University Press, 2009, Chapter 14.

Johnson, R., Hultman, C., and Zuber, R. "Currency Cocktails and Exchange Rate Stability." *Columbia Journal of World Business* 14 (Winter 1979): 117–126.

Madura, J., and Nosari, E. "Utilizing Currency Portfolios to Mitigate Exchange Rate Risk." *Columbia Journal of World Business* (Spring 1984): 96–99.

Panton, D., and Joy, M. "Empirical Evidence on International Monetary Market Currency Futures." *Journal of International Business Studies* (Fall 1978): 59–68.

Swanson, P., and Caples, S. "Hedging Foreign Exchange Risk Using Forward Exchange Markets: An Extension." *Journal of International Business Studies* (Spring 1987): 75–82.

Problems and Questions

1. Given the following:
   - $E_0 = \$1.50/BP$
   - $F_0 = \$1.50/BP$ (one-year forward contract)
   - $R_{US} = 2\%$ (annual)
   - $R_{BP} = 2\%$ (annual)
     a. Explain how you would speculate on the BP using the forward market if you expected the spot exchange rate to be $1.60/BP one year from now.
     b. Explain how you would speculate on the BP using the money market if you expected the spot exchange rate to be $1.60/BP one year from now (assume you can borrow and lend at $R_{US} = R_{BP} = 2\%$).
     c. Explain how you would speculate on the BP using the forward market if you expected the spot exchange rate to be $1.40/BP one year from now.
     d. Explain how you would speculate on the BP using the money market if you expected the spot exchange rate to be $1.40/FC one year from now (assume you can borrow and lend at $R_{US} = R_{BP} = 2\%$).

2. Mr. B just signed a contract to play professional basketball in Mexico for the Mexican Stars. The team owner has agreed to pay his living expenses for two years and an annual salary of 2,000,000 pesos, with 1,000,000 pesos to be paid one year from the present and the second-year 1,000,000 pesos to be paid two years from the present. Mr. B plans to play two years, then return to the United States. He would like to hedge the dollar value of his contract. Currently, the spot $/peso exchange rate is $0.05/peso and the Mexican risk-free rate is 6% (annual), the US risk-free rate is 2%. Forward rates offered by US and Mexican banks are governed by the IRPT.

   a. Explain how Mr. B could hedge the dollar value of his salary using forward contracts.

b. Suppose Mr. B could not find a bank to provide him with a forward contract. Explain how he could alternatively hedge his salary against exchange rate risk by using the money market. Assume Mr. B can borrow pesos at 6% and can invest dollars at 2%.

3. The Nancy Jewelry Company is a US company with jewelry stores located across the United States. In March, the company signs a contract with Swiss Watch, Inc. to purchase 100,000 watches the following March ($T = 1$ year) at the cost of 30SF per watch, with the payments to be made at the time of the March delivery. Currently, US and Swiss risk-free interest rates are both at 2% (annual), the \$/SF spot exchange rate is \$1.10/SF, and the \$/SF forward rates and the CME futures rate are governed by the IRPT.

   a. Explain how the Nancy Jewelry Company could hedge its dollars cost of the watches against exchange rate risk using forward contracts.
   b. Explain how the Nancy Jewelry Company could hedge its payment next March by using the money market. Assume it can borrow and lend dollars and Swiss francs at 2%.
   c. Explain how the Nancy Jewelry Company could hedge its March payment by taking a position in the CME's SF futures contract (contract size is 125,000 SF). Evaluate the hedge at possible spot exchange rates at the March expiration of \$1.20/SF and \$1.00/SF. Assume the watch payment occurs at the same time as the futures expiration and the expiring futures price is equal to the spot.

4. Suppose ESPN (Disney) is expecting revenues of 6,250,000 BP next April (one year from now: $T = 1$) from its United Kingdom Rugby sports productions division. Fearing that exchange rates could decrease when it converts its 6,250,000 BP, ESPN would like to hedge the dollar value of its revenue. Currently, the spot \$/£ exchange rate is \$1.50/£, the US risk-free rate is 3%, the British risk-free rate is 3%, and the one-year forward rate offered by US and British banks is determined by the IRPT.

   a. Explain how ESPN could hedge the dollar value of its revenue using a forward contract.
   b. Explain how ESPN could alternatively hedge its revenue of 6,250,000 BP against exchange-rate risk by using the money market. Assume ESPN can borrow BPs at 3% and dollars at 3%.
   c. Suppose in April, the BP futures contract trading on the CME is at \$1.50/£ (contract size = 62,500 BP). Show how ESPN could hedge its revenue against exchange-rate risk by using the contract expiring next April. Assume that at the futures expiration, ESPN will close its futures position at an expiring futures price equal to the spot exchange rate and convert its BP revenue at the spot exchange rate. Evaluate the position by assuming possible spot \$/£ exchange rate at expiration of \$1.45/£ and \$1.55/£.

5. Suppose Fox Sports owes the United Kingdom Rugby Association 12,500,000 BP as payment for the exclusive licensing right to produce Rugby matches on the European and US cable markets. Suppose the licensing payment is due next May (one year from now: $T = 1$). Fearing that exchange rates could increase when it

buys the pounds, Fox would like to hedge the dollar cost of buying the currency. Currently, the spot $/£ exchange rate is $1.50/BP, the US risk-free rate is 3%, the British risk-free rate is 3%, and the one-year forward rate offered by US and British banks is determined by the IRPT.

a. Explain how Fox Sports could hedge the dollar cost of purchasing BP using a forward contract.

b. Explain how Fox Sports could alternatively hedge its 12,500,000 BP purchase against exchange-rate risk by using the money market. Assume ESPN can borrow and lend BP at 3% and dollars at 3%.

c. Suppose in May, the BP futures contract trading on the CME is at $1.50/£ (contract size = 62,500 BP). Show how Fox could hedge its BP cost against exchange-rate risk by using the contract expiring next May. Assume that at the futures expiration, Fox will close its futures position at an expiring futures price equal to the spot exchange rate and buy its BP at the spot exchange rate. Evaluate the position by assuming possible spot $/£ exchange rate at expiration of $1.45/£ and $1.55/£.

6. A US investor just bought one share of Heineken stock for 200 euros when the dollar/euro spot exchange rate was $1.20/€. The investor expects the stock to pay a dividend worth 5 euros and to appreciate by 10% one year from now.

a. Calculate the one-year expected rate of return on the stock for an investment made in euros.

b. Calculate the possible one-year expected rates of return on the stock in terms of a dollar investment. Assume possible end-of-the-year exchange rates of $1.05/€, $1.10/€, $1.15/€, $1.20/€, and $1.25/€.

c. If the US risk-free rate were 7% (annual) and the Netherlands risk-free rate on euros were 5%, what would be the one-year forward rate a bank could provide the investor if it provides forward contracts based on the IRPT?

d. What would be the investor's possible expected rates of return if she hedged the dollar price of the stock (€200) by going short in a forward contract as determined by the IRPT? Evaluate at possible exchange rates of $1.05/€, $1.10/€, $1.15/€, $1.20/€, and $1.25/€.

7. Suppose the spot US dollar/euro exchange rate is $1.20/€, the US risk-free rate is 4% (annual) and the rate paid on euros is 2%.

a. Assuming the IRPT holds, what should the equilibrium 1-year $/€ forward rate be?

b. Suppose a US bank provides one of its business customers with a forward contract in which the customer agrees to sell to the bank 12 million euros one year later at a forward price equal to IRPT. Assuming the bank can borrow and lend dollars and euros at the above risk-free rates, explain how the bank would hedge its forward position.

c. Explain the type of forward contract the bank would provide the business customer and how it would hedge the contract if the business customer wanted to buy 12 million euros one year later.

8. Explain why a risk-neutral investor would be indifferent between a one-year US dollar investment in a risk-free security at 3% and a one-year British pound investment at 5% if the investor expected the $/£ spot exchange rate one year later to equal the forward rate as determined by the IRPT. In your explanation, assume the current spot exchange rate is $1.50/BP.

9. Suppose the US investor in Question 8 were risk averse, instead of risk neutral, and wants a risk premium of 1% (annual) for assuming the exchange-rate risk on the international investment.

    a. Find the expected spot exchange rate that would make the risk-averse investor indifferent between the US and British risk-free investments.

    b. Demonstrate that the investor would earn that return if this expected exchange rate is realized.

10. Given the following euro and British pound spot exchange rates: 0.80€/$1 and 0.70 £/$1:

    a. What is the equilibrium £/€?

    b. Describe the triangular arbitrage strategy a US arbitrageur would pursue if the BP price of a euro were 0.90£/€.

    c. Describe the triangular arbitrage strategy a US arbitrageur would pursue if the BP price of a euro were 0.85£/€.

Bloomberg Exercises

1. Select a currency of interest (use SECF (SECF <Enter>); Category: Currencies, Spots tab. Upload the currency's Menu screen (Ticker <Curncy> <Enter>), and evaluate it using the following screen:

    a. DES: Description
    b. GP: Price Graph
    c. FXFR: Spots/Forwards Monitor
    d. FXFA: FX-Interest Rate Arbitrage
    e. FRD: FX Forward Calculator
    f. CN: News: Currency

2. Use the SECF screen to find the tickers for a select currency's spot exchange rate, deposit rates, forward rates, and futures: SECF <Enter>; Category: "Currencies," type in currency name in the amber "Name" box and select tabs: Spots, Depos, Fwds, and Futr. Upload the menu screens for a selected spot exchange rate (e.g., GBP <Curncy> for BP/$ spot rate), deposit rates (e.g., BPDRC <Curncy> for BP 3-month deposit rate), forward rate (e.g., GBP3M <Curncy> for 3-month British pound forward rate), and futures (e.g., BPA <Curncy> for BP/$ active futures). On each of the menu screens, analyze some of its screens (e.g., DES and GP).

3. Access Bloomberg information for a CME-listed currency futures contract: Type CTM to bring up the "Contract Table Menu," click "Categories" and "Currencies," search for CME currency futures on the Menu (type CME in the amber Exchange

box), find the CME currency of interest and bring up the contract's menu screen (Ticker <Curncy>; e.g., BPA <Curncy> for British pound futures), and then use the Expiration screen (EXS) to find the ticker for the contract with the expiration month you want to analyze (Ticker <Curncy>; e.g., BPH7 <Curncy> for the March 2017 contract). View screens to examine: DES and GP.

4. Using the GP screen, examine the historical prices of the currency futures contract you selected in Exercise 3. Select a time period that the contract was active.

   a. Select a period in which you would have taken a long position and calculate the profit from opening and closing at the futures prices at the beginning and ending dates for your selected period. Calculate the losses if you had taken a short position.

   b. Select a period in which you would have taken a short position and calculate the profits from opening and closing at the futures prices at the beginning and ending dates for your selected period. Calculate the losses if you had taken a long position.

   c. Using the annotation bar, apply the "% Change" tool to calculate the percentage change for your select periods, and then click the "News" icon on the annotation bar to find relevant news events on or preceding the opening date.

   d. Examine the spot exchange rate for the period that your futures contract was active. The ticker for the index can be found on SECF. Use the Chart screen (Chart <Enter>) to create multigraphs for the prices on the futures contract and the spot exchange rate. On the Chart Menu screen, select Standard G chart; once you have loaded your securities, go to "Edit" to put your graphs in separate panels.

5. Using the Bloomberg HRA Regression screen estimate the relation between two currencies. Load your selected currency (e.g., GBP <Curncy> for the British pound), and then go to the HRA screen for the regression. On the HRA screen, enter the other currency as the independent variable in the amber box (e.g., AUD <Curncy>) and select the time period and periodicity (daily).

   a. Comment on the regression results and the relation (beta).

   b. Explain how you would form bullish and bearish intercommodity spreads with the futures contracts on the underlying currencies.

6. Using the Chart screen (Chart <Enter>), examine the intercommodity spread you formed in Exercise 5. Note than the contracts have to have the same expiration.

   a. Use the Chart screen (Chart <Enter>) to create multigraphs for the index futures contracts. On the Chart Menu screen, select Standard G chart; once you have loaded your securities, go to "Edit" to put your graphs in separate panels.

   b. Select a period in which you would have taken a bullish spread position and calculate the profit you would have realized from opening and closing at the futures prices at the beginning and ending dates for your selected period. Calculate the losses if you had taken a bearish intercommodity position.

c. Select a period in which you would have taken a bearish spread position and calculate the profit you would have realized from opening and closing at the futures prices at the beginning and ending dates for your selected period. Calculate the losses if you had taken a bullish position.

d. Using the annotation bar, apply the "% Change" tool to calculate the percentage change for your select periods, and then click the "News" icon on the annotation bar to find relevant news events on or preceding the opening date.

7. Examine an ex-post long hedging position for a future currency purchase.

   a. Select a futures contract and use the expiration date on the futures contract as the date of your purchase.

   b. Use the Chart screen (Chart <Enter>) to create multigraphs for the prices on the futures and spot exchange rate. On the Chart Menu screen, select Standard G chart; once you have loaded your futures and currency, go to "Edit" to put your graphs in separate panels.

   c. Select a beginning date that you would have implemented your hedge and a closing date near the futures expiration as the date for purchasing the currency and closing your hedge. Calculate the profit or loss on the futures position from opening and closing at the futures prices at the beginning and ending dates, the cost of purchasing the currency on the closing date, and the hedged cost (currency purchase minus futures profit). Compare your hedged cost to the unhedged cost. In retrospect, was the hedge a good strategy?

8. Examine an ex-post short hedging position for a future currency sale.

   a. Select a futures contract and use the expiration date on the futures as the date of your sale.

   b. Use the Chart screen (Chart <Enter>) to create multigraphs for the prices on futures and spot exchange rate. On the Chart Menu screen, select Standard G chart; once you have loaded your futures and currency, go to "Edit" to put your graphs in separate panels.

   c. Select a beginning date that you would have implemented your hedge and a closing date near the futures expiration as the date for the currency sale and closing your hedge. Calculate the profit or loss on the futures position from opening and closing at the futures prices at the beginning and ending dates, the revenue from selling the currency on the closing date, and the hedged revenue (currency sale plus futures profit). Compare your hedged revenue to the unhedged revenue. In retrospect, was the hedge a good strategy?

9. Select a currency exchange rate with the dollar (GBP <Curncy> for BP), a futures contract on the currency (e.g., British pound expiring in approximately three months), the deposit rate on the currency (e.g., GBP3M <Curncy> for a three-month deposit rate on BP), and the deposit rate on the US dollar (e.g., USDRC <Curncy> for three-month US dollar rates) that matches the maturity (e.g., three months) of your selected futures. Using the selected deposit rates, calculate the carrying-cost price of the futures. How close is it to the actual price?

CHAPTER 3

Equity Index Futures

The Kansas City Board of Trade was the first exchange to offer trading on a futures contract on an equity index when it introduced the Value Line Composite Index (VLCI) contract in 1983. This was followed by the introduction of the Standard & Poor's (S&P) 500 futures contract by the CME and the New York Stock Exchange (NYSE) index futures contract by the New York Futures Exchange (NYFE). Today, there are a number of futures index contracts available. Many of these contracts are on stock indexes, but there are also some on commodities (e.g., DJ-AIG Commodity Index and the GSCI index), bond indexes (e.g., Municipal Bond Index), and currencies (e.g., the US dollar index). Exhibit 3.1 shows Bloomberg Description and Price screens on an expiring CME's S&P 500 futures contract with an expiration of June 16, 2016. The futures contract price on the S&P 500 futures is 2,079 on June 16, 2016, the multiplier is $250, and the expiration date is 6/16/16.

Theoretically, an index futures contract, like the S&P 500 index, can be thought of as an agreement to buy (long) or sell (short) a portfolio of stocks composing the index in their correct proportions at specific price, f_0, on a specified delivery date T. Index futures contracts, however, have a *cash settlement* feature. With the cash settlement features, an index futures purchaser (long position holder) agrees to buy cash equal to the closing spot index (S_T) on the delivery date at the futures price f_0, to the index futures seller (short position holder), who in turn, agrees to sell the cash equal to the closing spot index (S_T) on the delivery date at the futures price f_0. To settle, if $S_T > f_0$, then the futures seller pays the futures holder a cash settlement of $S_T - f_0$; if $S_T < f_0$, then the futures buyer pays the futures seller a cash settlement of $S_T - f_0$. For example, on January 5, 2016, the June S&P 500

EXHIBIT 3.1   S&P 500 Futures Contract Bloomberg Description and Price Screens, SPA <Comdty>

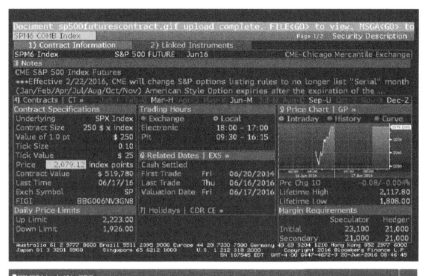

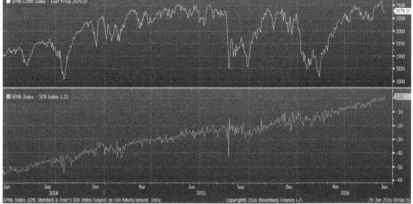

futures contract was trading at 2,004. A contract created on that date and held to the June 16 expiration when the spot index was at 2,079, would have been settled with the futures seller paying the futures buyer $18,750: Multiplier $(S_T - f_0) =$ $(\$250)(2,079 - 2,004) = \$18,750$. If the spot index on June 16 were less than 2,004, say 1,929, then the futures buyer would pay the futures seller $18,750: Multiplier $(S_T - f_0) = (\$250)(1,929 - 2,004) = -\$18,750$.

Like all exchange-traded futures contracts, there is a clearinghouse associated with the exchange. As such, most futures contracts are closed by holders taking opposite position. For example, on 2/11/16, the June S&P 500 futures contract was trading at 1,815. A futures buyer who had taken a long position to buy the index at 2,004 on 1/5/16 and then closed his position by going short on 2/11/16 at 1,815 would have had to pay the clearinghouse $47,250. On the other hand, a futures seller who took a long position to sell the index at 2,004 on 1/5/16 and then closed her position by

EXHIBIT 3.2   Long and Short Outright Positions on S&P 500 Contracts

	Clearinghouse Records for Long June S&P 500 Speculator
1/5/16	**Opening Position:** Speculator agrees to buy S&P 500 Index on June 16, 2016, for 2,004 ($250 multiplier).
2/11/16	**Closing Position:** Speculator agrees to sell S&P 500 Index on June 16, 2016, for $f_t = 1{,}815$ ($250 multiplier).
Settlement	Speculator pays clearinghouse $47,250. Closing payment to clearinghouse: Multiplier $(f_t - f_0) = (\$250)(1{,}815 - 2{,}004) = -\$47{,}250$

	Clearinghouse Records for Short June S&P 500 Speculator
1/5/16	**Opening Position:** Speculator agrees to sell S&P 500 Index on June 16, 2016, for 2,004 ($250 multiplier).
2/11/16	**Closing Position:** Speculator agrees to buy S&P 500 Index on June 16, 2016, for $f_t = 1{,}815$ ($250 multiplier).
Settlement	Speculator receives $47,250 from the clearinghouse. Closing receipt from clearinghouse: Multiplier $(f_0 - f_t) = (\$250)(2{,}004 - 1{,}815) = \$47{,}250$

going long on 2/11/16 at 1,815 would have receive $47,250 from the clearinghouse (see Exhibit 3.2).

The S&P 500 Bloomberg Description screen also shows the initial and maintenance (secondary) dollar margin requirements for speculative and hedging positions on the contract. With a contract value of $519,780 (= ($250)(2,079.12)), the initial margin is $23,100 for a speculator, which is an effective margin requirement of 4.44%.

Other index futures contracts have many of the same characteristics as the S&P 500 index options, with the size of index futures contracts equal to a multiple of the index value and with a cash-settlement feature. Some contracts, like the mini indexes, have smaller multipliers. Other contracts are based on sectors or more narrow-based indexes, and some are based on the volatility of the index or differences between indexes, instead of the price of the index. Exhibit 3.3 shows a number of equity index futures contracts listed on the Chicago Mercantile Exchange (CME), Chicago Board of Trade (CBT), and the Eurex.

The annual volume of trading on broad-based stock index futures trading has grown dramatically over the last 30 years. The growth in these derivatives' popularity can be attributed to their use as a stock portfolio management tool. In this chapter, we examine the speculative and hedging uses of these contracts, as well as the arbitrage strategy, known as program trading, which is used when index derivative contracts are not priced correctly.

EXHIBIT 3.3 Type of Equity Index Futures

Ticker	Description	Category Equity Index	Exchange	Options	Volume	Open Interest
ASDA Index	S&P 500 Annual Dividend Index Futures	Equity Index : EQIX	Chicago Mercantile Exchange : CME	No	740	47,336
ESA Index	S&P 500 E-mini	Equity Index : EQIX	Chicago Mercantile Exchange : CME	Yes	1,880,908	2,784,467
FAA Index	S&P MidCap 400 E-mini	Equity Index : EQIX	Chicago Mercantile Exchange : CME	Yes	17,850	83,455
FCYA Index	E-mini FTSE China 50 Index Future	Equity Index : EQIX	Chicago Mercantile Exchange : CME	No	5	60
FFEA Index	E-mini FTSE 100 Index Future	Equity Index : EQIX	Chicago Mercantile Exchange : CME	No	89	36
IBAA Index	Ibovespa, USD	Equity Index : EQIX	Chicago Mercantile Exchange : CME	No	6	146
ISDA Index	S&P 500 Quarterly Dividend Index Futures	Equity Index : EQIX	Chicago Mercantile Exchange : CME	No	20	842
IXAA Index	S&P E-mini Financial Select Sector Futures	Equity Index : EQIX	Chicago Mercantile Exchange : CME	No	94	5,004
IXCA Index	S&P E-mini Health Care Select Sector Futures	Equity Index : EQIX	Chicago Mercantile Exchange : CME	No	419	5,371
IXDA Index	S&P E-mini Materials Select Sector Futures	Equity Index : EQIX	Chicago Mercantile Exchange : CME	No	71	1,481
IXIA Index	S&P E-mini Industrial Select Sector Futures	Equity Index : EQIX	Chicago Mercantile Exchange : CME	No	34	8,784
IXPA Index	S&P E-mini Energy Select Sector Futures	Equity Index : EQIX	Chicago Mercantile Exchange : CME	No	130	2,507
IXRA Index	S&P E-mini Consumer Staples Select Sector Futures	Equity Index : EQIX	Chicago Mercantile Exchange : CME	No	83	25,399
IXSA Index	S&P E-mini Utilities Select Sector Futures	Equity Index : EQIX	Chicago Mercantile Exchange : CME	No	155	19,695
IXTA Index	S&P E-mini Technology Select Sector Futures	Equity Index : EQIX	Chicago Mercantile Exchange : CME	No	864	4,216
MNCA Index	CME E-Mini Nifty 50 Index Futures	Equity Index : EQIX	Chicago Mercantile Exchange : CME	No	535	104
NHA Index	Nikkei 225 Yen	Equity Index : EQIX	Chicago Mercantile Exchange : CME	Yes	50,404	68,076
NQA Index	NASDAQ 100 E-mini	Equity Index : EQIX	Chicago Mercantile Exchange : CME	Yes	253,877	226,860
NXA Index	Nikkei 225	Equity Index : EQIX	Chicago Mercantile Exchange : CME	Yes	15,962	33,758
RGYA Index	E-mini Russell 1000 Growth Index Futures	Equity Index : EQIX	Chicago Mercantile Exchange : CME	No	8	38
RSYA Index	E-mini Russell 1000 Index Futures	Equity Index : EQIX	Chicago Mercantile Exchange : CME	No	112	64
RVVA Index	E-mini Russell 1000 Value Index Futures	Equity Index : EQIX	Chicago Mercantile Exchange : CME	No	57	1,079
SPA Index	S&P 500	Equity Index : EQIX	Chicago Mercantile Exchange : CME	Yes	5,754	63,657
DJEA Index	DJ US Real Estate	Equity Index : EQIX	Chicago Board of Trade : CBT	No	328	14,680
DMA Index	DJ Industrial Average Mini	Equity Index : EQIX	Chicago Board of Trade : CBT	Yes	172,149	113,193
DNA Index	Bloomberg Commodity Index	Non-Equity Index : NEIX	Chicago Board of Trade : CBT	No	1,197	19,849

(Continued)

81

EXHIBIT 3.3 *(Continued)*

Ticker	Description	Category Equity Index	Exchange	Options	Volume	Open Interest
ATTA Index	ATX Index	Equity Index :EQIX	Eurex :EUX	No	1,357	39,338
AWA Index	Euro STOXX Construction	Equity Index :EQIX	Eurex :EUX	No	205	317
BHA Index	Euro STOXX Travel&Leisure	Equity Index :EQIX	Eurex :EUX	No	1	6,476
BJA Index	STOXX 600 Banks	Equity Index :EQIX	Eurex :EUX	No	16,661	64,446
BNA Index	Euro STOXX Food & Bev	Equity Index :EQIX	Eurex :EUX	No	355	2,207
BWA Index	Euro STOXX Ind Gds & Servs	Equity Index :EQIX	Eurex :EUX	No	282	164
CAA Index	Euro STOXX Banks	Equity Index :EQIX	Eurex :EUX	No	192,211	641,066
CEEA Index	CECEEUR Index	Equity Index :EQIX	Eurex :EUX	No	5,040	3,310
CUA Index	Euro STOXX Chemicals	Equity Index :EQIX	Eurex :EUX	No	34	432
DAA Index	DJ Euro STOXX Basic Res	Equity Index :EQIX	Eurex :EUX	No	41	2,229
DEDA Index	Euro Stoxx 50 DVD	Equity Index :EQIX	Eurex :EUX	Yes	22,887	958,912
DFWA Index	Mini-DAX Futures	Equity Index :EQIX	Eurex :EUX	No	22,972	3,823
DPA Index	TECDAX	Equity Index :EQIX	Eurex :EUX	No	315	4,340
DWA Index	Euro STOXX Personal & Household	Equity Index :EQIX	Eurex :EUX	No	148	2,204
EBA Index	Euro STOXX Auto	Equity Index :EQIX	Eurex :EUX	No	54	2,354
FCOA Index	Bloomberg Commodity Futures	Non-Equity Index :NEIX	Eurex :EUX	No	52	50
FVSA Index	VSTOXX Mini-Futures	Non-Equity Index :NEIX	Eurex :EUX	No	44,665	183,745
GPA Index	STOXX 600 Utilities	Equity Index :EQIX	Eurex :EUX	No	2,450	19,480
GXA Index	DAX Index	Equity Index :EQIX	Eurex :EUX	No	129,099	105,818
HGA Index	STOXX 600 Healthcare	Equity Index :EQIX	Eurex :EUX	No	2,496	17,296
HOA Index	Euro STOXX Healthcare	Equity Index :EQIX	Eurex :EUX	No	120	1,726
ITA Index	Euro STOXX Utilities	Equity Index :EQIX	Eurex :EUX	No	1,420	11,848
JAA Index	Euro STOXX Retail	Equity Index :EQIX	Eurex :EUX	No	423	544
JSA Index	STOXX 600 Basic Resources	Equity Index :EQIX	Eurex :EUX	No	1,795	23,116
JVA Index	STOXX 600 Insurance	Equity Index :EQIX	Eurex :EUX	No	449	6,124
KGA Index	STOXX 600 Oil & Gas	Equity Index :EQIX	Eurex :EUX	No	7,045	50,698

Source: Bloomberg, CTM Screen

Speculative Strategies

Outright Positions

As a speculative tool, equity index futures represent a highly liquid alternative to speculating on the overall stock market or on different types of stock indexes. In the case of equity index futures, bullish (bearish) speculators can take long (short) outright positions. Speculators that want to profit from directional changes in the market or a sector, but who do not want to assume the degree of risk associated with an outright position, can instead form a spread with stock index futures.

Exhibit 3.4 shows the Bloomberg Description screens and price graphs of the June 2016 E-Mini Health Care Sector futures index contract (IXCM6) and its underlying index—Health-Care index (IXV). The Health Care Spot index tracts the movement of the components of the S&P 500 index involved in health care services. The price graphs show the index and the June futures contract prices from 4/22/16 to 6/16/16 (the futures expiration date). From 4/22/16 to 5/6/16, the June futures decreased from 719.50 to 692. A bearish speculator who took a short position in one June contract on 4/22/16 and then closed it with a long position on 5/6/16 would have realized a profit of $2,750, while a bullish speculator who went long on 4/22/16 and closed with a short position on 5/6/16 would have lost $2,750 (see Exhibit 3.5). If the bullish speculator had opened his long position on 5/19/16 when the June contract was trading at 690.90 and closed it on 6/6/16 when the futures was at 727.60, he would have realized a profit of $3,670: Multiplier $(f_t - f_0) = (\$100)(727.60 - 690.90) = \$3,670$; while the bearish speculator would have lost $3,670: Multiplier $(f_0 - f_t) = (\$100)(690.90 - 727.60) = -\$3,670$.

Spreads

As discussed with commodity and currency speculative positions, futures spreads are formed by taking long and short positions on different futures contracts simultaneously. They are, in turn, used to reduce the risk associated with a pure outright position.

When the prices on more distant equity index futures contracts are more price sensitive to changes in its spot price than near-term futures, a spreader who is bullish on the index's market or sector could form an intracommodity spread by taking a long position in a longer-term index futures contract and a short position in a shorter-term one. If the index subsequently rises, the percentage gain in the long position on the distant contract will exceed the percentage loss on the short position on the nearby contract. In this case, the spreader will profit, but not as much as she would with an outright long position. On the other hand, if the index declines, the percentage losses on the long position will exceed the percentage gains from the short position. In this situation, the spreader will lose, but not as much as she would have if she had an outright long position. By varying the long-to-short ratios, the speculator can obtain different return-risk combinations. Like many currency futures, the prices of futures with different expirations might not deviate significantly from the spot price. If this is the case, then an intracommodity spread would not be an applicable speculative strategy.

EXHIBIT 3.4   Health Care Index and June Health Care Futures Contract Bloomberg Description and Price Screens

Health Care Sector Index

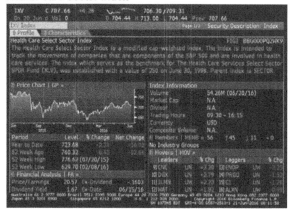

June E-Mini Health Care Sector Futures

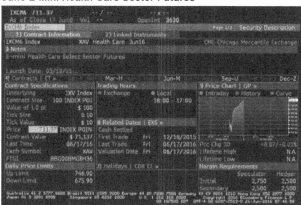

June Futures and Index Prices: 4/22/16–6/16/16

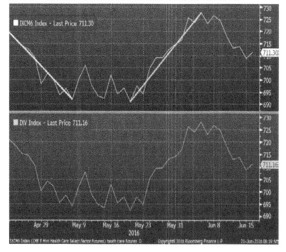

EXHIBIT 3.5   Long and Short Outright Positions on June E-Mini Health-Care Sector Contracts

	Clearinghouse Records for Long June Health-Care Sector Speculator
4/22/16	**Opening Position:**
	Speculator agrees to buy June E-Mini Health Care Sector futures on June 16, 2016, for 719.50 ($100 multiplier).
5/6/16	**Closing Position:**
	Speculator agrees to sell June E-Mini Health Care Sector futures on June 16, 2016, for 692 ($100 multiplier).
Settlement	Speculator pays clearinghouse $2,750.
	Closing payment to clearinghouse:
	Multiplier $(f_t - f_0) = (\$100)(692 - 719.50) = -\$2,750$
	Clearinghouse Records for Short June Health-Care Sector Speculator
4/22/16	**Opening Position:**
	Speculator agrees to sell June E-Mini Health Care Sector futures on June 16, 2016, for 719.50 ($100 multiplier).
5/6/16	**Closing Position:**
	Speculator agrees to buy June E-Mini Health Care Sector futures on June 16, 2016, for 692 ($100 multiplier).
Settlement	Speculators receive $2,750 from the clearinghouse.
	Closing receipt from clearinghouse:
	Multiplier $(f_0 - f_t) = (\$100)(719.50 - 692) = \$2,750$

Instead of an intracommodity spread, a spreader alternatively could form an intercommodity spread by taking opposite positions in different index futures. For example, suppose the relation between the Russell 2,000 index and the Russell 1,000 index is such that when the Russell 2,000 changes by 10%, the Russell 1,000 changes by 9%. A risk-averse investor who is bearish on the market could set up an intercommodity spread by going short in the Russell 2,000 contract and long in the Russell 1,000 contract. As discussed with commodity and currency spreads, intercommodity index futures spreads allow investors to attain lower return-risk combinations than pure speculative positions. Moreover, by changing the ratios from one long to one short or by forming intercommodity spreads with different correlations, spreaders can attain a number of different return-risk combinations.

Intercommodity Spread: Bloomberg Case

Exhibit 3.6 shows Bloomberg's HRA screen displaying the estimated regression relation between the Health Care Sector Index (IXV) and the Technology Index (IXT). The slope of the regression line is $\Delta IXV / \Delta IXT = 0.734$. An equity speculator expecting the overall market to increase (decrease) could form an intercommodity spread by going long (short) in a Technology Index futures and short (long) in Mini Health Care Index futures. Exhibit 3.7 shows the futures prices for the June 2016 E-Mini

EXHIBIT 3.6   Regression Relation Between Health Care Index and Technology Index

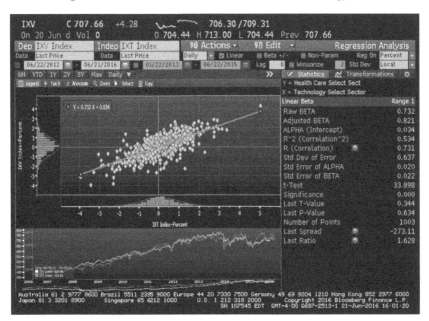

EXHIBIT 3.7   Prices on June Technology Index Futures and Short in June Health-Care Index
Futures: 1/1/ 2016 to 6/6/16

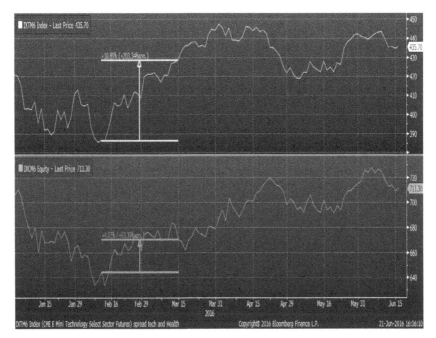

EXHIBIT 3.8   Intercommodity Spread: Long in June Technology Index Futures and Short in June Health Care Index Futures

	Clearinghouse Records for Bullish Intercommodity Spread
2/10/16	**Opening Position:**
	Speculator agrees to buy Technology Index on June 16, 2016, for $f_0 = 386.60$ ($100 multiplier).
	Speculator agrees to sell Health Care Index on June 16, 2016, for $f_0 = 644.40$ ($100 multiplier).
3/15/16	**Closing Position:**
	Speculator agrees to sell Technology Index on June 16, 2016, for $f_t = 428.70$ ($100 multiplier).
	Speculator agrees to buy Health Care Index on June 16, 2016, for $f_t = 670.60$ ($100 multiplier).
Settlement	**Long Technology Position:**
	Clearinghouse pays Speculator $4,210:
	Multiplier $(f_t - f_0) = (\$100)(428.70 - 386.60) = \$4,210$
	Short Health Care Position:
	Speculator pays clearinghouse $2,620:
	Multiplier $(f_0 - f_t) = (\$100)(644.40 - 670.60) = -\$2,620$
	Intercommodity Spread Position: $4,210 − $2,620 = $1,590

Technology index futures and the June 2016 E-Mini Health-Care index futures from 1/1/16 to 6/6/16 (expiration on the contracts).

Suppose a bullish speculator formed an intercommodity spread on 2/10/16 by going long in one June 2016 E-Mini Technology Index futures and short in one June 2016 E-Mini Health Care Index futures. From 2/10/16 to 3/15/16, the June Technology futures contract increased 10.89% from 386.60 to 428.70 and the June Health Care contract increased 4.07% from 644.40 to 670.60 (see Exhibit 3.8). If the spreader opened her spread on 2/10/16 and closed it on 3/15/16, she would have realized a profit of $4,210 on her long Technology Index futures position and a loss of $2,620 on her short Health Care futures position, resulting in a net gain of $1,590.

The spreader probably regretted that she did not take an outright long position in the Technology Index where she would have realized a $4,210 gain. Her short position in the Health Care Index, however, was taken to give her some protection if the market declined and both sectors decreased.

Hedging Equity Positions

One of the major uses of stock index derivatives is hedging stock portfolio positions. Several different types of hedging models can be applied to hedging portfolio positions. Depending on the underlying asset to be hedged, the most popular models are the *Naive Hedging Model* and the *Price-Sensitivity Model*.

Hedging Models

Naive Hedging Model

In many of the hedging cases we presented for commodities and currency positions, we assumed ideal conditions in which there was no quantity, quality, or timing risk extant. In such rare cases, a perfect hedge, in which the value of the spot position is unchanged at expiration, can be attained using a naive hedging model. In this model, the number of futures contracts (n_f) is found simply by dividing the current value of the spot position (V_0) by the price of the futures contract (f_0).

$$\text{Naive Hedge: } n_f = \frac{V_0}{f_0}$$

For example, a portfolio manager who wants to lock in the future value of a $50 million portfolio highly correlated with the overall market when the futures price on the S&P 500 futures contract is 2,000 ($250 multiplier) could do so by going short in n_f = 100 S&P 500 futures contracts:

$$n_f = \frac{V_0}{f_0} = \frac{\$50,000,000}{(2,000)(\$250)} = 100 \text{ contracts}$$

Under ideal conditions, the combined value of the portfolio and the cash flows from the futures position would be worth $50 million at the futures delivery date.

In practice, we would expect some quality, quantity, and timing risks to exist in hedging a portfolio with index futures. For example, the $50 million portfolio may not be perfectly positively correlated with the S&P 500 spot index (quality risk). With less than perfect positive correlation, the percentage changes in the portfolio value would differ from those of the index. In such a case, a naive hedging model will not be able to provide a perfect hedge. Also, in most hedging applications, the time period for hedging the portfolio differs from the time period on the futures contract (timing risk), and the relative prices of the portfolio and futures contract usually do not yield a hedge ratio with a round number like 25 (quantity risk). For a manager wanting to hedge a stock portfolio with index futures in which such hedging risk exists, the price-sensitivity model may be more effective in reducing price risk than the naive hedging model.

Stock Index Price-Sensitivity Model

The price-sensitivity model determines the number of stock index futures contracts that will minimize the variability of the profits from a hedged portfolio consisting of the stock portfolio and stock index futures contracts. In this model, the number of futures contracts or hedge ratio (n_f) that will minimize the variability is:

$$n_f = \beta \frac{V_0}{f_0}$$

where:

V_0 = current value of the stock portfolio.
f_0 = price on the futures contract.
β = beta of stock portfolio.

Thus, if a June S&P 500 futures contract is available at 2,000, a portfolio manager wanting to hedge a $50 million portfolio with a beta of 1.5 would need 150 short contracts:

$$n_f = \beta \frac{V_0}{f_0} = 1.50 \frac{\$50,000,000}{(2,000)(\$250)} = 150 \text{ contracts}$$

Short Hedge

Consider the case of a portfolio manager, who in January knows that he will have to liquidate his stock portfolio in June and decides to hedge the value of the stock portfolio by taking a short position in the June S&P 500 futures contract. Assume in this case that the portfolio is well-diversified (no unsystematic risk), has a beta of 1.25, and in January is worth $50,000,000 when the S&P 500 spot index (S_0) is at 2,000. Finally, suppose a June S&P 500 futures contract is priced at 2,000 with a $250 multiple. To hedge the portfolio, the manager would need to go short in 125 S&P 500 contracts:

$$n_f = \beta \frac{V_0}{f_0} = 1.25 \frac{\$50,000,000}{(2,000)(\$250)} = 125 \text{ contracts}$$

At the June expiration, the manager would liquidate his portfolio and receive or pay a cash settlement equal to the difference in the futures price (f_0) and the closing spot price on the S&P 500 (S_T) on the delivery day: $f_0 - S_T$. (The manager more likely would close the futures contract by going long in the expiring June contract trading near the spot price: $f_T = S_T$.) With the short position, any loss in the market would be offset by a gain on the futures position. However, any gain in the market would be negated by a loss on the futures position. This can be seen in Exhibit 3.9. In the exhibit, the first column shows five possible S&P 500 spot index values from 1,500 to 2,500; the second column shows the proportional change in S&P 500 from the 2,000 value of the index when the hedge was set up; column 3 shows the proportion changes in the portfolio given its beta of 1.25; column 4 shows the portfolio values that correspond with the index values; column 5 shows the cash flow at expiration from one future position; column 6 shows the cash realized from the 125 short index futures contract at the June expiration; and column 7 shows the value of the futures-hedged portfolio of $50,000,000.

In this example, we have a perfect hedge. Part of this is because we assumed the portfolio is well-diversified and the futures price and portfolio value are such that exactly 125 contracts are needed. In most cases, we would not expect such conditions to exist. Also, if the markets are efficient, we would not expect any difference to exist between locking in the June value of the portfolio with index futures and locking in the June portfolio value by selling the portfolio in January and investing the

EXHIBIT 3.9 Value of Futures-Hedged Stock Portfolio

(1)	(2)	(3)	(4)	(5)	(6)	(7)
S&P 500 Spot Index at Expiration: $S_T = f_T$	Proportional Change in the S&P 500: $(S_T - 2000)/2000$	Proportional Change in Portfolio Value $\beta g = 1.25$ $(S_T - 2000)/2000)$	Portfolio Value: $(1 + \beta g)\$50m$	Short Futures Cash Flow per Contract $f_0 - S_T = 2,000 - S_T$	Futures Cash Flow $125(\$250)$ $(2000 - f_T)$	Hedged Portfolio Value $(4) + (6)$
1,500	−0.25	−0.31250	$34,375,000	500	$15,625,000	$50,000,000
1,750	−0.125	−0.15625	$42,187,500	250	$7,812,500	$50,000,000
2,000	0.00	0.00	$50,000,000	0	$0.00	$50,000,000
2,250	0.125	0.15625	$57,812,500	−250	−$7,812,500	$50,000,000
2,500	0.25	0.31250	$65,625,000	−500	−$15,625,000	$50,000,000

$$n_f = \frac{\beta V_0}{f_0} = \frac{(1.25)(\$50,000,000)}{(\$250)(2,000)} = 125 \text{ contracts}$$

proceeds in a risk-free security for the period. Thus, if the portfolio manager actually knew he would be liquidating the portfolio in June, then selling 125 futures contracts in January and closing the contracts and liquidating the portfolio in June should be equivalent to selling the portfolio in January and investing the funds in a risk-free security for the period. If this equivalence did not hold, an arbitrage opportunity would exist. Exploiting such opportunities, in turn, is the basis of the index carrying cost model for determining the equilibrium price of index futures. This is examined later in this chapter.

Long Index Hedging Example

A portfolio manager who was planning to invest a future inflow of cash in a stock portfolio could lock in the purchase price of the portfolio by going long in a stock index futures contract. For example, suppose in January, the portfolio manager in the above example was anticipating an inflow of cash in June and was planning to invest the cash in a stock portfolio with a beta of 1.25 and currently worth $50,000,000. If the June S&P 500 futures contract is at $f_0 = 2,000$, the manager could hedge the portfolio purchase price by going long in 125 contracts:

$$n_f = \beta \frac{V_0}{f_0} = 1.25 \frac{\$50,000,000}{(2,000)(\$250)} = 125 \text{ contracts}$$

In June, the manager would buy the portfolio and receive or pay a cash settlement on the futures equal to the difference in the closing spot price on the S&P 500 (S_T) on the delivery day and the futures price: $S_T - f_0$. (Again, the manager more likely would close the futures contract by going short in the expiring June contract trading near the spot price: $f_T = S_T$.) With the long position, any higher portfolio cost due to a stock market increase would be offset by a gain on the long futures position. On the other hand, any lower portfolio cost because of a market decrease would be negated

EXHIBIT 3.10 Future Portfolio Purchase Hedged with Index Futures

(1) S&P 500 Spot Index: S_T	(2) Proportional Change in the S&P 500: $(S_T - 2000)/$ 2000	(3) Proportional Change in Portfolio Value $\beta g = 1.25$ $(S_T - 2000)/$ 2000	(4) Portfolio Costs $\$50m(1 + \beta g)$	(5) Long Futures Cash Flow per Contract $S_T - f_0 =$ $(S_T - 2000)$	(6) Futures Cash Flow $125(\$250)$ $(f_T - 2000)$	(7) Portfolio Costs with Futures $(4) - (6)$
1,500	−0.25	−0.31250	$34,375,000	−500	−$15,625,000	$50,000,000
1,750	−0.125	−0.15625	$42,187,500	−250	−$7,812,500	$50,000,000
2,000	0.00	0.00	$50,000,000	0	$0.00	$50,000,000
2,250	0.125	0.15625	$57,812,500	250	$7,812,500	$50,000,000
2,500	0.25	0.31250	$65,625,000	500	$15,625,000	$50,000,000

$$n_f = \frac{\beta V_0}{f_0} = \frac{(1.25)(\$50,000,000)}{(\$250)(2,000)} = 125 \text{ contracts}$$

by a loss on the long futures position. This is shown in Exhibit 3.10, where the long hedge position enables the manager to lock in a cost of $50 million for purchasing the portfolio and closing the futures position in June, regardless of the S&P 500 value.

Hedging Risk

The previous examples represent perfect hedging cases in which certain revenues or costs can be locked in at a future date. Most portfolio hedging is subject to quality, timing, and quantity risk. Quality risk exists when the commodity or asset being hedged is not identical to the one underlying the futures contract. In the above example, the portfolio with a beta of 1.25 was not identical to the S&P 500. The beta in the formula for n_f, in turn, adjusted the number of contracts to reduce the quality risk. Timing risk would exist in our long hedging example if the manager needed to invest in a portfolio at the beginning of June instead of at the futures' expiration at the end of June. To minimize timing risk or basis risk, portfolio hedgers often select futures contracts that mature before the hedged asset is to be bought or sold but as close as possible to that date. For very distant horizon dates, hedgers might follow a rolling-the-hedge-forward strategy by taking a futures position, then at expiration closing the position and taking a new one. Finally, because of the standardization of futures contracts, futures hedge is subject to quantity risk. As noted previously, the presence of quality, timing, and quantity risk means that pricing risk cannot be eliminated totally by hedging with futures contracts.

Bloomberg Case: Portfolio Hedging

Exhibit 3.11 summarizes the portfolio features of the Xavier Growth Fund and the Russell 1,000 Index as of 6/23/16. The information was accessed from Bloomberg's

EXHIBIT 3.11   Bloomberg Case: Xavier Growth Fund: Features Compared to Russell 1,000 Index

Indicator	Xavier Growth Fund	Russell 1,000 Index, RIY
Market Value: 6/23/16	$10,905,664	–
Dividend Yield	2.87	2.14
Price to Earnings Ratio (P/E)	19.13	19.97
Price to Cash Flow Ratio (P/CF)	10.94	10.97
Price to Book Ratio (P/B)	2.86	2.75
Current Ratio	1.20	1.38
Beta	0.85	1.00

Portfolio screen (PORT) as of 6/23/16. The fund's holdings consisted of 10 Blue Chip stocks (15,000 shares in each stock), a dividend yield of $2.87/share compared to the Russell 1,000 Index dividend yield of $2.14 and a beta of 0.85. On 6/23/16, the fund had a market value of $10,905,664. Exhibit 3.12 shows the values of the fund and the prices on the Russell 1,000 index and a June Mini-Russell Futures Contract (contract size = $50) from 9/17/16 to 6/16/16 (expiration date on the futures). From 12/1/15 to 1/20/16, the fund decreased 7.29% from $10.249 million to $9.501 million, the Russell 1,000 Index decreased 12.08% from 1,166.65 to 1,025.68, and the June Russell 1,000 futures contract decreased 11.17% from 1,158.60 to 1,029.20.

EXHIBIT 3.12   Values of Xavier Growth Fund, Russell 1,000, and June Mini-Russell 1,000 Futures Contract from 9/17/15 to 6/16/16

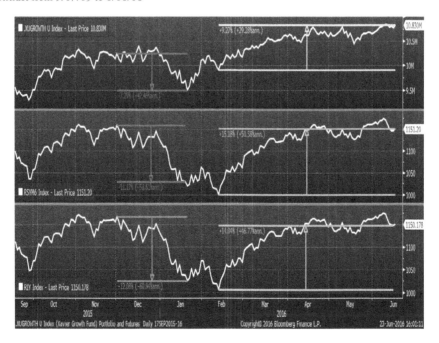

Using the price-sensitivity model, the Xavier Growth Fund's value could have been hedged on 12/1/15 by going short in 150 June contracts:

$$n_f = \beta \frac{V_0}{f_0} = 0.85 \frac{\$10.249 \, \text{million}}{(1,158.60)(\$50)} = 150 \, \text{contracts}$$

As shown in Exhibit 3.13, the hedged portfolio value would have been $10.4715 million on 1/20/16 instead of $9.501 million.

Portfolio Exposure—Market Timing

Instead of hedging a portfolio's value against market or systematic risk, suppose a manager wanted to change her portfolio's exposure to the market. For example, a stock portfolio manager who is very confident of a bull market may want to give her portfolio more exposure to the market by increasing the portfolio's beta. Changing a portfolio's beta to profit from an expected change in the market is referred to as *market timing*.

Without index futures and derivatives, the beta of a portfolio can be changed only by altering the portfolio's allocation of securities. With index futures, though, a manager can change the portfolio beta, β_0, to a new one, referred to as a target beta, β_{TR}, simply by going long or short in equity index futures contracts. The number of futures contracts needed to move the portfolio beta from β_0 to β_{TR} can be determined using the price-sensitivity model in which:

$$n_f = \frac{V_0}{f_0} \, (\beta_{TR} - \beta_0)$$

EXHIBIT 3.13   Xavier Growth Fund Hedged with June Mini-Russell 1,000 Futures Contracts

	Fund Values and Opening and Closing Clearinghouse Records for June Mini-RIY Index
12/1/15	**Xavier Growth Fund Value = $10.249 million**
	Futures Opening Position:
	Fund agrees to sell 150 Mini-Russell 1,000 futures contracts on June 16, 2016 for 1,158.60 ($50 multiplier).
2/11/16	**Xavier Growth Fund Value = $9.501 million**
	Futures Closing Position:
	Fund agrees to buy 150 Mini-Russell 1,000 futures contracts on June 16, 2016 for 1,029.20 ($50 multiplier).
Settlement	Speculators receive $970,500 from clearinghouse:
	$(N_f)(\text{Multiplier}) \, (f_0 - f_t) = (150)(\$50)(1,158.60 - 1,029.20) = \$970,500.$
	Hedged Portfolio Value:
	$9.501 million + 0.9705 million = $10.4715 million
	Unhedged portfolio value: $9.501 million

where

if $\beta_{TR} > \beta_0$, long in futures
if $\beta_{TR} < \beta_0$, short in futures

Market-Timing Example

Consider the case of a stock portfolio manager who in September is confident the market will increase over the next three months, and as a result, wants to change her portfolio's beta from its current value of $\beta_0 = 1$ to $\beta_{TR} = 1.25$. Suppose the portfolio currently is worth \$100 million, the spot S&P 500 index is at 2,000, and the price on the December S&P 500 futures contract is 2,000. To adjust the portfolio beta from 1 to 1.25, the manager would need to buy $n_f = 50$ December S&P 500 index futures:

$$n_f = \frac{V_0}{f_0}(\beta_{TR} - \beta_0) = \frac{\$100,000,000}{(2,000)(\$250)} \ (1.25 - 1) = 50$$

As shown in Exhibit 3.14, if the market increases, the manager earns higher rates of return from the futures-adjusted portfolio than from the unadjusted portfolio. If the market declines, though, she incurs greater losses with the adjusted portfolio than with the unadjusted. For example, on the futures expiration, if the market increased by 10%, the portfolio values would have increased from \$100 million to \$110 million (a 10% increase, reflecting a $\beta = 1$), and the spot index and closing futures price would have increased to $f_T = S_T = 2,000(1.10) = 2,200$, generating an additional cash flow of \$2.5 million from the long futures position (\$2,500,000 = (50)(\$250)(2,200 − 2,000)) and increasing the portfolio value to \$112.5 million (a 12.5% increase, reflecting a $\beta = 1.25$). In contrast, on the futures expiration, if the market decreased by 10%, the portfolio would have decreased from \$100 million to \$90 million (a 10% decrease, reflecting a $\beta = 1$), and the spot index and closing futures price would have decreased to $f_T = S_T = 2,000(0.90) = 1,800$, generating a loss of \$2.5 million from the long futures position (\$2,500,000 = (50)(\$250)(1,800 − 2,000)) and decreasing the portfolio value to \$87.5 million (a 12.5% decrease, reflecting a $\beta = 1.25$). Thus, the futures-enhanced portfolio is consistent with the characteristics of a portfolio with a β of 1.25.

Bloomberg Case: Market Timing

In our Bloomberg portfolio hedging case, we showed how the Xavier Growth Fund maintained it value of approximately \$10 million by going short in 150 June Russell 1,000 futures contracts. From 2/11/16 to 6/16/16, the fund increased 9.27% from \$9.911 million to \$10.83 million, the Russell 1,000 Index increased 14.12% from 1,005.89 to 1,147.89, and the June Russell 1,000 futures contract increased 15.18% from 999.50 to 1,151.20. Suppose on 2/11/16, the Xavier Growth Fund's managers decided to increase the portfolio's exposure in anticipation of a market increase.

EXHIBIT 3.14 Market Timing

(1)	(2)	(3)	(4)	(5)
S&P 500 Spot Index: $S_T = f_T$	Proportional Change: $g = (S_T - 2,000)/2,000$	Portfolio Value $100m(1 + g)$	Futures Profit $(50)($250) [f_T - 2,000]$	Portfolio Value with Futures (3) + (4)
1,600	−0.20	$80,000,000	−$5,000,000	$75,000,000
1,800	−0.10	$90,000,000	−$2,500,000	$87,500,000
2,000	0.00	$100,000,000	0	$100,000,000
2,200	0.10	$110,000,000	$2,500,000	$112,500,000
2,400	0.20	$120,000,000	$5,000,000	$125,000,000

S&P 500 Spot Index: S_T	Portfolio Rates of Return and $\beta = \Delta$ Portfolio Rate/Δg			
	(6)	(7)	(8)	(9)
	Portfolio Rate: [Col (3)/$100m] − 1	β Col(6)/Col(2)	Futures-Enhanced Portfolio Rate: [Col (5)/$100m] − 1	β Col(8)/Col(2)
1,600	−0.20	1.00	−0.25	1.25
1,800	−0.10	1.00	−0.125	1.25
2,000	0.00	1.00	0	1.25
2,100	0.10	1.00	0.125	1.25
2,200	0.20	1.00	0.25	1.25

It increased its beta from 0.85 to 1.25 by going long in June Russell Index futures. Using the price-sensitivity model, the fund would have needed to go long in 79 June contracts:

$$n_f = \frac{V_0}{f_0}(\beta_{TR} - \beta_0) = \frac{\$9,911,000}{(999.50)(\$50)}(1.25 - 0.85) = 79 \text{ contracts}$$

As shown in Exhibit 3.15, the futures-enhanced portfolio value would have been worth $11.429 million on 6/16/16 instead of $10.83 million. This represents an 11.51% increase compared to 5.677% without the futures.

Speculating on Unsystematic Risk

The price movements of an individual stock are affected by both systematic factors (market factors that affect all stocks) and unsystematic factors (factors unique to the securities of a particular industry or firm). Suppose an investor is very confident that firm or industry factors in the future will lead to a stock price increase. However,

EXHIBIT 3.15 Xavier Growth Fund Futures-Enhanced Portfolio: Portfolio and June Mini-Russell 1,000 Futures Contracts

	Fund Values and Opening and Closing Clearinghouse Records for June Mini-RIY Index
2/11/16	**Xavier Growth Fund Value = $10.249 million**
	Futures Opening Position:
	Fund agrees to buy 79 Mini-Russell 1,000 futures contracts on June 16, 2016 for 999.50 ($50 multiplier).
6/16/16	**Xavier Growth Fund Value = $10.83 million**
	Futures Closing Position:
	Fund agrees to sell 79 Mini-Russell 1,000 futures contracts on June 16, 2016 for 1,151.20 ($50 multiplier).
Settlement	Speculators receive $970,500 from clearinghouse:
	$(n_f)(\text{Multiplier})\,(f_t - f_0) = (79)(\$50)(1,151.20 - 999.50) = \$599,215.$
	Hedged Portfolio Value:
	$10.83 million + 0.599215 million = $11.429215 million
	Portfolio value without futures: $10.83 million

suppose that the investor is also bearish about the market, fearing that a general price decline in all securities would partially negate the anticipated positive impacts on the stock's price resulting from the specific firm or industry events. The investor would therefore like to eliminate the stock's systematic factors, leaving his investment exposed only to the unsystematic factors. With index futures, an investor can accomplish this by hedging away the systematic risk of the stock.

Speculating on Unsystematic Risk: Example

To illustrate how speculating on unsystematic risk works, consider the case of a hedged fund that in June identifies the ABC company as a good candidate for a takeover by a leveraged buyout firm. Based on this expectation, suppose the hedge fund is considering purchasing 100,000 shares of ABC stock, but is hesitant because it is afraid the stock market could decline over the next three months (the time period its managers believe the takeover could happen). To hedge against the systematic risk, the fund could go short in September index futures. In this case, suppose ABC stock has a beta of 1.10 and is trading at $50 per share, the spot S&P 500 is at 2,000, and the September S&P 500 futures contract is at 2,000. The hedge fund could speculate on the stock's unsystematic risk while hedging the systematic risk by buying 100,000 shares of ABC stock and going short in eleven December index futures contracts:

$$n_f = \beta\,\frac{V_0}{f_0} = (1.10)\,\frac{(100,000)(\$50)}{(2,000)(\$250)} = 11 \text{ short contracts}$$

To see the possible impacts of using this strategy, consider the following four scenarios occurring in mid-September:

- **Scenario A:** The takeover of ABC and a bull market cause the price of ABC stock to increase by 20% to $60.00 and the spot S&P 500 to increase 10% to 2,200.
- **Scenario B:** No takeover of ABC and a bull market cause ABC stock to increase by 11% to $55.50 and the spot S&P 500 to increase 10% to 2,200.
- **Scenario C:** The takeover of ABC and a bear market cause ABC stock to increase by 10% to $55.00 and the spot S&P 500 to decrease by 10% to 1,800.
- **Scenario D:** No takeover of ABC and a bear market cause ABC stock to decrease by 11% to $44.50 and the spot S&P 500 to decrease 10% to 1,800.

Exhibit 3.16 shows the values and rates of return for both the futures-hedged stock position and the unhedged stock position for each of the four cases. As shown, the highest returns are earned on the hedged stock if Scenario C occurs: The takeover takes place during a bear market. In this case, the hedge fund would gain both from speculating on the takeover and from the short futures position, earning a 21% rate of

EXHIBIT 3.16   Speculating on Unsystematic Risk

(1) Scenario	(2) Futures Profit (11)($250) $[2,000 - f_T]$	(3) Stock Value (Stock Price) (100,000 Shares)	(4) Stock Value Hedged with Futures: (2) + (3)
A **Takeover and Bull Market:** ABC Stock = $60 $S_T = f_T = 2,200$	−$550,000	$6,000,000	$5,450,000
B **No Takeover and Bull Market:** ABC Stock = $55.50 $S_T = f_T = 2,200$	−$550,000	$5,550,000	$5,000,000
C **Takeover and Bear Market:** ABC Stock = $55 $S_T = f_T = 1,800$	$550,000	$5,500,000	$6,050,000
D **No Takeover and Bear Market:** ABC Stock = $44.50 $S_T = f_T = 1,800$	$550,000	$4,450,000	$5,000,000

	Rates of Return	
Scenario	$Rate = \dfrac{Col.(3)}{(100,000)(\$50)} - 1$	$Rate = \dfrac{Col.(4)}{(100,000)(\$50)} - 1$
A	9.00%	20.00%
B	0.00%	11.00%
C	21.00%	10.00%
D	0.00%	−11.00%

return. If the fund did not hedge, then its rate of return would have been only 10%. A positive rate of return of 9% on the hedged stock position is also realized in Case A, in which there is a takeover during a bull market. Since the trust department has hedged away the systematic factors, the hedged returns are not as high as the unhedged position of 20% in this scenario. In Scenario B, in which there is no takeover and the market increases, the hedged return is zero compared to the unhedged return of 11%. Finally, in Scenario D in which there is no takeover and the market declines, the hedged stock return is zero, while the unhedged return loses 11%. Thus, the best scenario for the hedge fund is Scenario C, in which both of the fund's expectation occur—takeover and bear market.

Carrying-Cost Model for an Equity Index

Like all futures pricing, the equilibrium futures price on a stock index futures contract is determined by the cost-of-carry model. For an equity index, its equilibrium futures price is equal to the net costs of carrying a spot index portfolio or proxy portfolio to expiration at time T. For the case of a discrete dividend payment on the portfolio worth D_T at expiration, the equilibrium futures price is

$$f_0^* = S_0(1 + R_f)^T - D_T$$

where

S_0 = current spot index value
D_T = value of the stock index dividends at time T
R_f = Annual risk-free rate
T = Time to expiration as a proportion of a year

For the continuous dividend case, the equilibrium futures price is

$$f_0^* = S_0 e^{(R_f - \psi)T}$$

where

ψ = Annual dividend yield

If the equilibrium condition does not hold, an arbitrage opportunity will exist by taking a position in the spot portfolio and an opposite one in the futures contract. For example, if the market price on the futures contract (f_0^M) exceeds the equilibrium price, an arbitrageur could earn a riskless profit of $f_0^M - f_0^*$ with an *index arbitrage* strategy in which she borrows S_0 dollars at the risk-free rate of R_f, buys the spot index portfolio for S_0, and locks in the selling price on the portfolio at time T by going short in the index futures at f_0^M.

Index Arbitrage

An index arbitrage strategy requires identifying a position in the underlying index portfolio. To go long in the S&P 500 would require the purchase of the index's

500 stocks in their correct proportions and the correct reinvestment of each stock's dividends for the futures period. In practice, arbitrageurs can take positions in smaller proxy portfolios. A proxy portfolio could be formed with a small number of securities whose allocations in the portfolio were determined so as to maximize the correlation between the portfolio's returns and the spot index. A proxy portfolio also might be formed with a highly diversified mutual fund or ETF, such as a spider. The proxy portfolio, mutual fund, or ETF can be viewed as a position in the index. For example, if the spot S&P 500 were at 2,000, then a highly diversified portfolio with a current value of $5 million, dividends expected to be worth $250,000 one year later, and a beta of one could be viewed as equivalent to a hypothetical S&P 500 spot portfolio consisting of $N_0 = 2,500$ hypothetical shares of the index, with each share priced at $S_0 = \$2,000$, and with an expected dividends per share of $100 ($D_T = \$250,000/2,500$):

$$V_0^P = N_0 S_0$$

$$V_0^P = (2,500)(\$2,000) = \$5,000,000$$

$$D_T = \frac{\text{Total expected dividends}}{N_0} = \frac{\$250,000}{2,500} = \$100$$

The proxy portfolio, in turn, can be used to determine the carrying-cost price of the index futures contract, as well as the arbitrage strategies when an index futures contract is mispriced. For example, suppose the S&P 500 spot index were currently at 2,000, the risk-free rate was at 5%, and there was an S&P 500 futures contract expiring in one year ($T = 1$). In terms of the carrying-cost model, the equilibrium price on the S&P 500 futures contract using the proxy portfolio's dividend per share of $100 would be $2,000:

$$f_0^* = S_0(1 + R_f)^T - D_T$$

$$f_0^* = \$2,000\,(1.05)^1 - \$100 = \$2,000$$

If the market futures price is above the equilibrium, for example at $f_0^M = \$2,025$, an arbitrageur could receive a cash flow of $25 (= $2,025 − $2,000) per index share at expiration with an index arbitrage strategy formed by borrowing $2,000 at 5%, buying an S&P 500 spot index share, and going short in the S&P 500 futures contract at $2,025. This arbitrage can also be formed with the $5 million proxy portfolio by:

1. Borrowing $5,000,000 at 5%.
2. Purchasing the proxy portfolio for $5,000,000.
3. Going short in 10 S&P 500 futures contracts (Index shares/multiplier = 2,500/250 = 10 S&P 500 futures contracts; given the contracts' $250 multiplier) expiring in one year.

EXHIBIT 3.17   Index Arbitrage Using Proxy Portfolio When the S&P 500 Index Futures Are Overpriced

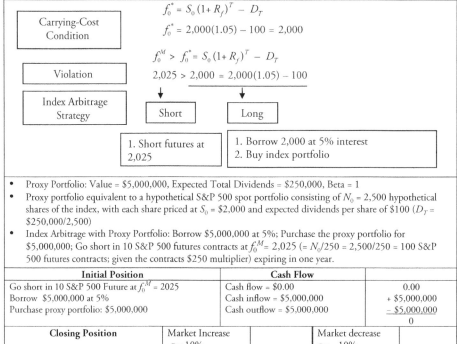

- Proxy Portfolio: Value = $5,000,000, Expected Total Dividends = $250,000, Beta = 1
- Proxy portfolio equivalent to a hypothetical S&P 500 spot portfolio consisting of N_0 = 2,500 hypothetical shares of the index, with each share priced at S_0 = $2,000 and expected dividends per share of $100 ($D_T$ = $250,000/2,500)
- Index Arbitrage with Proxy Portfolio: Borrow $5,000,000 at 5%; Purchase the proxy portfolio for $5,000,000; Go short in 10 S&P 500 futures contracts at f_0^M = 2,025 (= N_0/250 = 2,500/250 = 100 S&P 500 futures contracts; given the contracts $250 multiplier) expiring in one year.

Initial Position	Cash Flow	
Go short in 10 S&P 500 Future at f_0^M = 2025	Cash flow = $0.00	0.00
Borrow $5,000,000 at 5%	Cash inflow = $5,000,000	+ $5,000,000
Purchase proxy portfolio: $5,000,000	Cash outflow = $5,000,000	− $5,000,000
		0

Closing Position	Market Increase g = 10% $S_T = f_T$ =2,000(1.10) $S_T = f_T$ =2,200		Market decrease g = −10% S_T = 2,000(0.90) = 1,800	
Close futures: (10)(250)(2025 − f_T)	= (10)(250)(−175)	− $437,500	= (10)(250)(225)	$562,500
Sell Proxy Portfolio: $5,000,000(1 + g)	= $5,000,000(1.10)	$5,500,000	= $5,000,000(0.90)	$4,500,000
Receive Dividends: $250,000	= $250,000	$250,000	= $250,000	$250,000
Repay Debt: $5,000,000(1.05)	= − $5,250,000	− $5,250,000	= − $5,250,000	− $5,250,000
		$62,500		$62,500

As shown in Exhibit 3.17, the arbitrageur would realize a cash flow of $62,500 at expiration (arbitrage cash flow per the index times the number of hypothetical index shares defining the proxy portfolio: ($25)(2,500) = $62,500. At expiration, the arbitrageur would sell her portfolio, close her expiring futures positions, receive the portfolio's dividends, and repay her $5,250,00 debt (= $5,000,000 (1.05)). She, in turn, would receive $62,500 provided the proxy portfolio is perfectly correlated with the S&P 500 and she receives the expected dividends. For example, if one year later the market increased by 10% (g = 0.10) such that the S&P 500 were at 2,200 (= 2,000(1.10)), then the portfolio (if it were perfectly correlated) would be worth $5,500,000 (= $5,000,000(1.10)), $250,000 in dividends would be received, the cost of debt would be $5,250,000 (= $5,000,000(1.05)), and there would be a loss of $437,500 from closing the short futures position by going long in expiring S&P

futures at $f_T = S_T = 2,200$: $(10)(250)$ $(f_0^M - S_T) = (10)(\$250)$ $(2,025 - 2,200) =$ $-\$437,500$. Thus, the net cash flow in this case would be $62,500 at a spot index and closing futures price of 2,200. Moreover, with an arbitrage of $62,500, arbitrageurs would try to set up this index arbitrage strategy with the proxy portfolio and index futures. By their actions, though, they would try to go short in the S&P futures causing the price of futures to decrease until it equaled the carrying-cost value of 2,000. At that price, the arbitrage is zero.

In contrast, if the market decreased by 10% ($g = -0.10$) one year later, then the spot S&P 500 and expiring futures contract would be at 1,800 (= (2,000)(0.90)). In this case, the proxy portfolio (if it were perfectly correlated) would be worth $4,500,000 (= ($5,000,000) (0.90)), $250,000 in dividends would be received, the cost of debt still would be $5,250,000 (= $5,000,000(1.05)), and there would be a gain of $562,500 from closing the short futures positions by going long in the expiring S&P futures at $f_T = S_T = 1,800$: $(10)(\$250)$ $(f_0^M - S_T) = (10)(\$250)$ $(2,025 - 1,800) = \$562,500$. Thus, at a spot index and closing futures price of 1,800, the net cash flow would again be $62,500. In fact, for any spot index, there is an arbitrage profit of $62,500, provided the proxy portfolio is perfectly correlated and expected dividends of $250,000 are received.

If the market futures price is below the equilibrium price of $2,000, for example at $f_0^M = \$1,975$, an arbitrageur could receive a cash flow of $25 (= $2,000 − $1,975) per index share at expiration with an index arbitrage strategy formed by selling short an S&P 500 spot index share at $2,000, investing $2,000 in risk-free security at 5%, and going long in the S&P 500 futures contract at $1,975. This arbitrage can be set up with the $5 million proxy portfolio by

1. Selling short the proxy portfolio for $5,000,000
2. Investing $5,000,000 in a risk-free security at 5%
3. Going long in 10 S&P 500 futures contracts at 1,975 (= Index Shares/Multiplier = 2,500/250 = 10 S&P 500 futures contracts; given the contracts' $250 multiplier) expiring in one year

As shown in Exhibit 3.18, the arbitrageur would realize a cash flow of $62,500 at expiration. At expiration, the arbitrageur would close her short position by buying the portfolio, close her expiring futures positions, pay the portfolio's dividends to share lenders on the short position, and receive $5,250,000 from the investment (= $5,000,000 (1.05)). An arbitrage profit of $62,500 is shown in Exhibit 3.18 for cases in which the market increased by 10% and decreased by 10%. Again, for any spot index, an arbitrage of $62,500 is realized provided the proxy portfolio is perfectly correlated with the index and expected dividends of $250,000 are received. With an arbitrage of $62,500, arbitrageurs would try to set up this index arbitrage strategy with the proxy portfolio and index futures. By their actions, though, they would try to go long in the S&P futures, causing the price of futures to increase until it equaled the carrying-cost value of $2,000. At that price, the arbitrage is zero.

EXHIBIT 3.18   Index Arbitrage Using Proxy Portfolio When the S&P 500 Index Futures Are Underpriced

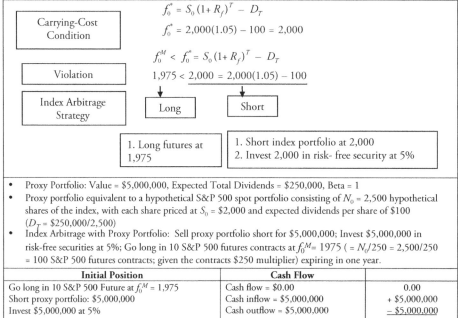

- Proxy Portfolio: Value = $5,000,000, Expected Total Dividends = $250,000, Beta = 1
- Proxy portfolio equivalent to a hypothetical S&P 500 spot portfolio consisting of N_0 = 2,500 hypothetical shares of the index, with each share priced at S_0 = $2,000 and expected dividends per share of $100 ($D_T$ = $250,000/2,500)
- Index Arbitrage with Proxy Portfolio: Sell proxy portfolio short for $5,000,000; Invest $5,000,000 in risk-free securities at 5%; Go long in 10 S&P 500 futures contracts at f_0^M = 1975 (= N_0/250 = 2,500/250 = 100 S&P 500 futures contracts; given the contracts $250 multiplier) expiring in one year.

Initial Position	Cash Flow	
Go long in 10 S&P 500 Future at f_0^M = 1,975	Cash flow = $0.00	0.00
Short proxy portfolio: $5,000,000	Cash inflow = $5,000,000	+ $5,000,000
Invest $5,000,000 at 5%	Cash outflow = $5,000,000	− $5,000,000
		0

Closing Position	Market Increase g = 10% $S_T = f_T$ =2,000(1.10) $S_T = f_T$ =2,200		Market decrease g = −10% S_T = 2,000(0.90) = 1,800	
Close futures: (10)(250)(f_T − 1,975)	= (10)(250)(225)	$562,500	=(10)(250)(−175)	−$437,500
Buy proxy portfolio: $5,000,000 (1 + g)	= $5,000,000(1.10)	−$5,500,000	= $5,000,000(0.90)	−$4,500,000
Pay dividends on portfolio: $250,000	= $250,000	−$250,000	= $250,000	−$250,000
Investment value: $5,000,000(1.05)	= $5,250,000	$5,250,000	= $5,250,000	$5,250,000
		$62,500		$62,500

Bloomberg Case: Pricing Equity Index Futures

Exhibit 3.19 summarizes the portfolio features of the Xavier Equity Index Fund relative to the Russell 1,000 Growth Index. The information was accessed from Bloomberg's Portfolio screen (PORT). On 2/11/16, the fund's holdings consisted of 30 Dow stocks (3,000 shares in each stock), a dividend yield of $2.87/share, compared to the Russell 1,000 Growth Index's dividend yield of $1.79, and a beta of approximately one (β = 0.97). Exhibit 3.20 shows the values of the fund, the Russell 1,000 Growth index, and a June Mini-Russell Growth Index futures contract (contract size = $50) from 9/17/16 to 6/16/16 (expiration date on the futures).

On 2/11/16, the fund had a market value of $6,860,160, the Russell 1,000 Growth Index was at 886.829, and the June futures contract on the index was at 881.79. Given the fund's value and index price, the Xavier Equity Index Fund could

EXHIBIT 3.19 Features of Xavier Equity Index Fund and Russell 1,000 Growth Index (RLG)

Indicator	Xavier Index Fund	Russell Growth Index
Market Value, 2/11/16	$6,860,160	886.829
Dividend Yield, 2/11/16	2.87	1.79
Price to Earnings Ratio (P/E)	17.09	21.55
Price to Cash Flow Ratio (P/CF)	11.91	13.89
Price to Book Ratio (P/B)	3.09	5.55
Total Debt to Common Equity	194.55	111.29
Current Ratio	1.32	1.41
Beta	0.97	

EXHIBIT 3.20 Values of Xavier Equity Index Fund, Russell 1,000 Growth Index (RLG), and June Mini-Russell 1,000 Growth Index Futures Contract (RGYM6) from 12/1/15 to 6/16/16

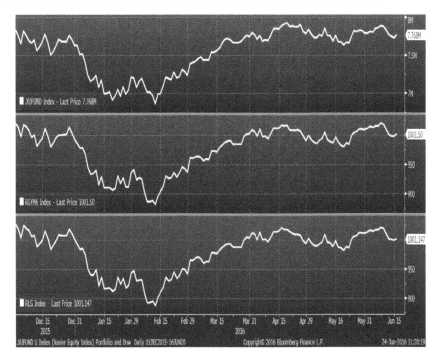

be viewed as a portfolio consisting of 7,736 index shares priced at 886.829 per share and with an dividend yield of $\psi = \$2.87$ per share:

$$N_0 = \frac{V_0}{S_0} = \frac{\$6,860,160}{886.829} = 7,736 \text{ shares}$$

$$V_0^P = N_0 S_0$$

$$V_0^P = (7,736)(\$886.829) = \$6,860,160$$

On 2/22/16, there were 125 days to expiration on the June contract ($T = 125/365 = 0.3425$) and the Eurodollar money market rate was at 0.85%. Using the continuous carrying-cost model, the value of the June Mini-Russell Growth Index futures Contract would have been 880.71:

$$f_0^* = S_0\, e^{(R^A - \psi)T}$$

$$f_0^* = 886.829\, e^{(0.0085 - 0.0287)0.3425}$$

$$f_0^* = 880.71$$

This carrying cost value of 880.71, in turn, almost matches the closing price of the June Mini-Russell Growth Index futures contract price of 881.80 on 2/11/16, suggesting there would have been no arbitrage opportunities by taking positions in the Xavier Equity Index Fund and the June Russell 1,000 Growth Index.

Program Trading and the Triple Witching Hour

Introduced to the financial vernacular in the 1980s, *program trading* refers to the use of computer programs in constructing and executing security portfolio positions. Program trading often involves using programs to: (1) monitor real time data of stocks, futures, and option prices to identify any mispricing of a stock portfolio values relative to the values of index futures or option positions; (2) define appropriate arbitrage strategies given mispriced portfolios and futures and option positions; and (3) execute orders so securities can be bought or sold quickly and simultaneously when arbitrage advantages exist. The index arbitrage involving proxy portfolio just described is an example of a program trading strategy.

Since the price of an expiring futures contract is equal to the spot index price at expiration, program traders who have implemented an index arbitrage strategy often will wait until the expiration day on the futures contract to close their positions. As a result, on or near the delivery day of the index futures contract, an abnormally large volume of trading can often occur on the exchanges as program traders, other arbitrageurs, and hedgers close their futures positions and liquidate or purchase large blocks of stock. This reversing of positions has often caused large swings to occur in stock prices, with the fluctuations being particularly dramatic on the *triple witching hour*—the last hour of trading on the day when index futures, stock index options, and options on stock index futures all expire.

Non-Equity Indexes

In this chapter, we have focused on equity index futures. As noted in the introduction, there are futures contracts on indexes such as ones on commodities indexes (e.g., DJ-AIG Commodity Index and the GSCI index), bond indexes (e.g., Municipal Bond Index), and currencies (e.g., the US dollar index). Some relatively new indexes have been introduced by the CME, CBT, CBOE, Eurex, and other derivative exchange (see Exhibit 3.21). Based on volume, one of the more popular non-equity index futures contracts is the contract on CBOE's Volatility Index (VIX). The index is based on volatility, measured by the implied volatility on stock options (discussed in Chapter 12). The Bloomberg Description pages for the CBOE's Volatility Index and futures contracts are shown in Exhibit 3.22.

EXHIBIT 3.21 Non-Equity Index Futures Contracts

Ticker	Description Non-Equity Indexes	Exchange	Volume 6/23/2016	Open Interest 6/23/2016
WLA Index	IDxIPCA	Bolsa De Mercadorias & Futuros: BMF	4,775	34,600
1UA Index	VIX Week 1 Futures	CBOE Futures Exchange: CBF	24	26
5UA Index	VIX Week 5 Futures	CBOE Futures Exchange: CBF	60	1,110
RXSA Index	Russell 2000 Volatility Index	CBOE Futures Exchange: CBF	10	254
UXA Index	CBOE Volatility Index (VIX)	CBOE Futures Exchange: CBF	275,200	383,959
DNA Index	Bloomberg Commodity Index	Chicago Board of Trade: CBT	143	19,983
GIA Index	Goldman Sachs Commodity	Chicago Mercantile Exchange: CME	32	11,723
FVSA Index	VSTOXX Mini-Futures	Eurex: EUX	89,102	205,427
ILBA Comdty	CILI Inflation Linked Bond	JSE Interest Rate Market: YLX	2	1,103
KVYA Index	KOSPI 200 Volatility Futures	Korea Exchange: KFE	83	279
RVIA Index	Russian Market Volatility	Moscow Exchange: RTS	33	292
JVIA Index	Nikkei 225 VI Futures	Osaka Exchange: OSE	55	1,741

EXHIBIT 3.22   CBOE's Volatility Index and Futures Contracts

CBOE Volatility Index, VIX

CBOE Volatility Index Futures, UXN6

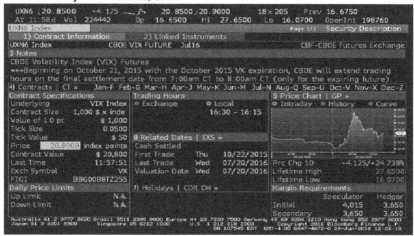

Conclusion

Since their introduction by the Kansas City Board of Exchange in the early 1980s, equity index futures, as well as spot and futures equity options, have become a valuable tool in managing stock portfolio positions. Equity index futures also provide a liquid way to speculate on the market—by forming different types of spreads. These derivative contracts also make it possible for stock portfolio managers to lock in future portfolio values. Managers also can use equity index futures to adjust the beta of a portfolio if they anticipate a bull or bear market, thus eliminating the need to reallocate their portfolio allocation. They can also use index futures to eliminate a stock's systematic risk, enabling them to speculate on unsystematic factors.

Given the myriad uses of equity index futures, it is not surprising that such instruments have grown since their introduction. Equally impressive as the growth in index futures, though, has been the growth of interest rate and debt futures. As we will examine in the next chapter, these contracts, like index futures, can be used in a number of ways to manage fixed-income positions.

BLOOMBERG: EQUITY INDEX FUTURES AND RELATED SCREENS

BLOOMBERG CTM SCREEN, UPLOADING, AND SPOT INDEX SCREENS

Bloomberg Commodity Screens, CTM
Exchange-listed equity-index contracts can be found by accessing the CTM screen: CTM <Enter>. Contracts can be found by category, exchange, and region. For example, to find an equity index contract offered by the CME, use the CME Exchange screen and click "Equity Index" from the dropdown menu in the "Category" column. Alternatively, click "Categories" and "Equity Index" and then type the name of the exchange (e.g., CME) in the amber Exchange box to find the contract of interest.

Uploading a Futures Contract
To upload a futures contract's menu screen enter: Ticker <Comdty> (e.g., SPA <Comdty> for the S&P 500 futures contract menu), and then use the Expiration screen (EXS) on the contract's menu page to find the ticker for the contract with the expiration month you want to analyze: Ticker <Comdty> (e.g., SPM7 <Comdty> for the March 2017 contract). The menu includes:

- CT: Contract Table
- EXS: Expiration Schedule
- GP: Price Graph
- GIP Intraday Graph
- FAIR: Fair Value Monitor
- FMON: Futures Monitor

SECF and Uploading an Equity Index
The SECF screen can be used to find indexes (SECF <Enter>; Category: Index/Stats; Eqty Tab. To upload an index's menu screen, enter: Ticker <Index> (e.g., SPX <Index>). The menu includes:

- Des: Description
- GP: Price Graph
- GIP: Intraday Graph
- COMP: Comparative Return
- HRA: Historical Regression
- CT: Futures Contracts Listed

(Continued)

ETFs

There are often ETFs that are constructed to be highly correlated to an index. The **SECF** screen can be used to find ETFs: SECF <Enter>; Category: Equity; ETFs tab; select Equity from "Focus" dropdown. To upload an ETF, enter Ticker <Equity> (e.g., SPY <Equity> for the Spider S&P 50). The menu includes:

- Des: Description
- GP: Price Graph
- HRA
- PORT: Portfolio Analysis of the ETF's underlying portfolio

BLOOMBERG PORTFOLIO SCREENS FOR EVALUATING PORTFOLIOS: PRTU AND PORT

PRTU

On the Bloomberg PRTU screen, you can set up a stock or fixed-income portfolio. Once loaded, you can analyze the portfolio using screens from the PMEN menu. See Appendix A for a description on how to construct portfolios using PRTU.

Historical Portfolio Returns

To analyze the past-return performances of a portfolio, a history of portfolio rates of return needs to be created in PRTU. With history, the historical performance of the portfolio can then be analyzed from the performance tab on the PORT screen.

Steps for Creating Historical Data for Portfolios in PRTU

1. Bring up the PRTU screen for your portfolio.
2. On the screen, change the date in the amber "Date" box (e.g., Month/Day/2006). You should see the securities disappear from the screen.
3. Click the "Actions" tab. From the "Actions" dropdown, select "Import" to bring up the import box.
4. On the import box, select "Portfolio" from the "Source" dropdown, the name of your portfolio from the "Name" dropdown, change the date (e.g., back to the current period), hit the "Import" tab, and then click "Save."

You should now have a portfolio with historical data.

PORT

On the Bloomberg Portfolio Risk & Analytics screen (PORT), you can evaluate a portfolio in depth. By using the screen tabs (e.g., "Holdings," "Characteristics," "Performance," and "Attributions"), you can evaluate the features, drivers, and historical performances of the portfolio, securities in the portfolio, and the portfolio's index.

PORT Tabs

1. For portfolio securities: Holdings tab, "by none."
2. For sector breakdown: Holdings tab, "by GIC Sectors."
3. For size: Holdings tab, "by Market Cap."
4. For portfolio features: Characteristics tab, "Main View," "Portfolio vs Index" (e.g., INDU), "by GIC Sectors."
5. For performance: Performance tab, "Main View," "Portfolio vs None."
6. For performance: Performance tab, "Total Return," "Portfolio vs Index" (e.g., INDU), Time = MTD, YTD, and Custom (for Custom, the select time period must match the period history of the portfolio created in PRTU).
7. For performance: Performance tab, "Statistical Summary," "Portfolio vs Index" (e.g., INDU).
8. For performance: Performance tab, "Seasonal Analysis."
9. Performance tab, "Period Analysis."
10. For portfolio features: Attribution tab, "Main View," "Portfolio vs None," Time = MTD, YTD, and Custom.
11. For portfolio features: Attribution tab, "Main View," "Portfolio vs None," Time = MTD, YTD, and Custom.
12. For portfolio features: Attribution tab, "Attribution Summary," "Portfolio vs None," Time + MTD, YTD, and Custom.
13. For portfolio features: Attribution tab, "Attribution Summary," "Portfolio vs Index" (e.g., INDU), Time = MTD, YTD, and Custom (see Exhibit 3.23).

EXHIBIT 3.23 Example of PORT Slides—Xavier Growth Fund

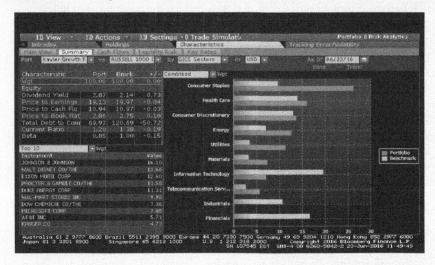

(Continued)

Other PMEN Screens for Portfolio Analysis

Other screens of note on the PMEN menu screen are Portfolio Display (PDSP), Portfolio News (NPH), Events Calendar (EVTS), Equity Relative Valuation (RVP), Expected Cash Flow (PCF), and Summary Reports (PRTS). Some of these screens can be found from the PMEN screen, by clicking a white heading (e.g., "Performance & Attributions"). Many of these screens have tabs for accessing different information, sending information to Excel, and downloading information to PDF and Excel reports.

Importing PRTU Portfolios to Other Screens

Once a portfolio is created, you can export it to other screens or import your portfolio if you are on another screen. For example, if you want to analyze a portfolio created in PRTU using relative valuation, instead of using the RVP function in PMEN, you could select a stock in the portfolio (e.g., Apple), access the stock's menu (AAPL <Equity> <Enter>), and then bring up the stock's RV menu. On the RV menu of the stock, you can then import the portfolio by selecting "Portfolio" from the dropdown "Comp Source" tab and the name of the portfolio from the dropdown "Name" menu. Similarly, you can also import the portfolio from other screens, such as CORR, PC, CACT, MOST, FMAP, EVTS, MRR, and MMAP screens, and also from Excel using the Bloomberg Excel Add-In.

BLOOMBERG CIXB AND OSA SCREENS

CIXB

The returns of a portfolio in EQS or PRTU can be evaluated using historical regression (HRA), comparative returns (COMP), and values (GP) by putting the portfolio into a CIXB basket, creating historical data, and then treating the portfolio as an index.

Steps:

1. CIXB <Enter>.
2. On the CIXB screen, name the ticker and the portfolio in the ".Ticker" and "Name" yellow box and hit <Enter> to update (.XUGROWTH for ticker and XU Growth for Name.
3. Click "Import" from the Actions dropdown tab.
4. On the "Import to CIXB" box, click "import from list" tab at bottom to bring up "Import from List" tab.
5. On "Import from List" tab: Select Portfolio (or EQS search or index) from the "Source" dropdown and the name of the portfolio (search or index) from the "Name" dropdown, and then click the "Import" tab. These steps will import the portfolio's stocks, shares, and prices to the CIXB screen.
6. On CIXB screen, click the "Create" tab to bring up a time period box for selecting the time period for price and return data. After selected the time period, hit "Save." This will activate a Bloomberg program for calculating the portfolio's daily historical returns.

7. The data will be sent to a report, RPT. To access this report, type "RPT" and hit <Enter>.
8. Upload the CIXB-created portfolio as an index: enter .Ticker <Index> (e.g., .XUGROWTH <Index>). On the menu screen, evaluate the portfolio: COMP, GP, and HRA (see Exhibit 3.24).

EXHIBIT 3.24   Example of Bloomberg CIXB Screen

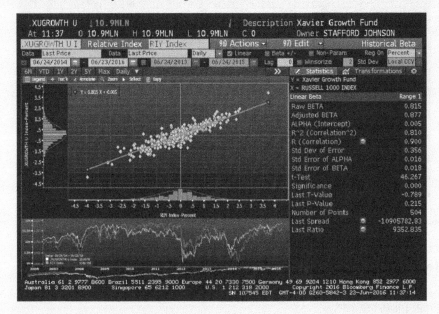

OSA: Hedging Portfolios Using OSA
On the OSA screen, you can import a portfolio and then use the "Hedge" tab to determine the number of index futures contracts needed to hedge your portfolio. The number of contracts is based on the beta of the portfolio.

Steps:

1. OSA <Enter>.
2. From the "Portfolio" dropdown, select a portfolio.
3. Click gray "Hedge" tab.
4. On the Hedge screen, select index (e.g., SPX) and ticker (e.g., SPZ3 for December S&P 500 futures).
5. The right corner box on the Hedge screen shows the portfolio value, beta, future price, contract size, and number of contracts: $n_f = \beta V/(f_0)250$ (see Exhibit 3.25).

(Continued)

EXHIBIT 3.25   Example of Bloomberg OSA Screen

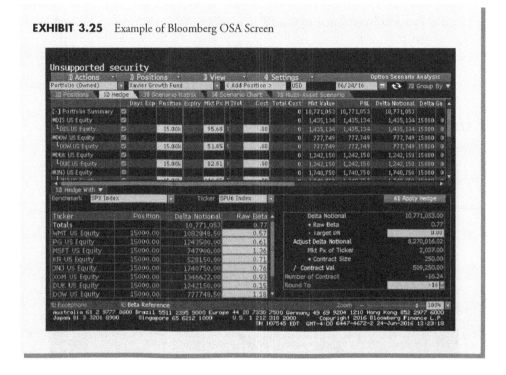

Selected References

Figlewski, S. "Hedging Performance and Basis Risk in Stock Index Futures." *Journal of Finance* 39 (July 1984): 657–669.

Figlewski, S., and Kin, S. "Portfolio Management with Stock Index Futures." *Financial Analysts Journal* 38 (January–February 1982): 52–60.

Johnson, R. Stafford, *Introduction to Derivatives: Options, Futures, and Swaps.* New York: Oxford University Press, 2009, Chapter 13.

Modest, D., and Sundaresan, M. "The Relationship Between Spot and Futures Prices in Stock Index Futures Markets: Some Preliminary Evidence." *Journal of Futures Markets* 3 (1983): 15–41.

Santoni, G. "Has Program Trading Made Stock Prices More Volatile?" *Review* (Federal Reserve Bank of St. Louis) 69: 18–29.

Stoll, H., and Whaley, R. "Expiration Day Effects of Index Options and Futures," Salomon Brothers Center for the Study of Financial Institutions. Monograph Series in Finance and Economics, Monograph 1986: 3.

Stoll, H., and Whaley, R. "Program Trading and Expiration Day Effects." *Financial Analysts Journal* 43 (March–April 1987): 16–23.

Problems and Questions

1. Explain how the clearinghouse would record the following:

   a. Mr. A buys a September S&P 500 futures contract from Ms. B for 2,000 on June 20.

   b. Mr. D buys a September S&P 500 futures contract from Mr. E for 2,100 on June 25.

    c. Ms. B buys a September S&P 500 futures from Mr. D for $2,200 on June 28.

    d. Mr. E buys a September S&P 500 futures from Mr. A for $2,500 on July 3.

    Show the clearinghouse's payments and receipts needed to close each position.

2. Suppose on March 1 you take a long position in a June S&P 500 futures contract at 2,000 with a $250 multiplier.

    a. How much cash or risk-free securities would you have to deposit to satisfy an initial margin requirement of 4.00%?

    b. Calculate the values of your commodity account on the following days, given the following futures prices:

        3/2   2,100
        3/3   2,000
        3/4   1,900
        3/5   1,800
        3/8   2,000
        3/9   2,100

    c. If the maintenance margin requirement specifies keeping the value of the commodity account equal to 100% of the initial margin requirement each day, how much cash would you need to deposit in your commodity account each day?

3. The Bryce Investment Trust Company plans to liquidate part of its stock portfolio in June. It would like to hedge the portfolio sale. The portfolio the company plans to sell is well diversified, has a beta of 1.5, and is currently worth $50 million. The S&P 500 spot index is currently at 2,000, and a June S&P 500 futures contract is currently at 2,000 with a $250 multiplier.

    a. Using the price-sensitivity model, determine how many S&P 500 futures contracts the Bryce Investment Trust Company would need in order to hedge the sale of this $50 million portfolio in June.

    b. Show in a table the values of the portfolio, futures cash flows, and the hedged portfolio values on the June expiration date for possible spot index values of 1,500, 2,000, and 2,500. Assume no quantity, quality, or timing risks.

4. The Keynes Investment Company is expecting a $20 million inflow of cash from one of its investment clients in June and is planning to invest the cash in a portfolio of stocks with a $\beta = 1$. Keynes Investments is concerned that there will be a strong bull market and would like to hedge its June investment with June S&P 500 futures contracts currently trading at 2,000 with a $250 multiplier. Currently, the S&P 500 spot index is at 2,000.

    a. Using the price-sensitivity model, determine how many S&P 500 futures contracts the Keynes Investment Company would need in order to lock in the purchase price of the portfolio at $20 million portfolio.

    b. Show in a table the values of the portfolio, futures cash flows, and the hedged portfolio values on the June expiration date for possible spot index values of 1,500, 2,000, and 2,500. Assume no quantity, quality, or timing risks.

5. The Hunter Investment Company manages a well-diversified equity fund. The current value of the portfolio it manages is $100 million and the portfolio has a

beta of 1.5. Hunter Investment is concerned about a bear market and would like to reduce its portfolio beta to one. Currently, the S&P 500 spot index is trading at 2,000 and a June S&P 500 futures contract is trading at 2,000, with a $250 multiplier.

a. Using the price-sensitivity model, determine how many S&P 500 futures contracts the Hunter Investment Company would need in order to reduce its portfolio beta from 1.5 to 1.0 in June.

b. Show in a table the values of the portfolio, futures cash flows, and the futures-adjusted portfolio values on the June expiration date for possible spot index values of 1,500, 2,000, and 2,500. Assume no quantity, quality, or timing risks.

c. Calculate the futures-adjusted portfolio values as a proportion of the initial $100 million portfolio value and the unadjusted portfolio values as a proportion of $100 million value for possible spot index values of 1,500, 2,000, and 2,500.

d. Calculate the proportional return for the futures-adjusted portfolio to the proportion changes in S&P from its initial value of 2,000. Calculate the proportional return for the unadjusted portfolio to the proportion changes in S&P from its initial value of 2,000. Comment on how the futures lower the portfolio's beta.

6. Kendall Investment Company just received information that General Pharmaceutical (GP) might be introducing a new acne drug in June. In response to the information, Kendall decided to buy 10,000 shares of GP, priced at $P_g = \$50$/share and with a β of 0.8. Kendall, however, is concerned that the market could decline by June, negating any increase in GP stock.

a. Explain how Kendall could construct a hedge with S&P 500 futures contract expiring in June to reduce its exposure to systematic risk. Assume the current spot index and the futures contract are both 2,000, with a 250 futures multiplier.

b. Evaluate the value of the stock and the futures for the following scenarios occurring one month later:

   • There is a bull market and the new drug is introduced with S_T increasing to 2,250 and P_g to $70.
   • There is a bear market and the new drug is introduced with S_T decreasing to 1,750 and P_g increasing to only $55.

c. Compare the periodic rates of return as a proportion of the stock investment $(($50)(10,000) = \$500,000)$ for each scenario that would result with and without the futures position.

7. Determine the equilibrium price of a December S&P 500 futures contract. Assume the current spot S&P 500 index is at 2,000, the annual risk-free rate is 2.00%, dividends worth $20.00 at the December expiration, and 90 days to expiration ($T = 0.25$). Comment on whether the market is normal or inverted.

8. The Zuber Hedge Fund has formed a proxy portfolio that it is using to identify arbitrage opportunities using index arbitrage strategies. The proxy portfolio is worth $100 million, has a beta of one, and dividends estimated to be worth $5 million one year later. The current S&P 500 spot index is at 1,250 and the annual risk-free rate is 5%.

   a. Define the Zuber Hedge Fund's portfolio as an investment in hypothetical shares in the S&P 500. What is the dividend per index share to be paid in one year?
   b. Determine the equilibrium price of an S&P 500 futures contract expiring in one year using Zuber's proxy portfolio.
   c. Describe the index arbitrage strategy Zuber could employ if the S&P 500 futures were trading at 1,260. (Note: The S&P 500 futures multiplier is $250.)
   d. Evaluate the index arbitrage from c at the futures' expiration by assuming the market increases by 10% and decreases by 10%. Assume the portfolio is perfectly correlated with the index.
   e. Describe program trading.
   f. What is the triple witching hour?

Bloomberg Exercises

1. Select an equity index such as the S&P 500 (SPX) or a sector index. To find your index, use SECF (SECF <Enter>); Category: Index/Stat. Upload the index's Menu screen (Ticker <Index> <Enter>), and evaluate it using the following screen:

   a. DES: Description
   b. GP: Price Graph
   c. CT: Futures Contract Table
   d. COMP: Comparative Returns
   e. HRA: Historical Regression

2. Access Bloomberg information on a broad-based CME or CBT equity index futures contract like the S&P 500 or the Dow Jones: type CTM to bring up the "Contract Table Menu," click "Categories" and "Equity Index," search for CME or CBT on the menu (type CME or CBT in the amber Exchange box), find the CME or CBT contract of interest, and bring up the contract's menu screen (Ticker <Comdty>; e.g., SPA <Comdty> for S&P 500 futures), and then use the Expiration screen (EXS) on the contract's menu page to find the ticker for the contract with the expiration month you want to analyze (Ticker <Comdty>; e.g., SPM7 <Comdty> for the March 2017 contract). View screens to examine: DES, GP, and FAIR.

3. Access Bloomberg information on a sector or narrow-based equity index futures contract, such as a sector index like the S&P E-Mini Technology Index (IXPA): type CTM to bring up the "Contract Table Menu," click "Categories" and "Equity Index," search for CME on the menu (type CME in the amber Exchange box),

find the CME contract of interest and bring up the contract's menu screen (Ticker <Index>; e.g., IXPA <Index> for S&P 500 Technology futures), and then use the Expiration screen (EXS) on the contract's menu page to find the ticker for contract with the expiration month you want to analyze (Ticker <Comdty>; e.g., IXTZ6 <Comdty> for the December 2016 contract). View screens to examine: DES, GP, and FAIR.

4. Using the GP screen, examine the historical prices of a broad-based equity index futures contract you selected in Exercise 2. Select a time period that the contract was active.

   a. Select a period in which you would have taken a long position and calculate the profit from opening and closing at the futures prices at the beginning and ending dates for your selected period. Calculate the losses if you had taken a short position.

   b. Select a period in which you would have taken a short position and calculate the profits from opening and closing at the futures prices at the beginning and ending dates for your selected period. Calculate the losses if you had taken a long position.

   c. Using the annotation bar, apply the "% Change" tool to calculate the percentage change for your select periods, and then click the "News" icon on the annotation bar to find relevant news events on or preceding the opening date.

   d. Examine the spot index for the period that your futures contract was active. The ticker for the index can be found on the futures Description screen. Use the Chart screen (Chart <Enter>) to create multigraphs for the prices on the futures contract and the underlying index. On the Chart Menu screen, select Standard G chart; once you have loaded your securities, go to "Edit" to put your graphs in separate panels.

   e. Estimate the current equilibrium price on the index futures contract using the FAIR screen and compare that price to the current market price. You may want to go to the Help page on the FAIR screen to learn more about how Bloomberg calculates its FAIR price. To access Help, click the "?" icon in the far right corner.

5. Using the GP screen, examine the historical prices of a narrow-based equity index futures contract you selected in Exercise 3. Select a time period that the contract was active.

   a. Select a period in which you would have taken a long position and calculate the profit from opening and closing at the futures prices at the beginning and ending dates for your selected period. Calculate the losses if you had taken a short position.

   b. Select a period in which you would have taken a short position and calculate the profits from opening and closing at the futures prices at the beginning and ending dates for your selected period. Calculate the losses if you had taken a long position.

   c. Using the annotation bar, apply the "% Change" tool to calculate the percentage change for your select periods, and then click the "News" icon on the annotation bar to find relevant news events on or preceding the opening date.

    d. Examine the spot index for the period that your futures contract was active. The ticker for the index can be found on the futures Description screen. Use the Chart screen (Chart <Enter>) to create multigraphs for the prices on the futures contract and the underlying index. On the Chart Menu screen, select Standard G chart; once you have loaded your securities, go to "Edit" to put your graphs in separate panels.

    e. Estimate the current equilibrium price on the index futures contract using the FAIR screen and compare that price to the current market price.

6. Using the Bloomberg HRA regression screen estimate the relation between a narrow-based index (e.g., a sector index) and broad-based index (e.g., S&P 500, SPX). Load your selected sector spot index (e.g., IXPA <Index> for S&P 500 Technology index), and then go to the HRA screen for the regression. On the HRA screen, enter the broad-based index as the independent variable in the amber box (e.g., SPX Index) and select the time period and periodicity (daily).

    a. Comment on the regression results and the relation (beta).

    b. Explain how you would form bullish and bearish intercommodity spreads with the futures contracts on the underlying indexes.

7. Using the Chart screen (Chart <Enter>), examine the intercommodity spread you formed in Exercise 6. Note than the contracts have to have the same expiration.

    a. Use the Chart screen (Chart <Enter>) to create multigraphs for the index futures contracts. On the Chart Menu screen, select Standard G chart; once you have loaded your securities, go to "Edit" to put your graphs in separate panels.

    b. Select a period in which you would have taken a bullish spread position and calculate the profit from opening and closing at the futures prices at the beginning and ending dates for your selected period. Calculate the losses if you had taken a bearish intercommodity position.

    c. Select a period in which you would have taken a bearish spread position and calculate the profit from opening and closing at the futures prices at the beginning and ending dates for your selected period. Calculate the losses if you had taken a bullish position.

    d. Using the annotation bar, apply the "% Change" tool to calculate the percentage change for your select periods, and then click the "News" icon on the annotation bar to find relevant news events on or preceding the opening date.

8. Examine an ex-post long hedging position for a future purchase of 1,000 shares of a selected ETF (e.g., S&P 500 Spider, SPY).

    a. Select a futures contract on the ETF you plan to purchase (e.g., one of the futures on the S&P 500 futures (SPA)) to hedge the S&P 500 Spider. Use the expiration date on the futures contract as the date of your ETF purchase.

    b. Use the "Chart" screen (Chart <Enter>) to create multigraphs for the prices on the futures and the ETF. On the Chart Menu screen, select the Standard G chart; once you have loaded your securities, go to "Edit" to put your graphs in separate panels.

    c. Select a beginning date that you would have implemented your hedge and a closing date near the futures expiration as the date for purchasing the ETFs and closing your hedge. Use the price-sensitivity model to determine the number of futures contracts needed to hedge the position.

    d. Calculate the profit or loss on the futures position from opening and closing at the futures prices at the beginning and ending dates, the cost of purchasing the 1,000 shares of the ETF on the closing date, and the hedged cost (ETF purchase minus futures profit). Compare your hedged cost to the unhedged cost. In retrospect, was the hedge a good strategy?

9. Examine an ex-post short hedging position for a future sale of 1,000 shares of a selected ETF (e.g., S&P 500 Spider, SPY).

    a. Select a futures contract on the ETF you plan to sell (e.g., one of the futures on the S&P 500 futures (SPA) to hedge the S&P 500 Spider. Use the expiration date on the futures contract as the date of your ETF sale.

    b. Use the "Chart" screen (Chart <Enter>) to create multigraphs for the prices on the futures and the ETF. On the Chart Menu screen, select the Standard G chart; once you have loaded your securities, go to "Edit" to put your graphs in separate panels.

    c. Select a beginning date that you would have implemented your hedge and a closing date near the futures expiration as the date for selling the ETFs and closing your hedge. Use the price-sensitivity model to determine the number of futures contracts needed to hedge the position.

    d. Calculate the profit or loss on the futures position from opening and closing at the futures prices at the beginning and ending dates, the revenue from selling the 1,000 shares of the ETF on the closing date, and the hedged revenue (ETF sale plus futures profit). Compare your hedged revenue to the unhedged revenue. In retrospect, was the hedge a good strategy?

10. Construct your own equity portfolio and then analyze it using PORT and as an index created from CIXB. Guidelines:

- In constructing you own portfolio, consider using the equity search screen (EQS), FMAP to identify stocks that make up different types of funds, or the stocks making up indexes.
- Make the number of shares for the stocks in your portfolio large enough so that your portfolio's market value is at least $10 million.
- Create historical data for your portfolio. See sections: "Bloomberg: Equity Index Futures and Related Screens" and "Steps for Creating Historical Data for Portfolios in PRTU."
- Import your portfolio in CIXB and create historical data. See sections: "Bloomberg: Equity Index Futures and Related Screens" and "Bloomberg CIXB and OSA Screens."

    a. Evaluate your portfolio in PORT (make sure the "View" is set for equity) using some of the following tabs:

      - Holdings tab, "by none"
      - Holdings tab, "by GIC Sectors"

- Holdings tab, "by Market Cap"
- Characteristics tab, "Main View," "Portfolio vs Index (e.g., INDU), "by GIC Sectors"
- Characteristics tab, "Main View," "Portfolio vs Index" (e.g., INDU), "by GIC Sectors"
- Performance tab, "Main View," "Portfolio vs None"
- Performance tab, "Total Return," "Portfolio vs Index" (e.g., INDU), Time = MTD, YTD, and Custom (for Custom, the select time period must match the period history of the portfolio created in PRTU).
- Performance tab, "Statistical Summary," "Portfolio vs Index" (e.g., INDU)
- Performance tab, "Seasonal Analysis"
- Performance tab, "Period Analysis"
- Attribution tab, "Main View," "Portfolio vs None," Time = MTD, YTD, and Custom
- Attribution tab, "Main View," "Portfolio vs None," Time = MTD, YTD, and Custom
- Attribution tab, "Attribution Summary," "Portfolio vs None," Time + MTD, YTD, and Custom
- Attribution tab, "Attribution Summary," "Portfolio vs Index" (e.g., INDU), Time = MTD, YTD, and Custom

b. Examine the portfolio as a basket created in CIXB: Upload the portfolio as an index (.Ticker <Index> <Enter>) and examine its historical values (GP) and regression relation with a market index (SPX).

11. Examine an ex-post short hedging position for the portfolio you created in Exercise 10.

a. Select one futures contract on S&P 500 (SPA) to hedge your portfolio. Use the expiration date on the futures contract as the date of your hedge value.

b. Use the "Chart" screen (Chart <Enter>) to create multigraphs for the prices on the futures and the portfolio (.Ticker of the portfolio you created in CIXB). On the Chart Menu screen, select the Standard G chart; once you have loaded your securities, go to "Edit" to put your graphs in separate panels.

c. Select a beginning date that you would have implemented your hedge and a closing date near the futures expiration as the date for closing your hedge. Use the price-sensitivity model to determine the number of futures contracts needed to hedge the portfolio.

d. Calculate the profit or loss on the futures position from opening and closing at the futures prices at the beginning and ending dates, the value of your portfolio on the closing date, and the hedged value (portfolio value plus futures profit). Compare your hedged value to the unhedged value. In retrospect, was the hedge a good strategy?

e. Use Bloomberg's OSA screen to determine the number of futures contracts you would need to hedge your portfolio. See section: "Bloomberg: Equity Index Futures and Related Screens" and "Bloomberg CIXB and OSA Screens."

12. Examine an ex-post portfolio beta enhancement or reduction (market-timing) strategy for the portfolio you created in Exercise 10.

    a. Select one futures contract on the S&P 500 (SPA) to go long or short. Use the expiration date on the futures contract as the date for closing the strategy.

    b. Use the Chart screen (Chart <Enter>) to create multigraphs for the prices on the futures and the portfolio (.Ticker of the portfolio you created in CIXB). On the Chart Menu screen, select the Standard G chart; once you have loaded your securities, go to "Edit" to put your graphs in separate panels.

    c. Select a beginning date that you would have implemented your futures adjusted portfolio and a closing date near the futures expiration as the date for closing your positions. Use the price-sensitivity model to determine the number of long or short futures contracts needed to move to your target beta.

    d. Calculate the profit or loss on the futures position from opening and closing at the futures prices at the beginning and ending dates, the value of your portfolio on the closing date, and the futures-adjusted value (portfolio value plus futures profit). Compare your futures-adjusted portfolio value to the unadjusted portfolio value.

13. Estimate the current equilibrium price on the S&P 500 equity index futures contract (SPA) based on the Spider S&P 500 ETF (SPY).

$$f_0^* = S_0 \, e^{(R_f - \psi)T}$$

Bloomberg information you need to access for determining the carrying-cost price:

- S_0, Price of the spider, which can be found on Bloomberg's GP screen for the Spider: SPY <Equity>, GP.
- Ψ, Dividend yield = DPS/Price per Share: Dividend yield can be found on the DVD screen.
- To find dividend per share (DPS): Load SPY (SPY <Cmdty>), type PORT to bring up the PORT screen, and click "Characteristics" and "Summary" tabs on the PORT screen.
- R_f, Risk-free rate: To estimate R_f, use a three-month LIBOR, which can be found on Bloomberg GP screen for US0003M or six-month LIBOR, which can be found on Bloomberg GP screen for US0006M.
- T = time to delivery as a proportion of a year.

Compare the actual price of the futures with the equilibrium price, and explain the index arbitrage position you would form.

CHAPTER 4

Interest Rate and Bond Futures and Forward Contracts

Futures and forward contracts on interest rates and bonds provide corporations, financial institutions, and others with a tool for hedging their fixed-income positions against adverse price movements, for speculating on expected interest rate changes, and for creating synthetic debt and investment positions to change the structure of their fixed-income position or to provide them with better rates than direct positions. Exhibit 4.1 lists various interest rates and bond futures contracts traded on the CBT, CME, Eurex, and other derivative exchanges. In this chapter, we examine these contracts, their speculative and hedging uses, and how they are priced. The material presented in Chapter 4 assumes an understanding of bond valuation and return.

Types of Interest Rate Futures and Forward Contracts

Today, the three most popular interest rate and bond futures contracts are on Eurodollar deposits, T-bonds, and T-notes.

Eurodollar Futures Contract

A Eurodollar deposit is a time deposit in a bank located or incorporated outside the United States. A Eurodollar interest rate is the rate that one large international bank is willing to lend to another large international bank. The average rate paid by a

EXHIBIT 4.1   Types of Interest Rate and Bond Futures Contracts

Ticker	Description	Options
Chicago Mercantile Exchange: CME Interest Rates		
BUAA Comdty	2yr Euro$ Bundle Future	Yes
BUBA Comdty	3yr Euro$ Bundle Future	Yes
BUDA Comdty	5yr Euro$ Bundle Future	Yes
DNA Comdty	Eurodollar, 3Mo AON	Yes
EDA Comdty	Eurodollar, 3Mo	Yes
ELX Futures: ELX	**Interest Rate**	
EMA Comdty	Eurodollar, 1 Month	Yes
GEA Comdty	Eurodollar, 3Mo	Yes
IEBA Comdty	Euribor, 3Mo	No
IUA Comdty	Eurodollar, E-mini	No
MYA Comdty	Euroyen, 3Mo	Yes
PKA Comdty	Eurodollar, Pack	No
WCA Comdty	Eurodollar, 1Mo AON	No
Y5A Comdty	Eurodollar, 5Yr Bundle	No
BNEA Comdty	Eurodollar, 2Yr Bundle	No
BNLA Comdty	Eurodollar, 3Yr Bundle	No
BNOA Comdty	Eurodollar, 4Yr Bundle	No
BNPA Comdty	Eurodollar, 5Yr Bundle	No
FEA Comdty	Eurodollar, 3Mo	No
PKEA Comdty	Eurodollar, Pack	No
ICE Futures Europe - Financials: ICF Interest Rates		
AGCA Comdty	Agency DTCC GCF Repo Index	No
AKRA Comdty	ERIS Euribor 10yr Interest Rate Future	No
ARWA Comdty	ERIS Euribor 5yr Interest Rate Future	No
BDAA Comdty	Eurodollar, 2Yr Bundle	No
ERA Comdty	Euribor, 3Mo	Yes
ESA Comdty	Euroswiss, 3 Mo	Yes
FKYA Comdty	Three Month Euribor Futures TAS	No
ICAA Comdty	ERIS Euribor 2yr Interest Rate Future	No
ICEA Comdty	Eris GBP 2yr Interest Rate Future	No
IDLA Comdty	Eris GBP 2yr Interest Rate Future	No
IDRA Comdty	Eris GBP 5yr Interest Rate Future	No
IDYA Comdty	Eris GBP 10yr Interest Rate Future	No
IRDA Comdty	ERIS Euribor 7yr Interest Rate Future	No
IUYA Comdty	ERIS Euribor 10yr Interest Rate Future	No
J A Comdty	Euroyen, Tibor 3Mo	No
KKTA Comdty	ERIS Euribor 30yr Interest Rate Future	No
KKYA Comdty	ERIS GBP 30yr Interest Rate Future	No
L A Comdty	Sterling, 90 Day	Yes
LEDA Comdty	Eurodollar, 3Mo	No
OBPA Comdty	ERIS Euribor 30yr Interest Rate Future	No
ODYA Comdty	ERIS Euribor 10yr Interest Rate Future	No
OMA Comdty	Eonia, 1Mo	No
PKSA Comdty	Eurodollar, Pack	No
TMOA Comdty	Eonia, 3Mo	No
TUCA Comdty	ERIS GBP 30-year 2% Coupon	No
TULA Comdty	ERIS Euribor 3yr Interest Rate Future	No
TUPA Comdty	ERIS GBP 7-year 1.75% Coupon	No
USTA Comdty	US Treasury DTCC GCF Repo Index	No
WGLA Comdty	Three Month Sterling Future TAS	No

EXHIBIT 4.1 *(Continued)*

Ticker	Description	Options
Global Markets	**Interest Rate**	
GMEUR02 Comdty	2 year tenor Constant Maturity Future on IRS	No
GMEUR03 Comdty	3 year tenor Constant Maturity Future on IRS	No
GMEUR04 Comdty	4 year tenor Constant Maturity Future on IRS	No
GMEUR05 Comdty	5 year tenor Constant Maturity Future on IRS	No
GMEUR30 Comdty	30 year tenor Constant Maturity Future on IRS	No
Eurex: EUX	**Interest Rate**	
EXA Comdty	EONIA Future	No
FPA Comdty	Euribor, 3Mo	Yes
OMEA Comdty	EUR Secured Funding Futures	No
Chicago Board of Trade: CBT Bond		
3YA Comdty	US Treasury Note, 3Yr	No
FVA Comdty	US Treasury Note, 5Yr	Yes
TUA Comdty	US Treasury Note, 2Yr	Yes
TYA Comdty	US Treasury Note, 10Yr	Yes
USA Comdty	US Treasury Long Bond	Yes
UXYA Comdty	US Ultra Treasury Note, 10Yr	Yes
WNA Comdty	US Treasury Ultra Bond	Yes
Eurex: EUX Bond		
BTAA Comdty	Mid-Term Euro-OAT Futures	No
BTSA Comdty	Short term Euro-BTP futures	No
DUA Comdty	Euro Schatz	Yes
FBA Comdty	Swiss CONF	No
IKA Comdty	Euro-BTP Future	No
KOAA Comdty	Euro-BONO-Futures Long-Term Spanish Government Bonds	No
MFBA Comdty	Mid Term Euro-BTP Futures	No
OATA Comdty	French Government Bond	Yes
OEA Comdty	Euro Bobl	Yes
RXA Comdty	Euro Bund	Yes
RXWA Comdty	EURO-BUND Weekly Options	Yes
UBA Comdty	Euro Buxl	No
ICE Futures Europe - Bond		
FWAA Comdty	Ultra Long Bund Future TAS	No
G A Comdty	Long Gilt	Yes
IGOA Comdty	Medium BTP Future Active Contract	No
IGRA Comdty	Long BTP Future Active Contract	No
IGSA Comdty	Short BTP Future Active Contract	No
SPAA Comdty	Long Spanish Government Bond Future Active Contract	No
SPOA Comdty	Medium Spanish Government Bond Future Active Contract	No
SPTA Comdty	Short Spanish Government Bond Future Active Contract	No
SWCA Comdty	Long Swiss Confederation Bond Future Active Contract	No
SWOA Comdty	Medium Swiss Confederation Bond Future Active Contract	No
TRAA Comdty	Ultra Long Bund Future Active Contract	No
TRLA Comdty	Long Bund Future Active Contract	No
TRPA Comdty	Medium Bund Future Active Contract	No
TRTA Comdty	Short Bund Future Active Contract	No
UGLA Comdty	Ultra Long Gilt	No
WBA Comdty	Short Gilt	No
WHBA Comdty	Short Gilt Futures TAS	No

sample of London Euro-banks is known as the London Interbank Offer Rate (LIBOR). The LIBOR is frequently used as a benchmark rate on bank loans and deposits.

The CME's futures contract on the Eurodollar deposit is a cash-settlement contract based on the delivery or purchase of a Eurodollar deposit with a face value of $1 million and a maturity of 90 days. Eurodollar futures are quoted in terms of an index. This index, I, is equal to 100 minus the annual percentage discount rate, R_D, for a 90-day Eurodollar rate, R_D:

$$I = 100 - R_D(\%)$$

Given a quoted index value or discount yield, the actual contract price on the contract is:

$$f_0 = \frac{100 - R_D\%(90/360)}{100} \$1,000,000$$

Exhibit 4.2 shows the Bloomberg Description screen for the December 2016 Eurodollar futures contract and its price and yield graphs from 6/29/15 to 6/24/16.

EXHIBIT 4.2   CME's December Eurodollar Futures Bloomberg Description Screens, Price and Yield Graphs

Prices on a December 2016 90-Day Eurodollar Futures (IMM Index)

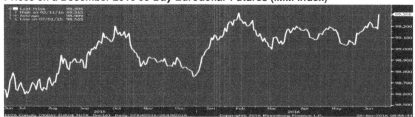

Implied Yields on December 90-Day Eurodollar Futures

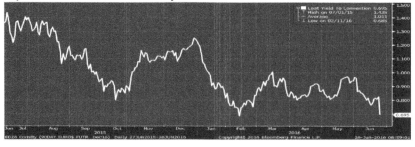

On 6/24/16, the December contract was trading at 99.305 or an annual discount yield of $R_D = 0.695\%$ $(= 100 - 99.305)$; the actual futures price was \$998,262.50 and the implied YTM_f was 0.708%:

$$f_0 = \frac{100 - R_D\%(90/360)}{100} \$1,000,000$$

$$f_0 = \frac{100 - (100 - 99.305)(90/360)}{100} \$1,000,000 = \$998,262.50$$

$$YTM_f = \left[\frac{F}{f_0}\right]^{365/91} - 1$$

$$YTM_f = \left[\frac{\$1,000,000}{\$998,262.50}\right]^{365/90} - 1 = 0.00708$$

Eurodollar futures contracts have cash settlements at delivery. When a Eurodollar futures contract expires, the cash settlement is determined by the futures price and the settlement price. The settlement price or expiration futures index price is 100 minus the average three-month LIBOR offered by a sample of designated Euro-banks on the expiration date:

Expiration futures price = 100 − LIBOR

The CME also offers Eurodollar bundles and packs. A Eurodollar bundle is the sale or purchase of one each of a series of consecutive Eurodollar futures contracts. The Bloomberg Description screen for a five-year Eurodollar bundle is shown in Exhibit 4.3.

EXHIBIT 4.3 CME's Five-Year Eurodollar Bundle Contract Bloomberg Description Screens

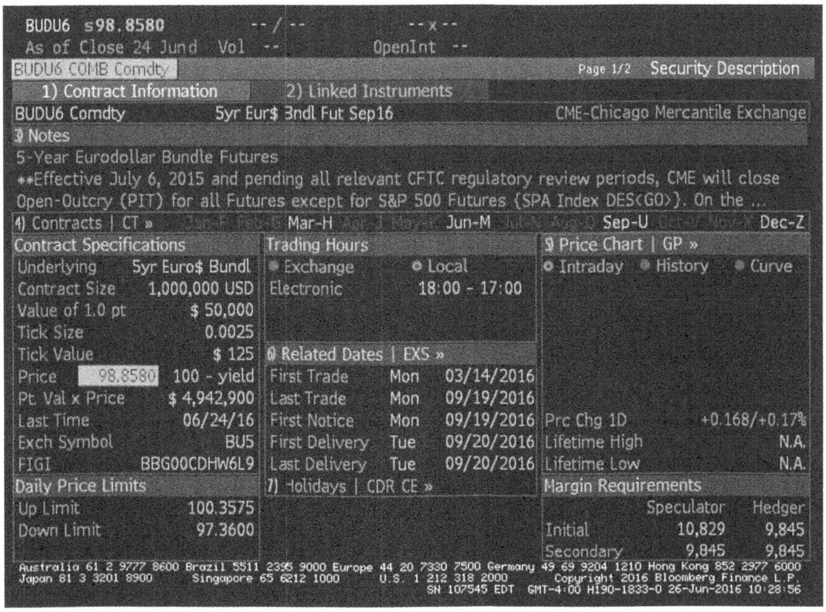

A Eurodollar PACK is the sale or purchase of an equally weighted, consecutive series of four Eurodollar futures, quoted on an average net change basis from the previous day's close. Bundles and packs are often used to lock in a rate of a floating-rate loan or investment. They are used instead of forming Eurodollar strips. A strip is a series of Eurodollar futures contracts. In addition to the CME's Eurodollar futures, there are also a number of other contracts traded on interest rates in other countries. For example, there are Euroyen, Euroswiss, and Euribor contracts (three-month LIBOR contract for the euro).

T-Bond and T-Note Futures Contracts

The most heavily traded bond futures contracts are the CBT's T-bond and T-note contracts. The T-bond contract calls for the delivery or purchase of a T-bond with a maturity of at least 15 years. The CBT has a conversion factor to determine the actual price received by the seller. The futures contract is based on the delivery of a T-bond with a face value of $100,000. To ensure liquidity, any T-bond with a maturity of 15 years is eligible for delivery, with a conversion factor used to determine the actual price of the deliverable bond. Since T-bonds futures contracts allow for the delivery of a number of T-bonds at any time during the delivery month, the CBT's delivery procedure on such contracts is more complicated than the procedures on other futures contracts. Exhibit 4.4 shows the price and yield graphs for the CBT's US Ultra-Treasury Bond. The underlying bond on this contract is a 30-year T-bond paying a 6% coupon. Exhibit 4.5 lists the bonds eligible to be delivered on this contract and their conversion factor.

EXHIBIT 4.4   CBT's September US Ultra-Treasury Bond Contract: Price and Yield Graphs

Prices on September 2016 US Ultra-Treasury Futures

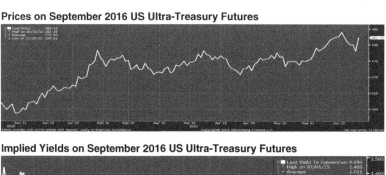

Implied Yields on September 2016 US Ultra-Treasury Futures

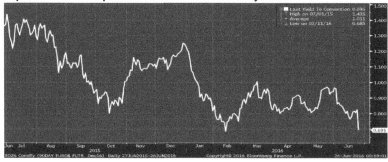

EXHIBIT 4.5 Deliverable Bonds and Conversion Factors on CBT's September US Ultra-Treasury Bond

1 Cash Security	2 Price	4 Conversion Factor	6 Gro/Bas (32nds)	7 Net/Bas (32nds)
T 3 1/8 11/15/41	115-26 3/4	0.6301	30.117	10.059
T 3 1/8 02/15/42	115-27 1/4	0.6285	39.952	19.753
T 3 3/4 11/15/43	129-11+	0.701	49.165	24.641
T 3 5/8 08/15/43	126-16+	0.6855	48.608	24.805
T 3 5/8 02/15/44	126-11 3/4	0.6831	57.861	34.052
T 3 05/15/42	113-07 1/4	0.6107	59.815	40.656
T 3 1/8 02/15/43	115-16 3/4	0.6223	65.629	45.415
T 3 3/8 05/15/44	120-23 3/4	0.6486	79.169	57.301
T 2 3/4 08/15/42	107-30	0.5765	90.122	72.63
T 2 7/8 05/15/43	110-04	0.5879	93.604	75.319
T 2 3/4 11/15/42	107-24	0.5748	94.042	76.666
T 3 1/8 08/15/44	115-07 3/4	0.6137	106.81	86.582
T 3 11/15/44	112-16 3/4	0.5955	126.008	106.815
T 3 05/15/45	112-15 3/4	0.5927	141.346	122.151
T 3 11/15/45	112-16 1/4	0.59	157.6	138.407
T 2 7/8 08/15/45	109-25 1/4	0.5743	162.209	143.777
T 2 1/2 02/15/45	101-26+	0.5264	186.956	171.228
T 2 1/2 02/15/46	101-24 3/4	0.5201	221.966	206.236
T 2 1/2 05/15/46	101-28 3/4	0.5186	234.719	219.109

Source: Bloomberg, DLV Screen

T-bond futures prices are quoted in dollars and 32nds for T-bonds with a face value of $100. The quoted price on the September Ultra-Treasury Bond futures is 182-11 (i.e., 182 11/32 or 182.34375). Given the face value of $100,000, the futures price would be $182,343.75. The actual price paid on the T-bond or revenue received by the seller in delivering the bond on the contract is equal to the quoted futures price times the conversion factor, CFA, on the delivered bond plus any accrued interest:

Seller's revenue = (Quoted futures price)(CFA) + Accrued interest

For example, the first deliverable bond listed in Exhibit 4.5 is a Treasury paying a $3\frac{1}{8}$ coupon, maturing on 11/15/41. The bond is priced at 115.6782, has a CFA of 0.6301, and an accrued interest of $0.78125 (= (3.125) (94/365)) based on a delivery date of 6/30. If this bond was selected as the deliverable one on the September futures and delivered on 9/30/16, the futures seller would receive $115.676 per $100 face value from the futures purchaser:

Seller's revenue on 9/30/16 = (182.34375)(0.6301) + 0.78125 = 115.676

T-note contracts are similar to T-bond contracts, except that they call for the delivery of T-notes. The most active T-note contracts on the CBT are contracts on

2-year, 5-year, and 10-year T-notes. T-note contracts have delivery procedures similar to T-bond contracts, except that some contracts require delivery of the most recently auctioned T-note. Exhibit 4.6 shows the Bloomberg Description screen and price and implied yields from 7/1/15 to 6/30/16 for the CBT's September 2016, five-year T-note contract, and Exhibit 4.7 shows the deliverable bonds and CFAs on the contract.

EXHIBIT 4.6   CBT's September Five-Year T-Note Contract Bloomberg Description Screens, Price and Yield Graphs

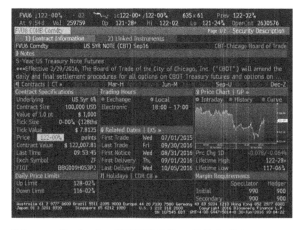

Prices on September 2016 US 5-Year T-Note Futures

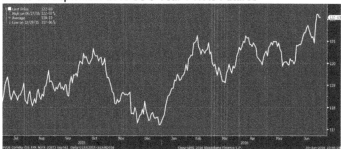

Implied Yields on September 2016 US 5-Year T-Note Futures

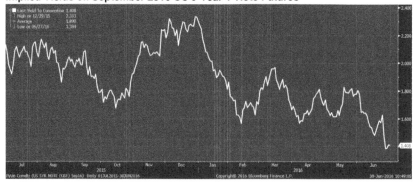

EXHIBIT 4.7 Deliverable Bonds and Conversion Factors on CBT's September Five-Year T-Note Contract

Cash Security	Price	Conversion Factor	Gro/Bas (32nds)	Net/Bas (32nds)
T 1 5/8 11/30/20	102-27 1/4	0.8408	7.716	−0.958
T 1 3/4 12/31/20	103-11 1/4	0.8426	16.686	7.061
T 1 3/8 01/31/21	101-21 3/4	0.8258	28.795	22.184
T 1 1/8 02/28/21	100-19 3/4	0.8133	43.61	39.021
T 1 1/4 03/31/21	101-02 3/4	0.8151	51.581	45.973
T 1 3/8 04/30/21	101-20 3/4	0.817	62.161	55.594
T 1 3/8 05/31/21	101-23 1/4	0.8141	75.986	69.355
T 1 1/8 06/30/21	100-14 3/8	0.8011	85.879	81.331

Forward Contracts—Forward Rate Agreements (FRA)

Forward contracts for interest rate products are private, customized contracts between two financial institutions or between a financial institution and one of its clients. Interest rate forward contracts predate the establishment of interest rate futures markets. A good example of an interest rate forward product is a *forward rate agreement*, FRA. This contract requires a cash payment or provides a cash receipt based on the difference between a realized spot rate such as the LIBOR and a prespecified rate. For example, the contract could be based on a specified rate of $R_k = 1\%$ (annual) and the three-month LIBOR (annual) in five months and a notional principal, *NP* (principal used only for calculation purposes) of $10 million. In five months, the payoff would be

$$\text{Payoff} = (NP) \frac{[\text{LIBOR} - R_k](91/365)}{1 + \text{LIBOR}\,(91/365)}$$

$$\text{Payoff} = (\$10,000,000) \frac{[\text{LIBOR} - 0.01](91/365)}{1 + \text{LIBOR}\,(91/365)}$$

If the LIBOR at the end of five months exceeds the specified rate of 1%, the buyer of the FRA (or long position holder) receives the payoff from the seller; if the LIBOR is less than 1%, the seller (or short position holder) receives the payoff from the buyer. Thus, if the LIBOR were at 1.5%, the buyer would be entitled to a payoff of $12,419 from the seller; if the LIBOR were at 0.5%, the buyer would be required to pay the seller $12,450. Note that the terminology is the opposite of futures. In a Eurodollar futures, the party with the long position hopes rates will decrease and prices will go up, whereas the short position holder hopes that rates will increase and prices will go down.

Speculating with Interest Rate and Bond Futures Contracts

Interest rate and bond futures contracts are used to speculate on expected interest rate changes. A long futures position can be taken when interest rates are expected to fall and a short futures position can be taken when rates are expected to rise. In the case of futures, speculating on interest rate changes by taking an outright or naked futures position represents an alternative to buying or short selling a bond on the spot market. Because of the risk inherent in such outright futures positions, though, some speculators form intracommodity and intercommodity spreads instead of taking a naked position.

Outright Positions

Exhibit 4.8 shows the Bloomberg price graphs for the September 2016 five-year T-note futures contract (FVU6) and the yields on a constant maturity five-year Treasury index (USGG5YR). From 12/29/15 to 4/7/16, yields on five-year Treasuries decreased 36.32% from 1.7849% to 1.1367% and prices on the September five-year T-note futures contracts increased from 117.21 to 121.24. A speculator that was expecting interest rates to decrease and who took a long position in the September contract on 12/29/15 and then closed it with a short position on 4/7/16 would have realized a profit of $4,030, or $4.03 per $100 face value, while a speculator that was expecting rates to decrease and who went short on 12/29/15 and closed the position with a long position on 4/7/16 would have lost $4,030 (see Exhibit 4.9).

EXHIBIT 4.8   Prices Graph on CBT September Five-Year T-Note Futures Contract (FVU6) and Yields on Five-Year T-Note (USGG5YR) Contracts 12/29/15 to 6/30/16

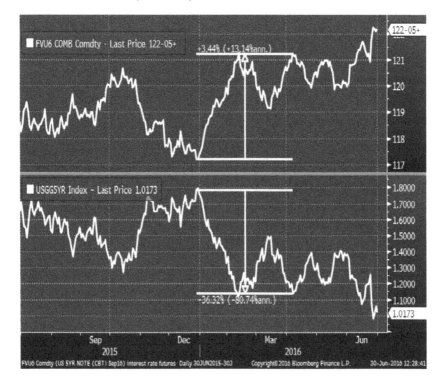

EXHIBIT 4.9 Long and Short Outright Positions on CBT September Five-Year T-Note Futures Contract

	Clearinghouse Records for Long September Five-Year T-Note Futures Speculator
12/29/15	**Opening Position:** Speculator agrees to buy September 2016 five-year T-note for 117.21 per $100 face value ($100,000 principal).
4/7/16	**Closing Position:** Speculator agrees to sell September 2016 five-year T-note for 121.24 per $100 face value ($100,000 principal).
Settlement	Clearinghouse pays Speculator $4,030. Closing receipt from clearinghouse: $(f_t - f_0) = (121.24 - 117.21) = 4.03$ per $100 face value $((121.24 - 117.21)/100)\,\$100,000 = \$4,030$
	Clearinghouse Records for Short September Five-Year T-Note Futures Speculator
12/29/15	**Opening Position:** Speculator agrees to sell September 2016 5-year T-note for 117.21 per $100 face value ($100,000 principal).
4/7/16	**Closing Position:** Speculator agrees to buy September 2016 5-year T-note for 121.24 per $100 face value ($100,000 principal).
Settlement	Speculator pays clearinghouse $4.030. Closing payment to clearinghouse: $(f_0 - f_t) = (117.21 - 121.24) = -4.03$ per $100 face value $((117.21 - 121.24)/100)\,\$100,000 = -\$4,030$

Duration, Rate-Anticipation Strategies, and Yield Curve Shifts

A bond's duration is defined as the percentage change in a bond's price ($\%\Delta P = \Delta P/P_0$) given a small change in yield (y). Mathematically, duration is obtained by taking the derivative of the equation for the price of a bond with respect to the yield, and then dividing by the bond's price and expressing the resulting equation in absolute value:

$$\text{Duration} = \frac{dP/P}{dy} = \frac{1}{(1+y)}\left(\sum_{t=1}^{M} t\,\frac{PV(CF_t)}{P_0^B}\right)$$

where:

dP/P_0 = percentage change in the bond's price
dy = small change in yield
M = number of periods to maturity
CF_t = Cash flow (coupon) at t

The bracketed expression in the duration equation is the weighted average of the time periods. Formally, the weighted average of the time periods is called *Macaulay's duration*, and the percentage change in the bond's price for a small change in yield in absolute value, is called the *modified duration*. Thus, the modified duration is equal to Macaulay's duration divided by $1 + y$.

Duration is a function of a bond's maturity (M) and coupons. Specifically, the greater a bond's maturity, the greater its duration, and therefore the greater its price sensitivity to interest rate changes. The smaller a bond's coupon rate, the greater its duration, and therefore the greater its price sensitivity to interest rate changes. Exhibit 4.10 shows the durations, prices, yields, and other features of newly issued US 3-month, 6-month, and 1-year T-bills, and 2-year, 3-year, 5-year, and 10-year T-notes, and 30-year T-bonds on 6/30/16.

Active strategies of selecting bonds or bond portfolios with specific durations based on interest rate expectations are referred to as *rate-anticipation strategies,* and when they involve simultaneously selling and buying bonds with different durations they are referred to as a *rate-anticipation swap*.

If a bond investor expected interest rates to decrease across all maturities by the same number of basis points, she could attain greater expected returns by purchasing bonds with larger durations or if she were managing a bond fund by reallocating her portfolio by selling shorter duration bonds and buying longer duration ones. In contrast, if a bond manager expected the interest rates to increase across all maturities by the same number of basis points, she could minimize her exposure to interest rate risk by changing her investments or portfolio to include more bonds with shorter durations. Alternatively, rate-anticipation strategies can be formed with futures positions on bonds with different durations. For example, a bond speculator expecting yields to decrease (increase) across all maturities could take an outright long (short) position in a CBT Ultra Long-Term Treasury futures contract. If yields on longer-term bonds decrease (increase), the speculator would profit from the increases (decreases) in spot and futures prices, and incur a loss if yields increase (decrease). If the speculator expected yields to decrease (increase) across all maturities, but did not want to be subject to the high return-risk position with contracts on longer-term bond, she could take a long (short) position on a futures contract on an intermediate-term Treasury, such as a five-year T-note, or on a Eurodollar futures contract.

EXHIBIT 4.10   Features of Treasury Issues

New Treasuries, 6/30/2016	Coupon and Maturity Date	Maturity Years	Yields to Maturity	Coupon Rate	Modified Duration
3-Month Bill	B 0 06/22/17	0.98	0.45	0.000	0.98
6-Month Bill	B 0 09/29/16	0.25	0.26	0.000	0.25
1-Year Bill	B 0 12/29/16	0.50	0.35	0.000	0.50
2-Year T-Note	T 0 5/8 06/30/18	2.00	0.59	0.625	1.98
3-Year T-Note	T 0 7/8 06/15/19	2.96	0.70	0.875	2.92
5-Year T-Note	T 1 1/8 06/30/21	5.00	1.01	1.125	4.85
7-Year T-Note	T 1 3/8 06/30/23	7.00	1.29	1.375	6.66
10-Year T-Note	T 1 5/8 05/15/26	9.87	1.49	1.625	9.08
30-Year T-Bond	T 2 1/2 05/15/46	29.87	2.30	2.500	21.12

In the financial literature, the relationship between the yields on financial assets and their terms to maturity is referred to as the *term structure of interest rates*. The term structure is often depicted graphically by a *yield curve*—a plot of the YTM against the terms to maturity for bonds that are otherwise alike. Yield curves constructed from US Treasury securities with different maturities are shown in Exhibit 4.11.

Interest rate anticipation strategies require forecasting not only general interest rate movements but also changes in the term structure of rates. Some rate-anticipation strategies are based on estimating the type of yield curve shift. Three types of yield curve shifts occur with some regularity: parallel shifts, shifts with twists, and shifts with humpedness. In a *parallel shift*, yields on all maturities change by the same magnitude. A *twist*, on the other hand, is a nonparallel shift. It implies either a flattening or steepening of the yield curve. If there is a flattening, the spread between long-term and short-term rates decreases; if there is a steepening, the spread increases. A shift with *humpedness* is also a nonparallel shift in which short-term and long-term rates change by different magnitudes than intermediate rates. An increase in both short and long-term rates relative to intermediate rates is referred to as a *positive butterfly*, and a decrease is known as a *negative butterfly*. If speculators expect a parallel shift in the yield curve, then using a rate-anticipation strategy based on the duration of the underlying bond as just described would be applicable. If a nonparallel shift is expected, speculative strategies are often based on intercommodity spreads. For example, if the yield curve is expected to flatten, with short-term rates increasing and intermediate-term rates decreasing, a speculator might consider taking a position in a Eurodollar futures contract or two-year Treasury contract and the opposite position in a futures contract on a 10-year T-note or 20-year T-bond.

EXHIBIT 4.11   Yield Curves: On-the-Run and Off-the-Run US Treasury Yield Curve (I111)

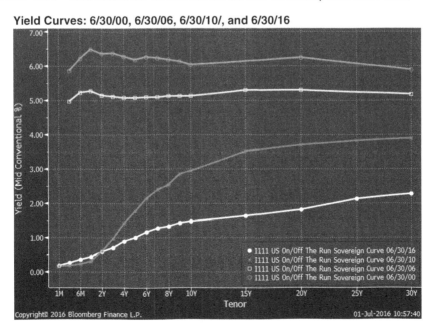

Spreads

Intracommodity Spread

As discussed with currency, commodity, and equity futures, intracommodity spreads are often based on the futures prices of longer-term contracts being more price sensitive to spot price changes than the futures prices on short-term contracts. If this is the case for, say, intermediate Treasuries, then a speculator who expects the interest rate on intermediate-term Treasury-notes to decrease in the future could form an intracommodity spread by going long in a longer-term T-note futures contract and short in a shorter-term one. This type of intracommodity spread will be profitable if the expectation of intermediate-term rates decreasing occurs. That is, the increase in the T-note price resulting from a decrease in intermediate-term rates will cause the price on the longer-term T-note futures to increase more than the shorter-term one. As a result, a speculator's gains from his long position in the longer-term futures will exceed his losses from his short position. If rates rise, though, losses will occur on the long position; these losses will be offset partially by profits realized from the short position on the shorter-term contract. On the other hand, if a bond speculator believes rates would increase but did not want to assume the risk inherent in an outright short position, she could form a spread with a short position in a longer-term contract and a long position in the shorter-term one.

Exhibit 4.12 shows the futures prices for the June 2016 and September 2016 futures contracts on the Ultra-Treasury Bond, along with price graph for a T-bond

EXHIBIT 4.12   Prices on June 2016 and September 2016 Ultra T-Bond Futures Contract and Deliverable Bond, Treasury, 3 3/4 4/15/41

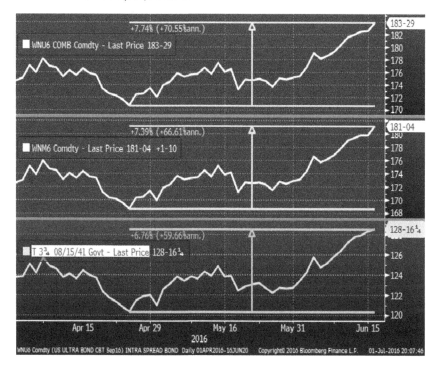

EXHIBIT 4.13 2-to-1 Intracommodity Spread: Long Two September T-Bond Futures and Short in One T-Bond Futures

	Clearinghouse Records for Two Long September T-Bond Futures Speculator
4/26/16	**Opening Position:**
	Speculator agrees to buy two September 2016 Ultra T-bonds for 170.6875 per $100 face value ($100,000 principal).
6/16/16	**Closing Position:**
	Speculator agrees to sell September 2016 Ultra T-bond for 183.906 per $100 face value ($100,000 principal).
Settlement	Clearinghouse pays Speculator $26,437.
	Closing receipt from clearinghouse:
	$2(f_t - f_0) = 2(183.906 - 170.6875) = 26.437$ per $100 face value
	$(26.437/100) \, \$100,000 = \$26,437$
	Clearinghouse Records for One Short June T-Note Futures Speculator
4/26/16	**Opening Position:**
	Speculator agrees to sell one June 2016 Ultra T-bond for 168.656 per $100 face value ($100,000 principal).
6/16/16	**Closing Position:**
	Speculator agrees to buy one June 2016 Ultra T-bond for 181.125 per $100 face value ($100,000 principal).
Settlement	Speculator pays clearinghouse $12,469.
	Closing payment to clearinghouse:
	$(f_0 - f_t) = (168.656 - 181.125) = -12.469$ per $100 face value
	$(-12.469/100) \, \$100,000 = -\$12,469$
Spread	**Cash Flow = $26,437 − $12,469 = $13,968**

with 3.75% coupon and maturity of 8/15/41. This bond was identified from Bloomberg Deliverable Bond screen (DLV) as the most likely to be delivered on the June contract. The deliverable bond had a CFA of 0.7108. From 4/26/16 to 6/16/16, the spot price on the deliverable bond increased 6.76% from 120.375 to 128.523, the June contract price increased 7.39% from 168.656 to 181.125, and the September contract price increased 7.74% from 170.6875 to 183.906. A spreader anticipating interest rates decreasing and long-term T-bond prices increasing during this period could have formed a 2-to-1 intracommodity spread by going long in two September contracts and short in one June contract. As shown in Exhibit 4.12, this spread would have generated a profit of $13,968.

Intercommodity Spread

Intercommodity spreads consist of long and short positions on futures contracts with the same expirations, but with different underlying assets. Such spreads can be used as rate-anticipation strategies to obtain a different return-risk position when a parallel shift in the yield curve is expected. Consider the case of a speculator who is forecasting a general decline in interest rates across all maturities—a downward parallel shift in the yield curve. Since bonds with greater durations are more price sensitive to interest rate changes than those with shorter maturities, the speculator could set up a rate-anticipation strategy by going long in a futures contract on a longer-term bond, such as the 30-year T-bond with the position partially hedged by going short in a futures contract on a shorter-term note, such as a two-year T-note. On the other hand, if an investor were forecasting an increase in rates across all maturities, she could go short in the T-bond futures contract and long in the T-note contract. Forming spreads with T-note and T-bond futures is sometimes referred to as the *NOB strategy* (notes over bonds). It should be noted that instead of forming a spread, investors can also take a position in a futures spread contract offered on the CBT, or other exchange (see Exhibit 4.1).

Exhibit 4.14 shows the Treasury yield curves for 5/29/15 and 4/7/16. For that period, the yields on 30-year T-bonds decreased 17.26% from 3.0215% to 2.5% and

EXHIBIT 4.14 Yield Curves on 5/29/15 and 4/7/16 for the On-the-Run and Off-the-Run US Treasury Yield Curve (I111), Prices on September 2016 5-Year T-Note and 30-Year T-Bond Futures Contracts

Yield Curves on 5/29/15 and 4/7/16

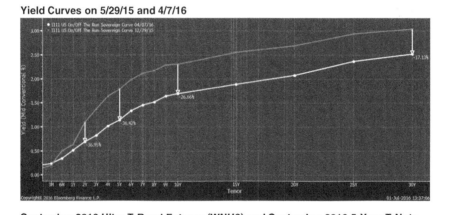

September 2016 Ultra T-Bond Futures (WNU6) and September 2016 5-Year T-Note Futures Prices, 12/29/15–7/1/16

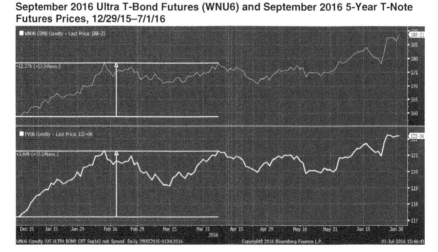

the yields on five-year notes decreased 35.10% from 1.7754% to 1.1523%. The exhibit also shows the Bloomberg price graphs for the September 2016 five-year T-note futures contract (FVU6) and the September Ultra T-Bond (30-year) contract. From 12/29/15 to 4/7/16, the price on the September five-year T-note futures contracts increased 3.44% from 117.21 to 121.24 and the price on the September Ultra-T-Bond increased 12.27% from 158.6875 to 178.15625. A speculator that was expecting this downward shift in the yield curve could have gone long in a number of futures contracts. With the greater duration on the underlying ultra T-bond than the five-year T-note, the speculator would have had a greater expected return but also greater risk by taking a long position in the T-bond futures than the five-year T-note futures contract. With an intercommodity spread formed by going long in the T-Bond futures and short positon in the T-note, the speculator could obtain different return-risk position between the two outright positions. Exhibit 4.15 shows an intercommodity spread formed with a long position in the September Ultra-bond contract and a short position in the September five-year T-note contract. If the spread was formed on 12/29/15 and closed on 4/7/2016, the spreader would have realized a profit of $19,468.75 on the long T-bond position and a loss of $4,030 on the short T-note position for a net gain of $15,438.75.

Another active bond strategy is a credit swap or quality swaps. Quality swaps often involve a *sector rotation* in which more funds are allocated to a specific quality sector in anticipation of a price change. For example, suppose a bond fund manager expected a recession accompanied by a flight to safety in which the demand for higher-quality bonds would increase and the demand for lower-quality ones would decrease. To profit from this expectation, the manager could change the allocation of her bond fund by selling some of her low-quality ones and buying more high-quality bonds. On the other hand, suppose the economy were in a recession, but the bond manager believed that it was near its trough and that economic growth would follow. To capitalize from this expectation, the manager could tilt her bond portfolio toward lower-quality bonds by selling some of her higher-quality bonds and buying lower-quality ones. In addition to sector rotations, quality swaps can also be constructed to profit from anticipated changes in yield spreads between quality sectors—credit spreads. Credit spreads tend to widen during periods of economic recession and narrow during periods of economic expansion. If the economy were at the trough of a recession and were expected to grow in the future, speculators or a hedge fund might anticipate a narrowing in the spread between lower- and higher-quality bonds.

Instead of taking positions in different quality bonds, speculators alternatively can form a quality swap by taking positions in futures contracts on bonds with different quality ratings. For example, a spread formed with futures contracts on a dollar-denominated Brazilian bond and US T-bond. A speculator forecasting an economic expansion in Brazil could, in turn, profit from an anticipated narrowing in the risk premium by forming an intercommodity spread consisting of a long position in dollar-denominated Brazilian bond (e.g., a contract on a 2018 Brazilian sovereign debt bond listed on the BMF—Bolsa de Mercadorias e Futuros; see Bloomberg: MIF <Comdty>) and a short position in a T-bond futures contract. It should be noted that unlike NOB strategies formed with Treasury contracts, quality

EXHIBIT 4.15   Intercommodity Spread: Notes over Bonds (NOB)—Long T-Bond Futures
and Short in Five-Year T-Note Futures

	Clearinghouse Records for Long September Ultra T-Bond Futures Speculator
12/29/15	**Opening Position:**
	Speculator agrees to buy September 2016 ultra T-bond for 158.6875 per $100 face value ($100,000 principal).
4/7/16	**Closing Position:**
	Speculator agrees to sell September 2016 ultra T-bond for 178.15625 per $100 face value ($100,000 principal).
Settlement	Clearinghouse pays Speculator $19,468.75.
	Closing receipt from clearinghouse:
	$(f_t - f_0) = (178.15625 - 158.6875) = 19.46875$ per $100 face value
	$(19.46875/100)\ \$100,000 = \$19,468.75$
	Clearinghouse Records for Short September Five-Year T-Note Futures Speculator
12/29/15	**Opening Position:**
	Speculator agrees to sell September 2016 five-year T-note for 117.21 per $100 face value ($100,000 principal).
4/7/16	**Closing Position:**
	Speculator agrees to buy September 2016 5-year T-note for 121.24 per $100 face value ($100,000 principal).
Settlement	Speculator pays clearinghouse $4,030.
	Closing payment to clearinghouse:
	$(f_0 - f_t) = (117.21 - 121.24) = -4.03$ per $100 face value
	$(-4.03/100)\ \$100,000 = -\$4,030$
Spread	**Cash Flow = $19,468.75 − $4,030 = $15,438.75**

swaps require a position in futures contract on a lower-quality bond. There are only
a few such contracts (usually on foreign bond), and often there is limited trading.
Such positions can be synthetically created by taking a position in a shorter-term
low-quality bond and an opposite position in a longer-term lower-quality bond. This
is known as a *locking-in strategy*.

Hedging with Interest Rate and Bond Futures Contracts

Long hedge positions on debt securities are used by money market managers,
fixed-income managers, and dealers to lock in their costs on future security purchases.
In contrast, short hedge positions are used by bond and money market managers,
investment bankers, and dealers who are planning to sell fixed-income securities in
the future, by banks and other intermediaries to lock in the rates they pay on future
deposits, and by corporate treasurers and other borrowers who want to lock in the
future rates on their loans or who want to fix the rates on the floating-rate loans.

Long Hedge

A long position in an interest rate futures contract can be used by money market and fixed-income managers to lock in the purchase price on a future investment. If interest rates at the future investment date are lower, then the price on the fixed-income securities will be higher, and as a result, the cost of buying the securities will be higher. With a long futures position, though, the manager would realize a profit when he closes his long futures position. With the profit from the futures, the manager would then be able to defray the additional cost of purchasing the higher-priced fixed-income securities. In contrast, if rates are higher, the cost of securities will be lower, but the manager would have to use part of the investment cash inflow to cover losses on his futures position. In either interest rate scenario, though, the manager would find that he can purchase approximately the same number of securities, given his hedged position.

Long Hedge Example: Future T-Note Purchase

Consider the case of a fixed-income manager who on 12/30/2015 anticipates an increase in cash of approximately $1 million in June from maturing bonds in her portfolio. Suppose the manager plans to buy five-year T-notes, but is concerned about rates decreasing and bond price rising over the next six months and would like to lock in the price on her future T-note purchase. On 12/30/2015, the price on the CME June five-year T-note was 117.6875 and the most likely to be delivered bond on the contract was a T-note with a $1\frac{3}{8}\%$ coupon and maturity of 8/31/2020 (see Exhibit 4.16). To lock in a June purchase price on her planned investment in T-notes, the manager would need to go long in 10 June T-note futures contracts. Examining Bloomberg's DLV screen, one finds that on June 16 (the expiration date) the $1\frac{3}{8}\%$ Treasury maturing on 8/31/2020 was on the deliverable bond list. On that date, this note had accrued interest of $0.475 per $100 face value and its CFA was 0.8317. Suppose on 6/16/16, a trader with a short position on the June contract delivered those bonds to the fixed-income manager. Give the note's CFA and futures price on the June contract of 117.6875, the manager would have paid $978,807 to the futures seller for ten $1\frac{3}{8}\%$ T-notes maturing on 8/31/2020 plus $4,750 of accrued interest—total cost of $983,557.

T-note Price per $100 face value:

$$\text{Cost} = (\text{Quoted futures price})(\text{CFA}) + \text{Accrued interest}$$
$$\text{Cost} = (117.6875)(0.8317) + 0.475$$
$$\text{Cost} = \$98.3557$$

Cost of 10 T-notes with $100,000 face value plus accrued interest

$$\text{Cost} = 10\,\frac{98.3557}{100}(\$100,000)$$
$$\text{Cost} = \$983,557$$

EXHIBIT 4.16 Yield on the Constant Maturity Five-Year Treasury Index, Prices on CBT June 2016 Five-Year T-Note Contract, and Prices on 1 3/8% Treasury with Maturity of 8/31/2020

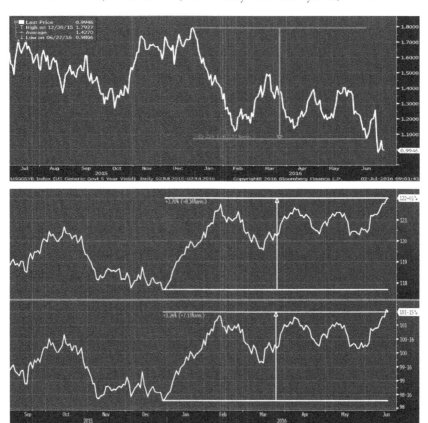

From 12/30/2015 to 6/15/2016, five-year Treasury yields decreased 40.23% from 1.7927% to 1.0715%, the June 2016 futures contract on the five-year T-note increased 3.82% from 117.6875 to 122.19, and the price on the $1\frac{3}{8}$% 8/31/20 Treasury increased from 98.4065 to 101.469. If the fixed-income manager purchased ten $1\frac{3}{8}$% T-note maturing on 8/31/2020 on the spot market at 101.469 and paid accrued interest of $0.475 (per $100 face value) and closed her long futures contract by going short in the expiring June contracts trading at 122.19, her net cost would have been $974,419:

$$\text{Cost of 10 T-notes} = 10\,(\text{Price of treasury} + \text{Accrued interest})$$

$$\text{Cost of 10 T-notes} = 10\left[\frac{101.469}{100}\right]\$100,000 + \$4,750$$

$$\text{Cost of 10 T-notes} = \$1,019,440$$

$$\text{Futures cash flow} = 10 \left[\frac{(f_T - f_0)}{100} \right] (\$100,000)$$

$$\text{Futures cash flow} = 10 \left[\frac{(122.19 - 117.6875)}{100} \right] (\$100,000) = \$45,025$$

$$\text{Net cost} = \$1,019,444 - \$45,025 = \$974,419$$

Thus, with the long futures position, the manager would have been able to lock in a T-note cost of $983,557 by purchasing the delivered bonds on the contract or for a net cost of $974,419 from buying her T-notes on the spot for $1,019,440 and receiving $45,025 from the clearinghouse. Without the hedge, the manager would have paid $1,019,440 for the T-notes on 6/16/2016. In retrospect, the manager would have been correct by locking in the price with the long futures position.

Long Hedge Example: Future Eurodollar Investment

Consider the case of a money market manager who on January 2, 2016, was expecting a cash inflow of $10 million on June 13, 2016, that he planned to invest for three months in certificates of deposit, CD, paying the LIBOR. Exhibit 4.17 shows the prices and discount yields on the June 2016 Eurodollar futures contract from 1/2/16 to 6/13/16. On 1/2/16, the June contract was trading at index price of 98.59 or an annual discount yield of $R_D = 1.41\%$ (=$100 - 98.59$) with the actual futures price for a $1,000,000 face value being $996,475 and the implied yield to maturity, YTM_f, being 1.0442%:

$$f_0 = \frac{100 - R_D\%(90/360)}{100} \$1,000,000$$

$$f_0 = \frac{100 - (100 - 98.59)(90/360)}{100} \$1,000,000 = \$996,475$$

$$YTM_f = \left[\frac{F}{f_0} \right]^{360/90} - 1$$

$$YTM_f = \left[\frac{\$1,000,000}{\$996,475} \right]^{365/90} - 1 = 0.01442$$

Suppose the money market manager was worried that short-term rates could decrease from January to June and decided to lock in the three-month rate on his September $10 million investment by going long in ten CME June Eurodollar futures at 98.59 ($R_D = 1.41\%$ or $f_0 = \$996,475$). If the LIBOR at the June expiration was lower, the money market manager would have to invest in a CD with a lower rate, but would have profited on the futures position and therefore would have more funds to invest at the lower rate. On the other hand, if the LIBOR at the June expiration was higher, then the money market manager would have to invest in a CD with a higher rate, but would have incurred a loss on the futures contracts that, in turn,

EXHIBIT 4.17   Prices and Yields on CME's June Eurodollar Futures

Prices on a June 2016 90-Day Eurodollar Futures (CME Index)

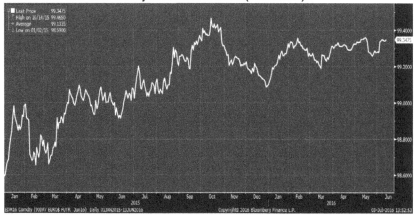

Implied Yields on December 90-Day Eurodollar Futures

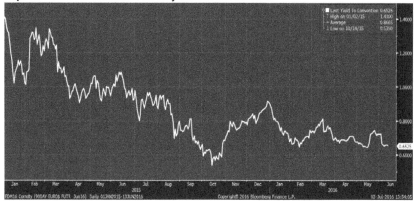

would have lowered the amount of funds he would have to invest at the higher rate. The impact that rates have on the amount of funds invested ($10 million plus or minus the closing futures position) and the rate paid on them will exactly offset each other, leaving the money market manager with a locked-in yield on the three-month CD investment to be made in June.

This hedge can be seen in Exhibit 4.18. The exhibit shows three possible LIBORs at the June 13 expiration along with their corresponding index prices and futures prices. As shown, at the lower discount rate of 0.91%, the fund would have a profit of $12,500 from its futures position to augment its $10 million investment. Investing $10,012,500 at the lower LIBOR rate of 0.91% would return a maturing cash flow three months later of $13,035,201 and provide a yield based on a $10 million investment of 1.42% (the same as the YTM implied on the futures contract). On the other hand, at the higher discount rate of 1.91%, the fund would incur a loss of $12,500 on its futures position, reducing its investment to $9,987,500. Investing $9,987,500 at the higher LIBOR rate of 1.91% would, however, return a maturing cash flow

EXHIBIT 4.18 Long Hedge with Eurodollar Futures Initial Position, January 3, 2016: Long in 10 June Eurodollar futures contracts at $R_D = 1.41$ (Index = 95.89, f_0 = $996,475) to hedge $10,000,000 CD investment in June

Position				Price on 6/13/2016
(1) Expiring June Futures Index Price	99.09	98.59	98.09	99.3475
(2) Expiring June Discount Yield, R_D	0.0091	0.0141	0.0191	0.006525
(3) Price on Expiring June Contract: $[(100 - R_D (0.25))/100]\$1,000,000$	$997,725	$996,475	$995,225	$998,369
(4) Profit on 10 Long Futures: $10(f_T - \$996,475)$	$12,500	$0	−$12,500	$18,938
(5) Investment Cash Flow	$10,000,000	$10,000,000	$10,000,000	$10,000,000
(6) Investment Cash Flow + Futures Cash Flow	$10,012,500	$10,000,000	$9,987,500	$10,018,938
(7) June LIBOR = R_D	0.0091	0.0141	0.0191	0.0065
(8) Maturity Cash Flow: (Row 7) $(1 + \text{June LIBOR})^{(90/360)}$	$10,035,201	$10,035,065	$10,034,852	$10,035,241
(9) Three-Month June to September Yield = (Row $(8)/\$10,000,000)^{360/90} - 1$	0.0142	0.0141	0.0140	0.0142

three months later of $10,034,852 and provide a yield based on a $10 million investment of 1.40% (approximately the same as the YTM implied on the futures contract). Note that at any rate, the yield would be approximately 1.4%. Thus, the money market manager by going long in January in a June Eurodollar futures contact priced at 98.59 would have been able to lock in a three-month yield on a June CD investment of 1.4%.

On June 13, 2016, the actual price and rate on the expiring June futures were 99.3475 and 0.6525%. As shown in the last column of Exhibit 4.18, at those prices, the manager would have realized a profit of $18,938 from his long futures position and would have been able to invest $10,018,938 at the lower LIBOR of 0.6525%. Based on a $10 million investment, his yield would have been 1.42%.

Short Hedge

Short hedges are used when corporations, governments, financial institutions, dealers, and underwriters are planning to sell bonds or borrow funds at some future date and want to lock in the rate. If interest rates have increased at the time the fixed-income securities are sold (or the loan starts), then the price on the fixed-income securities will be lower, and as a result, the revenue from selling the fixed-income securities will be less (or the rate on the loan is higher). With a short futures-hedged position, though, the security seller (or borrower) would be able to profit when he closes his short position by going long in a lower-priced expiring futures contract. With the profit from the futures, the seller would be able to offset the lower revenue from selling the securities (or defray the additional interest cost of the loan). In contrast, if rates decrease, the revenue from selling the securities at higher prices will be greater (or loan interest cost lower), but the security seller will have to use part of the investment cash inflow (or interest savings) to cover losses on his futures position. In either interest rate scenario, though, the manager will find less revenue variation from selling securities and closing his futures (or effective rate paid on loans), given his hedged position.

Short Hedge Example: Future T-Note Sale

To illustrate how a short hedge works, suppose the fixed-income manager in our earlier example anticipates on 12/30/2015 that instead of having cash, she will need cash in June and plans to obtain it by selling her holdings of 10 T-notes with coupon rates of $1^3/_8\%$ and maturities of 8/31/2020. On 12/30/2015, the price on a CME June five-year T-note was 117.6875 and the most likely to be delivered bond happened to be the $1^3/_8\%$ Treasury maturing on 8/31/2020 (see Exhibit 4.14). To lock in a June selling price on her T-notes, the manager would need to go short in 10 of the June T-note futures contracts. As previously noted, at the June expiration, the $1^3/_8\%$ Treasury maturing on 8/31/2020 was on the deliverable bond list, it had accrued interest of $0.475 per $100 face value, and its CFA was 0.8317. If the manager delivered 10 of her bonds on her short futures contracts, she would have received $983,557 in revenue:

> Seller's revenue per $100 face value:
>
> Seller's revenue = (Quoted futures price)(CFA) + Accrued interest
>
> Seller's revenue = (117.6875)(0.8317) + 0.475
>
> Seller's revenue = $98.3557

Seller's revenue on 10 T-notes with $100,000 face value:

$$\text{Revenue} = 10 \, \frac{98.3557}{100}(\$100,000)$$

$$\text{Revenue} = \$983,557$$

It was also noted previously that from 12/30/2015 to 6/15/2016, five-year Treasury yields decreased 40.23% from 1.7927% to 1.0715%, the June 2016 futures contract on the five-year T-note increased 3.70% from 117.6875 to 122.19, and the price on the $1^3/_8\%$ 8/31/20 Treasury increased from 98.4065 to 101.469. If the manager sold her T-notes on the spot market and closed the futures contract by going long in the expiring June contracts trading at 122.19 her net revenue would have been $974,419:

$$\text{Revenue from treasury sale} = 10 \text{ Price of treasury} + \text{Accrued interest}$$

$$\text{Revenue from treasury sale} = 10 \left[\frac{101.469}{100}\right] \$100,000 + \$4,750$$

$$\text{Revenue from treasury sale} = \$1,019,440$$

$$\text{Futures cash flow} = 10 \left[\frac{(f_0 - f_T)}{100}\right] (\$100,000)$$

$$\text{Futures cash flow} = 10 \left[\frac{(117.6875 - 122.19)}{100}\right] (\$100,000)$$

$$= -\$45,025$$

$$\text{Net revenue} = \$1,019,444 - \$45,025 = \$974,419$$

Note that while the treasurer is able to lock in her revenue of $983,557 by delivering her bonds on the contract or receiving a net revenue of $974,419 from selling her T-notes on the spot and paying the clearinghouse, she probably regrets she hedged the T-notes. Without the hedge and with rates decreasing, she could have sold her T-notes on 6/16/2016 for $1,019,440.

Hedging with a Short Eurodollar Futures Contract — Managing the Maturity Gap

An important use of short hedges is in minimizing the interest rate risk that financial institutions are exposed to when the maturity of their assets does not equal the maturity of their liabilities—called a *maturity gap*. As an example, consider the case of a small bank with a maturity gap problem in which its short-term loan portfolio has an average maturity greater than the maturity of the CDs that it is using to finance its loans. Specifically, suppose on September 15, 2015, the bank made loans of $100 million, all with maturities of 180 days (maturity date of 3/15/16) paying a rate equal to the six-month LIBOR plus 10 basis points. On 9/15/15, the six-month LIBOR was at 0.54% (see Exhibit 4.19), providing the bank with a return on its loans of 0.64% and cash flow from the loans of $100,319,490:

$$\text{Bank cash inflow on } 3/15/16 = \$100,000,000 (1.0064)^{180/360} = \$100,319,490$$

To finance the loans, suppose the bank's customers prefer 90-day CDs to 180-day CDs, and as a result, the bank sells $100 million worth of 90-day CDs on 9/15/15 at a rate equal to the three-month LIBOR of 0.33425% (see Exhibit 4.19). On 12/15/15, the bank would owe $100,083,525:

$$\text{Bank CD debt on } 12/15/15 = \$100,000,000 (1.0033452)^{90/360} = \$100,083,525$$

EXHIBIT 4.19   Six-Month LIBOR (US0006M), Three-Month LIBOR (US0006M), and Prices on
CME's December 2015 Eurodollar Futures (EDZ15) 9/15/2015 to 3/15/2016

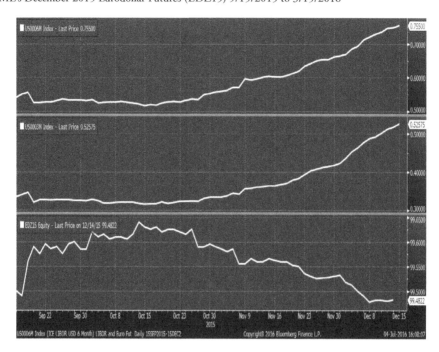

To finance this debt, the bank would have to sell $100,083,525 worth of 90-day
CDs at the three-month LIBOR on 12/15/15. In the absence of a hedge, the bank
would be subject to interest-rate risk. If short-term rates increase, the bank would
have to pay higher interest on its planned December CD sale, lowering its interest
spread; if rates decrease, the bank's spread would increase.

Suppose on 9/15/15, the bank was fearful of higher three-month LIBOR in
December and decided to minimize its exposure to interest rate risk by hedging its
$100,083,525 CD sale in September by going short in a December 2015 Eurodollar
futures contract. As shown in Exhibit 4.19, December 2015 Eurodollar futures were
trading at an index price of 99.5 ($R_D = 0.50\%$) on 9/15/15 with an implied YTM
on the futures of 0.5%. To hedge the liability, the bank would need to go short in
100.208786 December Eurodollar futures (assume perfect divisibility) and would
lock in an effective 3-month rate of 0.5%:

$$f_0(12/15/15) = \frac{100 - (0.5)(90/360)}{100}(\$1,000,000) = \$998,750$$

$$YTM_f(\text{December}) = \left[\frac{\$1,000,000}{\$998.750}\right]^{365/90} - 1 = 0.005$$

$$n_f = \frac{\$100,083,525}{\$998,750} = 100.208786 \text{ Short Eurodollar contracts}$$

When the 90-day CD issued on 9/15/15 matures on 12/15/15, the bank would issue new 90-day CDs at the prevailing LIBOR to finance the $100,083,525 maturing CD debt plus (minus) any loss (profit) from closing its expiring December 2015 Eurodollar futures position. If the three-month LIBOR were greater in December, the bank would have to pay a greater interest on the three-month CD that it would issue on 12/15/15, but it would realize a profit from closing its expiring Eurodollar futures contracts, decreasing the amount of funds it would need to finance at the higher rate. On the other hand, if the three-month LIBOR were lower in December, the bank would have lower interest payments on the three-month CD that it would issue in December, but it would also incur a loss on its futures position and therefore would have more funds that need to be financed at the lower rates. The impact that rates have on the amount of funds needed to be financed and the rate paid on them will exactly offset each other, leaving the bank with a fixed debt amount when the CDs issued in December mature on 3/15/16.

The bank's hedge can be seen in Exhibit 4.20, which shows three possible LIBORs at the 12/15/15 expiration date along with their corresponding index prices and futures prices and the bank's debt on it maturing December CD of $100,083,525. As shown in the exhibit, at the lower LIBOR of 0.25%, the bank would incur a loss of $62,631 on its futures position, which would increase its debt to $100,146,156. Issuing a new three-month CD on 12/15/15 for $100,146,156 at the lower LIBOR rate of 0.25% would, in turn, obligate the bank to a debt obligation on 3/15/16 of $100,208,689. Based on the December debt of $100,083,525, the effective rate paid on the futures-hedged debt would be 0.5% (the same as the YTM implied on the futures contract):

$$\text{Effective rate paid} =$$
$$\left[\frac{[\text{December CD Debt} - \text{Futures profit}] \, (1 + \text{LIBOR})^{0.25}}{\$100,083,525} \right]^{360/90} - 1$$

$$\text{Effective rate paid} = \left[\frac{[\$100,083,525 - (-\$62,631)](1.0025)^{0.25}}{\$100,083,525} \right]^{360/90} - 1$$

$$\text{Effective rate paid} = \left[\frac{\$100,208,689}{\$100,083,525} \right]^{360/90} - 1 = 0.005$$

On the other hand, at the higher LIBOR of 0.75%, the bank would have a profit of $62,631 on its futures position, which would lower its debt to $100,020,894. Issuing a new three-month CD on 12/15/15 for $100,020,894 at the higher LIBOR rate of 0.75% would, in turn, obligate the bank to a debt obligation on 3/15/16 of $100,207,908 (approximately the same as the debt on the lower rate case). Based on the bank's December debt $100,083,525, the effective futures-hedge rate paid on the debt would again be 0.5% (the same as the YTM implied on the futures contract):

Effective rate paid =

$$\left[\frac{[\text{December CD debt} - \text{Futures profit}]\,(1 + \text{LIBOR})^{0.25}}{\$100,083,525} \right]^{360/90} - 1$$

$$\text{Effective rate paid} = \left[\frac{[\$100,083,525 - \$62,631](1.0075)^{0.25}}{\$100,083,525} \right]^{360/90} - 1$$

$$\text{Effective rate paid} = \left[\frac{\$100,207,908}{\$100,083,525} \right]^{360/90} - 1 = 0.005$$

The effective hedged rate of 5% holds for any LIBOR. On 12/15/15, the actual price and discount rate on the expiring December futures was 99.4822 and 0.5178%. As shown in the last column of Exhibit 4.20, at those prices, the bank would have realized a profit of $4,459 from its short futures position and it would have needed to borrow $100,087,984 at the LIBOR of 0.5178%. Based on a $100,083,525 December debt obligation, the bank's effective rate is again approximately 0.5%.

To summarize: On 9/15/15, the bank provided six-month loans of $100,000,000 paying 0.64% financed by issuing three-month CDs on 9/15 paying 0.33425% to be refinanced on 12/15/15 by issuing a three-month CD with the rate of 0.5% rate locked with a short position in 100.208786 December Eurodollar taken on 9/15/15. With the 0.33425% rate the bank pays on its first CDs and 0.5% locked in rate of the second CD, the bank would pay an effective six-month rate of 0.4171%:

$$R(180\ days) = \left[(1.0033425)^{0.25}\,(1.005)^{0.25} \right]^{360/180} - 1 = 0.004171$$

The futures position, in turn, enabled the bank to create an effective six-month CD rate of 0.4171% and eliminate (or at least minimizing) its interest rate risk. The $100,000,000 six-month loans initiated on 9/15/15 paying 0.64% interest would have provided the bank with interest income of $319,490 (= $[(1.0064)^{0.5} - 1](\$100,000,000)$), while the financing cost would have been $208,833 (= $[(1.004171)^{0.5} - 1](\$100,000,000)$), which would have left the bank with a spread profit of $110,657 (see the last row of Exhibit 4.20). Note that on 12/15/15, three-month LIBOR was 0.52575 (see Exhibit 4.20). If the bank had not hedged the rate paid on its December debt of $100,083,525, then its debt obligation on 3/15/16 would have been $100,214,814 (= $(\$100,083,525)(1.0052575)^{0.25}$), and its spread profit would have been $104,676 (= $\$100,000,000\,(1.0064)^{0.5} - (\$100,083,525)$ $(1.0052575)^{0.25}$)—or $5,981 less than the locked-in spread.

Cross Hedging and the Price-Sensitivity Model

The above examples were presented as perfect hedging cases in which certain revenues or costs could be locked in at a future date. Whether it is a commodity, currency,

EXHIBIT 4.20   Hedging Maturity Gap Initial Position, 9/15/15: Short in 100.208786 December 2015 Eurodollar futures contracts at $R_D = 0.50\%$ (Index $= 99.5, f_0 = \$998,750$) to hedge the rate paid on December CD of $100,083,525

Position				Price on 12/15/2015
(1) Expiring December 2015 Futures Index Price	99.75	99.50	99.25	99.4822
(2) Expiring December Discount Yield, R_D	0.0025	0.0050	0.0075	0.005178
(3) Price on Expiring December Contract: $[(100 - R_D(0.25))/100]\$1,000,000$	$999,375	$998,750	$998,125	$998,706
(4) Profit on 101.21 Short Futures: 100.208786 $(\$998,750 - f_T)$	−$62,631	$0	$62,631	$4,459
(5) 12/15/15 Debt on Maturing CD: $100,083,525 $= \$100,000,000$ $(1.0034452)^{90/360}$	$100,083,525	$100,083,525	$100,083,525	$100,083,525
(6) Funds to Finance: Maturing Debt − Futures Profit, Row (5) − Row (4)	$100,146,156	$100,083,525	$100,020,894	$100,079,065.66
(7) December 3-Month LIBOR $= R_D$	0.0025	0.0050	0.0075	0.005178
(8) Debt on 3/15/16: (Row 7) $(1 + \text{December LIBOR})^{(90/360)}$	$100,208,689	$100,208,396	$100,207,908	$100,208,367
(9) Effective 3-Month (12/15/15 to 3/15/16) Rate Paid $=$ (Row $(8)/\$100,083,525)^{360/90} - 1$	0.005	0.005	0.005	0.005
(10) 3/15/16 Principal and Interest Received on Loan Made on 9/15/15: $100(1.0064)^{0.5}$	$100,319,490	$100,319,490	$100,319,490	$100,319,490
(11) Bank Profit: Row (10) − Row (8)	$110,801	$111,094	$111,582	$111,122

equity position, or a fixed-income position, the presence of quality risk, timing risk, and quantity risk makes perfect hedges the exception and not the rule. If a fixed-income position to be hedged has a futures contract with the same underlying asset, such as in the previous hedging cases, then a naive hedge usually will be effective in reducing interest rate risk. Many fixed-income positions, though, involve securities and interest rate positions in which a futures contract on the underlying security does not exist. In such cases, an effective cross hedge needs to be determined to minimize the price risk in the underlying spot position. Two commonly used models for cross hedging for fixed-income positions are the regression model and the price-sensitivity model. In the *regression model*, the estimated slope coefficient of the regression equation is used to determine the hedge ratio. The coefficient, in turn, is found by regressing the spot price on the bond to be hedged against the futures price.

The second hedging approach is to use the *price-sensitivity model* developed by Kolb and Chiang (1981) and Toers and Jacobs (1986). This model has been shown to be relatively effective in reducing the variability of debt positions. The model determines the number of futures contracts that will make the value of a portfolio consisting of a fixed-income security and an interest rate futures contract invariant to small changes in interest rates. The derivation of the model is presented in a number of derivative text. The optimum number of futures contracts that achieves this objective is:

$$n_f = \frac{Dur_S}{Dur_f} \frac{V_0}{f_0} \frac{(1 + YTM_f)^T}{(1 + YTM_S)^T}$$

where:

Dur_S = duration of the bond or bond portfolio
Dur_f = duration of the bond on the underlying contract (the cheapest-to-deliver bond)
V_0 = value of bond or the bond portfolio
f_0 = futures price
T = time to expiration on the futures as proportion of year
YTM_S = yield to maturity on the bond fund
YTM_f = yield to maturity implied on the futures contract

Hedging a Bond Portfolio

Suppose a bond portfolio manager is planning to liquidate part of his portfolio at a future date and fears higher interest rates in the future. To protect the portfolio value against the possibility of a rate increase and bond price decline, the manager could go short in an OTC T-bond or T-note offered by a dealer or short in a CBT T-note or ultra T-bond futures contract. If rates increase, the bond portfolio value will decrease, but the loss in value will be offset by profits realized from his futures position. If rates decrease, the bond portfolio value will increase, but the gain in value will be offset by losses from his futures position.

Exhibit 4.21 summarizes the portfolio features of the Xavier Bond Fund, the Bank of America/Merrill Lynch US Corporate and Government Bond Index (B0A0), and the CBT's June 2016 five-year T-note futures contract and its cheapest-to-deliver bond for dates 7/1/16 and 12/30/15. The information was accessed from Bloomberg's

EXHIBIT 4.21   Features of the Xavier Bond Fund, the BOA/ML Aggregate Investment Grade Index (BOA0), and the CBT June Five-Year T-Note Futures

	Xavier Bond Fund	Xavier Bond Fund	BOA/ML Investment Grade Index (BOA0)	BOA/ML Investment Grade Index (BOA0)	CBT June 2016 5-Year T-Note Futures	CBT June 2016 5-Year T-Note Futures
	12/30/2015	**7/1/2016**	**12/30/2015**	**7/1/2016**	**12/30/2015**	**7/1/2016**
Market Value	$11.925 million	$12.369 million	$16.213 billion	$17.176 billion	117.6875	122.19
Yield to Maturity (%)	2.98	2.16	2.51	1.80	1.76	1.73
Modified Duration	5.43	5.20	6.08	6.58	4.02	4.00
Coupon Rate (%)	3.73	3.73	3.23	3.19	1.38	1.38
Maturity (years)	5.60	6.33	8.33	8.87	4.66	4.10
Bloomberg Composite Ratings	A+	A+	AA	AA	AAA	AAA

For the futures, the market value is the futures price and yield to maturity is the implied YTM on the futures.
For the futures, the duration, coupon rate, and maturity are for a $1\,^3/_8$ T-note, maturing on 8/31/20.
This was most likely to be delivered bond on 12/30/15.
Source: Bloomberg

Portfolio screen (PORT). The fund's holdings consisted of 39 investment-grade corporates, Treasuries, and federal agency bonds. On 12/30/15, the value of the bond portfolio was $11,925,000 and it had a duration of 5.43 and yield to maturity of 2.98%. Suppose on 12/30/15, the managers of the Xavier Bond Fund decided to hedge the portfolio's value out of fear that interest rates would increase by going short in June 2016 futures contract on the five-year T-note. On 12/30/15, the most likely to-be-delivered bond on the futures was a $1\,^3/_8$% T-note maturing on 8/31/20, which had a duration of 4.02. Using the price-sensitivity model, the managers would have needed to go short in 136 June T-note contracts to hedge the portfolio's value against their anticipated interest rate increase:

$$n_f = \frac{Dur_S}{Dur_f} \frac{V_0}{f_0} \frac{(1 + YTM_f)^T}{(1 + YTM_S)^T}$$

$$n_f = \frac{5.43}{4.02} \frac{\$11,925,000}{\$117,687} \frac{(1.0176)^{(165/365)}}{(1.0298)^{(165/365)}}$$

$$n_f = 136 \;\; \text{Short contracts}$$

where:

Dur_S = duration of the bond fund = 5.43
Dur_f = duration of the cheapest-to-deliver bond = 4.02
V_0 = value of bond portfolio = $11.925 million
f_0 = futures price = 117.6875 per $100 face ($117,687 per $100,000 face)
T = time to expiration on the futures as proportion of year = 165/365
YTM_S = yield to maturity on the bond fund = 2.98%
YTM_f = yield to maturity implied on the futures contract = 1.76%

From 12/30/15 to 6/15/16, the five-year Treasury yield actually decreased 40.23% from 1.7927% to 1.0715%, and as a result, the value of Xavier Bond Fund increased 3.70% from $11.925 million to $12.369 (see Exhibit 4.22). If the Xavier Fund managers had hedged the portfolio, however, they would have incurred a loss of $612,340 on the June 2016 futures contract on the five-year T-note, which had increased 3.83%

EXHIBIT 4.22   Value of Xavier Bond Fund, Price of CBT June 2016 Five-Year T-Note Contract, and Yield on the Constant Maturity Five-Year Treasury Index

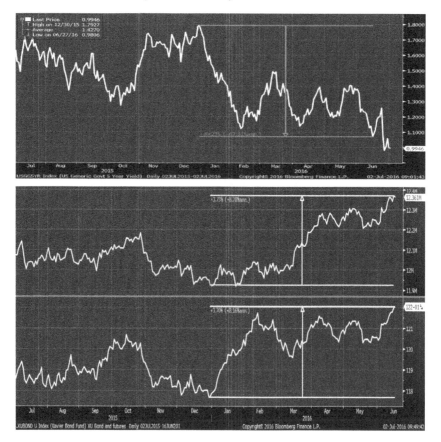

from 117.6875 to 122.19, leaving them with a hedged portfolio value of $11,756,660 (= $12,369,000 − $612,340):

$$Futures\ cash\ flow = n_f\ \frac{(f_0 - f_T)}{100}\ (\$100,000)$$

$$Futures\ cash\ flow = 136\ \frac{(117.6875 - 122.19)}{100}\ (\$100,000) = -\$612,340$$

Thus, the managers would have regretted that they hedged the value, although they did lock in a value for their portfolio close to the 12/31/15 value (see Exhibit 4.23).

Managing Asset and Liability Positions

Interest rate derivatives can also be used by financial and nonfinancial corporations to alter the exposure of their balance sheets to interest rate changes. The change can be done for speculative purposes (increasing the firm's exposure to interest rate changes) or for hedging purposes (reducing exposure). As an example, consider the case of a bond fund that manages its bond portfolio against Barclays' aggregate government-corporate index. Suppose the fund expects interest rates to decrease in the coming year across all maturities. To outperform the index, suppose the fund would like to lengthen the duration of its bond fund relative to the index's duration. The fund could do this

EXHIBIT 4.23 Xavier Bond Fund Hedged with June Five-Year T-Notes Futures Contracts

	Bond Fund Values and Opening and Closing Clearinghouse Records for CBT June 2016 Five-Year T-Note Contract
12/30/15	**Futures Opening Position:**
	Fund goes short in 136 CBT June 2016 T-note futures at 117.6875.
	Xavier Bond Fund Value = $11.925 million
6/16/16	**Xavier Bond Fund Value = $12.369 million**
	Futures Closing Position:
Settlement	Fund goes long in 136 CBT June 2016 futures at 122.19.
	Closing receipt from clearinghouse:
	$136(f_0 - f_T) = 136(117.6875 - 122.19) = -612.34$ per $100 face value
	$(-\$612.34/100)\ \$100,000 = -\$612,340$
	Hedged Bond Portfolio Value:
	$\$12,369,000 - \$612,340 = \$11,756,660$
	Bond Portfolio Value without Futures: $12,369,000

by swapping some of its shorter-term Treasuries in its portfolio for longer-term one. Given that longer-term (higher duration) bonds are more price sensitive to interest rate changes, the bond fund would find an interest rate decrease across all maturities would cause the value of its bond portfolio to increase proportionally more than the index if it made the swap. However, instead of increasing the duration of its bond portfolio by changing the fund's allocation from long-term to short-term Treasuries, the fund alternatively could take a long position in T-bond or T-note futures contracts. If rates, in turn, were to decrease across all maturities as expected, then the fund would realize not only an increase in the value of its bond portfolio, but also a profit from its long futures position—on the other hand, if rates were to increase, then the fund would see not only a decrease in the value of its bond portfolio but also losses on it futures position. Thus, by adding futures to its fund, the fund would be changing its bond portfolio's exposure to interest rates by effectively increasing its duration.

Instead of increasing its balance sheet's exposure to interest rate changes, a company may choose to reduce it. For example, if the above bond fund expected interest rates to increase, it could reduce its bond portfolio's duration by taking a short position in an interest rate futures contract. If it reduces the duration to zero, then it would being hedging the portfolio's value.

Using derivatives to change the exposure of an asset or liability to interest rates, exchange rates, or other market parameters without changing the original composition of the assets and liabilities is referred to as *off-balance-sheet restructuring*.

It should be noted that contracts on both bonds and equity indexes can be used to manage a fund's overall asset allocation. For example, a fund manager with a portfolio of bonds and equities that was anticipating a rising stock market and increasing interest rates might consider selling some of her bond holdings and purchasing more stock. With futures on T-bonds and T-notes and with equity indexes, the manager could alternatively consider forming an intercommodity spread by going short in a futures contract on a Treasury with a duration closest to her bond portfolio's duration and going long in an S&P 500 futures contract.

Enhancing the Interest Rate Exposure of a Bond Portfolio

Exhibit 4.21 summarizes the portfolio features of the Xavier Bond Fund, the BOA0 Bond Index (BOA0), and the CBT five-year T-note and its cheapest-to-deliver bond for dates 7/1/16 and 12/30/15. Compared to the bond index, the Xavier Bond Fund had a lower average maturity and slightly higher coupon rate than the index. As a result, it had a lower duration of 5.20 than the index's duration of 6.58. The Xavier Bond Fund was positioned to outperform the index under an increasing interest rate scenario and underperform under an increasing rate scenario. Exhibit 4.24

EXHIBIT 4.24   Xavier Bond Fund and BOA/ML Aggregate Performance

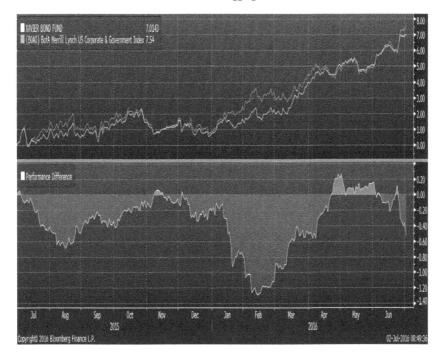

shows the total return (cumulative daily returns of price changes) of the fund relative to the index from 7/1/15 to 7/1/16. With its lower duration, the Xavier Bond Fund outperformed the index during the few periods when rates were increasing, but underperformed during periods of declining rates. With rates decreasing more frequently than increasing during this period, the fund had a lower total return than the index.

As noted, from 12/30/15 to 6/15/16, the five-year Treasury yield decreased 40.23% from 1.7927% to 1.0715% and the value of the Xavier Bond Fund increased 3.70% from \$11.925 million to \$12.369 and the June 2016 futures contract on the five-year T-note increased 3.82% from 117.6875 to 122.19 (see Exhibit 4.22). With its higher duration, the value of B0A0 index increased 5.9% from \$16.213 billion to \$17.176 billion. Suppose on 12/30/15, the managers of the Xavier Bond Fund decided to increase the fund's duration in anticipation of a decrease in interest rates by going long in the June T-note contract. On 12/30/15, the Xavier Bond Fund had a duration of 5.43 and yield to maturity of 2.98%, the bond index had a duration of 6.08, and the cheapest-to-deliver bond on the futures was a $1\frac{3}{8}$% T-note maturing on 8/31/2020, which had a duration of 4.02. Using the price-sensitivity model, the fund would have needed to go long in 16 June T-note contracts to increase its duration from 5.43 to the B0A0 index's duration of 6.08:

$$n_f = \frac{Dur_T - Dur_S}{Dur_f} \frac{V_0}{f_0} \frac{(1 + YTM_f)^T}{(1 + YTM_S)^T}$$

$$n_f = \frac{6.08 - 5.43}{4.02} \frac{\$11,925,000}{\$117,687} \frac{(1.0176)^{(165/365)}}{(1.0298)^{(165/365)}}$$

$$n_f = 16.2957 \approx 16 \ Long \ contracts$$

where:

Dur_T = target duration = 6.08
Dur_S = duration of the bond fund = 5.43
Dur_f = duration of the cheapest-to-deliver bond) = 4.02
V_0 = value of bond = \$11.925 million
f_0 = Futures price = 117.6875 per \$100 face (\$117,687 per \$100,000 face)
T = time to expiration on the futures as proportion of year = 165/365
YTM_S = yield to maturity on the bond fund = 2.98%
YTM_f = yield to maturity implied on the futures contract = 1.76%

As shown in Exhibit 4.25, the June T-note futures contracts would have provided the fund \$72,040 on 6/16/16 when the fund was worth \$12.369 million. Thus, the

EXHIBIT 4.25   Xavier Bond Fund and Futures-Enhanced Portfolio Value with June 2016 T-Note Futures Contracts

	Bond Fund Values and Opening and Closing Clearinghouse Records for CBT June 2016 Five-Year T-Note Contract
12/30/15	**Futures Opening Position:**
	Fund goes long in 16 CBT June 2016 T-note futures at 117.6875.
	Xavier Bond Fund Value = \$12.369 million (6/16/16) and \$11.925 million (12/30/15)
6/16/16	**Futures Closing Position:**
	Fund goes short in 16 CBT June 2016 futures at 122.19.
Settlement	Closing receipt from clearinghouse:
	$16(f_t - f_0) = 16(122.19 - 117.6875) = 72.04$ per \$100 face value
	$(72.04/100) \$100,000 = \$72,040$
	Enhanced Bond Portfolio Value:
	\$12,369,000 + 72,040 = \$12,441,040
	Percent Increase: 4.327%
	(\$12,441,040/\$11,925,000) − 1 = 0.04327
	Bond Portfolio Value without Futures: \$12,369,000
	Percent increase: 3.7%
	(\$12,369,000/\$11,925,000) − 1 = 0.037

fund's futures-enhanced portfolio value would have been worth $12.441 million instead of $12.369 million. This represents a 4.327% increase compared to the 3.7% that it would have realized without the futures. The increase in portfolio value and the long futures position is due to the 40.23% decrease in five-year Treasury yields from 12/30/15 to 6/15/16. It should be noted that if rates had increased, then the portfolio would have lost value and losses would have incurred on the long futures position. The futures position served to increase the bond fund's exposure to interest rates.

Synthetic Debt and Investment Position

There are some cases in which the rate on debt and investment positions can be improved or changed by creating synthetic positions with futures and other derivative securities such as swaps. These cases involve creating a synthetic fixed-rate loan by combining a floating-rate loan with short positions in Eurodollar contracts and creating a synthetic floating-rate loan by combining a fixed-rate loan with long positions in Eurodollar contracts. Similar synthetic fixed-rate and floating-rate investment positions can also be formed.

Synthetic Fixed-Rate Loan

A corporation wanting to finance its operations or its capital expenditures with fixed-rate debt has a choice of either a direct fixed-rate loan or a synthetic fixed-rate loan formed with a floating-rate loan and short positions in Eurodollar futures contracts, whichever is cheaper. Similarly, a company with an existing floating-rate loan can change to a fixed-rate loan by taking short positions in Eurodollar futures contracts. Consider the case of a corporation that can obtain a one-year $10 million fixed-rate loan from a bank at 4.0% or alternatively can obtain a one-year, floating-rate loan from a bank. In the floating-rate loan agreement, suppose the loan starts on date 9/20 at a rate of 3.0% and then is reset on 12/20, 3/20, and 6/20 to equal the spot LIBOR (annual) plus 250 basis points divided by four: (LIBOR + 0.025)/4.

To create a synthetic fixed-rate loan from this floating-rate loan, the corporation could go short in a series of Eurodollar futures contracts—*Eurodollar strip*. For this case, suppose the company goes short in a series of 10 contracts expiring at 12/20, 3/20, and 6/20 and trading at the following prices:

T	12/20	3/20	6/20
Index	99.00	98.50	98.00
R_D	1.00%	1.50%	2.00%
f_0	$997,500	$996,250	$995,000

The locked-in rates obtained using Eurodollar futures contracts are equal to 100 minus the index plus the basis points (bp) on the loan:

$$\text{Locked-in rate} = [100 - \text{Index}] + \text{bp}/100$$

$$12/20: R_{12/20} = [100 - 99.00] + 2.5\% = 3.50\%$$

$$3/20: R_{3/20} = [100 - 98.50] + 2.5\% = 4.00\%$$

$$6/20: R_{6/20} = [100 - 98.00] + 2.5\% = 4.5\%$$

For example, suppose on date 12/20, the settlement LIBOR is 1.50%, yielding a settlement index price of 98.5 and a closing futures price of $996,250. At that rate, the corporation would realize a profit of $12,500 (= (10)($1,250)) from its 10 short positions on the 12/20 futures contract:

$$f_T = \frac{(100 - (100 - 98.5)(0.25))}{100} \, \$1,000,000 = \$996,250$$

Profit on 12/20 contract = (10) ($997,500 − $996,250) = $12,500.

At the 12/20 date, though, the new interest that the corporation would have to pay for the next quarter would be set at $237,500:

$$12/20 \text{ Interest} = [(\text{LIBOR} + 0.025)/4](\$10,000,000)$$

$$12/20 \text{ Interest} = [(0.015 + 0.025)/4](\$10,000,000)$$

$$12/20 \text{ Interest} = \$100,000$$

Subtracting the futures profit of $12,500 from the $100,000 interest payment (and ignoring the time value factor) the corporation's hedged interest payment for the next quarter is $87,500. On an annualized basis, this equates to a 3.5% interest on a $10 million loan, the same rate as the locked-in rate:

$$Hedged\ rate = \frac{4(\$87,500)}{\$10,000,000} = 0.035$$

On the other hand, if the 12/20 LIBOR were 0.50%, then the quarterly interest payment would be only $75,000 (= (0.005 + 0.025)/4)($10,000,000)) = $75,000). This gain to the corporation, though, would be offset by a $12,500 loss on the futures contract (i.e., at 0.5%, f_T = $998,750, yielding a loss on the 12/20 contract of 10($997,500 − $998,750) = −$12,500). As a result, the total quarterly debt of the company again would be $87,500 ($75,000 + $12,500). Ignoring the time value factor, the annualized hedged rate the company pays would again be 3.5% (= [(4)($87,500)]/$10,000,000). Thus, the corporation's short position in the 12/20 Eurodollar futures contract at 99.00 enables it to lock in a quarterly debt obligation of $87,500 and a 3.5% annualized borrowing rate.

Given the other locked-in rates, the one-year fixed rate for the corporation on its floating-rate loan hedged with the Eurodollar futures contracts would be 3.749%:

$$\text{Synthetic fixed rate} = \left[(1.030)^{0.25}(1.035)^{0.25}(1.04)^{0.25}(1.045)^{0.25}\right]^1 - 1 = 0.03749$$

Thus, the corporation would gain by financing with a synthetic fixed-rate loan at 3.749% instead of a direct fixed-rate loan at 4.00%.

Note that it may be that the company already has a floating-rate obligation that it would like to convert to a fixed-rate obligation out of concern that rates would be increasing. It could do this easily by going short in a Eurodollar strip.

Synthetic Floating-Rate Loan

A synthetic floating-rate loan is formed by borrowing at a fixed rate and taking a long position in a Eurodollar futures contract. For example, suppose the corporation in the preceding example wanted a floating-rate loan instead of a fixed one. It could take the one offered by the bank at LIBOR plus 250 bp or it could form a synthetic floating-rate loan by borrowing at a fixed rate for one year and going long in a series of Eurodollar futures expiring at 12/20, 3/20, and 6/20. For example, suppose the corporation borrows at a fixed rate of 3.0% for one year with interest payments made quarterly at dates 12/20, 3/20, and 6/20 and then goes long in the series of Eurodollar futures to form a synthetic floating-rate loan. On date 12/20, if the settlement LIBOR were 1.5% (settlement index price of 98.5 and a closing futures price of $996,250), the corporation would lose $12,500 (= (10)($996,250 − $997,500) = −$12,500) from its 10 long positions on the 12/20 futures contracts, and it would pay $75,000 on its fixed-rate loan ((0.030/4)($10,000,000) = $75,000). The company's effective annualize rate would be 3.5% ([4($75,000 + $12,500)]/$10,000,000 = 0.035), which is 0.5% less than the rate paid on the floating-rate loan (LIBOR + 250 bp = 1.5% + 2.5% = 4%). If the settlement LIBOR on 12/20 were 0.5% (settlement index price of 99.5 and a closing futures price of $998,750), then the corporation would realize a profit of $12,500 (= (10)($998,750 − $997,500)) from the 10 long positions on the 12/20 futures contracts and would pay $75,000 on its fixed-rate loan. Its effective annualize rate would be 2.5% ((4)($75,000 − $12,500))/$10,000,000 = 0.03), which again is 0.5% less than the rate on the floating-rate loan (LIBOR + 250 bp = 0.5% + 2.5% = 3.0%).

Thus, the corporation would gain by financing with a synthetic floating-rate loan instead of the direct floating-rate one. Note that it may be that the company already has a fixed-rate rate obligation that it would like to convert to a floating-rate obligation to gain from an expected decrease in rates. It could do this easily by going long in a Eurodollar strip.

Synthetic Investments

Futures can also be used on the asset side to create synthetic fixed- and floating-rate investments. An investment company setting up a three-year unit investment trust offering a fixed rate could invest the trust funds either in three-year fixed-rate securities or a synthetic one formed with a three-year floating-rate note tied to the LIBOR and long positions in a series of Eurodollar futures, whichever yields the higher rate. Similarly, an investment fund with investment in floating-rate bonds could fix the rate on its investment by going long in Eurodollar strip. By contrast, an investor looking for a floating-rate security could alternatively consider a synthetic floating-rate investment consisting of a fixed-rate security and a short Eurodollar strip. Similarly, an investment fund with fixed-income bonds could convert them to floating-rate bonds by going short in a Eurodollar strip.

Pricing Interest Rate and Bond Futures

As discussed with commodity, currency, and equity index contracts, the price on a futures contract is governed primarily by the spot price of the underlying asset and can be explained by the carrying-cost model. For fixed-income securities, the carrying costs include the financing costs of holding the underlying asset to expiration and the benefits include the coupon interest earned from holding the security.

Pricing a T-Bill Futures Contract

Consider the pricing of a T-bill futures contract. (T-bill futures are often delisted. However, the more popular Eurodollar futures contracts are similar to T-bills except for their cash settlement features.) With no coupon interest, the underlying T-bill does not generate any benefits during the holding period and the financing costs are the only carrying costs. In terms of the model, the equilibrium relationship between the futures and spot price on the T-bill is:

$$f_0 = S_0 (1 + R_f)^T$$

where:

f_0 = contract price on the T-bill futures contract.
T = time to expiration on the futures contract.
S_0 = $S_0(T + 91)$ = current spot price on a T-bill identical to the T-bill underlying the futures ($M = 91$ days and $F = \$1,000,000$) except it has a maturity of $91 + T$.
R_f = risk-free rate or repo rate.
$S_0(1 + R_f)^T$ = financing costs of holding a spot T-bill.

If the carrying-cost equation does not hold, an arbitrage opportunity occurs. The arbitrage strategy is referred to as a *cash-and-carry arbitrage* and involves taking opposite positions in the spot and futures contracts. For example, suppose in April there is a June T-bill futures contract expiring in 60 days, and 151-day spot T-bills and the 60-day repo or risk-free rate are trading at the following price:

- 151-day T-bill is priced at $99.385953 per $100 face to yield 1.5%.
- 60-day risk-free rate or repo rate is at 1.25%.

Using the carrying-cost model, the equilibrium price of the September T-bill futures contract is $f_0 = \$995{,}891$, or $\$99.589112$ per $100 par value:

$$f_0 = S_0(1 + R_f)^T$$

$$f_0 = \$99.385953(1.0125)^{(60/365)} = \$99.589112$$

where:

$$S_0 = \frac{\$100}{(1.015)^{151/365}} = \$99.385953$$

If the market price on the T-bill futures contract were not equal to $\$99.589112$, then a cash-and-carry arbitrage opportunity would exist. For example, if the T-bill futures price is at $f_0^M = 100$, an arbitrageur could earn a risk-free profit of $\$4.108.88$ per $1 million face value or $\$0.410888$ per $100 face value ($\$100 - \$99.589112$) at the expiration date by executing the following strategy:

• Borrow $\$99.385953$ at the repo (or borrowing) rate of 1.25%, and then buy a 151-day spot T-bill for $S_0(151) = \$99.385953$.
• Take a short position in a T-bill futures contract expiring in 60 days at the futures price of $f_0^M = \$100$.

At expiration, the arbitrageur would earn $\$0.410888$ per $100 face value ($\$4{,}108.88$ per $1 million par) when she follows this strategy:

• Sell the T-bill on the spot futures contract at $100.
• Repay the principal and interest on the loan of $\$99.385953(1.0125)^{60/365} = \$99.589112$:

$$\pi_T = f_0^M - f_0^*$$

$$\pi_T = \$100 - \$99.385953(1.0125)^{(60/365)}$$

$$= \$100 - \$99.589112 = \$0.410888$$

$$\pi_T = \frac{0.410888}{100}(\$1{,}000{,}000) = \$4{,}108.88$$

In addition to the arbitrage opportunity when the futures is overpriced at $100, a money market manager currently planning to invest for 60 days in a T-bill at 1.25% could also benefit with a greater return by creating a synthetic 60-day investment by buying a 151-day bill and then going short at $100 in the T-bill futures contract expiring in 60 days. For example, using the above numbers, if a money market manager were planning to invest $\$99.385953$ for 60 days, she could buy a 151-day bill for that amount and go short in the futures priced at $100. Her return would be 3.818%, compared to 1.25% from the 60-day spot T-bill:

$$R = \left[\frac{\$100}{\$99.385953}\right]^{365/60} - 1 = 0.03818$$

Both the arbitrage and the investment strategies involve taking short positions in the T-bill futures. These actions would therefore serve to move the price on the futures down toward the equilibrium carrying-cost price of $99.589112. If the futures price is $99.589112, the rate on the synthetic 60-day investment would match the repo rate of 1.25%:

$$R = \left[\frac{\$99.589112}{\$99.385953} \right]^{365/60} - 1 = 0.0125$$

If the market price on the T-bill futures contract is below the equilibrium value, then the cash-and-carry arbitrage strategy is reversed. In our example, suppose the futures were priced at $99. In this case, an arbitrageur would go long in the futures, agreeing to buy a 91-day T-bill 60 days later, and would go short in the spot T-bill, borrowing the 151-day bill, selling it for 99.385953, and investing the proceeds at 1.25% for 60 days. Sixty days later (expiration), the arbitrageur would buy a 91-day T-bill on the futures for 99 (f_0^M), use the bill to close her short position, and collect 99.589112 from his investment, realizing a cash flow of $5,891.12 or $0.589112 per $100 par:

$$\pi_T = f_0^* - f_0^M$$

$$\pi_T = \$99.385953(1.0125)^{(60/365)} - \$99$$

$$= \$99.589112 - \$99 = \$0.589112$$

$$\pi_T = \frac{0.589112}{100}(\$1,000,000) = \$5,891.12$$

In addition to this cash-and-carry arbitrage, if the futures price is below the carrying-cost price of $99.589112, a money manager currently holding 151-day T-bills also could obtain an arbitrage by selling the bills for $99.385953, investing the proceeds at 1.25% for 60 days, and then going long in the T-bill futures contract expiring in 60 days. Sixty days later, the manager would receive $99.589112 from the investment and would pay $99 on the futures to reacquire the bills for a cash flow of 0.589112 per $100 par.

Other Equilibrium Conditions Implied by the Carrying-Costs Model

For T-bill futures and Eurodollar futures contracts, the equilibrium condition defined by the carrying-cost model in the equation can be redefined in terms of the following two equivalent conditions: (1) the rate on a spot T-bill (or actual repo rate) is equal to the rate on a synthetic T-bill (or implied repo rate); (2) the rate implied on the futures contract is equal to the implied forward rate.

Equivalent Spot and Synthetic T-Bill Rates

As illustrated in the previous example, a money market manager planning to invest funds in a T-bill for a given short-term horizon either can invest in the spot T-bill or construct a synthetic T-bill by purchasing a longer-term T-bill, then locking in its selling price by going short in a T-bill futures contract. In the preceding example, the manager either could buy a 60-day spot T-bill yielding a 1.25% rate of return and trading at $S_0 = \$99.796$ (=$100/(1.0125)^{60/365}$) or could create a long position in a synthetic 60-day T-bill by buying the 151-day T-bill trading at $S_0 = \$99.385953$, and then locking in the selling price by going short in the T-bill futures contract expiring in 60 days. If the futures price in the market exceeds the equilibrium value as determined by the carrying-cost model ($f_0^M > f_0^*$), then the rate of return on the synthetic T-bill (R_{syn}) will exceed the rate on the spot; in this case, the manager should choose the synthetic T-bill. As we saw, at a futures price of $100, the manager earned a rate of return of 3.818% on the synthetic, compared to only 1.25% from the spot. On the other hand, if the futures price is less than its equilibrium value ($f_0^M < f_0^*$), then R_{syn} will be less than the rate on the spot; in this case, the manager should purchase the spot T-bill. In an efficient market, money managers will drive the futures price to its equilibrium value as determined by the carrying-cost model. When this condition is realized, R_{syn} will be equal to the rate on the spot and the money manager would be indifferent to either investment. In our example, this occurs when the market price on the futures contract is equal to the equilibrium value of $99.589112. At that price, R_{syn} is equal to 1.25%:

$$R = \left[\frac{\$100}{\$99.589112} \right]^{365/60} - 1 = 0.0125$$

Thus, if the carrying-cost model holds, the rate earned from investing in a spot T-bill and the rate from investing in a synthetic will be equal. The rate earned from the synthetic T-bill is commonly referred to as the *implied repo rate*. Formally, the implied repo rate is defined as the rate where the arbitrage profit from implementing the cash-and-carry arbitrage strategy is zero:

$$\pi = f_0 - S_0 (1 + R_f)^T$$

$$0 = f_0 - S_0 (1 + R_f)^T$$

$$R_f = \left[\frac{f_0}{S_0} \right]^{1/T} - 1$$

The actual repo rate is the one we use in solving for the equilibrium futures price in the carrying-cost model; in our example, this was the rate on the 60-day T-bill (1.25%).

Thus, the equilibrium condition that the synthetic and spot T-bill be equal can be stated equivalently as the equality between the actual and the implied repo rates.

Implied Forward and Futures Rates

The other condition implied by the carrying-cost model is the equality between the rate implied by the futures contract, YTM_f, and the implied forward rate, R_I. The implied forward rate is the rate attained for a future date that is implied by current rates. This rate can be attained by a locking-in strategy consisting of a short position in a shorter-term bond and a long position in a longer-term one. In terms of our example, the implied forward rate on a 91-day T-bill investment to be made 60 days from the present, $R_I(91,60)$, is obtained by:

- Selling short the 60-day T-bill at $99.796 (or equivalently borrowing $99.796 at 1.25%)
- Buying $S_0(T)/S_0(T+91) = S_0(60)/S_0(151) = \$99.796/\$99.385952 = 1.0041258$ issues of the 151-day T-bill
- Paying $100 at the end of 60 days to cover the short position on the maturing bond (or the loan)
- Collecting $1.0041258(\$100) = \$100.41258$ at the end of 151 days from the long position

This locking-in strategy would earn an investor a return of $100.41258, 91 days after the investor expends $100 to cover the short sale; thus, the implied forward rate on a 91-day investment made 60 days from the present is 0.41258%, or annualized, 1.66517%:

$$R_I(91, 60) = \left[\frac{\$100.41258}{\$100} \right]^{365/91} - 1 = 0.0166517$$

Instead of locking in the implied forward rate of 1.66517% by shorting the 60-day bill and going long in the 151-day bill, an investor could simply purchase a 91-day T-bill on the futures contract. If the futures contract is priced at the equilibrium carrying-cost price, then the implied rate on the futures will be equal to the implied forward rate. In terms of our example, if $f_0 = \$99.589112$, then the implied futures rate will be 1.66517%:

$$YTM_f = \left[\frac{F}{f_0^*} \right]^{365/91} - 1 = \left[\frac{\$100}{\$99.589112} \right]^{365/91} - 1 = 0.0166517$$

Thus, if the carrying-cost model holds, then the rate implied on the futures contract will be equal to the implied forward rate.

Implied futures rate = Implied forward rate

$$YTM_f = R_I$$

$$\left[\frac{\$100}{f_0^*} \right]^{365/91} - 1 = \left[\frac{S(T)}{S(T+91)} \right]^{365/91} - 1$$

Note that solving this condition for f_0^*, one obtains the carrying-cost equation:

$$\left[\frac{\$100}{f_0^*} \right]^{365/91} - 1 = \left[\frac{S(T)}{S(T+91)} \right]^{365/91} - 1$$

$$f_0^* = \frac{S(T+91)\,\$100}{S(T)}$$

$$f_0^* = \frac{\dfrac{\$100}{(1+R_f)^{T+91}}}{\dfrac{\$100}{(1+R_f)^T}}\$100$$

$$f_0^* = \frac{\$100}{(1+R_f)^{T+91}}\frac{(1+R_f)^T}{\$100}\$100$$

$$f_0^* = \frac{\$100}{(1+R_f)^{T+91}}(1+R_f)^T$$

$$f_0^* = S_0\,(1+R_f)^T$$

where:

$$S_0 = S(T+91)$$

In summary, we have three equivalent equilibrium conditions governing futures prices on T-bill and Eurodollar futures contracts:

1. The futures price is equal to the costs of carrying the underlying spot security.
2. The rate on the spot is equal to the rate on the synthetic security (or the implied repo rate is equal to the actual repo rate).
3. The implied rate of return on the futures contract is equal to the implied forward rate. If any of these equivalent positions do not hold, then there would be an arbitrage opportunity by taking a position in futures (f_0) and an opposite position in the spot ($S_0(1+R_f)^T$).

Pricing a Eurodollar Futures Contract

In our example of the bank hedging its maturity gap with a Eurodollar futures contract on 9/15/15, we noted that on 9/15/15 the six-month spot LIBOR was 0.54%, the three-month LIBOR was 0.33425%, and the price on the December 2015 Eurodollar futures contract was 99.5 (index) or the actual price of $99.875 per $100 face value and implied YTM on the futures of 0.5%. Using a 30-day, 360-day day-count convention, the maturity on the December futures on 9/15/15 was $T = 90/360 = 0.25$, the maturity on three-month investment at the LIBOR was 12/15/15 and $T = 90/360 = 0.25$, and the maturity on a six-month investment at the LIBOR was 3/16/15 and $T + 90 = 180/360 = 0.50$. Using the carrying-cost model, the equilibrium price of the December Eurodollar futures contract on 9/15/15 would be $99.814 per $100 face value:

$$f_0^* = S_0\,(1+R_f)^T$$

$$f_0^* = \frac{\$100}{(1.0054)^{0.50}}(1.0033425)^{0.25} = \$99.814$$

Compared to the implied yield to maturity implied on the futures of 0.74747%, the implied forward rate on a three-month investment made three months from 9/15/15 would have been 0.7461%:

$$R_I = \left[\frac{S(0.25)}{S(0.50)}\right]^{1/0.25} - 1$$

$$R_I = \left[\frac{\$100/(1 + R_f)^{0.25}}{\$100/(1 + R_f)^{0.50}}\right]^{1/0.25} - 1$$

$$R_I = \left[\frac{(1 + R_f)^{0.50}}{(1 + R_f)^{0.25}}\right]^{1/0.25} - 1$$

$$R_I = \left[\frac{(1.0054)^{0.50}}{(1.0033425)^{0.25}}\right]^{1/0.25} - 1$$

$$R_I = 0.007461$$

Note that the small difference between the carrying-cost price and actual price may be attributed to the day-count convention or using the reported closing price instead of the asked price.

Equilibrium T-Bond Futures Price

Because of the uncertainties over the bond to be delivered and the time of the delivery, the pricing of a T-bond and T-note futures contract is more complex than the pricing of Eurodollar futures contracts. Like all futures, the price on the futures contract depends on the spot price (S_0) and the risk-free rate. If we assume that we know the cheapest-to-deliver bond and the time of delivery, the equilibrium futures price for a T-bond or T-note futures contract is

$$f_0^* = [S_0 - PV(C)](1 + R_f)^T$$

where:

S_0 = current spot price of the cheapest-to-deliver T-bond (clean price plus accrued interest)

$PV(C)$ = present value of coupons paid on the bond during the life of the futures contract

Example

Exhibit 4.26 shows the Bloomberg Description page on 7/8/16 for the CBT's December 10-Year T-note (TYZ6) contract and a listing of the cheapest-to-deliver bonds on that contract. The cheapest bond on 7/8/16 was the 2.5% T-note maturing

EXHIBIT 4.26   Bloomberg Description Screen and List of Deliverable Bonds on 7/8/16 for the December US 10-Year T-Note and Deliverable Bond

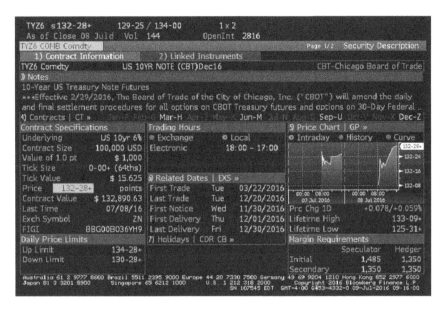

Cash Security	Price	Conversion Factor	Gro/Bas (32nds)	Net/Bas (32nds)
T 2 ½ 08/15/23	109-02 1/4	0.8139	29.14	−0.239
T 1 ³/₈ 06/30/23	101-08 1/4	0.7541	33.44	20.308
T 2 ³/₄ 11/15/23	111-00+	0.8217	58.221	25.172
T 2 ³/₄ 02/15/24	111-06	0.8164	86.259	53.307
T 2 ½ 05/15/24	109-16+	0.7966	116.959	87.534
T 2 ³/₈ 08/15/24	108-19 1/4	0.7836	142.991	115.441
T 2 ¼ 11/15/24	107-22	0.7702	170.725	144.901
T 2 02/15/25	105-22 1/4	0.7488	197.978	175.806

on 8/15/2023, with a conversion factor (CFA) of 0.8139. On 7/8/16, the 2.5% Treasury was trading at $108.844 with accrued interest of $1.01. Its next semiannual coupon payment of $1.25 was scheduled for 8/15/16 (see Exhibit 4.27). On 7/8/16, the yield on the three-month LIBOR was 0.66348% and the yield on the six-month LIBOR was 0.9349. To determine the carrying-cost value for the December 10-year T-note on 7/8/16, the following Bloomberg information was accessed:

- On 7/8/16, the cheapest-to-deliver bond on the December contract was the T-note paying 2.5% coupon with maturity of 8/15/23, CFA of 0.8139 (Bloomberg DLV screen), and trading on 7/8/16 at 108.844 (clean price) with accrued interest of 1.01 (Bloomberg YAS screen).
- On 7/8/16, the cheapest-to-deliver T-note's next semi-annual coupon of $1.25 was on 8/15/16, which was 38 days from 7/8/16; the next coupon comes on 3/15/17, which was 182 days from the 8/15/16 date (Bloomberg CSH screen).

- On 7/8/16, three-month LIBOR was at 0.66348% (Bloomberg GP screen for US0003M) and the six-month LIBOR was at 0.9349% (Bloomberg GP screen for US0006M).
- The first delivery date on the December 10-year T-notes futures was 12/1/16, its last delivery date was 12/30/16, and the last trade date on the contract was 12/20/16 (Bloomberg Description screen); the estimated delivery date was 12/20/16, which is 165 days from 7/8/16.

EXHIBIT 4.27 Bloomberg Description and YAS Screens on 7/8/16 for US Treasury with 2.5% Coupon and Maturity 8/15/23

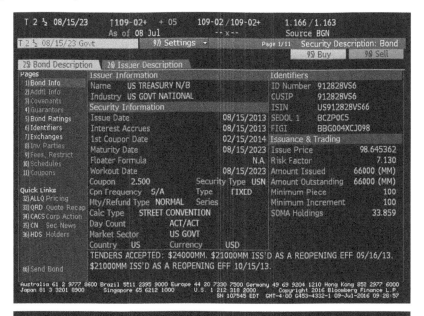

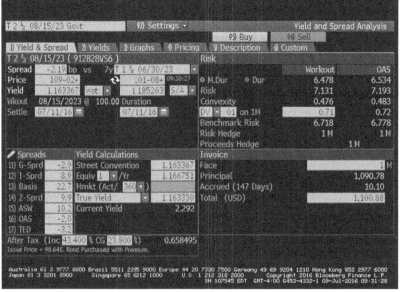

The spot price on 7/8/16 for the 2.5% deliverable was 109.9842 (clean price plus accrued interest) and the present value of a $1.25 coupon received 38 days later using the three-month LI BORF was 4.8957:

$$S_0 = \$108.844 + \$1.01 = \$109.9842$$

$$PV(C) = \frac{\$1.25}{(1.0066348)^{38/365}} = \$1.24914$$

Using the six-month LIBOR of 0.9349% as the risk-free rate for the 175-day period to the estimated delivery date, the equilibrium futures price on 7/8/16 in terms of the 2.5% deliverable T-note would have been 108.2127 per $100 face value:

$$f_0^* = [S_0 - PV(C)](1 + R_f)^T$$

$$f_0^* = [\$109.9842 - \$1.24914](1.009349)^{175/365} = \$109.22127$$

The quoted price on a futures contract written on the delivered bond would be stated net of accrued interest at the delivery date. The delivery date occurs 137 days after the last coupon payment (175 days − 38 days). Thus, at delivery, there would be 137 days of accrued interest. Given the 182-day period between coupon payments, the accrued interest would therefore be $0.941 (= (137/182)($1.25)). The future price for the delivered bond on the estimated delivery date (12/20/16) would be 108.28027 (=109.22127 − 0.941). Given a CFA of 0.8139, the equilibrium quoted futures price would be $133.0388:

Clean futures price on the deliverable bond (12/12/16)

$$= f_0^* - \text{Accrued interest}$$

Clean futures price on the deliverable bond(12/12/16)

$$= \$109.22127 - (137/182)\$1.25$$

Clean futures price on the deliverable bond (12/12/16)

$$= \$108.28027$$

$$\text{Quoted futures price} = \frac{\text{Clean futures price on deliverable bond}}{\text{CFA}}$$

$$\text{Quoted futures price} = \frac{\$108.28027}{0.8139} = \$133.0387885$$

At delivery, the holder of a short position in the December contract that was priced at $133.0387885 with the underlying deliverable bond being the 2.5% Treasury with CFA of 0.8139 would receive $109.22127 for delivering the bond at the equilibrium carry-cost price:

Seller's revenue = (Quoted futures price)(CFA) + Accrued interest

Seller's revenue = ($133.0387885)(0.8139) + $0.941

Seller's revenue = $108.28027 + $0.9141 = $109.22127

On 7/9/16, the last price on the December 10-year T-Note contract was, in turn, $132.891, the bid price was 129.781, and the ask price was 134.03. Thus, the carrying-cost value was very close to the last price.

Arbitrage

Like T-bill futures, cash-and-carry arbitrage opportunities will exist if the prices on T-bond futures are not equal to their carrying cost value. In the case of the December T-note future, its carrying cost price on 7/8/16 was $109.22127 (or its quoted price of $133.0387885):

$$f_0^* = [S_0 - PV(C)](1 + R_f)^T$$

$$f_0^* = [\$109.9842 - \$1.24914](1.009349)^{175/365} = \$109.22127$$

where:

$$S_0 = \$108.844 + \$1.01 = \$109.9842$$

$$PV(C) = \frac{\$1.25}{(1.0066348)^{38/365}} = \$1.24914$$

Suppose the December futures contract was priced at $f^M = \$111$ (quoted price of $135.4394 = ($111/0.8139) − $0.941)). To exploit this, an arbitrageur would:

- Take a short position in the December T-note futures at $f^M = \$111$.
- Buy the underlying cheapest-to-deliver bond (2.5% T-note maturing on 8/15/23) for $109.9842 (clean price plus accrued interest).
- Finance the T-note purchase by (1) borrowing $108.73506 (= $S_0 - PV(C)$ = $109.9842 − $1.24914) at 0.9349% for 175 days, and (2) borrowing $1.24919 ($PV(C)$ at 0.66348% for 38 days.

After setting up the arbitrage on 7/8/16, 38 days later the arbitrageur would receive a $1.25 coupon from the 2.5% T-note (8/15/16) that he would use to pay off the 38-day loan of $1.24914 (=1.24914(1.0066346)^{38/365}). At expiration, the arbitrageur would sell the bond on the futures contract at $f^M = \$111$ and pay off the financing cost on the 175-day loan of 109.22 (= $108.735506(1.009349)^{175/365}). This, in turn, would equate to an arbitrage profit of $f^M - f_0^* = \$111 − \$109.22 = \$1.78$ per $100 face value. This risk-free return would result in arbitrageurs pursuing this strategy of going short in the futures and long in the T-bond, causing the futures price to decrease to $109.22127 and the arbitrage disappears. If the futures price were below $109.22127, arbitrageurs would reverse the strategy, shorting the bond, investing the proceeds, and going long in the T-note futures contract.

It should be noted that if the futures price on a T-note or a bond futures contract is equal to the costs of carrying the underlying spot security, then the rate on the spot will be equal to the rate on the synthetic security formed with the futures, and the implied rate of return on the futures contract will be equal to the implied forward rate. If any of these equivalent positions do not hold, then there would be an arbitrage opportunity by taking a position in futures and an opposite position in the spot.

Conclusion

Introduced during the volatile interest rate periods of the 1970s and 1980s, interest rate derivatives have become one of the most popular derivative contracts. In this chapter, we have examined their speculative and hedging uses and how they are priced. As we have seen, these derivatives can be used by (1) financial institutions to manage the maturity gap between their assets and liabilities, (2) financial and nonfinancial corporations to fix the rates on their floating-rate loans, to create synthetic fixed-rate or floating-rate debt and investment positions, or to change their bond portfolio's interest rate exposure, and (3) fixed-income managers, money market managers, and dealers to lock in the future purchase or selling price of their fixed-income securities.

This completes our analysis of futures contracts. In the next chapter, we begin our analysis of option derivatives. The fundamental difference between futures and options contracts is that futures obligate the holder (seller) of the contract to purchase (or deliver) the underlying asset, whereas an options contract give the holder (seller) the right (responsibility) but not the obligation (liability) to deliver. By providing a right instead of an obligation, options can be used to create more speculative positions than futures, and they provide a tool to hedging against adverse price movements while still providing opportunities to gain from favorable price movement.

BLOOMBERG: BOND AND INTEREST RATE FUTURES AND RELATED SCREENS

BLOOMBERG COMMODITY SCREENS, CTM
Bond and interest rate future contracts can be found by accessing the CTM screen: CTM <Enter>. The contracts can be found by category, exchange, and region. For example, to find a bond or interest rate contract offered by the CBT, use the CTM Exchange screen and click "Bond" or "Interest Rates" from the dropdown menu in the "Category" column. Alternatively, click "Categories" and "Interest Rates" or "Bonds," type the name of the exchange (e.g., CBT or CME) in the amber Exchange box, and then find the contract of interest.

UPLOADING A FUTURES CONTRACT
To upload a futures contract's menu screen enter: Ticker <Comdty> (e.g., EDA <Comdty> for three-month Eurodollar contract), and then use the Expiration screen (EXS) on the contract's menu page to find the ticker for the contract with the expiation month you want to analyze: Ticker <Comdty> (e.g., EDH7 <Comdty> for the March 2017 contract). The menu includes:

- CT: Contract Table
- EXS: Expiration Schedule
- GP: Price Graph
- GIP Intraday Graph
- DLV: Cheapest-to-Deliver Bond

(Continued)

- FAC: Conversion Factor
- COC: Bond Cost of Carry
- FPA: Forward Price Analysis

BLOOMBERG BOND AND INTEREST RATE FUTURES AND RELATED SCREENS

- WIR: Monitors Eurodollar Packs
- IRDD: List of interest rate derivatives
- EDS: Eurodollar Markets verses futures
- YCRV or GC to access yield curves
- FWCV to determine implied forward rates
- US0003M, US0006M, US0009M, and US0012M (US0003M <Index> <Return>) to see historical 3-month, 6-month, 9-month, and 12-month LIBORs
- USGG2YR, USGG5YR, USFF10YR, and USGG30YR (USGG2YR <Index> <Enter>) to see historical 2-year, 5-year, 10-year, 20-year, and 30-year Treasury yields
- FIHR, Hedging screen, to calculate the number bond futures contracts needed to hedge the interest rate risk of a position in a bond you specify (To use, load a fixed-income security and then type FIHR.)

DLV

The DLV screen shows the trading between a conversion-factor or yield-based bond futures contract and its basket of deliverable bonds by ranking the basket in order of cheapest to deliver. The bond list displays all of the bonds that the party shorting the loaded futures contract can deliver to satisfy contract requirements upon expiration. The list ranks the bonds from the cheapest to the most expensive to deliver in terms of implied repo rate (see Exhibit 4.28).

EXHIBIT 4.28 Example of DLV Screen

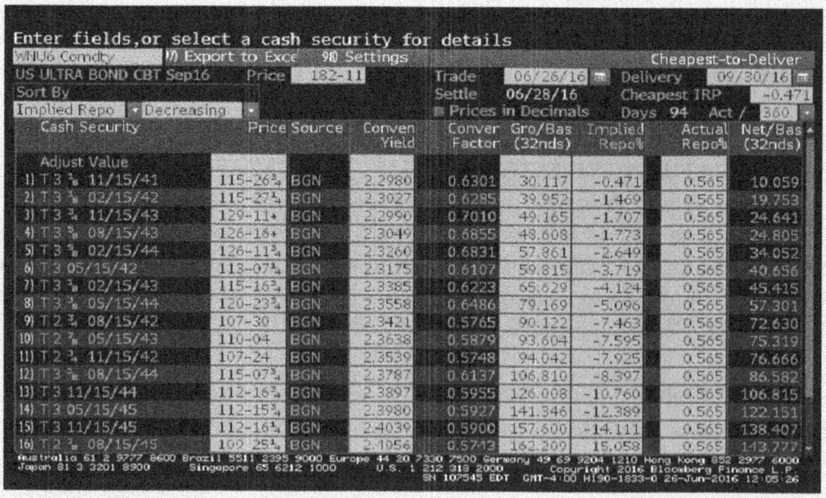

Enter fields,or select a cash security for details

WNU6 Comdty | 97) Export to Excel | 98) Settings | Cheapest-to-Deliver

US ULTRA BOND CBT Sep16 | Price 182-11 | Trade 06/26/16 | Delivery 09/30/16

Sort By | Settle 06/28/16 | Cheapest IRP -0.471

Implied Repo | Decreasing | Prices in Decimals | Days 94 Act / 360

Cash Security	Price	Source	Conven Yield	Conver Factor	Gro/Bas (32nds)	Implied Repo%	Actual Repo%	Net/Bas (32nds)
Adjust Value								
1) T 3 ⅛ 11/15/41	115-26¾	BGN	2.2980	0.6301	30.117	-0.471	0.565	10.059
2) T 3 ⅛ 02/15/42	115-27¼	BGN	2.3027	0.6285	39.952	-1.469	0.565	19.753
3) T 3 ¾ 11/15/43	129-11+	BGN	2.2990	0.7010	49.165	-1.707	0.565	24.641
4) T 3 ⅝ 08/15/43	126-16+	BGN	2.3049	0.6855	48.608	-1.773	0.565	24.805
5) T 3 ⅝ 02/15/44	126-11¾	BGN	2.3260	0.6831	57.861	-2.649	0.565	34.052
6) T 3 05/15/42	113-07¼	BGN	2.3175	0.6107	59.815	-3.719	0.565	40.656
7) T 3 ⅛ 02/15/43	115-16¾	BGN	2.3385	0.6223	65.629	-4.124	0.565	45.415
8) T 3 ⅜ 05/15/44	120-23¾	BGN	2.3558	0.6486	79.169	-5.096	0.565	57.301
9) T 2 ¾ 08/15/42	107-30	BGN	2.3421	0.5765	90.122	-7.463	0.565	72.630
10) T 2 ⅞ 05/15/43	110-04	BGN	2.3638	0.5879	93.604	-7.595	0.565	75.319
11) T 2 ¾ 11/15/42	107-24	BGN	2.3539	0.5748	94.042	-7.925	0.565	76.666
12) T 3 ⅛ 08/15/44	115-07¾	BGN	2.3787	0.6137	106.810	-8.397	0.565	86.582
13) T 3 11/15/44	112-16¾	BGN	2.3897	0.5955	126.008	-10.760	0.565	106.815
14) T 3 05/15/45	112-15¾	BGN	2.3980	0.5927	141.346	-12.389	0.565	122.151
15) T 3 11/15/45	112-16¼	BGN	2.4039	0.5900	157.600	-14.111	0.565	138.407
16) T 2 ⅞ 08/15/45	109-25¼	BGN	2.4056	0.5743	162.209	15.058	0.565	143.777

Australia 61 2 9777 8600 Brazil 5511 2395 9000 Europe 44 20 7330 7500 Germany 49 69 9204 1210 Hong Kong 852 2977 6000
Japan 81 3 3201 8900 Singapore 65 6212 1000 U.S. 1 212 318 2000 Copyright 2016 Bloomberg Finance L.P.
SN 107545 EDT GMT-4:00 H190-1833-0 26-Jun-2016 12:05:26

SWPM: BLOOMBERG SWAPS AND INTEREST RATE DERIVATIVES SCREEN

SWPM analyzes, creates, and values swaps and interest rate derivative contracts. The Forward Rate Agreement screen in SWPM can be used to set up and evaluate a forward rate agreement. To access the FRA on the SWPM screen, go to the red "Swaps & Options" tab, click "Vanilla," "FRA," and "Regular." This will bring up the Main screen that can be used to create the FRA. You can then change the settings on the Main screen.

BLOOMBERG PORTFOLIO SCREENS FOR EVALUATING PORTFOLIOS: PRTU AND PORT

On the Bloomberg PRTU screen, you can set up bond portfolios. Once loaded, you can analyze the portfolio using PORT and other screens from the PMEN menu. See Appendix A for a description on how to construct portfolios using PRTU and "Bloomberg: Equity Index Futures and Related Screens" in Chapter 3 (see Exhibit 4.29).

EXHIBIT 4.29   Example of PORT Screen: Xavier Bond Fund

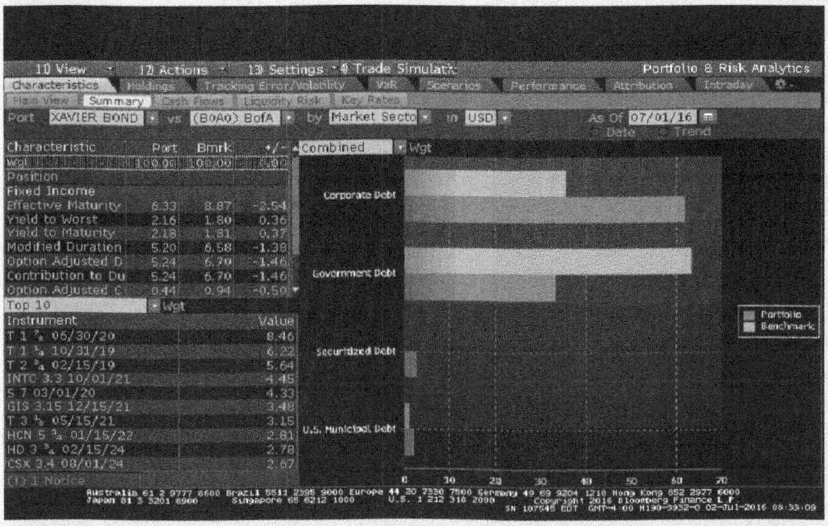

MARS

MARS provides risk management, stress-testing, and scenario analysis tools for portfolios. The tabs and sub-tabs allow you to perform advanced scenario and risk analyses, such as multiasset market data shifts, key rate risk analyses, and credit risk analyses. The "Hedging" tab allows you to hedge interest rate risk exposure for the portfolio and its entire term structure with futures and swaps (see Exhibit 4.30).

(Continued)

EXHIBIT 4.30   Example of MARS Screens

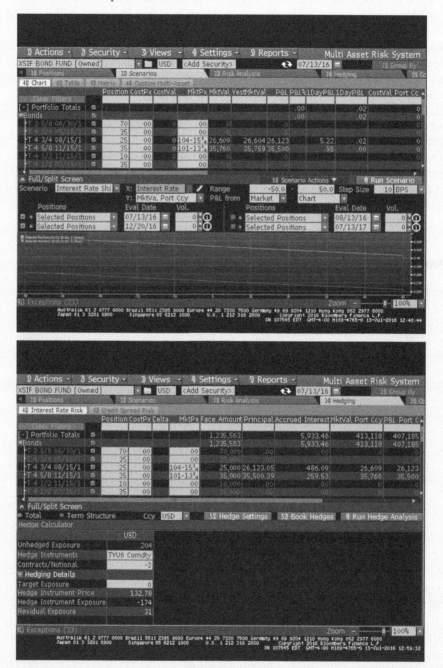

Selected References

Cox, J. C., J. E. Ingersoll. and S. A. Ross. "The Relation between Forward Prices and Futures Prices." *Journal of Financial Economics* 9 (1981): 321–346.

Haley, Charles W. "Forward Rate Agreements (FRA)." *The Handbook of Interest Rate Risk Management*. Edited by Jack Clark Francis and Avner Simon Wolf. New York: Irwin Professional Publishing, 1994.

Hull, J. *Options, Futures and Other Derivative Securities*. Englewood Cliffs, NJ: Prentice Hall, 2007.

Johnson, R. Stafford, *Introduction to Derivatives: Options, Futures, and Swaps*. New York: Oxford University Press, 2009, Chapter 15.

Livingston, M. "The Cheapest Deliverable Bond for the CBT Treasury Bond Futures Contract." *Journal of Futures Markets* 4 (1984): 161–172.

Problems and Questions

1. Suppose you took a short position in a June Eurodollar futures at $R_D = 2.50\%$. Determine the futures settlement prices and your position's profits and losses given the following LIBOR at the June futures' expiration: 2.00%, 2.5%, and 3.00%. Determine your profits and losses if you had taken a long position in the June contract at $R_D = 2.5\%$.

2. Explain how the clearinghouse would record the futures trades in a–d. Include the clearinghouse's payments and receipts needed to close each position.

   a. Mr. A buys a September T-bond futures contract from Ms. B for $105,000 on June 20.

   b. Mr. D buys a September T-bond futures contract from Mr. E for $104,500 on June 25.

   c. Ms. B buys a September T-bond futures contract from Mr. D for $104,250 on June 28.

   d. Mr. E buys a September T-bond futures contract from Mr. A for $106,000 on July 3.

3. Define a forward rate agreement (FRA). Provide your own example of a FRA.

4. Given a FRA with the following terms:

   - Notional principal = $20 million
   - Reference rate = LIBOR
   - Contract rate = $R_k = 2.00\%$ (annual)
   - Time period = 90 days
   - Day-count convention = Actual/365

   Show in a table the payments and receipts for long and short positions on the FRA given possible spot LIBORs at the FRA's expiration of 1.00%, 1.50%, 2.00%, 2.50%, and 3.00%.

5. Kendall National Bank is planning to make a $10 million short-term loan to Two-Dollar General. In the loan contract, Two-Dollar agrees to pay the principal and an interest of 2.50% (annual) at the end of 180 days. Since Kendall National sells more 90-day CDs than 180-day CDs, it is planning to finance the loan by selling a 90-day CD now at the prevailing LIBOR of 1.25%, and then 90 days later (mid-September) sell another 90-day CD at the prevailing LIBOR. The bank

would like to minimize its exposure to interest rate risk on its future CD sale by taking a position in a September Eurodollar futures contract trading at 98.5 (CME index).

   a. How many September Eurodollar futures contracts would Kendall National Bank need in order to effectively hedge its September CD sale against interest rate changes? Assume perfect divisibility.

   b. Determine the total amount of funds the bank would need to raise on its CD sale 90 days later if the LIBOR is 1.75% and if it is 1.25% (assume futures are closed at the LIBOR). What would the bank's debt obligations be at the end of 180-day period? What is the bank's effective rate for the entire 180-day period?

6. As an alternative to a nine-month, 4% fixed-rate loan for $10 million, the O'Brien Beverage Company is considering a synthetic fixed rate loan formed with a $10 million floating-rate loan from First National Bank and a Eurodollar strip. The floating-rate loan has a maturity of 270 days (0.75 of a year), starts on December 20, and the rate on the loan is set each quarter. The initial quarterly rate is equal to 3.5%/4, the other rates are set on 3/20 and 6/20 equal to one fourth of the annual LIBOR on those dates plus 100 basis points: (LIBOR % + 1%)/4. On December 20, the Eurodollar futures contract expiring on 3/20 is trading at 97 (IMM index) and the contract expiring on 6/20 is trading at 98 and the time separating each contract is 0.25/year.

   a. Explain how O'Brien could use the strip to lock in a fixed rate. Calculate the rate the O'Brien Company could lock in with a floating-rate loan and Eurodollar futures strip.

   b. Calculate and show in a table the company's quarterly interest payments, futures profits, hedged interest payments (interest minus futures profit), and hedged rate for each period (12/20, 3/20, and 6/20) given the following rates: LIBOR = 4% on 3/20 and LIBOR = 3% on 6/20.

7. Xavier Trust is planning to invest $10 million for one year. As an alternative to a one-year fixed-rate note paying 2.5%, XSIF is considering a synthetic investment formed by investing in a Second National Bank one-year floating-rate note (FRN) paying LIBOR plus 100 basis points and taking a position in a Eurodollar futures strip. The FRN starts on 12/20 at 3.00% (LIBOR = 2.00%) and is then reset the next three quarters on 3/20, 6/20, and 9/20. On December 20, the Eurodollar futures contract expiring on 3/20 is trading at 97 (IMM index), the contract expiring on 6/20 is trading at 98, and the contract expiring on 9/20 is trading at 98.50; the time separating each contract is 0.25/year and the reset dates on the floating-rate note and the expiration dates on the futures expiration are the same.

   a. Explain how Xavier Trust could use a strip to lock in a fixed rate. Calculate the rate Xavier could lock in with a floating-rate note and Eurodollar futures strip.

   b. Calculate and show in a table Xavier's quarterly interest receipts, futures profits, hedged interest return (interest plus futures profit), and hedged rate for each period (12/20, 3/20, 6/20, and 9/20) given the following rates: LIBOR = 3.5% on 3/20, LIBOR = 3% on 6/20, and LIBOR = 1% on 6/20.

8. Using the carrying-cost model, determine the equilibrium price of a forward contract on a 90-day zero coupon bond (ZCB) with a face value of $1 million and expiring in 180 days. Assume the price on a similar 270-day spot ZCB is $954,484 and the risk-free rate on 90-day investments is 6% (annual). Describe the cash-and-carry arbitrage that arbitrageurs could implement if the contract price is at $985,000 and at $980,000.

9. Given: (1) 121-day spot T-bill trading 98.318 to yield 5.25%; (2) 30-day risk-free rate of 5.15%; (3) a T-bill futures contract with an expiration of $T = 30$ days.

   a. What is the equilibrium T-bill futures price and its implied futures YTM (annualized)?
   b. Explain what a money market manager planning to invest funds for 30 days should do if the price on the T-bill futures were trading at 98.8. What rate would the manager earn?
   c. Explain the arbitrage a money market manager could execute if she were holding 121-day T-bills and the T-bill futures were trading at 98.

10. Given the following information related to a T-bond futures contract expiring in six months:

    • The best estimate of the cheapest-to-deliver bond on the T-bond futures contract pays an 8% coupon, is currently priced at 108 (clean price), has a conversion factor of 1.21; the bond's last coupon date was 30 days ago, and its next coupon is 152 days, with the coupon after that coming in the next 183 days.
    • The yield curve is flat at 5%.
    • The best estimate for the expiration on a T-bond futures contract is 180 days.

    Using the carrying-cost model, determine the equilibrium price on the T-bond futures contract.

Bloomberg Exercises

1. Select a US Treasury bond or note with an intermediate-term or long-term maturity (5 to 20 years). To find your bond, use the FIT screen or SECF (SECF <Enter>; Category: Fixed-Income; Govt Tab; select Maturity: 4–7 years or greater; select denomination: USD). Evaluate the bond using the following screens:

   a. DES to identify the bond's key features.
   b. YAS to determine the bond's price, invoice price, yield, and modified duration.
   c. CSHF to find the bond's cash flow.
   d. TDH and ALLQ to determine the liquidity on the bond based on it trading activity and bid-ask spreads.
   e. COC to determine the bond's cost of carry.
   f. FPA to conduct a forward price analysis.

2. Evaluate the current yield curve level and structure using the following screens:

    a. YCRV or GC to access yield curves.

    b. FWCV to determine implied forward rates.

    c. US0003M, US0006M, US0009M, and US0012M (US0003M <Index> <Return>) to see historical 3-month, 6-month, 9-month, and 12-month LIBORs.

    d. USGG2YR, USGG5YR, USFF10YR, and USGG30YR (USGG2YR <Index> <Enter>) to see historical 2-year, 5-year, 10-year, 20-year, and 30-year Treasury yields.

3. Access Bloomberg information on a CME Eurodollar futures contract: Type CTM to bring up the "Contract Table Menu," click "Categories" and "Interest Rates," search for CME on the Menu (type CME in the amber Exchange box), find the CME contract of interest, and bring up the contract's menu screen (Ticker <Comdty>; e.g., EDA <Comdty> for three-month Eurodollar contract), and then use the Expiration screen (EXS) on the contract's menu page to find the ticker for the contract with the expiation month you want to analyze (Ticker <Comdty>; e.g., EDH7 <Comdty> for the March 2017 contract). View screens to examine: DES and GP.

4. Using the GP screen, examine the historical prices of the Eurodollar futures contract you selected in Exercise 3 (select a time period that the contract was active).

    a. Select a period in which you would have taken a long position and calculate the profit from opening and closing at the futures prices at the beginning and ending dates for your selected period. Calculate the losses if you had taken a short position.

    b. Select a period in which you would have taken a short position and calculate the profits from opening and closing at the futures prices at the beginning and ending dates for your selected period. Calculate the losses if you had taken a long position.

    c. Using the annotation bar, apply the "% Change" tool to calculate the percentage change for your select periods, and then click the "News" icon on the annotation bar to find relevant news events on or preceding the opening date.

    d. Examine the spot LIBOR for the period that your futures contract was active. Begin typing US000 (e.g., US0003M for three-month LIBOR or US0006M for six-month LIBOR) to see the dropdown that will identify the ticker for the LIBOR with the maturity of underlying Eurodollar on your selected futures contract. Comment on the LIBOR and futures price relations for the period.

    e. Use the Chart screen (Chart <Enter>) to create multigraphs for the prices on the Eurodollar futures contract and the LIBOR. On the Chart Menu screen, select Standard G chart; once you have loaded your securities, go to "Edit" to put your graphs in separate panels.

    f. Select a spot LIBOR that matches the maturity (M) of your selected futures (e.g., US0006M for six-months) and determine its rate on the date you set up your hedge and the spot price of a Eurodollar CD ($\$100/1 + LIBOR^M$). Select a LIBOR that is closest to the time to expiation (T) on the futures contract at the time you set up your hedge (e.g., US0003M for three-month LIBOR). Using the carrying-cost model determine the futures equilibrium price:

$$f_0^* = S_0(1 + R_f)^T$$

Compare the equilibrium price with the actual price on the date you set up the hedge.

5. Access Bloomberg information on a T-bond futures contract: type CTM to bring up the "Contract Table Menu," click "Categories" and "Bonds," search for the CBT on the Menu (type CBT in the amber Exchange box area), find the CBT contract of interest and bring up its menu screen (Ticker <Comdty>; e.g., USA <Comdty> for T-Bonds), and then use the Expiration screen (EXS) on the contract's menu page to find the ticker for the contract with the expiation month you want to analyze (Ticker <Comdty>; e.g., USH7 <Comdty> for the March 2017 contract). View screens to examine: DES, DLV, and GP.

6. Using the GP screen, examine the historical prices of the T-bond futures contract you selected in Exercise 5 (select a time period that the contract was active).

   a. Select a period in which you would have taken a long position and calculate the profit from opening and closing at the futures prices at the beginning and ending dates for your selected period. Calculate the losses if you had taken a short position.

   b. Select a period in which you would have taken a short position and calculate the profits from opening and closing at the futures prices at the beginning and ending dates for your selected period. Calculate the losses if you had taken a long position.

   c. Using the annotation bar, apply the "% Change" tool to calculate the percentage change for your select periods, and then click the "News" icon on the annotation bar to find relevant news events on or preceding the opening date.

   d. Examine the constant maturity Treasury yield index for the period that your futures contract was active. Begin typing USGG (e.g., USGG20YR) to see the dropdown that will identify the ticker for the Treasury with the maturity of underlying Treasury on your selected futures contract. Comment on the yield and futures price relations for the period.

   e. Examine the prices and yields on the cheapest-to-deliver bond on the contract for the period that your futures contract was active. Begin typing "T" followed by maturity (e.g., 3/15/23) for a dropdown to see the ticker for the Treasury with the maturity of underlying Treasury on your selected futures contract. Comment on the yield and futures price relations for the period.

   f. Use the Chart screen (Chart <Enter>) to create multigraphs for the T-note, cheapest-to-deliver note, and constant maturity Treasury yield. On the Chart Menu screen, select the Standard G chart; once you have loaded your securities, go to "Edit" to put your graphs in separate panels.

7. Access Bloomberg information on a T-note futures contract: type CTM to bring up the "Contract Table Menu," click "Categories" and "Bonds," search for CBT

on the Menu (type CBT in the amber Exchange box area), find the CBT contract of interest, and bring up the contract's menu screen (Ticker <Comdty>; e.g., FVA <Comdty> for five-year Treasury), and then use the Expiration screen (EXS) on the contract's menu page to find the ticker for contract with the expiration month you want to analyze (Ticker <Comdty>; e.g., FV7 <Comdty> for the March 2017 contract). View screens to examine: DES, DLV, and GP.

8. Using the GP screen, examine the historical prices of the T-note futures contract you selected in Exercise 7 (select a time period that the contract was active).

   a. Select a period in which you would have taken a long position and calculate the profit from opening and closing at the futures prices at the beginning and ending dates for your selected period. Calculate the losses if you had taken a short position.

   b. Select a period in which you would have taken a short position and calculate the profits from opening and closing at the futures prices at the beginning and ending dates for your selected period. Calculate the losses if you had taken a long position.

   c. Using the annotation bar, apply the "% Change" tool to calculate the percentage change for your select periods, and then click the "News" icon on the annotation bar to find relevant news events on or preceding the opening date.

   d. Examine the yield on a constant maturity Treasury yield index for the period that your futures contract was active. Begin typing USGG (e.g., USGG10YR) to see the dropdown that will identify the ticker for the Treasury with the maturity of underlying Treasury on your selected futures contract. Comment on the yield and futures price relations for the period.

   e. Examine the prices and yields on the cheapest-to-deliver note on the contract for the period that your futures contract was active. Begin typing "T" followed by maturity (e.g., 3/15/23) for a dropdown to see the ticker for the Treasury with the maturity of underlying Treasury on your selected futures contract. Comment on the yield and futures price relations for the period.

   f. Use the Chart screen (Chart <Enter>) to create multigraphs for the T-note, the cheapest-to-deliver note, and constant maturity Treasury yield. On the Chart Menu screen, select the Standard G chart; once you have loaded your securities, go to "Edit" to put your graphs in separate panels.

9. Using the Chart screen (Chart <Enter>), examine an intercommodity Notes-over-Bonds (NOB) spread formed with a T-bond futures and T-note futures contracts similar to the ones you analyzed in Exercises 6 and 8. Note that the contracts have to have the same expiration.

   a. Use the Chart screen (Chart <Enter>) to create multigraphs for the T-bond, and T-note futures. On the Chart Menu screen, select Standard G chart; once you have loaded your securities, go to "Edit" to put your graphs in separate panels.

   b. Select a period in which you would have taken a long NOB spread position (long T-bond contract and short T-note contract) and calculate the profit from opening and closing at the futures prices at the beginning and ending dates for your selected period. Calculate the losses if you had taken a short NOB position (short T-bond contract and long T-note contract).

c. Select a period in which you would have taken a short NOB spread position (short T-bond contract and long T-note contract) and calculate the profit from opening and closing at the futures prices at the beginning and ending dates for your selected period. Calculate the losses if you had taken a long NOB position (long T-bond contract and short T-note contract).

d. Using the annotation bar, apply the "% Change" tool to calculate the percentage change for your select periods, and then click the "News" icon on the annotation bar to find relevant news events on or preceding the opening date.

10. Examine an ex-post long hedging position for a future T-bond or T-note purchase.

a. Select a futures contract and use one of the cheapest-to-deliver bonds or notes on the contract as the bond or note you plan to purchase, and use the expiration date on the futures contract as the date of your bond or note purchase.

b. Use the Chart screen (Chart <Enter>) to create multigraphs for the prices on the futures and cheapest-to-deliver bond. On the Chart Menu screen, select the Standard G chart. Once you have loaded your securities, go to "Edit" to put your graphs in separate panels.

c. Select a beginning date that you would have implemented your hedge and a closing date near the futures expiration as the date for purchasing the bond and closing your hedge. Calculate the profit or loss on the futures position from opening and closing at the futures prices at the beginning and ending dates, the cost of purchasing the cheapest-to-deliver bond on the closing date, and the hedged cost (bond purchase minus futures profit). Compare your hedged cost to the unhedged cost. In retrospect, was the hedge a good strategy?

11. Examine an ex-post short hedging position for a future T-bond or T-note sale.

a. Select a futures contract and use one of the cheapest-to-deliver bonds or notes on the contract as the bond or note you plan to sell and use the expiration date on the futures as the date of your bond or note sale.

b. Use the Chart screen (Chart <Enter>) to create multigraphs for the prices on futures and cheapest-to-deliver bond. On the Chart Menu screen, select the Standard G chart; once you have loaded your securities, go to "Edit" to put your graphs in separate panels.

c. Select a beginning date that you would have implemented your hedge and a closing date near the futures expiration as the date for the bond sale and closing your hedge. Calculate the profit or loss on the futures position from opening and closing at the futures prices at the beginning and ending dates, the revenue from selling the cheapest-to-deliver bond on the closing date, and the hedged revenue (bond sale plus futures profit). Compare your hedged revenue to the unhedged revenue. In retrospect, was the hedge a good strategy?

12. Examine an ex-post short hedging position in which you hedge the value of a holding of 1,000 issues of a selected option-free (bullet), investment-grade corporate bond of interest with a futures contract on a T-note or T-bond with a maturity

close to the maturity on your bond. Form your hedge, using the price-sensitivity model.

a. In selecting your bond, you may want to (1) use the Bloomberg SECF screen to find your bonds (SECF <Enter>; Category: Fixed-Income; Corp Tab; Maturity: 4–7 years or greater; denomination: USD), (2) use the bond search screen (SRCH <Enter>), or (3) select corporate bonds of interest (Ticker <Corp>; e.g., (IBM <CORP>). From the bond's menu screen, evaluate the bond in terms of its features (DES screen), prices (GP), price, yield, yield spread, full price, accrued interest, and duration (YAS screen).

b. Select a futures contract on a T-bond or T-note with a maturity close to the maturity of the selected bond you are to hedge and use the expiration date on the futures as the date of your hedge.

c. Determine the prices, yield to maturity, and duration on the cheapest to deliver. Begin typing "T" followed by maturity (e.g., 3/15/23) for a dropdown to see the ticker for the Treasury with the maturity of underlying Treasury on your selected futures contract.

d. Examine the constant maturity Treasury yield index for the period that your futures contract was active. Begin typing USGF (e.g., USGF20YR) to see the dropdown that will identify the ticker for the Treasury with the maturity of the underlying Treasury on your selected futures contract. Comment on the yield and futures price relations for the period.

e. Using the price-sensitivity model, calculate the number of futures contracts needed to hedge your position of 1,000 issues of your selected bond.

f. Use the Chart screen (Chart <Enter>) to create multigraphs for the prices on futures and the selected bond and the yield on the constant maturity Treasury. On the Chart Menu screen, select Standard G chart; once you have loaded your securities, go to "Edit" to put your graphs in separate panels.

g. Select a beginning date that you would have implemented your hedge and a closing date near the futures expiration as the date for the closing your hedge. Calculate the profit or loss on the futures position from opening and closing at the futures prices at the beginning and ending dates, the value of the 1,000 issue of the selected bond, and the hedged value (value of 1,000 issues plus or minus the futures closing position). Compare your hedged value to the unhedged value. In retrospect, was the hedge a good strategy?

13. Estimate the current equilibrium price on the T-bond futures contract you selected in Exercise 5 or the T-note contract you selected in Exercise 7:

$$f_0^* = [S_0 - PV(C)](1 + R_f)^T$$

Bloomberg information you need to access for determining the carrying-cost price:

- Cheapest-to-deliver bond on the futures contract and its conversion factor, CFA (Bloomberg DLV screen).
- Full price of the cheapest-to-deliver bond, (clean price) plus accrued interest (Bloomberg YAS screen, "Invoice" section).

- The time to the cheapest-to-deliver bond's next semi-annual coupon (Bloomberg CSH screen).
- The time from next coupon date to the next subsequent coupon date (Bloomberg CSH screen).
- 3-month LIBOR (Bloomberg GP screen for US0003M) and 6-month LIBOR (Bloomberg GP screen for US0006M).
- The first and last delivery dates and times on the T-notes futures and the last trade date (Bloomberg screen).
- Estimated delivery date (e.g., the last trade date) and time (Bloomberg Description screen).

14. Construct a portfolio of investment-grade corporate bonds and US Treasuries using the PRTU screen. After constructing the bond fund, evaluate the portfolio in PORT.

Guidelines:
- Use the Bloomberg search/screen function, SRCH, or SECF to identify the bonds for your portfolio.
- Make the number of issues for the bonds in your portfolio large enough so that your portfolio's market value is at least $10 million.
- Create historical data for your portfolio. See Chapter 3, sections: "Bloomberg: Equity Index Futures and Related Screens" and "Steps for Creating Historical Data for Portfolios in PRTU."

Import your portfolio in CIXB and create historical data. See Chapter 3, sections: "Bloomberg: Equity Index Futures and Related Screens" and "Bloomberg CIXB and OSA Screens." Evaluate your portfolio using PORT and as an index created in CIXB:

a. Evaluate your portfolio in PORT (make sure the "View" is set for Fixed Income) using some of the following tabs:
   - Holdings tab, "by none"
   - Holdings tab, "by Duration"
   - Characteristics tab, "Summary View"
   - Performance tab, "Main View"
   - Performance tab, "Total Return"

b. Examine the portfolio as a basket created in CIXB: Upload the portfolio as an index (.Ticker <Index> <Enter>) and examine its historical values (GP).

15. Examine an ex-post short hedging position for the portfolio you created in Exercise 14.

a. Select a futures contract on a CBT T-bond or T-note contract to hedge your portfolio. Use the expiration date on the futures contract as the date of your hedge value.

b. Use the Chart screen (Chart <Enter>) to create multigraphs for the prices on the futures and the portfolio (.Ticker of Portfolio you created in CIXB).

On the Chart Menu screen, select the Standard G chart; once you have loaded your securities, go to "Edit" to put your graphs in separate panels.

c. Select a beginning date that you would have implemented your hedge and a closing date near the futures expiration as the date for closing your hedge. Use the price-sensitivity model to determine the number of futures contracts needed to hedge the portfolio. Information on your portfolio characteristics can be found from your portfolio's PORT screen, "Characteristics" and "Summary" tabs. Information on the futures' cheapest-to-deliver bond can be found on the DES, YAS, and GP screens of the loaded bond (Bond Ticker <Corp>).

d. Calculate the profit or loss on the futures position from opening and closing at the futures prices at the beginning and ending dates, the value of your portfolio on the closing date, and the hedged value (portfolio value plus futures profit). Compare your hedged value to the unhedged value. In retrospect, was the hedge a good strategy?

e. Use Bloomberg's MARS screen to determine the number of futures contracts you would need to hedge your portfolio. See section: "MARS" in "Bloomberg: Bond and Interest Rate Futures and Related Screens."

16. Examine a duration enhancement or reduction strategy for the portfolio you created in Exercise 14.

a. Select one futures contract on a T-bond or T-note (e.g., TYA) to go long or short. Use the expiration date on the futures contract as the date for closing the strategy.

b. Use the Chart screen (Chart <Enter>) to create multigraphs for the prices on the futures and the portfolio (.Ticker of portfolio you created in CIXB). On the Chart Menu screen, select Standard G chart; once you have loaded your securities, go to "Edit" to put your graphs in separate panels.

c. Select a beginning date that you would have implemented your futures adjusted portfolio and a closing date near the futures expiration as the date for closing your position. Use the price-sensitivity model to determine the number of long or short futures contracts needed to move to your target duration.

d. Calculate the profit or loss on the futures position from opening and closing at the futures prices at the beginning and ending dates, the value of your portfolio on the closing date, and the future-adjusted value (portfolio value plus futures profit). Compare your futures-adjusted portfolio value to the unadjusted portfolio value.

PART 2

Options Markets and Strategies

CHAPTER 5

Fundamentals of Options Trading

In the early 1900s, a group of investment firms formed the Put and Call Brokers and Dealers Association. Through this association, an investor who wanted to buy an option could do so through a member who either would find a seller through other members or would sell (write) the option himself. This market was functional, but it lacked an adequate secondary market. In 1973, the Chicago Board of Trade formed the Chicago Board Options Exchange (CBOE). The CBOE was the first organized option exchange for the trading of options. Just as the CBT had served to increase the popularity of futures, the CBOE helped to increase the trading of options by making the contracts more marketable. Since the creation of the CBOE, organized exchanges in the United States, most of the organized futures exchanges, and many security exchanges outside the United States have also begun offering markets for the trading of options. As the number of exchanges offering options increased, so did the number of securities and instruments with options written on them. Today, option contracts exist not only on stocks but also on foreign currencies, equity indexes, futures contracts, and debt and interest rate-sensitive securities.

In addition to options listed on organized exchanges, there is an OTC market in currency, bonds, and interest-sensitive securities and products in the United States and a growing OTC market outside the United States. The derivative contracts offered in the OTC market include spot options and forward contracts on Treasury securities,

London Interbank Offered Rate (LIBOR)-related securities, and special types of interest rate products, such as interest rate calls and puts, caps, floors, and collars. OTC derivatives products are typically private, customized contracts between two financial institutions or between a financial institutions and one of its clients.

In this chapter, we begin our analysis of options by defining common option terms, discussing the fundamental option strategies, identifying some of the important factors that determine the price of an option, and examining the option exchange. This chapter will provide a foundation for the more detailed analysis of the markets, strategies, and pricing of options that will be examined in Chapters 6 to 11. In this chapter, we present examples of stock options and in Chapter 6, we will examine non-stock options such as equity index and futures options.

Option Terminology

By definition, an option is a security that gives the holder the right to buy or sell a particular asset at a specified price on, or possibly before, a specific date. A call option would be created, for example, if A paid $10.00 to B for a contract that gives A the right, but not the obligation, to buy one share of P&G from B for $100 on or before July 1. Similarly, a put option would be created if A paid B $10.00 for a contract for the right to sell one share P&G B for $100 on or before July 1.

Depending on the parties and types of assets involved, options can take on many different forms. Certain features, however, are common to all options. First, with every option contract there is a right, but not the obligation, to either buy or sell. Specifically, by definition a *call* is the right to buy a specific asset or security, whereas a *put* is the right to sell. Second, every option contract has a buyer and seller. The option buyer is referred to as the *holder*, and as having a *long* position in the option. The holder buys the right to *exercise* or evoke the terms of the option claim. The seller, often referred to as the option *writer*, has a *short* position and is responsible for fulfilling the obligations of the option if the holder exercises. Third, every option has an option price, exercise price, and exercise date. The price paid by the buyer to the writer for the option is referred to as the *option premium* (call premium and put premium). The *exercise price* or *strike price* is the price specified in the option contract at which the underlying asset can be purchased (call) or sold (put). Finally, the *exercise date* or period is the last day or time period the holder can exercise. Associated with the exercise date are the definitions of European and American options. A *European option* is one that can be exercised only on the exercise date, while an *American option* can be exercised at any time on or before the exercise date. Thus, from our previous example, A is the holder, B is the writer/seller, $10.00 is the option premium, $100 is the exercise or strike price, July 1 is the exercise date, and the option is American.

Exhibit 5.1 shows price quotes on a number of call and put options on Procter & Gamble stock as of 7/22/16 accessed from the Bloomberg OMON screen. Each option contract is characterized by its strike or exercise price, expiration, and whether it's a

EXHIBIT 5.1 P&G Call and Put Options, 7/22/16

Ticker	Calls Strike	Bid	Ask	Last	Ticker	Puts Strike	Bid	Ask	Last
				19-Aug-16 (27d); CSize 100					19-Aug-16 (27d); CSize 100
PG 8/19/16 C84	84.00	2.47	2.52	2.64	PG 8/19/16 P84	84.00	0.74	0.77	0.77
PG 8/19/16 C84.5	84.50	2.07	2.17	1.78	PG 8/19/16 P84.5	84.50	0.88	0.91	0.90
PG 8/19/16 C85	85.00	1.77	1.81	1.74	PG 8/19/16 P85	85.00	1.04	1.08	1.08
PG 8/19/16 C85.5	85.50	1.47	1.50	1.46	PG 8/19/16 P85.5	85.50	1.23	1.27	1.30
PG 8/19/16 C86	86.00	1.19	1.22	1.19	PG 8/19/16 P86	86.00	1.45	1.49	1.50
PG 8/19/16 C86.5	86.50	0.95	0.97	0.95	PG 8/19/16 P86.5	86.50	1.71	1.76	1.76
PG 8/19/16 C87	87.00	0.74	0.76	0.74	PG 8/19/16 P87	87.00	2.00	2.05	2.11
				16-Sep-16 (55d); CSize 100					16-Sep-16 (55d); CSize 100
PG 9/16/16 C77.5	77.50	8.35	8.65	8.30	PG 9/16/16 P77.5	77.50	0.28	0.30	0.30
PG 9/16/16 C80	80.00	6.00	6.35	5.85	PG 9/16/16 P80	80.00	0.45	0.48	0.48
PG 9/16/16 C82.5	82.50	3.90	4.10	4.01	PG 9/16/16 P82.5	82.50	0.78	0.80	0.81
PG 9/16/16 C85	85.00	2.20	2.24	2.22	PG 9/16/16 P85	85.00	1.44	1.48	1.49
PG 9/16/16 C87.5	87.50	0.93	0.96	0.92	PG 9/16/16 P87.5	87.50	2.65	2.76	2.86
PG 9/16/16 C90	90.00	0.30	0.33	0.29	PG 9/16/16 P90	90.00	4.50	4.75	4.80
PG 9/16/16 C92.5	92.50	0.08	0.10	0.10	PG 9/16/16 P92.5	92.50	6.75	7.25	0.00
				21-Oct-16 (90d); CSize 100					21-Oct-16 (90d); CSize 100
PG 10/21/16 C77.5	77.50	8.50	8.90	8.60	PG 10/21/16 P77.5	77.50	0.55	0.61	0.60
PG 10/21/16 C80	80.00	6.25	6.65	6.65	PG 10/21/16 P80	80.00	0.79	0.90	0.90
PG 10/21/16 C82.5	82.50	4.15	4.60	3.85	PG 10/21/16 P82.5	82.50	1.33	1.42	1.35
PG 10/21/16 C85	85.00	2.53	2.65	2.60	PG 10/21/16 P85	85.00	2.15	2.27	2.22
PG 10/21/16 C87.5	87.50	1.22	1.37	1.23	PG 10/21/16 P87.5	87.50	3.40	3.65	3.60
PG 10/21/16 C90	90.00	0.46	0.52	0.48	PG 10/21/16 P90	90.00	5.20	5.50	5.30
PG 10/21/16 C92.5	92.50	0.13	0.18	0.14	PG 10/21/16 P92.5	92.50	7.45	7.70	7.45
				18-Nov-16 (118d); CSize 100					18-Nov-16 (118d); CSize 100
PG 11/18/16 C70	70.00	14.45	16.65	0.00	PG 11/18/16 P70	70.00	0.27	0.52	0.00
PG 11/18/16 C75	75.00	11.00	11.35	0.00	PG 11/18/16 P75	75.00	0.54	0.79	0.68
PG 11/18/16 C80	80.00	6.50	6.85	0.00	PG 11/18/16 P80	80.00	1.22	1.35	1.26
PG 11/18/16 C85	85.00	2.89	3.00	2.94	PG 11/18/16 P85	85.00	2.73	2.78	2.81
PG 11/18/16 C90	90.00	0.73	0.85	0.78	PG 11/18/16 P90	90.00	5.45	5.85	0.00
PG 11/18/16 C95	95.00	0.04	0.20	0.00	PG 11/18/16 P95	95.00	8.45	11.95	0.00
PG 11/18/16 C100	100.00	0.00	0.07	0.00	PG 11/18/16 P100	100.00	13.30	16.85	0.00
				16-Dec-16 (146d); CSize 100					16-Dec-16 (146d); CSize 100
PG 12/16/16 C70	70.00	15.85	16.25	0.00	PG 12/16/16 P70	70.00	0.39	0.66	0.00
PG 12/16/16 C75	75.00	11.10	11.50	0.00	PG 12/16/16 P75	75.00	0.70	0.98	0.83
PG 12/16/16 C80	80.00	6.60	7.10	0.00	PG 12/16/16 P80	80.00	1.46	1.66	0.00
PG 12/16/16 C85	85.00	3.05	3.45	3.10	PG 12/16/16 P85	85.00	2.93	3.20	0.00
PG 12/16/16 C90	90.00	0.77	1.02	0.95	PG 12/16/16 P90	90.00	5.60	6.05	5.70
PG 12/16/16 C95	95.00	0.09	0.27	0.00	PG 12/16/16 P95	95.00	8.40	12.10	0.00
PG 12/16/16 C100	100.00	0.00	0.08	0.00	PG 12/16/16 P100	100.00	13.10	16.90	0.00

(continued)

EXHIBIT 5.1   (*Continued*)

20-Jan-17 (181d); CSize 100				20-Jan-17 (181d); CSize 100			
PG 1/20/17 C77.5	77.50	8.95	9.25	9.05	PG 1/20/17 P77.5	77.50	1.44	1.55	1.42
PG 1/20/17 C80	80.00	6.90	7.10	6.95	PG 1/20/17 P80	80.00	1.90	2.02	1.95
PG 1/20/17 C82.5	82.50	5.00	5.15	5.05	PG 1/20/17 P82.5	82.50	2.57	2.67	2.60
PG 1/20/17 C85	85.00	3.30	3.50	3.40	PG 1/20/17 P85	85.00	3.50	3.65	3.50
PG 1/20/17 C87.5	87.50	2.09	2.17	2.10	PG 1/20/17 P87.5	87.50	4.75	4.90	5.25
PG 1/20/17 C90	90.00	1.14	1.23	1.15	PG 1/20/17 P90	90.00	6.30	6.55	6.50
PG 1/20/17 C92.5	92.50	0.55	0.59	0.56	PG 1/20/17 P92.5	92.50	8.10	8.60	8.80

call or put. As shown on the call screen, on 7/22/16, P&G stock closed at $85.72, the P&G call option with an exercise price of 85 and expiration of September 16 closed at 2.22 and dealers were offering to sell the option (Ask) at 2.24 and to buy (Bid) the option at 2.20. The P&G put option with an exercise price of 85 and expiration of September 16 closed at 1.49, dealers' ask price was 1.48, and their bid was 1.44. Note, the contract size on the option is 100, meaning that the contract calls for buying or selling 100 options.

Fundamental Option Strategies

Many types of option strategies with interesting names such as *straddles, spreads, combinations,* and so forth, exist. The building blocks for these strategies are six fundamental option strategies: call and put purchases, call and put writes, and call and put writes in which the seller covers her position. The features of these strategies can be seen by examining the relationship between the price of the underlying security and the possible profits or losses that would result if the option either is exercised or expires worthless.

Call Purchase

To see the major characteristics of a call purchase, suppose an investor buys a call option on P&G stock with an exercise price (*X*) of $85 at a call premium (*C*) of $2.25. If the stock price reaches $95 and the holder exercises, a profit of $7.75 will be realized as the holder acquires a share of P&G for $85 by exercising and then selling it in the market for $95: a $10 capital gain minus the $2.25 premium. If the holder exercises when the stock is trading at $87.25, he will break even: The $2.25 premium will be offset exactly by the $2.25 gain realized by acquiring the stock from the option at $85 and selling in the market at $87.25. Finally, if the price of P&G is at $85 or below, the holder will not find it profitable to exercise, and as a result, will let the option expire, realizing a loss equal to the call premium of $2.25. Thus, the maximum loss from the call purchase is $2.25.

EXHIBIT 5.2   Call Purchase

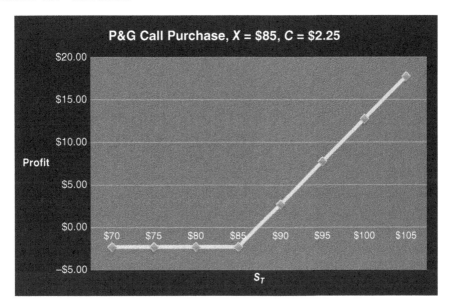

P&G Call on 7/22/2016: $T = 9/16/16$, $X = \$85$ $C = \$2.25$, Contract $= 100$ Calls		% Return Call	% Return Stock
Stock Price, S_T	Profit Per Call: Max $[S_T - \$85, 0] - 2.25$	Profit/($\$2.25$)	$(S_T/\$85) - 1$
$70	−$2.25	−100.00%	−17.65%
$75	−$2.25	−100.00%	−11.76%
$80	−$2.25	−100.00%	−5.88%
$85	−$2.25	−100.00%	0.00%
$90	$2.75	122.22%	5.88%
$95	$7.75	344.44%	11.76%
$100	$12.75	566.67%	17.65%
$105	$17.75	788.89%	23.53%
Break-Even Price	$87.25		

The investor's possible profit/loss and stock price combinations can be seen graphically in Exhibit 5.2 and the accompanying table. In the graph, the profits/losses are shown on the vertical axis and the market prices of the stock at the time of the exercise and/or expiration (signified as T: S_T) are shown along the horizontal axis. This graph is known as a *profit graph*. The line from the coordinate ($85, −$2.25) to the ($105, $17.75) coordinate and beyond shows all the profits and losses per call associated with each stock price. The horizontal segment shows a loss of $2.25, equal to the premium paid when the option was purchased. Finally, the horizontal intercept shows the break-even price at $87.25. The break-even price can be found algebraically by solving for the stock price at the exercise date (S_T) in which the profit (π) from the position is zero. The profit from the call purchase position is:

$$\pi = (S_T - X) - C_0$$

where C_0 is the initial ($t = 0$) cost of the call.

Setting π equal to zero and solving for S_T yields the break-even price of S_T^*:

$$S_T^* = X + C_0 = \$85 + \$2.25 = \$87.25$$

The profit graph in Exhibit 5.2 highlights two important features of call purchases. First, the position provides an investor with unlimited profit potential; second, losses are limited to an amount equal to the call premium. These two features help explain why some *speculators* prefer buying a call rather than the underlying stock itself. In this example, suppose that the price of P&G stock could range from $75 to $95 at expiration. If a speculator purchased P&G stock at $85, the profit from the stock would range from −$10 to +$10, or in percentage terms, from −11.76% to +11.76%. On the other hand, the return on the call option would range from +344.44% to −100%! Thus, the potential reward to the speculator from buying a call instead of the stock can be substantial—in this example, 344.44% compared to 11.76% for the stock, but the potential for loss also is large, −100% for the call versus −11.76% for the stock.

In addition to the profit graph, option positions also can be described graphically by *value graphs*. A value graph shows the option's value or cash flow at expiration, associated with each level of the stock price.

Naked Call Write

The second fundamental strategy involves the sale of a call in which the seller does not own the underlying stock. Such a position is known as a naked call write. To see the characteristics of this position, consider the P&G call option with the exercise price of $85 and the call premium of $2.25. The profits or losses associated with each stock price from selling the call are depicted in Exhibit 5.3 and its accompanying table. As shown, when the price of the stock is at $95, the seller suffers a $7.75 loss if the holder exercises the right to buy the stock from the writer at $85. Since the writer does not own the stock, she would have to buy it in the market at its market price of $95, and then turn it over to the holder at $85. Thus, the call writer would realize a $10 capital loss, minus the $2.25 premium received for selling the call, for a net loss of $7.75. When the stock is at $87.25, the writer will realize a $2.25 loss if the holder exercises. This loss will offset the $2.25 premium received. Thus, the break-even price for the writer is $87.25—the same as the holder's. This price also can be found algebraically

EXHIBIT 5.3   Naked Call Write

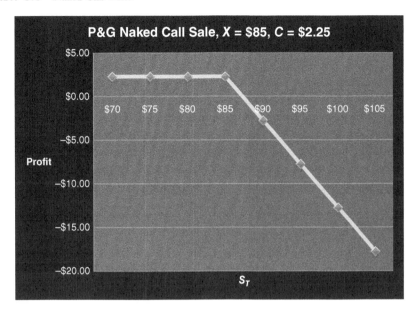

P&G Call on 7/22/2016: $T = 9/16/16$, $X = \$85$
$C = \$2.25$, Contract = 100 Calls

Stock Price, S_T	Profit Per Call: $\$2.25 - \text{Max} [S_T - \$85, 0]$
$70	$2.25
$75	$2.25
$80	$2.25
$85	$2.25
$90	−$2.75
$95	−$7.75
$100	−$12.75
$105	−$17.75
Break-Even Price	$87.25

by solving for the stock price in which the profit from the naked call write position is zero:

$$\pi = (X - S_T) + C_0$$
$$0 = (X - S_T) + C_0$$
$$S_T^* = X + C_0$$
$$S_T^* = \$85 + \$2.25 = \$87.25$$

Finally, at a stock price of $85 or less, the holder will not exercise, and the writer will profit by the amount of the premium, $2.25.

As highlighted in the graph, the payoffs to a call write are just the opposite of the call purchase; that is: gains/losses for the buyer of a call are exactly equal to the losses/gains of the seller. Thus, in contrast to the call purchase, the naked call write position provides the investor with only a limited profit opportunity equal to the value of the premium, with unlimited loss possibilities. Although this limited profit and unlimited loss feature of a naked call write may seem unattractive, the motivation for an investor to write a call is the cash or credit received and the expectation that the option will not be exercised. As we will discuss late in this chapter, though, there are margin requirements on an option write position in which the writer is required to deposit cash or risk-free securities to secure the position.

Covered Call Write

One of the most popular option strategies is to write a call on a stock already owned. This strategy is known as a *covered call write*. For example, an investor who bought P&G stock at $85 some time ago, and who did not expect its price to appreciate in the near future, might sell a call on P&G with an exercise price of $85. As shown in Exhibit 5.4, if P&G is greater than $85, the covered call writer loses the stock when the holder exercises, leaving the writer with a profit of only $2.25. The benefit of the covered call write occurs when the stock price declines. For example, if ABC stock declined to $75, then the writer would suffer an actual (if the stock is sold) or paper loss of $10. The $2.25 premium received from selling the call, though, would reduce this loss to just $7.75. Similarly, if the stock is at $82.75, a $2.25 loss will be offset by the $2.25 premium received from the call sale.

Put Purchase

Since a put gives the holder the right to sell the stock, profit is realized when the stock price declines. With a decline, the put holder can buy the stock at a low price in the stock market, and then sell it at the higher exercise price on the put contract. To see the features related to the put purchase position, consider the purchase of a P&G put option with an exercise price $85 and the put premium ($P$) of $2.25. If the stock price declines to $75, the put holder could purchase P&G at $75 and then use the put contract to sell the stock at the exercise price of $85. Thus, as shown by the profit graph in Exhibit 5.5, at $75 the put holder would realize a $7.75 profit (the $10 gain from buying the stock and exercising minus the $2.25 premium). The break-even price in this case would be $82.75:

$$\pi = (X - S_T) - P_0$$
$$0 = (X - S_T) - P_0$$
$$S_T^* = X - P_0$$
$$S_T^* = \$85 - \$2.25 = \$82.75$$

EXHIBIT 5.4 Cover Call Write

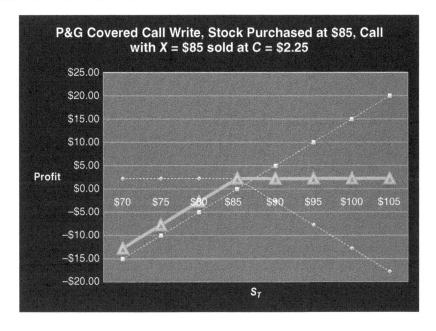

P&G Call on 7/22/2016: $T = 9/16/16$, $X = \$85$
$C = \$2.25$, Contract $= 100$ Calls

Stock Price, S_T	Profit Per Call: $\$2.25 - \text{Max} [S_T - \$85, 0]$	Profit on Stock: $S_T - \$85$	Total Profit
$70	$2.25	−$15.00	−$12.75
$75	$2.25	−$10.00	−$7.75
$80	$2.25	−$5.00	−$2.75
$85	$2.25	$0.00	$2.25
$90	−$2.75	$5.00	$2.25
$95	−$7.75	$10.00	$2.25
$100	−$12.75	$15.00	$2.25
$105	−$17.75	$20.00	$2.25
Break-Even Price	$87.25		

Finally, if the stock is $85 or higher at expiration, it will not be rational for the put holder to exercise. As a result, a maximum loss equal to the $2.25 premium will occur when the stock is trading at $85 or more.

Thus, similar to a call purchase, a long put position provides the buyer with potentially large profit opportunities (not unlimited, since the price of the stock cannot be less than zero), while limiting the losses to the amount of the premium. Unlike the call purchase strategy, the put purchase position requires the stock price to decline before profit is realized.

EXHIBIT 5.5   Put Purchase

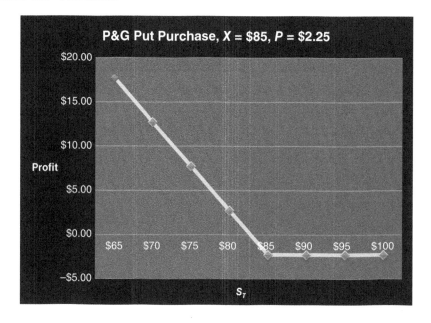

P&G Put on 7/22/2016: $T = 9/16/16$, $X = \$85$
$P = \$2.25$, Contract = 100 Puts

Stock Price, S_T	Profit Per Put: Max $[\$85 - S_T, 0] - 2.25$
$65	$17.75
$70	$12.75
$75	$7.75
$80	$2.75
$85	−$2.25
$90	−$2.25
$95	−$2.25
$100	−$2.25
Break-Even Price	$82.75

Naked Put Write

The exact opposite position to a put purchase (in terms of profit/loss and stock price relations) is the sale of a put, defined as the naked put write. This position's profit graph for the P&G 85 put is shown in Exhibit 5.6. Here, if P&G is at $85 or more, the holder will not exercise and the writer will profit by the amount of the premium, $2.25. In contrast, if P&G decreases, a loss is incurred. For example, if the holder exercises at $75, the put writer must buy the stock at $85. An actual $10 loss will occur if the writer elects to sell the stock and a paper loss if he holds on to it. This loss, minus

EXHIBIT 5.6   Naked Put Write

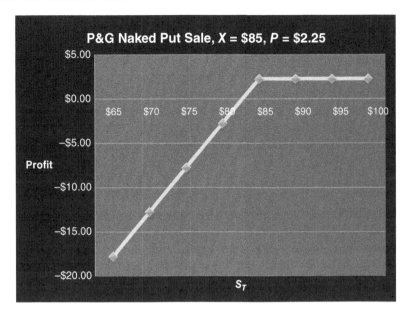

P&G Put on 7/22/2016: $T = 9/16/16$, $X = \$85$
$P = \$2.25$, Contract $= 100$ Puts

Stock Price, S_T	Profit Per Put: $\$2.25 - \text{Max } [\$85 - S_T, 0]$
$65	−$17.75
$70	−$12.75
$75	−$7.75
$80	−$2.75
$85	$2.25
$90	$2.25
$95	$2.25
$100	$2.25
Break-Even Price	$82.75

the $2.25 premium, yields a loss of $7.75 when the market price is $75. The break-even price in which the profit from the position is zero is $S_T^* = \$82.75$, the same as the put holder's:

$$\pi = (S_T - X) + P_0$$
$$0 = (S_T - X) + P_0$$
$$S_T^* = X - P_0$$
$$S_T^* = \$85 - \$2.25 = \$82.75$$

Covered Put Write

The last fundamental option strategy is the covered put write. This strategy requires the seller of a put to have a short stock position to cover her position. Because a put writer is required to buy the stock at the exercise price if the holder exercises, the only way she can cover the obligation is by selling the underlying stock short. For example, suppose a writer of a P&G 85 put shorts a share of P&G stock: borrows one share of the stock and then sells it in the market at $85/share. At expiration, if the stock price is less than the exercise price and the put holder exercises, the covered put writer will buy the share with the $85 proceeds obtained from the short sale, and then return the share that was borrowed to cover the short sale obligation. The put writer's obligation is thus covered and she profits by an amount equal to the premium of $2.25, as shown in Exhibit 5.7. In contrast, losses from the covered put write occur when the stock price is above $82.75 ($X - P_0$). When the stock price is $85 or greater, the put is worthless, since the holder would not exercise, but losses would occur from covering the short sale. For example, if the writer had to cover the short sale when P&G was trading at $95, she would incur a $10 loss (or $10 paper loss if she did not have to cover). This loss, minus the $2.25 premium the writer received, would equate to a net loss of $7.75. Finally, the break-even price for the covered put write in which profit is zero occurs at $87.25.

Other Option Strategies

Options can be combined with stock and other options to generate a number of different investment strategies. Two well-known strategies of note are straddles and spreads. In Chapter 7, we will examine these and other strategies in more detail.

Straddle

A straddle purchase is formed by buying both a call and put with the same terms—same underlying stock, exercise price, and expiration date. A straddle write, in contrast, is constructed by selling a call and a put with the same terms. Profit graphs and tables are shown in Exhibit 5.8 for a straddle purchase of a P&G call and put each with an exercise price of $85 and a premium of $2.25. The straddle purchase shown in the figure can be geometrically generated by vertically summing the profits on the call purchase position and put purchase position at each stock price. The resulting straddle purchase position is characterized by a V-shaped profit and stock price relation. Thus, the motivation for buying a straddle comes from the expectation of a large stock price movement in either direction. For example, at the stock price of $95, a $5.50 profit is earned: $10 gain on the call minus a $4.50 cost of the straddle purchase; similarly at $75, a $5.50 profit is attained: $10 gain on the put minus a $4.50 cost of the straddle. Losses on the straddle occur if the price of the underlying stock remains stable, with the maximum loss being equal to the costs of the straddle ($4.50) and

EXHIBIT 5.7   Covered Put Write

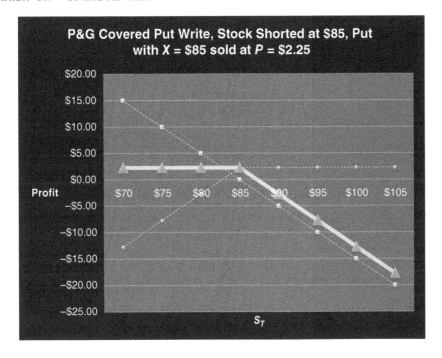

P&G Put on 7/22/2016: $T = 9/16/16$, $X = \$85$
$P = \$2.25$, Contract = 100 Puts

Stock Price, S_T	Profit Per Put: $\$2.25 - \text{Max} [\$85 - S_T, 0]$	Profit on Short Stock Position: $\$85 - S_T$	Total Profit
$70	−$12.75	$15.00	$2.25
$75	−$7.75	$10.00	$2.25
$80	−$2.75	$5.00	$2.25
$85	$2.25	$0.00	$2.25
$90	$2.25	−$5.00	−$2.75
$95	$2.25	−$10.00	−$7.75
$100	$2.25	−$15.00	−$12.75
$105	$2.25	−$20.00	−$17.75
Break-Even Price	$87.25		

occurring when the stock price is equal to the exercise price. Finally, the straddle is characterized by two break-even prices ($89.50 and $80.50).

In contrast to the straddle purchase, a straddle write yields an inverted V-shaped profit graph. The seller of a straddle is betting against large price movements. As shown in Exhibit 5.9, a maximum profit equal to the sum of the call and put premiums occurs when the stock price is equal to the exercise price; losses occur if the stock price moves past the break-even prices of $89.50 and $80.50.

EXHIBIT 5.8   Straddle Purchase

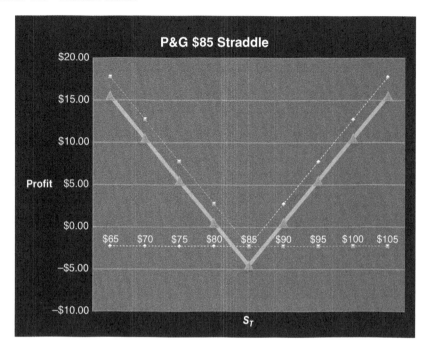

P&G Call and Put, $X = \$85$, $C = \$2.25$, and $P = \$2.25$

Stock Price S_T	Profit Per Call Max $[S_T - \$85, 0] -\$2.25$	Profit Per Put Max $[\$85 - S_T, 0] - \$2.25$	Total Profit
$65	−$2.25	$17.75	$15.50
$70	−$2.25	$12.75	$10.50
$75	−$2.25	$7.75	$5.50
$80	−$2.25	$2.75	$0.50
$85	−$2.25	−$2.25	−$4.50
$90	$2.75	−$2.25	$0.50
$95	$7.75	−$2.25	$5.50
$100	$12.75	−$2.25	$10.50
$105	$17.75	−$2.25	$15.50
Break-Even Prices	$80.50	$89.50	

Spread

A spread is the purchase of one option and the sale of another on the same underlying security but with different terms: different exercise prices, different expirations, or both. Two of the most popular spread positions are the bull spread and the bear spread. A bull call spread is formed by buying a call with a certain exercise price and selling

EXHIBIT 5.9   Straddle Write

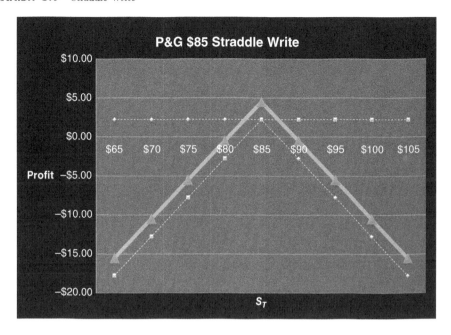

P&G Call and Put, $X = \$85$, $C = \$2.25$, and $P = \$2.25$

Stock Price S_T	Profit Per Call $\$2.25 - \text{Max} [S_T - \$85, 0]$	Profit Per Put $\$2.25 - \text{Max} [\$85 - S_T, 0]$	Total Profit
$65	$2.25	−$17.75	−$15.50
$70	$2.25	−$12.75	−$10.50
$75	$2.25	−$7.75	−$5.50
$80	$2.25	−$2.75	−$0.50
$85	$2.25	$2.25	$4.50
$90	−$2.75	$2.25	−$0.50
$95	−$7.75	$2.25	−$5.50
$100	−$12.75	$2.25	−$10.50
$105	−$17.75	$2.25	−$15.50
Break-Even Prices	$80.50	$89.50	

another call with a higher exercise price, but with the same expiration date. A bear call spread is the reversal of the bull spread; it consists of buying a call with a certain exercise price and selling another with a lower exercise price. (The same spreads also can be formed with puts.)

Exhibit 5.10 shows the profit graphs and tables at expiration for a bull spread formed with the purchase of one P&G 80 call for $6.00 per call and the sale of one 85 call for $2.25 (same expirations). Geometrically, the profit and stock price relation for the spread shown in the exhibit can be obtained by vertically summing the profits

EXHIBIT 5.10   Bull Spread

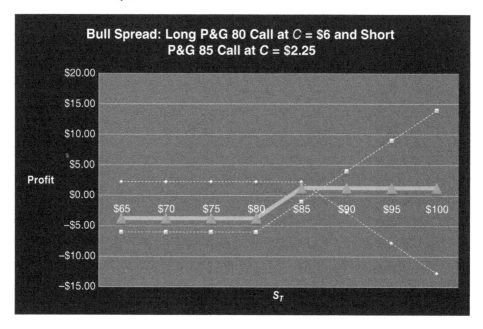

P&G Bull Call Spread: Short Call: $X = \$85$, $C = \$2.25$
Long Call: $X = \$80$, $C = \$6.00$

Stock Price S_T	Profit Per Short 85 Call $\$2.25 - \text{Max}\,[S_T - \$85, 0]$	Profit Per Long 80 Call $\text{Max}\,[S_T - \$80, 0] - \$6.00$	Total Profit
$65	$2.25	−$6.00	−$3.75
$70	$2.25	−$6.00	−$3.75
$75	$2.25	−$6.00	−$3.75
$80	$2.25	−$6.00	−$3.75
$85	$2.25	−$1.00	$1.25
$90	−$2.75	$4.00	$1.25
$95	−$7.75	$9.00	$1.25
$100	−$12.75	$14.00	$1.25
Break-Even Price	$83.75		

from the long 80 call position and the short 85 call position at each stock price. The bull spread is characterized by losses limited to $3.75 when the stock price is $80 or less, limited profits of $1.25 starting when the stock price hits $85, and a break-even price of $83.75.

A bear call spread results in the opposite profit and stock price relation as the bull spread: A limited profit occurs when the stock price is equal or less than the lower exercise price and a limited loss occurs when the stock price is equal or greater than the higher exercise price. Spreads are examined in more detail in Chapter 7.

Option Price Relations

Like futures contracts, the price of an option derives its value from the underlying security and is governed by arbitrage. In general, the price of an option is a function of the underlying security price, the time to expiration, the exercise price, and the volatility of the underlying security. The pricing of option contracts in terms of arbitrage forces is examined in Part 3. Here, we identify some of the factors that determine the price of an option.

Call Price Relations

The relationship between the price of a call and its expiration time, exercise price, and stock price can be seen by defining the call's intrinsic value and time value premium. By definition, the *intrinsic value* (IV) of a call at a time prior to expiration (let t signify any time prior to expiration), or at expiration (T again signifies expiration date) is the maximum (Max) of the difference between the price of the stock (S_t) and the exercise price or zero (since the option's price cannot have a negative value):

$$IV = \text{Max} \, [S_t - X, 0]$$

Thus, if a call had an exercise price of \$85 and the stock was trading at \$95, then the intrinsic value of the call would be \$10; if it were trading at \$85 or less, the IV would be zero. The intrinsic value can be used to define *in-the-money, on-the-money,* and *out-of-the-money* calls. Specifically, an in-the-money call is one in which the price of the underlying stock exceeds the exercise price; as a result, its IV is positive. When the price of the stock is equal to the exercise price, the call's IV is zero and the call is said to be on the money (or at the money). Finally, if the exercise price exceeds the stock price, the call would be out of the money and the IV would be zero:

Type	Condition	Example
In-the-money:	$S_t > X$, $IV > 0$	\$95 > \$85, IV = \$10
On-the-money:	$S_t = X$, $IV = 0$	\$85 = \$85, $\geq$ IV = 0
Out-of-the-money	$S_t < X$,- $IV = 0$	\$75 < \$85, = 0

For an American call option, the IV defines a boundary condition in which the price of a call has to trade at a value at least equal to its IV:

$$C_t \geq \text{Max} \, [S_t - X, 0]$$

If this condition does not hold ($C_t < \text{Max}[S_t - X, 0]$), an arbitrage opportunity exists. If $C_t < \text{Max}[S_t - X, 0]$, an arbitrageur could earn a riskless return by buying the call, exercising, and then selling the stock. For example, suppose an American call option on P&G stock with an exercise price of $85 was trading at $9.00 when the stock was trading at $95 (IV = Max($95 − $85, 0) = $10). In this situation, we have an asset (the stock) selling at two different prices: one is $95, offered in the stock market; the other is $94 ($9 call premium plus $85 exercise price), available in the option market. In this case, an arbitrageur could realize a riskless profit of $1.00 (excluding commissions) per call by: (1) buying the call at $9.00; (2) immediately exercising it (buying P&G stock at $85); and (3) selling the stock in the market for $95:

$S_t = \$95, X = \$85, C_t = \$9$	
Position	Cash Flow
Buy P&G 85 Call for $9	−$9.00
Exercise P&G 85 Call	−$85.00
(Buy Stock for $X = \$85$)	
Sell Stock in Market for $95	+$95.00
Profit	+1.00

Arbitrageurs seeking to profit from this opportunity would increase the demand for the P&G call, causing its price to go up until the call premium was at least $10 and the arbitrage opportunity disappeared. Thus, in equilibrium, the American call would have to trade at a price at least equal to its IV.

It is important to note that the exploitation of arbitrage opportunities by arbitrageurs ensures that the price of the option will change as the underlying stock price changes. For example, if P&G stock were to increase from $95 to $100, then in the absence of arbitrage, the price of the P&G 85 call would have to increase from at least $10 to at least $15, to $20 when the stock is at $105, and to $25 when the stock is at $110. Thus, arbitrageurs ensure that the call option derives its value from the underlying stock. Finally, note that since the above arbitrage strategy governing the price of an American option requires an immediate exercise of the call, the resulting IV boundary condition does not hold for European options (the condition governing European options will be discussed in Chapter 9).

The other component of the value of an option is the *time value premium* (TVP). By definition, the TVP of a call is the difference between the price of the call and the IV:

$$TVP = C_t - IV$$

If the call premium were $12 when the price of the underlying stock on the 85 call was $95, the TVP would be $2. The TVP decreases as the time remaining to expiration decreases. Specifically, if the call is near expiration, we should expect the call to trade at close to its IV; if, however, six months remain to expiration, then the price of the call should be greater and the TVP positive; if nine months remain, then the TVP should be even greater. In addition to the intuitive reasoning, an arbitrage argument also can be used to establish that the price of the call is greater with a greater time to expiration (this argument is presented in Chapter 9).

Combined, the IV and the TVP show that two factors influencing the price of a call are the underlying stock's price and the time to expiration:

$$C_t = IV + TVP$$

Call Price Curve

Graphically, the relationship between C_t and the TVP and IV can be seen in Exhibit 5.11. In the figure, graphs plotting the call prices and IV (on the vertical axis) against P&G stock prices (on the horizontal axis) are shown for the 85 P&G call option. The IV line shows the linear relationship between the IV and the stock price. The line emanates from a horizontal intercept equal to the exercise price. When the price of the stock is equal or less than the exercise price of $85, $IV = 0$; when the stock is priced at $S_t = 90, $IV = 5; when $S_t = 95, $IV = 10, and so on. The IV line, in turn, serves as a reference for the nonlinear call price curves. As we just noted, arbitrageurs ensure that the call price curve cannot go below the IV line. Furthermore, the IV line would be the call price curve if we are at expiration, since $TVP = 0$ and thus $C_T = IV$. The call price curves in the exhibit show the positive relationship between C_t and S_t. The vertical distance between a curve and the IV line, in turn, measures the TVP. Thus, the call price curve shown for the more distant expirations have greater time value premiums.

Note that the call and stock price relation is not a linear one. Specifically, if the price of the stock is very high relative to its exercise price—*a deep in-the-money call*—then the costs of acquiring the option would be relatively expensive (large intrinsic value), resulting in a lower demand. As a result, at relatively high stock prices, the time value premiums would be very small. In contrast, when the price of the stock is substantially below its exercise price—a *deep out-of-the-money call*—investors would most likely have very little confidence in the option being profitable. As a result, the demand and price of the call would be extremely low and the price of the call would be equal or approximately equal to zero. Moreover, with a low or zero demand for a deep out-of-money call, any incremental change in the stock price would have a negligible impact on the price of the call. The relationship between the call and stock prices when the stock price is either very low or very high is seen graphically in Exhibit 5.11. At the low stock prices, the call option curve approaches the horizontal axis, suggesting that the call is (or almost is) worthless, and that any marginal change in S_t has only a small impact on C_t. As the stock price increases, the call price curve begins to increase at an increasing rate, implying the TVP is increasing. This will continue until the stock is on- or near-the-money; at that point, the TVP is at a maximum. Finally, as the stock increases further, the TVP starts to decrease, and at very high stock prices the TVP is negligible and the call option curve approaches the minimum boundary line.

In summary, the graphs in Exhibit 5.11 show (1) there is a direct relationship between the price of the call and the stock price, as reflected by the positively sloped call price curves; (2) the call is above its IV, as shown by the call price curves being above the IV line; and (3) the price of the call is greater the longer the time to expiration, as reflected by the distance between call price curves with different expiration periods.

EXHIBIT 5.11   Call Graph: Call and Stock Price Relation

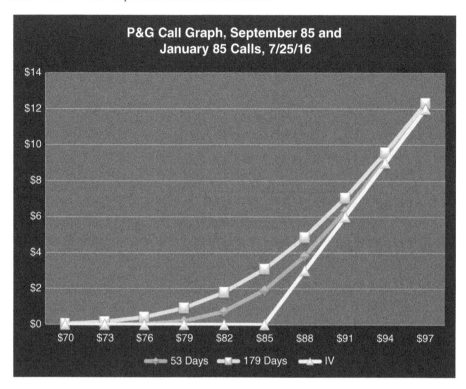

Date	7/25/2016	7/25/2016	7/25/2016
Price	September 16 P&G Call	January 20, 2017 P&G Call	Intrinsic Value
Days to Expiration	53 Days	179 Days	IV
$70	$0.0002	$0.0504	$0.00
$73	$0.0040	$0.1590	$0.00
$76	$0.04	$0.42	$0.00
$79	$0.20	$0.92	$0.00
$82	$0.74	$1.79	$0.00
$85	$1.91	$3.10	$0.00
$88	$3.83	$4.86	$3.00
$91	$6.33	$7.05	$6.00
$94	$9.15	$9.57	$9.00
$97	$12.10	$12.32	$12.00

Volatility

The call price curve shows the positive relation between a call price and the underlying security price and the time to expiration. An option's price also depends on the volatility of the underlying security.

Since a long call position is characterized by unlimited profits if the underlying security increases but limited losses if it decreases, a call holder would prefer more volatility rather than less. Specifically, greater variability suggests, on the one hand, a given likelihood that the security will increase substantially in price, causing the call to be more valuable. On the other hand, greater volatility also suggests a given likelihood of the security price will decrease substantially. However, given that a call's losses are limited to just the premium when the security price is equal to the exercise price or less, the extent of the price decrease would be inconsequential to the call holder. Thus, the market will value a call option on a more volatile security greater than a call on one with lower variability.

The positive relationship between a call's premium and its underlying security's volatility is illustrated in Exhibits 5.12 and 5.13. The exhibits show distributions for Stocks A and B and the corresponding distributions of the intrinsic values of a $100 call on the each of stocks. Each stock has an expected stock price of $100. The distribution for Stock A shown in Exhibit 5.12, though, has a volatility as measured in terms of the

EXHIBIT 5.12   Price and Variability Relation for Stock A, Volatility: $\sigma(\text{Return}) = 0.11$

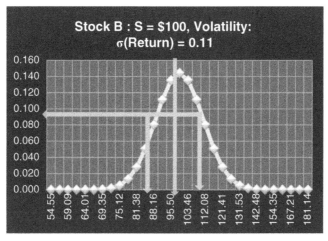
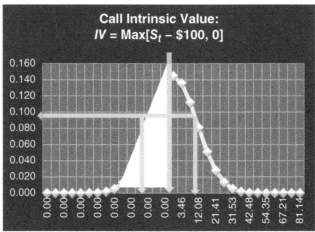

EXHIBIT 5.13 Price and Variability Relation for Stock B, Volatility: σ(Return) = 0.22

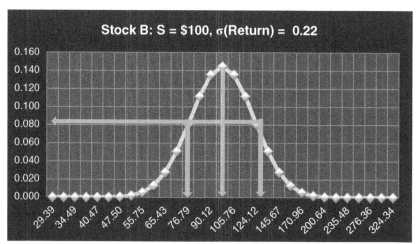

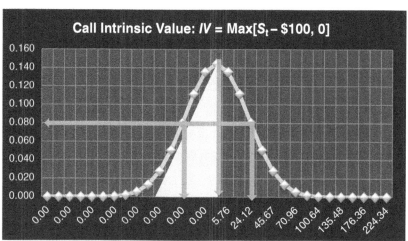

standard deviation of the stock's returns of σ(Return) = 0.11, while the distribution for Stock B shown in Exhibit 5.13 has greater volatility of σ(Return) = 0.22. Both distributions approach normal distribution with their variability characterized by equal chances of an increase by X% or decrease by X% by the end of the period. A call option on Stock B with the greater variability (Exhibit 5.13) is characterized by an equal chance it will either increase or decrease by greater percent by the end of the period than Stock A with the lower variability (Exhibit 5.12). For example, there is an equal probability of 0.09 that Stock B would be either $124.12 or $76.97 and the IV of its call option would be either $24.12 or zero at the end of the period, compared to possible stock values and IVs for A of only $112.08 and $88.16 and $12.08 and zero. Since, Stock B's call cannot perform worse than Stock A's call, and can do better, it follows there would be a higher demand and therefore price for the call option on Stock B than the call on Stock A. Thus, given the limited loss characteristic of an option, the more volatile the underlying security, the more valuable the option, all other factors being equal.

Put Price Relations

Analogous to calls, the price of a put at a given point in time prior to expiration (P_t) also can be explained by reference to its IV and TVP. In the case of puts, the IV is defined as the maximum of the difference between the exercise price and the stock price or zero:

$$IV = \text{Max } [X - S_t, 0]$$

Similar to calls, in-the-money, on-the-money, and out-of-the-money puts are defined as:

Type	Condition	Example
In-the-money:	$X > S_t, IV > 0$	$85 > $75, $IV = $10
On-the-money:	$X = S_t, IV = 0$	$85 = $85, $IV = 0$
Out-of-the-money	$X < S_t, IV = 0$	$75 < $85, $IV = 0$

Like call options, the IV of an American put option defines a boundary condition in which the price of the put has to trade at a price at least equal to its IV: $P_t \geq \text{Max } [X - S_t, 0]$. If this condition does not hold, an arbitrageur could buy the put, the underlying stock, and exercise to earn a riskless profit. For example, suppose P&G stock is trading at $75 and a P&G 85 put were trading at $9.00, below its IV of $10.00. Arbitrageurs could realize risk-free profits by (1) buying the put at $9.00; (2) buying P&G stock for $75; and (3) immediately exercising the put, selling the stock on the put for $85. Doing this, the arbitrageur would realize a risk-free profit of $1.00:

$S_t = $75, $X = $85, $P_t = $9 Position	Cash Flow
Buy P&G 80 Put for $9.00	−$9.00
Buy P&G Stock for $75.00 in the Market	−$75.00
Exercise P&G 85 Put	
(Sell Stock on the put for $X = $85.00)	+$85.00
Profit	+$1.00

As in the case of calls, arbitrageurs pursuing this strategy would increase the demand for puts until the put price was equal to at least the $10 difference between the exercise and stock prices. Thus, in the absence of arbitrage, an American put would have to trade at a price at least equal to its IV.

Similar to call options, the TVP for the put is defined as:

$$TVP = P_t - IV$$

Thus, the price of the put can be explained by the time to expiration and the stock price in terms of the put's TVP and IV:

$$P_t = IV + TVP$$

Put Price Curve

Exhibit 5.14 shows two negatively sloped put-price curves for a P&G 85 puts with different exercise periods, and a negatively sloped IV line going from the horizontal intercept (where $S_t = X = \$85$) to the vertical intercept where the IV is equal to the exercise price when the stock is trading at zero. When the price of P&G is

EXHIBIT 5.14 Put Graph: Put and Stock Price Relation

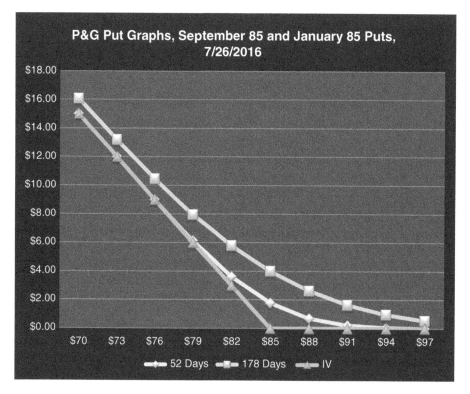

Date	7/26/2016	7/26/2016	7/26/2016
	September 2016	January 2017	Intrinsic
Price	P&G Put	P&G Put	Value
Days to Expiration	52 Days	178 Days	IV
$70	$15.0000	$16.0659	$15.00
$73	$12.0000	$13.1861	$12.00
$76	$9.0018	$10.4515	$9.00
$79	$6.1212	$7.9528	$6.00
$82	$3.6152	$5.7802	$3.00
$85	$1.7733	$3.9979	$0.00
$88	$0.6984	$2.6253	$0.00
$91	$0.2169	$1.6353	$0.00
$94	$0.0529	$0.9665	$0.00
$97	$0.0102	$0.5427	$0.00

equal or greater than the exercise price of $85, $IV = 0$; when P&G is priced at $S_t = \$80$, $IV = \$5.00$; when it is $75, $IV = \$10.00$, and so on. The graphs show four relationships:

1. The price of the put increases as the price of the underlying stock decreases, since the put's IV is greater the lower the stock price.
2. The price of the put is above its IV with time remaining to expiration (if the put is American), else arbitrage opportunities would ultimately push the price up to equal the IV.
3. The greater the time to expiration, the higher the TVP and thus the greater the put price.
4. The slope of the put price curve approaches the slope of the IV line for relatively low stock prices (*deep in-the-money puts*) and approaches zero for relatively large stock prices (*deep-out-of-the money puts*). That is, when a put is deep out-of-the-money, its price changes very little in response to an incremental change in the price of the stock, and it will be equal (or almost equal) to zero; when a put is deep in the money, its price will have a very small TVP and will come closer to equaling the intrinsic value as the stock price decreases.

Variability

Like calls, the price of a put option depends not only on the underlying security price and time to expiration but also on the volatility of the underlying security. Since put losses are limited to the premium when the price of the underlying security is greater than or equal to the exercise price, put buyers, like call buyers, will value puts on securities with greater variability more than those with lower variability.

Put-Call Parity

Consider a strategy of buying a share of stock for $50 and a put on the stock with exercise price of $50. The cash flow from this portfolio at expiration is shown in Exhibit 5.15. As shown in Column 7, this stock and put portfolio has a minimum value of $50 (the exercise price) for $S_T < \$50$, and a value equal to the stock for $S_T \geq \$50$. Thus, an investor who purchased the stock some time ago could eliminate the downside risk of the stock by buying a put. In this case, the stock value has been ensured not to fall below $50, the exercise price on the put. A combined stock and

EXHIBIT 5.15 Cash Flows on Call, Put, Stock, and Bond Positions at Expiration

Stock Price, S_T	Long Call	Bond	Bond and Call	Long Put	Stock	Stock and Put
$30	$0	$50	$50	$20	$30	$50
$40	$0	$50	$50	$10	$40	$50
$50	$0	$50	$50	$0	$50	$50
$60	$10	$50	$60	$0	$60	$60
$70	$20	$50	$70	$0	$70	$70

put position such as this is known as a *portfolio insurance* strategy. Portfolio insurance represents an example of how options can be used by hedgers.

Given the values of the stock and put portfolio, consider now a portfolio consisting of a bond with a face value of $50 and a 50 call on the stock. As shown in Column 4 of Exhibit 5.15, the values of this portfolio at time T are identical to the stock and put portfolio's values at each stock price. If the stock appreciates, the call becomes more valuable and the return on the bond is enhanced by the appreciation in the call price. On the other hand, if the stock falls below the exercise price, the call is worthless and the portfolio simply is equal to the face value of the bond ($50). A bond and call portfolio such as this is referred to as a *fiduciary call*, and it can be used as a substitute for buying the stock and put.

The equality between the stock-put portfolio and the bond-call portfolio may be expressed algebraically as:

$$S_t + P_t = C_t + B_t$$

This expression is commonly referred to as *put-call parity*. Since the two portfolios have exactly the same cash flows at expiration, their values at any time t must be identical, or else arbitrage opportunities will exist. For example, if the bond-call combination is cheaper than the stock-put portfolio, an arbitrageur can earn a profit without taking risk and without investing any of her own money. To expedite the strategy, the arbitrageur would have to buy the cheap portfolio (bond and call) and sell the expensive one (stock and put). The put-call parity condition is governed by the *law of one price*. This law says that in the absence of arbitrage, any investments that yield identical cash flows most be equally priced. Put-call parity and other boundary conditions are examined in more detail in Chapter 9.

Option Exchanges

As with all exchanges, the primary function of derivative exchanges offering options is to provide marketability to option contracts by linking brokers and dealers, standardizing contracts, establishing trading rules and procedures, guaranteeing and intermediating contracts through a clearinghouse, and providing continuous trading through electronic matching or with market makers, specialists, and locals.

Standardization

The option exchanges standardize contracts by setting expiration dates, exercise prices, and contract sizes on options. The expiration dates on options are defined in terms of an expiration cycle. For example, the March cycle has expiration months of March, June, September, and December. In a three-month option cycle, only the options with the three nearest expiration months trade at any time. Thus, as an option expires, the exchange introduces a new option. The exchanges also offer longer maturity contracts called LEAPS. On many option contracts, the expiration day is the Saturday after the third Friday of the expiration month; the last day on which the expiring option trades, however, is Friday.

In addition to setting the expiration date, the exchanges also choose the exercise prices for each option, with as many as six strike prices associated with each option when an option cycle begins. Once an option with a specific exercise price has been introduced, it will remain listed until its expiration date. The exchange can, however, introduce new options with different exercise prices at any time.

The standard size for a stock option contract is 100 calls. Thus, a per share quote of a P&G July 85 call at $2.50 means that a call buyer actually would be purchasing 100 calls at $2.50 per call ($250 investment), giving her the right to buy 100 shares of P&G at $85 per share (total exercise value of $8,500) on or before (if American) the September expiration date. Note that the CBOE and other option exchanges automatically adjust options for stock splits and stock dividends. For example, if ABC stock is trading at $50, and there is a put option on it with an exercise price of $60, then a 2-for-1 stock split would result in an automatic adjustment in which the number of contracts doubles and the exercise price is halved. Thus, the owner of one ABC 60 put contract (100 puts) would now have two ABC 30 puts (200 puts). Options also are adjusted automatically for stock dividends by changing the number of shares and the exercise price.

Option exchanges also impose exercise limits and position limits on an option's trading. These limits are intended to prevent an investor or groups of investors from having a dominant impact on a particular option. An *exercise limit* specifies the maximum number of option contracts that can be exercised in a specified period (e.g., five consecutive business days) by any investor or investor group. An exercise limit is determined by the exchange for each stock and non-stock option. A *position limit* sets the maximum number of options an investor can buy and sell on one side of the market; the limit for each stock and non-stock option is the same as the exercise limit. A *side of the market* is either a bullish or bearish position. An investor who is bullish could profit by buying calls or selling puts, while an investor with a bearish position would hope to profit by buying puts and selling calls.

Exhibit 5.16 shows the Bloomberg Description screen for the September 2016 P&G 85 call as of July 29, 2016. As shown, the call had an exercise price of $85, a contract size of 100 calls, was American, was last trading at $2.16, and had a position limit of 25 million shares.

The Option Clearing Corporation

Like futures exchanges, option exchanges, such as the CBOE, provide a clearinghouse (CH) or *option clearing corporation* (OCC), as it is commonly referred to on the option exchange. In the case of options, the OCC intermediates each transaction that takes place on the exchange and guarantees that all option writers fulfill the terms of their options if they are assigned. In addition, the OCC also manages option exercises, receiving notices and assigning corresponding positions to clearing members.

As an intermediary, the OCC functions by breaking up each option trade. After a buyer and seller complete an option trade, the OCC steps in and becomes the effective

EXHIBIT 5.16　Bloomberg Description Screen for September 2016 85 P&G Call

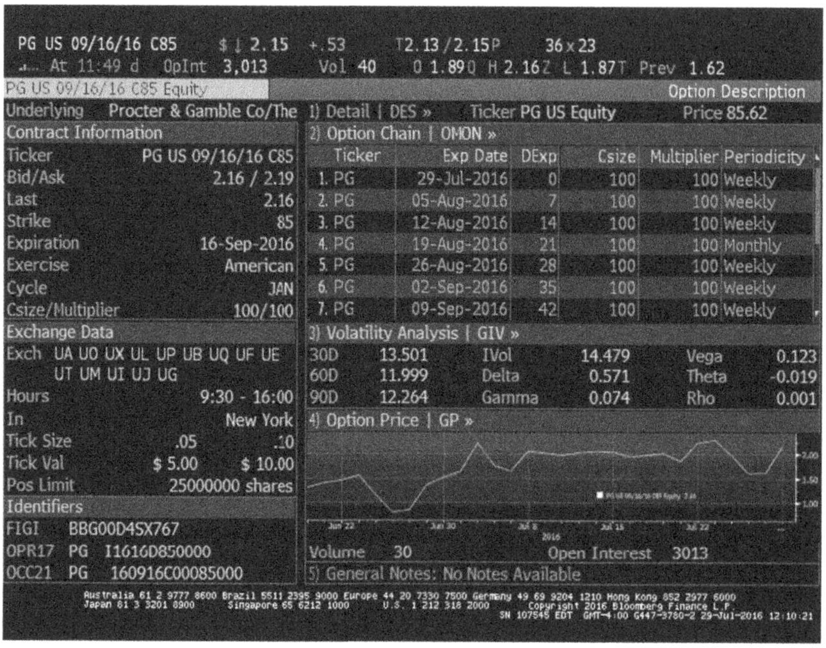

buyer to the option seller and the effective seller to the option buyer. At that point, there is no longer any relationship between the original buyer and seller. If the buyer of the option decides to exercise, he does so by notifying the OCC (through his broker). The OCC (who is the holder's effective option seller) will select one of the option sellers with a short position on the exercised security and assign that writer the obligation of fulfilling the terms of the exercise request.

By breaking up each option contract, the OCC makes it possible for option investors to close their positions before expiration. If a buyer (seller) of an option later becomes a seller (buyer) of the same option, the OCC's computer will note the offsetting position in the option investor's account and will therefore cancel both entries. Exhibit 5.17 shows the prices of the September P&G 85 call from 6/20/16 to 7/29/16, along with prices for September P&G 85 put and P&G stock. Suppose on June 30, Investor A bought a September 85 P&G call for $1.51 from Investor B when P&G was trading for $84.67. When the OCC breaks up the contract, it would have recorded Investor A's right to exercise with the OCC and Investor B's responsibility to sell P&G stock at $85 if a party long on the call contract decides to exercise and the OCC subsequently assigns B the responsibility. The transaction between A and B would lead to the following entry in the clearing firms records:

June 30 Clearinghouse Records for September P&G 85 Call

---

1. Investor A has the <u>right</u> to exercise.
2. Investor B has <u>responsibility.</u>

EXHIBIT 5.17   Prices on September P&G 85 Call, September P&G 85 Put, and P&G Stock, 6/20/16 to 7/29/16

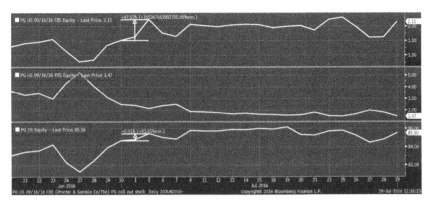

Suppose on July 5, when the price of P&G was trading at $85.50 and the price of the September P&G 85 call was trading at $2.22, Investor A decided to close her call position by selling a September 85 call at $2.22 to Investor C. After the OCC broke up this contract, it would have recorded a new entry showing Investor A with the responsibility of selling P&G stock at $X = \$85$ if assigned. This entry, however, would have canceled out Investor A's original entry, giving her the right to buy P&G stock at $X = \$85$:

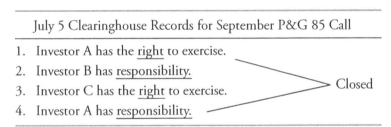

The OCC would have accordingly closed Investor A's position. Thus, Investor A bought the call for $1.51 and then closed her position by simply selling the call for $2.22 for a profit of $0.71. Her call sale, in turn, represents an offsetting position and is referred to as an *offset* or *closing sale*.

If seller B also had wanted to close his position on July 5, he could have done so by simply buying a September 85 P&G call for $2.22. For example, suppose Investor B feared that P&G stock would continue to increase and therefore decided to close his short position by buying a September 85 P&G call from Investor D for $2.22. After this transaction, the OCC would have again stepped in to break up the contract, and enter Investor B's and D's positions on its records. The OCC's records would have shown a new entry in which Investor B has the right to buy P&G at $85. This entry, in turn, would have canceled Investor B's previous entry in which he had a responsibility to sell P&G at $85 if assigned. The offsetting positions (the right to buy and the obligation to sell) would have canceled each other, and the OCC computer system simply would have erased both entries.

July 5 Clearinghouse Records for September P&G 85 Call

---

1. Investor B has <u>responsibility.</u>
2. Investor C has the <u>right</u> to exercise.   Closed
3. Investor B has the <u>right</u> to exercise.
4. Investor D has <u>responsibility.</u>

Since Investor B's second transaction serves to close his opening position, it is referred to as a *closing purchase*. In this case, Investor B loses $0.71 by closing: selling the call for $1.51 and buying it back for $2.22.

Operationally, the OCC functions similar to the futures exchanges clearinghouse through its members. Referred to as clearing firms, these members are typically investment firms that are members of the exchange. Each one maintains an account with the OCC, records and keeps track of the positions for each option buyer and seller the OCC places with it, maintains all margin positions, and contributes to the special fund used to guarantee assignment. To recapitulate, by breaking up each transaction, the OCC provides marketability to options by making it easier for investors to close their positions. The OCC also enhances the marketability of option contracts by guaranteeing that the terms of a contract will be fulfilled if a holder exercises.

Margin Requirements

To secure the OCCs underlying positions, exchange-traded option contracts have initial and maintenance margin requirements. The margin requirements on options apply only to the naked option writer. On most exchanges, the initial margin is the amount of cash or cash equivalents that must be deposited by the writer. In addition to the initial margin, the writer also has a maintenance margin requirement with the brokerage firm in which he has to keep the value of his account equal to certain percentage of the initial margin value. Thus, if the value of an option position moves against the writer, he is required to deposit additional cash or cash equivalents to satisfy his maintenance requirement.

In a covered call write position, the writer does not need to maintain a margin account, since she owns the underlying stock. The writer is required, however, to either keep the stock in escrow at the brokerage firm or if the stock is held at the writer's bank, have the bank issue an *escrow receipt,* which is a letter of guarantee from the bank to the brokerage firm stating it will deliver the writer's stock should there be an assignment. If the option expires or if the writer closes the position, she can have access to the stock. For a covered put position in which the writer has sold a put and the underlying stock short, the brokerage house generally requires the covered writer to maintain the usual margin requirements on a short sale.

Finally, for a spread, the short option position is considered covered by the long option. As a result, the margin requirements on the short position are not as large as a naked option write position. While spreads with different times to expiration and spreads with both different exercise prices and expirations are treated differently, as a general rule, if the spread results in a debit, the spreader must deposit the net cost of the spread in her margin account; if the spread results in a credit, the spreader must deposit the difference between the exercise prices.

Trading Cost

Through the option exchanges, brokers, dealers, market makers, specialists, and the OCC have created a network whereby an investor can buy and sell options in a matter of seconds. The cost of maintaining this complex system is paid for by investors through the commission costs they pay to their brokers, the bid-ask spread investors pay to market makers or specialists when they set up and then later close their positions, and the fees charged by the clearing firms of the OCC that are usually included in the brokerage commission and paid by their brokers.

In accordance with the Security Act Amendment of 1975, commissions on all security transactions are negotiable between the investor and the broker. The option buyer pays a commission when he buys the option and when he sells the option. If the option holder exercises, he is charged a commission for buying (calling) or selling (putting) the stock. Since the call (put) holder in exercising would eventually (initially) sell (buy) the stock, the total commission costs to exercise an option instead of closing it is relatively high.

Part of the commission fees investors pay their brokers goes to cover the fees charged by the clearing firms of the OCC for handling, recording, and intermediating option transactions. These fees range from $0.50 to $1.00 per contract. The OCC also imposes fees on market makers or specialists and other members for clearing their transactions. The fees are lower than those charged commission brokers handling the public's transactions.

The primary function of a market maker and specialist is to ensure a continuous market. To do this, they stand ready to buy and sell securities at their bid and ask prices. The bid-ask spread thus represents their compensation for providing liquidity. To the investor, though, the bid-ask spread represents another transaction cost involved in trading securities. If a market maker's bid price for P&G September 85 call is $2.16 and her ask price is $2.19 (see P&G description screen in Exhibit 5.16), an option buyer who paid $2.19 for the option, then immediately sold it for $2.16, would be paying the market maker $0.03 for the services of providing a continuous market.

An investor's dollar return from an option position takes the form of a capital gain or loss. For option buyers, taxable gains and losses result when they sell their options to close, when they sell stock from an exercised call, when they exercise a put, and when their options expire. For option writers, gains and losses occur when writers buy back their options to close, when they sell securities on an assigned call option, when they sell the securities obtained from an exercised put option that they have been assigned, and when the option expires.

Types of Option Transactions

The OCC provides marketability by making it possible for option investors to close their positions instead of exercising. In general, there are four types of trades investors of an exchange-traded option can make: opening, expiring, exercising, and closing transactions. The *opening transaction* occurs when investors initially buy or sell an option. An *expiring transaction,* in turn, is allowing the option to expire—that is, doing nothing when the expiration date arrives because the option is worthless (out of the money). If it is profitable, a holder can exercise. Finally, holders or writers of options can close their positions with *offsetting* or *closing transactions* or orders.

As a general rule, option holders should close their positions rather than exercise. If there is some time to expiration, an option holder who sells her option will receive a price that exceeds the exercise value. That is, if the holder sells the option, she will receive a price that is equal to an IV plus a TVP; if she exercises, however, her exercise value is only equal to the IV. As a result, by exercising instead of closing, she loses the TVP. Thus, an option holder in most cases should close her position instead of exercising. There are some exceptions to the general rule of closing instead of exercising. For example, if an American option on a stock that was to pay a high dividend exceeded the TVP on the option, then it would be advantageous to exercise.

Since many options are closed, the amount of trading and thus the marketability of a particular option can be determined by ascertaining the number of option contracts that are outstanding at a given point in time. The number of option contracts outstanding is referred to as *open interest.* Thus, in terms of closing transactions, open interest represents the number of closing transactions on an option that could be made before it expires. The exchange, in turn, keeps track of the amount of opening and closing transactions that occur. For example, an opening order to buy five calls would increase open interest by 5, and a closing order to sell five calls would lower open interest by 5. The open interest on the September 85 P&G call was 3,013 contracts on 7/29/16 (Exhibit 5.16).

Conclusion

In this chapter, we have provided an overview of options by defining option terms, examining fundamental option strategies, and defining some of the basic determinants of the price of an option. Most of our examples involved stock options. In the next chapter, we examine the markets for non-stock options.

BLOOMBERG: OPTIONS SCREENS

BLOOMBERG OMON
Listed options for a stock, index, currency, and futures can be found on the OMON screen. For a loaded security enter: OMON. OMON provides real-time pricing, market data, and data for exchange-traded call and put options for the selected underlying security. Other derivative screens for a loaded security of note include:

- CALL: Call Options
- PUT: Put Options
- CWS: Covered Option Write Screen
- GV: Volatility Graph
- HVT: Historical Volatility Table
- CT: Contract Table

UPLOADING AN OPTION CONTRACT

To upload an option menu screen, enter: Option's Ticker <Equity> (e.g., PG 9/16/16 C85 <Equity> for September 2016 P&G 85 call option; option tickers can be found on OMON. View screens to examine:

- DES: Description Screen
- GP: Price Graph

SECF FOR FINDING OPTIONS

The SECF screen can be used to find the tickers for an option contracts: SECF <Enter>; select "Equities" from the Category dropdown and select "Equity Options."

BLOOMBERG'S OPTION SCENARIO SCREEN, OSA

Profit and value graphs for options can be generated using the Bloomberg Option Scenario screen, OSA. To access OSA for a security, load the menu page of the security and type OSA (or click "OSA" from the menu). For example, for Procter & Gamble (PG) options:

1. Go to P&G equity menu screen: PG <Equity>.
2. Type "OSA."
3. On the OSA screen, click the "Positions" tab and then click "Add Listed Options" to bring up options listed on the stock. This brings up a screen showing the listed options from which to select (e.g., 1 call contract (100 calls) and 1 put contract (100 puts) on the October 2016 contract).
4. After selecting the positions, type 1 <Enter> (or click) to load positions and bring up the OSA Position screen.
5. On the Position screen, click the "Scenario Chart" tab at the top of the screen to bring up the profit graph. The profit graph shows profits for the strategy at expiration where the option price is trading at its intrinsic value and also at time periods prior where the option price is determined by an option-pricing model (described in Part 3). The profit graphs for different periods can be changed or deleted by using the select options at the top of the screen.
6. On the Scenario Chart screen, you can use the dropdown to change the y-axis from profits to "Market Value."
7. From the Position screen (click "Position" tab), you can select different positions and then click the "Scenario Chart" tab to view the profit graph (see Exhibit 5.18).

(Continued)

EXHIBIT 5.18   Example of Bloomberg Option Scenario Screen, OSA

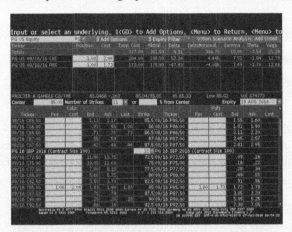

Profit Graphs for P&G Straddle, 7/27/2016

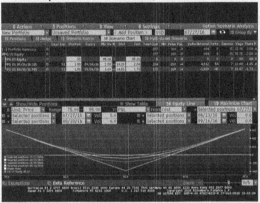

Call Price Curve and IV, 7/27/2016

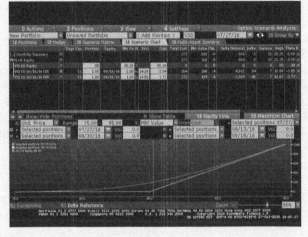

Selected References

Cox, J. C., and Rubinstein, M. *Option Markets*. Englewood Cliffs, NJ: Prentice-Hall, 1985.

Johnson, R. S. *Introduction to Derivatives: Options, Futures, and Swaps*. New York: Oxford University Press, 2009: Chapter 1.

Problems and Questions

1. Show graphically the profit and stock price relationships at expiration or if the option is exercised for the following fundamental option positions:

   a. Call Purchase
   b. Naked Call Write
   c. Covered Call Write
   d. Put Purchase
   e. Naked Put Write
   f. Covered Put Write

   In each case, assume the stock is trading at $50.00, the exercise price is $50.00, and the price of the call or put is at $3.00.

2. Show graphically the profit and stock price relationships at expiration for the following option positions. In each case, show the profit graph for each position at various stock prices and then aggregate the profits for the separate positions at each stock price to generate the profit graph for the total position.

   a. A straddle purchase formed with ABC call and put options, each with exercise prices of $60 and premiums of $5.
   b. A straddle write formed with ABC call and put options, each with exercise prices of $40 and premiums of $2.
   c. A covered call write formed by purchasing ABC stock at $48 and selling an ABC 50 call at $3.
   d. A call spread formed by buying an ABC 50 call at $3 and selling an ABC 55 put at $1.
   e. A put spread formed by buying an ABC 50 put at $1 and selling an ABC 55 put at $2.
   f. A stock insurance strategy formed by purchasing ABC stock at $50 and buying an ABC 50 put at $3.

3. Determine the break-even prices at expiration for the following:

   a. A straddle purchase formed with ABC call and put options, each with exercise prices of $60 and premiums of $5.
   b. A straddle write formed with ABC call and put options, each with exercise prices of $40 and premiums of $2.
   c. A covered call write formed by purchasing ABC stock at $45 and selling an ABC 50 call at $4.
   d. A covered put write formed by selling ABC stock short at $45 and selling an ABC 50 put at $6.
   e. A stock insurance strategy formed by purchasing ABC stock at $48 and buying an ABC 50 put at $4.

4. Compare and contrast buying stock with a call purchase strategy.

5. Compare and contrast selling stock short with a put purchase strategy.

6. Explain what arbitrageurs would do if the price of an American call on ABC stock with an exercise price of $50 were priced at $9 when the underlying price on ABC stock were trading at $60. What impact would their actions have in the option market on the call's price? Would arbitrageurs follow the same strategy if the call option were European? If not, why?

7. Explain what arbitrageurs would do if the price of an American put on ABC stock with an exercise price of $50 were priced at $9 when the underlying futures price on ABC stock were trading at $40. What impact would their actions have in the option market on the put's price?

8. Explain intuitively why call and put options are more valuable the greater their underlying security's variability.

9. Given a call and put with an exercise price of $60, a risk-free discount bond with face value of $60 and the same maturity as the options' expiration:

   a. Construct a table of expiration values (or cash flows) of a stock and put portfolio for stock values of $40, $50, $60, $70, and $80.

   b. Construct a table of expiration values (or cash flows) of a long bond and call values for stock values of $40, $50, $60, $70, and $80.

   c. Compare the cash flows for the stock and put portfolio with the call and bond portfolio. Comment on put-call parity.

10. Explain the role and functions of the Option Clearing Corporation.

11. Suppose in February Ms. X sold a June ABC 100 call contract to Mr. Z for $5, then later closed her position by buying a June ABC 100 for $7 from Mr. Y. Explain how the OCC would handle these contracts.

12. Explain the various types of option transactions.

13. Explain why option holders should, in most cases, close their options instead of exercising. Under what condition, would it be beneficial to exercise a call option early?

Bloomberg Exercises

1. Find descriptions, recent prices, and other information on the call and put options of a selected stock. From the loaded stock's menu screen, bring up:

   a. OMON

   b. CALL

   c. PUT

   d. GV, Volatility Graph

   e. HVT, Historical Volatility Table

   f. CT, Contract Table

2. Examine several of the call and put options you selected in Exercise 1 from screens shown on the option's menu screen: Option Ticker <Equity>. View screens on the option's menu: DES and GP.

3. Select a stock and bring up its equity screen: Stock Ticker <Equity>. Using the Bloomberg OSA screen, select a call and put option on the stock and evaluate the following option strategies on the stock with a profit graph:

a. Call purchase
b. Call sale
c. Put purchase
d. Put sale
e. Covered call write
f. Covered put write
g. Straddle purchase
h. Straddle sale

For a guide on using the OSA screen, see "Bloomberg's Option Scenario Screen" found in "Bloomberg: Options Screens."

4. Evaluate a covered write position for a selected stock using Bloomberg's Covered Option Write screen (CWS) for a loaded stock.

5. Use the Chart screen (Chart <Enter>) to create multigraphs for the historical prices of the stock, call, and put options you analyzed in Exercise 2. Select a time period that the contract was active. On the Chart Menu screen, select Standard G chart; once you have loaded your securities, go to "Edit" to put your graphs in separate panels.

a. Select a period in which you would have taken a call purchase position and calculate the profit from opening and closing at the call prices at the beginning and ending dates for your selected period. Calculate the losses if you had taken a naked call write position.

b. Select a period in which you would have taken a put purchase position and calculate the profits from opening and closing at the put prices at the beginning and ending dates for your selected period.

c. Select a period in which you would have taken a straddle purchase position and calculate the profits from opening and closing at the call and put prices at the beginning and ending dates for your selected period.

d. Select a period in which you would have taken a straddle write position and calculate the profits from opening and closing at the call and put prices at the beginning and ending dates for your selected period.

e. Using the annotation bar, apply the "% Change" tool to calculate the percentage change for some of your cases in (a) to (d), and then click the "News" icon on the annotation bar to find relevant news events on or preceding the opening date.

6. Use the GV screen for a loaded stock to evaluate its historical volatility, the stock price, and the price of an option on the stock (you can load your option on the screen). Examine the relations between the option price, stock price, and volatility.

CHAPTER 6

Non-Stock Options: Equity Index, Futures, OTC, and Embedded Options

Today, option contracts exist not only on stocks but also on futures contracts, foreign currencies, equity indexes, and debt and interest rate-sensitive securities. Given the number of futures contracts on commodities, equity indexes, currency, interest rates and bonds, there is an extensive market for options listed on those contracts. In addition to exchange-traded spot options and futures options, there is also a large over-the-counter (OTC) market in option contracts in the United States and a growing OTC market outside the United States. The option contracts offered in the OTC market include foreign currencies, Treasury securities, interest rate–related securities, and special types of interest rate products, such as interest rate calls and puts, caps, floors, and collars. These OTC options are primarily used by financial institutions and nonfinancial corporations to hedge their currency and interest rate positions. Finally, many equity and debt securities have embedded option characteristics. For example, the call and put features on corporate debt securities, the conversion clauses on convertible bonds, and the preemptive rights of existing stockholders are all embedded option characteristics associated with corporate securities.

In this chapter, we examine the different types of non-stock options available on both the organized exchanges and the OTC market. We begin, by first examining exchanged-traded equity-index options and the extensive market for futures options. This is followed by an analysis of OTC options. We then conclude the chapter by examining embedded options and the options created by corporations.

Equity-Index Options

Trading in equity index options began in March 1983 when the CBOE introduced an option on the Standard and Poor's 100 index (S&P 100). Because of its hedging uses by institutional investors, this option quickly became one of the most highly traded options. In late April 1983, the American Stock Exchange began offering trading on an option on the Major Market Index (MMI), an index similar to the Dow Jones Industrial Average (DJIA). The introduction of the AMEX's option soon was followed by the New York Stock Exchange's listing of the NYSE stock index option and the Philadelphia Exchange's Value Line index option (index of 1,700 stocks) and the National Over-the-Counter index option (index of 100 OTC stocks). Today, the most popular spot index options include options on the S&P 500, NASDAQ 100, Russell 2,000, and the S&P 500 Mini. Exhibit 6.1 shows a listing of dollar-denominated equity index

EXHIBIT 6.1 Equity Index Spot Options

Index Ticker	Name
SPX Index	S&P 500 Index
VIX Index	Chicago Board Options Exchange SPX Volatility Index
MXEF Index	MSCI Emerging Markets Index
MXWO Index	MSCI World Index
NDX Index	NASDAQ 100 Stock Index
SOX Index	Philadelphia Stock Exchange Semiconductor Index
MXEA Index	MSCI EAFE Index
BKX Index	KBW Bank Index
RIY Index	Russell 1000 Index
XAU Index	Philadelphia Stock Exchange Gold and Silver Index
RLV Index	Russell 1000 Value Index
OEX Index	S&P 100 Index
RLG Index	Russell 1000 Growth Index
OSX Index	Philadelphia Stock Exchange Oil Service Sector Index
RDXUSD Index	Russian Depositary Index USD
UTY Index	Philadelphia Stock Exchange Utility Index
M1EF Index	MSCI Emerging Markets Net Return USD Index
M1WO Index	MSCI World Net Return USD Index
RUY Index	Russell 2000 Index/Old
XSP Index	S&P 500 Mini
DJX Index	Dow Jones Industrial Average Chicago Board Options Exchange
RVX Index	CBOE Russell 2000 Volatility Index
HGX Index	Philadelphia Stock Exchange Housing Sector Index
SPXPM Index	S&P 500 PM Index
M1APJ Index	MSCI AC Asia Pacific ex Japan Net Return USD Index
M1MS Index	MSCI EM Asia Net Return USD Index
BVZ Index	CBOE Binary Options VIX
RIOB Index	FTSE Russia IOB Index
MNX Index	Chicago Board Options Exchange Mini NDX 100 Share Index
M1LA Index	MSCI EM Latin America Net Return USD Index
DMSCIEF1 Index	MSCI EM Index
M1EE Index	MSCI EM Europe Middle East and Africa Net Return USD Index
XEO Index	S&P 100 Index for European Style Options

EXHIBIT 6.2   S&P 500 and NASDAQ 100 Options, 8/23/16

2,200 S&P 500 December 2016 Call

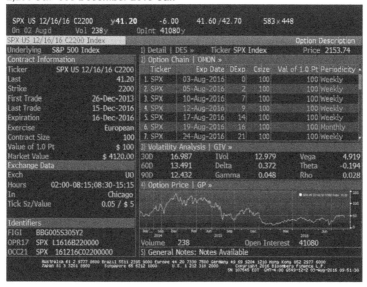

December 4,100 NASDAQ 100 Put

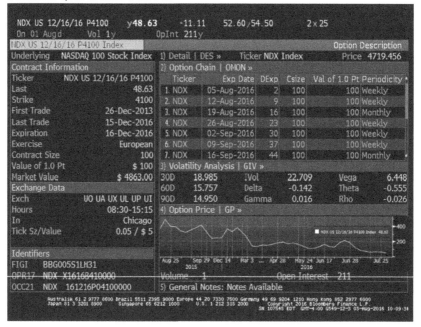

options, and Exhibit 6.2 shows the Description screens for the December 2,200 S&P 500 call and December 4,100 NASDAQ 100 put (NDX).

Theoretically, an index option can be thought of as an option to buy (call) or sell (put) a portfolio of stocks comprising the index in their correct proportions. Unlike stock options, index options have a cash settlement feature. When such an option is exercised, the assigned writer pays the exercising holder the difference between the exercise price and the spot index at the close of trading on the exercising day. Thus, an index option can be viewed as an option giving the holder the right to purchase (call) or sell (put) cash at a specific exercise price. Specifically, for an index call option:

> **Definition:** A call option on an index gives the holder the right to purchase an amount of cash equal to the closing spot index (S_t) on the exercising day at the call's exercise price. To settle, the exercising holder receives a cash settlement of $S_t - X$ from the assigned writer.

For example, the December 2,200 S&P 500 call shown in Exhibit 6.2 gives the holder the right to buy cash equal to the closing spot index on the exercising day for $2,200 (as discussed below, there also is a multiplier). If the holder exercises when the spot index is $2,300, he in effect is exercising the right to buy $2,300 of cash for $X = \$2,200$. With cash settlement, the assigned writer simply pays the holder $100.

The put option on an index, on the other hand, gives the holder the right to sell cash equal to the spot index value:

> **Definition:** A put option on an index gives the holder the right to sell cash equal to the closing spot index on the exercising date at the put's exercise price. To settle, the exercising holder receives a cash settlement amount of $X - S_t$ from the assigned writer.

Thus, the holder of the December 4,100 NASDAQ 100 put who exercises the put when the spot index is at $4,000 could view exercising as the equivalent to selling $4,000 cash to the assigned writer for $4,100. The writer would settle by paying the holder $X - S_t = \$100$.

The cash settlement feature of index options is one characteristic that differentiates them from stock options. Several other differentiating features of index options should be noted. First, the size of an index option is equal to a multiple of the index value. The S&P 500 and NASDAQ 100 index options, for example, have contract multiples of $100. Thus, the actual exercise price on the S&P 500 is $220,000 = (2,200)(\$100)$. Second, the expiration features on many index options are similar to stock options. However, some index options have a shorter expiration cycle (see the expiration cycle on the Description screens for the S&P call and NASDAQ put in Exhibit 6.2). The CBOE also offers longer maturity contracts on indexes—LEAPS. Third, American index options have an *end-of-the-day exercise* feature. When an index option is exercised, the closing value of the spot index on the exercising day is used to determine the cash settlement. Since the spot index is computed continuously throughout the day, it is possible for a holder to exercise an in-the-money call early in the day, only to have it closed at the end of the day out of the money (in such a case, the holder pays the writer the difference between X and S_t). Thus, an index option holder should wait until late in the day before giving his exercise notice. Fourth, a number of index options are European; this is the case for the S&P 500 and

NASDAQ 100 options shown in Exhibit 6.2. Fifth, the tax treatment on index option positions differs from stock options in that all realized and unrealized gains on index options that occur during the year are subject to taxes, and all realized and unrealized losses occurring during the year can offset an investor's capital gains. Finally, the margin requirements for index options are similar to those for stock options, except for covered write positions, which have the same margin requirements as naked index option positions.

Equity index options give speculators a tool for generating a number of different investment strategies. As we examined in Chapter 5 and will examine in more detail in Chapter 7, strategies such as outright call and put positions, straddles, and spreads can be formed with index options, making it possible for investors to speculate on expected bullish, bearish, or even stable markets with different return-risk exposures.

Call Price and Intrinsic Value

Like stock options, in the absence of arbitrage the price of an equity index option must be at least equal to its intrinsic value. Recall the arbitrage strategy used when an American call option on a stock was priced below its intrinsic value: the strategy required purchasing the call and the stock and exercising the option. When an index option is exercised, the assigned writer pays the exercising holder cash equal to the difference between the closing day spot index price and the exercise price. Because of this cash settlement feature, the arbitrage strategy for index options priced below their intrinsic values does not require taking an actual position in the underlying security. For example, if an American 2,200 S&P 500 call were trading at $50 at the close of trading and the closing spot index was at 2,260, then an arbitrageur could buy the call contract for $5,000 (50 times the $100 multiplier) and immediately exercise to receive a $6,000 cash settlement from the assigned writer to realize a $1,000 riskless profit. Such actions by arbitrageurs would push the price of the 2,200 S&P 500 call to at least its IV of 60 when the index is at 2,260. Exhibit 6.3 shows the *IV* line and the call price curve for the December 2016 S&P 500.

If an American NASDAQ 100 put with an exercise price of 4,100 were trading below its IV, say, at $90 when the NASDAQ 100 index was at 4,000, then an arbitrageur could buy the put contract for $9,000 (90 times the $100 multiplier) and immediately exercise to receive a $10,000 cash settlement from the assigned writer to realize a $1,000 riskless profit. Such actions by arbitrageurs would push the price of the 4,100 put to at least its IV of 100 when the index is at 4,000. Exhibit 6.3 shows the *IV* line and put price curve for the December 2016 NASDAQ 100 put.

It should be noted that the condition that the call and put must trade at prices at least equal to their IV holds only for American options; that is, to execute the above arbitrage strategies requires immediate exercise of the options. Many index options, however, are European, which cannot be exercised early. The minimum boundary conditions for a European call is $\text{Max}(S_t - PV(X), 0)$ and for a European put is $\text{Max}(PV(X) - S_t, 0)$. The proofs for these conditions are presented in Chapter 9.

EXHIBIT 6.3 Option Price Curves: December 2,220 S&P 500 Call and December 4,100 NASDAQ 100 Put

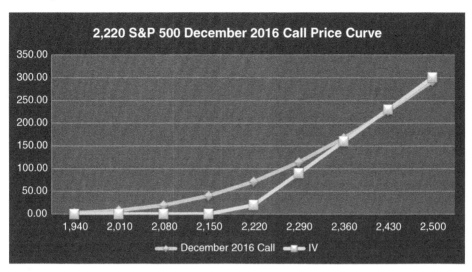

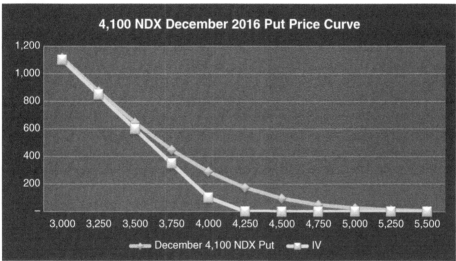

Spot Foreign Currency Options

In 1982, the Philadelphia Stock Exchange (PHLX) became the first organized exchange to offer trading in foreign currency options on the major currencies. The contract sizes for many of the options were equal to half the size of the currency's futures listed on the Chicago Mercantile Exchange (CME). With the emergence of futures options on currency, currency hedgers and speculators have opted to use futures options on currency more than the spot options. Today, there are listed currency options on some organized exchanges, but the market is thin.

Spot Bond and Interest Rate Options

The CBOE, AMEX, and PHLX did at one time offer options on actual Treasury securities and Eurodollar deposits. These spot options, however, proved to be less popular than futures options on these securities, and as a result, they were delisted. A number of non-US exchanges, though, do list options on actual debt securities, typically government securities.

Futures Options

A futures option gives the holder the right to take a position in a futures contract. Specifically, a call option on a futures contract gives the holder the right to take a long position in the underlying futures contract, and a put option on a futures contract gives the holder the right to take a short position in the underlying futures contract.

A call option on a futures contract gives the holder the right to take a long position in the underlying futures contract when she exercises and requires the writer to take the corresponding short position in the futures. Upon exercise, the holder of a futures call option in effect takes a long position in the futures contract at the current futures price and the writer takes the short position and pays the holder via the clearinghouse the difference between the current futures price and the exercise price. In contrast, a put option on a futures option entitles the holder to take a short futures position and the writer the long position. Thus, whenever the put holder exercises, he in effect takes a short futures position at the current futures price, and the writer takes the long position and pays the holder through the clearinghouse the difference between the exercise price and the current futures price. Like all option positions, the futures option buyer pays an option premium for the right to exercise, and the writer, in turn, receives a credit when he sells the option and is subject to initial and maintenance margin requirements on the option position.

In practice, when the holder of a futures call option exercises, the clearinghouse establishes for the exercising option holder a long futures position at the futures price equal to the exercise price and a short futures position for the assigned writer. Once this is done, margins on both positions are required, and the positions are marked to market at the current settlement price on the futures. When the positions are marked to market, then the exercising call holder's margin account on his long position will be equal to the difference between the futures price and the exercise price, $f_t - X$, while the assigned writer will have to deposit funds or monies worth $f_t - X$ to satisfy her maintenance margin on her short futures position. Thus, when a futures call is exercised, the holder takes a long position at f_t with a margin account worth $f_t - X$; if he were to immediately close the futures, he would receive cash worth $f_t - X$ from the clearinghouse. The assigned writer, in turn, is assigned a short position at f_t and must deposit $f_t - X$ to meet her margin. If the futures option is a put, then the same procedure applies, except the holder takes a short position at f_t (when the exercised position is marked to market), with a margin account worth $X - f_t$, and the writer is assigned a long position at f_t and must deposit $X - f_t$ to meet her margin.

Market

Before 1936, the US futures exchanges offered futures options for a number of years. In 1936, though, the instruments were banned when US security regulations were tightened following the 1929 stock market crash. Futures options continued to be offered on some foreign exchanges. The current US market for futures options began in 1982 when the Commodity Futures Trading Commission (CFTC) initiated a pilot program in which it allowed each futures exchange to offer one option on one of its futures contracts. In 1987, the CFTC gave the exchanges permanent authority to offer futures options. Currently, the most popular futures options are the options on the financial futures: SP 500, T-bond (CBT), T-note (CBT), Eurodollar deposit (CME), and the major foreign currencies (CME). In addition to options on financial futures contracts, futures options also are available on gold, precious metals, livestock, food and fiber, petroleum, and grains and oil. Many of these contracts have expiration months, position limits, and contract specifications similar to their underlying futures contracts. Some futures options contracts, though, do not have the same expiration date as their underlying futures contract. Exhibit 2.1 identifies which of the listed currency futures also have an option on the futures contract, Exhibit 3.1 shows a similar identification for equity indexes, and Exhibit 4.1 shows one for bond and interest rate futures contracts. Exhibit 6.4 shows a listing of select nonfinancial futures options contracts offered by CBT, CME, NYMEX, and ICE.

Equity Index Futures Options

Exhibit 6.5 shows the Bloomberg Description screen for a call option on the December S&P 500 futures contract. The option has an exercise price of 2,155, $250 multiplier, and expires at the same time as the futures contract (December 16). On 8/4/16, the futures options were priced at 70.10 or $17,525 (= (70.10)($250)).

Some of the characteristics of the S&P 500 futures options can be seen by examining the profit relationships for the fundamental strategies formed with these options. Exhibits 6.6a and 6.6b show the profit graphs for the call purchase and sale positions on the December S&P 500 futures option described in Exhibit 6.5, and Exhibit 6.6c and 6.6d show the profit graphs for put purchase and sale positions for the December S&P 500 futures put with an exercise price of 2,155, and put premium of 75.10 (prices on 8/4/16).

The call purchase strategy in Exhibit 6.6a reflects cases in which the holder exercises the call at expiration, if profitable. For example, at $f_T = 2,350$, the holder of the 2,155 futures calls would realize a cash flow of $48,750 and a profit of $31,225 (= $48,750 − (70.10)($250)). That is, upon exercising, the holder would assume a long position in the expiring S&P 500 futures at 2,350, which she subsequently would close by taking an offsetting short futures position at 2,350, and then receive $48,750 from the assigned writer: $(f_T − X)\$250 = (2,350 − 2,155)(\$250) = \$48,750$. If f_T is less than or equal to $X = \$2,155$, she would not exercise, resulting in a limited loss of $17,525. The opposite profit and futures price relation is attained for a naked call write position (Exhibit 6.6b). In this case, if the index is at 2,155 or less, the writer of

EXHIBIT 6.4 Select Nonfinancial Futures with Listed Options

Ticker	Description	Category	Type	Options
Chicago Board of Trade: CBT			Futures	Yes
BOA Comdty	Soybean Oil	Soy: SOY	Futures	Yes
CA Comdty	Corn	Corn: CORN	Futures	Yes
DLA Comdty	Ethanol, CME Futures	Refined Products: REFP	Futures	Yes
KWA Comdty	KC HRW Wheat	Wheat: WHET	Futures	Yes
OA Comdty	Oats	Other Grain: OGRN	Futures	Yes
RRA Comdty	Rice, Rough	Other Grain: OGRN	Futures	Yes
SA Comdty	Soybean	Soy: SOY	Futures	Yes
SMA Comdty	Soybean Meal	Soy: SOY	Futures	Yes
WA Comdty	Wheat	Wheat: WHET	Futures	Yes
NYMEX Exchange: NYM			Futures	Yes
BZAA Comdty	Crude Oil, Brent Last Day	Crude Oil: CRDO	Futures	Yes
CLA Comdty	Crude Oil, WTI	Crude Oil: CRDO	Futures	Yes
HNYA Comdty	Natural Gas Quadultimate Options	Natural Gas: NATG	Futures	Yes
HOA Comdty	NY Harbor ULSD Fut	Refined Products: REFP	Futures	Yes
HRCA Comdty	Steel, Hot-Rolled Coil	Base Metal: BMTL	Futures	Yes
NGA Comdty	Natural Gas	Natural Gas: NATG	Futures	Yes
PAA Comdty	Palladium	Precious Metal: PMTL	Futures	Yes
PLA Comdty	Platinum	Precious Metal: PMTL	Futures	Yes
XBA Comdty	Gasoline, RBOB	Refined Products: REFP	Futures	Yes
Chicago Mercantile Exchange: CME				
CHEA Comdty	Cheese	Foodstuff: FOOD	Futures	Yes
DAA Comdty	Milk	Foodstuff: FOOD	Futures	Yes
DRWA Comdty	Dry Whey Future	Foodstuff: FOOD	Futures	Yes
FCA Comdty	Cattle, Feeder	Livestock: LSTK	Futures	Yes
GIA Index	Goldman Sachs Commodity	Non-Equity Index: NEIX	Futures	Yes
KVA Comdty	Milk, Class IV	Foodstuff: FOOD	Futures	Yes
LBA Comdty	Lumber	Industrial Material: IMAT	Futures	Yes
LCA Comdty	Cattle, Live	Livestock: LSTK	Futures	Yes
LEA Comdty	Milk, Non-Fat Dry	Foodstuff: FOOD	Futures	Yes
LHA Comdty	Lean Hogs	Livestock: LSTK	Futures	Yes
M1A Index	HDD, Minneapolis Seasonal	Weather: WTHR	Futures	Yes
SPA Index	S&P 500	Equity Index: EQIX	Futures	Yes
V6A Comdty	Butter, Cash Settled	Foodstuff: FOOD	Futures	Yes
ICE Futures Europe - Commodities: ICE				
COA Comdty	Crude Oil, Brent	Crude Oil: CRDO	Futures	Yes
DFA Comdty	Coffee, Robusta 10 Tonne	Foodstuff: FOOD	Futures	Yes
ENA Comdty	Crude Oil, WTI	Crude Oil: CRDO	Futures	Yes
FNA Comdty	Natural Gas	Natural Gas: NATG	Futures	Yes
MOA Comdty	Emissions - EUA	Emissions: EMIS	Futures	Yes
NVA Comdty	Heating Oil	Refined Products: REFP	Futures	Yes
QCA Comdty	London Cocoa Future	Foodstuff: FOOD	Futures	Yes
QKA Comdty	Wheat	Wheat: WHET	Futures	Yes
QSA Comdty	Low Sulphur Gasoil Futures (G)	Refined Products: REFP	Futures	Yes
QWA Comdty	Sugar	Foodstuff: FOOD	Futures	Yes
XAA Comdty	Coal, Rotterdam Monthly	Coal: COAL	Futures	Yes
XOA Comdty	Coal, Richard Bay Monthly	Coal: COAL	Futures	Yes
XWA Comdty	Coal, Newcastle Monthly	Coal: COAL	Futures	Yes
YGPA Comdty	Gasoline	Refined Products: REFP	Futures	Yes

EXHIBIT 6.5   Description Screen for December S&P 500 Futures Call: $X = 2,155$, $C = 70.20$; 8/4/16

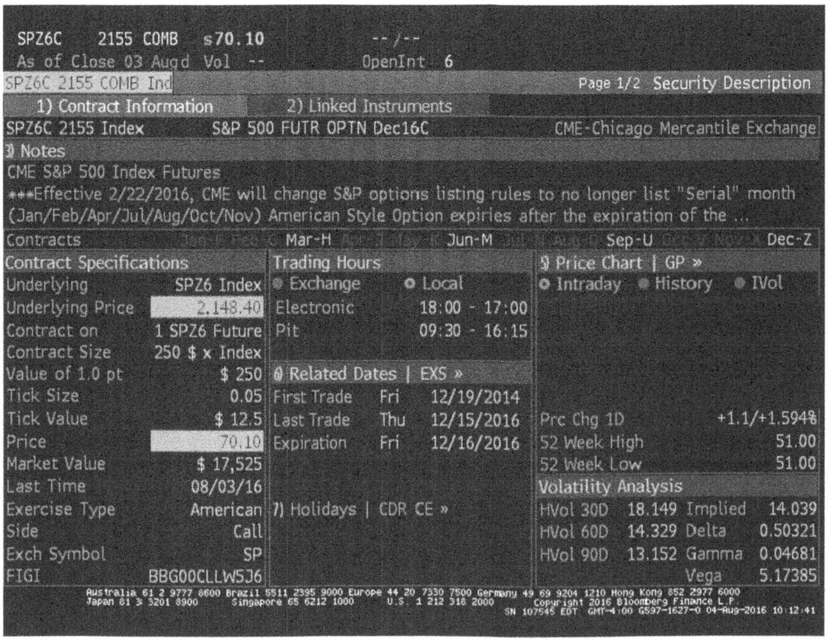

a 2,155 S&P 500 futures call would earn the premium of $17,525 (= (70.10)($250)) and if $f_T > 2,155$, he, upon assignment, would have to pay the difference between f_T and X and would have to assume the short position.

Exhibits 6.6c and 6.6d show the long and short put positions. In the case of a put purchase, if the holder exercises when f_T is less than X, then she will receive $X - f_T$ and a short futures position that she can offset. For example, if the put exercised when $f_T = 1,950$, then she would receive $51,250 (= (2,155 - 1,950)($250)) from the assigned writer and take the short position in the 1,950 December 500 futures contract, that she would close by taking a long position in the S&P 500 futures contract at 1,950. Her profit would be $32,475 (= $51,250 - (75.10)($250)). If f_T were greater than or equal to the $X = \$2,155$, she would not exercise, resulting in a limited losses of $18,775. The put writer's position would be just the opposite (Exhibit 6.6d).

Currency Futures Options

Exhibit 6.7 shows the Bloomberg Description screen and profit graph for a put option on the December British pound futures contract. The option has an exercise price of $1.30/BP, contract size of 62,500 BP (same as the underlying futures contract), and expiration of 12/9/16, which preceded the futures expiration of 12/16/16. On 8/4/16, the BP futures put option was priced at $0.0252/BP or $1,575 per contract (= ($0.0252/BP)(62,500 BP)).

EXHIBIT 6.6   Fundamental Futures Options Profit Graphs for December S&P 500 Futures

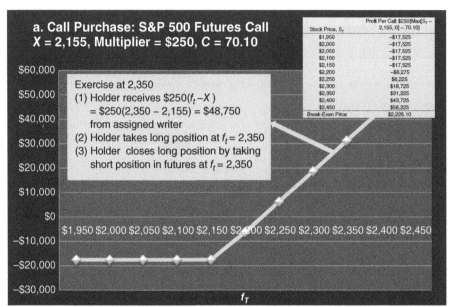

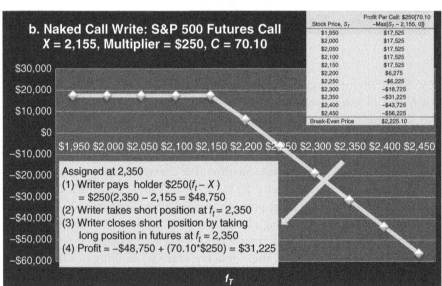

The profit graph and table in the exhibit show limited losses equal to the premium of $1,575 when the December British pound futures contract is priced at $f_t = \$1.30$ or greater, a break-even price of $1.2748/BP, and profits increasing as the future price decreases past its break-even price. If the put were exercised when $f_T = \$1.20/BP$, then the exercising holder would receive $6,250 (= ($1.30/BP − $1.20/BP)(62,500 BP)) from the assigned writer and take the short position in the December British pound

EXHIBIT 6.6 (*Continued*)

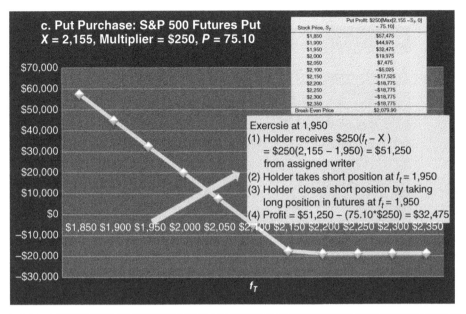

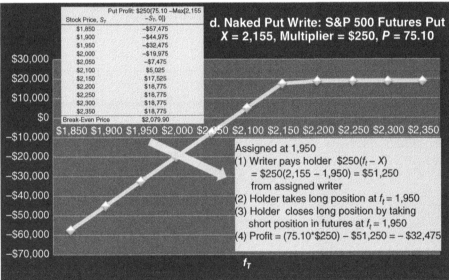

futures contract at $f_T = \$1.20/BP$, which he would close by taking a long position the December futures contract at $1.20/BP. His profit would be $4,675 (= $6,250 − $1,575).

Commodity and Energy Futures Options

There are an extensive number of futures options contracts on agriculture and livestock, energy and the environment, and metals offered by the CBT, CME, NYMEX, ICE,

EXHIBIT 6.7 Description Screen and Profit Graph for December British Pound Futures Put: $X = \$1.30$, $P = \$0.0252$, Size $= 62,500$ BP, 8/6/16

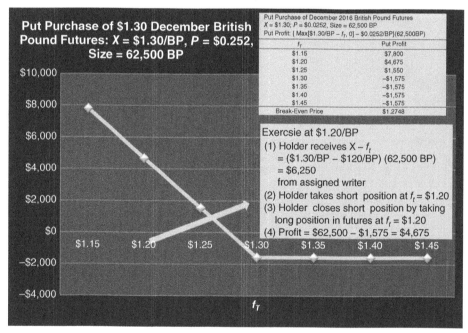

and other exchanges. Exhibit 6.8 shows the Bloomberg Description screen and profit graph for a call option on the CBT December corn futures contract. The option has an exercise price of $3.30/bu., contract size of 5,000 bu., and expiration date of 11/16/16 (the underlying futures contract's expiration delivery period is 12/01/16 to 12/16/16). On 8/8/16, the December corn futures call option was priced at $0.20/bu. or $1,000 per contract (= ($0.20/bu.)(5,000 bushels)).

EXHIBIT 6.8 Description Screen and Profit Graph for December Corn Futures Call: $X = \$3.30/\text{bu.}$, $C = \$0.20/\text{bu.}$, Size = 5,000 bushels, 8/8/16

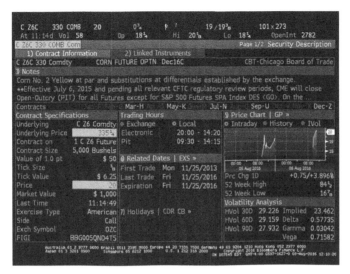

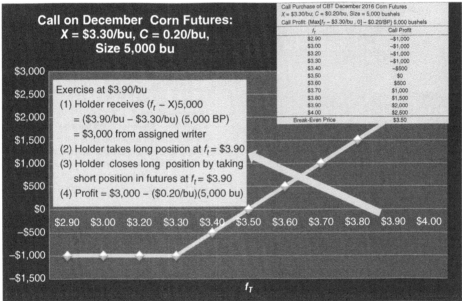

Exhibit 6.9 shows the Bloomberg Description screen and profit graph for a put option on the NYMEX December futures crude oil contract. The option has an exercise price of $45, contract size of 1,000 barrels, and expiration date of 11/16/16 (the underlying futures contract's expiration delivery period is 12/01/16 to 12/31/16). On 8/8/16, the December crude oil futures put option was priced at $3.95/brl. or $3,950 per contract (= ($3.95/brl.)(1,000 barrels)).

EXHIBIT 6.9 Description Screen and Profit Graph for December Crude Oil Futures Put:
$X = \$45.00/\text{brl.}$, $P = \$3.72$ brl., Size = 1,000 brl., 8/8/16

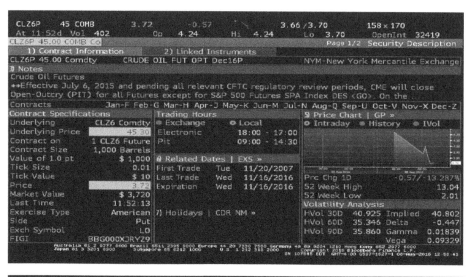

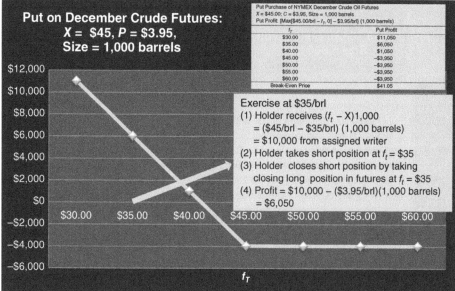

T-Note Futures Options

The CBT offers trading on futures options on T-bonds and T-notes with maturities of 2, 5, and 10 years. The premiums on the call and put option contracts on the T-bond and T-note futures are quoted as a percentage of the face value of the underlying bond or note. For example, a buyer of the 122 December 2016 five-year T-note futures call contract (see Exhibit 6.10) that is trading at 56 (or 0 56/64 or = 0.875) would pay

EXHIBIT 6.10 Description Screen and Profit Graphs for December Five-Year T-Note Futures: $X = \$122,000$, and Profit Graphs for Call Purchase, Naked Call Write, and Put Purchase with $C = \$2,130$, $P = \$2,130$

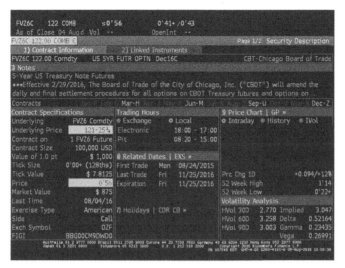

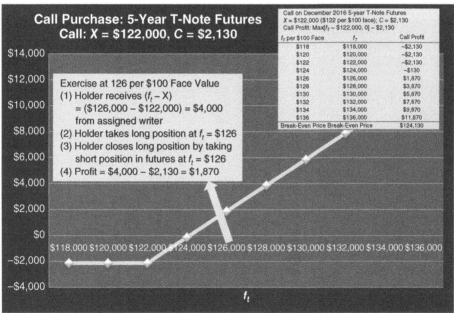

$875 for the option to take a long position in the December five-year T-note at an exercise price of $122,000 and expiration of 11/25/16 (note the T-note futures has a deliver period during the month of December and the option has an exercise date). If long-term rates were to subsequently drop, causing the December T-bond futures price to increase to $f_t = 125$, then the holder, upon exercising, would have a long position

EXHIBIT 6.10 (*Continued*)

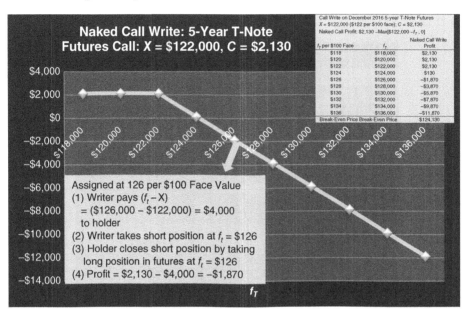

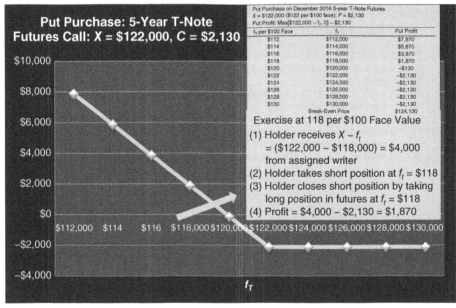

in the December T-note futures contract and a margin account worth $3,000. If she closed her futures contract at 125, she would have a profit of $2,125:

$$\text{Value of Margin} = \frac{f_t - X}{100}\ (\$100{,}000) = \left[\frac{125 - 122}{100}\right] \$100{,}000 = \$3{,}000$$

$$\pi = \$3{,}000 - \frac{56/64}{100}(\$100{,}000) = \$2{,}125$$

By contrast, if five-year T-note rates were stable or were to increase resulting in T-note prices below 122, then the call would be worthless and the holder would simply allow it to expire, losing the $875 premium. Exhibit 6.10 shows the profit graphs for the call purchase, call write, and put purchase positions.

Eurodollar Futures Options

The CME offers trading on short-term interest rate futures options on Eurodollar deposits and the 30-day LIBOR contracts. The maturities of the options correspond to the maturities on the underlying futures contracts, and the exercise quotes are based on the system used for quoting the futures contracts that was presented in Chapter 4. That is, the exercise prices on the Eurodollar contracts are quoted in terms of an CME index (I), which is equal to 100 minus the annual discount yield: $I = 100 - R_D$. Exhibit 6.11 shows the Bloomberg Description screen and profit graph for a December Eurodollar futures call with an exercise price of 99.25 ($R_D = 0.75$). The actual exercise price on the December futures contract is $998,125:

$$X = \frac{100 - R_D(0.25)}{100}(\$1,000,000)$$

$$X = \frac{100 - (100 - 99.25)(0.25)}{100}\$1,000,000 = \$998,125$$

The option premiums on Eurodollar futures options are quoted in terms of an index point system. For Eurodollars, the dollar value of an option quote is based on a $25 value for each basis point underlying a $1 million Eurodollar face value. The actual quotes are in percentage; thus, the 0.0225 quote for the December Eurodollar futures call shown in Exhibit 6.11 would imply a price of $25 times 2.25 basis points: ($25)(2.25) = $56.25. In addition, for the closest maturing month, the options are quoted to the nearest quarter of a basis point; for other months, they are quoted to the nearest half of a basis point.

An investor buying the 99.25 December call on 8/6/16 would therefore pay $56.25 for the right to take a long position in the CME's $1 million December Eurodollar futures contract at an exercise price of $998,125. If short-term rates were to subsequently drop, causing the March Eurodollar futures price to increase to an index price of 99.75 ($R_D = 0.25$ and $f_t = [[100 - (100 - 99.75)(0.25)]/100]($1,000,000) = \$999,375$), the holder, upon exercising, would have a long position in the CME December Eurodollar futures contract and a futures margin account worth $1,250. If she closed the long futures position at 99.75, she would realize a profit of $1,193.75:

$$\text{Value of margin} = f_t - X = \$999,375 - \$998,125 = \$1,250$$

$$\text{Value of margin} = \$25\,(\text{Futures index} - \text{Exercise index})$$

$$\text{Value of margin} = \$25[99.75 - 99.25](100) = \$1,250$$

$$\pi = \$1,250 - \$56.25 = \$1,193.75$$

EXHIBIT 6.11   Description Screen and Profit Graph for December Eurodollar Futures Call: $X =$ $998,125, $C = 56.25$, 8/6/16

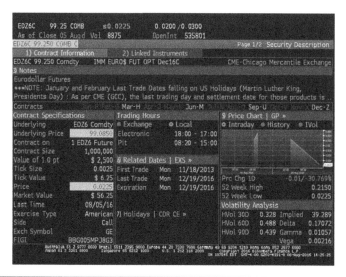

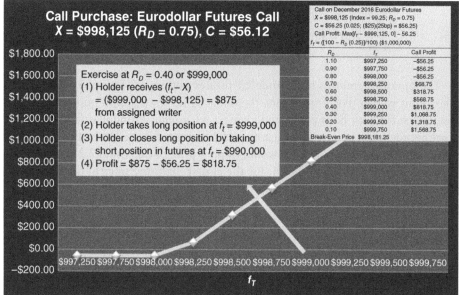

If short-term rates were at $R_D = 0.75\%$ and stayed there or increased, then the call would be worthless and the holder would simply allow the option to expire, losing her $56.125 premium. Exhibit 6.11 shows the profit graph and table for the December Eurodollar future call.

Differences between Futures and Spot Options

The pricing models for spot and futures options, which we examine in Part 3, show that the two instruments are equivalent if the options and the futures contract expire at the same time, the carrying-costs model governing futures prices holds, and the options are European. In contrast, spot and futures options will differ to the extent that these conditions do not hold. There are, however, several factors that serve to differentiate the two contracts. First, since most futures contracts are relatively more liquid than their corresponding spot security, it is usually easier to form hedging or arbitrage strategies with futures options than with spot options. Second, futures options often are easier to exercise than their corresponding spot. For example, to exercise an option on a T-bond or foreign currency futures contract, one simply assumes the futures position; exercising a spot T-bond or foreign currency option, though, requires an actual purchase or delivery. Finally, most futures options are traded on the same exchange as their underlying futures contract, while most spot options are traded on exchanges different from their underlying securities. This, in turn, makes it easier for futures options traders to implement arbitrage and hedging strategies than spot options traders. For these reasons, the market for futures options is more actively traded than that for spot options.

Futures Options Pricing Relations

Like a spot option, the price on an American futures call option at time t must be at least equal to the call's intrinsic value, IV, as defined by the price on the futures contract at time t:

$$C_t^a \geq IV_t = \text{Max}[f_t - X, 0]$$

If this condition does not hold, an arbitrageur could buy the call, exercise, and close the futures position. For example, if a $45 call on the NYMEX crude oil futures contract were trading at $4.00 when the futures contract was trading at $50, an arbitrageur could (1) buy the call at $4.00, (2) exercise the call to obtain $f_t - X = $50 - $45 = 5.00 from the assigned writer plus a long position in the December crude oil futures contract priced at $50.00, and (3) close the long futures position by immediately taking an offsetting short position at $50.00. Doing this, an arbitrageur would realize a riskless profit of $1.00 or $1,000 per contract (= ($1.00/brl.)(1,000 barrels)).

Thus, in the absence of arbitrage the price of a futures call must trade at a price at least equal to its IV and increase as the futures price increases when it is in the money. Prior to expiration, the call will also trade with a time value premium: $C = IV + TVP$. Exhibit 6.12 shows the IV line and the call price curve for the NYMEX December futures call with an exercise price of $45 and with 100 days to expiration.

Arbitrage also ensures that the price of an American futures put option at time t must be at least equal to the call's intrinsic value, IV:

$$P_t^a \geq IV_t = \text{Max}[X - f_t, 0]$$

If this condition does not hold, an arbitrageur could buy the put, exercise, and close the futures position. For example, if a $45 put on the NYMEX crude oil futures contract were trading at $4.00 when the futures contract was trading at $40, an

EXHIBIT 6.12 Futures Call Price Curve

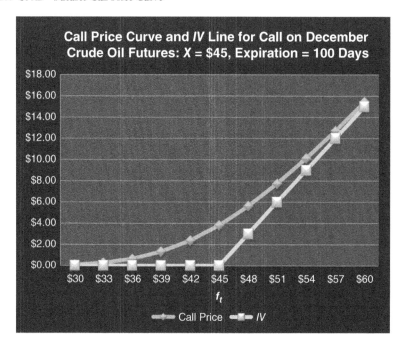

arbitrageur could (1) buy the put at $4.00, (2) exercise the put to obtain $X - f_t =$ $45 − $40 = $5.00 from the assigned writer plus a short position in the December crude oil futures contract priced at $40.00, and (3) close the short futures position by immediately taking an offsetting long position at $40.00. Doing this, an arbitrageur would realize a riskless profit of $1.00, or $1,000 per contract (= ($1.00/brl.)(1,000 barrels)). Thus, the price for a futures put must trade at a price at least equal to its IV, and increase as the futures price decreases when it is in the money. Exhibit 6.13 shows the *IV* line and the call price curve for the NYMEX December futures put with an exercise price of $45 and with 100 days to expiration.

Closing Futures Options

Like the OCC for spot options, the clearinghouses on the futures exchanges by intermediating each contract make it possible for option investors to close their positions instead of exercising. As a general rule, futures option holders should close their positions rather than exercise. If there is some time to expiration, an option holder who sells her option will receive a price that exceeds the exercise value: that is, if the holder sells the option, she will receive a price that is equal to an IV plus a TVP; if she exercises, however, her exercise value is only equal to the IV. As a result, by exercising instead of closing, she loses the TVP.

It should be noted that while the technicalities on exercising futures options are cumbersome, the profits and losses from closing a futures options are usually realized by simply buying (selling) and selling (buying) the option. Exhibit 6.14 shows the yields on five-year Treasuries from 4/1/16 to 8/10/16, along with the prices on

EXHIBIT 6.13 Futures Put Price Curve

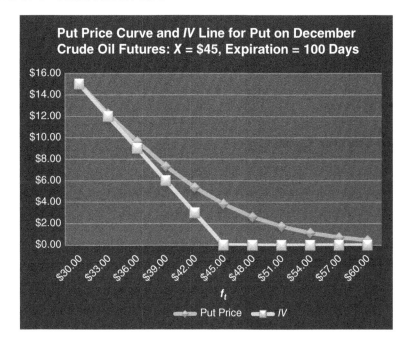

EXHIBIT 6.14 Price Graphs: Five-Year Constant Maturity US Treasury Yields (H15T5y), December 2016 Five-Year T-Note Futures (FVZ6), 122 December Five-Year T-Note Futures Call (FVZ6C122), and 122 December Five-Year T-Note Futures Put (FVZ6P122)

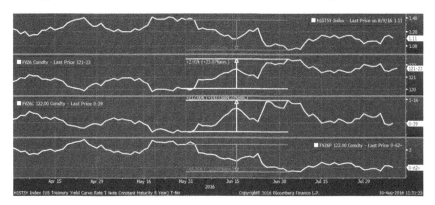

the December five-year T-note futures contract, and the 122 call and 122 put on the futures contract. From 5/31/16 to 7/5/16, the five-year Treasury yield dropped 31% from 1.37% to 0.95%. With the decrease in yields, the price on the December futures increased 18% from $120.07 per $100 face value to $122.23, the 122 December futures call increased 212% from $0.390625 (25/64) to $1.21875 (1 − 14), and the 122 December put decreased 68% from $2.3125 to $0.734375. A speculator who bought the call on 5/31/16 expecting the interest rate decrease and sold it on 7/5/16 would have made a profit of $828.125 on one contract, while a speculator who bought the put on 5/31/16 expecting rates to increase and closed the put on 7/15/16 would have lost $1,578.125 per contract.

$$\text{Call } \pi = \frac{1.21875 - 0.390625}{100}(\$100,000) = \$828.125$$

$$\text{Put } \pi = \frac{0.734375 - 2.3125}{100}(\$100,000) = \$1,578.125$$

Over-the-Counter Options

The OTC market consists of dealers who offer forward contracts, interest rate derivative products, and options on currency and debt securities. In the OTC option market, currency, bond, and interest rate option contracts are negotiable, with buyers and sellers entering directly into an agreement. In contrast to exchange-trade options, the dealers' market provides option contracts that are tailor-made to meet the holder's or writer's specific needs.

The OTC market does not have a clearinghouse to intermediate and guarantee the fulfillment of the terms of the option contract, nor market makers or specialists to ensure continuous markets; the options, therefore, lack marketability. Since each OTC option has unique features, the secondary market is limited. Prior to expiration, holders of OTC options who want to close their position may be able to do so by selling their positions back to the original option writers or possibly to an OTC dealer who is making a market in the option. This type of closing is more likely to occur if the option writer is a dealer that can hedge option positions and also if the option is relatively standard (e.g., OTC option on a T-bond). Because of this inherent lack of marketability, the premiums on OTC options are higher than exchange-traded ones. For example, the bid-ask spread on an OTC T-bond is typically twice that of an exchange-traded T-bond futures option. Finally, since there is no option clearing corporation to guarantee the option writer, OTC options also have different credit structures than exchange-traded options. Depending on who the option writer is, the contract may require initial and maintenance margins to be established.

OTC Currency Options

The OTC currency market is a dealer's market for currency. In this dealer's market, banks and investment houses provide tailor-made foreign currency option contracts for their customers, primarily multinational corporations. Compared to exchange-traded options, options in the OTC market are larger in contract size, often European, and are available on more currencies.

OTC Bond and Interest Rate Options

The OTC market for interest rate options is large, consisting of debt and interest-sensitive securities and products. Currently, security regulations in the United States prohibit off-exchange trading in options on futures. All US OTC options are therefore options on spot securities. The OTC markets in and outside the United States consist primarily of dealers who make markets in the underlying spot security, investment banking firms, and commercial banks. OTC options are primarily used by financial institutions and nonfinancial corporations to hedge their interest rate positions. The options contract offered in the OTC market include spot options on Treasury securities and special types of interest rate products, such as interest rate calls and puts, caps, floors, and collars.

OTC T-Bond and T-Note Options

When options are structured on Treasury securities, terms such as the specific underlying security, its maturity and size, the option's expiration, and the delivery are all negotiated. For OTC Treasury options, the underlying security is often a recently auctioned Treasury (on-the-run bond), although some selected existing securities (off-the-run securities) are used. In such cases, OTC dealers often offer or will negotiate contracts giving the holder the right to purchase or sell a specific T-bond or T-note. For example, a dealer might offer a T-bond call option to a fixed income manager, giving him the right to buy a specific T-bond maturing in year 2020 and paying a 3% coupon with a face value of $100,000. Because the option contract specifies a particular underlying bond, the maturity of the bond, as well as its value, will be changing during the option's expiration period. For example, a one-year call option on the 15-year bond, if held to expiration, would be a call option to buy a 14-year bond. Another feature of a spot T-bond or T-note option offered or contracted on the OTC market is that the underlying bond or note can pay coupon interest during the option period. As a result, if the option holder exercises on a non-coupon paying date, the accrued interest on the underlying bond must be accounted for. For a T-bond or T-note option, this is done by including the accrued interest as part of the exercise price. Like futures options, the exercise prices on a spot T-bond or T-note option is quoted as an index equal to a proportion of a bond with a face value of $100 (e.g., 105). If the underlying bond or note has a face value of $100,000, then the exercise price would be:

$$X = \left[\frac{\text{Index}}{100} \right] (\$100,000) + \text{Accrued interest}$$

Finally, the prices of spot T-bond and T-note options are typically quoted like futures T-bond options in terms of points and 32nds of a point. Thus, the price of a call option on a $100,000 T-bond quoted at $1\frac{5}{32}$ is $1,156.25 = (1.15625/100)($100,000).

Interest Rate Calls

In addition to option contracts on specific securities, the OTC market also offers a number of interest-rate option products. These products are usually offered by commercial or investment banks to their clients. Two products of note are the interest rate call and the interest rate put. An *interest rate call*, also called a *caplet*, gives the buyer a payoff on a specified payoff date if a designated interest rate, such as the LIBOR, rises above a certain exercise rate, R_X. On the payoff date, if the rate is less than R_X, the interest rate call expires worthless; if the rate exceeds R_X, the call pays off the difference between the actual rate and R_X, times a notional principal, NP, times the fraction of the year specified in the contract. For example, given an interest rate call with a designated rate of LIBOR, $R_X = 2\%$, $NP = \$20$ million, time period of 90 days, and day count convention of 90/360, the buyer would receive a \$50,000 payoff on the payoff date if the LIBOR were 3% (= $(0.03 - 0.02)(90/360)(\$20,000,000) = \$50,000$).

Interest rate call options are often written by commercial banks in conjunction with future loans they plan to provide to their customers. The exercise rate on the option usually is set near the current spot rate, with that rate often being tied to the LIBOR. For example, a company planning to finance a future \$10 million inventory 60 days from the present by borrowing from a bank at a rate equal to the LIBOR at the start of the loan could buy from the bank an interest rate call option with an exercise rate equal to, say, 2%, expiration of 60 days, and notional principal of \$10 million. At expiration (60 days later), the company would be entitled to a payoff if rates were higher than 2%. Thus, if the rate on the loan were higher than 2%, the company would receive a payoff that would offset the higher interest on the loan.

Interest Rate Puts

An *interest rate put*, also called a *floorlet*, gives the buyer a payoff on a specified payoff date if a designated interest rate is below the exercise rate, R_X. On the payoff date, if the rate is more than R_X, the interest rate put expires worthless; if the rate is less than R_X, the put pays off the difference between R_X and the actual rate times a notional principal, NP, times the fraction of the year specified in the contract. For example, given an interest rate put with a designated rate of LIBOR, $R_X = 2\%$, $NP = \$20$ million, time period of 90 days, and day-count of 90/360, the buyer would receive a \$50,000 payoff on the payoff date if the LIBOR were 1%: $(0.02 - 0.01)(90/360)(\$10,000,000) = \$50,000$.

A financial or nonfinancial corporation that is planning to make an investment at some future date could hedge that investment against interest rate decreases by purchasing an interest rate put option from a commercial bank, investment banking firm, or dealer. For example, suppose that instead of needing to borrow \$10 million, the previous company was expecting a net cash inflow of \$10 million in 60 days from its operations and was planning to invest the funds in a 90-day bank CD paying the LIBOR. To hedge against any interest rate decreases, the company could purchase an interest rate put (corresponding to the bank's CD it plans to buy) from the bank with the put having an exercise rate of, say, 2%, expiration of 60 days, and notional principal of \$10 million. The interest rate put would provide a payoff for the company if the LIBOR were less than 2%, giving the company a hedge against interest rate decreases.

EXHIBIT 6.15 Interest Rate Call Option Purchase

Interest Rate Call Purchase Profit Graph
X = 0.02, Reference rate = LIBOR, Period = 0.25,
NP = $10 million, Option Cost = $12,500

Interest Rate Call Purchase Profit Table
Exercise Rate = 2%, Reference Rate = LIBOR, NP = $10 million
Period = 0.25 year, Option cost = $12,500
Call Profit: {Max[LIBOR − 0.02 , 0] (0.25)($10,000,000)} − $12,500

LIBOR	Call Profit
0.0050	−$12,500
0.0075	−$12,500
0.0100	−$12,500
0.0125	−$12,500
0.0150	−$12,500
0.0175	−$12,500
0.0200	−$12,500
0.0225	−$6,250
0.0250	$0
0.0275	$6,250
0.0300	$12,500
0.0325	$18,750
0.0350	$25,000
0.0375	$31,250
0.0400	$37,500
Break-Even LIBOR	0.0250

Fundamental Interest Rate Call and Put Positions

The profit graphs for interest rate calls and puts can be defined in terms of the profit and interest rate relations for the option. Exhibit 6.15 shows the profit graph and table for an interest rate call with the following terms: Exercise rate = 2%, reference rate = LIBOR, NP = $10 million, time period as proportion of a year = 0.25, and the cost of the option = $12,500. As shown in the exhibit, if the LIBOR reaches 3.0% at expiration, the holder would realize a payoff of $25,000 (= (0.03 − 0.02)($10,000,000)(0.25)) and a profit of $12,500; if the LIBOR is 2.5%, the holder would break even with the $12,500 payoff equal to the option's cost; if the LIBOR is 2% or less, there would be no payoff and the holder would incur a loss equal to the call premium of $12,500. Just the opposite relationship between profits and rates exist for an interest rate put. Exhibit 6.16 shows the profit graph and table for an interest rate put with terms similar to those of the interest rate call.

Caps

A popular option offered by financial institutions in the OTC market is the *cap*. A plain-vanilla cap is a series of European interest rate call options—a portfolio of

EXHIBIT 6.16   Interest Rate Put Option Purchase

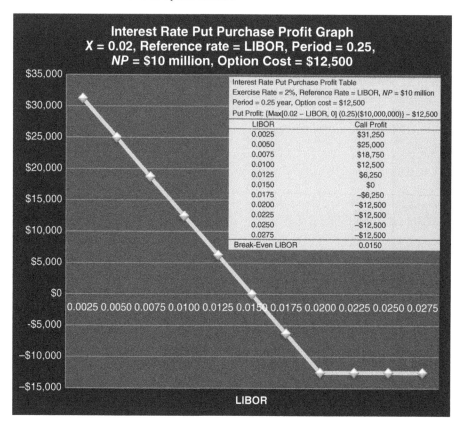

caplets. For example, a 2%, two-year cap on a three-month LIBOR, with a *NP* of $100 million, provides, for the next two years, a payoff every three months of (LIBOR − 0.02)(0.25)($100,000,000) if the LIBOR on the effective date exceeds 2% and nothing if the LIBOR equals or is less than 2%. (Typically, the payment is not on the effective date, but rather, on the delivery date three months later.) Caps are often written by financial institutions in conjunction with a floating-rate loan and are used by buyers as a hedge against interest rate risk. For example, a company with a floating-rate loan tied to the LIBOR could lock in a maximum rate on the loan by buying a cap corresponding to its loan. At each reset date, the company would receive a payoff from the caplet if the LIBOR exceeded the cap rate, offsetting the higher interest paid on the floating-rate loan; on the other hand, if rates decrease, the company would pay a lower rate on its loan while its losses on the caplet would be limited to the cost of the option. Thus, with a cap, the company would be able to lock in a maximum rate each quarter and still benefit with lower interest costs if rates decrease.

Floors

A plain-vanilla *floor* is a series of European interest rate put options—a portfolio of floorlets. For example, a 2%, two-year floor on a three-month LIBOR, with a NP of $100 million, provides, for the next two years, a payoff every three months of $(0.02 - \text{LIBOR})(0.25)(\$100,000,000)$ if the LIBOR on the effective date is less than 2% and nothing if the LIBOR equals or exceeds 2%. Floors are often purchased by investors as a tool to hedge their floating-rate investments against interest rate declines. Thus, with a floor, an investor with a floating-rate security is able to lock in a minimum rate each period, while still benefiting with higher yields if rates increase.

Convertible Securities

Warrants, rights, convertible bonds, and convertible preferred stock issued by corporation, financial institutions, and some government entities can be classified as convertible securities. These instruments are options giving the holder the right to buy or sell another security or to convert one security into another.

Warrants

A warrant is a call option giving the holder the right to buy a specified number of shares of another security at a specific price, on or before a specific date. Most warrants are sold by corporations, usually giving the holder the right to buy a specified number of shares of the company's common stock any time on or before expiration, with expiration ranging between three to five years. As such, warrants represent a long-term American call option written by the corporation. Like exchange-traded call options, warrants are protected against stock splits and dividends, but not cash dividends. Companies and financial institutions also issue warrants on their debt securities and preferred stock. Exhibit 6.17 shows a listing of select stock and bond warrants. Exhibit 6.18, in turn, shows the Bloomberg Description screen for a GM stock warrant, along with the price graphs for the warrant and GM stock. The GM warrant has an exercise price of $18.33, expiration of 7/10/19, and on 8/12/16, the warrant was priced at $13.70 when GM was trading at $31.63 ($IV = \$31.63 - \$18.33 = \$13.30$; $TVP = \$0.40$). On 12/17/13, the price of GM was trading at $42.53 and the $18.33 warrant was trading at $23.859. Exhibit 6.19, in turn, shows the profit graph for the GM warrant with a call price of $13.70, along with the warrant's call price curve.

Corporations often issue warrants as a *sweetener* with other securities (e.g., subordinate bond or preferred stock). When they are issued with another security, they can be either nondetachable or detachable. If the holder of a nondetachable warrant wants to sell the warrant, she would have to sell the accompanying security with it or exercise the warrant. A detachable warrant, however, can be sold separately. Most outstanding warrants trade on the over-the-counter market.

Most of the contractual characteristics (exercise price, expiration, etc.) of equity warrants are similar to those of call options on a stock. The fundamental difference between a call on a stock and a warrant on the same stock is that the writer of the warrant is the corporation, while the writer of a call option is an individual investor.

EXHIBIT 6.17 Select Warrants

Warrants on Stock

Ticker	Company Name	Expiration	Exercise	Ticker	Company Name	Expiration	Exercise
AIG/WS	American International Group	1/19/2021	$44.58	OXBRW	Oxbridge Re Holdings Ltd	3/26/2019	$7.50
CCNWW	CardConnect Corp	8/1/2021	$12.00	WBSFW	Webster Financial Corp	11/21/2018	$18.28
GM/WS/B	General Motors Co	7/10/2019	$18.33	BARCL14Z	Alliance Data Systems Corp	1/26/2018	$327.80
HCACW	Hennessy Capital Acquisition	9/11/2020	$11.50	GVCWBC18	Community West Bancshares	12/19/2018	$4.49
LMBHW	Limbach Holdings Inc	7/20/2021	$11.50	NXTDW	NXT-ID Inc	2/9/2019	$3.00
PACEW	Pace Holdings Corp	10/29/2020	$11.50	SUNWW	Sunworks Inc	3/9/2020	$4.15
TACOW	Del Taco Restaurants Inc	6/30/2020	$11.50	PLAFW	Platform Specialty Products	10/31/2016	$11.50
KMI/WS	Kinder Morgan Inc/DE	5/25/2017	$40.00	0654464W	Gevo Inc	5/19/2020	$5.50
CFCOW	CF Corp	7/8/2021	$11.50	GEVWW	FNB Corp/PA	1/9/2019	$11.52
TRCHW	Tejon Ranch Co	8/31/2016	$40.00	GVFNB19	Nautilus Marine Acquisition	7/15/2016	$11.50
WFC/WS	Wells Fargo & Co	10/28/2018	$33.90	NMARW	Gran Colombia Gold Corp	3/18/2019	$3.25
APOPW	Cellect Biotechnology Ltd	7/29/2021	$7.50	TPWRF	Cambridge Capital Acquisition	12/17/2018	$11.50
EAG1W	Double Eagle Acquisition	10/16/2020	$11.50	ABN25878	ETX Energy LLC	11/15/2024	$0.01
GP1AW	GP Investments Acquisition	5/26/2022	$11.50	KOOIW	BellSouth Telecommunications	10/15/2031	$0.00
SHLDW	Sears Holdings Corp	12/15/2019	$25.69	IRIGW	Clean Diesel Technologies Inc	6/3/2020	$2.65
DRIOW	DarioHealth Corp	3/8/2021	$5.63	NWGULFW1	EveryWare Global Inc	5/13/2018	$6.00
ZIONZ	Zions Bancorporation	11/14/2018	$36.27	111W	Great Southern Bancorp Inc	12/5/2018	$9.57
BLVDW	Boulevard Acquisition Corp II	9/25/2020	$11.50	CDSTW	India Globalization Capital Inc	3/6/2017	$5.00
TGLSW	Tecnoglass Inc	12/16/2016	$8.00	EVRWQ	US Shale Solutions Inc	9/1/2024	$0.01
KODK/WS	Eastman Kodak Co	9/3/2018	$14.93	GVGSBC18	Woodbine Holdings LLC	5/18/2016	$0.01
BTX/WS	BioTime Inc	10/1/2018	$4.55	IGCIW	Daimler North America Corp	1/18/2031	$0.00

SGYPW	Synergy Pharmaceuticals Inc	12/6/2016	$5.50	SHALESW2	Goodrich Petroleum Corp	3/12/2025	$4.66
RNVAW	Rennova Health Inc	12/30/2020	$1.94	WBBNZ	Banner Corp	11/21/2018	$10.89
XGTIW	xG Technology Inc	7/18/2018	$6.87	126W	Old Second Bancorp Inc	1/16/2019	$13.43
TROXW	Tronox Ltd	2/14/2018	$51.37	ABN25877	Overseas Shipholding Group	8/5/2039	$0.01
SBNYW	Signature Bank/New York NY	12/12/2018	$30.21	GDPUS1	Talbots Inc/The	4/6/2015	$14.85
NETEW	Net Element Inc	10/2/2017	$7.50	GVBANR18	Daimler North America Corp	1/18/2031	$112.25
USCXW	US Concrete Inc	8/31/2017	$26.68	GVOSBC19	Charlotte Russe Holding Inc	12/18/2050	$12.00
ETRMW	EnteroMedics Inc	9/28/2016	$4.65	OVSPW	Central European Media Enterp	5/4/2050	$86.96
ONSIW	Oncobiologics Inc	2/18/2017	$6.60	TLB/WS	Capitol Acquisition Corp	11/8/2012	$7.50
MSTPW	Mast Therapeutics Inc	6/14/2018	$0.65	123W	Ascend Telecom Holdings Ltd	9/17/2018	$11.50
ONSIZ	Oncobiologics Inc	2/18/2017	$8.50	ASCEW	Enven Energy Corp	11/6/2020	$15.00

Warrants on Bonds

113W	Goldman Sachs Group	2/15/2033	$103.78	120W	Goldman Sachs Group	2/15/2033	$104.46
116W	Prudential Financial Inc	7/15/2033	$96.46	121W	BellSouth LLC	10/15/2031	$111.02
122W	Credit Suisse USA Inc	7/15/2032	$109.55	124W	Walt Disney	3/1/2032	$101.54
112W	Goldman Sachs Group	2/5/2033	$3.78	125W	Goldman Sachs Group Inc/The	2/15/2034	$104.44
118W	AT&T Corp	11/15/2031	$115.98	4620743Z	Provident Financing Trust I	3/15/2038	$1,000.00

EXHIBIT 6.18   GM Warrant (Gm/WS/B0: $X =$ \$18.33, Expiration = 7/10/19), Bloomberg Description Page, 8/12/16, Price Graph of GM Warrant and GM Stock, 8/12/11 to 8/12/16

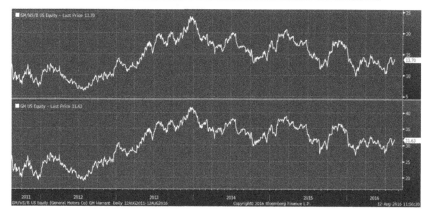

This difference implies that when a warrant holder exercises, the corporation must issue new shares of stock. When the company, in turn, sells the shares on the warrant contract, it will receive cash from the warrant holders, which it can use to finance its capital formation; however, the company also will have its stock diluted. In contrast, when an exchange-traded call option on the stock is exercised, the writer sells his shares (if the writer is covered) or buys existing shares in the market (if naked) and sells them to the holder. Thus, exercising a call neither dilutes the company's stock nor increases its cash flows.

To illustrate the differences between warrants and call options, consider the case of the Zuber Corporation that owns crude oil wells, currently worth \$100 million. Assume the Zuber Corporation is an all-equity company, has one million shares of stock outstanding (n_0). To see the implications of a call option on the Zuber Corporation, suppose that one of Zuber's major shareholders sells a call option to a large investment

EXHIBIT 6.19 Warrant Profit Graph and Price Graph

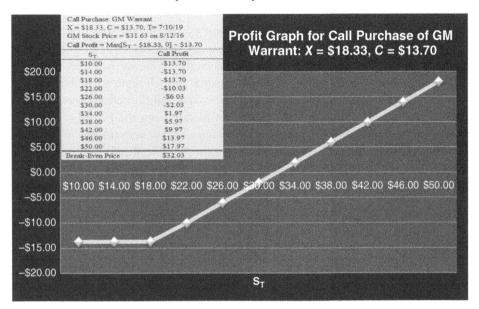

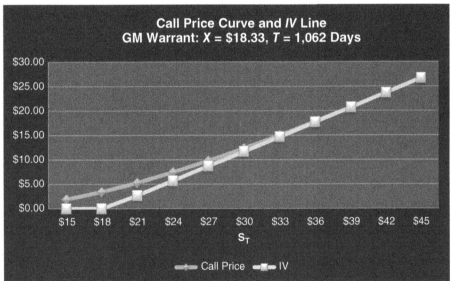

fund giving them the right to buy 100,000 shares of Zuber stock at $X = \$110$ per share. After selling the call option, suppose the value of the Zuber Company increases from $100 million to $120 million, initially raising the price of a share of Zuber stock from $100 to $120. If, after the increase in value, the Investment Fund exercised their call option, the large shareholder would simply sell its 100,000 shares to the fund at $110 per share. For the Zuber Corporation the exercise of this call option would have no impact on the company's total number of shares of one million shares.

Now suppose that instead of a large Zuber shareholder selling a call option when the company is worth $100 million, the Zuber Corporation sells a warrant to the Investment Fund, giving them the right to buy $n_w = 100{,}000$ shares at $110 per share. Again suppose that the value of the company increases to $120 million, and the Investment Fund exercises their warrant. When they exercise, the Zuber Corporation will have to create 100,000 new shares of stock and sell them to the Fund. This, in turn, will dilute the company's equity shares. This dilution effect, however, will be offset partially by the receipt of $11 million in cash from the Fund (= (100,000 shares)($110 per share)). Thus, in this case the exercise of the warrant affects the number of shares of the Zuber Corporation and its value. Specifically, the new value of the Zuber Corporation (V^Z) is $131 million: value of Zuber before the warrant exercise, V_0, plus the cash from the exercised warrant:

$$V^Z = V_0 + \text{Cash from the exercised warrant}$$

$$V^Z = \$120 \text{ million} + \$11 \text{ million} = \$131 \text{ million}$$

and the Zuber Corporation now has $n_0 + n_w = 1{,}100{,}000$ shares of stock, with the value of each share worth $119.09:

$$\frac{\text{Total Stock Value}}{\text{Total Shares}} = \frac{V^Z}{n_0 + n_w} = \frac{\$131{,}000{,}000}{1{,}100{,}000} = \$119.09$$

For the Investment Fund, the dilution effect associated with the warrant causes the gain from exercising the warrant to be less than the gain from exercising the call. That is, the Investment Fund's gain from exercising the call is $1,000,000 (= 100,000($120 − $110)), while its return from exercising the warrant is only $909,000 (=100,000($119.09 − $110). Formally, the difference between the two options can be seen by comparing their intrinsic values (IV_C and IV_W):

$$IV_C = \text{Max} \left[\frac{V_0}{n_0} - X, 0 \right]$$

$$IV_W = \text{Max} \left[\frac{V_0 + X n_w}{n_0 + n_w} - X, 0 \right]$$

IV_W expressed in terms of IV_C is:

$$IV_W = \left[\frac{n_0}{n_0 + n_w} \right] IV_C$$

The term $n_0/(n_0 + n_w)$ is a dilution factor. In the example, it is equal to 1,000,000/ 1,100,000 = 0.909. Thus, the equation for IV_W shows that the intrinsic value of a warrant is equal to the intrinsic value of a call option on the same underlying stock times the dilution factor. Since warrants and call options on the same stock are perfectly correlated (that is, they both derive their values from the same asset), the current warrant price (W_0), in turn, should be equal to the current call value times the dilution factor:

$$W_0 = \left[\frac{n_0}{n_0 + n_w} \right] C$$

Rights

Most state laws give the shareholders of a corporation the right to maintain their shares of ownership in the corporation. This *preemptive right* means that when a company issues new shares of stock, the existing shareholders must be given the first right of refusal. Corporations can accomplish this by issuing each shareholder a certificate, known as a *right* (or subscription warrant). From World War II through the 1960s, two-thirds of all common stock issues were rights offerings. Beginning in the late 1960s, though, US firms began to obtain shareholders' approval to eliminate preemptive rights. When a company does issue rights, the right entitles the existing shareholder to buy new issues of common stock at a specified price, known as the *subscription price*, for a specified period of time before the stock is sold to the general public. To maintain ownership proportionality, each share of stock receives one right, and to facilitate the new stock sale, the subscription price usually is set below the current stock price. After a company issues rights to its shareholders, the existing shares of stock sell cum rights (buyers of the stock are entitled to the right) to a specified ex-rights date, after which the stock sells without the right.

A right is similar to a warrant. Technically, it is a call option issued by the corporation, giving the holder the right to buy stock at a specified price (subscription price) on or before a specific date. Like warrants, when a right is exercised, new shares are created and the company has additional capital. Also, like warrants, rights can be sold in a secondary market. Rights differ from warrants in that their expiration periods are shorter (e.g., one to three months compared to three to five years for a warrant), and their exercise prices usually are set below their stock prices, while warrants usually have exercise prices above. Also, because of their short expiration periods, rights are usually not adjusted for stock-splits and stock dividends.

To illustrate the characteristics of rights, suppose the Zuber Corporation is planning to raise $10 million in equity to finance an oil well purchase. The company is currently worth $100 million, has no debt, and has one million shares of stock outstanding (n_0), with each share trading at $100. Because of the preemptive rights of shareholders, suppose Zuber plans to finance its $10 million investment with a rights offering in which its existing shareholders will be given the opportunity to buy new shares of stock at a subscription price of $80, with each shareholder to receive one right for each share he owns. With its planned $10 million investment expenditure and a subscription price of $80, Zuber would need to sell 125,000 new shares:

$$\text{Number of new shares} = N_n = \frac{\text{Investment expenditure}}{\text{Subscription price}}$$

$$N_n = \frac{\$10,000,000}{\$80/\text{Share}} = 125,000 \text{ shares}$$

Since one right is given for each existing share and Zuber has one million existing shares, eight rights would be therefore needed (N_R) to purchase one new share:

$$N_R = \frac{1,000,000}{125,000} = 8 \text{ rights}$$

Thus, shareholders would surrender eight rights and $80 to buy one new shares. This rights offering, in turn, would provide Zuber $10 million cash to finance its investment and would create 125,000 additional shares.

The intrinsic value of the right (IV_R) is equal to the difference between the market price of the stock (S_T) and the subscription price (X_S) divided by the number of rights needed to purchase one share:

$$IV_R = \frac{S_T - X_S}{N_R}$$

With 125,000 additional shares and $10 million cash inflow, the estimated price of Zuber stock would be $97.78:

$$S_T = \frac{\text{Current equity value} + \text{Investment value}}{\text{Old shares} + \text{New shares}}$$

$$S_T = \frac{\$100,000,000 + \$10,000,000}{1,000,000 + 125,000} = \$97.78$$

With an $80 subscription price, eight rights would be worth $17.78 ($97.78 − $80), and one right would be worth $2.22:

$$IV_R = \frac{S_T - X_S}{N_R} = \frac{\$97.78 - \$80.00}{8} = \$2.22$$

Exhibit 6.20 shows a subscription right issued by Empire Resorts Inc. on 1/4/16, along with the Bloomberg Description screen for Empire Resorts and the price graphs for Empire's stock and the right around the right's trading period from 1/15/16 to 2/5/16. The Empire right had a subscription price of $14.40 for every 0.4748644 shares. That is, each Empire shareholder received one subscription right for each 0.4748644 shares, with the right entitling them to purchase a new share issue for $14.40. The number of new shares offered was 20.13889 million. At $14.40/share, the offering was expected to raise $290 million for Empire Resorts. As specified in Empire's Rights Prospectus, the purpose of the funding was to finance the purchase of the N.Y. State Gaming License and to finance the development and operation of Montreign Resort. For most of the trading period, the price of Empire stock traded below the right's subscription price of $14.40. On 1/21/16, Empire stock did trade at $14.79, making the *IV* of the right equal to $0.821287:

$$IV_R = \frac{S_T - X_S}{N_R} = \frac{\$14.79 - \$14.40}{0.4748644} = \$0.821287$$

EXHIBIT 6.20   Rights of Empire Resort Inc.: Empire Right: Subscription Price = $14.40, One right for 0.4748644 Shares

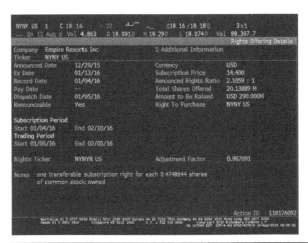

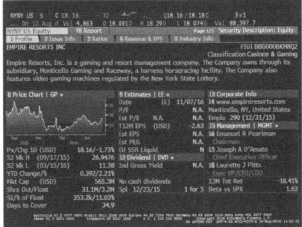

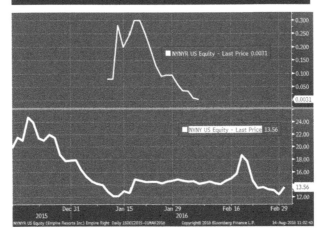

The price of the right on 1/21/16, however, was $0.30, lower than the *IV*, reflecting the dilution effect.

Convertible Bonds

A *convertible bond* is similar to a bond with a nondetachable warrant. Like a regular bond it pays interest and principal, and like a warrant it can be exchanged for a specified number of shares of common stock. Convertible bonds often are sold as subordinate issues by smaller, riskier companies. The conversion feature of the bond, in turn, serves as a "sweetener" to the debt issue. To investors, convertible bonds offer the potential for high rates of return if the corporation does well, while still providing a downside protection as a bond. Convertible bonds usually sell at a lower yield than similar non-convertible bonds and usually are callable. Exhibit 6.21 lists some convertible bonds and their features.

Convertible Bond Terms

Exhibit 6.22 shows the Bloomberg Description and Yield Analysis (YAS) screens for a convertible bond issued by Centerpoint Energy (CNP). The convertible bond pays a coupon of 4.1837%, matures on 09/15/29, can be converted at any time into one share of Centerpoint common stock, and is callable at any time at a call price of $100 per face value. The convertible features of the bond can be described in terms of its conversion ratio, conversion price, conversion value, and straight debt value.

The *conversion ratio* (*CR*) is the number of shares of stock that can be acquired when the bond is tendered for conversion. The Centerpoint convertible's conversion ratio is one share of its stock for each bond. It should be noted that on some convertible bonds, the conversion ratio can change over time. Also, some convertible bonds allow conversion to be done either by tendering over the bond or paying a specified amount of cash (or some combination). For example, a convertible could stipulate that 25 shares of stock can be obtained in exchange for the bond or cash equal to a specific proportion of the company's stock value, whichever is smaller.

The *conversion price* (*CP*) is the bond's par value divided by the conversion ratio: $CP = F/CR$. The conversion price of the Centerpoint convertible is $100. The conversion price is applicable only when the bond is trading at par. Many convertible bond contracts, though, specify changes in the conversion ratio over time by specifying changes in the conversion price instead of the conversion ratio.

The *conversion value* (*CV*) is the convertible bond's value as a stock. At a given point in time (*t*), the conversion value is equal to the product of the conversion ratio times the market price of the stock (S_t): $CV_t = (CR) S_t$. On 8/12/16, Centerpoint stock was trading at $22.57. With a *CR* of one, the conversion value of Centerpoint convertible bond was therefore the same as the stock price.

The *straight debt value* (*SDV*) is the convertible bond's value as a nonconvertible bond. The SDV is found by discounting the convertible's cash flows by the yield on an

EXHIBIT 6.21 Select Convertible Bonds

Name	Ticker	Coupon	Maturity	Maturity Type	Announce	Collateral Type	Issued Amount
DISH Network Corp	DISH	3.375	8/15/2026	CONVERTIBLE	8/3/2016	SR UNSECURED	3,000,000,000
Microchip Technology Inc	MCHP	1.625	2/15/2025	CONVERTIBLE	2/6/2015	SR SUBORDINATED	1,725,000,000
Cobalt International Energy Inc	CIE	3.125	5/15/2024	CONVERTIBLE	5/8/2014	SR UNSECURED	1,300,000,000
Bristol-Myers Squibb Co	BMY	0.153	9/15/2023	CONV/PUT/CALL	9/25/2003	SR UNSECURED	1,200,000,000
Comcast Holdings Corp	CMCSA	2.000	10/15/2029	CONV/CALL	10/12/1999	COMPANY GUARNT	1,150,000,000
Liberty Media Corp	LMCA	1.375	10/15/2023	CONVERTIBLE	10/11/2013	SR UNSECURED	1,000,000,000
CenterPoint Energy Inc	CNP	4.184	9/15/2029	CONV/CALL	9/15/1999	SUBORDINATED	1,000,000,000
DP World Ltd	DPWDU	1.750	6/19/2024	CONV/PUT	6/12/2014	SR UNSECURED	1,000,000,000
SL Green Operating Partnership LP	SLG	3.000	3/30/2027	CONV/PUT/CALL	3/21/2007	SR UNSECURED	750,000,000
Vantage Drilling International	VTG	1.000	12/31/2030	CONVERTIBLE	2/1/2016	SECURED	749,983,373
Comcast Holdings Corp	CMCSA	2.000	11/15/2029	CONV/CALL	11/2/1999	SUBORDINATED	657,141,625
Teva Pharmaceutical Finance Co LLC	TEVA	0.250	2/1/2026	CONV/PUT/CALL	1/27/2006	COMPANY GUARNT	575,000,000
Omnicare Inc	OCR	3.750	12/15/2025	CONVERTIBLE	12/1/2010	COMPANY GUARNT	575,000,000
Hospitality Properties Trust	HPT	3.800	3/15/2027	CONV/PUT/CALL	4/5/2007	SR UNSECURED	575,000,000
SunEdison Inc	SUNE	3.375	6/1/2025	CONVERTIBLE	5/13/2015	SR UNSECURED	450,000,000
General Cable Corp	BGC	4.500	11/15/2029	CONVERTIBLE	10/26/2009	SUBORDINATED	429,463,000
Medicines Co/The	MDCO	2.750	7/15/2023	CONVERTIBLE	6/7/2016	SR UNSECURED	402,500,000
Caesars Entertainment Inc	CZR	0.680	4/15/2024	CONV/PUT/CALL	11/8/2004	COMPANY GUARNT	375,000,000
Carrizo Oil & Gas Inc	CRZO	4.375	6/1/2028	CONV/PUT/CALL	5/22/2008	COMPANY GUARNT	373,750,000
ON Semiconductor Corp	ON	2.625	12/15/2026	CONV/PUT/CALL	12/2/2011	COMPANY GUARNT	356,930,000
SEACOR Holdings Inc	CKH	2.500	12/15/2027	CONV/PUT/CALL	12/6/2012	SR UNSECURED	350,000,000
WESCO International Inc	WCC	6.000	9/15/2029	CONV/CALL	7/27/2009	COMPANY GUARNT	345,000,000
SEACOR Holdings Inc	CKH	3.000	11/15/2028	CONV/PUT/CALL	11/7/2013	SR UNSECURED	230,000,000
Meritor Inc	MTOR	4.000	2/15/2027	CONV/PUT/CALL	6/8/2007	COMPANY GUARNT	200,000,000
BearingPoint Inc	BGPT	5.000	4/15/2025	CONV/PUT/CALL	4/22/2005	SR SUB NOTES	200,000,000
Powerwave Technologies Inc	PWAV	1.875	11/15/2024	CONV/PUT/CALL	4/14/2005	SUBORDINATED	200,000,000
BearingPoint Inc	BGPT	2.750	12/15/2024	CONV/PUT/CALL	12/17/2004	SUBORDINATED	200,000,000
Powerwave Technologies Inc	PWAV	1.875	11/15/2024	CONV/PUT/CALL	11/5/2004	SUBORDINATED	200,000,000
Stillwater Mining Co	SWC	1.875	3/15/2028	CONV/PUT/CALL	7/16/2009	SR UNSECURED	181,500,000

(continued)

EXHIBIT 6.21 (*Continued*)

Name	Ticker	Coupon	Maturity	Maturity Type	Announce	Collateral Type	Issued Amount
Goodrich Petroleum Corp	GDPM	3.250	12/1/2026	CONV/PUT/CALL	12/1/2006	COMPANY GUARNT	175,000,000
Bill Barrett Corp	BBG	5.000	3/15/2028	CONV/PUT/CALL	3/5/2008	COMPANY GUARNT	172,500,000
NorthStar Realty Finance LP	NRF	7.250	6/15/2027	CONV/PUT/CALL	6/12/2007	COMPANY GUARNT	172,500,000
Mesa Air Group Inc	MESA	2.115	2/10/2024	CONV/PUT/CALL	2/5/2004	COMPANY GUARNT	171,409,000
Globalstar Inc	GSAT	5.750	4/1/2028	CONV/PUT/CALL	4/10/2008	SR UNSECURED	150,000,000
Trico Marine Services Inc/United States	TRMA	3.000	1/15/2027	CONV/PUT/CALL	5/23/2007	SR UNSECURED	150,000,000
Powerwave Technologies Inc	PWAV	3.875	10/1/2027	CONV/PUT/CALL	9/18/2007	SUBORDINATED	150,000,000
Orbital Sciences Corp	OA	2.438	1/15/2027	CONV/PUT/CALL	3/26/2007	SR SUBORDINATED	143,750,000
Convergys Corp	CVG	5.750	9/15/2029	CONVERTIBLE	9/9/2009	JR SUBORDINATED	125,000,000
WCI Communities Inc/Old	WCI	4.000	8/5/2023	CONV/PUT/CALL	7/31/2003	COMPANY GUARNT	125,000,000
Covad Communications Group Inc	DVW	3.000	3/15/2024	CONV/PUT/CALL	3/5/2004	SR UNSECURED	125,000,000
RAIT Financial Trust	RAS	7.000	4/1/2031	CONV/PUT/CALL	3/15/2011	SR UNSECURED	115,000,000
Lexington Realty Trust	LXP	6.000	1/15/2030	CONV/PUT/CALL	1/20/2010	COMPANY GUARNT	115,000,000
Playboy Enterprises Inc	PLA	3.000	3/15/2025	CONV/PUT/CALL	3/10/2005	SR SUBORDINATED	115,000,000
Midway Games Inc	MWY	7.125	5/31/2026	CONV/PUT/CALL	5/25/2006	SR UNSECURED	75,000,000
Midway Games Inc	MWY	7.125	5/31/2026	CONV/PUT/CALL	10/5/2006	SR UNSECURED	75,000,000
Globalstar Inc	GSAT	8.000	4/1/2028	CONV/PUT/CALL	5/20/2013	COMPANY GUARNT	54,600,000
Agenus Inc	AGEN	5.250	2/1/2025	CONV/PUT/CALL	1/20/2005	SR UNSECURED	50,000,000
BELLUS Health Inc	BLUCN	6.000	11/15/2026	CONVERTIBLE	11/3/2006	SR UNSECURED	42,085,000
Toreador Resources Corp	ZAZA	7.000	10/1/2025	CONV/PUT/CALL	2/1/2010	SR UNSECURED	31,631,000
IRC Retail Centers Inc	IRC	5.000	11/15/2029	CONV/PUT/CALL	6/29/2010	SR UNSECURED	29,215,000

EXHIBIT 6.22   Centerpoint Energy Convertible Bond (CNP CUSIP: US15189T20690): Coupon = 4.1837%, Maturity = 09/15/16, CR = 1.00), Bloomberg Description and YAS Screens, 8/12/16

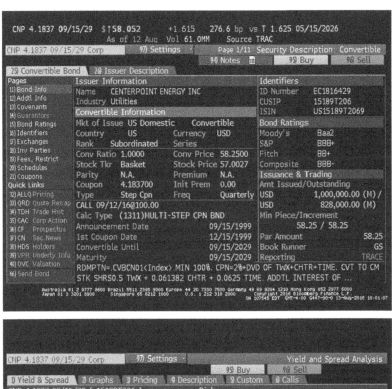

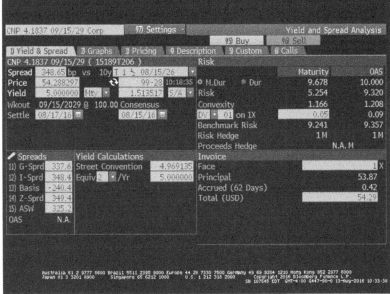

identical, but nonconvertible bond. Thus, in the case of the Centerpoint convertible, if a 4.1837%, callable bonds, with the same BBB quality ratings, and similar maturity were trading to yield 5.00%, then the current SDV of the Centerpoint convertible would be $54.29 per $100 face value (see the YAS screen in Exhibit 6.22).

Minimum and Maximum Convertible Bond Prices

Arbitrage forces ensure that the minimum price of a convertible bond (B_t^{CB}) is the greater of either its straight debt value or conversion value. Thus, the minimum price of a convertible bond is:

$$\text{Min } B_t^{CB} = \text{Max}[CV_t, SDV_t]$$

If a convertible bond is priced less than its conversion value, arbitrageurs could buy it, convert to shares of stock, and then sell the shares in the market to earn an arbitrage profit of $CV - B_t^{CB}$. Arbitrageurs seeking such opportunities would push the price of the convertible up until it is at least equal to its conversion value. Similarly, if a convertible is priced below its SDV, then one could profit by buying the convertible and selling it as a regular bond or by shorting a regular bond and buying the convertible. Thus, the minimum boundary condition for the ABC convertible bond is defined by the maximum of its CV or SDV.

In addition to a minimum price, if the convertible bond has a call feature, the exercise price at which the issuer can redeem the bonds (X_B) places a maximum limit on the price of the convertible. That is, for most issuers it is advantageous for them to buy back the convertible bond once its price is equal to the exercise price. Buying back the bond, in turn, frees the company to sell new stock and debt at prices higher than the stock or straight debt values associated with the convertible. Thus, the maximum price of a convertible bond is its exercise price. The actual price of a convertible usually will sell at a premium above its minimum value, but below the maximum.

On 8/12/16, the Centerpoint convertible bond was trading at $58.25, relatively close to its SDV of $54.29 (at YTM of 5%); this was significantly above its conversion value of $22.57 and significantly below its call value. Centerpoint's convertible was therefore trading more like a bond.

Embedded Options

Many of the characteristics of exchange-traded and OTC options are embedded in the equity and debt securities of corporations. For example, the call and put features on corporate debt securities are options embedded in those corporate securities.

Callable Bonds

Many bonds have call features that give the issuer the right to buy back the bond from the bondholders at a specified price. This feature is a benefit to the issuer. If interest rates decrease in the market, then the issuer can reduce his interest costs of financing assets by borrowing funds at the lower rates and using the proceeds to call the bond issue. When a bond issue is called, bondholders sell their bonds back to the issuer, usually at a premium above the face value on the bond, the amount of the premium being specified in the bond indenture. Although the bondholders benefit from receiving the call premium, they also are in a situation in which they have to reinvest their funds in a market with lower interest rates.

Conceptually, when an investor buys a callable bond, she implicitly is selling a call option to the issuer, giving the issuer the right to buy the bond from the bondholder before maturity at a specified price. Theoretically, a callable bond can be priced as the value of an identical, but option-free (or bullet) bond minus the value of the call feature. The inclusion of option features in a bond contract also makes the evaluation of such bonds more difficult. A 10-year, 5% callable bond issued when interest rates are relatively high may be more like a 3-year bond, given that a likely interest rate decrease would lead the issuer to buy the bond back. Determining the value of such a bond requires taking into account not only the value of the bond's cash flow, but also the value of the call option embedded in the bond.

Putable Bond

A putable bond, or put bond, gives the holder the right to sell the bond back to the issuer at a specified exercise price (or put price), PP. In contrast to callable bonds, putable bonds benefit the holder: If the price of the bond decreases below the exercise price, then the bondholder can sell the bond back to the issuer at the exercise price. From the bondholder's perspective, a put option provides a hedge against a decrease in the bond price. If rates decrease in the market, then the bondholder benefits from the resulting higher bond prices, and if rates increase, then the bondholder can exercise, giving her downside protection. Given that the bondholder has the right to exercise, the price of a putable bond will be equal to the price of an otherwise identical option-free bond plus the value of the put option

Sinking-Fund Bonds

Many bonds have sinking fund clauses specified in their indenture requiring that the issuer make scheduled payments into a fund or buy up a certain proportion of the bond issue each period. Often when the sinking fund agreement specifies an orderly retirement of the issue, the issuer is given an option of either purchasing the bonds in the market or calling the bonds at a specified call price. This option makes the sinking fund valuable to the issuer. If interest rates are relatively high, then the issuer will be able to buy back the requisite amount of bonds at a relatively low market price. However, if rates are low and the bond price high, then the issuer will be able to buy back the bonds on the call option at the call price. Thus, a sinking fund bond with this type of call provision should trade at a lower price than an otherwise identical option-free bond.

Equity and Debt as Call Option Positions

The limited liability feature of common stock enables the stockholders of a leveraged corporation (a corporation with debt) to view their equity position as a call option on the assets of the corporation, with the corporation's creditors being viewed as the writers of the call option and the owners of the firm. That is, a company's stock in effect gives its shareholders the right to buy the firm from the company's creditors at an exercise price equal to the face value on the debt. If the company is successful, causing the value of the firm's assets to grow, then the shareholders will exercise their equity right and effectively buy back the company from the creditors at the exercise price equal to the debt's face value. If the value of the firm is less than the debt's face value, then the shareholders will choose not to exercise their option to reclaim the firm from the bondholders.

To illustrate, suppose a company has debt consisting only of a zero coupon bond with a face value of F and maturing at time T. The shareholders of the company can view their equity position as a call option in which they can buy the company from the bondholders at an exercise price equal to the face value of the debt, with an expiration date equal to the bond's maturity. As shown in Exhibit 6.23a, if the value of the firm's assets (V^A) exceeds F at maturity, $V_T^A > F$, the shareholders of the company would exercise their option and purchase the company from the bondholder at the exercise price of F. If $V_T^A < F$ at maturity, then the shareholders would not

EXHIBIT 6.23 Equity and Debt Values at Maturity

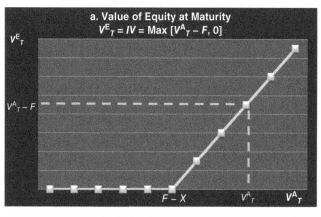

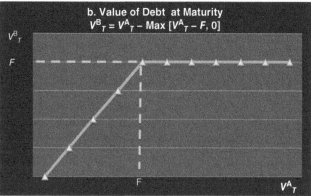

(or could not) exercise. Thus, at expiration the total value of equity of the company (V_T^E) would be:

$$V_T^E = \text{Max}[V_T^A - F, 0]$$

The bondholders' position can be viewed as a covered call write position in which they (1) own the assets of the firm and (2) have a short position on a call option on the firm's assets. As shown in Exhibit 16.23b, at expiration if $V_T^A < F$, the call (or equity) position is worthless, and the bondholders retain their ownership of the company. If $V_T^A \geq F$, however, then the shareholders will buy the company from the bondholders at the exercise price of F. In this case, the value of the bond (V_T^B) is equal to F. Thus, the value of the bondholders' position at maturity is equal to the minimum of either F or V_T^A:

$$V_T^B = \text{Min}[V_T^A, F]$$

This minimum condition can be stated equivalently in terms of the following maximum condition:

$$V_T^B = V_T^A - \text{Max}[V_T^A - F, 0]$$

That is:

	$\text{Min}[V_T^A, F]$	$V_T^A - \text{Max}[V_T^A - F, 0]$
If $V_T^A \geq F$	F	$V_T^A - [V_T^A - F] = F$
If $V_T^A < F$	V_T^A	$V_T^A - 0 = V_T^A$

The equations show the expiration value of the debt is equal to the value of the firm minus the intrinsic value of the call, which is equal to the expiration value of a covered call write position.

Prior to maturity, the value of the stock (V_T^E) would be equal to its intrinsic value plus a time value premium, and the value of the debt would be equal to the value of the firm minus the equity value. Exhibit 6.24 shows the values of equity and debt as functions of the value of the firm. In the graph, the *IV* line depicts the intrinsic value of the equity, the 45-degree line shows the maximum equity value, the curve in between shows the familiar call price curve, representing the value of the equity, and the vertical distance between the 45-degree line (V_T^A) and the equity curve (V_T^E) shows the value of the debt.

Conclusion

In this chapter, we have examined the characteristics of non-stock options: index, futures, OTC, convertible, and embedded options. Like stock options, these options provide instruments for financial managers and traders to take speculative, hedging, and fund management positions related to debt, currency, portfolios, and commodities. In the next two chapters, we examine the speculative and hedging uses of stock and non-stock options.

EXHIBIT 6.24 Equity and Debt Values Prior to Maturity

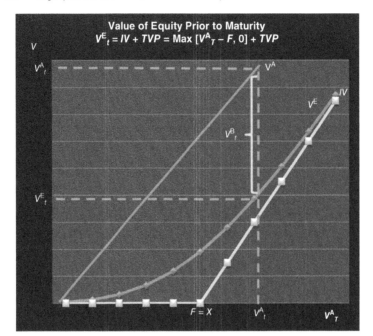

BLOOMBERG: OPTIONS SCREENS

UPLOADING FUTURES USING CTM AND THEN UPLOADING THE FUTURES OPTION FROM THE FUTURES SCREEN

- To find a futures contract from the CTM screen, use the CTM's Exchange screen and click "Equity Index," "Currencies," "Bond," "Interest Rate," or "Commodity" from the dropdown menu in the "Category" column. Alternatively, click "Categories," select type (e.g., index, currency, etc.), and then type the name of the exchange (e.g., CME or CBT) in the amber Exchange box to find the futures contract of interest and its ticker. *Note:* From the CTM screen, you can click "Yes" from the "Options" tab to see if the futures contract has an options contract on it.

- To upload the futures contract's menu screen, enter: Ticker <Comdty> (e.g., SPA <Comdty> for the S&P 500 futures contract menu, C A for corn; EDA for three-month Eurodollar; or FVA for a five-year T-note) or Ticker <Curncy> for currency futures (e.g., BPA <Curncy> for British pound futures).

- On the futures contract's menu screen, use the expiration screen (EXS) to find the ticker for the contract with the expiration month you want to analyze: Ticker <Comdty> (e.g., SPM7 <Comdty> for the March 2017 S&P 500 contract).

- On the selected futures menus screen, type OMON to find the options listed on the futures contract and their ticker.

- To bring up the futures option's menus page enter: Option's Ticker <Comdty> or Option's Ticker <Curncy> for currency futures options. The option's menu screens of note:
  - DES
  - GP
  - OSA
  - OSL: Option Strike List
  - OMON: Option Monitor
  - OMST: Most Active Options
  - OVL: Option Valuation
  - CALL: Call Options
  - PUT: Put Options
  - CWS: Covered Option Write Screen
  - GV: Volatility Graph
  - HVT: Historical Volatility Table
  - CT: Contract Table

FINDING FUTURES, FUTURES OPTIONS, INDEX OPTIONS, WARRANTS, AND CONVERTIBLE BONDS FROM THE SECF SCREEN

The SECF screen can be used to find the tickers for futures, futures options, spot index options, currency futures, currency futures options, and warrants: SECF <Enter>; select from the "Category" dropdown and from the tabs.

- For **commodity options**, click "Commodities" from the "Category" dropdown and then click the "Opt" tab.

- For **currency futures**, click "Currency" from the "Category" dropdown and then select "Active Futures" from the "futr" tab. Use OMON on the currency futures screen to find the currency futures options.

- For **futures indexes**, click "Index/Stat" from the "Category" dropdown and then click "futr" tab or click "opts." Use OMON on the futures screen to find the futures options.

- For **equity futures indexes**, click "Equity" from the "Category" dropdown and then click the "Equity Futures" tab. Use OMON on the futures screen to find the futures options.

- For options on **spot equity indexes**: Select "Equity" from the "Category" dropdown and click the "Index Options" tab.

- For **bond and interest rate futures contracts**, click "Fixed Income" from the "Category" dropdown, click "Futr" tab, and select "Active Futures" from the "Instrument" dropdown tab. You may also want to type in CME or CBT in the amber "Source" box to upload CME or CBT contracts. Use OMON on the futures screen to find the futures options.

- For **bond and interest rate futures option contracts**, click "Fixed Income" from the "Category" dropdown, click "Opt" tab, and select "Active Futures" from the

(Continued)

"Instrument" dropdown tab. You may also want to type in CME or CBT in the amber "Source" box to upload CME or CBT contracts. Use OMON on the futures screen to find the futures options.

- For **warrants**, click "Equity" from the "Category" dropdown, click the "Warrants" tab, and select type of warrants from the "Type" download.

- For **convertible bonds**, click "Fixed Income" from the "Category" dropdown, click the "Corporate" tab, and select "Convertible" from the "MtyType" download tab.

FINDING RIGHTS FROM THE IPO SCREEN

Rights can be found from the IPO screen:

- IPO <Enter>
- Click "Rights" box.
- Screen by "Offer Stage" (e.g., Trading), "Global Breakdown" (e.g., North America and United States), and "Industry" (e.g., All).
- Click the rights offering of interest to bring up a description of the right and its ticker.
- To upload the rights menu screen, enter "Ticker" <Equity> <Enter>.
- View screens to exam on the rights menu screen: DES and GP.

BLOOMBERG'S OPTION SCENARIO SCREEN

Profit and value graphs for futures options can be generated using the Bloomberg OSA screen. To access OSA for a security, load the menu page of the underlying futures contract and then type OSA (or click "OSA" from the menu).

1. To upload the futures contract's menu screen, enter: Ticker <Comdty> (e.g., SPA <Comdty> for the S&P 500 futures contract menu, C A for corn; EDA for three-month Eurodollar; or FVA for a five-year T-note) or Ticker <Curncy> for currency futures (e.g., BPA <Curncy> for British pound futures).
2. On the futures contract's menu screen, use the expiration screen (EXS) to find the ticker for the contract with the expiration month you want to analyze: Ticker <Comdty> (e.g., SPM7 <Comdty> for the March 2017 S7P 500 contract).
3. On the selected futures menus screen, type OSA.
4. On the OSA screen, click the "Positions" tab and then click "Add Listed Options" tab to bring up options listed on the futures. This brings up a screen showing the listed options from which to select (e.g., 1 call contract (100 calls) and 1 put contract (100 puts) on the October 2013 contract).
5. After selecting the positions, type 1 <Enter> (or click) to load positions and bring up the OSA position screen.
6. On the position screen, click the "Scenario Chart" tab at the top of the screen to bring up the profit graph. The profit graph shows profits for the strategy at expiration where the option price is trading at its intrinsic value and also at time periods prior where the option price is determined by an option-pricing model (described in Chapter 10). The profit graphs for different periods can be changed or deleted by using the select options at the top of the screen.

7. On the Scenario Chart screen, you can use the dropdown to change the axis from profits to "Market Value."

The OSA screen for a warrant can be uploaded from the Warrants menu screen.

CONVERTIBLE BOND SCREENS

- Convertible bonds can be found using **SECF** (see above). To find if a specific company has a convertible, you can bring up the **company's bond menu** (Ticker <Corp> <Enter>) and then select "Convertible" from the "Mty type" tab.
- **SRCH:** The bond search screen, SRCH, can also be used to find convertibles. On the SRCH screen, type in "Convertible" in the amber box. You may also want to narrow the search by also entering Country and Ratings. Click "Results" to see your search. To bring up the convertible's menu screen, enter: Convertible's ticker <Corp>.
- **CSCH: Convertible Bond Search:** You can use the CSCH screen to search for convertibles. You may want to screen by "Trading Activity" (e.g., Active), by Country, and by "Maturity Type" (e.g., convertible/callable or convertible/callable/putable). Click "Results" to see your search. To bring up the convertible's menu screen, enter the convertible's ticker <Corp>.
- View screens to examine on the convertible's menu page: DES, YAS, GP, CNVG (Convertible Bond Analysis), and OVCV (Convertible Valuation).

SWPM FOR CAPS AND FLOORS

SWPM: Bloomberg Swaps and Interest Rate Derivatives screen: SWPM analyzes, creates, and values swaps and interest rate derivative contracts. The Caps/Floors screen in SWPM can be used to create caps and floors and value them. To access the screen: go to the "Products" tab, click "Cap" under the "Options" dropdown. This will bring up the main screen that can be used to create the cap. You can then change the settings on the main screen. For a floor, click "Floor" from the "Products" tab.

1. Options: Notional Principal, Payment Frequency, Cap Strike Rate, Spread (the amount of basis points to add or subtract from the floating rate, LIBOR).
2. Forward Graph Options: SWPM determines future cash flows at each reset date based on the forward rate at that date. The user can select that yield curve from which the forward rates are to be determined. On the "Curve" screen ("Curve" tab), one can view the forward graph and make shift adjustment.
3. Discount Rate Option: SWPM also discounts cash flows to determine the market value (shown at the bottom of main screen; the user can also select which yield curve to be used for discounting).

TAB SCREENS

1. "Details" tab shows the detail of the cap.
2. "Resets" tab shows the reset rate at each effective date (forward LIBOR plus basis point you added to spread). One can change the rates from this tab.
3. "Cashflow" tab shows cash flows.

(Continued)

4. "Scenario" tab allows one to make scenario changes.
5. The cap is valued by using a forward rate curve and the Black futures option model (discussed in Part 3); each caplet is valued in the cash flow table.

IRDD: IRDD List Interest Rate Derivatives. Click the derivative of interest to go to the SWPM screen for evaluating that derivative.

Selected References

Abken, P. "Interest Rate Caps, Collars, and Floors." *Federal Reserve Bank of Atlanta Economic Review* 74, 6 (1989): 2–24.

Abken, P. A. "*Introduction to Over-the-Counter (OTC) Options.*" In J. C. Francis and A. S. Wolf, eds., *The Handbook of Interest Rate Risk Management.* New York: Irwin Professional, 1994, Chapter 25.

Black, F., and M. Scholes. "The Pricing of Options and Corporate Liabilities." *Journal of Political Economy* 81 (1973): 637–659.

Brenner, M., Courtadon, G., and M. Subrahmanyam. "Options on the Spot and Options on Futures." *The Journal of Finance* 40 (December 1985): 1303–1317.

Bhattacharya, A. K. "Interest-Rate Caps and Floors and Compound Options." In F. Fabozzi, ed., *The Handbook of Fixed Income Securities*, 6th ed. New York: McGraw-Hill, 2001.

Black, F., and M. Scholes. The Pricing of Options and Corporate Liabilities. *Journal of Political Economy* 81 (1973): 637–659.

Followill, R. "Relative Call Futures Option Pricing: An Examination of Market Efficiency." *The Review of Futures Markets* 6 (1987): 354–381.

Johnson, R. S. *Introduction to Derivatives: Options, Futures, and Swaps.* New York: Oxford University Press, 2009: Chapter 12.

Shastri, K., and K. Tandon. "Options on Futures Contracts: A Comparison of European and American Pricing Models." *The Journal of Futures Markets* 6 (Winter 1986): 593–618.

Thorp, E. "Options on Commodity Forward Contracts." *Management Science* 29 (October 1985): 1232–1242.

Wolf, A. "Fundamentals of Commodity Options on Futures." *Journal of Futures Markets* 2 (1982): 391–408.

Problems and Questions

1. Answer the following:

   a. What right does a September $5.00 wheat futures call option contract give the holder?

   b. What right does a September $5.00 wheat futures put option contract give the holder?

   c. What conditions are necessary to make the spot options and futures options equivalent?

   d. True or false: If the futures option contract and the underlying futures contract expire at the same time, then the futures options can be viewed as an option on the underlying spot security with the option having a cash settlement clause.

2. Explain the mechanics of exercising and closing an S&P 500 futures call options contract with an exercise price of 2,250 and multiplier of $250 when the

underlying futures contract is trading at 2,750. Explain the assigned writer's position and responsibility.

3. Explain the mechanics of exercising and closing an S&P 500 futures put options contract with an exercise price of 2,250 and multiplier of $250 when the underlying futures contract is trading at 2,000. Explain the assigned writer's position and responsibility.

4. Show graphically the profit and futures price relationships at expiration for the following positions on an S&P 500 futures options with an exercise price of 2,250, multiplier of $250, and call and put prices both equal to 75. Evaluate at futures prices at expiration or when the contract is exercised of 1,500, 1,750, 2,000, 2,250, 2,500, 2,750, and 3,000.

   a. Call purchase
   b. Put purchase
   c. Naked call write
   d. Naked put write
   e. Straddle purchase
   f. Straddle write

5. Explain what arbitrageurs would do if the price of a S&P 500 futures call with an exercise price of 2,500 ($250 multiplier) were priced at 45 when the underlying futures price was trading at 2,550. What impact would their actions have in the option market on the call's price?

6. Explain what arbitrageurs would do if the price of a S&P 500 futures put with an exercise price of 2,500 ($250 multiplier) were priced at 45 when the underlying futures price was trading at 2,450. What impact would their actions have in the option market on the put's price?

7. Explain the mechanics of exercising and closing a five-year T-note futures call options contract with an exercise price of $120,000 (for T-note with $100,000 face value) when the underlying futures contract is trading at $125,000. Explain the assigned writer's position and responsibility.

8. Explain the mechanics of exercising and closing a five-year T-note futures put options contract with an exercise price of $120,000 (for T-note with $100,000 face value) when the underlying futures contract is trading at $115,000. Explain the assigned writer's position and responsibility.

9. Show graphically the profit and futures price relationships at expiration for the following positions on five-year T-note futures options with an exercise price of $120,000 (for T-note with $100,000 face value), and a call and a put both priced at $2,000. Evaluate at futures prices at expiration or when the contract is exercised at $110,000, $115,000, $120,000, $125,000, $130,000, $135,000, and $135,000.

   a. Call purchase
   b. Put purchase
   c. Naked call write
   d. Naked put write
   e. Straddle purchase
   f. Straddle write

10. Explain what arbitrageurs would do if the price of a five-year T-note futures call with an exercise price of $120,000 were priced at $1,750 when the underlying futures price was trading at $122,000. What impact would their actions have in the option market on the call's price? Explain what arbitrageurs would do if the price of a five-year T-note futures put with an exercise price of $120,000 were priced at $1,750 when the underlying futures price was trading at $118,000. What impact would their actions have in the option market on the put's price?

11. What is the actual exercise price and premium for a September Eurodollar futures call with an exercise price quoted in terms of the CME index of 99.00 (R_D = 1.00%) and premium quoted at 0.05 (5 basis points). Explain the mechanics of exercising and closing the September Eurodollar futures call options contract when the futures contract is at R_D = 0.25%. Evaluate the option by generating a profit graph for a call purchase for R_D values at expiration or when exercised of 1.50%, 1.25%, 1.00%, 0.75%, 0.50%, and 0.25%.

12. What is the actual exercise price and premium for a September Eurodollar futures put with an exercise price quoted in terms of the CME index of 99.00 (R_D = 1.00%) and premium quoted at 0.05 (5 basis points). Explain the mechanics of exercising and closing the September Eurodollar futures put options contract when the futures contract is at R_D = 1.75%. Evaluate the option by generating a profit graph for a put purchase for R_D values at expiration or when exercised of 1.75%, 1.50%, 1.25%, 1.00%, 0.75%, 0.50%, and 0.25%.

13. Show graphically the profit and futures price relationships at expiration for the following positions on a September euro futures options with an exercise price of $1.115/euro, contract size of 125,000 euros, and call and put price of $0.02/€. Evaluate at futures prices at expiration or when the contract is exercised of $1.00/€, $1.05/€, $1.10/€, $1.15/€, $1.20/€, and $1.25/€.

    a. Call purchase
    b. Put purchase
    c. Naked call write
    d. Naked put write
    e. Straddle purchase
    f. Straddle write

14. Show graphically the profit and futures price relationships at expiration for the following positions on a November corn futures options with an exercise price of $3.20/bushel, size of 5,000 bushels, and call and put price of $0.20/bushel. Evaluate at futures prices at expiration or when the contract is exercised of $2.80, $2.90, $3.00, $3.10, $3.20, $3.30, $3.40, $3.50, 3.60, and $3.70.

    a. Call purchase
    b. Put purchase
    c. Naked call write
    d. Naked put write
    e. Straddle purchase
    f. Straddle write

15. Show graphically and in a table the profit and T-bond price relationships at expiration for the following positions on OTC T-bond options. In each case, assume that the T-bond spot call and put options each have exercise prices of $100,000 and premiums of $1,000, and that there is no accrued interest at expiration. Evaluate at spot T-bond prices of $90,000, $95,000, $100,000, $105,000, and $110,000.

   a. A straddle purchase formed with long positions in the T-bond call and put options.

   b. A straddle write formed with short positions in T-bond call and put options.

   c. A simulated long T-bond position formed by buying the T-bond call and selling the T-bond put.

   d. A simulated short stock position formed by selling the T-bond call and buying the T-bond put.

16. Show graphically and in a table the profit and LIBOR relationships at expiration for the following positions on interest rate options. In each case, assume that the interest rate call and put options each have exercise rates of 2%, a LIBOR reference rate, notional principals of $20 million, time period of 0.25 per year, and premiums of $25,000. Evaluate at spot discount yields at expiration of 0.5%, 1.0%, 1.5%, 2.00%, 2.50%, 3.00%, 3.50%, and 4.00%.

   a. An interest rate call purchase
   b. An interest rate put purchase
   c. An interest rate call sale
   d. An interest rate put sale

17. Cincy Land Developers is a real estate development company with a shopping mall development project currently valued at $20 million. The Cincy Company financed the project by borrowing from the Midwest Bank. The loan calls for a $25 million principal at the end of four years (no coupon interest). Show graphically the following relations:

   a. The value of Cincy's equity position at the loan's maturity as it relates to the value of its assets.

   b. The value of the creditors' position at the loan's maturity as it relates to the value of Cincy's assets.

   c. The current equity and debt values as they relate to the value of the assets.

18. Alcibiades Thoroughbred Inc. is a small horse syndicate that owns a three-year-old racehorse named Butterfly Spread. Based on Butterfly Spread's racing record and potential breeding value, the estimated value of the horse and therefore Alcibiades Thoroughbred Inc. is $1,000,000. Alcibiades has 10 shareholders, each with 100 shares (total shares = n = 1,000) and no debt. In addition, Alcibiades also has a warrant that it sold to Mr. Lucky giving him the right to buy 100 shares of Alcibiades for $1,300 per share.

   a. What would be the intrinsic value of Mr. Lucky's Alcibiades warrant if Butterfly Spread won the Bluegrass Stakes, a major stakes race, causing the value of the horse and ABC Inc. to increase to a value of $2,000,000?

    b. Instead of an Alcibiades warrant, suppose one of the Alcibiades equity holders sold a call option to Mr. Lucky giving him the right to buy 100 shares of Alcibiades stock at $1,300 per share. What would be the IV of the call if Butterfly Spread won the Bluegrass Stakes?

    c. Explain intuitively the difference between the call's IV and the warrant's IV.

    d. Show the algebraic relationship between the values of a warrant and a call.

19. Brandy Inc. is a $100 million oil company. The company has one million shares outstanding and no debt. Expecting the price of oil to increase, Brandy Inc. is planning to raise $10 million through a rights offering to finance the purchase of an oil well. The company has decided to make the subscription price on a new share $75, and, to comply with the state's preemption right, the company will issue one right for each share.

    a. Determine the number of rights that will be needed to buy one new share.

    b. What is the intrinsic value of each right?

20. Given the following features of the ABC convertible bond

- Coupon rate (annual) = 5%
- Face value = F = $1,000
- Maturity = 10 years
- Callable at $1,100
- YTM on a comparable, nonconvertible bond = 6%
- Conversion ratio = 10 shares
- Current stock price = S_0 = $95

    Calculate the following:

    a. ABC's conversion price

    b. ABC's conversion value

    c. ABC's straight debt value

    d. Minimum price of the convertible

    e. The arbitrage strategy if the price of the convertible was $925

Bloomberg Exercises

1. Find descriptions, recent prices, and other information on call and put options for some of the following: an equity index, commodity futures options, index futures options, currency futures options, Eurodollar futures options, and T-note futures option. For information on how to find futures and futures options from the SECF and CTM screens and how to upload the futures options and index options contracts, see section "Bloomberg: Options Screens." From the loaded option's menu screen, bring up:

    a. OMON

    b. CALL

    c. PUT

    d. GV, Volatility Graph

    e. HVT, Historical Volatility Table

    f. GP

2. Using the Bloomberg OSA screen, evaluate the following option strategies with a profit graph for some of the call and put options you selected in Exercise 1:
   a. Call purchase
   b. Call sale
   c. Put purchase
   d. Put sale
   e. Covered call write
   f. Covered put write
   g. Straddle purchase
   h. Straddle sale

   For a guide on using the OSA screen, see "Bloomberg's Option Scenario Screen" found in "Bloomberg: Options Screens."

3. Select several of the options you evaluated in Exercise 1 and bring up their screens. Using the Bloomberg OSA screen, select a call and put on each of the futures options and create a call price curve and put price curve for the current date and *IV* line using the expiration date. For a guide on using the OSA screen, see "Bloomberg's Option Scenario Screen" found in "Bloomberg: Options Screens."

4. Find descriptions, recent prices, and other information on an equity warrant. To search for warrants, go to the SECF screen. On the screen, click "Equity" from the "Category" dropdown, click the "Warrants" tab, and select type of warrants from the "Type" download. Using the Bloomberg OSA screen, evaluate the warrant purchase with a profit graph.

5. Find descriptions, recent prices, and other information on a recent rights offering. To search for warrants, go to the IPO screen. On the screen, Click "Rights" box, and screen by "Offer Stage" (e.g., Trading), "Global Breakdown" (e.g., North America and United States), and "Industry" (e.g., All). Click the rights offering of interest to bring up a description of the right and its ticker. To upload the rights menu screen, enter "Ticker" <Equity> <Enter>. View screens to exam on the rights menu screen: DES and GP.

6. Find descriptions, recent prices, and other information on a convertible bond. Use SECF, SRCH, or CSCH to search for convertible bonds. Upload the convertible's menu screen (convertible's Ticker <Corp>). View screen to examine: DES, GP, YAS.

7. Use the Bloomberg SWPM screen to create and analyze a cap. Tabs to include in your analysis: Details, Resets, Cashflows, and Curves.

8. Use the Bloomberg SWPM screen to create and analyze a floor. Tabs to include in your analysis: Details, Resets, Cashflows, and Curves.

CHAPTER 7

Option Strategies

In Chapter 5, we defined the six fundamental option strategies and the straddle and spread in terms of their profit and security price relationships near expiration. As we noted in Chapter 5, one of the important features of an option is that it can be combined with positions in the underlying security and other options to generate a number of different investment strategies. For example, a speculator who expected a stock to increase in the future but didn't want to assume the risk inherent in a call purchase position could form a bull call spread. In contrast, a speculator who expected a stock to be stable over the near term could, in turn, try to profit by forming a straddle write. Thus, by combining different option positions, speculators can obtain positions that match their expectation and their desired risk-return preference. In this chapter, we extend the discussion of option strategies in Chapter 5 to a more detailed analysis of the fundamental strategies and introduce some new ones that can be used for either speculation or hedging.

Call Purchases

Investors often view the call purchase as a leveraged alternative to purchasing stock. As we discussed in Chapter 5, compared to a long stock position, the purchase of a call yields higher expected returns, but like buying stock on margin, it also is more risky. For example, as shown in the profit graph and table for an Amazon call purchase in Exhibit 7.1, Amazon stock purchased at $625.90 on 9/30/15 yields a 19.83% rate of return (excluding any dividends) if its price reaches $750, while the Amazon call option with an exercise price of $600, February expiration (2/15/16), and trading at

EXHIBIT 7.1   Profit Graph and Table for February 2016, 600 Call Contract on Amazon

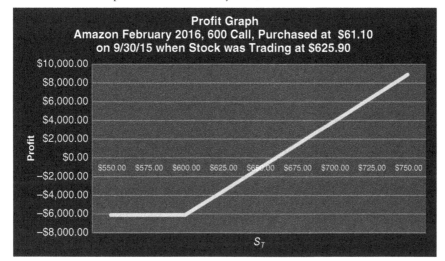

		Return % Call	Return % Stock
Stock Price at T	Profit	Profit / ($61.10 * 100)	$(S_T / \$625.90) - 1$
$550.00	−$6,110.00	−100.00%	−12.13%
$575.00	−$6,110.00	−100.00%	−8.13%
$600.00	−$6,110.00	−100.00%	−4.14%
$625.00	−$3,610.00	−59.08%	−0.14%
$650.00	−$1,110.0	−18.17%	3.85%
$675.00	$1,390.00	22.75%	7.84%
$700.00	$3,890.00	63.67%	11.84%
$725.00	$6,390.00	104.58%	15.83%
$750.00	$8,890.00	145.50%	19.83%

Break-Even Price = $661.10

a premium of $61.10 on 8/30/15 would yield a rate of return of 145.50% (($750 − $600)/$61.10) if it were exercised or sold at its intrinsic value of $150 at the 2/15/16 expiration. In contrast if the stock would have decreased to $600 (near expiration), then the loss on the stock would be 4.14%, compared to a 100% loss on the call. Thus, like a leveraged stock purchase, a long call position yields a higher return-risk combination than a stock purchase.

In addition to providing investors with a short-run alternative to a long stock position, call purchases also can be used by investors as a way to purchase stock when they are temporarily illiquid. For example, suppose an investor has funds tied up in illiquid securities at a time when she wanted to buy the stock of a company that is expected to release unexpectedly good earnings information. The investor could acquire the stock first by buying a call option on it, then, after becoming liquid, exercising the option.

Follow-up Strategies

A call purchase position is used when the price of the stock is expected to increase. Once an investor has selected a call option on a stock, she must monitor the position and determine what to do with the option if the price of the stock changes differently than she expected. Strategies used after setting up an initial option position are known as *follow-up actions*. These strategies, in turn, can be classified as either *aggressive follow-up strategies*, used when the price of the stock moves to a profitable position, and *defensive follow-up strategies*, employed when the stock price moves to an actual or potentially unprofitable position.

Aggressive Follow-Up Strategies

To see the types of aggressive strategies one can use, consider the case of an investor who purchased an Amazon February 2016, 600 call contract for $61.10 on 9/30/15 when Amazon was trading at $625.90. Exhibit 7.2 shows the Bloomberg price graphs for Amazon stock, its February 600 call, February 625 call, and February 625 put. As shown in the graph, the price of Amazon increased to $673.25 on 11/11/15, causing the February 600 call to increase to $91.75, the 625 call to increase to 74.90, and the 625 put to decrease to $27.10. Faced with this positive development, the Amazon call buyer would have had a number of alternatives open to her.

First, the investor could have *liquidated* by selling the 600 call for $91.75, realizing a profit of $3,065 (= ($91.75 − $61.10)(100)). The advantage of liquidating is certainty: the investor would know that even if the stock price declined, she will still have earned $3,065. The disadvantage of liquidating, of course, is the opportunity loss if the stock increased in price.

If the investor had strongly felt that Amazon would continue to rise, then a second follow-up strategy is simply to *do nothing*. As shown in Exhibit 7.2, if the stock reached $750 at expiration ($T$) then the investor would realize a profit of $8,890 by selling the call at a price equal to its intrinsic value of $150—this is $5,825 more than if she had liquidated. Of course, if the price of the stock had decreased after reaching $673.25 and moved to $600 or less, then the investor would have lost the premium of $6,110 and would have regretted not liquidating the call back when the stock was at $673.25.

If the call purchaser wanted to gain more than just $3,065—in case the stock continued to rise—but did not want to lose if the stock declined, she could have followed up the call purchase strategy by creating a *spread*. Recall that a call spread is formed by buying and selling a call option simultaneously on the same stock, but with different terms. In the case of aggressive follow-up strategies, a spread often is created by selling a call with a higher exercise price. In terms of our example, suppose the investor sold the Amazon February 625 call contract for $74.90 when the stock was at $673.75. As shown Exhibit 7.2, at expiration the investor would realize a limited profit of $3,880 if the price of Amazon were $625 or above and limited profit of $1,380 if the stock were $600 or less, Thus, the spread would have yielded the investor less profit than the liquidating strategy if the stock price were to increase, but unlike the do-nothing strategy, the spread would lock in a profit if the stock decreased.

If, after the price of the stock reached $673.75, the expectation was that the price would continue to rise, then the investor might want to consider following up with a roll-up strategy. As the name implies, a *roll-up strategy* requires moving to a higher exercise price. This can be accomplished in several ways. For example, our investor could have sold her 600 call contract for $9,175, and then used the proceeds to buy 1.225 February 625 calls at $74.90 (assume perfect divisibility). As shown in the

EXHIBIT 7.2   Aggressive Follow-Up Strategies for Amazon Call Purchase

Prices of Amazon, February 600 Call, February 625 Call, and February 625 Put

Profit Table on 11/11/15 Follow-Up Positions formed on 600 Call Purchased on 9/30/15

Stock Price at Expiration, 2/15/16	**Liquidate**: Sell 600 Call for $91.75 on 11/11/15	**Do Nothing**	**Spread**: 600 Call Purchased at $61.10 on 9/30/15; 625 Call Sold for $74.90 on 11/11/15	**Roll up**: Sell the 600 Call Contract for $9,175 and Buy 1.225 February 625 Call Contracts	**Combination**: 600 Call Purchased at $61.10 on 9/30/15; 625 Put Purchased for $27.10 on 11/11/15
$550	$3,065.00	−$6,110.00	$1,380.00	−$6,110.00	$664,680.00
$575	$3,065.00	−$6,110.00	$1,380.00	−$6,110.00	$664,680.00
$600	$3,065.00	−$6,110.00	$1,380.00	−$6,110.00	$664,680.00
$625	$3,065.00	−$3,610.00	$3,880.00	−$6,110.00	$417,180.00
$650	$3,065.00	−$1,110.00	$3,880.00	−$3,047.50	$169,680.00
$675	$3,065.00	$1,390.00	$3,880.00	$15.00	−$1,320.00
$700	$3,065.00	$3,890.00	$3,880.00	$3,077.50	$1,180.00
$725	$3,065.00	$6,390.00	$3,880.00	$6,140.00	$3,680.00
$750	$3,065.00	$8,890.00	$3,880.00	$9,202.50	$6,180.00
$775	$3,065.00	$11,390.00	$3,880.00	$12,265.00	$8,680.00
$800	$3,065.00	$13,890.00	$3,880.00	$15,327.50	$11,180.00
$825	$3,065.00	$16,390.00	$3,880.00	$18,390.00	$13,680.00

Source: Bloomberg OSA Screens

exhibit, this roll-up strategy would have provided the investor with a relatively substantial gain near expiration if the stock were to have increased in price, but also would have resulted in losses if the stock were to have declined. To minimize the range in potential profits and losses, the investor alternatively could have implemented a roll-up strategy by selling the 60 call and then using only a portion of profit to buy 625 calls.

Finally, the call purchaser could set up a combination as a follow-up strategy. A combination purchase is a long position in a call and a put on the same stock with different terms. For aggressive follow-up strategies, a combination could be formed by buying a put with a higher exercise price. The impact of this combination strategy is shown in the exhibit for the case in which our investor bought a February 625 put for $27.10.

Note: It is important to remember that there is no optimum follow-up strategy; rather, the correct follow-up depends ultimately on where the investor thinks the stock eventually will close, and on how strongly she believes in that forecast.

Defensive Follow-Up Strategies

If, after purchasing a call, the price of the stock decreases, the investor then needs to consider defensive follow-up strategies.

To see the types of defensive strategies one can use, consider the case of an investor who purchased Macy's February 2016, 60 call on 8/12/15 for $6.80 when Macy's was trading at $64.11. Exhibit 7.3 shows the Bloomberg price graphs for Macy's stock, its

EXHIBIT 7.3   Defensive Follow-Up Strategies for a Macy Call

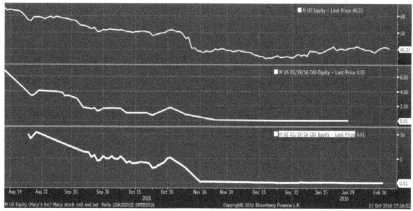

Prices of Macy's, February 60 Call, February 50 Call, and February 625 Put

Profit Table on 9/30 Follow-Up Positions Formed on 60 Call Purchased on 8/12/15

Stock Price at Expiration, 2/15/16	Liquidate: Sell 60 Call for $1.61 on 9/30/15	Do Nothing	Spread: 60 Call Purchased at $6.80 on 8/12/15; 50 Call Sold for $5.35 on 9/30/15
$30	−$519	−$680	−$145
$35	−$519	−$680	−$145
$40	−$519	−$680	−$145
$45	−$519	−$680	−$145
$50	−$519	−$680	−$145
$55	−$519	−$680	−$645
$60	−$519	−$680	−$1,145
$65	−$519	−$180	−$1,145
$70	−$519	$320	−$1,145
$75	−$519	$820	−$1,145
$80	−$519	$1,320	−$1,145

Source: Bloomberg OSA Screens

February 60 call, and its February 50 call. As shown in the graph, shortly after trading at $64.11 on 8/12/15, the price of Macy's decreased significantly on poor earnings forecast and analysts' sell recommendations, falling to $51.32 on 9/30/15, causing the 60 call to decrease to $1.61 and the February 50 call to trade at $5.35.

Faced with this negative development, the call investor could have considered several alternative follow-ups. As shown in Exhibit 7.3, if the holder *liquidated*, she would have realized a loss of $519 compared to the $680 loss that she would have incurred if she did nothing and the price of the stock was below the exercise price at expiration. In contrast to the *do-nothing strategy*, liquidating does eliminate potential profit if the stock price reverses itself. If the investor thought that the price decline was a signal of further price decreases, she could have created a *spread*. As shown in the exhibit, if the holder combined the long position in the 60 call with a short position in a 50 call trading on 9/30 for $5.35, the investor would have limited her losses to $145 if the stock reached $50 or less. However, if the stock increased to $60 or higher, the investor would lose $1,145. If the investor believed Macy's stock could go either up or down, she could combine her 60 call with a 60 put to form a straddle.

Call Purchases in Conjunction with Other Positions

Simulated Put

Purchasing a call and selling the underlying stock short on a one-to-one basis yields the same type of profit and stock price relationship as a put purchase. This strategy is known as a *simulated put*.

The profit and stock price relation at expiration is shown in Exhibit 7.4 for an investor who sold 100 shares of Delta Airlines stock short at $48.93 per share and purchased a Delta March 49 call contract at $2.73 on January 6, 2016. The total profit and stock price relations at expiration are plotted in the table's accompanying figure. As can be seen, the simulated put strategy yields the same relationship as the purchase of a 49 put at $2.80.

Two strategies with the same profit and stock price relationships are referred to as *equivalent strategies*. Note, however, that while the put purchase and the simulated put formed with a long call and short stock position are equivalent in terms of their profit and stock price relations, they are not identical. Given the put-call parity relation discussed in Chapter 5, the equilibrium price of the 49 put is not likely to be $2.80 when the 49 call is priced at $2.73. Thus, the short sale and call purchase strategy do not yield an identical long 49 put position. To form an identical long put position with a put price consistent with put-call parity, a *synthetic put*, requires not only buying the call and shorting the stock but also buying a bond with a face value equal to the exercise price. The equality between the put position and the short stock, long call, and long bond position can be expressed algebraically as:

$$P_0 = C_0 - S_0 + B_0$$

or

$$\{+P\} = \{+C, +B, -S\}$$

where B_0 is the price of the bond with a face value of X and where the $+$ sign indicates a long position and $-$ indicates a short position.

EXHIBIT 7.4   Simulated Put: Long Call and Short Stock

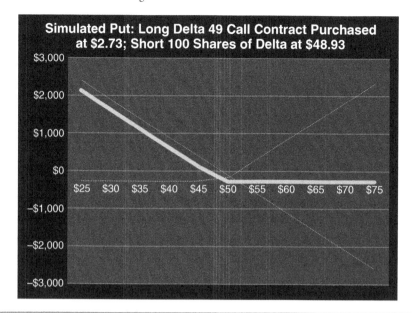

Stock Price	Call Profit: 100 Calls Purchased at $2.73	Short Stock Position Profit: 100 Shares Shorted at $48.93	Total Profit
$25	−$273	$2,393	$2,120
$30	−$273	$1,893	$1,620
$35	−$273	$1,393	$1,120
$40	−$273	$893	$620
$45	−$273	$393	$120
$50	−$173	−$107	−$280
$55	$327	−$607	−$280
$60	$827	−$1,107	−$280
$65	$1,327	−$1,607	−$280
$70	$1,827	−$2,107	−$280
$75	$2,327	−$2,607	−$280

For short-run investments, the put purchase is a better strategy than a simulated or synthetic put. The simulated put requires the investor to post collateral on the stock shorted, to pay dividends to the share lender if they are declared, and to pay the higher commission costs. The simulated put, though, is worth keeping in mind as a hedge or follow-up strategy for a short sale. For example, an investor who went short in a stock as a long-run bearish strategy might purchase a call to offset potential losses if the price of the stock increased due to an unexpected good earnings announcement. Such a strategy would represent an insurance strategy on a short stock position.

Simulated Straddle

The purchase of two calls for each share of stock shorted {+2C, −S} yields a strategy equivalent to a straddle purchase. This strategy is defined as a *simulated straddle*.

To illustrate, suppose in our previous example the investor bought two Delta Airline 49 call contracts at $2.73 per call after going short in 100 shares of the Delta at $48.93. As shown in the table and figure in Exhibit 7.5, the investor would obtain a V-shaped profit and stock price relation. He would have a loss equal to $453 when the stock price equals $50, two break-even prices at $43.47 and $55.53, and virtually unlimited profit potential if the stock price increases or decreases past the respective upper and lower break-even prices.

Similar to the simulated put, a simulated straddle is less attractive as a short-run investment than its equivalent straddle strategy because of the higher commission costs, required dividend coverage on the short sale, and collateral associated with the short sale. However, like the preceding comparison of the put and simulated put, the simulated straddle is a strategy worth keeping in mind as a possible follow-up strategy for a short stock position.

EXHIBIT 7.5 Simulated Straddle Short Stock and Long Two Call Contracts

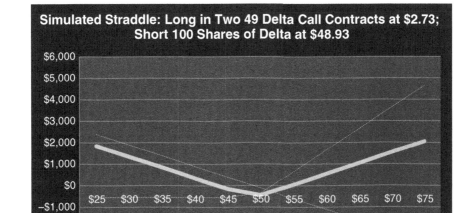

Stock Price	Call Profit: 200 Calls Purchased at $2.73	Short Stock Position Profit: 100 Shares Shorted at $48.93	Total Profit
$25.00	−$546	$2,393	$1,847
$30.00	−$546	$1,893	$1,347
$35.00	−$546	$1,393	$847
$40.00	−$546	$893	$347
$43.47	−$546	$546	$0
$45.00	−$546	$393	−$153
$50.00	−$346	−$107	−$453
$54.53	$560	−$560	$0
$55.00	$654	−$607	$47
$60.00	$1,654	−$1,107	$547
$65.00	$2,654	−$1,607	$1,047
$70.00	$3,654	−$2,107	$1,547
$75.00	$4,654	−$2,607	$2,047

Naked Call Writes

The second fundamental strategy we examined in Chapter 5 was the naked call write. The profit graph and table for a naked call write is shown in Exhibit 7.6. The exhibit shows the profits at different stock prices at expiration from selling a Kroger call contract with an exercise price of $37.50 and expiration of October 2016 purchased on 3/25/16 at $4.50 when Kroger was trading at $37.50. As highlighted in the profit graph, the naked call write is characterized by a limited profit and unlimited loss characteristic. As a result, this strategy is not very popular among option investors. However, it does have some attractive features. One such characteristic is that the option loses its time value premium as time passes. For example, if a writer sold a call, she could profit some time later if the price of the stock did not change. That is, the writer would be able to buy back the call at a lower price because of the lower time value premium. Of course, if the stock increased in price, then the writer would lose if the increase in intrinsic value exceeded the decrease in the time value premium.

It should be remembered, however, that in order to establish a naked call write, an investor must post collateral in the form of cash or risk-free securities as a security in the event the call is exercised and she is assigned.

EXHIBIT 7.6   Naked Call Write Short October 37.50 Kroger Call Contract purchased at 4.50

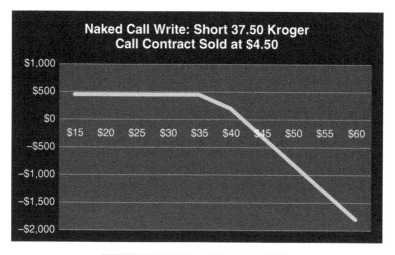

Stock Price	Call Profit: Short 100 October 37.50 Calls sold at $4.50
$20.00	$450
$25.00	$450
$30.00	$450
$35.00	$450
$40.00	$200
$42.00	$0
$45.00	−$300
$50.00	−$800
$55.00	−$1,300
$60.00	−$1,800

Follow-Up Strategies: Rolling Credit

Although a naked call write is less attractive than other strategies because of its limited profit and unlimited loss characteristic, one interesting tactical or defensive follow-up strategy that could be used with a naked call write is the *rolling-credit strategy*. Under this strategy, if the stock price increases, the naked call writer sells calls with higher exercise prices and then uses the proceeds (or credit) to close the initial short position by buying the calls back. This strategy then is repeated every time the stock increases to a new, uncomfortable level. The hope, in turn, is that the stock eventually will stabilize or preferably decrease in price, and the writer will realize a profit approximately equal to the call sales.

For the rolling-credit strategy to work, three conditions must hold. First, the stock price eventually must stop rising. If the stock does not stop, then, with continuous follow-ups, the writer will realize losses when the stock exceeds the break-even price on the option position with the highest possible exercise price. Second, even if the stock eventually stops rising, a rolling-credit writer must have sufficient collateral (the collateral requirements increase exponentially as the stock price increases). Finally, the success of the rolling-credit strategy requires that the writer not be assigned. Since the writer has no control over assignment, he needs to select options that have a small chance of being exercised. In summary, the rolling-credit strategy, on the surface, appears to be a simple strategy, as well as an easy way of making money. However, for the strategy to work, the aforementioned conditions must hold. If they do not, then the rolling-credit writer can incur substantial losses, perhaps more than he initially had been prepared for.

If the stock price stays below the exercise price or decreases, the naked call writer may want to pursue an aggressive follow-up action. Such actions could include any of the following:

- Closing the present position and moving to a short position in a call with a lower exercise price
- Closing the short position and using the proceeds to buy a put if he is relatively more bearish
- Closing and buying a call with a low exercise price if he feels the stock has bottomed out
- Simply liquidating the position

As noted above, there is no optimum follow-up strategy but rather, a number of strategies available that an investor can use, depending on what price he feels the stock eventually will reach.

Covered Call Writes

The third fundamental option strategy is the covered call write—namely, long in the stock and short in the call, {+S, −C}. This strategy is popular among institutional investors who see it as a way of hedging a long stock position against an anticipated small stock price decrease or as a way of enhancing the return on a particular stock. For example, suppose an investor already owned a stock in which he did not expect to

EXHIBIT 7.7   Covered Call Write: Long 100 Shares of Kroger purchased at $37.50, Short October
37.50 Call Contracts at 4.50

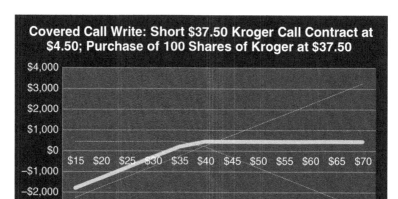

Stock Price	Call Profit: Short 100 October 37.50 Calls Sold at $4.50	Long Stock Position Profit: 100 Shares Purchased $37.50	Total Profit
$15.00	$450	−$2,250	−$1,800
$20.00	$450	−$1,750	−$1,300
$25.00	$450	−$1,250	−$800
$30.00	$450	−$750	−$300
$33.00	$450	−$450	$0
$35.00	$450	−$250	$200
$40.00	$200	$250	$450
$45.00	−$300	$750	$450
$50.00	−$800	$1,250	$450
$55.00	−$1,300	$1,750	$450
$60.00	−$1,800	$2,250	$450
$65.00	−$2,300	$2,750	$450
$70.00	−$2,800	$3,250	$450

appreciate in the near term. By writing a call, the investor would be able to increase
the total return if the stock price stays the same or decreases only slightly. If the stock
increases significantly, though, the capital gains on the stock position would be offset
by losses on the short call position. Exhibit 7.7 shows the profit graph and table of a
covered call write formed by owning 100 shares of Kroger purchased at $37.50 and
selling an October $37.50 call contract at $4.50.

As a short-run investment strategy, a covered call write has a lower return-risk
trade-off than a long stock position. This may be seen by comparing columns 3 and 4 in

Exhibit 7.7. Column 3 shows the profits for each stock price obtained from purchasing 100 shares of Kroger stock at $37.50; column 4 shows the profits for a covered call position formed by purchasing 100 shares of Kroger at $37.50 and selling an October $37.50 Kroger call contract at $4.50. As shown in the exhibit, if at expiration the stock had declined from $37.50 to $33.00, the investor would realize a profit of $450 from the call premium, which would offset the $450 actual (if stock is sold) or paper loss from the stock. If the stock price stayed at $37.50 or increased beyond it, then the covered call writer would receive a profit of only $450. For example, if the stock were at $60 at expiration, the option would be trading at its intrinsic value of $22.50. To close the option position, the writer would have to pay $2,250 to buy the 100 calls, which would negate the $2,250 actual or paper gain he would earn from the stock. Thus, the investor would be left with a profit equal to just the call premium of $450.

All covered writes require selling a call against the stock owned. This strategy, though, can be divided into two general types: an out-of-the-money covered call write and an in-the-money covered call write. The out-of-the-money write yields a higher return-risk trade-off than an in-the-money-write. It should be noted that the investor is not limited to constructing covered call writes from the options available on the exchange. The investor could construct a covered call write using a portfolio of written calls with different exercise prices. Finally, note that as with all option positions, if the price of the underlying stock changes unexpectedly, then an investor may want to pursue a follow-up strategy.

Ratio Call Writes

A ratio call write is a combination of a naked call write and a covered call write. It is constructed by selling calls against more shares of stock than one owns: for example, selling two calls for each share of stock purchased or owned {+S, −2C}. The table and figure in Exhibit 7.8 summarize the profit and stock price relations for a ratio call write formed by purchasing 100 shares of Kroger stock for $37.50 per share and selling two October $37.50 call contracts at $4.50 per call. As shown in the exhibit, this ratio call write strategy generates an inverted V-shaped profit and stock price relation, with two break-even prices and a maximum profit of $650 occurring when the price of the stock is between $35 and $40. Moreover, different ratio call write strategies (differing by their ratios) generate similar characteristics, provided the ratio is greater than 1. For example, a comparison of the 3:1 ratio call write shown in Exhibit 7.9 to the 2:1 ratio write show in 7.8 shows that going from 2:1 to 3:1, the break-even prices go from $28.50 and $46.50 to $24 and $44.25, respectively, and the maximum profit increases from $650 to $1,100. As a result, an investor, by varying the ratio, can obtain a number of inverted V-shaped relations (not perfectly inverted V graphs), with each ratio call write differing in terms of its maximum profit, the magnitude of its gains and losses at each stock price, and its break-even prices.

EXHIBIT 7.8 2:1 Ratio Call Write

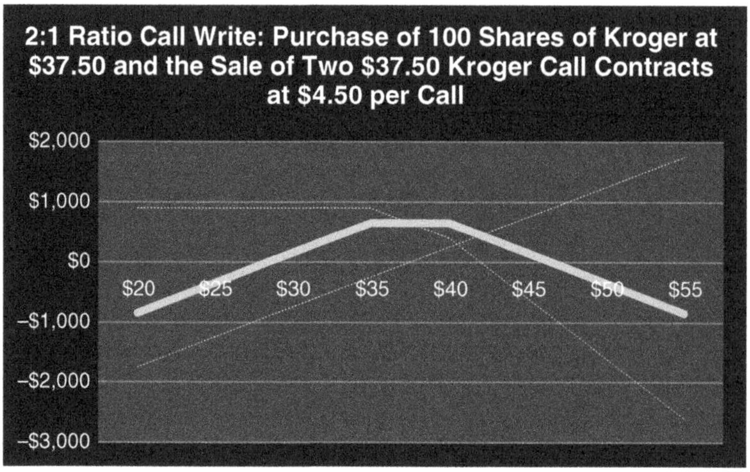

2:1 Ratio Call Write: Purchase of 100 Shares of Kroger at $37.50 and the Sale of Two $37.50 Kroger Call Contracts at $4.50 per Call

Stock Price	Call Profit: Short 200 October 37.50 Calls Sold at $4.50	Long Stock Position Profit: 100 Shares Purchased at $37.50	Total Profit
$15.00	$900	−$2,250	−$1,350
$20.00	$900	−$1,750	−$850
$25.00	$900	−$1,250	−$350
$28.50	$900	−$900	$0
$30.00	$900	−$750	$150
$33.00	$900	−$450	$450
$35.00	$900	−$250	$650
$40.00	$400	$250	$650
$45.00	−$600	$750	$150
$46.50	−$900	$900	$0
$50.00	−$1,600	$1,250	−$350
$55.00	−$2,600	$1,750	−$850
$60.00	−$3,600	$2,250	−$1,350

Put Purchases

Just as a call purchase can be viewed as an alternative to a leveraged stock purchase, a put purchase can be thought of as a leveraged alternative to a short sale. This is illustrated in Exhibit 7.10, which shows that if Boeing stock was sold short at $132 on 3/25/16, it would have provided an investor with a 24.24% rate of return as expressed as a proportion of a 100% margin if the stock had declined to $100 (0.2424 = ($132 − $100)/$132), and a 17.42% loss if it had increased to $155. In contrast, the purchase of a $130 put on 3/25/16 when the option was trading at a premium of $10.40 would have yielded a 188.46% rate of return (1.8846 = ($130 − 100)/$10.40) if the stock were at $100, but a 100% loss if the stock were at $130 or higher. Thus, for short-run investments, investors who are bearish on a stock will find the purchase of a

EXHIBIT 7.9   3:1 Ratio Call Write

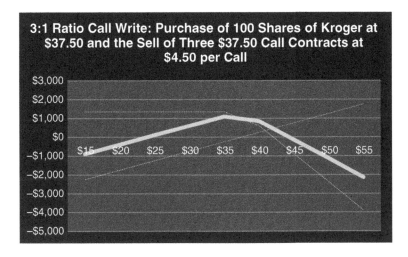

Stock Price	Call Profit: Short 300 October 37.50 Calls Sold at $4.50	Long Stock Position Profit: 100 Shares Purchased $37.50	Total Profit
$10.00	$1,350	−$2,750	−$1,400
$15.00	$1,350	−$2,250	−$900
$20.00	$1,350	−$1,750	−$400
$24.00	$1,350	−$1,350	$0
$25.00	$1,350	−$1,250	$100
$30.00	$1,350	−$750	$600
$33.00	$1,350	−$450	$900
$35.00	$1,350	−$250	$1,100
$40.00	$600	$250	$850
$44.25	−$675	$675	$0
$45.00	−$900	$750	−$150
$50.00	−$2,400	$1,250	−$1,150
$55.00	−$3,900	$1,750	−$2,150
$60.00	−$5,400	$2,250	−$3,150

put represents a higher return-risk alternative to the short sale. In addition, the short sale carries with it an obligation to cover dividends, which the put does not (although its price does decrease at the stock's ex-dividend date), and total commission costs are higher for short sales than put purchases.

Put Purchase Strategies

A put purchase strategy is used when the price of a stock is expected to decline. Bearish investors should keep two points in mind in selecting puts. First, an out-of-the-money put provides a higher return-risk investment than an in-the-money put. For example, suppose that ABC stock is at $59, an out-of-the-money ABC June 55 put is trading

EXHIBIT 7.10 Put Purchase and Short Stock Position

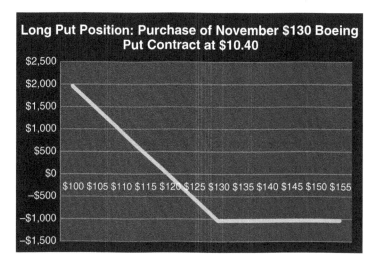

Boeing Put on 3/25/2016: $T = 11/18/16$, $X = \$130$, $P = \$10.40$, Contract = 100 Puts; Boeing Stock = \$132		Return on Put	Return on Short Position on 100% Initial Margin
Stock Price	Profit	Profit / (\$10.40*100)	(\$132 − S_T)/ \$132
\$100	\$1,960	188.46%	24.24%
\$105	\$1,460	140.38%	20.45%
\$110	\$960	92.31%	16.67%
\$115	\$460	44.23%	12.88%
\$120	−\$40	−3.85%	9.09%
\$125	−\$540	−51.92%	5.30%
\$130	−\$1,040	−100.00%	1.52%
\$135	−\$1,040	−100.00%	−2.27%
\$140	−\$1,040	−100.00%	−6.06%
\$145	−\$1,040	−100.00%	−9.85%
\$150	−\$1,040	−100.00%	−13.64%
\$155	−\$1,040	−100.00%	−17.42%

Break-Even Price = \$119.60

at \$1, and an in-the-money ABC June 60 put is at \$3. If the price of ABC decreases to \$50 near expiration, then the 55 put could be sold at its intrinsic value of \$5, yielding a rate of return of 400% ((\$5 −\$1)/\$1), while the 60 put could be sold at its intrinsic value of \$10 to yield a rate of 233% ((\$10 − \$3)/\$3). In contrast, if ABC drops to only \$55, then the out-of-the-money 55 put would be worthless, while the 60 put would yield a profit of \$2 (at \$60 or higher, both puts yield 100% losses). Thus, an out-of-the-money put offers higher potential rewards but also higher risk than an in-the-money put. Second, it is important to keep in mind that in-the-money puts tend to lose their value faster than out-of-the-money puts when the price of the stock increases. This is because when the price of the underlying stock increases over time, the in-the-money put loses both its intrinsic value and its time value premium, while the out-of-the-money losses just its time value premium.

Follow-Up Strategies

Once an investor has purchased a put, she needs to be able to identify the possible follow-up actions that can be pursued if the stock price changes are different from what she expects. Aggressive follow-up actions can be taken if the stock decreases more than expected, and defensive actions can be used if the stock increases in price.

Aggressive Follow-Up Strategies

To see the types of aggressive strategies one can use, consider the case of an investor who purchased the Devon Energy, April 2016, 24 put contract for $1.94 on 1/29/16 when Devon was trading at $27.90. Exhibit 7.11 shows the Bloomberg price graphs

EXHIBIT 7.11   Price Graphs: Devon Energy, Devon April 24 Put, Devon April 20 Put, and Devon April 26 Put, 1/15/16 to 3/28/16

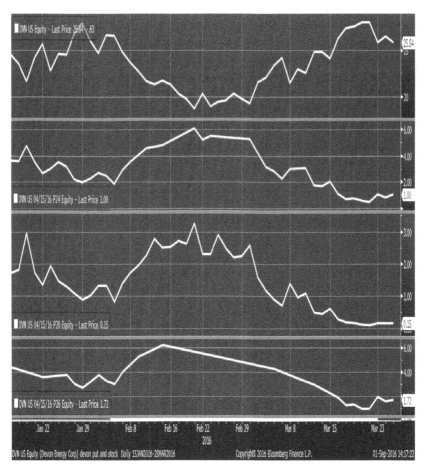

for Devon Energy stock, its April 24 put, April 20 put, and April 26 put. As shown in the graph, the price of Devon decreased to $26.59 on 2/2/16, causing the April 24 put to increase to $2.72 and the April 20 put to increase to $1.34. Faced with this positive development, the Devon put buyer would have had a number of alternatives open to her. First, she could have *liquidated* by selling the 24 put for $2.72, realizing a profit of $78.00 (= ($2.72 − $1.94)(100)). The advantage of liquidating is certainty: The investor would know that even if the price of the stock increased, she will still have earned $78.00. The disadvantage of liquidating, of course, is the opportunity loss if the stock decreased in price. If the investor had strongly felt that Devon Energy would continue to decrease, then a second follow-up strategy is to *do nothing*. As shown in Exhibit 7.12, if the stock reached $20 at expiration ($T$) then the investor would have realized a profit of $206 by selling the put at a price equal to its intrinsic value of $4.00—this is $128 more than if she had liquidated.

If the put purchaser wanted to gain more than just $206—in case the stock continues to decline—but did not want to lose if the stock increased, she could have followed up the put purchase strategy by creating a *spread*. In the case of aggressive follow-up strategies, a spread often is created by selling a put with a lower exercise price. In terms of our example, suppose the investor sold the April 20 put contract for $1.34 when the stock was at $26.59. As shown in exhibit, at expiration the investor would realize a limited profit of $340 if the price of Devon were $20 or less and limited loss of $60 if the stock were $24 or greater, Thus, the spread would have yielded the investor less profit than the liquidating strategy if the stock price were to decrease, but unlike the do-nothing strategy, the spread would lock in a smaller loss if the stock increased.

If, after the price of the stock reached $26.59, the expectation was that the price would continue to fall, then the investor might want to consider a roll-down follow-up strategy. This could have been done by selling the 24 put contracts for $272 and

EXHIBIT 7.12   Aggressive Follow-Up Strategies for April 24 Put Purchase

Devon Energy: April 24 Put Contract purchased at $1.94 on 1/29/2016 when Stock was selling at $27.90

Stock Price at Expiration, 4/15/16	Liquidate: Sell 24 Put for $2.72 on 2/2/16	Do Nothing	Spread: 24 put Purchased at $1.94 on 1/15/16; 20 put Sold for $1.34 on 2/3/16	Roll Down: Sell the 24 Put Contract for $2.72 and buy 2.03 April 20 put Contracts at $1.34
$15.00	$78	$706	$340	$821
$17.50	$78	$456	$340	$314
$20.00	$78	$206	$340	−$194
$22.50	$78	−$44	$90	−$194
$25.00	$78	−$194	−$60	−$194
$27.50	$78	−$194	−$60	−$194
$30.00	$78	−$194	−$60	−$194
$32.50	$78	−$194	−$60	−$194
$35.00	$78	−$194	−$60	−$194

using the proceeds to buy 2.03 April 20 puts at $1.34 (assume perfect divisibility). This roll-down strategy would have provided the investor with a relatively substantial gain near expiration if the stock were to have decreased in price, but also would have resulted in losses if the stock were to have increased. To minimize the range in potential profits and losses, the investor alternatively could have implemented a roll-down strategy by selling the 24 puts and then using only the profit to buy 0.582 April 20 puts at 1.34.

Defensive Follow-Up Strategies

If, after purchasing a put the price of the stock unexpectedly increases, an investor needs to consider defensive follow-up strategies. For example, from 2/3/16 to 2/19/16, Devon Energy's stock decreased from $26.59 to $18.65, the April 24 put increased from $2.72 to $6.06 and the April 20 put increased from $1.34 to $3.25. Suppose on 2/19/16 an investor bearish about Devon bought the April 24 put at $6.06. As shown in Exhibit 7.11, from 2/19/16 to 3/7/16, Devon increased from $18.65 to $24.19, causing the April 20 put to decrease from $6.06 to $2.22 and the April 20 put to fall from $3.25 to $0.71. Faced with this negative development, the put investor could have *liquidated*, incurring a loss of $384 (= ($2.22 − $6.06)(100)). This contrast to a $606 loss that he would have incurred if he did nothing and the price of the stock stayed above the $24 exercise price near expiration (see Exhibit 7.13). In contrast to this *do-nothing strategy*, liquidating does eliminate potential profit if the stock price reverses itself. If the investor thought that the price increase was a signal of further price increases, he could have created a *spread* to minimize his losses (if the stock were to increase). As shown in Exhibit 7.13, if the holder combined the long position in the April 24 put with a short position in the April 26 put trading on 3/7/16 for 3.97, the investor would have limited his losses to $409 if the stock reached $24 or less at expiration. However, if the stock increased to $26 or higher, the investor would have lost only $209. Finally, if the

EXHIBIT 7.13 Defensive Follow-Up Strategies for April 24 Put Purchased at $6.06

Stock Price at Expiration, 4/15/16	Liquidate: Sell 24 Put for $2.22 on 3/7/16	Do Nothing	Spread: April 24 Put Purchased at $6.06 on 2/19/16; April 26 Put Sold for $3.97 on 3/7/16
$15.00	−$384	$294	−$409
$17.50	−$384	$44	−$409
$20.00	−$384	−$206	−$409
$22.50	−$384	−$456	−$409
$25.00	−$384	−$606	−$309
$27.50	−$384	−$606	−$209
$30.00	−$384	−$606	−$209
$32.50	−$384	−$606	−$209
$35.00	−$384	−$606	−$209

investor believed Devon's stock could go either up or down, he could have combined his put with a 24 call to form a straddle or sold the put and used the proceeds to buy a call.

Put Purchases in Conjunction with a Long Stock Position

Simulated Call

Purchasing a put and owning the underlying stock on a one-to-one basis, {+P, +S}, yields the same type of profit and stock price relation as a call purchase—*simulated call*. In Exhibit 7.14, the profits at expiration for various stock prices are shown for

EXHIBIT 7.14   Long Stock and Put Position Simulated Call and Stock Insurance

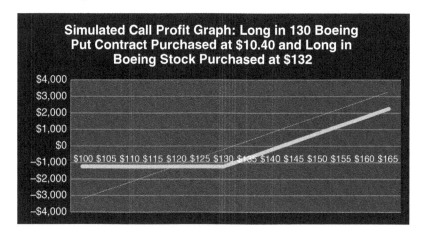

Boeing Put on 3/25/2016: $T = 11/18/16$, $X = \$130$,
$P = \$10.40$, Contract = 100 Puts; Boeing Stock = $132

Stock Price	Put Profit = Max(0, $130 − S_T$) − $10.40)100	Stock Profit = (S_T − $132)100	Total Profit
$100	$1,960	−$3,200	−$1,240
$105	$1,460	−$2,700	−$1,240
$110	$960	−$2,200	−$1,240
$115	$460	−$1,700	−$1,240
$120	−$40	−$1,200	−$1,240
$125	−$540	−$700	−$1,240
$130	−$1,040	−$200	−$1,240
$135	−$1,040	$300	−$740
$140	−$1,040	$800	−$240
$145	−$1,040	$1,300	$260
$150	−$1,040	$1,800	$760
$155	−$1,040	$2,300	$1,260
$160	−$1,040	$2,800	$1,760
$165	−$1,040	$3,300	$2,260

a long put and stock position consisting of 100 shares of Boeing stock purchased at $132 per share and an April 130 put contract purchased at $10.40. As can be seen in the table and the accompanying figure in the exhibit, the combined put and stock position yields the same relation as the purchase of a 130 April call contract at $12.40. Note, however, that more often than not, calls and puts with identical terms are not likely to be equally priced. To form an identical long call position with a call price consistent with put-call parity, a *synthetic call*, requires not only buying the put and stock, but also shorting a bond with a face value equal to the exercise price (i.e., borrow an amount equal to the present value of exercise price: $PV(X) = B_0$):

$$C_0 = P_0 + S_0 - B_0$$

or as

$$\{+C\} = \{+P, +S, -B\}$$

Portfolio Insurance

As we discussed in Chapter 5, the combined stock and put position is known as a *portfolio insurance* or *stock insurance strategy*. The features of such a strategy are best seen by examining the position's cash flows and value graph, shown in the table and figure in Exhibit 7.15. As shown, the 130 Boeing put provides downside protection against the stock falling below $130, while allowing for the upside profit potential if the stock increases. Thus, for the cost of the put premium of $1,040, an investor can obtain insurance against decreases in the stock's price. Hedging a stock portfolio positions with index put options is a popular hedging strategy used by portfolio managers. Portfolio insurance using index options are examined in more detail in Chapter 8.

Naked Put Writes

The naked (or uncovered) put write strategy provides only limited profit potential if the stock price increases with the chances of large losses if the stock price decreases. The position as defined in terms of its profit and stock price relationship near expiration is equivalent (though not identical) to the covered call write. Besides being similar to the covered call write, the naked put write strategy also is like the naked call write in that it provides an opportunity for investors to profit from the decrease over time in the option's time value premium. For example, the Boeing April $130 put selling in March for $10.40 when Boeing stock was trading at $132 would, with no change in the stock price, trade at its intrinsic value of $2.00 at expiration. Thus, a profit of $8.40 would have been earned by the naked put writer from the decrease in the time value premium.

Similar to the naked call write, naked put write strategies with in-the-money puts provide higher return-risk combinations than those with out-of-the-money puts.

EXHIBIT 7.15   Value Graph and Table of Long Stock and Put Positions: Stock Insurance

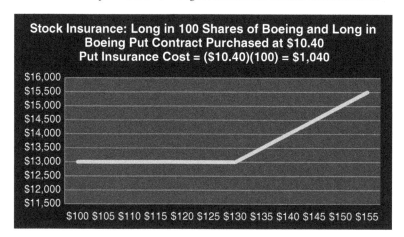

Boeing Put on 3/25/2016: $T = 11/18/16$, $X = \$130$, $P = \$10.40$,
Contract = 100 Puts; Boeing Stock = $132

Stock Price	Stock Value $= S_T 100$	Put Value $= \text{Max}(\$130 - S_T, 0)100$	Hedged Stock Value $=$ Stock Value + Put Value
$100	$10,000	$3,000	$13,000
$105	$10,500	$2,500	$13,000
$110	$11,000	$2,000	$13,000
$115	$11,500	$1,500	$13,000
$120	$12,000	$1,000	$13,000
$125	$12,500	$500	$13,000
$130	$13,000	$0	$13,000
$135	$13,500	$0	$13,500
$140	$14,000	$0	$14,000
$145	$14,500	$0	$14,500
$150	$15,000	$0	$15,000
$155	$15,500	$0	$15,500

Thus, the more the put is in the money, the greater return-risk possibilities (at expiration) available from a naked put write position.

Finally, the defensive rolling credit follow-up strategy defined for the naked call write position can be applied to the naked put write strategy for cases in which the stock decreases in price. For example, if Boeing stock decreased from $132 to $130, causing the April 130 put to go from $10.40 to $12.30, the writer of the April 130 put could roll down by selling, say, Boeing April 128 puts, and then using the proceeds (or credit) to close the April 130 puts. Like the rolling credit strategy for the uncovered call write position, this strategy needs to be repeated each time the stock decreases to a new, uncomfortable level. In turn, the put writer will profit from this follow-up strategy provided the stock eventually stops decreasing, the option is not exercised, and the writer has sufficient collateral to cover each follow-up adjustment.

Covered Put Writes

The covered put write strategy involves selling a put and shorting the underlying stock: {−P, −S}. It is equivalent (but not identical) to the naked call write, providing limited profit potential if the stock declines and unlimited loss possibilities if the price of the stock increases. The naked call write, however, has a smaller commission cost and lower collateral requirements than the covered put write. As a short-run speculative strategy, the covered put write is not as good as the naked call write and, as such, is seldom used as a strategy by option traders.

Analogous to a covered call write, a covered put write can be used as a hedging strategy for a short stock position or as a way of increasing returns for an investor who is short in the stock. For example, an investor who was short in Boeing stock at $132 and was worried about an increase in the price of the stock above $132 could offset some of the losses resulting from a stock price increase by selling a put option on Boeing. The premium received from the put sale would then serve to partially offset losses on the short positions if the stock increased. If the stock decreased, though, then the short seller would find her profits from her short position offset by losses on her short put position.

Ratio Put Writes

The ratio put write is a combination of a covered put write and a naked put write. It is formed by selling puts against shares of stock shorted at a ratio different than 1:1, for example, selling two puts for each share of stock shorted: {−2P, −S}. In terms of its profit and stock price relationship near expiration, the ratio put write is equivalent to the ratio call write. Like the ratio call write, the ratio put position is characterized by an inverted V-shaped profit and stock relation, two break-even prices, and a maximum profit occurring when the stock price is equal to the exercise price. The major difference between these equivalent strategies is that the ratio call write requires an investment to purchase the stock, while the ratio put write requires posting collateral to cover the short sale.

The ratio put write position can be reversed. This strategy is known as a *reverse hedge* with puts. The strategy yields a V-shaped profit and stock price relation and is equivalent to the straddle purchase.

Call Spreads

As discussed in Chapter 5, a call spread is a strategy in which one simultaneously buys one call option and sells another on the same stock but with different terms. There are three types of spreads:

1. The *vertical* (or *money* or *price*) *spread*, in which the options have the same expiration dates but different exercise prices

2. The *horizontal* (or *time* or *calendar*) spread, in which the options have the same exercise price but different expiration dates
3. The *diagonal spread*, which combines the vertical and horizontal spreads by having options with both different exercise prices and expiration dates

Vertical (Money) Spreads

The most popular vertical or money spreads are the bull, bear, ratio, and butterfly spreads.

Bull and Bear Call Spreads

The bull money call spread is suited for investors who are bullish about a security. The strategy is formed by going long in a call with a given exercise price and short in another call on the same underlying security with a higher exercise price. For example, on 5/20/16 the S&P 500 was at 2,040, an August S&P 500 2,030 call was trading at 70.20, and an August S&P 500 2,050 call was trading at 57.60 ($100 multiplier). To form a bull spread on those S&P 500 calls, a spreader would have bought the 2,030 call and sold the 2,050 calls: {+C(2,030), −C(2,050)}. As shown in Exhibit 7.16, this bull money spread is characterized by losses limited to $1,260 if the S&P 500 was trading at 2,030 (the low exercise price) or less at expiration, and limited profits of $740, if the S&P were trading at 2,050 (the high exercise price) or higher at expiration.

The bear money call spread is the exact opposite of the bull spread. It is formed by buying a call at a specific exercise price and selling a call on the same stock but with a lower strike price. In terms of the previous example, if the spreader bought the S&P 500 2,050 call at $57.60 and sold the 2,030 call at 70.20: {+C(2,050), −C(2,030)}, then as shown in Exhibit 7.17 and its accompanying figure, her profit would be limited to $1,260 if the S&P 500 were $2,030 or less, and her loss would be $740 if the S&P 500 were $2,050 or higher.

Ratio Money Spreads

The bull and bear spreads are balanced spreads or 1:1 money spreads. A *ratio money spread*, in turn, is formed by taking long and short positions in options that have not only different exercise prices but also ratios different than 1:1. The ratio money spread can be formed, for example, either by taking a long position in the low exercise call and a short position in the high one in different ratios, or by going short in the low exercise call and long in the high one in different ratios. For a given ratio, these two spreads yield exactly opposite results.

Using the previous example, a ratio money spread could be formed by buying one August S&P 500 2,030 call at 70.20 and selling two August S&P 500 2,050 calls at 57.60: {+C(2,030), −2C(2,050)}. As shown in Exhibit 7.18, this 1:2 ratio money spread is characterized by a limited profit of $4,500 if the S&P 500 is at the exercise price of 2,030 or less, profit increasing from $4,500 at 2,030 to $6,500 at 2,050, and then decreasing profit and losses occurring if the S&P 500 declines from 2,050. Hence,

EXHIBIT 7.16 Bull Call Spread

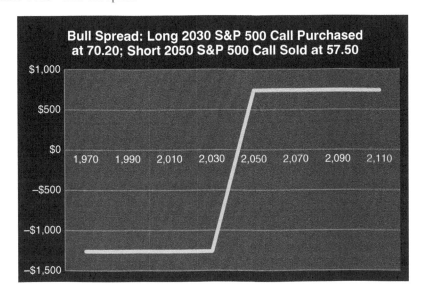

S&P 500 Call Spread: August 2,030 Call Trading at 70.20
August 2,050 Call Trading at 57.50; Multiplier = 100

S&P 500 Index, S_T	Long 2030 Call: $\{Max(S_T - 2{,}030{,}0) - 70.20\}(100)$	Short 2050 Call: $\{-Max(S_T - 2{,}050{,}0) + 57.60\}(100)$	Total Profit
1,970	−$7,020	$5,760	−$1,260
1,990	−$7,020	$5,760	−$1,260
2,010	−$7,020	$5,760	−$1,260
2,030	−$7,020	$5,760	−$1,260
2,050	−$5,020	$5,760	$740
2,070	−$3,020	$3,760	$740
2,090	−$1,020	$1,760	$740
2,110	$980	−$240	$740

the motivation for this strategy would be if an investor expected the market to go to 2,050 or decline.

In general, the characteristics of the money spread can be varied by changing the spread's ratio. This can be seen by comparing the profit and S&P 500 index relations for the 1:2 money spread with the 1:3 spread in which the profit hits a maximum of $12,260 when the S&P 500 is at 2,050, stabilizes at a profit of $10,260 when the index is at 2,030 or less, and declines if the index declines from 2,050. This ratio money spreads would be an alternative for a bearish investor to the bear spread. The profit graphs of the three spreads are shown in Exhibit 7.18.

Butterfly Money Spreads

The *butterfly spread* (also referred to as the *sandwich spread*) is a combination of the bull and bear spreads. Specifically, a *long butterfly money call spread* is formed by buying

EXHIBIT 7.17   Bear Call Spread

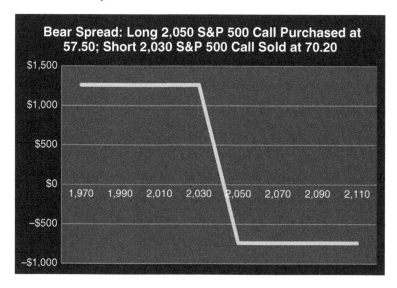

S&P 500 Call Spread: August 2,030 Call Trading at 70.20
August 2,050 Call Trading at 57.50; Multiplier = 100

S&P 500 Index, S_T	Short 2030 Call: $\{-\text{Max}(S_T - 2{,}030{,}0) + 70.20\}(100)$	Long in 2050 Call: $\{\text{Max}(S_T - 2050,\ 0) - 57.60\}(100)$	Total Profit
1,970	$7,020	−$5,760	$1,260
1,990	$7,020	−$5,760	$1,260
2,010	$7,020	−$5,760	$1,260
2,030	$7,020	−$5,760	$1,260
2,050	$5,020	−$5,760	−$740
2,070	$3,020	−$3,760	−$740
2,090	$1,020	−$1,760	−$740
2,110	−$980	$240	−$740

one call at a low exercise price, selling two calls at a middle exercise price, and buying one call at a high exercise price. To see the profit and stock price relations that a long butterfly generates, consider a spread formed with the Philadelphia Stock Exchange Gold & Silver Index (XAU): an index that includes the leading companies involved in the mining of gold and silver. On May 24, 2016, the XAU index was at 85.10, the August 70 XAU call was trading at 19.20, the August XAU 85 call was at 10.00, and the August XAU 100 call was at 4.70 (multiplier = $100). Suppose an investor formed a butterfly spread with these call options: long in one 70 call, short in two 85 calls, and long in one 100 call: $\{+C(70),\ -2C(85),\ +C(100)\}$. As shown in Exhibit 7.19, this long butterfly spread would generate an inverted V-shaped profit and index price relation, with limited losses at high and low index prices. The maximum profit of $1,100 occurs when the index equals the middle exercise price of 85 and the limited losses of $390 start when the index price is equal to the high (100) and low (70) exercise prices.

EXHIBIT 7.18   Ratio Call Spreads and Bear Money Spreads

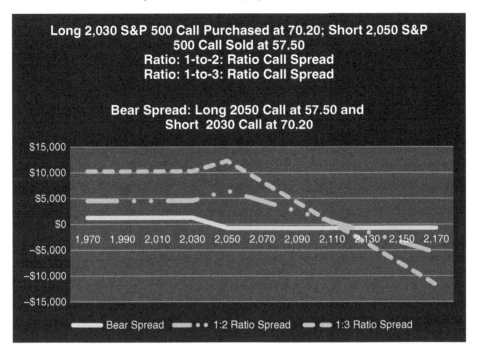

Long 2,030 S&P 500 Call Purchased at 70.20; Short 2,050 S&P 500 Call Sold at 57.50
Ratio: 1-to-2: Ratio Call Spread
Ratio: 1-to-3: Ratio Call Spread

Bear Spread: Long 2050 Call at 57.50 and Short 2030 Call at 70.20

S&P 500 Call Spread: August 2,030 Call Trading at 70.20

August 2,050 Call Trading at 57.50; Multiplier = 100

1	2	3	4
S&P 500 Index, S_T	Bear Spread	1:2 Ratio Spread	1:3 Ratio Spread
1,970	$1,260	$4,500	$10,260
1,990	$1,260	$4,500	$10,260
2,010	$1,260	$4,500	$10,260
2,030	$1,260	$4,500	$10,260
2,050	−$740	$6,500	$12,260
2,070	−$740	$4,500	$8,260
2,090	−$740	$2,500	$4,260
2,110	−$740	$500	$260
2,130	−$740	−$1,500	−$3,740
2,150	−$740	−$3,500	−$7,740
2,170	−$740	−$5,500	−$11,740

The long butterfly money spread is, in turn, a strategy that can be used if one expects the index to be near the middle exercise price near expiration. The long butterfly spread is an alternative to a short straddle. Compared to the short straddle formed with call and puts with the middle exercise price (e.g., 85), the butterfly provides limited losses, but lower maximum profit. See Exhibit 7.19.

EXHIBIT 7.19 Long Butterfly Spread and Short Straddle

Philadelphia Stock Exhange Gold & Silver Index, AUX

AUX 70 Call Trading at 19.20; AUX 85 Call Trading at 10; AUX 100 Call Trading at 4.70; AUX 85 Put Trading at 7.70

1	2	3	4	5	6	7	8
Philadelphia Stock Exchange Gold & Silver Index, AUX	Long One 70 AUX Call: {(Max(S_T − 70,0) − 19.20}(100)	Short Two 85 AUX Calls: 2{−(Max(S_T − 85, 0) + 10}(100)	Long One 100 AUX Call: {(Max(S_T −100),0) − 4.70}(100)	Long Butterfly Col(2) + Col(3) + Col(4)	Short One 85 AUX Call: {Max(S_T − 85,0) − 10}(100)	Short One 85 AUX Put: {Max(85 − S_T,0) − 7.70}(100)	Short 85 Straddle
45	−$1,920	$2,000	−$470	−$390	$1,000	−$3,230	−$2,230
50	−$1,920	$2,000	−$470	−$390	$1,000	−$2,730	−$1,730
55	−$1,920	$2,000	−$470	−$390	$1,000	−$2,230	−$1,230
60	−$1,920	$2,000	−$470	−$390	$1,000	−$1,730	−$730
65	−$1,920	$2,000	−$470	−$390	$1,000	−$1,230	−$230
70	−$1,920	$2,000	−$470	−$390	$1,000	−$730	$270
75	−$1,420	$2,000	−$470	$110	$1,000	−$230	$770
80	−$920	$2,000	−$470	$610	$1,000	$270	$1,270
85	−$420	$2,000	−$470	$1,110	$1,000	$770	$1,770
90	$80	$1,000	−$470	$610	$500	$770	$1,270
95	$580	$0	−$470	$110	$0	$770	$770
100	$1,080	−$1,000	−$470	−$390	−$500	$770	$270
105	$1,580	−$2,000	$30	−$390	−$1,000	$770	−$230
110	$2,080	−$3,000	$530	−$390	−$1,500	$770	−$730
115	$2,580	−$4,000	$1,030	−$390	−$2,000	$770	−$1,230
120	$3,080	−$5,000	$1,530	−$390	−$2,500	$770	−$1,730
125	$3,580	−$6,000	$2,030	−$390	−$3,000	$770	−$2,230

EXHIBIT 7.19 (*Continued*)

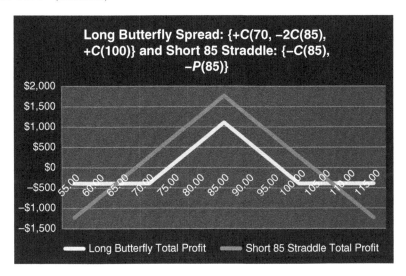

A *short butterfly money call spread* is the exact opposite of the long butterfly. It is formed by selling a low exercise call, buying two middle exercise calls, and selling a high exercise call. Exhibit 7.20 illustrates the profit and stock price relations for the short butterfly spread formed by going short in one 70 XAU call, long in two XAU 85 calls, and short in one XAU 100 call: $\{-C(70), +2C(85), -C(100)\}$. As shown in the graph, the short butterfly yields a V-shaped profit and security price relation with limited profits starting when the underlying security price is at the high and low exercise prices. The short butterfly spread is an alternative to a long straddle. Compared to a long straddle formed with call and puts with the middle exercise price (e.g., 85), the short butterfly provides limited profits, but a lower minimum loss.

Horizontal (Time) Spreads

The horizontal (or time or calendar) spread is formed by simultaneously buying and selling options that are identical except for the time to expiration. For example, a horizontal spread could be formed by selling an ABC June 50 call at $5 and buying a September 50 call at $9. A number of different types of time spreads exist. For example, a spreader may want to form a ratio time spread by going long in one long-term call and short in two short-term calls. An option investor also could form a butterfly time spread with three options with the same exercise prices but with different exercise dates.

Since horizontal, as well as diagonal, spreads have different exercise dates, it is impossible to know with certainty the value of the long-term option position at the expiration date of the short-term option position. As a result, time and diagonal spreads

EXHIBIT 7.20 Short Butterfly Spread and Long Straddle

Philadelphia Stock Exhange Gold & Silver Index, AUX

AUX 70 Call Trading at 19.20; AUX 85 Call Trading at 10; AUX 100 Call Trading at 4.70; AUX 85 Put Trading at 7.70

1	2	3	4	5	6	7	8
Philadelphia Stock Exhange Gold & Silver Index, AUX	Short One 70 AUX Call: $\{-(\text{Max}(S_T - 70,0) + 19.20\}(100)$	Long Two 85 AUX Calls: $2\{(\text{Max}(S_T - 85,0) - 10\}(100)$	Short One 100 AUX Call: $\{-(\text{Max}(S_T -100),0) + 4.70\}(100)$	Short Butterfly Col(2) + Col(3) + Col(4)	Long One 85 AUX Call: $\{\text{Max}(S_T - 85,0) - 10\}(100)$	Long One 85 AUX Put: $\{\text{Max}(85 - S_T,0) - 7.70\}(100)$	Long 85 Straddle
45	$1,920	−$2,000	$470	$390	−$1,000	$3,230	$2,230
50	$1,920	−$2,000	$470	$390	−$1,000	$2,730	$1,730
55	$1,920	−$2,000	$470	$390	−$1,000	$2,230	$1,230
60	$1,920	−$2,000	$470	$390	−$1,000	$1,730	$730
65	$1,920	−$2,000	$470	$390	−$1,000	$1,230	$230
70	$1,920	−$2,000	$470	$390	−$1,000	$730	−$270
75	$1,420	−$2,000	$470	−$110	−$1,000	$230	−$770
80	$920	−$2,000	$470	−$610	−$1,000	−$270	−$1,270
85	$420	−$2,000	$470	−$1,110	−$1,000	−$770	−$1,770
90	−$80	−$1,000	$470	−$610	−$500	−$770	−$1,270
95	−$580	$0	$470	−$110	$0	−$770	−$770
100	−$1,080	$1,000	$470	$390	$500	−$770	−$270
105	−$1,580	$2,000	−$30	$390	$1,000	−$770	$230
110	−$2,080	$3,000	−$530	$390	$1,500	−$770	$730
115	−$2,580	$4,000	−$1,030	$390	$2,000	−$770	$1,230
120	−$3,080	$5,000	−$1,530	$390	$2,500	−$770	$1,730
125	−$3,580	$6,000	−$2,030	$390	$3,000	−$770	$2,230

EXHIBIT 7.20 (*Continued*)

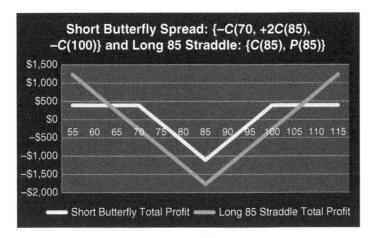

do not lend themselves to the same type of profit and security price analysis associated with the strategies we have analyzed to this point. We can, however, estimate profit and stock price relations by using the option pricing model to estimate the price of the longer-term option for each possible stock price at the expiration of the shorter-term one. We will discuss time and diagonal spreads following our examination of option pricing models.

Put Spreads

Horizontal, vertical, and diagonal put spreads are formed the same way as their corresponding call spreads, and they produce the same profit and stock price relation as their corresponding call spreads. For example, a call bear spread is formed by selling a call with a lower exercise price and buying one with a higher, and a put bear spread is also formed by selling a low exercise put and buying a higher exercise one. Both strategies yield the same profit and stock price relation. Similarly, a calendar put spread is constructed like its corresponding call by buying (or selling) a short-term put and selling (buying) a longer-term one.

In general, our preceding discussion on call spreads also applies to put spreads. It should be kept in mind that even though the put and call spreads are equivalent in terms of profit and stock price relation, differences do exist. For instance, with a bear put spread, the higher exercise price put will sell for more than the lower exercise one, leading to a debit position. The bear call spread, however, will have a higher premium associated with its lower exercise price option and a lower premium associated with its higher exercise call, thus leading to an initial credit position. In contrast, the bull put spread will yield a net credit position and the bull call spread a net debit one. Also, in comparing equivalent call and put spreads, it is important to note that the time value premium for puts may respond differently to stock price changes than do the time premiums for calls, thus leading to different uses of calendar put and calendar call spread strategies.

Straddle, Strip, and Strap Positions

The straddle is one of the more well-known option strategies. As previously described, a straddle purchase is formed by buying both a put and a call with the same terms—same underlying security, exercise price, and expiration date: {+C, +P}. A straddle write, in contrast, is formed by selling a call and a put with the same terms: {−C, −P}. For the straddle positions, the ratio of calls to puts is 1:1. Changing the ratio, in turn, yields either a strip or strap option strategy. Specifically, the *strip* is formed by having more puts than calls, and the *strap* is constructed with more calls than puts.

Straddle Purchases

The straddle purchase yields a V-shaped profit and security price relation near expiration with two break-even prices and the maximum loss equal to the sum of the call and put premium that occurs when the security is equal to the options' exercise price. In Exhibit 7.20, Columns (6), (7), and (8), the profit and index relation is shown for a straddle purchase consisting of an AUX August 85 call purchased for $10 and the August 85 put bought for $7.70.

The straddle purchase (or long straddle) is equivalent to the simulated straddle and the reverse hedge strategy. Since the simulated straddle and reverse hedge strategies involve security positions, they have the disadvantage of higher commission cost compared to the straddle purchase. Thus, the straddle purchase is the preferable short-run strategy.

The straddle purchase, as with all strategies that are characterized by V-shaped profit and security price relations, is well-suited for cases in which an investor expects substantial change in the price of the stock to occur but is not sure whether the change will be positive or negative. Although all long straddles are characterized by V-shaped profit graphs, different straddles on the same stock—differing in terms of their maximum loss, their break-even prices, and the rate of change in profits per change in stock prices (i.e., slopes)—can be generated by purchasing either an out-of-the-money call and in-the-money put, an out/in (call/put) straddle, or an in/out straddle.

Since many straddle strategies are based on anticipated events that could occur before the options' expiration date, they lend themselves to follow-up actions. As an example, suppose that when the Philadelphia Gold & Silver Index was at 85, an investor purchased the 85 AUX straddle. Then suppose that after the straddle was purchased, but before the options expired, leading economic indicators were released that augured for an economic slowdown, causing the Philadelphia Gold & Silver Index to increase, the AUX 85 call to increase, and the AUX 85 put to decrease.

Given this new situation, the investor could: (1) liquidate, if he felt the index was at a maximum and would stay there; (2) sell the call and keep the put, if he believed the market overreacted to the announcement and that therefore the index would decline; (3) sell the put and hold the call, if he believed the index would increase even further; or (4) roll-up the call (put) by liquidating the straddle and using the profit to buy AUX calls (put) with higher exercise prices. As always, determining what follow-up strategy to choose depends on the investor's expectation after an event and his confidence in his expectation.

Straddle Writes

The straddle write (or short straddle) yields an inverted V-shaped profit and security price relation near expiration, with two break-even prices and a maximum profit equal to the sum of the call and put premiums occurring when the price of the stock is equal to the options' exercise price. The short straddle is equivalent to the ratio call write strategy, discussed earlier. In Exhibit 7.19, Columns (6), (7), and (8), the profit and index price relation is shown for a straddle sale consisting of an AUX August 85 call sold for $10 and an AUG August put sold for $7.70.

The straddle write and other equivalent strategies yielding inverted V-shaped profit graphs are ideal for cases in which one either expects little change to occur in the price of the security, or, given the security's variability, is confident the price of the stock will fall within the range of the break-even prices. Thus, in contrast to the straddle purchaser, the straddle writer does not anticipate an event occurring in the near term that would affect the price of the underlying stock.

If an event does occur that increases or decreases the stock price, the writer may need to consider defensive follow-up action. For example, in our previous case in which the Philadelphia Gold & Silver Index increased, a straddle writer who sold the straddle expecting little changes could consider liquidating the short straddle, thus limiting his losses, possibly closing the call by buying it back, or closing the put position. A number of strategies, both defensive and aggressive, can be employed, including positions with different exercise prices and exercise dates.

Strips and Straps

Strips and straps are variations of the straddle. They are formed by adding an additional call position (strap) or an additional put position (strip) to a straddle. Specifically, the strip purchase (sale) consists of the long (short) straddle position plus the purchase (sale) of an extra put(s); the strap purchase (sale) consists of the long (short) straddle plus the additional purchase (sale) of a call(s). In Exhibit 7.21, the profit and index price relations for long straddle, strip, and strap positions formed with an AUX 85 call trading at $10 and an AUX 85 put trading for $7.70 are shown. In Exhibit 7.22, the short positions for the strip, strap, and straddle formed with the same options are shown.

EXHIBIT 7.21   Long Straddle, Strip, and Strap

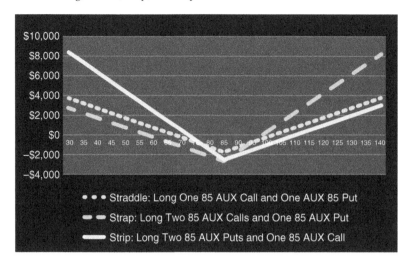

Philadelphia Stock Exhange Gold & Silver Index, AUX
AUX 85 Call Trading at 10; AUX 85 Put Trading at 7.70

Philadelphia Stock Exhange Gold & Silver Index, AUX	Straddle: Long One 85 AUX Call and One AUX 85 Put	Strap: Long Two 85 AUX Calls and One 85 AUX Put	Strip: Long Two 85 AUX Puts and One 85 AUX Call
40	$2,730	$1,730	$6,460
45	$2,230	$1,230	$5,460
50	$1,730	$730	$4,460
55	$1,230	$230	$3,460
60	$730	−$270	$2,460
65	$230	−$770	$1,460
70	−$270	−$1,270	$460
75	−$770	−$1,770	−$540
80	−$1,270	−$2,270	−$1,540
85	−$1,770	−$2,770	−$2,540
90	−$1,270	−$1,770	−$2,040
95	−$770	−$770	−$1,540
100	−$270	$230	−$1,040
105	$230	$1,230	−$540
110	$730	$2,230	−$40
115	$1,230	$3,230	$460
120	$1,730	$4,230	$960
125	$2,230	$5,230	$1,460
130	$2,730	$6,230	$1,960

In comparing the three long positions, a number of differences should be noted. First, as we move from the straddle to the strip the break-even prices move up, and as we move from the straddle to the strap, the break-even prices move down. Secondly, compared to the symmetrical returns on the straddle, the strip and strap positions

EXHIBIT 7.22 Short Straddle, Strip, and Strap

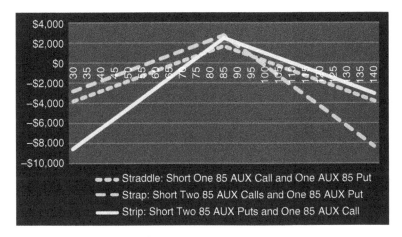

Philadelphia Stock Exhange Gold & Silver Index, AUX

AUX 85 Call Trading at 10; AUX 85 Put Trading at 7.70

Philadelphia Stock Exhange Gold & Silver Index, AUX	Straddle: Short One 85 AUX Call and One AUX 85 Put	Strap: Short Two 85 AUX Calls and One 85 AUX Put	Strip: Short Two 85 AUX Puts and One 85 AUX Call
40	−$2,730	−$1,730	−$6,460
45	−$2,230	−$1,230	−$5,460
50	−$1,730	−$730	−$4,460
55	−$1,230	−$230	−$3,460
60	−$730	$270	−$2,460
65	−$230	$770	−$1,460
70	$270	$1,270	−$460
75	$770	$1,770	$540
80	$1,270	$2,270	$1,540
85	$1,770	$2,770	$2,540
90	$1,270	$1,770	$2,040
95	$770	$770	$1,540
100	$270	−$230	$1,040
105	−$230	−$1,230	$540
110	−$730	−$2,230	$40
115	−$1,230	−$3,230	−$460
120	−$1,730	−$4,230	−$960
125	−$2,230	−$5,230	−$1,460
130	−$2,730	−$6,230	−$1,960

provide asymmetrical payoffs. The strip's rate of increase in profit exceeds that of the straddle when the stock decreases from its maximum-loss price and equals the straddle's rate when the stock increases. Thus, a strip is particularly well-suited for cases in which (like a straddle) an investor expects a stock either to increase or decrease in response to an event, but also expects that the stock response if the event is negative will be greater than its response if the event is positive. A strap, on the other hand, has a greater rate

EXHIBIT 7.23　Straps with Different Ratios

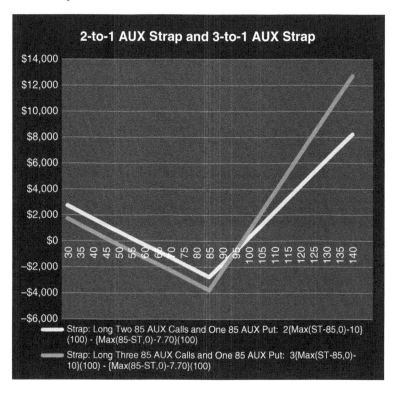

of increase in profit than the straddle when the stock increases and the same rate when the stock decreases.

Comparing the three short positions in Exhibit 7.22, the writer obtains wider ranges in the break-even prices and a greater maximum profit from selling a strip and strap than a straddle. A strip's losses, however, increase at a greater rate than a straddle write's losses when the stock price decreases from the maximum profit price and at the same rate when the stock increases. The opposite results occur in the case of the strap write.

Finally, note that the characteristics of strips and straps can be changed by varying the ratios. This is illustrated in Exhibit 7.23, in which the long strap position with a 2:1 call-to-put ratio is compared to a 3:1 strip.

Combinations

A *combination* is a position formed with a call and a put on the same underlying stock but with different terms: that is, either different exercise prices (referred to as a money or a vertical combination), exercise dates (called a time, calendar, or horizontal combination), or both (diagonal combination). The most common combinations are the ones formed with different exercise prices—money combinations, often called *strangles*.

EXHIBIT 7.24 Long Combination

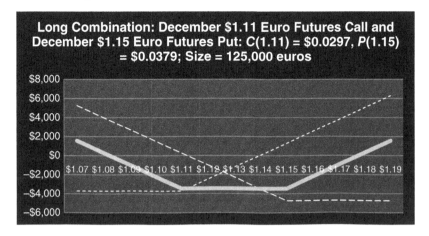

CME Euro Futures Options Combination

$1.11 December Futures Euro Call Trading at $0.0297

$1.15 December Futures Put Trading at $0.0379

December Futures Trading at $1.12425 on 9/1/2106

Long One $1.11 December Euro Futures Call: Profit$\{(\text{Max}(f_T - \$1.11),0) - \$0.0297\}(125{,}000)$

Long One $1.15 December Euro Futures Put: Profit $\{(\text{Max}(\$1.15 - f_T),0) - \$0.0379\}(125{,}000)$

Euro Futures, f_T	Profit: Long $1.11 December Futures Call	Profit: Long $1.15 December Futures Put	Long Combination: Total Profit
$1.07	−$3,713	$5,262	$1,550
$1.08	−$3,713	$4,012	$300
$1.09	−$3,713	$2,762	−$950
$1.10	−$3,713	$1,512	−$2,200
$1.11	−$3,713	$262	−$3,450
$1.12	−$2,463	−$988	−$3,450
$1.13	−$1,213	−$2,238	−$3,450
$1.14	$37	−$3,488	−$3,450
$1.15	$1,287	−$4,738	−$3,450
$1.16	$2,537	−$4,738	−$2,200
$1.17	$3,787	−$4,738	−$950
$1.18	$5,037	−$4,738	$300
$1.19	$6,287	−$4,738	$1,550

In Exhibit 7.24, the profit and index price relations are shown for a long money combination (a long strangle) constructed with a December $1.11 euro futures call contract trading at $0.0297/€ on 9/1/16 and a December $1.15 euro futures put contract trading at $0.0379/€ (contract size = 125,000 euros) on 9/1/16. When the underlying December euro futures trading at $1.12425/€ on 9/1/16 the long combination consists of an in-the-money call and an in-of-the-money put; that is, a 1.11/1.15 (call/put), in/in combination. As shown, the combination position is characterized by a limited loss $3,450 over a range of futures prices between the exercises prices ($1.11 and $1.15), and virtually unlimited profit potential if the underlying futures price increases or decreases. Short money combinations yield just the opposite—limited profit over a range of underlying security prices and potential losses if the underlying price changes substantially in either direction. In Exhibit 7.25,

EXHIBIT 7.25   Short Combination

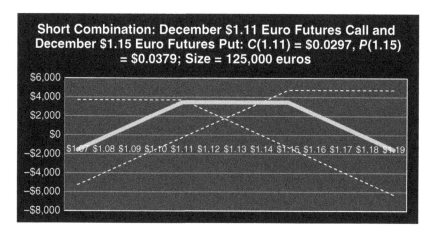

CME Euro Futures Options Combination

$1.11 December Futures Euro Call Trading at $0.0297

$1.15 December Futures Put Trading at $0.0379

December Futures Trading at $1.12425 on 9/1/2106

Short One $1.11 December Euro Futures Call: Profit{$0.0297 − (Max($f_T$ − $1.11),0)}(125,000)

Short One $1.15 December Euro Futures Put: Profit{$0.0397 − (Max($1.15 − f_T),0)}(125,000)

Euro Futures, f_T	Profit: Short $1.11 December Futures Call	Profit: Short $1.15 December Futures Put	Short Combination: Total Profit
$1.07	$3,713	−$5,262	−$1,550
$1.08	$3,713	−$4,012	−$300
$1.09	$3,713	−$2,762	$950
$1.10	$3,713	−$1,512	$2,200
$1.11	$3,713	−$262	$3,450
$1.12	$2,463	$988	$3,450
$1.13	$1,213	$2,238	$3,450
$1.14	−$37	$3,488	$3,450
$1.15	−$1,287	$4,738	$3,450
$1.16	−$2,537	$4,738	$2,200
$1.17	−$3,787	$4,738	$950
$1.18	−$5,037	$4,738	−$300
$1.19	−$6,287	$4,738	−$1,550

the profit and futures price relations are shown for a short money combination (a short strangle) constructed with the $1.11 December euro futures call and $1.15 euro futures put. Like straddles, different combinations on the same underlying security can be formed with in-the-money and out-of-the-money calls and puts: out/in (call/put), in/out, and out/out combinations.

Condors

Condors are formed with four call and/or put options on the same security but with different terms. They are a special type of butterfly spread involving bull and bear spreads with different exercise prices. Condors can be constructed in a number of ways. Exhibit 7.26 shows several ways in which a long condor can be formed with call and put options with four exercise prices: X_1, X_2, X_3, and X_4, in which $X_1 < X_2 < X_3 < X_4$. The long condor is similar to a short money combination, providing limited profit over a range of stock prices, and possible losses if the stock price changes in either direction. Different from the combination, the losses on the long condor are limited. This limited loss feature, in turn, makes the condor less risky than the combination. A short condor position is formed by simply reversing the long condor's positions. The short condor, in turn, has the opposite characteristics of the long position.

Simulated Stock Positions

Given that options can be used in different combinations to obtain virtually any profit and security price relation, it should not be too surprising to find that options can be used to form synthetic securities such as long and short security positions. A *simulated long position* is formed by buying a call and selling a put with the same terms. Similarly, a *simulated short position* is constructed by selling a call and buying a put with the same terms.

EXHIBIT 7.26 Condors

Long Condor	
Calls:	Long X_1 and X_4; Short X_2 and X_3
Puts:	Long X_1 and X_4; Short X_2 and X_3
Calls and Puts:	Long X_1 Call, Short X_2 Call, Short X_3 Put, Long X_4 Put
Calls and Puts:	Long X_1 Put, Short X_2 Put, Short X_3 Call, Long X_4 Call
Short Condor	
Calls:	Short X_1 and X_4; Long X_2 and X_3
Puts:	Short X_1 and X_4; Long X_2 and X_3
Calls and Puts:	Short X_1 Call, Long X_2 Call, Long X_3 Put, Short X_4 Put
Calls and Puts:	Short X_1 Put, Long X_2 Put, Long X_3 Call, Short X_4 Call

Simulated Long Positions

In Exhibit 7.27, the profit and stock price relations are shown for a simulated long position formed by buying a Tesla December 225 call at $22.25 and selling a Tesla December 225 put at $28.90. The simulated relations in this example are similar to buying 100 shares of Tesla at $223 per share (Tesla's price on May 26, 2016), but

EXHIBIT 7.27   Simulated Long Stock Position

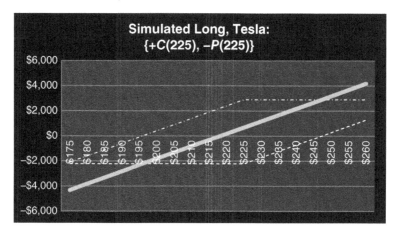

Tesla Motors: On May 27, 2016, Stock Trading at $223
TSLA Call: $X = 225, $C_0 = 22.25$; TSLA Put: $X = 225, $P_0 = 28.90

Tesla Motors Stock Prices at T, S_T	Long $225 TSLA Call: $\{(\text{Max}(S_T - 225),0) -22.25\}(100)$	Short $225 TSLA Put: $\{-(\text{Max}(225 - S_T,0) +28.90\}(100)$	Simulated Long: Total Profit	Long Tesla Stock at $223 Total Profit
$175	-$2,225	-$2,110	-$4,335	-$4,800
$180	-$2,225	-$1,610	-$3,835	-$4,300
$185	-$2,225	-$1,110	-$3,335	-$3,800
$190	-$2,225	-$610	-$2,835	-$3,300
$195	-$2,225	-$110	-$2,335	-$2,800
$200	-$2,225	$390	-$1,835	-$2,300
$205	-$2,225	$890	-$1,335	-$1,800
$210	-$2,225	$1,390	-$835	-$1,300
$215	-$2,225	$1,890	-$335	-$800
$220	-$2,225	$2,390	$165	-$300
$225	-$2,225	$2,890	$665	$200
$230	-$1,725	$2,890	$1,165	$700
$235	-$1,225	$2,890	$1,665	$1,200
$240	-$725	$2,890	$2,165	$1,700
$245	-$225	$2,890	$2,665	$2,200
$250	$275	$2,890	$3,165	$2,700
$255	$775	$2,890	$3,665	$3,200
$260	$1,275	$2,890	$4,165	$3,700

not identical. This is because the costs of the positions are different. In the example, it would cost $22,300 to buy 100 shares while the simulated long position would have a net cost equal to the difference in call and put premiums (net gain of $665); plus there is a margin requirement. Also, the long stock position could provide dividends that the simulated position does not. However, on an ex-dividend date the prices of the stock, call, and put all will change. Finally, the option position has a fixed life that ends at expiration, while an investor can hold the stock indefinitely. As we will discuss in Chapter 9, to attain an identical position (a synthetic position) requires that a long bond position be included with the long call and short put positions. Although the positions are not identical, the long call and short put positions on Tesla provide a very close profit and stock price relation to a long position in the stock.

Simulated Short Positions

In Exhibit 7.28, the profit and stock price relations are shown for a simulated short position formed by selling a Tesla December 225 call at $22.25 and buying a Tesla December 225 put at $28.90. The differences in the short position set up by selling 100 shares of Tesla stock short at $223 and the simulated short position are similar to the differences in the corresponding long positions. The simulated short position and stock position have different prices; the simulated short position has different margin requirements and commission costs than the short stock position; the short stock position requires dividend coverage while the simulated position does not, and the simulated short position has an expiration date, while the short stock position does not. To form an identical short stock position (synthetic short position), in turn, requires adding a bond position.

Splitting the Strikes

The above-simulated long and short positions can be altered by setting up strategies similar to the ones above but with different terms—exercise prices, dates, or both. When the differing term is the exercise price, the strategy is referred to as *splitting the strikes*.

In splitting the strike, an investor would go long in a call with a high exercise price and short in a put with a lower exercise price (usually both out-of-the-money) if she were bullish, and would do the opposite (write a call with a low exercise and buy a put with a high) if she were bearish. The profit and stock price relation for a bullish *splitting the strikes* position with Tesla options is shown in Exhibit 7.29, and the bearish position is shown in Exhibit 7.30. The positions are formed with the December 225 call trading at $22.25 and a December 215 put trading at $24.10, when Tesla stock was trading at $223 (5/27/16). As shown in the exhibits, the bullish and bearish positions provide a range of stock prices in which profits or losses are fixed and also smaller losses and profits at each stock price than their respective long and short stock positions.

EXHIBIT 7.28   Simulated Short Stock Position

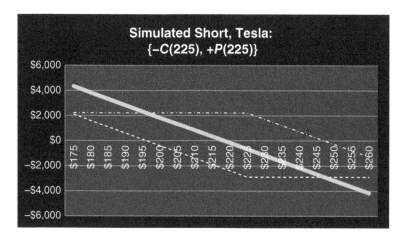

Tesla Motors: On May 27, 2016, Stock Trading at $223

TSLA Call: $X = \$225$, $C_0 = 22.25$; TSLA Put: $X = \$225$, $P_0 = \$28.90$

Tesla Motors Stock Prices at T, S_T	Short $225 TSLA Call: $\{-(\text{Max}(S_T - 225), 0) + 22.25\}(100)$	Long $225 TSLA Put: $\{(\text{Max}(221 - S_T, 0) - 28.90\}(100)$	Simulated Short: Total Profit
$175	$2,225	$2,110	$4,335
$180	$2,225	$1,610	$3,835
$185	$2,225	$1,110	$3,335
$190	$2,225	$610	$2,835
$195	$2,225	$110	$2,335
$200	$2,225	-$390	$1,835
$205	$2,225	-$890	$1,335
$210	$2,225	-$1,390	$835
$215	$2,225	-$1,890	$335
$220	$2,225	-$2,390	-$165
$225	$2,225	-$2,890	-$665
$230	$1,725	-$2,890	-$1,165
$235	$1,225	-$2,890	-$1,665
$240	$725	-$2,890	-$2,165
$245	$225	-$2,890	-$2,665
$250	-$275	-$2,890	-$3,165
$255	-$775	-$2,890	-$3,665
$260	-$1,275	-$2,890	-$4,165

Conclusion

One important feature of an option is it can be combined with other options and the underlying security to produce many different profit and security price relations. In this chapter, we have examined how many of these strategies are formed and their characteristics. Box 7.1 summarizes many of the strategies that were analyzed in this

EXHIBIT 7.29 Splitting the Strike, Bullish Position

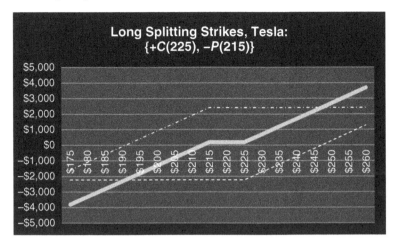

Tesla Motors: On May 27, 2016, Stock Trading at $223

TSLA Call: $X = \$225$, $C_0 = 22.25$; TSLA Put: $X = \$215$, $P_0 = \$24.10$

Tesla Motors Stock Prices at T, S_T	Long $225 TSLA Call: $\{(Max(S_T - 225), 0) - 22.25\}(100)$	Short 215 TSLA Put: $\{-(Max(215 - S_T, 0) + 24.10\}(100)$	Long Splitting Strikes: Total Profit
$175	−$2,225	−$1,590	−$3,815
$180	−$2,225	−$1,090	−$3,315
$185	−$2,225	−$590	−$2,815
$190	−$2,225	−$90	−$2,315
$195	−$2,225	$410	−$1,815
$200	−$2,225	$910	−$1,315
$205	−$2,225	$1,410	−$815
$210	−$2,225	$1,910	−$315
$215	−$2,225	$2,410	$185
$220	−$2,225	$2,410	$185
$225	−$2,225	$2,410	$185
$230	−$1,725	$2,410	$685
$235	−$1,225	$2,410	$1,185
$240	−$725	$2,410	$1,685
$245	−$225	$2,410	$2,185
$250	$275	$2,410	$2,685
$255	$775	$2,410	$3,185
$260	$1,275	$2,410	$3,685

chapter. Since the value of an option at expiration is equal to its intrinsic value, our analysis of option strategies was done in terms of the position's profit and stock price relation at expiration. Option strategies also can be evaluated in terms of their profit and stock price relation prior to expiration and in terms of how the position changes in value in response to changes in such parameters as time to expiration and the variability of the underlying stock. These descriptions of option strategies are based on option

EXHIBIT 7.30   Splitting the Strike, Bearish Position

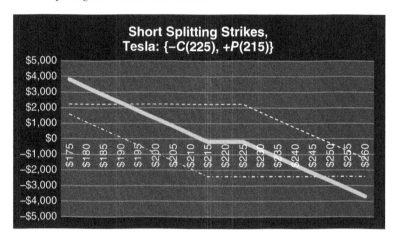

Tesla Motors: On May 27, 2016, Stock Trading at $223

TSLA Call: $X = \$225$, $C_0 = 22.25$; TSLA Put: $X = \$215$, $P_0 = \$24.10$

Tesla Motors Stock Prices at T, S_T	Short $225 TSLA Call: $\{-(\text{Max}(S_T - 225), 0) + 22.25\}(100)$	Long 215 TSLA Put: $\{(\text{Max}(215 - S_T, 0) - 24.10\}(100)$	Short Splitting Strikes: Total Profit
$175	$2,225	$1,590	$3,815
$180	$2,225	$1,090	$3,315
$185	$2,225	$590	$2,815
$190	$2,225	$90	$2,315
$195	$2,225	−$410	$1,815
$200	$2,225	−$910	$1,315
$205	$2,225	−$1,410	$815
$210	$2,225	−$1,910	$315
$215	$2,225	−$2,410	−$185
$220	$2,225	−$2,410	−$185
$225	$2,225	−$2,410	−$185
$230	$1,725	−$2,410	−$685
$235	$1,225	−$2,410	−$1,185
$240	$725	−$2,410	−$1,685
$245	$225	−$2,410	−$2,185
$250	−$275	−$2,410	−$2,685
$255	−$775	−$2,410	−$3,185
$260	−$1,275	−$2,410	−$3,685

pricing models. In Part 3, we will examine how call and put options are priced and how option strategies can be evaluated using the option pricing model. In the next chapter, we complete our analysis of option positions by examining the hedging positions that can be constructed with options.

BOX 7.1: SUMMARY OF DIFFERENT OPTION POSITIONS

1. **Simulated Put**: Long in a call and short in a security on a 1:1 basis.
2. **Simulated Straddle**: Long two calls for each positon shorted.
3. **Ratio Call Write**: Short in call and long in security, with more calls than securities owned.
4. **Stock Insurance or Simulated Call**: Long in put and long in security.
5. **Ratio Put Write**: Selling puts against securities shorted at a ratio different from 1:1.
6. **Vertical or Money Spread**: Long and short in calls with different exercise prices (similar positions formed with puts).
7. **Horizontal or Time Spread**: Long and short in calls with different exercise dates (similar positions formed with puts).
8. **Diagonal Spread**: Long and short in calls with different exercise prices and dates (similar positions formed with puts).
9. **Bull Call Spread**: Long in call with low X and short in call with high X.
10. **Bull Put Spread**: Long in put with low X and short in put with high X.
11. **Bear Call Spread**: Long in call with high X and short in call with low X.
12. **Bear Put Spread**: Long in put with high X and short in put with low X.
13. **Ratio Money Spread**: Long and short positions in options with different exercise prices and/or times and also with ratios different than 1:1.
14. **Long Butterfly Spread**: Long in call with low X, short in 2 calls with middle X, and long in call with high X (similar position formed with puts).
15. **Short Butterfly Spread**: Short in call with low X, long in 2 calls with middle X, and short in call with high X (similar position formed with puts).
16. **Straddle Purchase**: Long call and put with similar terms.
17. **Strip Purchase**: Straddle purchase with additional puts (e.g., long call and long 2 puts).
18. **Strap Purchase**: Straddle purchase with additional calls (e.g., long 2 calls and long put).
19. **Straddle Sale**: Short call and put with similar terms.
20. **Strip Sale**: Straddle sale with additional puts (e.g., short 1 call and short 2 puts).
21. **Strap Sale**: Straddle sale with additional calls (e.g., short 2 calls and short 1 put).
22. **Long Vertical or Money Combination**: Long in call and put with different exercise prices (short positions formed by going short in call and put).
23. **Long Horizontal or Time Combination**: Long in call and put with different exercise dates (short positions formed by going short in call and put).
24. **Long Diagonal Combination**: Long in call and put with different exercise prices and dates (short positions formed by going short in call and put).
25. **Money Combination Purchase**: Long call and put with different exercise prices.
26. **Money Combination Sale**: Short call and put with different exercise prices.
27. **Condors**: Four call and/or put options on the same security but with different terms.

BLOOMBERG: OPTION SCENARIO ANALYSIS
SCREEN—OSA

Profit and value graphs for options can be generated using the Bloomberg OSA screen. To access OSA for a security, load the menu page of the security and type OSA (or click "OSA" from the menu).

FOR STOCK

1. Go to equity menu screen (e.g., PG <Equity> <Return>).
2. Type "OSA."
3. On the OSA screen, click the "Positions" tab and then click the "Add Listed Options" tab to bring up options listed on the stock. This brings up a screen showing the listed options from which to select (e.g., 1 call contract (100 calls) and 1 put contract (100 puts)).
4. After selecting the positions, type 1 <Enter> (or click) to load positions and bring up the OSA position screen.
5. On the position screen, click the "Scenario Chart" tab at the top of the screen to bring up the profit graph. The profit graph shows profits for the strategy at expiration where the option price is trading at its intrinsic value and also at time periods prior where the option price is determined by an option-pricing model. The profit graphs for different periods can be changed or deleted by using the select options at the top of the screen.
6. From the position screen (click "Position" tab), you can select different positions and then click the "Scenario Chart" tab to view the profit graph.
7. The Scenario screen (gray "Scenario" tab) shows the profit table; click "Maximize Chart" tab to see just the graph.

FOR S&P 500 FUTURES OPTIONS

1. Select an S&P 500 futures option and bring up its equity screen (e.g., SPA <Comdty>) to bring up S&P futures.
2. Type EXS to bring up futures with different expirations.
3. Select a futures and bring up is menu screen: futures ticker <Comdty> (e.g., SPH7 <Comdty> for March 17 S&P futures).
4. On the future screen, type OSA.
5. On the OSA screen, select "Listed Options" from the red "Positions" dropdown tab to bring up listed futures options.

FOR CBT T-NOTE FUTURES OPTIONS

1. Select a CBT T-note futures (e.g., five-year T-note: FVA <Comdty>.
2. Type EXS to find expirations (e.g., FVH7 <Comdty> to load the March 2017 five-year T-Note futures).
3. On the selected futures screen, type OSA to bring up the OSA screen, and select "Listed Options" on the contract from the red "Positions" dropdown tab to bring up listed futures options and then select options to include in your evaluation.
4. Using the Bloomberg OSA screen and "Scenario Chart" tab, you can evaluate option strategies.

FOR COMMODITY FUTURES OPTIONS

1. Use CTM to identify commodities that have option contracts: Enter CTM; select the commodity futures (e.g., corn) and then select "Yes" on the "Options" tab to see futures with options contracts on them.
2. Upload futures contract with options (e.g., C A <Comdty> for corn).
3. Type EXS to find expirations (e.g., C H7 <Comdty> to load March 2017 corn futures).
4. On the selected futures screen, type OSA to bring up the OSA screen, and select "Listed Options" on the contract from the red "Positions" dropdown tab to bring up listed futures options and then select options to include in your evaluation.
5. Use the Bloomberg OSA screen and "Scenario Chart" tab to evaluate option strategies.

FOR CURRENCY FUTURES OPTIONS

1. Use CTM to identify currency futures that have option contracts: Enter CTM; select "Currencies" and then select "Yes" on the "Options" tab to see currency futures with options contracts on them.
2. Upload futures contract with options (e.g., BPA <Curncy> for British Pound futures).
3. Type EXS to find expirations (e.g., BPH7 <Curncy> to load March 2017 British Pound futures).
4. On the selected futures screen, type OSA to bring up the OSA screen, and select "Listed Options" on the contract from the red "Positions" dropdown tab to bring up listed futures options and then select options to include in your evaluation.
5. Use the Bloomberg OSA screen and "Scenario Chart" tab to evaluate option strategies.

FOR INDEX OPTIONS

1. Use SECF to identify indexes that have option contracts: Enter SECF; Select index/Stats from "Category" dropdown; click "Opts" tab for a listing of index options and their tickers.
2. Load index options: Ticker <Index>.
3. Type OSA to bring up the OSA screen, and select "Listed Options" on the contract from the red "Positions" dropdown tab to bring up listed index options and then select options to include in your evaluation. Evaluate positions using "Scenario Chart" and "Scenario Chart."

Selected References

Chaput, J. S., and L. H. Ederington. "Option Spread and Combination Trading." *Journal of Derivatives* 10, 4 (Summer 2003): 70–88.

McMillan, L. G. *Options as a Strategic Investment*, 4th ed. Upper Saddle River, NJ: Prentice-Hall, 2001.

Problems and Questions

Note: A number of the problems can be done in Excel

1. Evaluate the strategies below in terms of their profit and stock price relationships at expiration. In your evaluation, include a profit table that breaks down each strategy and identify the name of the strategy. Assume each stock position has 100 shares and each option contract represents 100 shares of stock:

   a. The short sale of XYX stock at $60 per share and the purchase of two XYZ March 60 call contracts at $3 per call. Evaluate at expiration stock prices of 40, 45, 50, 54, 60, 66, 70, and 80.

   b. The purchase of ABC stock at $75 per share and the sale of an XYZ December 70 call contract at $8. Evaluate at expiration stock prices of 60, 65, 67, 70, 74, 75, 80, 85, and 90.

   c. The purchase of 100 shares of XYZ stock at $39 per share and the sale of two XYZ October 40 call contracts at $6. Evaluate at expiration stock prices of 20, 27, 35, 40, 45, 53, and 60.

   d. The purchase of an XYZ September 50 call contract at $12 and the sale of an XYZ September 60 call contract at $6. Evaluate at expiration stock prices of 40, 45, 50, 55, 56, 60, 65, and 70.

   e. The purchase of one XYZ July 50 call contract at $12, the sale of two July 60 call contracts at $6, and the purchase of one XYZ July 70 call contract at $3. Evaluate at expiration stock prices of 40, 50, 53, 56, 60, 64, 67, 70, and 80.

   f. The purchase of one XYZ September 50 call contract at $12 and the sale of two XYZ 60 September call contracts at $5. Evaluate at expiration stock prices of 40, 45, 50, 52, 55, 60, 65, 68, 70, and 75.

   g. The purchase of XYZ stock at $35 per share and the purchase of an XYZ September 35 put contract for $3. Evaluate at expiration stock prices of 20, 25, 30, 35, 38, 40, 45, and 50.

   h. The purchase of an XYZ July 70 call contract at $3 and the purchase of an XYZ July 70 put contract at $2. Evaluate at expiration stock prices of 50, 60, 65, 70, 75, 80, and 90.

   i. The sale of an XYZ June 65 call contract at $4 and the sale of an XYZ June 65 put contract at $3. Evaluate at expiration stock prices of 50, 55, 58, 60, 65, 70, 72, 75, and 80.

   j. The purchase of an XYZ 40 call contract at $3 and the purchase of two XYZ 40 put contracts at $2 each. Evaluate at expiration stock prices of 25, 30, 35, 36.5, 40, 45, 47, 50, and 55.

   k. The sale of two 40 XYZ call contracts at $3 each and the sale of one XYZ 40 put contract at $2. Evaluate at expiration stock prices of 20, 25, 30, 32, 35, 40, 44, 45, and 50.

   l. The purchase of an XYZ 40 call contract at $3 and the purchase of an XYZ 35 put contract at $3. Evaluate at expiration stock prices of 20, 25, 29, 30, 35, 40, 45, 46, 50, and 55.

   m. The sale of an XYZ 70 call contract at $4 and the sale of an XYZ 60 put contract at $3. Evaluate at expiration stock prices of 40, 50, 53, 57, 60, 65, 70, 73, 77, 80, and 90.

   n. The sale of an XYZ 60 put contract at $2 and the purchase of an XYZ 70 put contract at $7, when XYZ stock is trading at 65. Evaluate at expiration stock prices of 50, 55, 60, 65, 70, 80, and 90.

   o. The sale of an XYZ 40 put contract at $3 and the purchase of an XYZ 40 call contract at $3. Evaluate at expiration stock prices of 30, 35, 40, 45, and 50.

   p. The purchase of an XYZ 50 put contract at $2 and the sale of XYZ 60 call contract at $1, when XYZ stock is trading at 53. Evaluate at expiration stock prices of 40, 45, 49, 50, 55, 60, 65, and 70.

2. Evaluate the following index option positions in terms of their profit and spot index relations at expiration. In your evaluation include a profit table and graph that breaks down each strategy.

   a. A long straddle formed with a 2,500 S&P 500 call trading at 50 and a 2,500 S&P 500 put trading at 50. Evaluate at spot index prices of 2,200, 2,300, 2,400, 2,500, 2,600, 2,700, 2,800, 2,900 and 3,000.

   b. A simulated long index position formed by purchasing a 2,500 S&P 500 call at 50 and selling a 2,500 S&P 500 put at 50. Evaluate at spot index prices of 2,200, 2,300, 2,400, 2,500, 2,600, 2,700, 2,800, 2,900 and 3,000.

3. Evaluate the following currency futures option strategies in terms of their profit and exchange rate relations at expiration. In your evaluation include a profit table and graph that breaks down each strategy.

   a. The purchase of a 150 (cents) British pound September futures call contract for 10 (cents) and the purchase of a 150 (cents) BP September futures put contract for 5 cents (contract size 62,500 British pounds). Evaluate at $/BP futures prices at the option's September expiration of $1.30/BP, $1.35, $1.40, $1.45, $1.50, $1.55, $1.50, $1.65, and $1.70.

   b. The sale of a 150 (cents) British pound September call contract for 10 (cents) and the sale of a 150 (cents) BP September put contract for 5(contract size = 62,500 BP). Evaluate at $/BP futures prices at the option's September expiration of $1.30/BP, $1.35, $1.40, $1.45, $1.50, $1.55, $1.50, $1.65, and $1.70.

4. Suppose shortly after you purchased an XYZ September 50 call contract at $3 per call, the price of XYX increased to $57 causing the price of your call to rise to $9 per call. Evaluate in terms of their profit and stock price relations the following follow-up actions you could pursue:

   a. Liquidate

   b. Do nothing

   c. Spread by selling the XYX 60 call trading at $3 per call

   d. Roll up by selling your 50 call and using the profit to buy two XYZ calls at $3 per call

Evaluate the strategies at expiration stock prices of $40, $45, $50, $55, $60, $65, $70, $75, and $80.

5. Suppose shortly after you purchased an XYZ December 60 call for $3 the price of the stock decreased to $56 per share on speculation of a future announcement of low quarterly earnings for the XYZ Company, which you believe is warranted. Explain how you could profit at expiration by changing your potentially unprofitable call position to a potentially profitable spread position based on the stock decreasing. Assume there is an XYZ September 50 call available at $8 and evaluate the spread at expiration stock prices of $45, $50, $55, $60, $65, and $70.

6. Suppose after selling an XYZ December 50 call for $3 when the stock was at $50, the price of the stock increases to $55. Assume at the $55 stock price, the December 50 call is trading at $6 and there is an XYX December 55 call available that is trading at $2.50. Believing that XYZ stock will stay at $55 at least until expiration, show how you could change your current unprofitable position to a potentially profitable one by implementing a rolling-credit strategy. How would your collateral requirements change?

7. Compare and contrast the following strategies:

    a. Call Purchase and Leveraged Stock Purchase
    b. Put Purchase and Synthetic Put
    c. In-the-Money Covered Call Write and Out-of-the-Money Covered Call Write
    d. Ratio Call Writes with different ratios of short calls to shares of stock
    e. Bull Spread and Bear Spread

8. Suppose after you purchased an XYZ December 40 put at $2 the price of XYZ stock dropped from $40 per share to $35 per share, causing the 40 put to increase to $6. Evaluate in terms of profit and stock price relations the following follow-up strategies:

    a. Liquidation
    b. Do Nothing
    c. Spread by selling a 35 put contract at $2
    d. Roll down by selling the 40 put and purchasing two 35 puts at $2

        Evaluate at expiration stock prices of $20, $25, $30, $35, $38, $40, $45 and $50.

9. Compare and contrast the following positions:

    a. Put Purchase and Short Sale
    b. Naked Put Write and Covered Call Write
    c. Covered Put Write and Naked Call Write
    d. Straddle, Strip, and Strap Purchases

10. List a number of strategies that will yield an Inverted V-shaped profit and stock price relationship at expiration.

11. List a number of strategies that will yield a V-shaped profit and stock price relationship at expiration.

Bloomberg Exercises

1. Select a stock and bring up its equity screen: Stock Ticker <Equity>. Using the Bloomberg OSA screen, select several call and put options on the stock and evaluate some of the following option strategies on the stock with a profit graph:

   a. Simulated Put: Long in a call and short in a stock on a 1:1 basis.

   b. Simulated Straddle: Long two calls for each share of stock shorted.

   c. Ratio Call Write: Short in call and long in stock, with more calls than shares owned.

   d. Stock Insurance or Simulated Call: Long in put option and long in stock.

   e. Ratio Put Write: Selling puts against shares of stock shorted at a ratio different than 1:1.

   f. Bull Call Spread: Long in call with low X and short in call with high X.

   g. Bull Put Spread: Long in put with low X and short in put with high X.

   h. Bear Call Spread: Long in call with high X and short in call with low X.

   i. Bear Put Spread: Long in put with high X and short in put with low X.

   j. Long Butterfly Spread: Long in call with low X, short in 2 calls with middle X, and long in call with high X (similar position formed with puts).

   k. Short Butterfly Spread: Short in call with low X, long in 2 calls with middle X, and short in call with high X (similar position formed with puts).

   l. Straddle Purchase: Long call and put with similar terms.

   m. Strip Purchase: Straddle purchase with additional puts (e.g., long call and long 2 puts).

   n. Strap Purchase: Straddle purchase with additional calls (e.g., long 2 calls and long put).

   o. Straddle Sale: Short call and put with similar terms.

   p. Strip Sale: Straddle sale with additional puts (e.g., short 1 call and short 2 puts).

   q. Strap Sale: Straddle sale with additional calls (e.g., short 2 calls and short 1 put).

   r. Money Combination Purchase: Long call and put with different exercise prices.

   s. Money Combination Sale: Short call and put with different exercise prices.

   For a guide on using the OSA screen, see "Bloomberg's Option Scenario Analysis Screen—OSA."

2. Using the Chart screen (Chart <Enter>), examine the historical prices of the stock and one of its call and puts options you selected in Exercise 1. Select a time period that the options were active.

   a. Use the Chart screen (Chart <Enter>) to create multigraphs for the stock, call, and put. On the Chart Menu screen, select the Standard G chart; once you have loaded your securities, go to "Edit" to put your graphs in separate panels.

   b. Select a period in which you would have taken a long call position and calculate the profit from opening and closing at the call prices at the beginning and ending dates for your selected period. Calculate the losses if you had taken a long put position.

   c. Select a period in which you would have taken a long put option position and calculate the profit from opening and closing at the put prices at the beginning and ending dates for your selected period. Calculate the losses if you had taken a long call position.

   d. Using the annotation bar, apply the "% Change" tool to calculate the percentage change for your select periods, and then click the "News" icon on the annotation bar to find relevant news events on or preceding the opening date.

3. Select an S&P 500 futures option and bring up its equity screen: SPA <Comdty> to bring up S&P futures; type EXS to bring up futures with different expirations; select a futures and bring up is menu screen: futures ticker <Comdty> (e.g., SPH7 <Comdty> for March 17 S&P futures); on the futures screen, type OSA; on the OSA screen, select "Listed Options" from the red "Positions" dropdown tab to bring up listed futures options.

   Using the Bloomberg OSA screen, evaluate some of the following option strategies that would reflect a bullish position on the market with a profit graph:

   a. Call purchase.

   b. Stock Insurance or Simulated Call: Long in put option and long in the futures.

   c. Bull Call Spread: Long in call with low X and short in call with high X.

   d. Bull Put Spread: Long in put with low X and short in put with high X.

   e. Strap Purchase: Straddle purchase with additional calls (e.g., long 2 calls and long 1 put).

4. Using the Chart screen (Chart <Enter>), examine the historical prices of the S&P futures and some of the futures call and futures put options you selected in Exercise 3. Select a time period that the contracts were active.

   a. Use the Chart screen (Chart <Enter>) to create multigraphs for the futures, call futures, and put futures. On the Chart Menu screen, select the Standard G chart; once you have loaded your securities, go to "Edit" to put your graphs in separate panels.

   b. Select a period and calculate the profit or loss from opening and closing a long call position at the futures call prices at the beginning and ending dates for your selected period.

   c. Comment on any follow-up actions you could have taken during the period to change your position to a profitable one if you had a loss or more profitable one if you had a profit.

5. Select a CBT T-note futures (e.g., five-year T-note: FVA <Comdty>; EXS to find expirations; FVH7 <Comdty> to load March 2017 five-year T-Note futures). On the selected futures screen, type OSA to bring up the OSA screen, and select "Listed Options" on the contract from the red "Positions" dropdown tab to bring up listed futures options and then select the futures options to include in your evaluation.

Using the Bloomberg OSA screen and "Scenario Chart" tab, evaluate some of the following option strategies that would reflect a bearish position in which you expected interest rates to rise and bond prices to decrease:

a. Put Purchase.
b. Simulated Put: Long in a call and short in the futures on a 1:1 basis.
c. Bear Call Spread: Long in call with high X and short in call with low X.
d. Bear Put Spread: Long in put with high X and short in put with low X.
e. Strip Purchase: Straddle purchase with additional puts (e.g., long call and long 2 puts).

6. Using the Chart screen (Chart <Enter>), examine the historical prices of the T-note futures and some of the futures call and futures puts options you selected in Exercise 5. Select a time period that the contracts were active.

   a. Use the Chart screen (Chart <Enter>) to create multigraphs for the futures, call futures, and put futures. On the Chart Menu screen, select the Standard G chart; once you have loaded your securities, go to "Edit" to put your graphs in separate panels.
   b. Select a period and calculate the profit or loss from opening and closing a long put position at the futures put prices at the beginning and ending dates for your selected period.
   c. Comment on any follow-up actions you could have taken during the period to change your position to a profitable one if you had a loss or more profitable if you had a profit.

7. Select a currency futures option. Use CTM to identify the currency futures that have option contracts: Enter CTM; select "Currencies" and then select "Yes" on the "Options" tab to see currency futures with options contracts on them. Upload the currency futures contract with the selected options (e.g., BPA <Curncy> for British pound futures). Type EXS to find expirations (e.g., BPH7 <Curncy> to load March 2017 British pound futures). On the selected futures screen, type OSA to bring up the OSA screen, and select "Listed Options" on the contract from the red "Positions" dropdown tab to bring up listed futures options and then select the options to include in your evaluation.

   Using the Bloomberg OSA screen and "Scenario Chart" evaluate some of the following option strategies that would reflect an expectation of a future event (e.g., Brexit vote, an election, a Central Bank announcement) that could cause the dollar price of your selected currency to increase or decrease significantly:

   a. Straddle Purchase: Long call and put with similar terms.
   b. Simulated Straddle: Long two calls for each a short futures position.
   c. Money Combination Purchase: Long call and put with different exercise prices.

8. Using the Chart screen (Chart <Enter>), examine the historical prices of currency futures and the futures call and futures put options you selected in Exercise 7. Select a time period that the contracts were active.

   a. Use the Chart screen (Chart <Enter>) to create multigraphs for the futures, call futures, and put futures. On the Chart Menu screen, select the Standard

       G chart; once you have loaded your securities, go to "Edit" to put your graphs in separate panels.

    b. Select a period and calculate the profit or loss from opening and closing a long straddle position at the futures call and put prices at the beginning and ending dates for your selected period.

    c. Comment on any follow-up actions you could have taken during the period to change your position to a profitable one if you had a loss or more profitable if you had a profit.

    d. Using the annotation bar, apply the "% Change" tool to calculate the percentage change for your select periods, and then click the "News" icon on the annotation bar to find relevant news events on or preceding the opening date.

9. Select a commodity futures option (e.g., a CBT commodity futures option). Use CTM to identify commodities that have option contracts: Enter CTM; Select commodity futures (e.g., corn) and then select "Yes" on the "Options" tab to see futures with options contracts on them; type EXS to find expirations (e.g., C H7 <Comdty> for March 2017 corn); upload futures options. On the selected futures screen, type OSA to bring up the OSA screen, and select "Listed Options" on the contract from the red "Positions" dropdown tab to bring up listed futures options and then select the options to include in your evaluation.

    Using the Bloomberg OSA screen and "Scenario Chart" evaluate some of the following option strategies that would reflect an expectation of a stable price trend for the selected commodity:

    a. Straddle Sale: Short call and put with similar terms.

    b. Ratio Call Write: Short in call and long in the futures, with more calls than futures positions.

    c. Long Butterfly Spread: Long in call with low X, short in 2 calls with middle X, and long in call with high X (similar position formed with puts).

    d. Money Combination Sale: Short call and put with different exercise prices.

10. Using the Chart screen (Chart <Enter>), examine the historical prices of commodity futures and the futures call and futures puts options you selected in Exercise 9. Select a time period that the contracts were active.

    a. Use the "Chart" screen (Chart <Enter>) to create multigraphs for the futures, call futures, and put futures. On the Chart Menu screen, select the Standard G chart; once you have loaded your securities, go to "Edit" to put your graphs in separate panels.

    b. Select a period and calculate the profit or loss from opening and closing a short straddle position at the futures call and put prices at the beginning and ending dates for your selected period.

    c. Comment on any follow-up actions you could have taken during the period to change your position to a profitable one if you had a loss or more profitable if you had a profit.

    d. Using the annotation bar, apply the "% Change" tool to calculate the percentage change for your select periods, and then click the "News" icon on the annotation bar to find relevant news events on or preceding the opening date.

11. Select a narrow-based spot index (e.g., S&P Small Cap 600, GNA <Index>). Use SECF to identify indexes that have option contracts: Enter SECF; select index/Stats from "Category" dropdown; click "Opts" tab for a listing of index options and their tickers. Load index options: Ticker <Index>. On the selected index screen, type OSA to bring up the OSA screen, and select "Listed Options" on the contract from the red "Positions" dropdown tab to bring up listed index options and then select the options to include in your evaluation.

    Using the Bloomberg OSA screen, evaluate some of the following option strategies that would reflect a bullish position on the market with a profit graph:

    a. Call Purchase.
    b. Bull Call Spread: Long in call with low X and short in call with high X.
    c. Bull Put Spread: Long in put with low X and short in put with high X.
    d. Strap Purchase: Straddle purchase with additional calls (e.g., long 2 calls and long put).

12. Using the Chart screen (Chart <Enter>), examine the historical prices of futures and futures call and put options you selected in Exercise 11. Select a time period that the contract was active.

    a. Use the "Chart" screen (Chart <Enter>) to create multigraphs for the futures, call futures, and put futures. On the Chart Menu screen, select Standard G chart; once you have loaded your securities, go to "Edit" to put your graphs in separate panels.
    b. Select a period in which you would have taken a long call position and calculate the profit from opening and closing at the futures call prices at the beginning and ending dates for your selected period. Calculate the losses if you had taken a long put position.
    c. Select a period in which you would have taken a long put option position and calculate the profit from opening and closing at the futures put prices at the beginning and ending dates for your selected period. Calculate the losses if you had taken a long call position.
    d. Using the annotation bar, apply the "% Change" tool to calculate the percentage change for your select periods, and then click the "News" icon on the annotation bar to find relevant news events on or preceding the opening date.

CHAPTER 8

Option Hedging

As we noted in Chapter 1, the Chicago Board of Trade was established to provide farmers, dealers, and food processors a way of hedging against price risk by entering forward contracts to buy or sell a commodity at a future date at a price specified today. While futures contracts enable businesses, farmers, and other economic entities to hedge the costs or revenues from unfavorable price movements, they also eliminate the benefits realized from favorable price movements. One of the differences of using options instead of futures contracts as a hedging tool is that the hedger, for the price of the option, can obtain protection against adverse price movements while still realizing benefits if the underlying asset moves in a favorable direction. Some of the important uses of options in hedging are from purchasing stock, index, futures options, and OTC put options as a way of attaining downside protection on the future sale of a portfolio, currency, bond, or commodity and by purchasing call options as a strategy for capping the costs of future purchases. In this chapter, we examine hedging equity, commodity, currency, and fixed-income positions with spot and futures options.

Hedging Stock Portfolio Positions

Creating a Floor for a Stock Portfolio Using Index Options

An equity portfolio insurance strategy is a hedging position in which an equity portfolio manager protects the future value of her fund by buying spot or futures index put options. The index put options, in turn, provide downside protection against a stock market decline, while allowing the fund to grow if the market increases. As an example, consider an equity fund manager who on May 27, 2016, planned to sell a portion of a stock portfolio in mid-August to meet an anticipated liquidity need. Suppose the portfolio the manager planned to sell was well-diversified and highly correlated with the S&P 500, had a beta (β) of 1.25, and currently was worth $V_0 = \$100$ million. On May 27, the spot S&P 500 was at 2,100. Suppose the manager on that date expected a bullish market to prevail in the future with the S&P 500 rising. As a result, the manager would have been hoping to benefit from selling her portfolio in August at a higher value. At the same time, though, suppose the manager was also concerned that the market could be lower in mid-August and did not want to risk selling the port-folio in a market with the index lower than 2,100. On May 27, an August S&P 500 put option with an exercise price of 2,100 and multiplier of 100 was trading at 54.40. As a strategy to lock in a minimum value from the portfolio sale if the market decreased, while obtaining a higher portfolio value if the market increased, suppose the manager set up a portfolio insurance strategy by buying August S&P 500 2,100 puts. To form the portfolio insurance position, the manager would have needed to buy 595.2381 August S&P 500 puts (assume perfect divisibility) at a cost of $3,238,095:

$$N_p = \beta \frac{V_0}{X}$$

$$N_p = 1.25 \frac{\$100,000,000}{(2100)(\$100)} = 595.2381 \text{ puts}$$

$$\text{Cost} = (595.2381)(\$100)(54.40) = \$3,238,095$$

Exhibit 8.1 shows for spot index values ranging from 1,860 to 2,460, the man-ager's revenue that would have resulted from selling the portfolio at the option's August expiration date and closing her puts by selling them at their intrinsic values. Note, for each index value shown in Column 1, there is a corresponding portfolio value (shown in Column 4) that reflects the proportional change in the market given the portfolio beta of 1.25. For example, if the spot index were at 1,860 at expiration, then the market as measured by the proportional change in the index would have decreased by 11.43% from its May 27 level of 2,100 ($-0.1143 = (1,860 - 2,100)/2,100$). Since the well-diversified portfolio has a beta of 1.25, it would have decreased by 14.29% (β (%Δ S&P 500) $= 1.25(-0.1143) = -0.1429$), and the portfolio would, in turn, have been worth only $85,714,280—85.714% of its May 26 value of $100 million. Thus, if the market were at 1,860, the corresponding portfolio value would be $85,714,286 ($= (1 + \beta$ (%Δ S&P 500)$V_0 = (1 + 1.25(-0.1143)(\$100,000,000)))$). On the other hand, if the spot S&P 500 index were at 2,460 at the August expiration, then the market would have increased by 17.14% ($= (2,460 - 2,100)/2,100$) and the portfolio would have increased by 21.43% ($=1.25(0.1714)$) to equal $121,428,571 ($=1.2143$ ($100,000,000)). Thus, when the market is at 2,460, the portfolio's corre-sponding value is $121,428,571. Given the corresponding portfolio values, Column 5 in Exhibit 8.1 shows the intrinsic values of the S&P 500 put corresponding to the spot index values, and Column 6 shows the corresponding cash flows that would be received by the portfolio manager from selling the 595.2381 expiring August index

EXHIBIT 8.1 Stock Portfolio Value Hedged with S&P 500 Puts

Portfolio Hedged with S&P 500 Index Puts; Portfolio: Initial Value = $100,000,000, β = 1.25;

S&P 500 Put: X = 2100, Multiplier = 100, Premium = 54.40; Hedge: 595.2381 Puts; Cost = (595.2381)(54.40)($100) = $3,238,095

Short S&P 500 Call: X = 2100, Multiplier = 100, Premium = 24.10; Hedge: 595.2381; Revenue = (595.2381)(24.10)($100) = $1,434,524

Range Forward: Long 595.2381 Put Contracts and Short 595.2381 Call Contracts; Net cost = $3,328,095 − $1,434,524 = $1,893,571

1	2	3	4	5	6	7	8	9	10
S&P 500 at T, S_T	Proportional Change in S&P 500: $g = (S_T − 2100)/2100$	Proportional Change in Portfolio: $\beta g = 1.25g$	Portfolio Value: $V_T = (1+\beta g)$ $100m	Put Value P_T = IV = Max $[2100 − S_T, 0]$	Value of Puts: CF = (595.2381) ($100) (IV)	Hedged Portfolio Value	Short Call Value: IV = Max$[S_T − 2310, 0]$	Value of Short Call: 595.2381 (100)IV	Ranged Forward: Hedged Portfolio Value = (4) + (6) − (9)
1860	−0.1143	−0.1429	$85,714,286	240	$14,285,714	$100,000,000	$0	$0	$100,000,000
1890	−0.1000	−0.1250	$87,500,000	210	$12,500,000	$100,000,000	$0	$0	$100,000,000
1920	−0.0857	−0.1071	$89,285,714	180	$10,714,286	$100,000,000	$0	$0	$100,000,000
1950	−0.0714	−0.0893	$91,071,429	150	$8,928,571	$100,000,000	$0	$0	$100,000,000
1980	−0.0571	−0.0714	$92,857,143	120	$7,142,857	$100,000,000	$0	$0	$100,000,000
2010	−0.0429	−0.0536	$94,642,857	90	$5,357,143	$100,000,000	$0	$0	$100,000,000
2040	−0.0286	−0.0357	$96,428,571	60	$3,571,429	$100,000,000	$0	$0	$100,000,000
2070	−0.0143	−0.0179	$98,214,286	30	$1,785,714	$100,000,000	$0	$0	$100,000,000
2100	0.0000	0.0000	$100,000,000	0	$0	$100,000,000	$0	$0	$100,000,000
2130	0.0143	0.0179	$101,785,714	0	$0	$101,785,714	$0	$0	$101,785,714
2160	0.0286	0.0357	$103,571,429	0	$0	$103,571,429	$0	$0	$103,571,429
2190	0.0429	0.0536	$105,357,143	0	$0	$105,357,143	$0	$0	$105,357,143
2220	0.0571	0.0714	$107,142,857	0	$0	$107,142,857	$0	$0	$107,142,857
2250	0.0714	0.0893	$108,928,571	0	$0	$108,928,571	$0	$0	$108,928,571
2280	0.0857	0.1071	$110,714,286	0	$0	$110,714,286	$0	$0	$110,714,286
2310	0.1000	0.1250	$112,500,000	0	$0	$112,500,000	$0	$0	$112,500,000
2340	0.1143	0.1429	$114,285,714	0	$0	$114,285,714	$30	$1,785,714	$112,500,000
2370	0.1286	0.1607	$116,071,429	0	$0	$116,071,429	$60	$3,571,429	$112,500,000
2400	0.1429	0.1786	$117,857,143	0	$0	$117,857,143	$90	$5,357,143	$112,500,000
2430	0.1571	0.1964	$119,642,857	0	$0	$119,642,857	$120	$7,142,857	$112,500,000
2460	0.1714	0.2143	$121,428,571	0	$0	$121,428,571	$150	$8,928,572	$112,500,000

Portfolio Insurance: Portfolio Hedged with S&P 500 Index Puts; Portfolio: Initial Value = $100,000,000, β = 1.25; S&P 500 Put: X = 2100, Multiplier = 100, Premium = 45.70; Hedge: 595 Puts; Cost = (595.2381)(54.40)($100) = $3,238,095

puts at their intrinsic values. As shown in the exhibit, if the spot S&P 500 is less than 2,100 at expiration, the manager would have realized a positive cash flow from selling her index puts, with the put revenue increasing proportional to the proportional decreases in the portfolio values, providing, in turn, the requisite protection in value. On the other hand, if the S&P 500 spot index is equal to or greater than 2,100, the manager's put options would be worthless, but her revenue from selling the portfolio would be greater, the greater the index. Thus, if the market were 2,100 or less at expiration, the value of the hedged portfolio (stock portfolio value plus put values) would be $100 million; if the market were above 2,100, the value of the hedged portfolio would increase as the market rises. Thus, for the $3,238,095 cost of the put options, the fund manager would have attained on May 27 a $100 million floor for the value of the portfolio in mid-August, while benefiting with greater portfolio values if the market increased.

Creating a Cap for a Stock Portfolio Purchase Using Index Options

In addition to protecting the value of a portfolio, spot and futures index options also can be used to hedge the costs of future stock portfolio purchases. For example, suppose on May 27 the above portfolio manager was anticipating a cash inflow of $100 million in August, which she planned to invest in a well-diversified portfolio with a β of 1.25 that was currently worth $100 million when the current spot S&P 500 index was at 2,100. On May 27, an August S&P 500 call option with an exercise price of 2,100 and multiplier of 100 was trading at 45.70. As a strategy to cap the portfolio purchase in case the market increases, the manager could have purchased 595.2381 August S&P 500 2100 calls (assume perfect divisibility) at a cost of $2,720,238:

$$N_C = \beta \frac{V_0}{X}$$

$$N_p = 1.25 \frac{\$100,000,000}{(2100)(\$100)} = 595.2381 \text{ calls}$$

$$\text{Cost} = (595.2381)(\$100)(45.70) = \$2,720,238$$

As shown in Exhibit 8.2, if the spot index were 2,100 or higher at the August expiration, the corresponding cost of the portfolio would be higher; the higher portfolio costs, though, would have been offset by profits from the index calls. For example, if the market were at 2,370 in September, then the well-diversified portfolio with a β of 1.25 would cost $121,428,571; the additional $16,071,429 cost of the portfolio would be offset, though, by the $16,071,429 cash flow obtained from the selling 595.2381 August 2,100 index calls at their intrinsic value of 270. Thus, as shown in the exhibit, for index values of 2,100 or greater, the hedged costs of the portfolio would be $100 million. On the other hand, if the index is less than 2,100, the manager would have been able to buy the well-diversified portfolio at a lower cost, with the losses on the index calls limited to just the premium. Thus, for the $2,720,238 costs of the index call option, the manager on May 27 could have

EXHIBIT 8.2 Stock Portfolio Purchase Hedged with S&P 500 Calls

Portfolio Purchase with Cost Hedged with S&P 500 Index Calls; Portfolio: Initial Value at Time of Hedge = $100,000,000, $\beta = 1.25$

S&P 500 Call: $X = 2,100$, Multiplier = 100, Premium = 45.70; Hedge: 595.2381 Calls; Cost = (595.2381)(45.70)($100) = $2,720,238

Short S&P 500 Put: $X = 1,910$, Multiplier = 100, Premium = 24.10; Hedge: 595.2381; Revenue = (595.2381)(24.10)($100) = $1,434,524

Range Forward: Long 595.2381 Call Contracts and Short 595.2381 Put Contracts; Net Cost = $2,720,238 − $1,434,524 = $1,285,714

1	2	3	4	5	6	7	8	9	10
S&P 500 at T, S_T	Proportional Change in S&P 500: $g = (S_T - 2100)/2100$	Proportional Change in Portfolio: $\beta g = 1.25g$	Portfolio Cost: $V_T = (1 + \beta g)\$100\text{m}$	Call Value $C_T = IV = \text{Max}[S_T - 2100,0]$	Value of Calls: $CF = (595.2381)(\$100)(IV)$	Hedged Portfolio Cost: Col (4) − Col (6)	Short Put Value: $= IV = \text{Max}[1910 - S_T, 0]$	Value of Short Put: 595.2381 (100) IV	Range Forward: Hedged Portfolio Cost: (4) − (6) − (9)
1770	−0.1571	−0.1964	$80,357,143	0	$0	$80,357,143	−$140	−$8,333,333	$88,690,476
1800	−0.1429	−0.1786	$82,142,857	0	$0	$82,142,857	−$110	−$6,547,619	$88,690,476
1830	−0.1286	−0.1607	$83,928,571	0	$0	$83,928,571	−$80	−$4,761,905	$88,690,476
1860	−0.1143	−0.1429	$85,714,286	0	$0	$85,714,286	−$50	−$2,976,191	$88,690,476
1890	−0.1000	−0.1250	$87,500,000	0	$0	$87,500,000	−$20	−$1,190,476	$88,690,476
1910	−0.0905	−0.1131	$88,690,476	0	$0	$88,690,476	$0	$0	$88,690,476
1920	−0.0857	−0.1071	$89,285,714	0	$0	$89,285,714	$0	$0	$89,285,714
1950	−0.0714	−0.0893	$91,071,429	0	$0	$91,071,429	$0	$0	$91,071,429
1980	−0.0571	−0.0714	$92,857,143	0	$0	$92,857,143	$0	$0	$92,857,143
2010	−0.0429	−0.0536	$94,642,857	0	$0	$94,642,857	$0	$0	$94,642,857
2040	−0.0286	−0.0357	$96,428,571	0	$0	$96,428,571	$0	$0	$96,428,571
2070	−0.0143	−0.0179	$98,214,286	0	$0	$98,214,286	$0	$0	$98,214,286
2100	0.0000	0.0000	$100,000,000	0	$0	$100,000,000	$0	$0	$100,000,000
2130	0.0143	0.0179	$101,785,714	30	$1,785,714	$100,000,000	$0	$0	$100,000,000
2160	0.0286	0.0357	$103,571,429	60	$3,571,429	$100,000,000	$0	$0	$100,000,000
2190	0.0429	0.0536	$105,357,143	90	$5,357,143	$100,000,000	$0	$0	$100,000,000
2220	0.0571	0.0714	$107,142,857	120	$7,142,857	$100,000,000	$0	$0	$100,000,000
2250	0.0714	0.0893	$108,928,571	150	$8,928,571	$100,000,000	$0	$0	$100,000,000
2280	0.0857	0.1071	$110,714,286	180	$10,714,286	$100,000,000	$0	$0	$100,000,000
2310	0.1000	0.1250	$112,500,000	210	$12,500,000	$100,000,000	$0	$0	$100,000,000
2340	0.1143	0.1429	$114,285,714	240	$14,285,714	$100,000,000	$0	$0	$100,000,000
2370	0.1286	0.1607	$116,071,429	270	$16,071,429	$100,000,000	$0	$0	$100,000,000

(Continued)

337

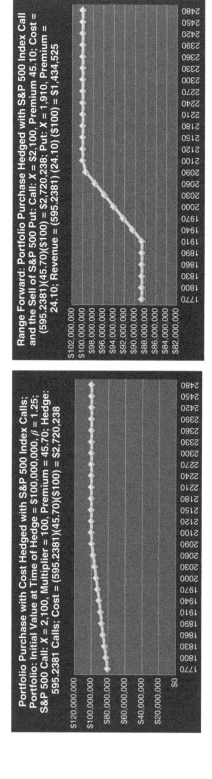

EXHIBIT 8.2 (*Continued*)

capped the maximum cost of the portfolio in mid-August at $100 million, while still benefiting with lower costs if the market declined.

Range Forward Contracts

Using put options to provide a floor and call options to provide a cap involves the cost of buying the underlying options. By limiting some of the upside potential for floors or downside benefits for caps, the cost of buying the options can be defrayed by selling options with a different exercise price. In Chapter 7, we define a splitting the strikes strategy consisting of long (short) call and short (long) put positions with different exercise prices. The premium on the short position, in turn, defrays part of the cost of the long position. Sometimes options to sell can be selected such that there is little cost, or even a profit. This position is sometimes referred to as a *range forward contract* or *zero-cost collar*.

A *short-range forward contract* consists of a long position in a put with a low exercise price, X_1, and a short position in a call with a higher exercise price, X_2. An investor holding the underlying security or portfolio and planning to sell it at time T could take a short-range forward contract to guarantee that the price of the stock or portfolio would be sold at a price between the exercise prices at the options' maturity. Exhibit 8.3 shows the structure of a range forward contract for the sale of Tesla stock at the options' August expiration. The contract is formed with a long position in the August 215 put (cost of $24.10 on May 27) and a short position in an August 225 call (sold for $22.25). As shown in the exhibit, the position ensures that the sale of Tesla in mid-August will be between $215 and $225.

In Exhibit 8.1, Columns (8), (9), and (10) show:

1. The intrinsic values of a short call position on a 2,310 August S&P 500.
2. The expiration cash flow from selling 595.2381 call contracts at 24.10; the calls raised $1,434,524 (= (595.2381)($100)(24.10)) to defray the cost of purchasing 595.2381 put contracts to hedge the $100 million portfolio.
3. The values of the portfolio with the long put and short call positions.

As shown in Column 10, this range forward contract provides a minimum portfolio value of $100 million if the S&P 500 is 2,100 or less and a maximum value of $112.5 million if the S&P 500 is 2,310 or greater. Thus, the portfolio ranges in value between $100 million and $112.5 million. In contrast to the portfolio insurance position in which there is upside potential and downside protection, the range forward provides a range of portfolio values between $100 million and $112.5 million, with a limit on the upside potential. However, the cost of the range forward positon is $1,893,571 (= $3,328,095 − $1,434,524), while the cost of the portfolio insurance position is $3,238,095.

In contrast to a short-range forward contract, a *long-range forward contract* consists of a short position in a put with a lower exercise price, X_1, and a long position in a call with a higher exercise price, X_2. An investor planning to purchase the options' underlying security at time T could take a long-range forward contract to guarantee

EXHIBIT 8.3 Selling Stock at T with a Short-Range Forward Contract Long in Put with X_1 and Short in Call with X_2

Position	Cash Flows at Expiration		
	$S_T < X_1$	$X_1 \leq S_T \leq X_2$	$S_T > X_2$
Stock Sale	S_T	S_T	S_T
Short X_2 Call	0	0	$-(S_T - X_2)$
Long X_1 Put	$X_1 - S_T$	0	0
	X_1	S_T	X_2

TSLA Call: $X = \$225$, $C_0 = 22.25$; TSLA Put: X = 215, $P_0 = \$24.10$

Tesla Motors Stock Prices at T, S_T	Cash Flow of Short \$225 TSLA Call: $-(\text{Max}(S_T - 225),0)$	Cash Flow of Long 215 TSLA Put: $(\text{Max}(215 - S_T,0))$	$S_T - P_T + C_T$
$185	$0	$30	$215
$190	$0	$25	$215
$195	$0	$20	$215
$200	$0	$15	$215
$205	$0	$10	$215
$210	$0	$5	$215
$215	$0	$0	$215
$217	$0	$0	$217
$219	$0	$0	$219
$221	$0	$0	$221
$223	$0	$0	$223
$225	$0	$0	$225
$230	−$5	$0	$225
$235	−$10	$0	$225
$240	−$15	$0	$225
$245	−$20	$0	$225
$250	−$25	$0	$225
$255	−$30	$0	$225

that the purchase price of the stock would be between the exercise prices at the options' maturity. Exhibit 8.4 shows the structure of a long-range forward contract for the purchase of the Tesla stock at the options' August expiration. The contract is formed with a long position in the August 225 call (cost of $22.25 on May 27) and a short position in an August 215 put (sold for $24.10). As shown in the exhibit, the position ensures that the purchase of Tesla in mid-August will be between $215 and $225.

In Exhibit 8.2, Columns (8), (9), and (10) show:

1. The intrinsic values of a long call position in a 2,100 August S&P 500.
2. The expiration cash flow from selling 595.2381 put contracts with an exercise price of 1,910 at 24.10; the puts sold raised $1,434,524 (= (595.2381)($100)(24.10)) to defray part of the cost of purchasing the 595.2381 call contracts to hedge the $100 million portfolio purchase.
3. The cost of the portfolio with the long call and short put positions.

EXHIBIT 8.4 Purchasing Stock at *T* with a Long-Range Forward Contract: Short in Put with X_1 and Long in Call with X_2

Position	Cash Flows at Expiration		
	$S_T < X_1$	$X_1 \leq S_T \leq X_2$	$S_T > X_2$
Stock Purchase	$-S_T$	$-S_T$	$-S_T$
Long X_2 Call	0	0	$S_T - X_2$
Short X_1 Put	$-(X_1 - S_T)$	0	0
	$-X_1$	$-S_T$	$-X_2$

TSLA Call: $X = \$225$, $C_0 = 22.25$; TSLA Put: $X = \$215$, $P_0 = \$24.10$

Purchase of Tesla Motors Stock Prices at *T*, S_T	Cash Flow of Long 225 TSLA Call: Max $(S_T - 225),0)$	Cash Flow of Short 215 TSLA Put: $-(Max(215 - S_T,0)$	Cost of Tesla with Long Range Forward Contract: $-S_T + P_T - C_T$
$185	$0	−$30	−$215
$190	$0	−$25	−$215
$195	$0	−$20	−$215
$200	$0	−$15	−$215
$205	$0	−$10	−$215
$210	$0	−$5	−$215
$215	$0	$0	−$215
$217	$0	$0	−$217
$219	$0	$0	−$219
$221	$0	$0	−$221
$223	$0	$0	−$223
$225	$0	$0	−$225
$230	$5	$0	−$225
$235	$10	$0	−$225
$240	$15	$0	−$225
$245	$20	$0	−$225
$250	$25	$0	−$225
$255	$30	$0	−$225

As shown, this long-range forward contract provides a minimum portfolio cost of $88,690,476 if the S&P 500 is 1,910 or less and a maximum cost of $100 million if the S&P 500 is 2,100 or greater. Thus, the cost of the portfolio ranges between $88,690,476 and $100 million. In contrast to the portfolio cap position in which there is downside lower cost potential, the long-range forward provides a range of portfolio costs between $88,690,476 and $100 million, with a limit on the downside cost potential. However, the cost of the range forward position is $1,285,714 (= $2,720,238 − $1,434,524), while the cost of the capped portfolio position is $2,720,238.

Note that when the exercise prices are the same, then the range forward positions becomes a simulated long or short stock position that can be used to lock in the purchase or sales price at a specific price. This makes the range forward contract a regular forward contract.

Portfolio Exposure—Market Timing and Beta Convexity

Instead of hedging a portfolio's value against market risk, suppose a manager wanted to change her portfolio's exposure to the market. As we discussed in Chapter 3, an equity portfolio manager who is very confident of a bull (bear) market can increase (decrease) her portfolio's exposure to the market by increasing (decreasing) the portfolio's beta, β_0, to a new target beta, β_{TR}, by going long (short) in equity index futures contracts. The manager also could increase (decrease) her portfolio's exposure by buying index calls (puts). The number of option contracts needed to move the portfolio beta from β_0 to β_{TR} can be determined using the price-sensitivity model in which:

$$n_{\text{Options}} = \frac{V_0}{X} \, (\beta_{TR} - \beta_0)$$

where

if $\beta_{TR} > \beta_0$, Long equity index call options

if $\beta_{TR} < \beta_0$, Long equity index put options

Changing a portfolio's market exposure with options instead of futures provides an asymmetrical gain and loss relation, referred to as a convex beta. For example, when calls (puts) are purchased to increase (decrease) the target beta, the option-adjusted portfolio has a β_{TR} for market increases (decreases) and β_0 for market decreases (increases). The cost of obtaining this asymmetrical or convex beta relation is the cost of the options.

For example, suppose on May 27, 2016, the equity fund manager in our earlier example was very bullish and wanted to increase her beta from 1.25 to 2.00. On May 27, the portfolio had a value of $V_0 = \$100$ million, and there was an August S&P 500 call with an exercise price of 2,100 trading at 45.70. To increase the portfolio's beta to 2.00, the manager would have needed to buy 357.142857 August S&P 500 calls for $1,632,143:

$$n_{\text{Call}} = \frac{V_0}{X} \, (\beta_{TR} - \beta_0)$$

$$n_{\text{Call}} = \frac{\$100,000,000}{(2,100)(100)} \, (2.00 - 1.25) = 357.142857$$

$$\text{Cost} = (357.142857)(45.70)(100) = \$1,632,143$$

As shown in Exhibit 8.5, if the market increases from 2,100, the manager earns higher proportional gains from the call-enhanced portfolio than from the unadjusted portfolio. As shown in the exhibit, the proportional increases in the call-enhanced portfolio for proportional increases in the market reflect a beta of 2.00. On the other hand, if the market decreases from 2,100, then proportional declines in the portfolio for declines in the market reflect a beta of 1.25.

EXHIBIT 8.5 Call-Enhanced Portfolio—Asymmetrical Betas

Portfolio Enhanced with S&P 500 Index Calls; Portfolio: Initial Value = $100,000,000, $\beta = 1.25$; Target: $\beta_{TR} = 2.00$

S&P 500 Call: X = 2,100, Multiplier = 100, Premium = 45.70; Hedge: 357.142857 Calls; Cost = (357.142857)(45.70)($100) = $1,632,143

1	2	3	4	5	6	7	8	9
S&P 500 at T, S_T	Proportional Change in S&P 500: $g = (S_T - 2100)/2100$	Proportional Change in Portfolio: $\beta g = 1.25g$	Portfolio Value: $V_T = (1+\beta g)$ $100m	Call Value $C_T =$ Max $IV =$ Max $[S_T - 2,100, 0]$	Value of Calls: CF $= (357.142857)$ ($100) (IV)	Enhance Hedged Value: Col (4) + Col (6)	Proportional Change: [Col (7)/$100m] − 1	Beta: Col (8)/ Col (2)
1,910	−0.0905	−0.1131	$88,690,476	0	$0	$88,690,476	−0.1131	1.2500
1,940	−0.0762	−0.0952	$90,476,190	0	$0	$90,476,190	−0.0952	1.2500
1,970	−0.0619	−0.0774	$92,261,905	0	$0	$92,261,905	−0.0774	1.2500
2,000	−0.0476	−0.0595	$94,047,619	0	$0	$94,047,619	−0.0595	1.2500
2,030	−0.0333	−0.0417	$95,833,333	0	$0	$95,833,333	−0.0417	1.2500
2,060	−0.0190	−0.0238	$97,619,048	0	$0	$97,619,048	−0.0238	1.2500
2,090	−0.0048	−0.0060	$99,404,762	0	$0	$99,404,762	−0.0060	1.2500
2,100	0.0000	0.0000	$100,000,000	0	$0	$100,000,000	0.0000	1.2500
2,120	0.0095	0.0119	$101,190,476	20	$714,286	$101,904,762	0.0190	2.0000
2,150	0.0238	0.0298	$102,976,190	50	$1,785,714	$104,761,905	0.0476	2.0000
2,180	0.0381	0.0476	$104,761,905	80	$2,857,143	$107,619,048	0.0762	2.0000
2,210	0.0524	0.0655	$106,547,619	110	$3,928,571	$110,476,190	0.1048	2.0000
2,240	0.0667	0.0833	$108,333,333	140	$5,000,000	$113,333,333	0.1333	2.0000
2,270	0.0810	0.1012	$110,119,048	170	$6,071,429	$116,190,476	0.1619	2.0000
2,300	0.0952	0.1190	$111,904,762	200	$7,142,857	$119,047,619	0.1905	2.0000
2,330	0.1095	0.1369	$113,690,476	230	$8,214,286	$121,904,762	0.2190	2.0000
2,360	0.1238	0.1548	$115,476,190	260	$9,285,714	$124,761,905	0.2476	2.0000
2,390	0.1381	0.1726	$117,261,905	290	$10,357,143	$127,619,048	0.2762	2.0000
2,420	0.1524	0.1905	$119,047,619	320	$11,428,571	$130,476,190	0.3048	2.0000
2,450	0.1667	0.2083	$120,833,333	350	$12,500,000	$133,333,333	0.3333	2.0000

In contrast, suppose on May 27, the equity fund manager was very bearish and wanted to decrease her beta from 1.25 to 0.75. On May 27, the August S&P 500 put with an exercise price of 2,100 was trading at 54.40. To decrease the portfolio's beta to 0.75, the manager would have needed to buy 238.095238 August S&P 500 puts for $1,295,238:

$$n_{\text{Put}} = \frac{V_0}{X} \left(\beta_{TR} - \beta_0 \right)$$

$$n_{\text{Put}} = \frac{\$100,000,000}{(2,100)(100)} (0.75 - 1.25) = -238.095238$$

$$\text{Cost} = (238.095238)(54.40(100) = \$1,295,238$$

As shown in Exhibit 8.6, if the market decreases from 2,100, the manager earns smaller proportional losses from the put-hedged portfolio than from the unadjusted portfolio. As shown in the exhibit, the proportional decreases in the put-hedged portfolio for proportional decreases in the market reflect a beta of 0.75. On the other hand, if the market increases from 2,100, then proportional increases in the portfolio for increases in the market reflect a beta of 1.25.

Hedging Currency and Commodity Positions

Hedging Currency Positions with Futures Options

Until the introduction of currency options, exchange-rate risk usually was hedged with foreign currency forward or futures contracts. Hedging with these instruments made it possible for foreign exchange participants to lock in the local currency values of their international revenues or expenses. However, with exchange-traded currency futures options and dealer's options, hedgers, for the cost of the options, can obtain not only protection against adverse exchange rate movements, but (unlike forward and futures positions) benefits if the exchange rates move in favorable directions.

To illustrate currency hedging with options, consider the case presented in Chapter 3 of a US investment fund expecting a payment of £10 million in principal on its Eurobonds next September. The fund hedged its future BP receipt by going short in 160 CME September BP futures trading at $f_0 = \$1.50/\text{BP}$ ($N_f = £10,000,000/£62,500 = 160$ BP). With this futures hedge, the fund at expiration would sell its £10 million on the spot market at the spot exchange rate, and then close its futures position by going long in an expiring September BP futures contract at an expiring future price equal (or approximately equal) to the spot exchange rate ($f_T = E_T$). This futures hedge, in turn, locked in a US dollar receipt of $15 million.

For the costs of BP futures put options, the US fund could also protect its dollar revenues from possible exchange rate decreases when it converts, while still benefiting if the exchange rate increases by purchasing BP put futures options—a currency-insured position. For example, suppose a September BP futures put with an exercise price of $X = \$1.50/£$ were available at $P_0 = \$0.02/£$. Given the

EXHIBIT 8.6 Put-Hedged Portfolio—Asymmetrical Betas

Portfolio Hedged with S&P 500 Index Puts; Portfolio: Initial Value = $100,000,000, $\beta = 1.25$; Target: $\beta_{TR} = 0.75$

S&P 500 Put: $X = 2,100$, Multiplier = 100, Premium = 54.40; Hedge: 238.095238 Puts; Cost = $(238.095238)(54.40)(\$100) = \$1,295,238$

1	2	3	4	5	6	7	8	9
S&P 500 at T, S_T	Proportional Change in S&P 500: $g = (S_T - 2100)/2100$	Proportional Change in Portfolio: $\beta g = 1.25g$	Portfolio Value: $V_T = (1+\beta g)$ $100m	Put Value $P_T =$ $IV =$ Max $[2,100 - S_T, 0]$	Value of put: CF $= (238.095238)$ ($100) (IV)	Put Hedged Value: Col (4) + Col (6)	Proportional Change: [Col (7)/ $100m] − 1	Beta: Col (8)/ Col (2)
1,910	−0.0905	−0.1131	$88,690,476	190	$4,523,810	$93,214,286	−0.0679	0.7500
1,940	−0.0762	−0.0952	$90,476,190	160	$3,809,524	$94,285,714	−0.0571	0.7500
1,970	−0.0619	−0.0774	$92,261,905	130	$3,095,238	$95,357,143	−0.0464	0.7500
2,000	−0.0476	−0.0595	$94,047,619	100	$2,380,952	$96,428,571	−0.0357	0.7500
2,030	−0.0333	−0.0417	$95,833,333	70	$1,666,667	$97,500,000	−0.0250	0.7500
2,060	−0.0190	−0.0238	$97,619,048	40	$952,381	$98,571,429	−0.0143	0.7500
2,090	−0.0048	−0.0060	$99,404,762	10	$238,095	$99,642,857	−0.0036	0.7500
2,100	0.0000	0.0000	$100,000,000	0	$0	$100,000,000	0.0000	0.7500
2,120	0.0095	0.0119	$101,190,476	0	$0	$101,190,476	0.0119	1.2500
2,150	0.0238	0.0298	$102,976,190	0	$0	$102,976,190	0.0298	1.2500
2,180	0.0381	0.0476	$104,761,905	0	$0	$104,761,905	0.0476	1.2500
2,210	0.0524	0.0655	$106,547,619	0	$0	$106,547,619	0.0655	1.2500
2,240	0.0667	0.0833	$108,333,333	0	$0	$108,333,333	0.0833	1.2500
2,270	0.0810	0.1012	$110,119,048	0	$0	$110,119,048	0.1012	1.2500
2,300	0.0952	0.1190	$111,904,762	0	$0	$111,904,762	0.1190	1.2500
2,330	0.1095	0.1369	$113,690,476	0	$0	$113,690,476	0.1369	1.2500
2,360	0.1238	0.1548	$115,476,190	0	$0	$115,476,190	0.1548	1.2500
2,390	0.1381	0.1726	$117,261,905	0	$0	$117,261,905	0.1726	1.2500
2,420	0.1524	0.1905	$119,047,619	0	$0	$119,047,619	0.1905	1.2500
2,450	0.1667	0.2083	$120,833,333	0	$0	$120,833,333	0.2083	1.2500

345

contract size of 62,500 British pounds, the US fund would need to buy 160 put contracts (N_p = £10,000,000/£62,500 = 160) at a cost of $200,000 (Cost = (160)(£62,500)(0.02/£)) to set up a floor for the dollar value of its £10,000,000 receipt in September. Exhibit 8.7 shows the dollar cash flows the US fund would receive in September from converting its receipts of £10,000,000 to dollars at the spot exchange rate (E_T) and closing its 160 futures put contracts at a price equal to the put's intrinsic value.

As shown in the exhibit, if the exchange rate is less than X = $1.50/£, the company would receive less than $15,000,000 when it converts its £10,000,000 to dollars; these lower revenues, however, would be exactly offset by the cash flows from the put position. For example, at a spot exchange rate of $1.30/£ the company would receive only $13 million from converting its £10 million, but would receive a cash flow of $2 million from the puts ($2,000,000 = 160 Max[(($1.50/£) − ($1.30/£), 0] (£62,500)); this would result in a combined receipt of $15 million. Thus, if the exchange rate is $1.50/£ or less, the company would receive $15 million. On the other hand, if the exchange rate at expiration exceeds $1.50/£, the US fund would realize a dollar gain when it converts the £10 million at the higher spot exchange rate, while its losses on the put would be limited to the amount of the premium. Thus, by hedging with currency futures put options, the US investment fund is able to obtain exchange-rate risk protection in the event the exchange rate decreases while still retaining the potential for increased dollar revenues if the exchange rate rises.

It should be noted that if the investment fund wanted to defray part of the cost of its put-insured currency position, it could sell British pound calls with a higher exercise price to form a short-range forward contract. Column (8) in Exhibit 8.7 shows the range forward position formed by combining the put-insured currency position with a short position of 160 BP futures call contracts with an exercise price of $1.70 and premium $0.015/BP. With the short call position providing the investment fund $150,000, the cost of range forward contract is only $50,000 compared to the put-insured cost of $200,000. The short-range forward position, however, limits the dollar revenue to a range between $15 million and $17 million, limiting the upside potential gains once the exchange rate increases past $1.70/BP.

Suppose that instead of receiving foreign currency, a US company had a foreign liability requiring a foreign currency payment at some future date. To protect itself against possible increases in the exchange rate while still benefiting if the exchange rate decreases, the company could hedge the position by taking a long position in a currency futures call option. For example, suppose a US company owed £10 million, with the payment to be made in September. To benefit from the lower exchange rates and still limit the dollar costs of purchasing £10,000,000 in the event the $/£ exchange rate rises, suppose the company bought 160 British pound futures call options with X = $1.50/£ ($N_c$ = £10,000,000/£62,500 = 160) at a cost of 0.02/£ (total cost = $200,000 = (160)(£62,500)(0.02/£)). Exhibit 8.8 shows the costs of purchasing £10 million at different exchange rates and the cash flows from selling 160 September British pound futures call contracts at expiration at a price equal to the call's intrinsic value.

EXHIBIT 8.7 Hedging £10 Million Cash Inflow with a British Pound Futures Put Option and Short-Range Forward Contract

September 10 Million British Pound Receipt Hedged with BP Futures Put

September BP Put: $X = \$1.50$, Size $= 62,500$ BP, Premium $= \$0.02$/BP

Purchase 160 BP Futures Puts at \$0.02/BP; $N_p = 160 = 10,000,000$ BP/62,500 BP; Cost $= (160)(62,500$ BP$)(\$0.02$/BP$) = \$200,000$

Sale of 160 BP Call Contracts: $X = \$1.70$/BP; Premium $= \$0.015$; Revenue $= (160)(62,500$BP$)(\$0.015) = \$150,000$

Range Forward: Long 160 Puts and Short 160 Calls: Cost $= \$200,000 - \$150,000 = \$50,000$

Expiration: Futures and Futures Options Expire at the Same Time: $f_T = E_T$

1	2	3	4	5	6	7	8
$f_T = E_T$	Dollar Receipt from Converting 10 Million BP on Spot: E_T (10,000,000 BP)	Put Value $P_T = IV$ = Max[\$1.50 − f_T,0]	Value of Puts: CF = (160)(62,500 BP) (IV)	Currency-Insured Position: (2) + (4)	Short Call Value: C_T = −IV = −Max [f_T − \$1.70, 0]	Value of Short Calls: CF = (160)(62,500 BP) (IV)	Dollar Revenue with Short Range Forward: (2) + (4) + (7)
$1.00	$10,000,000	$0.50	$5,000,000	$15,000,000	$0.00	$0	$15,000,000
$1.10	$11,000,000	$0.40	$4,000,000	$15,000,000	$0.00	$0	$15,000,000
$1.20	$12,000,000	$0.30	$3,000,000	$15,000,000	$0.00	$0	$15,000,000
$1.30	$13,000,000	$0.20	$2,000,000	$15,000,000	$0.00	$0	$15,000,000
$1.40	$14,000,000	$0.10	$1,000,000	$15,000,000	$0.00	$0	$15,000,000
$1.50	$15,000,000	$0.00	$0	$15,000,000	$0.00	$0	$15,000,000
$1.55	$15,500,000	$0.00	$0	$15,500,000	$0.00	$0	$15,500,000
$1.60	$16,000,000	$0.00	$0	$16,000,000	$0.00	$0	$16,000,000
$1.65	$16,500,000	$0.00	$0	$16,500,000	$0.00	$0	$16,500,000
$1.70	$17,000,000	$0.00	$0	$17,000,000	$0.00	$0	$17,000,000
$1.80	$18,000,000	$0.00	$0	$18,000,000	−$0.10	−$1,000,000	$17,000,000
$1.90	$19,000,000	$0.00	$0	$19,000,000	−$0.20	−$2,000,000	$17,000,000
$2.00	$20,000,000	$0.00	$0	$20,000,000	−$0.30	−$3,000,000	$17,000,000
$2.10	$21,000,000	$0.00	$0	$21,000,000	−$0.40	−$4,000,000	$17,000,000

EXHIBIT 8.8 Hedging Cost with a British Pound Futures Call Option and Long-Range Forward Contract

September 10 Million British Pound Expense Hedged with BP Futures Call

September BP Call: $X = \$1.50$, Size = 62,500 BP; Premium = $0.02/BP

Purchase 160 BP Futures Call Contracts at \$0.02/BP; $N_C = 160 = 10,000,000$ BP/62,500 BP; Cost = $(160)(62,500 \text{ BP})(\$0.02/\text{BP}) = \$200,000$

Sale of 160 BP Put Contracts: $X = \$1.30$/BP; Premium = \$0.015; Revenue = $(160)(62,500 \text{BP})(\$0.015) = \$150,000$

Range Forward: Long 160 calls and short 130 puts: Cost = \$200,000 − \$150,000 = \$50,000

Expiration: Futures and Futures Options Expire at the Same Time: $f_T = E_T$

1	2	3	4	5	6	7	8
$f_T = E_T$	Dollar Cost of purchasing 10 milion BP on Spot: E_T (10,000,000 BP)	Call Value $C_T = \text{Max}[f_T - \$1.50, 0]$ IV	Value of Calls: $CF = (160)(62,500$ BP) (IV)	Cap-Insured Position: (2) − (4)	Short Put Value: $P_T = -IV = -\text{Max}[\$1.30 - f_T, 0]$	Value of Short Calls: $CF = (160)(62,500$ BP) (IV)	Dollar BP Cost with Long Range Forward: (2) − (4) − (7)
$1.00	$10,000,000	$0.00	$0	$10,000,000	−$0.30	−$3,000,000	$13,000,000
$1.10	$11,000,000	$0.00	$0	$11,000,000	−$0.20	−$2,000,000	$13,000,000
$1.20	$12,000,000	$0.00	$0	$12,000,000	−$0.10	−$1,000,000	$13,000,000
$1.30	$13,000,000	$0.00	$0	$13,000,000	$0.00	$0	$13,000,000
$1.35	$13,500,000	$0.00	$0	$13,500,000	$0.00	$0	$13,500,000
$1.40	$14,000,000	$0.00	$0	$14,000,000	$0.00	$0	$14,000,000
$1.45	$14,500,000	$0.00	$0	$14,500,000	$0.00	$0	$14,500,000
$1.50	$15,000,000	$0.00	$0	$15,000,000	$0.00	$0	$15,000,000
$1.60	$16,000,000	$0.10	$1,000,000	$15,000,000	$0.00	$0	$15,000,000
$1.70	$17,000,000	$0.20	$2,000,000	$15,000,000	$0.00	$0	$15,000,000
$1.80	$18,000,000	$0.30	$3,000,000	$15,000,000	$0.00	$0	$15,000,000
$1.90	$19,000,000	$0.40	$4,000,000	$15,000,000	$0.00	$0	$15,000,000
$2.00	$20,000,000	$0.50	$5,000,000	$15,000,000	$0.00	$0	$15,000,000
$2.10	$21,000,000	$0.60	$6,000,000	$15,000,000	$0.00	$0	$15,000,000

As shown in the exhibit, for cases in which the exchange rate is greater than $1.50/£, the company has dollar expenditures exceeding $15 million; the expenditures, though, are exactly offset by the cash flows from the calls. On the other hand, when the exchange rate is less than $1.50/£, the dollar costs of purchasing £10 million decreases as the exchange rate decreases, while the losses on the call options are limited to the option premium.

If the US company wanted to defray part of the cost of the currency cap position, it could sell British pound puts with a lower exercise price to form a long-range forward contract. Column (8) in Exhibit 8.8 shows the range forward position formed by combining the cap-insured currency position with a short position of 160 BP futures put contracts with an exercise price of $1.30 and premium $0.015/BP. With the short put position providing $150,000, the cost of the long-range forward contract is $50,000 compared to the cap-insured cost of $200,000. The long-range forward position, in turn, limits the dollar cost to a range between $13 million to $15 million, limiting the lower dollar cost potential when the exchange rate falls below $1.30.

Hedging Commodity Positions with Futures Options

In Chapter 1, we presented the case of an oil refinery that locked in the cost of purchasing 100,000 barrels of crude oil in July by taking long position in 100 New York Mercantile Exchange (NYMEX)–listed July crude oil contracts (size = 1,000 barrels) at $35.24/barrel. Suppose, the company's treasury department was confident that crude oil prices would be declining in the future but still wanted some protection in case prices increase. For the costs of 100 NYMEX futures crude oil call options expiring in July, the company could obtain this objective of capping the costs of purchasing the crude oil in July, while still benefiting if crude oil costs decrease. For example, suppose the oil refinery purchases 100 crude oil futures calls with an exercise price of $35 and expiring in February at the same time as crude oil futures for $3.00 per barrel. The refining company's futures call option hedge position is shown in Exhibit 8.9. As shown, for the $300,000 cost of the options (contract size on the underlying crude oil futures is 1,000 barrels), the futures call option position serves to cap the refinery's cost of crude at $3,500,000 while allowing them to realized lower costs if crude prices are less than $35. For example, at $30 the company would pay $3 million for the 100,000 barrels of crude with its loss on the option limited to the $300,000 costs of the futures calls. On the other hand, if crude oil costs are greater than $35, the greater crude oil costs are offset by greater cash flows from the futures call options. For example, if crude prices were at $50, the $5 million cost of 100,000 barrels would be offset by $1.5 million cash flow from the closing of the call options. For this insurance, the refiner pays $300,000 for the futures calls. If the company wanted to defray part of the cost, it could form a long-range forward contract by selling crude oil futures call contracts with a lower exercise price.

In Chapter 1, we also presented the case of a corn farmer who went short in September corn contracts (contract size is 5,000 bushels) to lock in his revenue from his corn sale in September. Suppose another farmer planned to sell 100,000 bushels of

EXHIBIT 8.9   Hedging a Crude Oil Purchase with a Call Option on Crude Oil Futures

July Purchase of 100,000 Barrels of Crude Oil on the Spot

Purchase 100 July Crude Oil Contracts: $X = \$35/\text{brl}$, Premium = $\$3.00/\text{brl}$; Contract Size = 1,000 Barrels

$N_c = 100,000 \text{ brl}/1,000 \text{ brl} = 100$; Cost = $(100)(\$3.00/\text{brl})(1,000 \text{ Barrels}) = \$300,000$

Expiration: At Futures Option's Expiration, Assume: $f_T = S_T$

1	2	3	4	5
$f_T = S_T$	Cost: Purchase of 100,000 Barrels of Crude Oil on the Spot Market: S_T (100,000 barrels)	Call Value: $C_T = IV =$ Max$[f_T - \$35, 0]$	Value of Calls: $CF =$ 100 (1,000 barrels) (IV)	Hedged Cost: (2) − (4)
$20.00	$2,000,000	$0.00	$0	$2,000,000
$25.00	$2,500,000	$0.00	$0	$2,500,000
$30.00	$3,000,000	$0.00	$0	$3,000,000
$35.00	$3,500,000	$0.00	$0	$3,500,000
$40.00	$4,000,000	$5.00	$500,000	$3,500,000
$45.00	$4,500,000	$10.00	$1,000,000	$3,500,000
$50.00	$5,000,000	$15.00	$1,500,000	$3,500,000
$55.00	$5,500,000	$20.00	$2,000,000	$3,500,000
$60.00	$6,000,000	$25.00	$2,500,000	$3,500,000
$65.00	$6,500,000	$30.00	$3,000,000	$3,500,000

corn in September but expected corn prices to increase but wanted protections against an unexpected price decrease. Accordingly, the farmer could obtain downside protection by purchasing a put option on a corn futures contract. Exhibit 8.9 shows this put insurance strategy in which the farmer purchases 20 September put options on a corn futures contract with $X = \$2.40$, size = 5,000 bushels, and $P = \$0.20$/bu. As shown in Exhibit 8.10, if corn prices decrease, the farmer's lower revenue is offset by greater cash flows from the puts. In contrast, if corn prices increase, the farmer realizes greater revenues. For this insurance, the farmer pays \$20,000. If the farmer wanted to defray part of the cost, he could form a short-range forward contract by selling corn futures put contracts with a lower exercise price.

Note that there is no hedging risk in both of the hedging cases. With many commodity futures options having expirations different from the expiration on the underlying futures contract or having an expiration period, hedging with futures options often involves timing risk as well as quantity risk.

Hedging Fixed-Income Positions with Options

As examined in Chapter 4, a fixed-income manager planning to invest a future inflow of cash in high-quality, intermediate-term bonds could hedge the investment against possible higher bond prices and lower rates by going long in T-note futures contracts. If intermediate-term rates were to decrease, the higher costs of purchasing the bonds would then be offset by profits from his futures positions. On the other hand, if rates increased, the manager would benefit from lower bond prices, but he would also have to cover losses on his futures position. Thus, hedging future fixed-income investments with futures locks in a future price and return and therefore eliminates not only the costs of unfavorable price movements but also the benefits from favorable movements. However, by hedging with either exchange-traded futures call options on a T-note, T-bond, Eurodollar deposit, or with an OTC spot call option on a debt security, a hedger can obtain protection against adverse price increases while still realizing lower costs if security prices decrease.

For cases in which bond or money market managers are planning to sell some of their securities in the future or who want to hedge their security values, hedging can be done by going short in a T-note, T-bond, or Eurodollar futures contracts. If rates were higher at the time of the sale, the resulting lower bond prices and therefore revenue from the bond sale would be offset by profits from the futures positions (just the opposite would occur if rates were lower). The hedge also can be set up by purchasing an exchange-traded futures put options on Treasuries and Eurodollar contracts or an OTC spot put option on a debt security. This hedge would provide downside protection if bond prices decrease while earning values if security prices increase.

Short hedging positions with futures and put options can be used not only by holders of fixed-income securities planning to sell their instruments before maturity, but also by bond issuers, borrowers, and debt security underwriters. A company planning to issue bonds or borrow funds from a financial institution at some future date, for example, could hedge the debt position against possible interest rate increases by

EXHIBIT 8.10 Hedging a Corn Sale with a Corn Futures Put Option

September Sale of 100,000 Bushels of Corn on the Spot

Purchase 20 September Corn Futures Put Contracts: $X = \$3.30/\text{bu}$, Premium $= \$0.20/\text{bu}$; Contract Size $= 5,000$ bu

$N_p = 100,000 \text{ bu}/5,000 \text{ bu} = 20$; Cost $= (20)(\$0.20/\text{bu})\$5,000 \text{ bu}) = \$20,000$

Expiration: At Futures Option's Expiration, assume: $f_T = S_T$

1	2	3	4	5
$f_T = S_T$	Revenue: Sale of 100,000 Bushels of Corn on the Spot Market: S_T (100,000 bu)	Put Value $P_T = IV =$ Max[$3.30 $- f_T$,0]	Value of Puts: $CF = 20$ (5,000 bu) (IV)	Hedged Revenue: (2) + (4)
$2.40	$240,000	$0.90	$90,000	$330,000
$2.50	$250,000	$0.80	$80,000	$330,000
$2.70	$270,000	$0.60	$60,000	$330,000
$2.90	$290,000	$0.40	$40,000	$330,000
$3.10	$310,000	$0.20	$20,000	$330,000
$3.30	$330,000	$0.00	$0	$330,000
$3.50	$350,000	$0.00	$0	$350,000
$3.70	$370,000	$0.00	$0	$370,000
$3.90	$390,000	$0.00	$0	$390,000
$4.10	$410,000	$0.00	$0	$410,000

going short in debt futures contracts or cap the loan rate by buying an OTC put or exchange-traded futures put. Similarly, as we examined in Chapter 4, a bank that finances its short-term loan portfolio of one-year loans by selling 90-day CDs could manage the resulting maturity gap by also taking short positions in Eurodollar futures or futures options. Finally, an underwriter or a dealer who is holding a debt security for a short-period of time could hedge the position against interest rate increases by going short in an appropriate futures contract or by purchasing a futures put option.

Note that many debt and fixed-income positions involve securities and interest rate positions in which a futures contract on the underlying security does not exist. In such cases, an effective cross hedge needs to be determined to minimize the price risk in the underlying spot position. As noted in Chapter 4, one commonly used model for bond and debt positions is the *price-sensitivity model* developed by Kolb and Chiang and Toevs and Jacobs. For option hedging, the number of options (call for long hedging positions and puts for short hedging positions) using the price-sensitivity model is:

$$n_{\text{Options}} = \frac{Dur_S}{Dur_{\text{option}}} \frac{V_0}{X} \frac{(1 + YTM_f)^T}{(1 + YTM_S)^T}$$

where

Dur_{option} = duration of the bond underlying the option contract
Dur_S = duration of the bond being hedged
V_0 = current value of bond to be hedged
YTM_S = yield to maturity on the bond being hedged
YTM_f = yield to maturity implied on the underlying futures contract

Hedging a T-Note Purchase with T-Note Futures Calls

In Chapter 4, we presented the case of a fixed-income manager who on 12/30/15 planned to buy 10 five-year T-notes in June from an anticipated $1 million cash inflow resulting from maturing bonds in her portfolio. Concerned about rates decreasing and bond price rising over the next six months, the manager hedged the purchase by going long in 10 CME June five-year T-note futures contracts at a futures price of 117.6875. The most likely-to-deliver bond on the contract was a T-note with a $1^3/_8$% coupon, maturity of 8/31/20, conversion factor (CFA) of 0.8371, and accrued interest on the delivery date of $0.457 (see Exhibit 4.16). With this long futures position, the manager was able to lock in a T-note cost of $983,557 by purchasing the delivered bonds on the contract and paying the accrued interest:

T-Note Price per $100 Face Value:

Cost = (Quoted futures price)(CFA) + Accrued interest

Cost = (117.6875)(0.8317) + 0.475

Cost = $98.3557

Cost of 10 T-notes with $100,000 face value plus accrued interest:

$$\text{Cost} = 10 \; \frac{98.3557}{100}(\$100,000)$$

$$\text{Cost} = \$983,557$$

Alternatively, the manager could have a realized the $983,557 cost by buying her T-notes on the spot at the futures expiration and closing her expiring futures position.

Suppose on 12/30/15, the manager wanted to still hedge against the possibility of rates decreasing, but believed that rates would increase, causing five-year T-note prices to fall. In this case, the manager, for the cost of 10 June five-year T-notes call futures contracts, could cap the June cost of purchasing 10 T-notes in June while benefiting with lower bond cost if bond prices decreased as she expected. On 12/30/15, there was a CME call on the June five-year T-note with an exercise price of 118 selling for $750 per contract. Suppose that the manager purchased the call options in order to set a cap on the cost of buying the five-year notes in June. Exhibit 8.11 shows:

1. The hedged cost of buying the 10 T-notes with a $1^3/_8\%$ coupon and maturity of 8/31/20 at different spot prices between $S_T = 92$ and 105.
2. The corresponding June futures prices, where the futures prices are equal to the prices of the cheapest-to-deliver $1^3/_8\%$ note divided by underlying futures contract's conversion factor of 0.8371 ($f_T = (S_T + AI)/CFA$; $AI = 0.303$ on the option's expiration of 5/20/16).
3. The cash flow from selling ten 118 call options on the June futures contract at their intrinsic value.
4. The call hedged costs of buying the $1^3/_8\%$ T-notes on the option expiration and selling the calls at their IV.

As shown in the exhibit, the hedge caps the upper cost between $966,912 and $981,077 if bond prices are above 98.1406 (futures price of 118) and yields are less than 1.84476%, while allowing the manager to purchase bonds at lower prices if the bond price is at 98.1406 or less and the yield is at 1.84476% or greater.

Hedging a T-Note Sale with T-Note Futures Puts

To illustrate how a short hedge works, suppose the fixed-income manager on 12/30/15 in the preceding example anticipated needing cash in June and planned to obtain it by selling her holdings of 10 T-notes with coupon rates of $1^3/_8\%$ and maturity of 8/31/20 (same as the futures cheapest-to-deliver bond). Suppose the manager this time believed that five-year rates would decrease and bond prices would rise, but still wanted to hedge against the possibility that rates could increase and bond prices fall when she sold her 10 T-notes in June. Suppose on 12/30/15 the manager purchased CME puts on the June five-year T-note futures with an exercise price of 118 for

EXHIBIT 8.11 Hedging the Purchase of 10 Five-Year T-Notes with 10 Five-Year T-Note Futures Call Options

Cheapest-to-Deliver T-Note: 1 3/8 8/31/20: On 5/20/16 (Futures Expiration), Accrued Interest (AI) = $0.303 per $100 face; Conversion Factor = CFA = 0.8317

Futures Price at T: (Cheapest-to-Deliver T-Note Price + AI)/Conversion Factor = $(S_T + AI)/CFA$

Call Options on June 5-Year T-Note Futures with X = 118, Expiration = 5/20/15, Premium on 12/30/15 = 0 − 48; [(48/64/100)($100,000)] = $750

1	2	3	4	5	6	7	8
YTM	Price of T-Note: 1 3/8 8/31/20, S_T	Cost of 10 T-Notes with $100,000 Face plus Accrued Interest: 10 [(S_T + $0.303)/100] $100,000	Futures Prices at T, f_T: (S_T + AI)/(CFA) = (S_T + AI)/ (0.8317)	Call Value C_T = IV = Max [f_T − 118,0]	Cash Flow from Selling 10 June Futures Calls at IV: (10) (IV/100) ($100,000)	Futures Call Hedge: Cost of Buying T-Notes minus Cash Flow from Futures Call: (3) − (6)	Hedged Cost Savings: (3) − (9)
3.39891%	92	$923,030	110.98	$0.00	$0	$923,030	$0
3.13518%	93	$933,030	112.18	$0.00	$0	$933,030	$0
2.87466%	94	$943,030	113.39	$0.00	$0	$943,030	$0
2.89617%	95	$953,030	114.59	$0.00	$0	$953,030	$0
2.63588%	96	$963,030	115.79	$0.00	$0	$963,030	$0
2.37866%	97	$973,030	116.99	$0.00	$0	$973,030	$0
2.12446%	98	$983,030	118.20	$0.20	$1,953	$981,077	$1,953
1.84476%	98.1406	$984,436	118.36	$0.36	$3,643	$980,793	$3,643
1.87319%	99	$993,030	119.40	$1.40	$13,976	$979,054	$13,976
1.62480%	100	$1,003,030	120.60	$2.60	$26,000	$977,030	$26,000
1.37924%	101	$1,013,030	121.80	$3.80	$38,023	$975,007	$38,023
1.36426%	102	$1,023,030	123.00	$5.00	$50,047	$972,983	$50,047
0.89632%	103	$1,033,030	124.21	$6.21	$62,070	$970,960	$62,070
0.65885%	104	$1,043,030	125.41	$7.41	$74,094	$968,936	$74,094
0.42348%	105	$1,053,030	126.61	$8.61	$86,118	$966,912	$86,118

$750 per contract in order to set a floor on the revenue from here June bond sale. Exhibit 8.12 shows:

1. The hedged revenue from selling the 10 T-notes with a $1^3/_8$% coupon and maturity of 8/31/20 at different spot prices between $S_T = 92$ and 105.
2. The corresponding June futures prices, where the futures prices are equal to the sum of the prices of the cheapest-to-deliver $1^3/_8$% note plus the AI of 0.303 divided by the underlying futures contract's conversion factor of 0.8371 ($f_T = S_T + AI)/CFA$).
3. The cash flow from closing ten 118 put options on the June futures contract at their intrinsic value.
4. The call hedged revenue from selling the $1^3/_8$% T-notes at the option expiration date and selling the puts at their IV.

As shown in the exhibit, the hedge creates a floor on the revenue between $983,030 and $993,219 if bond prices are less than 98.1406 (futures price of 118) and yields are greater than 1.84476%, while allowing the manager to sell her bonds at higher prices if bond prices are greater than 98.1406 and yields are less than 1.84476%.

Hedging a Bond Portfolio with T-Bond Futures Puts

In Chapter 4, we examined the case of the managers of the Xavier Bond Fund hedging the June value of their portfolio on 12/30/15 by going short in the June 2016 five-year T-note futures contract. The fund's portfolio consisted of 39 investment-grade corporates, treasuries, and federal agency bonds. On 3/15/16, the value of the bond portfolio was $11,637,935 with a duration of 5.31 and yield to maturity of 2.78% (see Exhibit 4.21 for portfolio description on 12/30/15). Suppose on 3/15/15, the managers believed that rates would decrease and bond prices would rise, but still wanted to hedge against the possibility that rates could increase and bond prices fall, and accordingly decided to set a floor on their portfolio by buying the CME put on the June five-year T-note with an exercise price of 120 and trading at 0-59 or $921.875 per contract. The most likely-to-deliver bond on the underlying futures was the $1^3/_8$% T-note maturing on 8/31/20; this bond had a duration of 4.02. Using the price-sensitivity model, the managers would have needed to purchase 127 June T-note futures puts with an exercise price of 120 for a cost of $117,078:

$$n_p = \frac{Dur_S}{Dur_f} \frac{V_0}{X} \frac{(1 + YTM_f)^T}{(1 + YTM_S)^T}$$

$$n_p = \frac{5.31}{4.02} \frac{\$11,637,934}{\$120,000} \frac{(1.0176)^{(141/365)}}{(1.0278)^{(141/365)}}$$

$$n_p = 127 \text{ Put contracts}$$

EXHIBIT 8.12 Hedging the Sale of 10 Five-Year T-Notes with 10 Five-Year T-Note Futures Put Options

Cheapest-to-Deliver T-Note: 1 3/8 8/31/20: On 5/20/16 (Futures Expiration), Accrued Interest (AI) = $0.303 per $100 Face; Conversion Factor = CFA = 0.8317

Futures Price at T: (Cheapest-to-Deliver T-Note Price + AI)/Conversion Factor = (S_T + AI)/CFA

Put Options on June 5-Year T-Note Futures with X = 118, Expiration = 5/20/15, Premium on 12/30/15 = 0 − 48; [(48/64)/100]($100,000) = $750

1	2	3	4	5	6	7	9
YTM	Price of T-Note: 1 3/8 8/31/20, S_T	Revenue from Selling 10 T-Notes with $100,000 Face plus Accrued Interest: 10 [$(S_T + \$0.303)/100$] $100,000	Futures Prices at T, f_T: $(S_T + AI)/(CFA)$ = $(S_T + AI)/(0.8317)$	Put Value P_T = IV = Max[118 − f_T,0]	Cash Flow from Selling 10 June Futures Puts at IV: (10) (IV/100) ($100,000)	Futures Put Hedge: Revenue from Selling Cash T-Notes plus Cash Flow from Futures Puts: (3) + (6)	Hedged Value Savings: (7) − (4)
3.39891%	92	$923,030	110.98	$7.02	$70,189	$993,219	$70,189
3.13518%	93	$933,030	112.18	$5.82	$58,165	$991,195	$58,165
2.87466%	94	$943,030	113.39	$4.61	$46,142	$989,172	$46,142
2.89617%	95	$953,030	114.59	$3.41	$34,118	$987,148	$34,118
2.63588%	96	$963,030	115.79	$2.21	$22,095	$985,125	$22,095
2.37866%	97	$973,030	116.99	$1.01	$10,071	$983,101	$10,071
2.12446%	98	$983,030	118.20	$0.00	$0	$983,030	$0
1.84476%	98.1406	$984,436	118.36	$0.00	$0	$984,436	$0
1.87319%	99	$993,030	119.40	$0.00	$0	$993,030	$0
1.62480%	100	$1,003,030	120.60	$0.00	$0	$1,003,030	$0
1.37924%	101	$1,013,030	121.80	$0.00	$0	$1,013,030	$0
1.36426%	102	$1,023,030	123.00	$0.00	$0	$1,023,030	$0
0.89632%	103	$1,033,030	124.21	$0.00	$0	$1,033,030	$0
0.65885%	104	$1,043,030	125.41	$0.00	$0	$1,043,030	$0
0.42348%	105	$1,053,030	126.61	$0.00	$0	$1,053,030	$0

where

Dur_S = duration of the bond fund = 5.31
Dur_f = duration of the cheapest-to-deliver bond = 4.02
V_0 = value of bond portfolio = $11,637,934
X = 120
Put premium per contract = $921.875
Future conversion factor on cheapest-to-deliver bond = CFA = 0.8371
T = time to expiration on the option as proportion of year = 141/365
YTM_S = yield to maturity on the bond fund = 2.78%
YTM_f = yield to maturity implied on the futures contract = 1.76%

$$\text{Put cash flow} = n_p \frac{\text{Max}(X - f_T)}{100} (\$100,000)$$

$$\text{Put cash flow} = 127 \frac{(120 - f_T)}{100} (\$100,000)$$

$$\text{Put hedge cost} = (127)(\$921.875) = \$117,078$$

Exhibit 8.13 shows:

1. The portfolio values and accrued interest on the option's expiration of 5/20/16 given different interest rate shifts ranging from 50 basis point decreases to 50 basis point increases, and the portfolio's corresponding yields to maturity and values.
2. The prices of the most-likely-to-deliver bond ($1^3/_8$% 8/31/20) on 5/20/16 given the different interest rate shifts and corresponding Treasury yields.
3. The corresponding June futures prices, where the futures prices are equal to the prices of the cheapest-to-deliver $1^3/_8$% T-note plus its accrued interest (AI) divided by the underlying futures contracts conversion factor of 0.8371 ($f_T = (S_T + AI)/CFA$).
4. The cash flow from closing the 127 June 120 futures put options on the June futures expiration.
5. The put hedged value: the portfolio value plus accrued interest and cash flows from selling the puts at their IV.

As shown in the Exhibit 8.13, the hedge creates a floor for the portfolio value of around $11.9 million if rates increase by 10 basis point or more, while the portfolio gains in value if interest rates increase.

It should be noted that for a 50 basis points increase in rates, the puts provide a portfolio savings of $194,388 (= Hedge value − Unhedged value = $11,983,853 − $11,789,467), while for a 20 bp increase, the savings is only $7,177 (= Hedge value − Unhedged value = $11,991,595 − $11,984,418). With the cost of the insurance at $117,078, the managers may have concluded that this protection was not large enough, given the costs of the puts. Alternatively, they may have found a better hedging strategy would be to set up a range forward contract by selling a call with a higher exercise price to defray part of the cost of the puts.

EXHIBIT 8.13 Hedging the Value of a Portfolio with T-Note Futures Put Options

Portfolio: Value on 3/15/16 = $11,637,934, Duration = 5.31, YTM = 2.78%

Cheapest-to-Deliver T-Note: 1 3/8 8/31/20: On 5/20/16 (Options Expiration), Accrued Interest (AI) = $0.303 per $100 Face

Futures Price at T: (Cheapest-to-Deliver T-Note Price + AI)/Conversion Factor = (S_T + AI)/CFA

Put Options on June 5-Year T-Note Futures with X = 120, Expiration = 5/20/15, Premium on 3/15/16 = ((59/64)/100)($100,000) = $921.875

Hedge: n_p = 127 Puts; Cost = (127)($921.875) = $117,078

Call Options on June 5-Year T-Note Futures with X = 120, Expiration = 5/20/15, Premium on 3/15/16 = ((59/64)/100)($100,000) = $921.875

Call Enhanced Portfolio: n_C = 40 Call; Cost = (40)($921.875) = $36,875

1	2	3	4	5	6	7	8	9	10
Interest Rate Shift (Basis Points)	YTM	Portfolio Value	Accrued Interest	Portfolio Value + Accrued Interest	T-Note YTM	T-Note Price	T-Note Accrued Interest	Futures Prices at T; $f_T = (S_T + AI)/CFA$; CFA = 0.8317	Put Value $P_T = IV =$ Max $[120 - f_T, 0]$
50	2.96%	$11,699,113	$90,354	$11,789,467	1.8070%	$98.228	$0.303	118.47	$1.53
40	2.89%	$11,763,539	$90,354	$11,853,893	1.7070%	$98.637	$0.303	118.96	$1.04
30	2.76%	$11,828,553	$90,354	$11,918,907	1.6070%	$99.043	$0.303	119.45	$0.55
20	2.66%	$11,894,064	$90,354	$11,984,418	1.5070%	$99.454	$0.303	119.94	$0.06
10	2.56%	$11,960,925	$90,354	$12,051,279	1.4070%	$99.867	$0.303	120.44	$0.00
0	2.46%	$12,027,519	$90,354	$12,117,873	1.3070%	$100.585	$0.303	121.30	$0.00
-10	2.36%	$12,094,783	$90,354	$12,185,137	1.2070%	$100.698	$0.303	121.44	$0.00
-20	2.26%	$12,163,085	$90,354	$12,253,439	1.1070%	$101.117	$0.303	121.94	$0.00
-30	2.16%	$12,232,131	$90,354	$12,322,485	1.0070%	$101.537	$0.303	122.45	$0.00
-40	2.06%	$12,119,786	$90,354	$12,210,140	0.9070%	$101.960	$0.303	122.96	$0.00
-50	1.96%	$12,188,950	$90,354	$12,279,304	0.8070%	$102.384	$0.303	123.47	$0.00

359

EXHIBIT 8.13 (Continued)

Interest Rate Shift (Basis Points)	11 Cash Flow from Selling 127 June Futures Puts at IV: (127)(IV/100)($100,000)	12 Futures Put Hedge: Value of Portfolio plus Accrued Interest plus Cash Flow from Futures Puts: (5) + (11)	13 Hedged Portfolio Value Saved: (5) − (12)	14 Call Value C_T = IV = Max[f_T−120,0]	15 Cash Flow from Selling 40 June Futures Calls at IV: (40)(IV/100)($100,000)	16 Futures Call Enhanced Portfolio: Value of Portfolio plus Accrued Interest plus Cash Flow from Futures Calls: (5) + (15)	17 Proportional Change in the Enhanced Portfolio: [Col (16)/$11,637,934]−1	18 Proportional Change in the Portfolio: [Col(5)/ $11,637,934]−1
50	$194,386.20	$11,983,853	$194,386	$0.00	$0.00	$11,789,467	0.01302	0.01302
40	$131,932.19	$11,985,825	$131,932	$0.00	$0.00	$11,853,893	0.01856	0.01856
30	$69,936.28	$11,988,844	$69,936	$0.00	$0.00	$11,918,907	0.02414	0.02414
20	$7,176.87	$11,991,595	$7,177	$0.00	$0.00	$11,984,418	0.02977	0.02977
10	$0.00	$12,051,279	$0	$0.44	$55,887.94	$12,107,167	0.04032	0.03552
0	$0.00	$12,117,873	$0	$1.30	$165,526.03	$12,283,399	0.05546	0.04124
−10	$0.00	$12,185,137	$0	$1.44	$182,781.05	$12,367,918	0.06272	0.04702
−20	$0.00	$12,253,439	$0	$1.94	$246,762.05	$12,500,201	0.07409	0.05289
−30	$0.00	$12,322,485	$0	$2.45	$310,895.76	$12,633,381	0.08553	0.05882
−40	$0.00	$12,210,140	$0	$2.96	$375,487.56	$12,585,628	0.08143	0.04917
−50	$0.00	$12,279,304	$0	$3.47	$440,232.05	$12,719,536	0.09294	0.05511

Changing a Bond Portfolio's Duration

In Chapter 4, we showed how the Xavier Bond Fund increased the fund's duration from 5.43 to 6.08 in anticipation of a decrease in interest rates by going long in 16 June T-note contract. Instead of using futures to change its portfolio's exposure to interest rate, the managers could have alternatively used futures options. A bond portfolio manager who is very confident of an interest rate decrease (increase) could increase (decrease) her bond portfolio's exposure by increasing (decreasing) the portfolio's duration, Dur_0, to a new target duration, Dur_{TR}, by going long (short) in a bond futures contracts. The manager also could increase (decrease) her portfolio's exposure by buying futures calls (puts). The number of option contracts needed to move the portfolio duration from Dur_0 to Dur_{TR} can be determined using the price-sensitivity model in which:

$$n_{Options} = \frac{Dur_{TR} - Dur_S}{Dur_f} \frac{V_0}{X} \frac{(1 + YTM_f)^T}{(1 + YTM_S)^T}$$

where

if $Dur_{TR} > Dur_0$, long in Call Options

if $Dur_{TR} < Dur_0$, Long in Put Options

Changing interest rate exposure with options instead of futures provides an asymmetrical gain and loss exposure—a convex duration. For example, when calls (puts) are purchased to increase (decrease) the target duration, the option-adjusted portfolio has a β_{TR} for interest rate decreases (decreases) and Dur_0 for interest rate increases (decreases). The cost of obtaining this asymmetrical relation is the cost of the options.

For example, suppose on 3/15/15, the Xavier Bond Fund manager strongly believed that rates would decrease and bond prices would rise, and as a result decided to use call options to increase the bond portfolio's duration from 5.31 to 7.00. On 3/15/16, the CME call on the June five-year T-note with an exercise price of 120 was trading at 0-59 or $921.875 per contract. (The most likely-to-deliver bond on the futures was the $1^3/_8$% T-note maturing on 8/31/20; this bond had a duration of 4.02.) Using the price-sensitivity model, the managers would have needed to purchase 40 June T-note futures calls with an exercise price of 120 for a cost of $36,875:

$$n_C = \frac{Dur_{TR} - Dur_S}{Dur_f} \frac{V_0}{X} \frac{(1 + YTM_f)^T}{(1 + YTM_S)^T}$$

$$n_C = \frac{7.00 - 5.31}{4.02} \frac{\$11,637,934}{\$120,000} \frac{(1.0176)^{(141/365)}}{(1.0278)^{(141/365)}}$$

$$n_C = 40.3667 \text{ Call contracts}$$

$$\text{Cost} = (40)(\$921.875) = \$36,875$$

As shown in Columns 14 to 18 in Exhibit 8.13, for downward yield curve shifts the call-enhanced portfolio has a significant greater proportional returns than the unadjusted portfolio, reflecting a greater duration, while for upward shift the returns are the same with the calls out of the money.

Managing the Maturity Gap with Eurodollar Futures Puts

In Chapter 4 we presented the case of a small bank with a maturity gap problem in which it made short-term loans with maturities of 180 days financed by a series of 90-day CDs sold now and 90 days later. In the absence of a hedge, the bank was subject to interest-rate risk. To minimize its exposure to interest rate risk the bank hedged its CD sale 90 days later by going short in a Eurodollar futures contract (see Exhibit 4.20). Instead of hedging its future CD sale with Eurodollar futures, the bank could alternatively buy put options on Eurodollar futures. By hedging with puts, the bank would be able to lock in or cap the maximum rate it pays on it future CD. If the LIBOR exceeds the implied yield on the underlying futures, the bank would have to pay a higher rate on its CD used to finance the maturing debt, but it would profit from its Eurodollar futures put position, with its put profits being greater, the higher the rates. The put profit would serve to reduce the funds the bank would need to pay the maturing CD, in turn, offsetting the higher rate it would have to pay on its new CD. Thus, the bank would be able to lock in a maximum rate that it would pay on its debt obligation. On the other hand, if the rate is less than or equal to the implied yield on the futures, then the bank would be able to finance its maturing debt at lower rates, while its losses on its futures puts would be limited to the premium it paid for the options. As a result, for lower rates the bank would realize a lower interest rate paid on its debt obligation 90 days later and therefore a lower rate paid over the 180-day period. Thus, for the cost of the puts, hedging the maturity gap with puts allows the bank to lock in a maximum rate on its debt obligation, with the possibility of paying lower rates if interest rates decrease.

Using Options to Set a Cap or Floor on a Cash Flow

In Chapter 4, we examined how a series or strip of Eurodollar futures contracts could be used to create a fixed or floating rate on the cash flow of an asset or liability. When there is a series of cash flows, such as a floating-rate loan or an investment in a floating-rate note, a strip of interest rate options can similarly be used to place a cap or a floor on the cash flow. For example, a company with a one-year floating-rate loan starting in September at a specified rate and then reset in December, March, and June to equal the spot LIBOR plus BP, could obtain a cap on the loan by buying a series of Eurodollar futures puts expiring in December, March, and June. At each reset date, if the LIBOR exceeds the discount yield on the put, the higher LIBOR applied to the loan will be offset by a profit on the nearest expiring put, with the profit increasing the greater the LIBOR; if the LIBOR is equal to or less than the discount yield on the put, the lower LIBOR applied to the loan will only be offset by the limited cost of the put. Thus, a strip of Eurodollar futures puts used to hedge a floating-rate loan places a ceiling on the effective rate paid on the loan.

In the case of a floating-rate investment, such as a floating-rate note tied to the LIBOR or a bank's floating rate loan portfolio, a minimum rate or floor can be obtained by buying a series of Eurodollar futures calls, with each call having an expiration near the reset date on the investment. If rates decrease, the lower investment return will be offset by profits on the calls; if rates increase, the only offset will be the limited cost of the calls.

Setting a Cap on a Floating-Rate Loan with a Series of Eurodollar Puts

As an example of a cap, suppose Northwestern Bank offers Ryan's Department Store a $20 million floating-rate loan to finance its inventory over the next two years. The loan has a maturity of two years, starts on December 20, and is reset the next seven quarters. The initial quarterly rate on the loan is equal to 2%/4 (the current LIBOR of 1% plus 100 bp), the other rates are set on the quarterly reset dates equal to one fourth of the annual LIBOR on those dates plus 100 basis points: (LIBOR % + 1%)/4. Suppose Ryan's wants to cap the loan by purchasing a strip of CME Eurodollar futures puts consisting of the seven put futures options. The top panel in Exhibit 8.14 shows seven Eurodollar futures puts each with an exercise price of $995,000 (IMM $X = 98$; $R_D = 2$) and with expirations coinciding with the reset dates on the loan.

Given these Eurodollar futures puts, Ryan's could cap the floating-rate loan by buying a strip of 20 Eurodollar futures puts for a total cost of $80,500. The lower panel in Exhibit 8.14 shows the put-hedged rates on the loan and the unhedged rates for an increasing interest rate scenario in which the LIBOR increases from 1% on March 20 to 4% seven quarters later. The numbers in the exhibit show for each period, Ryan's quarterly interest payments, option cash flow, option values at the interest payment date, hedged interest payments (interest minus option cash flow), and hedged rate as a proportion of a $20 million loan. The scenarios shown assume that the options' expiration dates coincide with the reset dates. As shown, the put options allow Ryan's to cap its loan at 3.00%, when the LIBOR is greater than 2%, while benefiting with lower rates on its loan when the LIBOR is less than 2%.

Setting a Floor on a Floating-Rate Investment with a Series of Eurodollar Calls

As a an example of a floor, suppose Kendall Trust is planning to invest $20 million in a Northwestern Bank two-year floating-rate note paying LIBOR plus 100 basis points. The investment starts on 12/20 at 2% (when the LIBOR = 1%) and is then reset the next seven quarters. Suppose Kendall Trust would like to establish a floor on the rates it obtains on the floating-rate note with a strip of the seven CME Eurodollar futures call options shown in the top panel in Exhibit 8.15. Each of the Eurodollar futures calls has an exercise price of $995,000 (IMM $X = 98$; $R_D = 2$) and expirations coinciding with the reset dates on the floating-rate note.

EXHIBIT 8.14 Capping a Floating-Rate Loan with Eurodollar Futures Puts: Loan Starts on 12/12 at 2% (1% + 100 Bp); Reset Next Seven Quarters at LIBOR + 100 BP; Strip of Seven Eurodollar Futures Puts Each with X = $995,000; Expirations Coinciding with Loan Reset Dates

T	3/20/T1	6/20/T1	9/20/T1	12/20/T1	3/20/T2	6/20/T2	9/20/T2	
X	$995,000	$995,000	$995,000	$995,000	$995,000	$995,000	$995,000	
P_0	2	2.1	2.2	2.3	2.4	2.5	2.6	
Cost of 20 Puts: 20 ($250)($P_0$)	$10,000	$10,500	$11,000	$11,500	$12,000	$12,500	$13,000	Total Cost = $80,500

1	2	3	4	5	6	7	8	9
Date	LIBOR %	Futures and Spot Price $S_T = f_T$	Put Cash Flow at Option's Expiration 20(Max[$995,000 − f_T, 0]	Value of Put Cash Flow at Payment Date (Put CF at T)(1+LIBOR)$^{0.25}$	Quarterly Interest at Payment Date 0.25 [[(LIBOR + 0.01)] ($20m)	Hedged Debt Col 6 − Col 5	Hedged Rate [(4)(Col 7)]/ $20m	Unhedged Rate LIBOR + 100bp
12/20	1.00							
3/20	1.00	$997,500	$0		$100,000	$100,000.00	0.020	0.020
6/20	1.50	$996,250	$0	$0.00	$100,000	$100,000.00	0.020	0.020
9/20	2.00	$995,000	$0	$0.00	$125,000	$125,000.00	0.025	0.025
12/20	2.50	$993,750	$25,000	$0.00	$150,000	$150,000.00	0.030	0.030
3/20	3.00	$992,500	$50,000	$25,154.81	$175,000	$149,845.19	0.030	0.035
6/20	3.50	$991,250	$75,000	$50,370.85	$200,000	$149,629.15	0.030	0.040
9/20	4.00	$990,000	$100,000	$75,647.81	$225,000	$149,352.19	0.030	0.045
12/20				$100,985.34	$250,000	$149,014.66	0.030	0.050

Expiring futures (or settlement price): $f_T = S_T = \dfrac{100 - (LIBOR(0.25))}{100}$ ($1,000,000)

EXHIBIT 8.15 Setting A Floor on a Floating-Rate Investment with Eurodollar Futures Call: Floating-Rate Note Starts on 12/12 At 2% (1% + 100 Bp); Reset Next Seven Quarters At LIBOR + 100 BP; Strip of Seven Eurodollar Futures Calls Each with X = $995,000; Expirations Coinciding with Reset Dates on the Floating-Rate Note

T	3/20/T1	6/20/T1	9/20/T1	12/20/T1	3/20/T2	6/20/T2	9/20/T2	
X	$995,000	$995,000	$995,000	$995,000	$995,000	$995,000	$995,000	
C_0	2	2.1	2.2	2.3	2.4	2.5	2.6	
Cost of 20 Calls: 20($250)($C_0$)	$10,000	$10,500	$11,000	$11,500	$12,000	$12,500	$13,000	Total Cost = $80,500

1	2	3	4	5	6	7	8	9
Date	LIBOR %	Futures and Spot Price $S_T = f_T$	Call Cash Flow at Option's Expiration 20(Max[f_T − $995,000,0]	Value of Call Cash Flow at Receipt Date (Call CF at T)(1+LIBOR)$^{0.25}$	Quarterly Interest at Receipt Date 0.25 [(LIBOR + 0.01)] ($20m)	Hedged Interest Revenue Col 6 + Col 5	Hedged Rate [(4)(Col 7)]/$20m	Unhedged Rate LIBOR + 100bp
12/20	1.00							
3/20	1.00	$997,500	$50,000		$100,000	$100,000.00	0.020	0.020
6/20	1.50	$996,250	$25,000	$50,124.53	$100,000	$150,124.53	0.030	0.020
9/20	2.00	$995,000	$0	$25,093.23	$125,000	$150,093.23	0.030	0.025
12/20	2.50	$993,750	$0	$0.00	$150,000	$150,000.00	0.030	0.030
3/20	3.00	$992,500	$0	$0.00	$175,000	$175,000.00	0.035	0.035
6/20	3.50	$991,250	$0	$0.00	$200,000	$200,000.00	0.040	0.040
9/20	4.00	$990,000	$0	$0.00	$225,000	$225,000.00	0.045	0.045
12/20				$0.00	$250,000	$250,000.00	0.050	0.050

Expiring futures (or settlement price): $f_T = S_T = \frac{100-(LIBOR)(0.25)}{100}$ ($1,000,000)

365

To set the floor on the floating note, Kendall would need to buy 20 Eurodollar call strips for a total cost of $80,500. The lower panel of Exhibit 8.15 shows Kendall Trust's quarterly interest receipts, option cash flow, option values at the interest payment dates, hedged interest revenue (interest plus option cash flow), and hedged rate as a proportion of a $20 million investment for each period with the assumption that the reset dates and option expiration dates coincide. The assumed LIBOR rate shown in the exhibit reflect an increasing interest rate scenario in which the LIBOR increases from 1% on March 20 to 4% seven quarters later. As shown, the call options allow Kendall to attain a floor on investment rate of 3% when the LIBOR is 2% or less with the benefit of higher yields when the LIBOR is greater than 3%.

Setting a Cap on a Floating-Rate Loan with a Series of Caplets — Cap

As noted in Chapter 6, a popular option offered by financial institutions is the cap: a series of European interest rate call options—a portfolio of caplets. For example, a 2.5%, two-year cap on a three-month LIBOR, with a NP of $100 million, provides, for the next two years, a payoff every three months of (LIBOR − 0.025)(0.25)($100,000,000) if the LIBOR on the reset date exceeds 2.5% and nothing if the LIBOR equals or is less than 2%. Caps are often written by financial institutions in conjunction with a floating-rate loan and are used by buyers as a hedge against interest rate risk.

As an example, suppose the Jones Development Company borrows $100 million from Southern Bank to finance a two-year construction project. Suppose the loan is for two years, starting on March 1 at a known rate of 2.5% (1% LIBOR plus 150 bp) then resets every three months—6/1, 9/1, 12/1, and 3/1—at the prevailing LIBOR plus 150 BP. In entering this loan agreement, suppose the Jones Company is uncertain of future interest rates and therefore would like to lock in a maximum rate, while still benefiting from lower rates if the LIBOR decreases. To achieve this, suppose the Jones Company buys a cap corresponding to its loan from Southern Bank for $150,000, with the following terms:

- The cap consist of seven caplets with the first expiring on 6/1/Y1 and the others coinciding with the loan's reset dates
- Exercise rate on each caplet = 2.5%
- NP on each caplet = $100 million
- Reference rate = LIBOR
- Time period to apply to the payoff on each caplet = 90/360
- Payment date on each caplet is at the loan's interest payment date, 90 days after the reset date
- The cost of the cap = $150,000

On each reset date, the payoff on the corresponding caplet would be

$$\text{Payoff} = (\$100,000,000)\,(\text{Max}[\text{LIBOR}-0.025,\ 0])(90/360)$$

With the 2.5% exercise rate or cap rate, the Jones Company would be able to lock in a maximum rate each quarter equal to the cap rate plus the basis points on the loan (4%), while still benefiting with lower interest costs if rates decrease. This can be seen in Exhibit 8.16, where the quarterly interests on the loan, the cap payoffs, and the hedged and unhedged rates are shown for different assumed LIBORs at each reset date on the loan. For the four reset dates from 6/1/Y2 to the end of the loan, the LIBOR exceeds 2.5%. In each of these cases, the higher interest on the loan is offset by the payoff on the cap yielding a hedged rate on the loan of 4.0% (the 4% rate excludes the $150,000 cost of the cap). For the first two reset dates on the loan, 6/1/Y1, 9/1/Y1, and 12/1/Y1, the LIBOR is less than the cap rate. At these rates, there is no payoff on the cap, but the rates on the loan are lower with the lower LIBORs.

Setting a Floor on a Floating-Rate Investment with a Series of Floorlets — Floor

As explained in Chapter 6, a plain-vanilla floor is a series of European interest rate put options—a portfolio of floorlets. For example, a 2.5%, two-year floor on a three-month LIBOR, with a NP of $100 million, provides, for the next two years, a payoff every three months of $(0.025 - \text{LIBOR})(0.25)(\$100,000,000)$ if the LIBOR on the reset date is less than 2.5% and nothing if the LIBOR equals or exceeds 2.5%. Floors are often purchased by investors as a tool to hedge their floating-rate investments against interest rate declines. Thus, with a floor, an investor with a floating-rate security is able to lock in a minimum rate each period, while still benefiting from higher yields if rates increase.

As an example, suppose Southern Bank in the above example wanted to establish a minimum rate or floor on the rates it was to receive on the two-year floating-rate loan it made to the Jones Development Company. To this end, suppose the bank purchased from another financial institution a floor for $100,000 with the following terms corresponding to its floating-rate asset:

- The floor consist of seven floorlets with the first expiring on 6/1/Y1 and the others coinciding with the reset dates on the bank's floating-rate loan to the Jones Company
- Exercise rate on each floorlet = 2.5%
- NP on each floorlet = $100 million
- Reference rate = LIBOR
- Time period to apply to the payoff on each floorlet = 90/360
- The cost of the floor = $100,000; it is paid at beginning of the loan, 3/1/Y1

On each reset date, the payoff on the corresponding floorlet would be

$$\text{Payoff} = (\$100,000,000)\,(\text{Max}[0.025 - \text{LIBOR}, \ 0])(90/360)$$

With the 2.5% exercise rate, Southern Bank would be able to lock in a minimum rate each quarter equal to the floor rate plus the basis points on the floating-rate asset (4%), while still benefiting with higher returns if rates increase. In Exhibit 8.17, Southern Bank's quarterly interests received on its loan to Jones, its floor payoffs, and its hedged and unhedged yields on its loan asset are shown for different assumed LIBORs

EXHIBIT 8.16 Hedging a Floating-Rate Loan with a Cap

Loan: Floating Rate Loan; Term = 2 years; Reset Dates: 6/1, 9/1, 12/1; Time Frequency = 0.25; Rate = LIBOR + 150bp; Payment Date = 90 days after reset date

Cap: Cost of Cap = $150,000; Cap Rate = 2.5%; Reference Rate = LIBOR; Time Frequency = 0.25;

Caplets' Expiration: On loan reset dates, starting at 6/1/Y1; Payoff made 90 days after reset date

1	2	3	4	5	6	7
Reset Date	Assumed LIBOR	Loan Interest on Payment Date (LIBOR + 150bp)(0.25)($100m)	Cap Payoff on Payment Date Max[LIBOR − 0.025,0](0.25)($100m)	Hedged Interest Payment Col. (3) − Col. (4)	Hedged Rate 4 [Col (5)/$100m]	Unhedged Rate LIBOR + 150bp
3/1/Y1[n]	0.010					
6/1/Y1	0.010	$625,000	$0	$625,000	0.025	0.025
9/1/Y1	0.015	$625,000	$0	$625,000	0.025	0.025
12/1/Y1	0.020	$750,000	$0	$750,000	0.030	0.030
3/1/Y2	0.025	$875,000	$0	$875,000	0.035	0.035
6/1/Y2	0.030	$1,000,000	$0	$1,000,000	0.040	0.040
9/1/Y2	0.035	$1,125,000	$125,000	$1,000,000	0.040	0.045
12/1/Y2	0.040	$1,250,000	$250,000	$1,000,000	0.040	0.050
3/1/Y3		$1,375,000	$375,000	$1,000,000	0.040	0.055

[n] There is no cap on this date

EXHIBIT 8.17 Hedging a Floating-Rate Investment with a Floor

Asset: Floating rate loan made by bank; Term = 2 years; Reset Dates: 3/1, 6/1, 9/1, 12/1;

Time Frequency = 0.25; Rate = LIBOR + 150BP; Payment Date = 90 days after reset date

Floor: Cost of Floor = $100,000; Floor Rate = 2.5%; Reference Rate = LIBOR; Time Frequency = .25;

Floorlets' Expirations: On loan reset dates, starting at 6/1/Y1; Payoff made 90 days after reset date

1	2	3	4	5	6	7
Reset Date	Assumed LIBOR	Interest Received on Payment Date (LIBOR + 150bp)(0.25)($100m)	Floor Payoff on Payment Date Max[0.025−LIBOR,0] (0.25)($100m)	Hedged Interest Income Col. (3) + Col. (4)	Hedged Rate 4 [Col (5)/$100M]	Unhedged Rate LIBOR + 150bp
3/1/Y1[n]	0.010					
6/1/Y1	0.010	$625,000	$0	$625,000	0.025	0.025
9/1/Y1	0.015	$625,000	$375,000	$1,000,000	0.040	0.025
12/1/Y1	0.020	$750,000	$250,000	$1,000,000	0.040	0.030
3/1/Y2	0.025	$875,000	$125,000	$1,000,000	0.040	0.035
6/1/Y2	0.030	$1,000,000	$0	$1,000,000	0.040	0.040
9/1/Y2	0.035	$1,125,000	$0	$1,125,000	0.045	0.045
12/1/Y2	0.040	$1,250,000	$0	$1,250,000	0.050	0.050
3/1/Y3		$1,375,000	$0	$1,375,000	0.055	0.055

[n] There is no floor on this date

369

at each reset date. For the first three reset dates on Southern Bank's loan to Jones, 6/1/Y1, 9/1/Y1, and 12/1/Y1, the LIBOR is less than the floor rate of 2.5%. At these rates, there is a payoff on the floor that compensates Southern Bank for the lower interest it receives on the loan; this results in a hedged rate of return on the bank's loan asset of 4% (the cost of the floor excluded). For the five reset dates from 6/1/Y1 to the end of the loan, the LIBOR equals or exceeds the floor rate. At these rates, there is no payoff on the floor, but the rates the bank earns on its loan to Jones are greater, given the greater LIBORs.

Collars and Corridors

A *collar* is a combination of a long position in a cap and a short position in a floor with different exercise rates. The sale of the floor is used to defray the cost of the cap. For example, the Jones Development Company in our previous case could reduce the cost of the cap it purchased to hedge its floating-rate rate loan by selling a floor. By forming a collar to hedge its floating-rate debt, the Jones Company, for a lower net hedging cost, would still have protection against a rate movement against the cap rate, but it would have to give up potential interest savings from rate decreases below the floor rate. For example, suppose the Jones Company decided to defray the $150,000 cost of its 2.5% cap by selling a 1% floor for $75,000, with the floor having similar terms to the cap (effective dates on floorlet = reset dates, reference rate = LIBOR, NP on floorlets = $100 million, and time period for rates = 0.25). By using the collar instead of the cap, Jones reduces its hedging cost from $150,000 to $75,000, and the company can still lock in a maximum rate on its loan of 4%. However, when the LIBOR is less than 1%, the company has to pay on the 1% floor, offsetting the lower interest costs it would pay on its loan. See Exhibit 8.18.

An alternative financial structure to a collar is a corridor. A *corridor* is a long position in a cap and a short position in a similar cap with a higher exercise rate. The sale of the higher exercise-rate cap is used to partially offset the cost of purchasing the cap with the lower strike rate. For example, the Jones Company, instead of selling a 1% floor for $75,000 to partially finance the $150,000 cost of its 2.5% cap, could sell a 3.5% cap for, say, $75,000. If cap purchasers, however, believe there was a greater chance of rates increasing than decreasing, they would prefer the collar to the corridor as a tool for financing the cap. In practice, collars are more frequently used than corridors.

A *reverse collar* is a combination of a long position in a floor and a short position in a cap with different exercise rates. The sale of the cap is used to defray the cost of the floor. For example, suppose that Southern Bank in our above floor example decided to reduce the $100,000 cost of the 2.5% floor it purchased to hedge the floating-rate loan it made to the Jones Company by selling a 4% cap for $50,000, with the cap having similar terms to the floor. By using the reverse collar instead of the floor, Southern Bank reduces its hedging cost from $100,000 to $50,000, and the bank can still lock in a minimum rate on its investment of 2.5%. However, when the LIBOR is greater than 4%, the bank rates on the investment are fixed at 5.5%, offsetting the higher interest it would have received. See Exhibit 8.19. Finally, note that instead of financing a floor with a cap, an investor could form a *reverse corridor* by selling another floor with a lower exercise rate.

EXHIBIT 8.18 Hedging a Floating-Rate Loan with a Collar

Loan: Floating Rate Loan; Term = 2 years; Reset Dates: 3/1, 6/1, 9/1, 12/1; Time Frequency = 0.25; Rate = LIBOR + 150bp; Payment Date = 90 days after reset date

Cap Purchase: Cost of Cap = $150,000; Cap Rate = 2.5%; Reference Rate = LIBOR; Time Frequency = 0.25;

Caplets' Expiration: On loan reset dates, starting at 6/1/Y1; Payoff made 90 days after reset date.

Floor Sale: Sale of Floor = $75,000; Floor Rate = 1%; Reference Rate = LIBOR; Time Frequency = 0.25;

Floorlets' Expiration: On loan reset dates, starting at 61/Y1; Payoff Date = 90 days after reset date.

1	2	3	4	5	6	7	8
Reset Date	Assumed LIBOR	Loan Interest (LIBOR + 150bp) (.25)($100M)	Cap Payoff Max [LIBOR − 0.025,0] (0.25)($100m)	Floor Payment Max[0.01 − LIBOR,0] (0.25)($100m)	Hedged Interest Payment Col. (3) − Col. (4) + Col (5)	Hedged Rate 4 [Col (6)/$100m]	Unhedged Rate LIBOR + 150bp
3/1/Y1[n]	0.010						
6/1/Y1	0.005	$625,000	$0	$0	$625,000	0.025	0.025
9/1/Y1	0.0075	$500,000	$0	$125,000	$625,000	0.025	0.020
12/1/Y1	0.010	$562,500	$0	$62,500	$625,000	0.025	0.0225
3/1/Y2	0.020	$625,000	$0	$0	$625,000	0.025	0.025
6/1/Y2	0.0225	$875,000	$0	$0	$875,000	0.035	0.035
9/1/Y2	0.030	$937,500	$0	$0	$937,500	0.0375	0.0375
12/1/Y2	0.035	$1,125,000	$125,000	$0	$1,000,000	0.040	0.045
3/1/Y3		$1,250,000	$250,000	$0	$1,000,000	0.040	0.050

[n] Loan interest, cap payoff, and floor payment made on payment date

371

EXHIBIT 8.19   Hedging a Floating-Rate Investment with Reverse Collar

Asset: Floating rate loan made by bank; Term = 2 years; Reset Dates: 3/1, 6/1, 9/1, 12/1;

Time Frequency = 0.25; Rate = LIBOR + 150bp; Payment Date = 90 days after reset date

Floor Purchase: Cost of Floor = $100,000; Floor Rate = 2.5%; Reference Rate = LIBOR; Time Frequency = 0.25;

Floorlets' Expirations: On loan reset dates, starting at 6/1/Y1; Payoff made 90 days after reset date.

Cap Sale: Revenue from Cap = $50,000; Cap Rate = 4%; Reference Rate = LIBOR; Time Frequency = 0.25;

Caplets' Expiration: On loan reset dates, starting at 6/1/Y1; Payoff made 90 days after reset date.

1	2	3	4	5	6	7	8
Reset Date	Assumed LIBOR	Interest Received (LIBOR + 150bp)(0.25) ($100m)	Floor Payoff Max[0.025−LIBOR,0] (0.25)($100m)	Cap Payment Max[LIBOR−0.04,0] (0.25)($100m)	Hedged Interest Income Col. (3) + Col. (4) − Col (5)	Hedged Rate 4 [Col (5)/$100M]	Unhedged Rate LIBOR + 150bp
3/1/Y1[n]	0.01000						
6/1/Y1	0.01500	$625,000	$0	$0	$625,000	0.025	0.025
9/1/Y1	0.02000	$750,000	$250,000	$0	$1,000,000	0.040	0.030
12/1/Y1	0.02750	$875,000	$125,000	$0	$1,000,000	0.040	0.035
3/1/Y2	0.03000	$1,062,500	$0	$0	$1,062,500	0.0425	0.043
6/1/Y2	0.04000	$1,125,000	$0	$0	$1,125,000	0.045	0.045
9/1/Y2	0.04500	$1,375,000	$0	$0	$1,375,000	0.055	0.055
12/1/Y2	0.05000	$1,500,000	$0	$125,000	$1,375,000	0.055	0.060
3/1/Y3		$1,625,000	$0	$250,000	$1,375,000	0.055	0.065

[n] Loan interest, floor payoff, and cap payment made on payment date

Conclusion

Stock, index, currency, commodity, and bond futures and spot options are valuable tools in managing security and portfolio positions. These derivative contracts make it possible for stock and fixed-income portfolio managers to obtain portfolio insurance or to cap the cost of buying a security in the future. Managers also can use derivatives to adjust the beta of a portfolio if they anticipate a bull or bear market, or the duration of a fixed-income portfolio, if they are anticipating an interest rate increase or decrease, thus eliminating the need to reallocate their portfolio allocation. Finally, futures options on commodities and currencies provide a tool for setting caps and floors for commodity and currency purchases and sale.

In our examination of option strategies and hedging positions in this and the last chapter, we have assumed a price for the option. As we examined earlier with futures pricing, the pricing of options is based on arbitrage. In Part 3, we examine option pricing models.

BLOOMBERG HEDGING SCREENS

OSA: EVALUATING A COMMODITY PURCHASE POSITION HEDGED WITH FUTURES OPTIONS

A future commodity sale or valuation (purchase) hedged by setting up a floor (cap) on the value (cost) with a put (call) or a short (long) range forward contract can be evaluated by uploading the spot commodity and then using the OSA screen.

1. Select a commodity such as corn or crude oil to evaluate the option hedging positions.
   - Select a commodity that has futures option contracts on it.
2. Use the SECF screen to find the tickers for futures, futures options, and spots.
   - For futures options: SECF <Enter>; select "Commodities" from the "Category" dropdown and then click the "Opt" tab.
   - For spot positions: select "Commodities" from the "Category" dropdown and then select "Spot" from the "Instrument" tab (e.g., Crude Oil and West Texas Crude, USCRWTIC; WEATTKHR for USDA No. 1 Hard Red Wheat).
3. Upload the spot commodity's menu screen: Commodity Ticker <Comdty> or Commodity Ticker <Index> (e.g., USCRWTIC <Index> for West Texas Crude or WEATTKH <Comdty>).
4. Bring up the OSA screen for the loaded commodity and select a position (e.g., 5,000 bushels of wheat to sell or 10,000 barrels to buy –10,000).
5. From the red "Positions" tab, click "Add Listed Options" and then the futures ticker in the upper-right amber area box (e.g., W A for wheat futures and CLA for crude oil futures). Select the call and put options on the futures needed to evaluate floors, caps, and long and short-range forward contracts.
6. On OSA set the number of puts (calls) needed to set a floor (cap) for the commodity and the number of short calls (puts) for short (long) range forward contacts.

(Continued)

7. Click "Scenario Chart" tab and input information in the setting: market value, range (−20% to 20%), and evaluation dates (see Exhibit 8.20).

EXHIBIT 8.20 Evaluating a Commodity Purchase Position Hedged with Futures Options

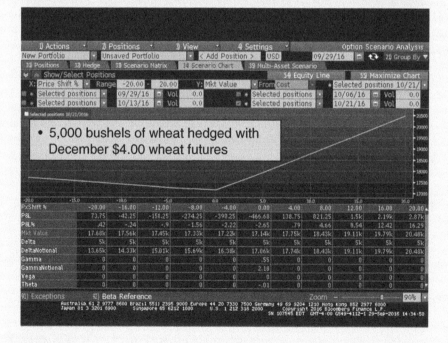

OSA: IMPORTING EQUITY PORTFOLIOS INTO BLOOMBERG'S OPTION SCENARIO SCREEN AND ADDING OPTIONS—PORTFOLIO INSURANCE AND RANGE FORWARD CONTRACTS

On the OSA screen, you can import a portfolio and then add option positions to evaluate a portfolio insurance position for a portfolio you created in PRTU:

- OSA <Enter>.

- From the "Portfolio" dropdown, select a portfolio.

- From the red "Positions" tab, click "Add Listed Options" and then enter an index like the S&P 500 (SPX) in the upper-right amber area box.

- Select the options on the index and then click 1<GO>.

- On the OSA screen, click portfolio summary box to include all stocks and options.

- Scroll down to the options and set the number of puts needed to ensure the portfolio, and for a short-range forward position, the number of short calls.

- Click "Scenario Chart" tab and input information in the settings boxes: profit/loss, market value, range (e.g., −20% to +20%), and evaluation dates (see Exhibit 8.21).

MARS: BOND HEDGING WITH FUTURES AND FUTURES OPTIONS USING THE MARS PLATFORM

Case: Importing Cheapest-to-Deliver-Note into Bloomberg's MARS Screen and Adding T-Note Futures and Futures Options

Multi Asset Risk System (MARS) provides scenario analysis tools. It allows you to analyze hedging interest rate risk exposure for a bond or portfolio with futures and options. On the MARS screen, you can import a bond or bond portfolio and then add futures and option positions. To evaluate a futures and options hedge for a T-note, such as the cheapest-to-deliver note on T-note futures:

- Load futures contract (e.g., FVH7 for March 2017 five-year T-note futures).

- On the futures screen, bring up the DLV screen to identify the cheapest-to-deliver note and its conversion factor (CFA).

- Bring up the cheapest-to-deliver bond's screen (enter Bond Ticker <Govt>); use YAS to find the bond's duration, current price, and YTM.

- MARS <Enter> to bring up the MARS screen and enter the bond's ticker in the amber "Add by ticker" box (you can type the name of the security to get a dropdown list (e.g., T 3/31/21)).

- From the red "Security" tab, click "Add Listed Options" and then enter the futures ticker in the upper-right amber area box (e.g., FVH7 for the March T-note futures) to bring up futures options.

- Select options and then click 1<GO>.

- On the MARS screen, enter the futures ticker in the amber "Add by ticker" box (you can type the name of the security to get a dropdown list (e.g., FVH7 for the March 2017 T-note futures).

(Continued)

- Set positions on the loaded cheapest-to-deliver note equal to 100 to make the holdings match the size of the underlying T-note on the futures and options ($100,000 face).

- For hedging analysis, set the positions on the futures to equal the conversion factor (e.g., CFA = 0.8317).

- Click "Scenario" tab and enter your setting: interest rate shifts, mkt. value, range (−50% to + 50%), and evaluation dates (include the expiration date on the futures option).

- Click "Run Scenario" tab.

EXHIBIT 8.21   Importing Equity Portfolios into Bloomberg's Option Scenario Screen and Adding Options

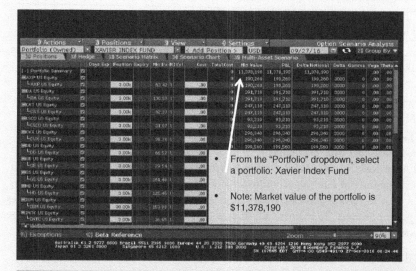

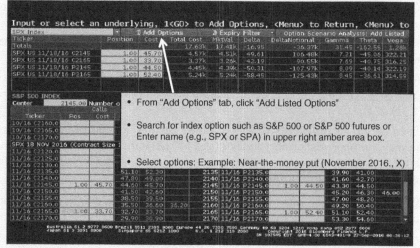

EXHIBIT 8.21 *(continued)*

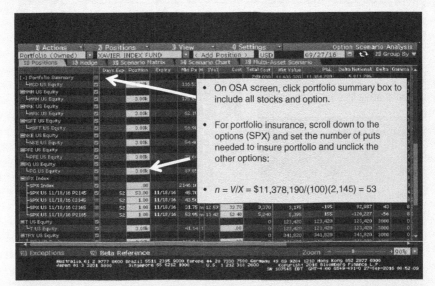

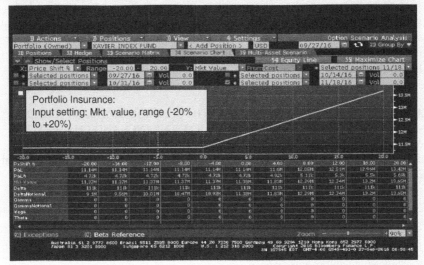

(Continued)

EXHIBIT 8.21   *(continued)*

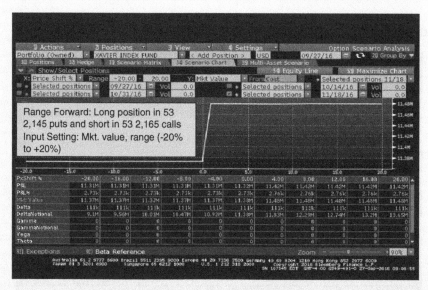

- Hedged positions to analyze: Bond position, futures position, bond position hedged with short futures, bond position hedged with long futures put, bond purchase position evaluated at the expiration date on futures or option (make the bond position negative to reflect cost), bond purchase hedge with long futures, bond purchase hedged with long futures call (see Exhibit 8.22).

MARS: IMPORTING BOND PORTFOLIOS INTO BLOOMBERG'S MARS SCREEN AND ADDING OPTIONS—BOND PORTFOLIO INSURANCE AND CHANGING MARKET EXPOSURE

On the MARS screen, you can import a portfolio and then add option positions to evaluate a portfolio insurance position for a portfolio you created in PRTU:

- MARS <Enter>.
- From the "Portfolio" dropdown, download a portfolio.
- From the red "Security" tab, click "Add Listed Options" and then enter the options in the upper-right amber area box.
- Select options and then click 1<GO>.
- To add the futures contract, enter the futures ticker in the amber "Add by ticker" box.
- On MARS screen, click portfolio summary box to include all securities.

- Scroll down to loaded options and set the number of puts or calls needed to insure the portfolio or change its exposure (you may want to use the price-sensitivity model).

- Click "Scenario" tab and input setting: interest rate shifts, mkt. value, range (–20% to +20%), and evaluation dates (see Exhibit 8.23).

EXHIBIT 8.22 Importing Cheapest-to-Deliver-Note into Bloomberg's MARS Screen and Adding T-Note Futures and Futures Options

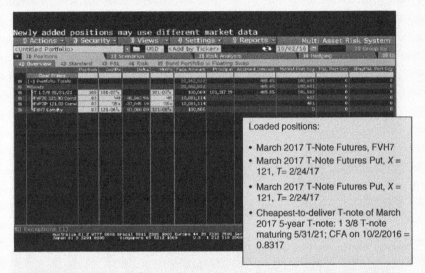

Loaded positions:

- March 2017 T-Note Futures, FVH7
- March 2017 T-Note Futures Put, X = 121, T= 2/24/17
- March 2017 T-Note Futures Put, X = 121, T= 2/24/17
- Cheapest-to-deliver T-note of March 2017 5-year T-note: 1 3/8 T-note maturing 5/31/21; CFA on 10/2/2016 = 0.8317

Scenario: Unhedged Bond Position

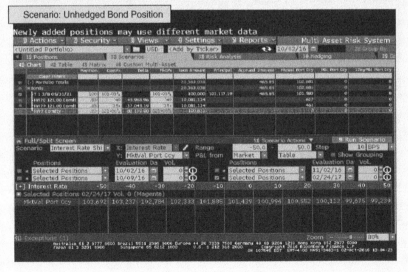

(Continued)

EXHIBIT 8.22 *(continued)*

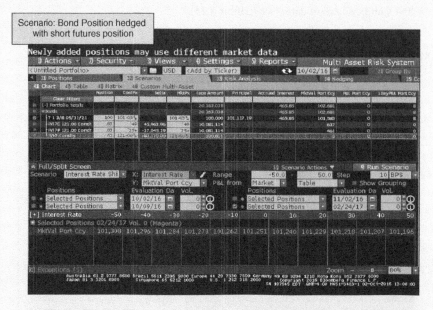

Scenario: Bond Position hedged with short futures position

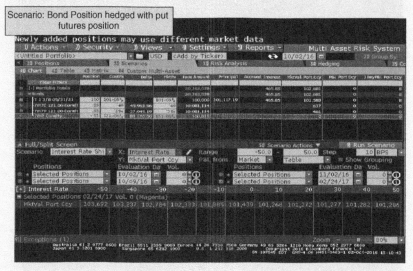

Scenario: Bond Position hedged with put futures position

EXHIBIT 8.23 Importing Bond Portfolios into Bloomberg's MARS Screen and Adding Options

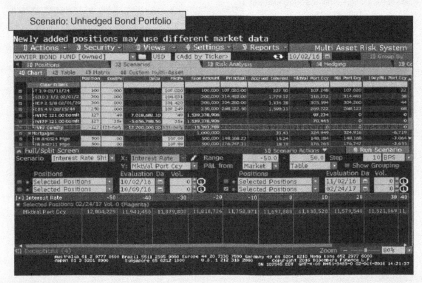

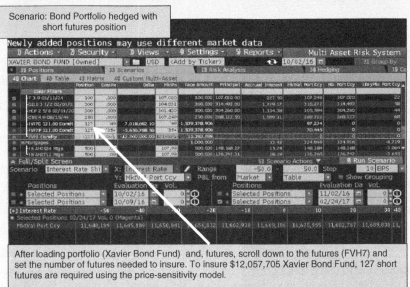

After loading portfolio (Xavier Bond Fund) and, futures, scroll down to the futures (FVH7) and set the number of futures needed to insure. To insure $12,057,705 Xavier Bond Fund, 127 short futures are required using the price-sensitivity model.

(Continued)

EXHIBIT 8.23   *(continued)*

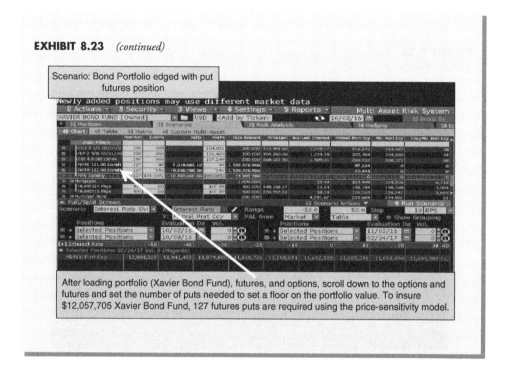

After loading portfolio (Xavier Bond Fund), futures, and options, scroll down to the options and futures and set the number of puts needed to set a floor on the portfolio value. To insure $12,057,705 Xavier Bond Fund, 127 futures puts are required using the price-sensitivity model.

Selected References

Clarke, R., and R. Arnott. "The Cost of Portfolio Insurance: Tradeoffs and Choices." *Financial Analysts Journal* 43 (November–December 1987): 35–47.

Etzioni, E. "Rebalance Disciplines for Portfolio Insurance." *Journal of Portfolio Management* 13 (Fall 1986): 59–62.

Figlewski, S. "Hedging Performance and Basis Risk in Stock Index Futures." *Journal of Finance* 39 (July 1984): 657–669.

Figlewski, S., and S. Kin. "Portfolio Management with Stock Index Futures." *Financial Analysts Journal* 38 (January-February 1982): 52–60.

Grant, D. "How to Optimize with Stock Index Futures." *Journal of Portfolio Management* 8 (Spring 1982): 32–36.

Gressis, N., G. Glahos, and G. Philippatos. "A CAPM-Based Analysis of Stock Index Futures." *Journal of Portfolio Management* 10 (Spring 1984): 47–52.

Kolb, R. W., and R. Chiang. "Improving Hedging Performance Using Interest Rate Futures." *Financial Management* 10 (Fall 1981): 72–79.

Leland, H. "Who Should Buy Portfolio Insurance?" *Journal of Finance* 35 (May 1980): 581–594.

Madura, J., and T. Veit. "Use of Currency Options in International Cash Management." *Journal of Cash Management* (January-February 1986): 42–48.

Madura, J., and E. Nosari. "Utilizing Currency Portfolios to Mitigate Exchange Rate Risk." *Columbia Journal of World Business* (Spring 1984): 96–99.

McCable, G., and C. Franckle. "The Effectiveness of Rolling the Hedge Forward in the Treasury Bill Futures Market." *Financial Management* 12 (Summer 1983): 21–29.

O'Brien, T. "The Mechanics of Portfolio Insurance?" *Journal of Portfolio Management* (Spring 1988): 40–47.

Pozen, R. "The Purchase of Protective Puts by Financial Institutions." *Financial Analysts Journal* 34 (July/August 1978): 47–60.

Rendleman, R., and C. Carabini. "The Efficiency of the Treasury Bill Futures Market." *Journal of Finance* 34 (September 1979): 895–914.

Resnick, B., and E. Hennigar. "The Relation Between Futures and Cash Prices for US Treasury Bonds." *Review of Research in Futures Markets* 2 (1983): 282–299.

Senchak, A., and J. Easterwood. "Cross Hedging CD's with Treasury Bill Futures." *Journal of Futures Markets* 3 (1983): 429–438.

Siegel, D., and D. Siegel. *Futures Markets*. Chicago: Dryden Press, 1990, 203–342 and 493–504.

Stokes, H., and H. Neuburger. "Interest Arbitrage, Forward Speculation and the Determination of the Forward Exchange Rate." *Columbia Journal of World Business* 4 (1979): 86–99.

Swanson, P., and S. Caples. "Hedging Foreign Exchange Risk Using Forward Exchange Markets: An Extension." *Journal of International Business Studies* (Spring 1987): 75–82.

Toevs, A., and D. Jacob. "Futures and Alternative Hedge Methodologies." *Journal of Portfolio Management* (Spring 1986): 60–70.

Viet, T., and W. Reiff. "Commercial Banks and Interest Rate Futures: A Hedging Survey." *Journal of Futures Markets* 3 (1983): 283–293.

Virnola, A., and C. Dale. "The Efficiency of the Treasury Bill Futures Market: An Analysis of Alternative Specifications." *Journal of Financial Research* 3 (1980): 169–188.

Problems and Questions

Note: A number of problems can be done in Excel.

1. The Bryce Investment Trust Company plans to liquidate part of its stock portfolio in June. The company is bullish but would like to set a floor on the portfolio sale as a defensive strategy. The portfolio it plans to sell is well diversified, has a beta of 1.5, and is currently worth $100 million. The S&P 500 index is currently at 2,250 and a June S&P 500 spot put option with an exercise price of 2,250 and multiplier of $100 is currently at 50.

   a. Using the price-sensitivity model, determine how many S&P 500 spot put contracts the Bryce Investment Trust Company would need in order to set a floor on the sale of its $100 million portfolio in June. What is the cost of the puts?

   b. Show in a table the proportional changes in the S&P 500 from its current level of 2,250, the proportional changes in the portfolio, the values of the portfolio corresponding to the spot index, the put option values, the put position's cash flow, and the put hedged portfolio values on the June expiration date for possible spot index values of index values for possible spot index values starting at 1,980 with 30 point steps to 2,850.

2. Suppose the Bryce Investment Trust Company in Problem 1 would like to defray part of the cost of the portfolio put insurance by setting up a short-range forward contract by selling a June S&P 500 spot call option with an exercise price of 2,500, multiplier of $100, and premium of 35.

    a. Using the price-sensitivity model, determine how many June S&P 500 call contracts the Bryce Investment Trust Company would need to sell to form a short-range forward contract with its long June put position. What is the revenue from the calls and the net cost of the short-range forward contract?

    b. Show in a table the proportional changes in the S&P 500 from its current level of 2,250, the proportional changes in the portfolio, the values of the portfolio corresponding to the spot index, the long put option values, the long put position's cash flow, the short call option values, the short call position's cash flow, and the short-range forward portfolio values on the June expiration date for possible spot index values starting at 1,980 with 30 point steps to 2,850.

3. The Keynes Investment Company is expecting a $100 million inflow of cash in June and is planning to invest the cash in a portfolio of stocks with a $\beta = 1.5$. Keynes Investments is concerned there will be a strong bull market and would like to cap its June portfolio investment cost with June S&P 500 spot call options with an exercise price of 2,250, multiplier of $100, and premium of 35. Currently, the S&P 500 index is at 2,250.

    a. Using the price-sensitivity model, determine how many S&P 500 spot call contracts the Keynes Investment Trust Company would need in order to set a $100 million cap on the purchase of its portfolio in June. What is the cost of the call?

    b. Show in a table the proportional changes in the S&P 500 from its current level of 2,250, the proportional changes in the portfolio, the values of the portfolio corresponding to the spot index, the call option values, the call position's cash flow, and the call-hedged portfolio cost on the June expiration date for possible spot index values of index values for possible spot index values starting at 1,900 with 25 point steps to 2,500.

4. Suppose the Keynes Investment Company in Problem 3 would like to defray part of the cost of its cap by setting up a long-range forward contract with a short position in June S&P 500 spot put options with an exercise price of 2,000, multiplier of $100, and premium of 35.

    a. Using the price-sensitivity model, determine how many June S&P 500 put contracts the Keynes Investment Company would need to sell to form a long-range forward contract with its long June call position. What is the revenue from the put and the net cost of the long-range forward contract?

    b. Show in a table the proportional changes in the S&P 500 from its current level of 2,250, the proportional changes in the portfolio, the values of the portfolio corresponding to the spot index, the long call option values, the long call position's cash flows, the short put option values, the short put position's cash flow, and the long-range forward portfolio cost on the June expiration date for possible spot index values starting at 1,900 with 25 point steps to 2,500.

5. The Hunter Investment Company manages a well-diversified equity fund. The current value of the portfolio it manages is $100 million and the portfolio has a beta of 1.0. Hunter Investment is bullish about the market and would like to increase its portfolio beta to 1.5 if the market is 2,250 or greater in June, while keeping its beta at one if the market is less than 2,250. Currently, the S&P 500 spot index is trading at 2,250 and a June S&P 500 spot call contract with an exercise price of 2,250 and $100 multiplier is trading at 50.

   a. Using the price-sensitivity model, determine how many S&P 500 call contracts the Hunter Investment Company would need in order to increase its portfolio beta to 1.5 in June if the market is 2,250 or greater while keeping its portfolio at one if the market is 2,250 or less.

   b. Show in a table the proportional changes in the S&P 500 from its current level of 2,250, the proportional changes in the portfolio, the values of the portfolio corresponding to the spot index, the long call option values, the long call position's cash flow, the call-enhanced portfolio values, and the proportion changes in the call-enhanced portfolio from its $100 million current value, proportion changes in the call-enhanced portfolio value to the proportional changes in S&P 500. Evaluate for possible spot index values on the June expiration date starting at 2,000 with 25 point steps to 2,600.

   c. Comment on the convexity of the call-enhanced portfolio's beta.

6. Suppose ESPN (Disney) is expecting revenues of £6,250,000 next April (one year from now: $T = 1$) from its United Kingdom Rugby sports productions division. ESPN expects the dollar price of the British pound to increase when it converts its £6,250,000 but would like to set a floor on the dollar value of its revenue. Currently, the spot $/£ exchange rate is $1.50/£, and there is a put option on the April BP futures contract with an exercise price of $1.50/£, contract size of £62,500 trading at $0.02/£.

   a. Explain how ESPN could set a floor on it dollar revenue in June with the British pound futures put option. How many contracts would they need to set up the floor?

   b. Show in a table ESPN's April dollar revenue from converting £6,250,000, the intrinsic values of the BP future put, the long put position's cash flow, and the put-insured dollar revenue on April expiration date for possible spot exchange rates of $1.00/£, $1.20/£, $1.50/£, $1.50/£, $1.60/£, $1.70/£, and $1.90/£. Assume the expiring futures price is equal to the spot $/£ exchange rate.

7. ESPN owes the United Kingdom Rugby Association £6,250,000 as payment for the exclusive licensing right to produce rugby matches on the European and US cable markets. ESPN expects the dollar price of the British pound to decrease when it buys £6,250,000 to pay for its obligation but would like to set a cap on the dollar cost of its British pounds. Currently, the spot $/£ exchange rate is

$1.50/£, and there is a call option on the April BP futures contract with an exercise price of $1.50/BP and contract size of 62,500 BP trading at $0.02/£.

   a. Explain how ESPN could cap the dollar cost of its British pounds in April with the British pound futures call option. How many contracts would ESPN need to buy to set up the cap?

   b. Show in a table ESPN's April dollar cost from purchasing £6,250,000, the intrinsic values of the BP futures call, the long call position's cash flow, and the call-capped dollar cost on the April expiration date for possible spot exchange rates of $1.00/£, $1.20/£, $1.50/£, $1.50/£, $1.60/£, $1.70/£, and $1.90/£. Assume the expiring futures price is equal to the spot $/£ exchange rate.

8. Ms. Hunter is the chief financial officer for Atlanta Developers. In January, she estimates that the company will need to purchase 300,000 square feet of plywood in June to meet its material needs on one of its office construction jobs. Ms. Hunter is confident that plywood prices will be decreasing in the future but does not want to assume the price risk if plywood prices were to increase. Suppose there is a June plywood futures call with $X = \$0.20/sq.$ ft. (contract size is 5,000 square feet), selling at $C = \$0.02$, and expiring at the same time as the June underlying plywood futures contract. Explain how Ms. Hunter could cap the company's June plywood costs with a position in the June plywood futures call. Evaluate the cap by showing in a table Ms. Hunter's hedged costs at the plywood futures option's expiration date by buying the plywood on the spot market and closing the futures call options at their intrinsic value. Evaluate at possible spot prices of 0.14/sq. ft., 0.16/sq. ft., 0.18/sq. ft., 0.20/sq. ft., 0.22/sq. ft., 0.24/sq. ft., 0.26/sq. ft., and 0.28/sq. ft.

9. In May, Mr. Smith planted a wheat crop that he expects to harvest in September. He anticipates the September harvest to be 100,000 bushels. While he expects wheat prices to increase, he would still like downside protection against any unexpected decrease in wheat prices. Suppose there is a September wheat futures put contract available with an exercise price of $X = \$4.40/bu.$ (contract size of 5,000 bushels), expiring at the same time as underlying September wheat futures, and currently trading at $0.05. Explain how Mr. Smith could obtain downside protection by buying the put. Show in a table Mr. Smith's hedged revenue at the futures' expiration date from closing the futures put at the intrinsic value and selling his 100,000 bushels of wheat on the spot market at possible spot prices of $3.60/bu., $3.80/bu., $4.00/bu., $4.20/bu., $4.40/bu., $4.60/bu., $4.80/bu., and $5.00/bu.

10. A fixed-income fund manager plans to sell 20 $100,000 face value T-bonds from her government fund in March. The T-bonds she plans to sell pay 3% interest and are currently priced at 105. At the anticipated selling date, the bonds will have 15 years to maturity and no accrued interest. The manager believes that long-term rates could decrease but does not want to risk selling the bonds at lower prices if rates increase. For $20,000, the manager can purchase an OTC T-bond option on

her bonds from a dealer at an exercise price equal the current price and expiration coinciding with her March T-bond sales date.

   a. Describe the OTC option and its terms.

   b. Show in a table the manager's option-hedged revenue (do not include option cost) for possible spot T-bond prices at the March sale of 98, 99, 100, 101, 102, 103, 104, 105, 106, 107, 108, 109, and 110. Assume the manager will exercise her option, if it is feasible (instead of closing), and that she will sell her bonds in the market, if it is not feasible.

11. Suppose the fixed-income fund manager in Question 10 were expecting a cash flow of $2,000,000 in March and planned to invest the cash flow in twenty T-bonds each with a face value of $100,000. Suppose the T-bonds she plans to buy pay 3% interest, have 15 years to maturity, and are currently priced at 105. At the anticipated purchase date, assume such bonds will have no accrued interest. The manager believes that long-term rates could increase but does not want to risk buying the bond at higher prices if rates decrease. For $20,000, the manager can purchase an OTC T-bond option on the 20 bonds from a dealer at an exercise price equal the current price and expiration coinciding with her March T-bonds purchase date:

   a. Describe the OTC option and its terms.

   b. Show in a table the manager's option-hedged cost (do not include option cost) for possible spot T-bond prices at the March purchase date of 98, 99, 100, 101, 102, 103, 104, 105, 106, 107, 108, 109, and 110. Assume the manager will exercise her option, if it is feasible (instead of closing), and that she will buy her bonds in the market, if it is not feasible.

12. The O'Brien Beverage Company is considering capping a two-year $10 million floating-rate loan from First National Bank with a strip of Eurodollar puts. O'Brien's floating-rate loan starts on December 20 with the rate on the loan reset each quarter. The initial quarterly rate is equal to 3.5%/4, the other rates are set each quarter on 3/20, 6/20, 9/20, and 12/20 over the next seven quarters to equal one fourth of the annual LIBOR on those dates plus 100 basis points: (LIBOR % + 1%)/4. The top panel in Table 8.1 shows seven Eurodollar futures put contracts with expirations coinciding with O'Brien's floating-rate loan available and their premiums on December 20. Each futures put has an exercise price of $993,750 ($X = 98.5$ CME index).

   a. Explain how the O'Brien Beverage Company could attain a cap on its floating-rate loan with the put options shown in Table 8.1. What is the cost of the put strip?

   b. Complete Table 8.1, showing the company's quarterly interest payments, option cash flow, hedged interest payments (interest minus option cash flow), and hedged rate as a proportion of a $10 million loan (do not include option cost) given the LIBOR rates shown in the table.

TABLE 8.1

T	3/20/T1	6/20/T1	9/20/T1	12/20/T1	3/20/T2	6/20/T2	9/20/T2	
X	$993,750	$993,750	$993,750	$993,750	$993,750	$993,750	$993,750	
P_0	4	4.2	4.4	4.6	4.8	5	5.2	
Cost of 10 Puts:								Total Cost =

1	2	3	4	5	6	7	8	9
Date	LIBOR %	Futures and Spot Price $S_T = f_T$	Put Cash Flow at Option's Expiration $10(\text{Max} [\$993,750 - f_T, 0])$	Value of Put Cash Flow at Payment Date $(\text{Put CF at T}) (1+\text{LIBOR})^{.25}$	Quarterly Interest at Payment Date $[(\text{LIBOR} + 0.01)]$ ($:	Hedged Debt Col 6 − Col 5	Hedged Rate $[(4)(\text{Col }7)]/ \$10\text{m}$	Unhedged Rate LIBOR + 100bp
12/20	1.50							
3/20	1.50	$996,250	$0		$62,500	$62,500.00	0.025	0.025
6/20	2.00	$995,000	$0	$0.00	$62,500	$62,500.00	0.025	0.025
9/20	2.50							
12/20	3.00							
3/20	3.50							
6/20	4.00							
9/20	4.50							
12/20								

13. Northern Trust is considering setting a floor on a two-year $10 million investment in a floating-rate note (FRN) from First National Bank with a strip of Eurodollar calls. The FRN pays LIBOR plus 100 basis points, starts on December 20 with the initial quarterly rate equal to 3.5%/4 and the other rates reset each quarter on 3/20, 6/20, 9/20, and 12/20 over the next seven quarters to equal to one fourth of the annual LIBOR on those dates plus 100 basis points: (LIBOR % + 1%)/4. The top panel in Table 8.2 shows on December 20 seven Eurodollar futures call contracts with expirations coinciding with First National Bank's FRN and their premium on December 20. The exercise price on each call is $993,750 ($X = 98.5$ CME index).

   a. Explain how the Northern Trust could attain a floor on its floating-rate note with the call options shown in Table 8.2. What is the cost of the call strip?

   b. Complete Table 8.2, showing Northern Trust's quarterly interest receipt, option cash flow, hedged interest receipt (interest plus option cash flow), and hedged rate as a proportion of a $10 million investment (do not include option cost) for each period, given the LIBOR rates shown in the table.

14. Suppose Eastern Bank offers Gulf Refinery a $150 million floating-rate loan along with a cap to finance the purchase of its drilling equipment. The floating-rate loan has a maturity of two years, starts on December 20, and is reset the next

TABLE 8.2

T	3/20/T1	6/20/T1	9/20/T1	12/20/T1	3/20/T2	6/20/T2	9/20/T2	
X	$993,750	$993,750	$993,750	$993,750	$993,750	$993,750	$993,750	
C_0	4	4.2	4.4	4.6	4.8	5	5.2	
Cost of 10 Calls:								Total Cost = $80,500

Date	LIBOR %	Futures and Spot Price $S_T = f_T$	Call Cash Flow at Option's Expiration $10(Max[f_T - \$993{,}750, 0]$	Value of Call Cash Flow at Receipt Date (Call CF at T) $(1+LIBOR)^{.25}$	Quarterly Interest at Receipt Date 0.25 $[(LIBOR + 0.01)]$ ($10m)	Hedged Interest Revenue Col 6 + Col 5	Hedged Rate [(4)(Col 7)]/ $10m	Unhedged Rate LIBOR + 100bp
12/20	1.50							
3/20	1.50	$996,250	$25,000		$62,500	$62,500.00	0.025	0.025
6/20	2.00	$995,000	$12,500	$25,093.23	$62,500	$87,593.23	0.035	0.025
9/20	2.50							
12/20	3.00							
3/20	3.50							
6/20	4.00							
9/20	4.50							
12/20								

seven quarters. The initial quarterly rate is equal to 2.5%/4 and the other rates are reset quarterly to equal to one fourth of the annual LIBOR on those dates plus 150 basis points: (LIBOR % + 1.5%)/4. The cap Eastern Bank is offering Gulf has the following terms:

- Seven caplets with expiration dates of 3/20, 6/20, and 9/20.
- The cap rate on each caplet is 2.5%.
- The time period for each caplet is 0.25 per year.
- The payoffs for each caplet are at the interest payment dates of the loan.
- The reference rate is the LIBOR.
- Notional principal is $150 million.
- The cost of the cap is $300,000.

Complete Table 8.3, showing the company's quarterly interest payments, caplet cash flows, hedged interest payments (interest minus caplet cash flow), and hedged and unhedged rate as a proportion of a $150 million loan (do not include cap cost) for each period, given LIBOR rates starting at 1% on 3/1/Y1 and then increasing each period by 50 bp.

15. Southern Trust is planning to invest $150 million in a Commerce Bank two-year floating-rate note paying LIBOR plus 150 basis points. The floating-rate note has a maturity of two years, starts on December 20, and is reset the next seven quarters. The initial quarterly rate is equal to 2.5%/4 and resets quarterly to equal

TABLE 8.3

Loan: Floating Rate Loan; Term = 2 years; Reset Dates: 3/1, 6/1, 9/1, 12/1;

Time Frequency = 0.25; Rate = LIBOR + 150bp; Payment Date = 90 days after reset date

Cap: Cost of Cap = \$300,000; Cap Rate = 2.50%; Reference Rate = LIBOR;
Time Frequency = 0.25;

Caplets' Expiration: On loan reset dates, starting at 6/1/Y1; Payoff made 90 days after reset date

1	2	3	4	5	6	7
Reset Date	Assumed LIBOR	Loan Interest on Payment Date (LIBOR + 150bp)(0.25) (\$150m)	Cap Payoff on Payment Date Max [LIBOR−0.025,0] (0.25) (\$150m)	Hedged Interest Payment Col. (3) − Col. (4)	Hedged Rate 4 [Col (5)/ \$150m]	Unhedged Rate LIBOR + 150bp
3/1/Y^n	0.010					
6/1/Y1	0.010	\$937,500	\$0	\$937,500	0.0250	0.0250
9/1/Y1	0.015	\$937,500	\$0	\$937,500	0.0250	0.0250
12/1/Y1						
3/1/Y2						
6/1/Y2						
9/1/Y2						
12/1/Y2						
3/1/Y3						

[n]There is no cap on this date

to one fourth of the annual LIBOR on those dates plus 150 basis points: (LIBOR % + 1.5%)/4. Commerce Bank is offering Southern Trust a floor with the following terms:

• Seven floorlets with expiration dates of 3/20, 6/20, and 9/20.
• The floor rate on each caplet is 2.5%.
• The time period for each caplet is 0.25 per year.
• The payoffs for each floorlet are at the interest payment dates on the FRN.
• The reference rate is the LIBOR.
• Notional principal is \$150 million.
• The cost of the floor is \$200,000.

Complete Table 8.4, showing the Southern Trust's quarterly interest receipts, floorlet cash flows, hedged interest receipts (interest plus floorlet cash flow), and hedged and unhedged rate as a proportion of a \$150 million investment (do not include floor cost) for each period given LIBOR rates starting at 1% on 3/1/Y1 and then increasing each period by 50 bp.

TABLE 8.4

Investment: $150 million in floating-rate note; Term = 2 years; Reset Dates: 3/1, 6/1, 9/1, 12/1;

Time Frequency = 0.25; Rate = LIBOR + 150BP; Payment Date = 90 days after reset date

Floor: Cost of Floor = $200,000; Floor Rate = 2.5%; Reference Rate = LIBOR; Time Frequency = .25;

Floorlets' Expirations: On loan reset dates, starting at 6/1/Y1; Payoff made 90 days after reset date

1	2	3	4	5	6	7
Reset Date	Assumed LIBOR	Interest Received on Payment Date (LIBOR + 150bp)(0.25) ($150m)	Floor Payoff on Payment Date Max [0.025−LIBOR,0] (0.25)($150m)	Hedged Interest Payment Col. (3) + Col. (4)	Hedged Rate 4 [Col (5)/ $150m]	Unhedged Rate LIBOR + 150bp
3/1/Y1[n]	0.010					
6/1/Y1	0.010	$937,500	$0	$937,500	0.025	0.025
9/1/Y1	0.015	$937,500	$562,500	$1,500,000	0.040	0.025
12/1/Y1						
3/1/Y2						
6/1/Y2						
9/1/Y2						
12/1/Y2						
3/1/Y3						

[n] There is no floor on this date

Bloomberg Exercises

1. Using the Bloomberg OSA screen, evaluate a stock insurance position and a short-range forward contract for a selected stock. Assume you own 100 shares of the stock and plan to sell it or hedge its value at the options' expiration. Bloomberg sequence: Stock Ticker <Equity>; OSA; load call and put options (for short-range forward position, select a call with a higher exercise price than the put used to create your floor); on the OSA screen, select "Market Value" and the expiration date as your evaluation dates.

2. Using the Bloomberg OSA screen, evaluate a cap and long-range forward contract on a stock purchase of a selected stock. Assume you plan to buy 100 shares of the stock at the expiration of the options. Bloomberg sequence: Stock Ticker <Equity>; OSA; load call and put options (for long-range forward position, select a put with a lower exercise price than the call used to cap the purchase); on the OSA screen, make the stock position negative to indicate purchase (e.g., −100); on OSA screen select "Market Value" (negatives values indicate cost) and the expiration date as one of your evaluation dates.

3. Using the Bloomberg OSA screen, evaluate an insurance and short-range forward position to hedge the futures value of 100 shares of a selected equity ETF (e.g., S&P 500 Spider, SPY). If there are listed options on the ETF's options, use them; otherwise, use the S&P spot or futures index options and the price-sensitivity model to determine the number of option contracts needed to set up the hedge. Bloomberg sequence: ETF Ticker <Equity>; OSA; load call and put options (for short-range forward position, select a call with a higher exercise price than the put used to create your floor); on the OSA screen select "Market Value" and the expiration date as your evaluation dates.

4. Evaluate a future sale of a commodity such as wheat with a floor and short-range forward positions.

   a. Select a commodity that has a futures options contracts on it.

   b. Use the SECF screen to find the tickers for futures, futures options, and spot contracts.

      • For futures options: SECF <Enter>; select "Commodities" from the "Category" dropdown; and then click the "Opt" tab.

      • For spot position: select "Commodities" from the "Category" dropdown and then select "Spot" from the "Instrument" tab.

   c. Upload the spot commodity's menu screen: Commodity Ticker <Comdty> or Commodity Ticker <Index> (e.g., WEATTKHR <Index> for wheat).

   d. Bring up the OSA screen for the loaded commodity and select a position (e.g., 5,000 bushels to sell). Evaluate the position at different dates (Click "Scenario Chart" tab).

   e. From the red "Positions" tab on OSA, click "Add Listed Options" and then the futures ticker in the upper-right amber area box (e.g., W A for CBT wheat futures contracts).

   f. Select the call and put options on the futures needed to evaluate the insurance and short-range forward contracts.

   g. On the OSA screen, set the number of long puts needed to insure the commodity sale and the number of short calls needed to set up the short-range forward position.

   h. Click "Scenario Chart" tab and input setting: profit/loss, market value, range (−20% to 20%), and evaluation dates.

5. Evaluate a future purchase of a selected commodity like crude oil with a cap and long-range forward position using Bloomberg's OSA screen.

   a. Select a commodity that has futures options contracts on it.

   b. Use the SECF screen to find the tickers for futures, futures options, and spot contracts.

      • For futures options: SECF <Enter>; select "Commodities" from the "Category" dropdown and then click the "Opt" tab.

      • For spot position: select "Commodities" from the "Category" dropdown and then select "Spot" from the "Instrument" tab (e.g., USCRWTIC for Crude Oil and West Texas Crude).

    c. Upload the spot commodity's menu screen: Commodity Ticker <Comdty> or Commodity Ticker <Index> (e.g., USCRWTIC <Index> for West Texas Crude).

    d. Bring up the OSA screen for the loaded commodity and select a position (e.g., −10,000 for 10,000 barrels to buy). Evaluate the position at different dates (Click "Scenario Chart" tab).

    e. From the red "Positions" tab on OSA, click "Add Listed Options" and then the futures ticker in the upper-right amber area box (e.g., CLA for crude oil futures).

    f. Select the call and put options on the futures needed to evaluate the cap and long-range forward contract.

    g. On the OSA screen, set the number of calls needed to cap the cost of the commodity and the number of short puts for the long-range forward contract.

    h. Click "Scenario Chart" tab and input setting: Market value, range (−20% to 20%), and evaluation dates. *Note:* Negative values indicate the cost of the commodity.

6. Access Bloomberg information on a currency futures contract with options: type CTM to bring up the "Contract Table Menu," click "Categories" and "Currency," search for CME-listed futures on the Menu (type CME in the amber Exchange box area), find the CME contract of interest and bring up the contract's menu screen (Ticker <Comdty>; e.g., BPA <Curncy> for British pound futures), and then use the Expiration screen (EXS) on the contract's menu page to find the ticker for the contract with the expiration month you want to analyze (Ticker <Curncy>; e.g., BPH7 <Curncy> for the March 2017 contract). View screens to examine: DES, DLV, and GP.

7. On the futures' screen, use OSA to load the currency futures' options contracts. Using OSA, generate profit graphs for the following positions:

    a. Long position in the futures and futures put

    b. Short position in the futures and futures call

    c. Long position in the futures and short position in the call

    d. Short position in the futures and short position in the put

8. Evaluate an equity mutual fund position with at least 10,000 shares that is to be sold or valued at a future date and hedged with a floor and short-range forward positions.

    a. Use the SECF screen to find the fund: SECF <Enter>; select "Funds" from the "Category" dropdown and then click the "Open End" tab and select Equity from the "Focus" dropdown. You may want to limit your search to US funds that are dollar-denominated and with a broad-based or narrow-based fund objective.

    b. Upload the fund's menu screen and evaluate its features (include its beta) using PORT ("Characteristics" and "Summary" tabs) or HRA.

    c. Bring up the OSA screen for the loaded fund and select a position (e.g., 10,000 shares). Evaluate the position at different dates (Click "Scenario Chart" tab).

d. From the red "Positions" tab on OSA, click "Add Listed Options" and then type in the ticker for the S&P 500 (SPX) or S&P 500 futures (SPA), or another selected equity spot or futures index with options, in the upper-right amber area box.

e. Select the call and put options on the futures needed to evaluate the insurance and short-range forward contracts. Use the price-sensitivity model to determine the number of options.

f. On the OSA screen, set the number of long puts needed to ensure the portfolio and the number of short calls for the short-range forward contract.

g. Click "Scenario Chart" tab and input setting: profit/loss, market value, range (−20% to 20%), and evaluation dates.

Using the OSA screen, evaluate a call-enhanced strategy. On the OSA screen, input a number of long call contracts to enhance the fund's value if the market increases.

9. Construct your own equity portfolio and then analyze it using PORT and also as an index created using the CIXB screen. Guidelines:

   • In constructing your own portfolio, use the Equity Search screen (EQS), the FMAP screen to identify stocks that make up different types of funds, or the SECF screen to identify stocks making up a fund or equity index.

   • Make the number of shares for the stocks in your portfolio large enough so that your portfolio's market value is at least $10 million.

   • Create historical data for your portfolio. See sections in Chapter 3: "Bloomberg: Equity Index Futures and Related Screens" and "Steps for Creating Data in PRTU."

   • Import your portfolio in CIXB and create historical data. See sections in Chapter 3: "Bloomberg: Equity Index Futures and Related Screens" and "Bloomberg CIXB and OSA Screens."

10. Using the Bloomberg OSA screen, evaluate an insurance and short-range forward position to hedge the futures value of the portfolio you constructed in Exercise 9 (or another portfolio you have constructed with a market value of at least $10 million). Use S&P 500 spot or futures options (for the short-range forward position, select a call with a higher exercise price than the put's exercise price used to create your floor), and use the price-sensitivity model to determine the number of options. See the section "Bloomberg Hedging Screens" for a guide in loading portfolios and options in OSA.

Using the OSA screen, evaluate a call-enhanced strategy. On the OSA screen, input a number of long call contracts to enhanced the portfolio's value if the market increases.

11. Access Bloomberg information on a T-notes futures contract with options. Bloomberg sequence: type CTM to bring up the "Contract Table Menu," click "Categories" and "Bonds," search for CBT-listed contracts on the menu (type CBT in the amber Exchange box area), find the CBT contract of interest, and bring up the contract's menu screen (Ticker <Comdty>; e.g., FVA <Comdty> for five-year Treasury), and then use the expiration screen (EXS) on the contract's

menu page to find the ticker for the contract with the expiration month you want to analyze (Ticker <Comdty>; e.g., FVH7 <Comdty> for the March 2017 contract). View screens to examine: DES, DLV, and GP.

12. Using the OSA screen, generate profit graphs on the futures options you selected in Exercise 11 for the following positions:

    a. Long position in the futures and futures put
    b. Short position in the futures and futures call
    c. Long position in the futures and short position in the call
    d. Short position in the futures and short position in the put

13. Using the Bloomberg MARS screen, load the futures, futures put, futures call, and cheapest-to-deliver notes on the T-note futures contract you analyzed in Exercise 11. For a guide, see sections "Bloomberg Hedging Screens" and "MARS: Bond Hedging with Futures and Futures Options Using the MARS Platform." Using MARS, evaluate and compare the following positions on the futures options' expiration date for interest rate shifts ranging between –50 bps and +50 bps:

    a. Unhedged bond position
    b. Bond position hedged with a short futures contract
    c. Bond position hedged with a long futures put contract
    d. Bond purchase position evaluated at the expiration date on the futures or option (make the bond position negative to reflect cost)
    e. Bond purchase hedged with a long futures contract
    f. Bond purchase hedged with a long futures call contract

14. Construct a portfolio of investment-grade corporate bonds and US Treasuries using the PRTU screen. After constructing the bond fund, evaluate the portfolio in PORT. Guidelines:

    • Use the Bloomberg search/screen function, SRCH, or SECF to identify the bonds for your portfolio.
    • Make the number of issues for the bonds in your portfolio large enough so that your portfolio's market value is at least $10 million.

    a. Evaluate the characteristic of your portfolio in PORT: "Characteristics" tab, "Summary View."
    b. Access Bloomberg information on a T-notes futures contract with options that has a maturity close to the average maturity of your portfolio. Bloomberg sequence: type CTM to bring up the "Contract Table Menu," click "Categories" and "Bonds," search for CBT on the Menu (type CBT in the amber Exchange box area), find the CBT contract of interest, and bring up the contract's menu screen (Ticker <Comdty>; for example, FVA <Comdty> for five-year Treasury), and then use the expiration screen (EXS) on the contract's menu page to find the ticker for the contract with the expiration month you want to analyze (Ticker <Comdty>; e.g., FVH7 <Comdty> for the March 2017 contract). View screens to examine: DES, YAS, DLV, and GP.

15. Using the Bloomberg MARS screen, load the futures, futures put, futures call, and bond portfolio you analyzed in Exercise 14. For a guide, see sections

"Bloomberg Hedging Screens" and "MARS: Importing Bond Portfolios into Bloomberg's MARS Screen and Adding Options—Bond Portfolio Insurance and Changing Market Exposure." Use the price-sensitivity model to determine the number of futures options contracts you would need to hedge the value of the portfolio. Using MARS, evaluate and compare the following positions on the futures options' expiration date for interest rate shifts ranging between –50 bps and +50 bps:

a. Unhedged bond portfolio position
b. Bond portfolio position hedged with short futures contracts
c. Bond portfolio position hedged with long futures put contracts
d. Bond portfolio position with an enhanced exposure to interest rate changes with long futures positions
e. Bond portfolio position with an enhanced exposure to interest rate changes with long futures call positions

16. Access Bloomberg information on a CME Eurodollar futures contract. Bloomberg sequence: Type CTM to bring up the "Contract Table Menu," click "Categories" and "Interest Rates," search for CME-listed contracts on the menu screen (type CME in the amber Exchange box), find the CME contract of interest, and bring up the contract's menu screen (Ticker <Comdty>; e.g., EDA <Comdty> for the 3-month Eurodollar contract), and then use the expiration screen (EXS) on the contract's menu page to find the ticker for the contract with the expiration month you want to analyze (Ticker <Comdty>; e.g., EDH7 <Comdty> for the March 2017 contract). View screens to examine DES and GP.

17. On the futures screen, use OSA to load the futures' options contracts for the options you selected in Exercise 16. Using OSA, generate profit graphs for the following positions:

a. Long position in the futures and futures put
b. Short position in the futures and futures call
c. Long position in the futures and short position in the call
d. Short position in the futures and short position in the put

PART 3

Option Pricing

CHAPTER 9

Option Boundary Conditions and Fundamental Price Relations

In this chapter, we begin our analysis of option pricing by examining the boundary conditions for minimum prices of options, the price relationships between options with different exercise prices and times to expiration, and how dividends influence the price of an option. In our analysis, we will examine each relationship separately. In Chapter 10, we will integrate many of the relationships by deriving the binomial option-pricing model.

To facilitate our discussion, the symbols for the call premium (C) and put premium (P) will be expressed (when it is helpful) in the following functional form: $C = C(X, T)$ or $P = P(X, T)$. Since some relations are applicable for European options, while others hold only for American, an a or c superscript (C^a or C^e) will be used when clarification is necessary. Similarly, when needed, the subscript 0 will be used to indicate the current period, T, to indicate the option's expiration period or date, and t to signify any time period between the present ($t = 0$) and expiration ($t = T$). We begin by examining the boundary conditions associated with stock options; although most of the conditions examined also hold for non-stock options. We then examine the boundary conditions associated with index, currency, debt, and futures options.

Call Boundary Conditions

Minimum American Call Price

As examined in Chapter 5, if a call option is American, then the call cannot trade at a price below its intrinsic value (IV). If it did, arbitrageurs could realize riskless returns by buying the call, exercising it, and selling the stock. For example, suppose a Boeing 130 American call is trading at $4 when the stock is trading at $135. Given these prices, an investor could buy the stock in the open market at a cost of $135 or alternatively buy the call and exercise it immediately at a cost of only $134 ($4 + $130 = $134). The investor would opt to acquire the stock indirectly through the option market. This action would lead to an increase in the demand for the call until the price of the call was equal to at least $5. In addition, with the call trading at $4, there also would be arbitrage opportunities from executing the arbitrage strategy: buy the call and exercise it immediately at a cost of $134, then sell the Boeing share for $135. In implementing this strategy, arbitrageurs would push the call premium up until it is at least equal to the intrinsic value of $5 and the arbitrage profit is zero:

$$C_t^a \geq \text{Max}[S_t - X, 0]$$

The intrinsic value defines a boundary or limit that governs the price of an American call. The IV, however, is not the minimum price of an American call on a non–dividend-paying stock. For example, suppose in the preceding example the Boeing 130 American call was trading at $6.00 when the stock was at $135 and that the call's expiration was one year. Further, suppose there was a riskless zero coupon bond available in the market with a face value equal to the call's exercise price of $130, maturity of one year, and trading at discount rate of $R_f = 2\%$. In this case, an arbitrageur could receive a cash inflow of $1.55 by buying the call at $6.00, buying the bond for $PV(X) = PV(\$130) = \$130/1.02 = \$127.45$, and selling the stock short at $135 (i.e., $135 − $6.00 − $127.45 = $1.55). At expiration, if Boeing's stock price is equal to or greater than the $130 exercise price ($S_T \geq X$), the arbitrageur could use the proceeds from the maturing bond principal ($130) to exercise the call, and then use the acquired stock to cover the short position; the net cash flow in this case is zero. On the other hand, if the stock price is less than $130, the call would be worthless. In this case, the arbitrageur would only need to use a portion of the $130 from the bond's principal to buy the stock and cover the short position, realizing a cash inflow of $135 − S_T. Thus, if the call is trading at $6.00, an arbitrageur receives an initial cash inflow of $1.55, and at expiration receives additional cash if $S_T < \$130$, and is able to cover the short position such that there are no losses if $S_T \geq \$130$. Given this risk-free opportunity, arbitrageurs would try to buy the call, in turn, pushing its price up until the initial cash flow (CF_0) is at least zero. This would occur when the price of the American call is equal to the difference in the stock price and the present value of the exercise price. That is:

$$CF_0 = S_0 - PV(X) - C_0^a \leq 0$$

$$C_0^a \geq S_0 - PV(X)$$

$$C_0^a \geq \text{Max}[S_0 - PV(X), 0], \text{ to preclude negative prices}$$

Thus, in our example, the arbitrageurs would push the price of the American call to at least \$7.55:

$$C_0^a \geq \text{Max}[S_0 - PV(X), 0]$$

$$C_0^a \geq \$135 - \frac{\$130}{1.02} = \$7.55$$

This boundary condition $\text{Max}[S_t - PV(X), 0]$, in turn, defines the minimum price of an American call at any time t ($\text{Min}[C_t^a]$):

$$\text{Min} C_t^a = \text{Max}[S_t - PV(X), 0]$$

Formal Proof of the Boundary Conditions

The above boundary condition was established by showing that if the condition is violated, then an arbitrage opportunity exists that will provide an initial positive cash flow with no liabilities at expiration when the position is closed. As a rule, the arbitrage strategy underlying any boundary condition can be defined in terms of the violation of the condition, with the arbitrageur going long in the lower-valued position and short in the higher-valued one. Thus, in a case in which the minimum price condition for the American call is violated ($C_0^a < \text{Max}[S_0 - PV(X), 0]$), the arbitrage strategy, as we saw above, should consist of a long position in the call and short position in ($S_0 - PV(X)$):

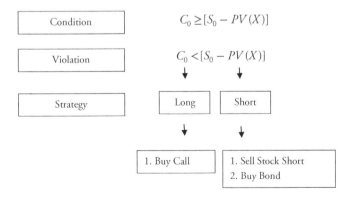

This strategy would provide an initial positive cash flow of

$$CF_0 = S_0 - PV(X) - C_0^a > 0,$$

and as shown in Exhibit 9.1, there would be no liabilities when the position is closed at expiration. That is, at expiration, if $S_T \geq X$, then the long bond and call positions will exactly cover the short stock position. On the other hand, if $S_T < X$, the total cash flow is positive: the call is worthless, but the principal of X received on the bond exceeds the cost of S_T to close the short stock position. Given this riskless opportunity, the price condition is then established by arguing that if the market is efficient, then arbitrageurs, in seeking the opportunity, would drive the price of the call to a level where the initial cash flow is at least zero:

$$CF_0 = S_0 - PV(X) - C_0^a \leq 0$$

$$C_0^a \geq S_0 - PV(X)$$

$$C_0^a \geq \text{Max}[\, S_0 - PV(X),\, 0\,], \text{ to preclude negative prices}$$

EXHIBIT 9.1   Proof of Boundary Condition: $C_0^a \geq S_0 - PV(X)$

Boundary Condition	Boundary Condition Violation	Arbitrage Strategy $C_0^a < (S_0 - PV(X))$		Details
$C_0^a \geq S_0 - PV(X)$	$C_0^a < S_0 - PV(X)$	1. Long Call 2. Short $(S_0 - PV(X))$	1. $\{+C_0^a\}$ 2. $\{-(S_0 - PV(X))\}$ $= \{-S_0, +PV(X)\}$	1. Buy Call 2. Buy Bond 3. Short Stock

Initial Positive Cash Flow of $CF_0 = S_0 - PV(X) - C_0^a > 0,$

No Liabilities at *T*:

Cash Flows at *T* **from of a Long Call,**

Long Bond, and Short Stock Portfolio

	Initial Cash Flow		Cash Flow at Expiration	
Strategy	Position	$S_T < X$	$S_T = X$	$S_T > X$
Long Call	$-C_0$	0	0	$(S_T - X)$
Long Bond	$-PV(X)$	X	X	X
Short Stock	S_0	$-S_T$	$-S_T$	$-S_T$
	$-C_0 - PV(X) + S_0\ (X - S_T) > 0$		0	0

Note: To preclude arbitrage, the current cash flow $-C_0 - PV(X) + S_0$ must be negative:
$-C_0 - PV(X) + S_0 < 0$ or $C_0 > S_0 - PV(X)$

The minimum price of an American call at any time t, is therefore

$$\text{Min}\,C_t^a = \text{Max}[S_t - PV(X),\,0]$$

Note that the minimum price for the American option was established by an arbitrage portfolio that required closing the positions in the call, bond, and stock at the call's expiration date. Since the call is closed at expiration, the distinction between American and European is not important in defining the minimum price. Thus, the minimum price of a European call option on a stock not paying a dividend can be determined by the same arbitrage argument used for the American option: Hence, the

$$\text{Min}\,C_t^e = \text{Max}[S_t - PV(X),\,0]$$

Boundary and Minimum Price Conditions for Calls on Dividend-Paying Securities

The prices of American and European call options on securities are affected by any income received on the underlying securities, such as dividends on stocks, coupon interest on bonds, and interest earned on currency invested. In the preceding example, an arbitrage profit could be realized when the Boeing 130 call was trading below $7.55, by going long in the call, long in the bond, and short in the stock. Suppose the 130 call, though, were trading below its minimum at $6.00, but the stock was expected to go ex-dividend in three months, with the value of the dividend at that date expected to be worth $D = \$2.00$. In this case, the arbitrage strategy of shorting Boeing, going long in a bond, and going long in the call, if implemented, would earn an initial cash flow of $1.55 ($135 − ($130/1.02) − $6.00). At the end of three months, though, an arbitrageur would have an obligation to pay $2.00 to the share lender to cover the dividend payment on the short stock position. Since this dividend obligation exceeds the initial excess cash of $1.55, the strategy is no longer a free lunch. The dividend payment in this example suggests that the boundary condition of $S_0 - PV(X)$ holds only for cases in which the underlying stock does not pay a dividend. In general, dividends have a negative impact on call values, with the minimum call price decreasing, the greater the anticipated dividend payments. In addition, if the dividend is expected to be relatively high, an early exercise advantage for arbitrageurs may exist; if so, the minimum value of the American call will be greater than the European one. The boundary and the minimum price conditions governing American and European call options on dividend-paying stocks are presented in a number of derivative books.

Note: Early Exercise of an American Call

In most cases, a call holder should close her position by selling the call instead of exercising. That is, prior to expiration, the call holder who sells receives the intrinsic value and the time value premium as part of the selling price, while the call holder who exercises receives just the call's intrinsic value. An exception to this rule occurs when the call's underlying stock goes *ex-dividend* during the period and the expected dividend exceeds the call's time value premium.

Stock exchanges specify an ex-dividend date for a stock. Investors who purchase shares of the stock before the ex-dividend date are entitled to receive the dividend, *cum-dividend,* while those who buy on or after the ex-dividend date are not. On the ex-dividend date, the price of the stock should decrease by an amount approximately equal to the dividend, since those who buy the stock at such time do not receive the dividend. Given the decrease in the price of the stock, a holder of an in-the-money call on that stock may find it profitable to exercise the call just before the stock goes ex-dividend.

As a formal argument, consider a call holder's alternative cash flow positions on the ex-dividend date from exercising just prior to the ex-dividend date and not exercising. If the holder exercises *just prior* to the ex-dividend date, then her cash flow on the ex-dividend date would be equal to the value of the stock on that date plus the value of the dividend (D) she is entitled to on the stock's date of record minus the exercise cost of X to buy the stock. If the stock is worth S_t just prior to the ex-dividend date, and we assume that the stock decreases by an amount equal to the value of the dividend on the ex-divided date, then the price of the stock on ex-dividend date would be worth $S_t - D$. Thus, the holder's cash flow on the ex-dividend date (CF^{ex}) from exercising just before is equal to the call's intrinsic value just prior to the ex-dividend date: $S_t - X$:

$$CF^{ex} = (S_t - D) + D - X$$
$$CF^{ex} = S_t - X$$

Alternatively, if the call holder does not exercise, then her cash flow, C^{ex}, on the ex-dividend date would be equal to the price of the call on the date, which would be equal to the call's intrinsic value plus its time value premium:

$$C^{ex} = IV + TVP$$
$$C^{ex} = [(S_t - D) - X] + TVP$$

In comparing the two positions, a call holder should exercise if the cash flow on the ex-dividend date from exercising just before exceeds the call value on the ex-dividend date. This will be the case when $D > TVP$, provided the call is in the money on the ex-dividend date:

$$S_t - X > S_t - D - X + TVP$$
$$D > TVP$$

In this case, the early exercise advantage exists because the dividend the holder is entitled to after exercising exceeds the time value premium she is giving up.

If the size of the dividend is such that the call is out of the money on the ex-dividend date ($D > S_t - X$), then the holder should exercise early if $S_t - X > TVP$. This occurs when $S_t - X > TVP$:

$$S_t - X > \text{Max}[S_t - D - X, 0] + TVP$$
$$S_t - X > TVP, \quad \text{for the case of } D > S_t - X$$

This condition suggests that call options that would be likely candidates for early exercise would be those with low TVP and/or high dividend payments.

Call Options with Different Exercise Prices

Suppose the August Boeing 130 European call is trading at $7.00 while an August Boeing 135 European call is at $8.00. Intuitively, we should expect the price of the call with the lower exercise price of $130 to be greater than the one with the higher exercise price of $135, since the former gives the holder the right to buy Boeing stock at a lower price. To profit from this price imbalance, an arbitrageur could buy the 130 call and sell the 135 one (i.e., set up a bull spread). As shown in Exhibit 9.2, at expiration, the arbitrageurs/spreaders would earn a profit regardless of the price of Boeing stock. By exploiting this opportunity, though, they would increase the price of the 130 call and lower the price of the 135 call until $C_0^e(130) > C_0^e(135)$ and the

EXHIBIT 9.2 Profit and Stock Price Relation for a Bull Spread Boeing 130 Call Contract Purchased at $7 and Boeing 135 Call Contract Sold at $8

Boeing 130 Call Trading at $7 and Boeing 135 Call Trading at $8

Stock Price	Profit: Long 130 Call Purchased at $7: {Max[$S_T - 100,0$] − $7}(100)	Profit: Short 135 Call Sold at $8: {$8 − Max[$S_T - \$135, 0$]}(100)	Total Profit
$100	−$700	$800	$100
$105	−$700	$800	$100
$110	−$700	$800	$100
$115	−$700	$800	$100
$120	−$700	$800	$100
$125	−$700	$800	$100
$130	−$700	$800	$100
$135	−$200	$800	$600
$140	$300	$300	$600
$145	$800	−$200	$600
$150	$1,300	−$700	$600
$155	$1,800	−$1,200	$600

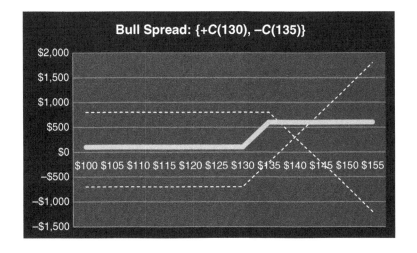

arbitrage opportunity disappears. Thus, arbitrageurs would ensure that the price of a lower exercise-priced call is greater than a higher-priced one:

$$C_t^e(X_1) > C_t^e(X_2), \text{ for } X_2 > X_1$$

In addition to the intuitive reasoning, a more formal arbitrage argument also can be used to establish the condition: $C_0^e(X_1) > C_0^e(X_2)$. Specifically, if this condition is violated, $C_0^e(X_1) < C_0^e(X_2)$, then arbitrageurs would be able to earn riskless profit by forming a bull call spread by going long in the X_1 call and short in the X_2 call. This strategy would provide an initial positive cash flow of

$$CF_0 = C_0^e(X_2) - C_0^e(X_1) > 0$$

and as shown in Exhibit 9.3, there would be no liabilities when the position is closed at expiration. That is, at expiration, there are three possible cases: $S_T < X_1$, $X_1 \leq S_T \leq X_2$, and $S_T > X_2$. If $X_1 \leq S_T \leq X_2$ or $S_T > X_2$, then the cash flows from the bull spread will be positive; if $S_T < X_1$, then the spread's cash flows will be zero. An arbitrage opportunity would therefore exist if there were no costs incurred in setting up the bull spread. To preclude this free lunch, the initial cash flows of the bull spread must therefore be negative:

$$CF_0 = -C_0^e(X_1) + C_0^e(X_2) < 0$$

or

$$C_t^e(X_1) > C_t^e(X_2), \text{ for } X_2 > X_1$$

EXHIBIT 9.3 Proof of Boundary Condition: $C_0^e(X_1) > C_0^e(X_2)$

Boundary Condition	Boundary Condition Violation	Arbitrage Strategy $C_0^e(X_1) < C_0^e(X_2)$	
		Details	
$C_0^e(X_1) >$ $C_0^e(X_2)$	$C_0^e(X_1) < C_0^e(X_2)$	1. Long in the X_1 Call 2. Short in the X_2 Call	Buy X_1 Call, Sell X_2 Call

Initial positive cash flow of $CF_0 = C_0^e(X_2) - C_0^e(X_1) > 0$

No liabilities at T when bull spread is closed

Position	Current Cash Flow	Cash Flow at Expiration		
		$S_T < X_1$	$X_1 \leq S_T \leq X_2$	$S_T > X_2$
Long X_1 Call	$-C_0^e(X_1)$	0	$S_T - X_1$	$S_T - X_1$
Short X_2 Call	$C_0^e(X_2)$	0	0	$-(S_T - X_2)$
	$-C_0^e(X_1) + C_0^e(X_2)$	0	$(S_T - X_1) > 0$	$(X_2 - X_1) > 0$

Note: To preclude arbitrage, the initial cash flow must be negative.
Thus: $-C_0^e(X_1) + C_0^e(X_2) < 0$ or $C_0^e(X_1) > C_0^e(X_2)$

The condition that $C_0^e(X_1) > C_0^e(X_2)$ also holds for an American option in which early exercise is possible. If it did not, then an arbitrageur/spreader again could take a long position in the call with the lower exercise price and a short position in the call with the higher exercise price. If he could hold the positions to expiration, then the same arbitrage profit discussed above for the European calls could be earned. However, it is possible the spreader could be assigned on the short position. If this did occur, then the arbitrageur/spreader would have to buy the stock in the market at S_t and sell it to the option holder at X_2 for a loss on the short position of $X_2 - S_t$. However, the spreader can more than offset this loss by simply selling his lower exercise price call at $C_t^a(X_1)$ $= S_t - X_1 + TVP$. Since $X_2 > X_1$, the cash flow from closing would exceed the cost of the assignment. Thus, if there were an early exercise at time t, the arbitrageur/spreader would still be able to earn a positive cash flow. Hence, an American option like the European is governed by the condition that $C_0^a(X_1) > C_0^a(X_2)$.

Price Limits on Calls with Different Exercise Prices

In addition to the condition that $C(X_1) > C(X_2)$, a second condition related to exercise prices is that the difference in the call premiums cannot be greater than the present value of the difference in the calls' exercise prices for European calls

$$C_t^e(X_1) - C_t^e(X_2) < PV(X_2 - X_1)$$

and greater than the difference in the calls' exercise prices for American calls,

$$C_t^a(X_1) - C_t^a(X_2) < X_2 - X_1$$

For the case of the European calls, if the price-limit condition does not hold (i.e., $C^e(X_1) - C^e(X_2) > PV(X_2 - X_1)$), then there would be an arbitrage opportunity by:

1. Going long in a bond with a face value of $X_2 - X_1$ and maturing at the option's expiration date: $\{+PV(X_2 - X_1)\}$
2. Going short in the X_1 call: $\{-C(X_1)\}$
3. Going long in the X_2 call: $\{+C(X_2)\}$

This strategy would yield an initial positive cash flow of $C_0^e(X_1) - C_0^e(X_2) - PV(X_2 - X_1)$, and as shown in Exhibit 9.4, there would be no liabilities at expiration when the position is closed; that is, the cash flows would be either positive or zero, but not negative when the position is closed. To preclude this arbitrage, the initial cash flow must therefore be negative:

$$C_t^e(X_1) - C_t^e(X_2) < PV(X_2 - X_1), \textit{ for } X_2 > X_1$$

Thus, in the case of the Boeing 130 and 135 options, if they were European, their expirations were one year, and the risk-free rate were 2%, then the difference in the

EXHIBIT 9.4   Proof of Boundary Condition: $C_0^e(X_1) - C_0^e(X_2) < PV(X_2 - X_1)$

Boundary Condition	Boundary Condition Violation	Arbitrage Strategy $C_0^e(X_1) - C_0^e(X_2) > PV(X_2 - X_1)$	
		Short	Long
$C_0^e(X_1) - C_0^e(X_2)$ $< PV(X_2 - X_1)$	$C_0^e(X_1) - C_0^e(X_2)$ $> PV(X_2 - X_1)$	Short in $[C_0^e(X_1) - C_0^e(X_2)]$ Long in $PV(X_2 - X_1)$	1.Sell X_1 call 2. Buy X_2 call 3.Buy bond with face value of $X_2 - X_1$

- **This strategy yields an initial positive cash flow of** $C_0^e(X_1) - C_0^e(X_2) - PV(X_2 - X_1)$
- **At expiration there are no liabilities**

Cash Flow at T from Bear Spread and Bond with Face Value of $X_2 - X_1$

	Cash Flow at Expiration		
Position	$S_T < X_1$	$X_1 \leq S_T \leq X_2$	$S_T > X_2$
Short in X_1 Call	0	$-(S_T - X_1)$	$-(S_T - X_1)$
Long in X_2 Call	0	0	$(S_T - X_2)$
Long in Bond	$X_2 - X_1$	$X_2 - X_1$	$X_2 - X_1$
	$(X_2 - X_1) > 0$	$(X_2 - S_T) > 0$	0

To preclude arbitrage initial cash flow must therefore be negative:

$$C_t^e(X_1) - C_t^e(X_2) < PV(X_2 - X_1), \text{ for } X_2 > X_1$$

prices of a Boeing 130 European call and 135 European calls should not be greater than \$4.90; otherwise there would be an arbitrage:

$$C_t^e(130) - C_t^e(135) < PV(\$135 - \$130) = \frac{\$5.00}{1.02} = \$4.90$$

The above condition is applicable for European calls. Suppose an arbitrageur is long in the bond and has a bear spread formed with American calls ($\{-C_0^a(X_1), +C_0^a(X_2)\}$) and both calls are exercised early at time t. The arbitrageur, in turn, would incur a negative cash flow of $X_2 - X_1$ at time t (buying the stock for X_2 and selling it on the assignment for X_1) that she could finance by borrowing $X_2 - X_1$ dollars at a rate R for the remainder of the period $(T - t)$. At expiration, closing the loan would cost $(X_2 - X_1)(1 + R)^{T-t}$. Since $(X_2 - X_1)(1 + R)^{T-t}$ is greater than the bond's principal cash flow of $(X_2 - X_1)$ received at T, the arbitrageur's strategy would no longer be riskless. Thus, the price limit condition for European calls needs to be adjusted for American calls. This can be done by defining the price limit in terms of an arbitrage portfolio consisting of the bear spread and a riskless bond purchased for $X_2 - X_1$, instead of $PV(X_2 - X_1)$. This bond investment would have a face value of

$(X_2 - X_1)(1 + R)^T$ at expiration, which would equal the maximum cost of covering the bear spread, regardless of when the spread is exercised. Thus, for American call options, the price limits condition would be:

$$C_t^a(X_1) - C_t^a(X_2) < X_2 - X_1, \text{ for } X_2 > X_1$$

Call Price and Time to Expiration Relations

Intuitively, the greater the time to expiration on an option, the greater should be its value. An arbitrage argument involving a time spread can also be used to establish the condition. Specifically, suppose that a Delta 50 American call expiring in six months ($T_2 = 0.5$ per year) is selling for $C_0^a(0.5) = \$5$, while a Delta American 50 call expiring in three months ($T_1 = 0.25$) is selling at a higher price of $C_0^a(0.25) = \$7$. An arbitrageur/spreader could realize a \$2 cash flow immediately by forming a time spread: Buy the longer-term call and sell the shorter-term one. If the shorter-term Delta call is ever exercised, whether at expiration or before, the arbitrageur can simply exercise the longer-term Delta call to meet the assignment; that is, she can buy the Delta at $X = \$50$ on the longer-term option, then deliver it on the shorter-term call's assignment for \$50. Thus, once the arbitrage is set, there are no further liabilities. Given this riskless opportunity, arbitrageurs in the market would buy the longer-term call, increasing its demand and price, and sell the shorter-term call, depressing its price, until $C_0^a(0.5) > C_0^a(0.25)$ and the arbitrage opportunity disappears. Thus:

$$C_t^a(T_2) > C_t^a(T_1), \text{ for } T_2 > T_1$$

It should be noted that this particular strategy is not applicable to European options since the spreader cannot exercise her longer-term call early to cover the expiring shorter-term call.

Put Boundary Conditions

Minimum Price of a Put

As discussed in Chapter 5, the minimum value of an American put (on a stock that pays no dividends) is the put's intrinsic value. This condition is governed by arbitrage. For example, suppose Boeing 130 puts are trading at \$4.00 when Boeing stock is at \$125. An arbitrageur could achieve a \$1.00 risk-free profit by buying the stock and the put for \$129 and then selling the stock immediately at \$130 by exercising the put. By executing this strategy, arbitrageurs would increase the demand for the put, causing its price to increase until the arbitrage profit disappears. The minimum put price where the arbitrage return is zero is the put's intrinsic value:

$$\text{Min}P_t^a = IV = \text{Max}[X - S_t, 0]$$

The arbitrage strategy governing the minimum price of an American put requires an early exercise, and as a result does not apply to European puts. The minimum price of a European put on a stock that pays no dividends can be established by comparing an investment in a bond with a face value of X to an investment in a portfolio of the stock and put. In Exhibit 9.5, the end-of-the-period cash flows are presented for the stock and put investment and an investment in a bond with a face value of X, maturing at the expiration date on the put. As shown, if $S_T \leq X$, then the stock and put portfolio would yield the same cash flow as the bond (X); on the other hand, if $S_T > X$, the put would be worthless but the stock would be worth more than the face value of the bond. Thus, since the put and stock portfolio yield the same cash flows at expiration as the bond investment in some cases ($S_T \leq X$) and a greater cash flow in others ($S_T > X$), it should be valued higher by investors:

$$P_t^e + S_t > PV(X)$$

Solving the inequality for P_t^e and expressing it with a constraint that P_t^e cannot be negative defines the minimum price of a European put:

$$P_t^e > \text{Max}[\, PV(X) - S_t, 0\,]$$
$$\text{Min} P_t^e = \text{Max}[\, PV(X) - S_t, 0\,]$$

An arbitrage argument also can be used to establish the minimum price of a European put. Similar to the arbitrage strategy we presented earlier for determining the minimum price of a call, if a European put is below its minimum price ($P_t^e < PV(X) - S_t$), then arbitrageurs would be able to earn riskless profit by going long in the put, short in a risk-free bond with a face value of X and maturity of T, and long in the stock. This strategy would provide an initial positive cash flow of

$$CF_0 = PV(X) - S_0 - P_0^e > 0$$

EXHIBIT 9.5   Comparison of Bond with Put and Stock Portfolio

	Cash Flows at Expiration		
Position	$S_T < X$	$S_T = X$	$S_T > X$
Investment 1:			
Bond Purchase with Face Value of X	X	X	X
Investment 2:			
Put Purchase	$X - S_T$	0	0
+	+	+	+
Stock Purchase	S_T	S_T	S_T
	X	X	S_T
Investor Preference	**Indifferent**	**Indifferent**	**Investment 2**

Note: Investment 1 (long bond) provides the same cash flow (X) at expiration whether the stock goes up or down. Investment 2: {+P, +S} provides a cash flow of X when $S_T \leq X$, and a greater flow of S_T if the stock price at expiration is greater than X. Hence, Investment 2 dominates 1 and should have a higher value at $t = 0$.

and as shown in Exhibit 9.6, there would be no liabilities when the position is closed at expiration. That is, if $S_T \leq X$ at expiration, the stock and put portfolio would yield a cash flow equal to X, which would just cover the short bond, and if $S_T > X$, the put would be worthless, but the stock's cash flow would exceed the proceeds needed to cover the bond, yielding a net cash flow of $S_T - X > 0$. This arbitrage opportunity would, in turn, force the price of the put to increase until it is at least equal to $PV(X) - S_t$.

It should be noted that since $PV(X) < X$, the minimum price of a European put is less than an American: Min $P_0^e <$ Min P_0^a. In contrast, for call options on stocks that pay no dividends during the options' lives, the minimum prices of American and European calls are the same.

Minimum Price Conditions for Puts on Income-Paying Securities

Like European and American call options, the prices of American and European puts are affected by any income received on the underlying security. In the case of dividend-paying stocks, the price of a put option is a positive function of dividends: as dividends increase, both American and European put prices increase. This contrasts to the case of an inverse price and dividend relation for European and American

EXHIBIT 9.6 Proof of Boundary Condition: $P_0^e \geq PV(X) - S_0$

Boundary Condition	Boundary Condition Violation	Arbitrage Strategy $P_0^e < PV(X) - S_0$		Details
		Long	Short	
$P_0^e \geq PV(X) - S_0$	$P_0^e < PV(X) - S_0$	1. Long Put	1. $\{+P_0^a\}$	1. Buy Put
		2. Short $(PV(X) - S_0)$	2. $-(PV(X) - S_0)$ $=\{-PV(X), +S_0\}$	2. Short Bond
				3. Buy Stock

- **This strategy provide an initial positive cash flow of**
  $CF_0 = PV(X) - S_0 - P_0^e > 0$
- **There are no liabilities when the position is closed at expiration**

Cash Flow at Expiration from Long Stock and Put and Short Bond Position

Position	Expiration Cash Flow		
	$S_T < X$	$S_T = X$	$S_T > X$
Long Stock	S_T	S_T	S_T
Long Put	$X - S_T$	0	0
Short Bond	$-X$	$-X$	$-X$
	0	0	$(S_T - X) > 0$

call options. It should also be noted that the minimum price of an American put is greater than its European counterpart, regardless of whether the stock pays a low or a high dividend, or no dividend at all. This also contrasts to the case of call options in which it is possible for American and European call values to be equal (i.e., no early exercise advantage) when dividends are relatively low (below the threshold dividend). The impacts of dividends on the minimum prices of American and European put options are presented in a number of derivative texts.

Price Relation of Puts with Different Exercise Prices

Intuitively, the put with the higher exercise price (X_2) should have a higher price than the one with the lower exercise price (X_1), since the former gives the put holder the right to sell the underlying security at a higher price. In addition to the intuitive reasoning, if the put with the higher exercise price is not priced higher, then in the case of European puts, arbitrageurs can earn riskless profit by forming a bear put spread—buying the higher exercise priced put for $P_0^e(X_2)$ and selling the lower exercise priced put for $P_0^e(X_1)$. For example, if a Boeing August 130 European put is trading at $5 and a Boeing 135 European put is selling for $4 $(P_0^e(130) > P_0^e(135))$, then, as shown in Exhibit 9.7, an arbitrage return is earned at expiration by purchasing the 135 put and selling the 130 put. In turn, with this arbitrage opportunity arbitrageurs/spreaders will push the price of the 135 put up and the price of the 130 put down until $P_0^e(135) > P_0^e(130)$ and the arbitrage profit disappears.

In addition to the intuitive reasoning, an arbitrage argument also can be used to establish the condition $P_0^e(X_2) > P_0^e(X_1)$. Specifically, if this condition is violated, $(P_0^e(X_2) < P_0^e(X_1))$, then arbitrageurs would be able to earn riskless profit by forming a bear put spread by going long in the X_2 put and short in the X_1 put. This strategy would provide an initial positive cash flow of

$$CF_0 = P_t^e(X_1) - P_t^e(X_2) > 0$$

and as shown in Exhibit 9.8, there would be no liabilities when the position is closed at expiration. That is, there are three possible cases at expiration: $S_T < X_1$, $X_1 \leq S_T \leq X_2$, and $S_T > X_2$. If $X_1 \leq S_T \leq X_2$ or $S_T < X_1$, then the cash flows from the bear spread would be positive; if $S_T > X_2$, then the spread's cash flows would be zero. An arbitrage opportunity would therefore exist if there were no costs incurred in setting up the bull spread. To preclude this free lunch, the initial cash flows of the bull spread would therefore have to be negative:

$$CF_0 = -P_0^e(X_2) + P_0^e(X_1) < 0$$

or

$$P_t^e(X_2) > P_t^e(X_1), \ for \ X_2 > X_1$$

EXHIBIT 9.7 Profit and Stock Price Relation for a Bear Spread: Boeing 135 Put Purchased at $4 and Boeing 130 Put Contract Sold for $5

Boeing 130 Put Trading at $5 and Boeing 135 Put Trading at $4

Stock Price	Profit: Short 130 Put Sold for $5: $\{-\text{Max}[\$130 - S_T, 0] + \$5\}(100)$	Profit: Long 135 Put Purchased at $4: $\{\text{Max}[\$135 - S_T, 0] - \$4\}(100)$	Total Profit
$100	−$2,500	$3,100	$600
$105	−$2,000	$2,600	$600
$110	−$1,500	$2,100	$600
$115	−$1,000	$1,600	$600
$120	−$500	$1,100	$600
$125	$0	$600	$600
$130	$500	$100	$600
$135	$500	−$400	$100
$140	$500	−$400	$100
$145	$500	−$400	$100
$150	$500	−$400	$100
$155	$500	−$400	$100

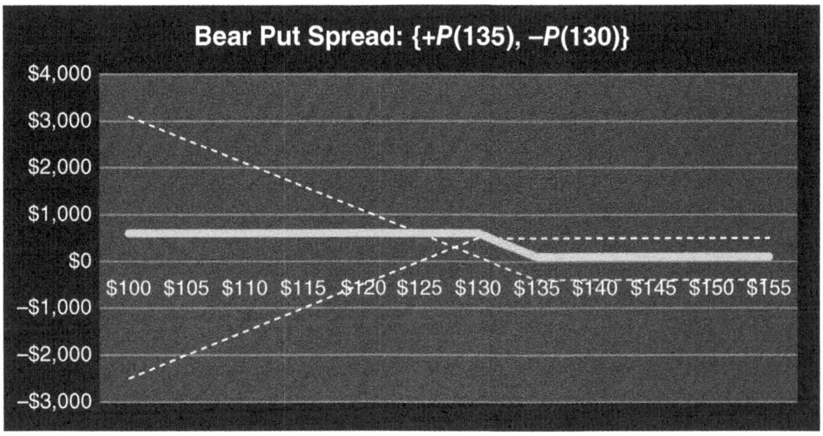

The condition that $P_t^e(X_2) > P_t^e(X_1)$ also holds for American puts. If the price on an American put with a lower exercise price exceeds a similar one with a higher strike price, then, as before, a risk-free profit could be earned from the bear put spread. Prior to expiration, if the bear put spreader is assigned the lower exercise price put in which she is short, then the spreader could buy the stock on the assignment at X_1 and use her long put position to sell the stock for X_2 to earn an arbitrage profit of $X_2 - X_1$. Thus, even with early exercise, an arbitrage profit still can be realized from a bear put spread when $P_0^a(X_1) > P_0^a(X_2)$. Thus:

$$P_t^a(X_2) > P_t^a(X_1), \text{ for } X_2 > X_1$$

EXHIBIT 9.8   Proof of Boundary Condition: $P_0^e(X_2) > P_0^e(X_1)$

Boundary Condition	Boundary Condition Violation	Arbitrage Strategy $P_0^e(X_2) < P_0^e(X_1)$	
		Long	Short
$P_0^e(X_2) > P_0^e(X_1)$	$P_0^e(X_2) < P_0^e(X_1)$	1. Long in the X_2 put	Buy X_2 Put
		2. Short in the X_1 Put	Sell X_1 put

- This strategy would provide an initial positive cash flow of $CF_0 = P_t^e(X_1) - P_t^e(X_2) > 0$
- There are no liabilities when the position is closed at expiration

	Cash Flows at Expiration		
Position	$S_T < X_1$	$X_1 \le S_T \le X_2$	$S_T > X_2$
Short X_1 Put	$-(X_1 - S_T)$	0	0
Long X_2 Put	$X_2 - S_T$	$X_2 - S_T$	0
	$X_2 - X_1 > 0$	$X_2 - S_T > 0$	0

To preclude arbitrage the initial cash flow must be negative:
$CF_0 = -P_0^e(X_2) + P_0^e(X_1) < 0$ or $P_t^e(X_2) > P_t^e(X_1)$, for $X_2 > X_1$

Price Limits on Puts with Different Exercise Prices

For European puts, the price difference between two puts that are identical except for their exercise prices must be less than the difference in the present values of the two puts' exercise prices:

$$P_t^e(X_2) - P_t^e(X_1) < PV(X_2 - X_1)$$

If this condition does not hold ($P_0^e(X_2) - P_0^e(X_1) > PV(X_2 - X_1)$), then an arbitrage opportunity exists by going long in a riskless bond with a face value of $X_2 - X_1$ and maturity of T and by constructing a bull spread, shorting the X_2 put and going long in the X_1 put. This strategy would provide an initial positive cash flow of

$$CF_0 = P_0^e(X_2) - P_0^e(X_1) - PV(X_2 - X_1) > 0$$

and as shown in Exhibit 9.9, there would be no liabilities at expiration when the position is closed. To preclude this free lunch, the initial cash flow must be negative:

$$CF_0 = P_0^e(X_2) - P_0^e(X_1) - PV(X_2 - X_1) < 0$$
$$P_0^e(X_2) - P_0^e(X_1) < PV(X_2 - X_1)$$

Thus, if the rate on a risk-free rate is 2%, then the price difference between the Boeing 135 and 130 puts expiring in one year should be $4.90:

$$P_0^e(135) - P_0^e(130) = PV(\$135 - \$130) = \frac{\$5.00}{1.02} = \$4.90$$

EXHIBIT 9.9 Proof of Boundary Condition: $P_0^e(X_2) - P_0^e(X_1) < PV(X_2 - X_1)$

Boundary Condition	Boundary Condition Violation	Arbitrage Strategy $P_0^e(X_2) - P_0^e(X_1) > PV(X_2 - X_1)$	
		Short	Long
$P_0^e(X_2) - P_0^e(X_1)$ $< PV(X_2 - X_1)$	$P_0^e(X_2) - P_0^e(X_1) >$ $PV(X_2 - X_1)$	Short in $[P_0^e(X_2) - P_0^e(X_1)]$ Long in $PV(X_2 - X_1)$	1. Sell X_2 put 2. Buy X_1 put 3. Buy bond with face value of $X_2 - X_1$

- This strategy would provide an initial positive cash flow of
  $CF_0 = P_0^e(X_2) - P_0^e(X_1) - PV(X_2 - X_1) > 0$
- There are no liabilities at expiration when the position is closed.

Cash flow at T from closing Bull Put Spread and Bond with Face Value of $X_2 - X_1$

	Cash Flows at Expiration		
Position	$S_T < X_1$	$X_1 \leq S_T \leq X_2$	$S_T > X_2$
Long X_1 Put	$X_1 - S_T$	0	0
Short X_2 Put	$-(X_2 - S_T)$	$-(X_2 - S_T)$	0
Long Bond	$X_2 - X_1$	$X_2 - X_1$	$X_2 - X_1$
	0	$S_T - X > 0$	$X_2 - X_1 > 0$

To preclude arbitrage, the initial cash flow must be negative:

$CF_0 = P_0^e(X_2) - P_0^e(X_1) - PV(X_2 - X_1) < 0$
$P_0^e(X_2) - P_0^e(X_1) < PV(X_2 - X_1)$

If the bull spread in the above arbitrage portfolio were formed with American puts that were exercised early at time t, then the arbitrageur would lose $X_2 - X_1$. If we assume the arbitrageur finances this short fall by borrowing $X_2 - X_1$ dollars at rate R for the remainder of the period, then at expiration she would owe $(X_2 - X_1)$ $(1 + R)^{T-t}$ on the debt: an amount that exceeds the face value on the bond. To ensure a free lunch the arbitrageur would need to buy a bond that yields a cash flow at expiration that is at least equal to $(X_2 - X_1)(1 + R)^{T-t}$. This can be done by purchasing a riskless zero-coupon bond with a face value of $(X_2 - X_1)(1 + R)^T$ for the price of $X_2 - X_1$. Since $(X_2 - X_1)(1 + R)^T > (X_2 - X_1)(1 + R)^{T-t}$, the arbitrageur would thus have a bond that can generate a return at least as good as the put spread and often better. To avoid arbitrage, the American puts would have to be priced such that:

$$P_0^a(X_2) - P_0^a(X_1) < X_2 - X_1$$

Put Price and Time to Expiration Relation

Like an American call, an American put with a greater time to expiration should be valued more than an identical put with a shorter time to expiration, since the former has a better chance of being in the money. Thus, for two puts on the same security and with the same exercise price but with different times, the following boundary condition holds:

$$P_t^a(T_2) > P_t^a(T_1), \text{ for } T_2 > T_1$$

If the price of a longer-term put were less than the price of a shorter-term put, an arbitrage opportunity would exist with a time spread. For example, suppose a Boeing 130 put expiring in one year ($T_2 = 1$ per year) is trading at \$5.00, while a Boeing 130 put expiring in six months ($T_1 = 0.5$) is selling for \$6.00: $P_0^a(130,1.0) < P_0^a(130, 0.5)$. Given this situation, a \$1.00 arbitrage opportunity exist by forming a time spread consisting of a short position in the higher-priced, short-term put and a long position in the lower-priced, long-term put. If the spreader is assigned on the shorter-term 130 put, whether at expiration or before, she can simply buy the Boeing stock at \$130 on the assignment and then sell the stock for \$130 by exercising her longer-term 130 put. Thus, if the longer-term put is priced below the shorter-term one, a spreader is sure of earning a riskless return. As spreaders exploit this opportunity, however, they will push the price of the longer-term put up (as they try to buy it) and depress the price of the shorter-term one (as they try to sell) until $P_0^a(T_2) > P_0^a(T_1)$.

It should be noted that since a longer-term European put cannot be exercised when a shorter-term European put expires, the above arbitrage/spread strategy cannot be applied to ensure the above condition holds for European puts.

Put and Call Boundary Conditions

Put-Call Parity

Since the prices of options on the same underlying security are derived from that security's value, the put price and call price are also related to each other. The relationship governing put and call prices is known as put-call parity. This relation was first defined in Chapter 5 by observing there were equivalent cash flows from a protective put {+S, +P}, and a fiduciary call, {+C, +PV(X)}. The put-call parity condition can also be proved in terms of the price conditions governing a *conversion* or *reversal* position. A conversion is a long position in the security, a short position in a European call, and long position in a European put: {+S, +P, −C}. A *reversal* is the opposite of a conversion: a short position in the stock, a long position in the European call, and short position in a European put: {−S, −P, +C}.

As shown in Exhibit 9.10, a conversion generates a certain cash flow at expiration equal to the exercise price. In the absence of arbitrage, the risk-free conversion position must be worth the same as a risk-free zero-coupon bond with a face value of X, maturing at the end of the option's expiration period:

$$P_0^e - C_0^e + S_0 = PV(X)$$

By reversing the conversion strategy, we create a reversal. As shown in Exhibit 9.11, a reversal results in a required fixed payment equal to X at expiration. To preclude

EXHIBIT 9.10 Conversion: $\{+S_0, + P_0^e, -C_0^e\}$

	Cash Flows at Expiration		
Position	$S_T < X$	$S_T = X$	$S_T > X$
Long Stock	S_T	S_T	S_T
Long Put	$X - S_T$	0	0
Short Call	0	0	$-(S_T - X)$
	X	X	X

arbitrage, a reversal should be equal to a short position in a bond $(-PV(X))$. Thus, the same put-call parity condition can be derived from a reversal position:

$$-P_0^e + C_0^e - S_0 = -PV(X)$$
$$P_0^e - C_0^e + S_0 = PV(X)$$

If the put-call parity condition does not hold, then an arbitrage opportunity will exist. For example, suppose the Boeing 130 call and put expiring in one year were trading for $5 each, when Boeing stock was selling for $130. Furthermore, suppose the risk-free rate were 2% so that a one-year zero-coupon bond with a face value of $X = \$130$ was worth $127.45. In this case, the put-call parity equilibrium condition is violated:

$$P_0^e - C_0^e + S_0 > PV(X)$$
$$\$5.00 - \$5.00 + \$130.00 > \frac{\$130}{1.02}$$
$$\$130.00 > \$127.45$$

The actual bond is cheap ($127.45), relative to the synthetic bond $\{+S, +P_0^e, -C_0^e\}$ ($130.00) and the put-call parity condition is violated: $P_0^e - C_0^e + S_0 > PV(X)$. Arbitrageurs could exploit this price imbalance by buying the bond and shorting the synthetic bond (long stock, long put, and short call). This strategy would yield an immediate cash flow of $P_0^e - C_0^e + S_0 - PV(X) = \$5.00 - \$5.00 - \$130.00 - \$127.45$

EXHIBIT 9.11 Reversal: $\{-S_0, -P_0^e, +C_0^e\}$

	Expiration Cash Flow		
Position	$S_T < X$	$S_T = X$	$S_T > X$
Short Stock	$-S_T$	$-S_T$	$-S_T$
Short Put	$-(X - S_T)$	0	0
Long Call	0	0	$(S_T - X)$
	$-X$	$-X$	$-X$

= \$2.55, and as shown in Exhibit 9.12, there would be no liabilities when the position is closed at expiration. That is, at expiration, the \$130.00 cash flow from the bond would be exactly equal to the cash flow needed to cover the short synthetic bond position. In implementing this strategy, arbitrageurs, though, would alter the demands and supplies of calls and puts, causing their prices to change until the put-call parity equality condition is reached.

A similar argument may be used if the actual bond is expensive relative to the synthetic one. For example, suppose the Boeing 130 call and put expiring in one year were trading again for \$5.00 each, but Boeing stock was selling for \$125.00. In this case, the put-call parity equilibrium condition is again violated:

$$P_0^e - C_0^e + S_0 > PV(X)$$

$$\$5.00 - \$5.00 + \$125.00 < \frac{\$130}{1.02}$$

$$\$125.00 < \$127.45$$

The actual bond is expensive (\$127.45), relative to the synthetic bond $\{+S, +P_0^e, -C_0^e\}$ (\$125.00). Arbitrageurs, in turn, could exploit this price imbalance by shorting the expensive real bond and buying the cheap synthetic one. This strategy

EXHIBIT 9.12   Proof of Put-Call Parity Condition: $P_0^e - C_0^e + S_0 = PV(X)$

Boundary Condition	Boundary Condition Violation	Arbitrage Strategy $P_0^e - C_0^e + S_0 > PV(X)$	
		Short	Long
$P_0^e - C_0^e + S_0 = PV(X)$	$P_0^e - C_0^e + S_0 > PV(X)$	Short in $[P_0^e - C_0^e + S_0]$	1. Sell put
		Long in $PV(X_2)$	2. Buy call
			3. Short stock
			3. Buy bond with face value of X

• **This strategy would yield an immediate cash flow of $P_0^e - C_0^e + S_0 - PV(X) > 0$**
• **There are no liabilities when the position is closed at expiration**

Cash Flow from Closing Short Stock and Put Positions and Long Bond and Call Positions

	Expiration Cash Flow		
Position	$S_T < X$	$S_T = X$	$S_T > X$
Short Stock	$-S_T$	$-S_T$	$-S_T$
Short Put	$-(X - S_T)$	0	0
Long Call	0	0	$(S_T - X)$
Long Bond	X	X	X
	0	0	0

EXHIBIT 9.13 Proof of Put-Call Parity Condition: $P_0^e - C_0^e + S_0 = PV(X)$

Boundary Condition	Boundary Condition Violation	Arbitrage Strategy $P_0^e - C_0^e + S_0 < PV(X)$	
		Long	Short
$P_0^e - C_0^e + S_0$ $= PV(X)$	$P_0^e - C_0^e + S_0 < PV(X)$	Long in $[P_0^e - C_0^e + S_0]$ Short in PV(X)	1. Buy put 2. Sell call 3. Buy stock 3. Short bond with face value of X

- **This strategy would yield an immediate cash flow of** $PV(X) - P_0^e + C_0^e - S_0 - PV(X) > 0$
- **There are no liabilities when the position is closed at expiration.**

Cash Flow from Closing Long Stock and Put Positions and Short Bond and Call Positions

	Cash Flows at Expiration		
Position	$S_T < X$	$S_T = X$	$S_T > X$
Long Stock	S_T	S_T	S_T
Long Put	$X - S_T$	0	0
Short Call	0	0	$-(S_T - X)$
Short Bond	$-X$	$-X$	$-X$
	0	0	0

would yield an immediate cash flow with no liabilities when the position is closed at expiration (see Exhibit 9.13).

The Price of a European Call and Put in Terms of Put-Call Parity

The put-call parity condition can be used to determine the equilibrium price of a European put, given the equilibrium price of a European call and the interest rate; or the equilibrium price of a call, given the equilibrium price of the put and the interest rate. That is, from the put-call parity equation:

$$C_0^e = P_0^e + S_0 - PV(X)$$
$$P_0^e = C_0^e - S_0 + PV(X)$$

The right-hand side of the call equation shows the value of a portfolio consisting of long positions in the put and stock and a short position in the bond. This position is referred to as a *synthetic call* since it replicates the cash flows from a European call. Similarly, the right-hand side of the put equation represents a portfolio consisting of long positions in the call and bond and a short position in the stock. Since this portfolio replicates the cash flows from a European put, it is referred to as a *synthetic put*.

Put-Call Parity for European Options on a Stock with a Dividend

If there are ex-dividend dates during the period the option positions are held, then, as shown in Exhibit 9.14, the conversion will yield a riskless cash flow equal to the exercise price plus the value of dividends at expiration date (D_T). Since the conversion is risk free, its equilibrium value will be equal to the value of a risk-free zero-coupon bond with a face value equal to X plus the value of the dividend at the options' expiration date:

$$P_0^e - C_0^e + S_0 = PV(X + D_T)$$

Put-Call Parity Prices for American Calls and Puts

The put-call parity condition depends on the relationships among the values of options, the price of the underlying stock, and the rate of return on a risk-free bond. The model holds strictly for European options and not for American options.

Box Spread

In the put-call parity model, call and put premiums are related by real and synthetic stock positions. Another way of relating call and put prices is by a box spread.

A long box spread consists of a call bull money spread and put bear money spread. A long box spread formed with European options yields a certain return at expiration equal to the difference in the exercise prices (see Exhibit 9.15). Since arbitrage ensures $C(X_1) > C(X_2)$ and $P(X_2) > P(X_1)$ for $X_2 > X_1$, a long box spread represents an investment expenditure, in which

$$\text{Cost of box spread} = C_0^e(X_1) - C_0^e(X_2) + P_0^e(X_2) - P_0^e(X_1)$$

In contrast, a short box spread or reverse box spread is a combination of call bear money spread and put bull money spread. In contrast to the long box spread, the short box spread generates a credit for the investor at the initiation of the strategy, and

EXHIBIT 9.14 Conversion with Dividend-Paying Stock

	Expiration Cash Flow		
Position	$S_T < X$	$S_T = X$	$S_T > X$
Long Put	$X - S_T$	0	0
Short Call	0	0	$-(S_T - X)$
Long Stock	S_T	S_T	S_T
Dividend	D_T	D_T	D_T
	$X + D_T$	$X + D_T$	$X + D_T$

EXHIBIT 9.15 Long Box Spread: $\{+C(X_1), -C(X_2), -P(X_1), +P(X_2)\}$

	Cash Flows at Expiration		
Position	$S_T < X_1$	$X_1 \leq S_T \leq X_2$	$S_T > X_2$
Long X_1 Call	0	$S_T - X_1$	$S_T - X_1$
Short X_2 Call	0	0	$-(S_T - X_2)$
Short X_1 Put	$-(X_1 - S_T)$	0	0
Long X_2 Put	$X_2 - S_T$	$X_2 - S_T$	0
	$X_2 - X_1$	$X_2 - X_1$	$X_2 - X_1$

requires a fixed payment at expiration equal to the difference in the exercise prices (see Exhibit 9.16).

Since the return on a long box spread is riskless, in equilibrium we would expect the price of the spread to be equal to the price on a risk-free zero coupon bond with a face value of $X_2 - X_1$ maturing at the same time as the options expire:

$$C_0^e(X_1) - C_0^e(X_2) + P_0^e(X_2) - P_0^e(X_1) = PV(X_2 - X_1)$$
$$C_0^e(X_1) - C_0^e(X_2) + P_0^e(X_2) - P_0^e(X_1) - PV(X_2 - X_1) = 0$$

Similarly, a short box spread represents a riskless loan with a fixed payment of $X_2 - X_1$ required on the short spread at expiration. Thus in equilibrium, the credit received from the spread should equal the proceeds from a loan requiring payment of $X_2 - X_1$ at maturity, $PV(X_2 - X_1)$. Thus:

$$-C_0^e(X_1) + C_0^e(X_2) - P_0^e(X_2) + P_0^e(X_1) = -PV(X_2 - X_1)$$

If we assume borrowing and lending rates are the same, then in equilibrium the short and long box spread condition yield the same equilibrium equation. If the box

EXHIBIT 9.16 Short Box Spread: $\{-C(X_1), +C(X_2), +P(X_1), -P(X_2)\}$

	Expiration Cash Flow		
Position	$S_T < X_1$	$X_1 \leq S_T \leq X_2$	$S_T > X_2$
Short X_1 call	0	$-(S_T - X_1)$	$-(S_T - X_1)$
Long X_2 Call	0	0	$S_T - X_2$
Long X_1 Put	$X_1 - S_T$	0	0
Short X_2 Put	$-(X_2 - S_T)$	$-(X_2 - S_T)$	0
	$-(X_2 - X_1)$	$-(X_2 - X_1)$	$-(X_2 - X_1)$

EXHIBIT 9.17   Proof of Box Spread Condition: $C_0^e(X_1) - C_0^e(X_2) + P_0^e(X_2) - P_0^e(X_1) = PV(X_2 - X_1)$

Boundary Condition	Boundary Condition Violation	Arbitrage Strategy $C_0^e(X_1) - C_0^e(X_2) + P_0^e(X_2) - P_0^e(X_1) < PV(X_2 - X_1)$	
		Long	Short
$C_0^e(X_1) - C_0^e(X_2) +$ $P_0^e(X_2)$ $-P_0^e(X_1) = PV(X_2 - X_1)$	$C_0^e(X_1) - C_0^e(X_2) +$ $P_0^e(X_2)$ $-P_0^e(X_1) < PV(X_2 - X_1)$	Long in $[C_0^e(X_1) - C_0^e(X_2) +$ $P_0^e(X_2) - P_0^e(X_1)]$ Short in PV $(X_2 - X_1)$	1. Buy X_1 call 2. Sell X_2 call 3. Buy X_2 put 4. Sell X_1 put 5. Short bond with face value of $X_2 - X_1$

- **Strategy yields a positive cash flow of $PV(X_2 - X_1) - [C_0^e(X_1) - C_0^e(X_2) + P_0^e(X_2) - P_0^e(X_1)]$**
- **At expiration, there are no liabilities**

Cash Flows from Closing Short Box Spread and Long Bond

	Expiration Cash Flow		
Position	$S_T < X_1$	$X_1 \leq S_T \leq X_2$	$S_T > X_2$
Short X_1 call	0	$-(S_T - X_1)$	$-(S_T - X_1)$
Long X_2 Call	0	0	$S_T - X_2$
Long X_1 Put	$X_1 - S_T$	0	0
Short X_2 Put	$-(X_2 - S_T)$	$-(X_2 - S_T)$	0
Long Bond	$X_2 - X_1$	$X_2 - X_1$	$X_2 - X_1$
	0	0	0

spread equation does not hold, then, as shown in Exhibits 9.17 and 9.18, arbitrage opportunities will exist.

As we did with the put-call parity model, the box spread equation can be solved in terms of any of the options' prices to define that option's equilibrium price. For example, solving for $C_0^e(X_1)$ we obtain:

$$C_0^e(X_1) = C_0^e(X_2) - P_0^e(X_2) + P_0^e(X_1) + PV(X_2 - X_1)$$

This equation shows the equilibrium price of the X_1 call depends on the value of bond $(PV(X_2 - X_1))$, a synthetic stock position formed with the higher exercise priced call and put, $(C_0^e(X_2) - P_0^e(X_2))$, and the price of the lower exercise priced put, $(P_0^e(X_1))$. If the equilibrium price for this option does not hold, then an arbitrage opportunity exists.

It should be noted that like the put-call parity relation, the box spread is defined in terms of the option values at expiration. As a result, the above equilibrium relations hold strictly for European and not for American options.

EXHIBIT 9.18 Proof of Box Spread Condition: $C_0^c(X_1) - C_0^c(X_2) + P_0^e(X_2) - P_0^e(X_1) = PV(X_2 - X_1)$

Boundary Condition	Boundary Condition Violation	Arbitrage Strategy $C_0^c(X_1) - C_0^c(X_2) + P_0^e(X_2) - P_0^e(X_1) > PV(X_2 - X_1)$	
		Short	Long
$C_0^c(X_1) - C_0^c(X_2) +$ $P_0^e(X_2) - P_0^e(X_1) =$ $PV(X_2 - X_1)$	$C_0^c(X_1) - C_0^c(X_2) +$ $P_0^e(X_2) - P_0^e(X_1)$ $> PV(X_2 - X_1)$	Short in $[C_0^c(X_1) - C_0^c(X_2) +$ $P_0^e(X_2) - P_0^e(X_1)]$ Long in $PV(X_2 - X_1)$	1. Sell X_1 call 2. Buy X_2 call 3. Sell X_2 put 4. Buy X_1 put 5. Long bond with face value of $X_2 - X_1$

- **Strategy yields an initial positive cash flow of** $-PV(X_2 - X_1) + [C_0^e(X_1) - C_0^e(X_2) + P_0^e(X_2) - P_0^e(X_1)]$
- **At expiration, there are no liabilities**

Cash Flows from Closing Long Box Spread and Short Bond

Position	Cash Flows at Expiration		
	$S_T < X_1$	$X_1 \leq S_T \leq X_2$	$S_T > X_2$
Long X_1 Call	0	$S_T - X_1$	$S_T - X_1$
Short X_2 Call	0	0	$-(S_T - X_2)$
Short X_1 Put	$-(X_1 - S_T)$	0	0
Long X_2 Put	$X_2 - S_T$	$X_2 - S_T$	0
Short Bond	$-(X_2 - X_1)$	$-(X_2 - X_1)$	$-(X_2 - X_1)$
	0	0	0

Boundary Conditions Governing Non-Stock Options

The arbitrage pricing relationships governing stock options can be extended to establish the boundary conditions and price relationships for index options, futures, and currencies.

Put-Call Parity for Spot Index and Spot Portfolio

Determining boundary conditions such as the put-call parity model for an index option requires defining arbitrage strategies involving positions in the underlying portfolio. To go long in the S&P 500 would require the simultaneous purchase of the index's 500 stocks in their correct proportions and the correct reinvestment of each stock's dividends for the option period. In practice, arbitrageurs can take positions in smaller proxy portfolios. In Chapter 3, we discussed index arbitrage and how a proxy portfolio could be formed with a small number of securities whose allocations in the portfolio were determined so as to maximize the correlation between the portfolio's returns and the spot index. A proxy portfolio also might be formed with a highly diversified mutual fund or ETF, such as a spider. The proxy portfolio, mutual fund, or ETF can be viewed as a position in the index. For example, suppose there is a highly diversified portfolio worth $5 million, paying dividends expected to be worth $250,000 one year later, and having a beta of one. If the spot S&P 500 were at 2,000, this portfolio could be viewed as equivalent to a hypothetical S&P 500 spot portfolio consisting of $N_0 = 2,500$ hypothetical shares of the index, with each share priced at $S_0 = \$2,000$ and with expected dividends per share of $100 ($D_T = \$250,000/2,500$):

$$V_0^P = N_0 S_0$$
$$V_0^P = (2,500)(\$2,000) = \$5,000,000$$

$$D_T = \frac{\text{Total expected dividends}}{N_0} = \frac{\$250,000}{2,500} = \$100$$

The proxy portfolio, in turn, can be used to determine arbitrage strategies not only for index futures but also index spot and futures option when they are mispriced. For example, suppose the S&P 500 spot index were currently at 2,000, the risk-free rate was at 5%, and the price of a European 2,000 S&P 500 index spot call expiring in one year was trading at 75. The put-call parity condition with dividends would require that the price of a European 2,000 S&P 500 put expiring in one year to also be equal to 75 (note: this is because the dividend yield and risk-free are both equal to 5%):

$$P_0^{e*} = C_0^e - S_0 + PV(X + D_T)$$
$$P_0^{e*} = 75 - 2,000 + \frac{2,000 + 100}{1.05} = 75$$

If the put were underpriced at 60, then an arbitrage could be formed by buying the put, selling the call, buying the index, and shorting the bond:

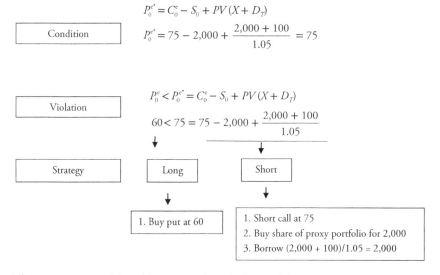

This strategy would yield an initial cash flow of $15 per index share, with no liabilities at expiration when the position is closed.

EXHIBIT 9.19 Arbitrage Using Proxy Portfolio when the Put-Call-Parity Condition for Index Options Is Violated

Condition	$P_0^{e^*} = C_0^e - S_0 + PV(X + D_T)$
	$P_0^{e^*} = 75 - 2{,}000 + \dfrac{2{,}000 + 100}{1.05} = 75$
Violation	$P_0^e < P_0^{e^*} = C_0^e - S_0 + PV(X + D_T)$
	$60 < 75 = 75 - 2{,}000 + \dfrac{2{,}000 + 100}{1.05}$

Strategy	1. Buy put at 60	1. Short call at 75
		2. Buy share of proxy portfolio for 2,000
		3. Borrow 2,000 + 100/1.05 = 2,000

Proxy Portfolio: Value = $5,000,000, Expected Total Dividends = $250,000, Beta = 1

Initial Position	Cash Flow	
Put Purchase: Buy 25 S&P 500 2,000 puts at 60	Cash Outflow = (25)(100)(60)	– $150,000
Call Sale: Sell 25 S&P 500 2,000 calls at 75	Cash Inflow = (25)(100)(75)	+ $187,500
Purchase Proxy Portfolio: $5,000,000	Cash Outflow = $5,000,000	– $5,000,000
Borrow $PV(X)$: Borrow $5,250,000/1.05	Cash Inflow = $1,179,245	+ $5,000,000
		+ $37,500

Closing Position	Market Increase $g = 10\%$ $S_T = 2{,}000(1.10)$ $= 2{,}200$		Market Decrease $g = -10\%$ $S_T = 2{,}000(0.90)$ $= 1{,}800$	
Sell 25 puts at $IV = \text{Max}[2000 - S_T, 0]$	= (25)(100)(0)	0	= (25)(100)(200)	$500,000
Buy 25 calls at $IV = \text{Max}[S_T - 2000, 0]$	= –(25)(100)(200)	–$500,000	= –(25)(100)(0)	0
Sell Proxy Portfolio: $5,000,000(1 + g)$	= $5,500,000	$5,500,000	= $5,500,000	$4,500,000
Receive Dividends: $250,000	= $250,000	$250,000	= $250,000	$250,000
Repay Debt: $5,000,000(1.05)	= –$5,250,000	–$5,250,000	= –$5,250,000	–$5,250,000
		0		0

This arbitrage can also be realized with the $5 million proxy portfolio. Since the proxy portfolio is equivalent to 2,500 hypothetical shares of the index when the index is at 2,000, an arbitrageur could:

1. Buy 25 puts (index shares/100 multiplier = 2,500/100) at 60
2. Sell 25 calls at 75 (index shares/100 multiplier = 2,500/100)
3. Borrow $5 million = ($5,000,000 + $250,000)/1.05 ($PV(X + D_T)$) = Index times hypothetical shares = (2,000)(2,500)
4. Invest $5 million in the proxy portfolio

As shown in Exhibit 9.19, the arbitrageur would realize an initial cash flow of $37,500 (initial arbitrage cash flow per the index times the number of hypothetical index shares defining the proxy portfolio: 15(2,500) = $37,500). At expiration, the arbitrageur would sell her portfolio, close her option positions, receive the portfolio's dividends, and repay her $5,250,000 debt. She, in turn, would have no liabilities provided the proxy portfolio is perfectly correlated with the S&P 500. For example, if one year later the market increased by 10% ($g = 0.10$) such that the S&P 500 were at $2,200 = (2,000(1.10))$, then

1. The portfolio (if it were perfectly correlated) would be worth $5,500,000 (= $5,000,000(1.10)).
2. $250,000 in dividends would be received.
3. The cost of debt would be $5,250,000 (= $5,000,000(1.05)).
4. The 2,000 puts would be worthless.
5. It would cost $500,000 to close the short 2,000 calls at their intrinsic value of 20: $(25)(100) \text{Max}[S_T - X, 0] = (25)(100)\text{Max}[2,200 - 2,000, 0] = \$500,000$.

The net cash flow in this case would be zero. Thus, there would be no liability at a spot index of 2,200.

In contrast, if the market decreased by 10% ($g = -0.10$) one year later such that spot S&P 500 was at 1,800 (= (2,000)(0.90)), then:

1. The proxy portfolio (if it were perfectly correlated) would be worth $4,500,000 (= ($5,000,000)(0.90)).
2. $250,000 in dividends would be received.
3. The cost of debt still would be $5,250,000 (= $5,000,000(1.05)).
4. The 2,000 calls would be worthless.
5. The long position in the 2,000 puts would generate a cash flow of $500,000 when the arbitrageur sold them at their intrinsic value of $500,000: $(25)(100) \text{Max}[X - S_T, 0] = (25)(100)\text{Max}[2,000 - 1,800, 0] = \$500,000$.

The net cash flow would again be zero. Thus, there would be no liability at a spot index of 1,800. In fact, for any spot index, there are no liabilities, provided the proxy portfolio is perfectly correlated and expected dividends of $250,000 are received (see Exhibit 9.19).

By earning an initial cash flow of $37,500, with no liabilities at expiration, arbitrageurs would try to set up this arbitrage strategy with the proxy portfolio and index options. By their action, though, they would decrease the call price and increase the put price until the initial cash flow were zero or equivalently where the put-call parity condition defining index options is met.

Put-Call Parity for Currency Spot Options

Since foreign currency can be invested in interest-bearing securities, the boundary conditions governing currency options are similar to stock and stock index options that pay dividends. Recall that the put-call parity model for stock options was derived by determining the European call and put prices in which the arbitrage profit from a conversion (or reversal) strategy was zero. For European currency options, a conversion is formed by:

1. Taking a long position in the foreign currency in which $E_0/(1 + R_{FC})^T$ dollars are converted to foreign currency and invested in a foreign risk-free security at a rate on the foreign currency of R_{FC}. E_0 = dollar price of foreign currency (FC): $E_0 = \$/FC$.
2. Forming a synthetic short position in foreign currency by taking a short position in a European currency call and a long position in a European currency put.

As shown in Exhibit 9.20, at expiration the foreign currency conversion yields a certain cash flow equal to the exercise price on the options. As a result, in equilibrium the value of the conversion should be equal to the present value of a domestic (US dollar) riskless bond (Rate of $R_\$$) with a face value equal to X. Thus, the put-call parity relation for European spot currency options is:

$$P_0^e - C_0^e + \frac{E_0}{(1 + R_{FC})^T} = \frac{X}{(1 + R_{f(\$)})^T}$$

$$P_0^e = C_0^e - \frac{E_0}{(1 + R_{FC})^T} + \frac{X}{(1 + R_{f(\$)})^T}$$

$$C_0^e = P_0^e + \frac{E_0}{(1 + R_{FC})^T} - \frac{X}{(1 + R_{f(\$)})^T}$$

Put-Call Futures Parity

When an asset has both an option and a futures contract, the put, call, futures, and spot prices all are related to each other. The relation between options and futures can be seen in terms of the put-call-futures parity model.

The put-call-futures parity model is similar to the put-call parity model. As the name implies, though, the put-call-futures parity model is derived using a futures position on the option's underlying asset instead of a position in the spot asset. The model's conversion strategy consists of a long position in a futures contract price at f_0 and a synthetic short futures position formed by buying a European put and selling a European call on the futures' underlying spot security, with the options having the same expiration date as the futures contract. As shown in Exhibit 9.21, with the price of the expiring futures contract (f_T) equal to the spot price on the underlying asset (S_T) at expiration, the value of the conversion formed with a long

EXHIBIT 9.20 Foreign Currency Conversion

Position
1. Convert $E_0/(1+R_{FC})^T$ dollars to $(1+R_{FC})^{-T}$ units of foreign currency (FC) and invest in foreign risk-free security at rate R_{FC}; the investment is worth one FC and E_T dollars at expiration.
2. Sell FC spot call and buy FC spot put

Position	Dollar Value of Conversion at Expiration		
	$E_T < X$	$E_T = X$	$E_T > X$
Dollar Value of Foreign Investment	E_T	E_T	E_T
Short Call	0	0	$-(E_T - X)$
Long Put	$X - E_T$	0	0
	X	X	X

EXHIBIT 9.21   Put-Call-Futures Parity: Conversion: $\{+f_0, +P_0^e, -C_0^e\}$

Position	Investment	Expiration Cash Flow		
		$S_T < X$	$S_T = X$	$S_T > X$
Long Futures	0	$S_T - f_0$	$S_T - f_0$	$S_T - f_0$
Long Put	P_0^e	$X - S_T$	0	0
Short Call	$-C_0^e$	0	0	$-(S_T - X)$
		$X - f_0$	$X - f_0$	$X - f_0$
	$P_0^e - C_0^e$			

position in a futures contract is $X - f_0$ at expiration, regardless of the spot price. Thus, the equilibrium value of the conversion with a futures position is equal to the value of a riskless zero discount bond with a face value of $X - f_0$ and maturity of T:

$$P_0^e - C_0^e + V_0^F = PV(X - f_0)$$

$$P_0^e - C_0^e + 0 = PV(X - f_0)$$

$$P_0^e - C_0^e = \frac{X - f_0}{(1 + R_f)^T}$$

where the initial value of the futures contract (V_0^F) is zero. If the equilibrium condition for put-call-futures parity does not hold, then an arbitrage opportunity will exist by taking a position in the put and futures contract and an opposite position in the call and a riskless bond with face value equal to $X - f_0$.

Equivalence Between Put-Call-Spot and Put-Call-Futures Parity Models

The put-call-futures parity model defines the equilibrium relationship between call, put, and futures prices. If the carrying-costs model holds, then the put-call-futures parity model and the put-call parity model defined for the underlying spot will be equivalent. The equivalence of the models can be shown algebraically simply by substituting the carrying-cost equation for f_0 in the put-call futures parity condition to obtain the put-call parity equation defined in terms of the spot asset. If the applicable carrying-costs model is $f_0 = S_0(1 + R)^T$ (such as a futures on a Eurodollar contract), then:

$$P_0^e - C_0^e = \frac{X - f_0}{(1 + R_f)^T}$$

$$P_0^e - C_0^e = \frac{X - S_0(1 + R_f)^T}{(1 + R_f)^T}$$

$$P_0^e - C_0^e = \frac{X}{(1 + R_f)^T} - S_0$$

Note that for foreign currency positions, the put-call-spot parity and put-call-futures parity also includes the foreign interest rate. That is, the foreign currency put-call-futures model is:

$$P_0^e - C_0^e + \frac{E_0}{(1 + R_{FC})^T} = \frac{X}{(1 + R_{f(\$)})^T}$$

and the carrying-cost for currency futures (interest rate parity) is

$$f_0 = E_0 \left[\frac{1 + R_{f(\$)}}{1 + R_{FC}} \right]^T$$

Thus, substituting the carrying cost for currency futures for f_0 in the put-call futures we obtain the foreign currency put-call-parity condition derived above:

$$P_0^e - C_0^e = \frac{(X - f_0)}{(1 + R_{f(\$)})^T}$$

$$P_0^e - C_0^e = \left[X - E_0 \left[\frac{1 + R_{f(\$)}}{1 + R_{FC}} \right]^T \right] \frac{1}{(1 + R_{f(\$)})^T}$$

$$P_0^e - C_0^e + \frac{E_0}{(1 + R_{FC})^T} = \frac{X}{(1 + R_{f(\$)})^T}$$

Finally, in the case of stock index future, the carrying cost is $f_0 = S(1 + R_f)^T - D_T$. Substituting into put-call futures parity, we obtain the put-call spot parity condition for stock index options:

$$P_0^e - C_0^e + V_0^F = \frac{X - f_0}{(1 + R_f)^T}$$

$$P_0^e - C_0^e + 0 = \frac{X - f_0}{(1 + R_f)^T}$$

$$P_0^e - C_0^e = \frac{X - (S_0(1 + R_f)^T - D_T)}{(1 + R_f)^T}$$

$$P_0^e - C_0^e = \frac{X + D_T}{(1 + R_f)^T} - S_0$$

$$P_0^e - C_0^e = PV(X + D_T) - S_0$$

The equivalence between put-call spot and put-call futures suggests that arbitrage strategies can be implemented by taking positions in the futures contract instead of underlying spot position. To see this, consider the previous example in which the 2,000 S&P 500 index put was underpriced at 60 when it should have been priced at

75 (by put-call parity). Instead of using the \$5 million proxy portfolio, an arbitrageur could have alternatively taken:

1. Long position in the underpriced put at 60
2. Short position in call at 75
3. Long position in an S&P 500 futures at a carrying cost price of 2,000 ($f_0 = S_0 (1 + R_f)^T - D_T = 2,000(1.05) - 100$; assuming the dividend yield on the index equals the dividend yield on the proxy portfolio)
4. Short bond position of $PV(X - f_0)$, which is zero in this case where $X = f_0$.

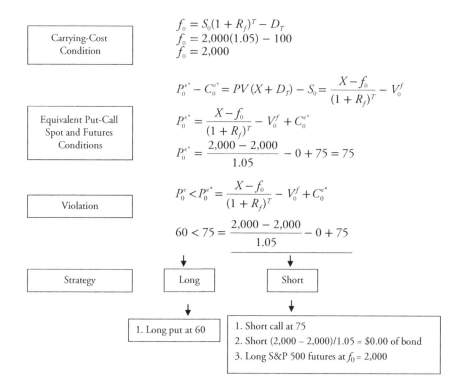

This strategy would yield an initial cash flow of \$15 per futures index share (without the futures multiplier of 250 and option multiplier of 100), with no liabilities at expiration when the position is closed. That is, at expiration, the arbitrageur would close her long futures position at an expiring futures price equal to the spot and close the call and put options (the arbitrageur would also have had to close a bond position if X had not been equal to f_0). She, in turn, would have no liabilities. For example, suppose one year later the market increased by 10% ($g = 0.10$) such that the S&P 500 were at $2,200 = (2,000(1.10))$. In this case, the arbitrageur would find the 2,000 puts out of the money and the long futures position at $f_T = S_T = 2,220$ providing a \$200 cash inflow ($f_T - f_0 = 2,200 - 2,000 = 200$), which would cover the loss on the short call S&P 500 call position of $IV = 200$ ($= \text{Max}[S_T - X, 0] = \text{Max}[2200 - 2000, 0] = 200$).

The net cash flow in this case would be zero. Thus, there would be no liability at a spot index of 2,200. In contrast, suppose the market decreased by 10% ($g = -0.10$) one year later, such that the spot S&P 500 would be at 1,800 ((2,000)(0.90)). In this case, the 2,000 S&P 500 call would be worthless and closing the long futures position would cost the arbitrageur 200 ($f_T - f_0 = 1{,}800 - 2{,}000 = -200$), but the 2,000 S&P 500 puts would be worth 200 ($f_T - f_0 = 1{,}800 - 2{,}000 = 200$). The net cash flow would again be zero. Thus, there would be no liability at a spot index of 1,800. In fact, for any spot index, there are no liabilities. Thus, by earning an initial cash flow of $15 per share, with no liabilities at expiration, arbitrageurs would try to set up this arbitrage strategy with the futures and index options. By their action, though, they would decrease the call price and increase the put price until the initial cash flow were zero or equivalently where the put-call spot parity and equivalent put-call futures parity condition defining index options are met.

Futures Options Price Conditions

Many of the option price relations and the arbitrage strategies governing spot option prices also apply to futures options. For example, as we noted in Chapter 6, the price on an American futures call option at time t must be at least equal to the call's intrinsic value as defined by the price on the futures contract at time t (f_t). Some of the arbitrage strategies described for spot options, such as the price relationships between spot options with different exercise prices and times to expirations are the same for futures options. Differences between spot and futures options do exist, however. For example, the minimum price of a European futures call is obtained by comparing a long futures position with a long position in the futures option and an investment in a riskless bond with a face value of $f_0 - X$. This contrasts with a spot or cash option in which the comparison is with a long position in the spot security and a call and bond with face value equal to X.

Like put-call spot and put-call-futures parity conditions, the put-call parity model for futures options can be derived from a conversion strategy consisting of a long position in the futures contract with a contract price of f_0 and a synthetic short futures position formed by purchasing a European futures put and selling a European futures call with an exercise price of X. As shown in Exhibit 9.22, if the options and the futures contract expire at the same time, then the conversion would be worth $X - f_0$ at expiration, regardless of the price on the futures contract. Since the conversion yields a riskless return, in equilibrium its value would be equal to the present value of a riskless bond with a face value of $X - f_0$:

$$P_0^e - C_0^e + V_0^f = \frac{X - f_0}{(1 + R_f)^T}$$

$$P_0^e - C_0^e + 0 = PV(X - f_0)$$

Note that this put-call parity condition for futures options is the same as the put-call-futures parity equilibrium condition. This equivalence should not be too surprising, since the values of the futures contract, spot options, and futures options all

EXHIBIT 9.22   Put-Call-Parity for Futures Options: Conversion: $\{+f_0, +P_0^e, -C_0^e\}$

Position	Investment	Expiration Cash Flow		
		$f_T < X$	$f_T = X$	$f_T > X$
Long Futures	0	$f_T - f_0$	$f_T - f_0$	$f_T - f_0$
Long Futures Put	P_0^e	$X - f_T$	0	0
Short Futures Call	$-C_0^e$	0	0	$-(f_T - X)$
	$P_0^e - C_0^e$	$X - f_0$	$X - f_0$	$X - f_0$

derive their values from the same underlying security and at expiration the prices on the expiring futures contract is equal to the spot price. Furthermore, if the carrying-cost model holds and the futures and options expire at the same time, then the put-call parity model for the European spot options will also be equal to put-call futures parity and put-call futures options parity.

Conclusion

Arbitrage involves buying and selling equivalent positions that are not equally priced. The exploitation of such opportunities by arbitrageurs serves to change the relative supplies and demands of the securities forming the positions until equilibrium is attained in which the positions are equally valued. In this chapter, we have explored how arbitrage strategies involving positions with options, underlying securities, and bonds govern the minimum and maximum option prices, the relative values of options with different exercise prices and times to expiration, and the relative values of puts and calls. The actual price of an option will be constrained by the boundary conditions identified in this chapter. In the next chapter, we examine the option pricing models, which are used to determine the equilibrium price of an option.

BLOOMBERG: CHART SCREEN, OMON, CALL, AND PUT

CHART
On the Chart screen, you can identify many of the relations and boundary conditions examined in this chapter by examining the historical prices for stock, index, and futures contracts and their call and put options with different expirations and exercise prices. On the Chart Menu screen, you can create multigraphs using the Standard G chart with your graphs in separate panels to evaluate the boundary relations. On the graph screens, you can edit the graph by going to the "Edit" dropdown tab. From the Edit dropdown, you can place graphs in separate panels (Securities and Data) and change colors and lines (Chart Colors and Lines) (see Exhibit 9.23).

EXHIBIT 9.23   Chart Screen

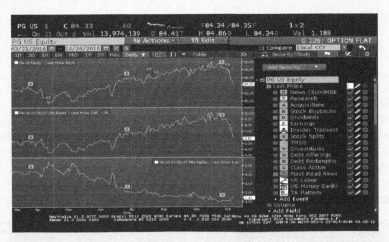

Information on Dividend Flag (D)

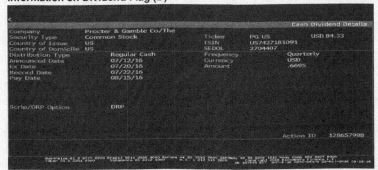

Information on "Most Read Information" Flag

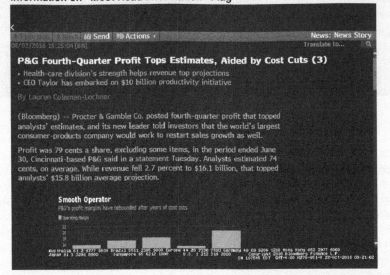

(*Continued*)

A useful tool on the chart page, as well as the GP screen, is the news and event identification flag. News and events such as dividends, "Most Read News," and insider trades can be flagged on the graph with the details access by clicking the flag. To create flags, click the flag icon on the top right side of the Chart or GP screen and then click the event.

OMON, CALL, AND PUT

Option price relations can be seen by looking at real-time pricing, market data, and data for exchange-traded call and put options found on OMON, CALL, and PUT. On the screen, you can compare option prices with different expirations and exercise prices (see Exhibit 9.24).

EXHIBIT 9.24   OMON

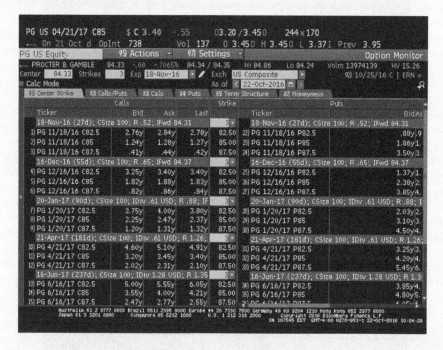

Selected References

Bodurtha, J., and G. Courtadon. "Efficiency Tests of the Foreign Currency Options Market." *Journal of Finance* 41 (March 1986): 151–162.

Cox, John C., and M. Rubinstein. *Option Markets*. Englewood Cliffs, NJ: Prentice-Hall, 1985: 127–163.

Galai, D. "Empirical Tests of Boundary Conditions for CBOE Options." *Journal of Financial Economics* 6 (June–September 1978): 187–211.

Galai, D. "A Survey of Empirical Tests of Option Pricing Models." In *Option Pricing*, edited by M. Brenner. Lexington, Mass.: Lexington Books, 1983, 45–80.

Hull, John C., *Options, Futures, and Other Derivatives,* 5th ed. Upper Saddle River, NJ: Prentice Hall, 2003, Chapter 8.

Johnson, L. "Foreign Currency Options, Ex Ante Exchange Rate Volatility, and Market Efficiency: an Empirical Test." *The Financial Review* (November 1986): 433–450.

Johnson, R. S. *Introduction to Derivatives: Options, Futures, and Swaps.* New York: Oxford University Press, 2009, Chapter 4.

Klemkosky, R., and B. Resnick. "Put-Call Parity and Market Efficiency." *Journal of Finance* 34 (December 1979): 1141–1155.

Klemkosky, R., and B. Resnick. "An *Ex Ante* Analysis of Put-Call Parity." *Journal of Financial Economics* 8 (1980): 363–378.

Merton, R. "The Relationship Between Put and Call Option Prices: Comment." *The Journal of Finance* 28 (March 1973): 183–184.

Merton, R. "Theory of Rational Option Pricing." *Bell Journal of Economics* 4 (Spring 1973): 141–183.

Stoll, H. "The Relationship Between Put and Call Option Prices." *Journal of Finance* 24 (May 1969): 319–332.

Problems and Questions

1. Prove the following conditions using an arbitrage argument. In your proof, show the initial positive cash flow when the condition is violated and prove that there are no liabilities at expiration:

   a. $C_t^a \geq \text{Max}[S_t - X, 0]$
   b. $C_t^e \geq \text{Max}[S_t - PV(X), 0]$
   c. $P_t^a \geq \text{Max}[X - S_t, 0]$
   d. $P_t^e \geq \text{Max}[PV(X) - S_t, 0]$
   e. $C_t^e(X_1) > C_t^e(X_2)$
   f. $P_t^e(X_2) > P_t^e(X_1)$
   g. $C_t^e(X_1) - C_t^e(X_2) < PV(X_2 - X_1)$
   h. $P_t^e(X_2) - P_t^e(X_1) < PV(X_2 - X_1)$
   i. $C_t^a(T_2) > C_t^a(T_1)$
   j. $P_t^a(T_2) > P_t^a(T_1)$
   k. $P_t^e + S_t = P_t^e + PV(X)$
   l. $C_t^e(X_1) - C_t^e(X_2) + P_t^e(X_2) - P_t^e(X_1) = PV(X_2 - X_1)$

2. Prove the following:

   a. End-of-period conversion value $= X$
   b. End-of-period reversal value $= -X$
   c. End-of-period long box spread value $= X_2 - X_1$
   d. End-of-period short box spread value $= -(X_2 - X_1)$

3. Prove mathematically the following condition for the early exercise of a call by a call holder: $D > TVP$.

4. Suppose just prior to going ex-dividend, XYZ stock is trading at $65 and is expected to go ex-dividend with a dividend expected to be worth $2.50 on the ex-dividend date. What advice would you recommend to a holder of an XYZ 60 American call option trading with a TVP of $1?

5. Suppose XYZ stock is trading $60, XYZ 60 European calls expiring in one year are trading at $3, and the annual risk-free rate is 3%. Using the put-call parity model determine the equilibrium price of an XYZ 60 European put expiring in one year.

6. Suppose XYZ stock is trading at $60, XYZ 60 European puts expiring in one year are trading at $2, and the annual risk-free rate is 3%. Using the put-call parity model, determine the equilibrium price of an XYZ 60 European call expiring in one year.

7. Determine the equilibrium price of a December S&P 500 call, given the S&P 500 put is trading at 50. Assume the spot SP 500 index is at 2,500, the risk-free rate is 5.00%, dividend per index share on the S&P 500 is $125 at the December expiration and one year.

8. PI Hedge Fund has formed a proxy portfolio that it is using to identify arbitrage opportunities using put-call parity relations. The proxy portfolio is highly correlated with the S&P 500 with a beta of 1, is currently worth $25 million, and is expected to pay dividends worth $1.25 million at the end of one year. The current S&P 500 index is at 2,500 and the risk-free rate is 5%.

   a. Define the PI Hedge Fund's proxy portfolio as an investment in hypothetical shares in the S&P 500. What is the dividend per index share?

   b. Determine the equilibrium price of a 2,500 S&P 500 index put expiring in one year given a 2,500 S&P 500 call expiring in one year trading at 50.

   c. Describe the arbitrage strategy PI could employ if the S&P 500 put were trading at 40.

   d. Evaluate PI's arbitrage strategy from c at the index's expiration by first assuming the market increases by 10%, then assuming it decreases by 10%. Assume the portfolio is perfectly correlated with the market.

9. Explain what arbitrageurs would do if the price of an American S&P 500 futures call with an exercise price of 2,100 were priced at 45 when the underlying futures price was trading at 2,150. What impact would their actions have in the futures option market on the call's price?

10. Explain what arbitrageurs would do if the price of an American S&P 500 futures put with an exercise price of 2,200 were priced at 45 when the underlying futures price was trading at 2,150. What impact would their actions have in the futures option market on the put's price?

11. Prove the following boundary conditions using an arbitrage argument. In your proof, show the initial positive cash flow when the condition is violated and prove there are no liabilities at expiration or when the positions are closed.

   a. European futures call option: $C_t \geq \text{Max}[PV(f_t - X), \ 0]$
   b. European futures put option: $P_t \geq \text{Max}[PV(X - f_t), \ 0]$
   c. Put-call futures parity for European futures options: $P_t - C_t = (X - f_t)/(1 + R_f)$

Bloomberg Exercises

1. Option price relations can be seen by looking at real-time pricing, market data, and data for exchange-traded call and put options found on OMON, CALL, and PUT. Using the OMON screen for selected a stock, examine to see if the following price relations hold:

   a. $C_t \geq \text{Max}[S_t - X, 0]$
   b. $P_t \geq \text{Max}[X - S_t, 0]$
   c. $C_t(X_1) > C_t(X_2)$
   d. $P_t^e(X_2) > P_t^e(X_1)$
   e. $C_t(X_1) - C_t(X_2) < X_2 - X_1$
   f. $P_t(X_2) - P_t(X_1) < X_2 - X_1$
   g. $C_t(T_2) > C_t(T_1)$
   h. $P_t(T_2) > P_t(T_1)$
   i. $P_t + S_t = P_t + PV(X)$
   j. $C_t^e(X_1) - C_t^e(X_2) + P_t^e(X_2) - P_t^e(X_1) = PV(X_2 - X_1)$

2. Use the Chart screen (Chart <Enter>) to generate historical prices of a selected stock and its call and put options with different expirations and expiration. Select a period in which the options were active. Create multigraphs on the Chart Menu screen using the Standard G chart with your graphs in separate panels. Evaluate the following boundary relations:

   a. Stock, call, and put prices
   b. The prices of call options with different exercise prices
   c. The prices of call options with different expirations
   d. The prices of put options with different exercise prices
   e. The prices of put options with different expirations

   Comment on the price relations. Remember that dividends may impact the stock and options near ex-dividend dates.

3. Use the Chart screen (Chart <Enter>) to generate historical prices for the S&P 500 spot, and call and put options on the index with different expirations and

expiration. Select a period in which the options were active. Create multigraphs on the Chart Menu screen using the Standard G chart with your graphs in separate panels. Evaluate the following boundary relations:

a. Index, call, and put prices
b. The prices of call options with different exercise prices
c. The prices of call options with different expirations
d. The prices of put options with different exercise prices
e. The prices of put options with different expirations

    Comment on the price relations.

4. Use the Chart screen (Chart <Enter>) to generate historical prices for a selected stock and its call and put options with the same expiration and exercise price. Using the "Flag" selection tool (click "Flag" icon tab), analyze the impact of the following events on the price of the stock, call, and put:

a. Ex-dividend date (click the "Dividends" flag and then identify the date by clicking the flag that appears on the graph).
b. "Most Read News"
c. Insiders transaction

CHAPTER 10

The Binomial Option Pricing Model

The two most widely used models for determining the equilibrium price of an option are the Black and Scholes (B-S) option pricing model (OPM) and the binomial option pricing model (BOPM). Black and Scholes derived their model in 1973 in a seminal paper in the *Journal of Political Economy*. The BOPM was discussed first by Stone (1973) and Sharpe (1978), then formalized by Cox, Ross, and Rubinstein (1979) and Rendleman and Bartter (1979). The models are similar in a number of ways. The major differences are the assumptions each makes concerning the underlying security price's fluctuations over time. In the BOPM, the time to expiration is partitioned into a discrete number of periods, each with the same length. In each period, the stock is assumed to follow a binomial process in which it either increases or decreases. The model then determines the equilibrium price of the option in which the cash flows from an arbitrage strategy consisting of positions in the security, option, and bond are zero for each discrete period. The B-S OPM, on the other hand, assumes a continuous process in which the time intervals are partitioned into infinitely small periods or, equivalently, the number of periods to expiration is assumed to approach infinity. In this continuous model, the price of the option is determined by assuming that the same arbitrage strategy used in the BOPM is implemented and revised continuously. Thus, the BOPM should be viewed as a first approximation of the B-S OPM. As the lengths of the intervals in the BOPM are made smaller, the discrete process merges into the continuous one and the BOPM and the B-S OPM converge.

In this and the next three chapters, we will examine the binomial and B-S option pricing models. In this chapter, we derive the binomial model for stock call and put options, and in Chapter 11, we examine the B-S model. In Chapter 12, we examine models for pricing equity index and futures options, and in Chapter 13, we examine the models for pricing bond and interest rate options.

In examining the BOPM, we begin by first deriving the model for call and put options under the assumption there is only one period to expiration. With this background, the single-period model will then be extended to the more realistic multiple-period case. Since the BOPM is based on arbitrage relations, we also will examine in this chapter the arbitrage strategies that market makers and other traders can pursue when the option's market price does not equal the BOPM value.

Single-Period BOPM

Single Period BOPM for Call Options

The equilibrium price of an option is based on the *law of one price*. This law states that two assets or portfolios with identical future cash flows must sell for the same price in order to avoid arbitrage opportunities. For example, if a call trades for $5 while a portfolio that exactly replicates the payoffs from a call trades for $10, we have an arbitrage opportunity. The price imbalance will create excess demand for the call and excess supply for the replicating portfolio forcing their respective prices to converge to a single value. Both the B-S model and BOPM are based on valuing options in terms of replicating a portfolio, thereby using the law of one price to establish the equilibrium price. For calls this price is found by equating the price of the call to the value of a replicating portfolio; that is, a portfolio constructed so that its possible cash flows are equal to the call's possible payouts.

Valuing a Call Option with a Replicating Portfolio

To construct a replicating portfolio, assume initially that options expire in one period, and at the end of the period, there are only two possible states. In this one-period, two-state case, assume that at the end of the period, a stock, currently priced at $S_0 = \$50$, will be worth either $S_u = \$55$ if the upstate occurs, or $S_d = \$47.50$ if the downstate occurs. Equivalently stated, assume that the stock will either increase to equal a proportion u times its initial price, where u is the relative stock price, S_u/S_0 ($u = 1.1$ in this case), or it will decrease to equal a proportion d times its initial value, S_d/S_0 ($d = 0.95$ in this case). See Exhibit 10.1a.

Next, consider a one-period European call option on the stock with an exercise price of $50. If the upstate occurs, the call will be worth its intrinsic value of $C_u = \$5$, and if the downstate occurs, the call will be worthless, $C_d = 0$ (see Exhibit 10.1a).

Third, assume there is a risk-free security to which funds can be lent (invested) or borrowed (sold short) for the period at a rate of R_f. To preclude arbitrage opportunities assume $d < r_f < u$, where $r_f = (1 + R_f)$. That is, if $r_f > u$, there would be arbitrage profits

EXHIBIT 10.1 Single-Period Binomial Values of Stock, Call, and Replicating Portfolio: $S_0 = \$50$, $u = 1.1$, $d = 0.95$, $R_f = 0.025$

a. Stock and Call Price

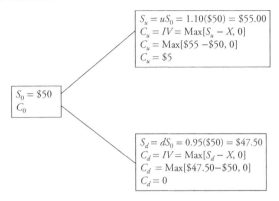

$$S_u = uS_0 = 1.10(\$50) = \$55.00$$
$$C_u = IV = \text{Max}[S_u - X, 0]$$
$$C_u = \text{Max}[\$55 - \$50, 0]$$
$$C_u = \$5$$

$$S_0 = \$50$$
$$C_0$$

$$S_d = dS_0 = 0.95(\$50) = \$47.50$$
$$C_d = IV = \text{Max}[S_d - X, 0]$$
$$C_d = \text{Max}[\$47.50 - \$50, 0]$$
$$C_d = 0$$

b. Replicating Portfolio

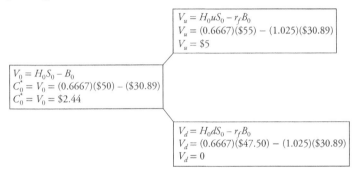

$$V_u = H_0 uS_0 - r_f B_0$$
$$V_u = (0.6667)(\$55) - (1.025)(\$30.89)$$
$$V_u = \$5$$

$$V_0 = H_0 S_0 - B_0$$
$$C_0^* = V_0 = (0.6667)(\$50) - (\$30.89)$$
$$C_0^* = V_0 = \$2.44$$

$$V_d = H_0 dS_0 - r_f B_0$$
$$V_d = (0.6667)(\$47.50) - (1.025)(\$30.89)$$
$$V_d = 0$$

by shorting the stock and buying the risk-free security; if $r_f < d$, there would be riskless profit by buying the stock and shorting the bond. To satisfy this condition, let us assume a period risk-free rate of 2.5% ($r_f = 1.025$) in our example.

With two securities (the stock and the risk-free security) and two states, a replicating portfolio with cash flows at the end of the period that exactly match the call's cash flows of the call can be formed by buying H_0 shares of stock at a price of S_0 partially financed by borrowing B_0 dollars at the risk-free rate. The current value of this portfolio, V_0, is:

$$V_0 = H_0 S_0 - B_0$$

(where the negative sign signifies borrowing) and, contingent upon the future state, at the end of the period the portfolio will have one of the following two possible values (see Exhibit 10.1b):

$$V_u = H_0 uS_0 - r_f B_0$$

$$V_d = H_0 dS_0 - r_f B_0$$

Given these two possible values, the replicating portfolio is found by solving for the unknowns, H_0 and B_0, that make the two possible portfolio values, V_u and V_d, equal to the two possible call values, C_u and C_d, in their respective states. Mathematically, this can be found by solving for the H_0 and B_0 values in which:

$$H_0 u S_0 - r_f B_0 = C_u$$

$$H_0 d S_0 - r_f B_0 = C_d$$

The solutions are:

$$H_0^* = \frac{C_u - C_d}{u S_0 - d S_0}$$

$$B_0^* = \frac{C_u(d S_0) - C_d(u S_0)}{r_f(u S_0 - d S_0)}$$

H_0^* is the ratio of the range in possible call values to stock values, often referred to as the *hedge ratio* or *delta value*. In our example:

$$H_0^* = \frac{C_u - C_d}{u S_0 - d S_0} = \frac{\$5 - 0}{\$55 - \$47.50} = 0.66667$$

$$B_0^* = \frac{C_u(d S_0) - C_d(u S_0)}{r_f(u S_0 - d S_0)} = \frac{(\$5)(\$47.50) - (0)(\$55)}{1.025[\$55 - \$47.50]} = \$30.89$$

Thus, to replicate the two possible call payouts one would need to purchase 0.6667 shares (assume perfect divisibility) of the stock at $50 per share, partially financed by borrowing $30.89. At the end of the period, this portfolio would replicate the two possible call payoffs of $5 or $0. That is:

$$V_u = (0.6667)(\$55) - (1.025)(\$30.89) = \$5$$

$$V_d = (0.6667)(\$47.50) - (1.025)(\$30.89) = 0$$

Finally, by the law of one price we can determine the equilibrium price of the call, C_0^*, by setting the current call value equal to the current value of the replicating portfolio:

$$C_0^* = H_0^* S_0 - B_0^*$$

For our example, the equilibrium call price is therefore $2.44 (see Exhibit 10.1b):

$$C_0^* = (0.6667)(\$50) - (\$30.89) = \$2.44$$

Single-Period Arbitrage Call Strategy

If the market price of the call, C_0^M, is not equal to C_0^*, then an arbitrage portfolio consisting of a position in the call and an opposite position in the replicating portfolio can be formed to take advantage of this mispricing opportunity. For example, if the call price in our illustrative example were $3.44 instead of $2.44, arbitrageurs could sell the expensive call for $3.44 and go long in the replicating portfolio (buy 0.6667 shares of stock at $50 and borrow $30.89 at 2.5%) to earn a positive cash flow of $1. As shown in Exhibit 10.2, at expiration, the cash flow at either stock price from closing the short call position and the long replicating portfolio position would cancel each other out and the initial profit of $1.00 would be worth $1.025. Thus, arbitrageurs would earn $1.025 with no cash outflows. As arbitrageurs try to sell calls at $3.44, however, they would push the price of the call down until it is equal to $2.44. At that price, the arbitrage opportunity is gone.

On the other hand, if the call is priced below $2.44, then the call is cheap relative to the replicating portfolio. In this case, arbitrage opportunities will exist by going long in the call and short in the replicating portfolio. For example, if $C_0^M = \$1.44$, then, as shown in Exhibit 10.3, arbitrageurs could buy the call and take a short position in the replicating portfolio (sell 0.6667 shares of stock short at $50 and invest $30.89 in a risk-free security) to earn a positive cash flow (or credit) of $1.00. At expiration, the cash flows at either stock price from closing the long call position and the short replicating portfolio position would again cancel each other out and the initial profit

EXHIBIT 10.2 Overpriced Call Arbitrage Strategy, Single-Period Case

$$S_0 = \$100, u = 1.1, d = .95, R_f = 0.025, X = \$50,$$
$$C_0^* = \$2.44, H_0^* = 0.6667, B_0^* = \$30.89, C_0^M = \$3.44$$

Initial Position	Cash Flow	Cash Flow
Sell Call	$C_0^M = \$3.44$	$3.44
Buy H_0^* Shares of Stock at $50	$-H_0^*(S_0) = -(0.6667)(\$50)$	−$33.33
Borrow B_0^* Dollars	$B_0^* = \$30.89$	$30.89
Initial Cash flow	$C_0^M - (H_0^* S_0 - B_0^*) = \$3.44 - \$2.44$	$1.00
	Cash Flow at Expiration	
Closing Position	$S_u = \$55$	$S_d = \$47.50$
	$C_u = \$5$	$C_d = 0$
Call: *IV*	−$5.00	0
Stock: (0.6667) S_T	$36.66	$31.66
Debt: ($30.89)(1.025)	−$31.66	−$31.66
	0	0
Value of Initial Cash Flow = $1(1.025)	$1.025	$1.025

EXHIBIT 10.3   Underpriced Call Arbitrage Strategy, Single-Period Case

$$S_0 = \$100, \; u = 1.1, \; d = .95, \; R_f = 0.025, \; X = \$50,$$
$$C_0^* = \$2.44, \; H_0^* = 0.6667, \; B_0^* = \$30.89, \; C_0^M = \$1.44$$

Initial Position	Cash Flow	Cash Flow
Buy Call	$-C_0^M = -\$1.44$	$-\$1.44$
Sell H_0^* Shares of Stock Short at \$50	$H_0^*(S_0) = (0.6667)(\$50)$	$\$33.33$
Invest B_0^* Dollars	$-B_0^* = -\$30.89$	$-\$30.89$
Initial Cash Flow	$(H_0^* S_0 - B_0^*) - C_0^M = \$3.44 - \$1.44$	$\$1.00$

	Cash Flow at Expiration	
Closing Position	$S_u = \$55$	$S_d = \$47.50$
	$C_u = \$5$	$C_d = 0$
Call: IV	$\$5.00$	0
Stock: $-(0.6667)\,S_T$	$-\$36.66$	$-\$31.66$
Investment: $(\$30.89)(1.025)$	$\$31.66$	$\$31.66$
	0	0
Value of Initial Cash Flow = $\$1(1.025)$	$\$1.025$	$\$1.025$

of \$1.00 would be worth \$1.025. Thus, arbitrageurs would earn \$1.025 with no cash outflows. As arbitrageurs try to buy calls at \$1.44, though, they would push the price of the call up until it is equal to \$2.44. At that price, the arbitrage opportunity is gone. Thus, in this binomial construct, arbitrage forces ensure that the price of the call will be equal to the value of the replicating portfolio.

Rewriting the Equilibrium Call Price Equation

The equation for the equilibrium price of the call can be rewritten by substituting the values of H_0^* and B_0^* into equilibrium equation:

$$C_0^* = H_0^* S_0 - B_0^*$$

$$C_0^* = \left[\frac{C_u - C_d}{(uS_0 - dS_0)} \right] S_0 - \left[\frac{C_u(dS_0) - C_d(uS_0)}{r_f(uS_0 - dS_0)} \right]$$

$$C_0^* = \frac{r_f S_0 [C_u - C_d] - [C_u(d) - C_d(u)] S_0}{r_f S_0 (u - d)}$$

$$C_0^* = \frac{1}{r_f} \left[\left(\frac{r_f - d}{u - d} \right) C_u + \left(\frac{u - r_f}{u - d} \right) C_d \right]$$

$$C_0^* = \frac{1}{r_f}[pC_u + (1-p)C_d]$$

where

$$p = \frac{r_f - d}{u - d}$$

$$1 - p = \frac{u - d}{u - d} - \frac{r_f - d}{u - d} = \frac{u - r_f}{u - d}$$

In terms of our illustrated example:

$$C_0^* = \frac{1}{1.025}[(0.50)(\$5.00) + (0.50)(0)] = \$2.44$$

where

$$p = \frac{1.025 - 0.95}{1.10 - .095} = 0.50$$

Risk-Neutral Pricing

The value of a risky asset is equal to the present value of the asset's expected cash flow, discounted at the risk-adjusted rate (k). In our one-period, two-state case, the values of the call and stock would be:

$$S_0 = \frac{E(S_T)}{(1+k)} = \frac{q(uS_0) + (1-q)(dS_0)}{1+k} = \frac{q(\$55) + (1-q)(\$47.50)}{1+k}$$

$$C_0 = \frac{E(C_T)}{(1+k)} = \frac{q(C_u) + (1-q)(C_d)}{1+k} = \frac{q(\$5.00) + (1-q)(0)}{1+k}$$

where q is the objective probability of the stock increasing in one period, and $(1-q)$ is the probability of it decreasing.

A risk-neutral market is defined as one in which investors will accept the same expected return ($E(k)$) from a risky investment as they would from a risk-free one. That is: $E(k) = R_f$; or equivalently the risk premium (RP) is zero: $RP = E(k) - R_f = 0$. In a risk-neutral market, the prices of all assets (risky and risk-free) are priced without regards to risk and determined by discounting the expected future payouts at the risk-free rate. In our option pricing example, if we assume a risk-neutral market, then the price of our stock and call would be:

$$S_0 = \frac{E(S_T)}{(1+k)} = \frac{q(uS_0) + (1-q)(dS_0)}{r_f} = \frac{q(\$55) + (1-q)(\$47.50)}{1.025}$$

$$C_0 = \frac{E(C_T)}{(1+k)} = \frac{q(C_u) + (1-q)(C_d)}{r_f} = \frac{q(\$5.00) + (1-q)(0)}{1.025}$$

Given the current price of the stock ($S_0 = \$50$) and the risk-free security ($R_f = 2.5\%$), if we solve mathematically for the probabilities q we obtain

$$\$50 = \frac{q(\$55) + (1-q)(\$47.50)}{1.0125}$$

$$q = 0.5$$

Or in parameter terms:

$$S_0 = \frac{q(uS_0) + (1-q)(dS_0)}{r_f}$$

$$q = \frac{r_f - d}{u - d}$$

The q value is the same as the p term derived from the BOPM replication approach. As such, the p parameter in the BOPM is often referred to as a *risk-neutral probability*. Substituting the risk-neutral probability into the one-period call equations, we obtain:

$$C_0^* = \frac{1}{r_f}[qC_u + (1-p)C_d] = \frac{1}{1.0125}[0.50(\$5.00) + (0.50)(0)] = \$2.44$$

The present value of the expected stock price is also equal to its current value using the risk-neutral probabilities:

$$S_0 = PV(E(S_t)) = \frac{E(S_T)}{r_f}$$

$$S_0 = \frac{1}{r_f}[puS_0 + (1-p)dS_0]$$

$$S_0 = \frac{1}{1.025}[(0.50)(\$55) + (0.50)(\$47.50)] = \$50$$

Thus, the equilibrium prices of options can be obtained by assuming that the option values are determined as though they and other securities are trading in a risk-neutral market. The reason options can be valued as though they were trading in a risk-neutral market is that they are redundant securities. In financial theory, a redundant security is one in which the security's possible outflows can be replicated by another security or portfolio. This implies that the redundant security can be valued by its arbitrage relation with the replicating asset, and not by investor preferences or the probabilities that investors assign to possible future outcomes. As we saw in deriving the BOPM, since we can replicate an option's payouts with a portfolio of its stock and a bond, the option is a redundant security, and therefore can be valued as though it were trading in a risk-neutral market. The risk-neutral pricing approach for pricing option is presented in more detail in Appendix 10A.

Single Period BOPM for Put Options

Similar to the pricing of a call option through a replicating portfolio, the equilibrium value of a European put also can be found by determining the value of a replicating put portfolio.

Valuing Put Options through a Replicating Portfolio

Consider again the one-period, two-state case in which a stock can either increase to equal $uS_0 = 1.1 (\$50) = \$55$ or decrease to equal $dS_0 = 0.95(\$50) = \$47.50$. A put on the stock that expires at the end of the period would, therefore, be worth either $P_u = \text{Max}[X - S_u, 0] = \text{Max}[\$50 - \$55, 0] = 0$, or $P_d = \text{Max}[X - S_d, 0] = [\$50 - \$47.50, 0] = \$2.50$. See Exhibit 10.4a.

Given the two possible stock prices and put values, a replicating put portfolio can be formed by purchasing H_0^P shares of stock and investing I_0 dollars in a risk-free

EXHIBIT 10.4 Single-Period Binomial Values of Stock, Put, and Replicating Portfolio: $S_0 = \$50$, $u = 1.1$, $d = 0.95$, $R_f = 0.025$

a. Stock and Put Values

$S_u = uS_0 = 1.10(\$50) = \$55.00$
$P_u = \text{Max}[X - S_u, 0]$
$P_u = \text{Max}[\$50 - \$55, 0] = 0$

$S_0 = \$50$
P_0

$S_d = dS_0 = 0.95(\$50) = \$47.50$
$P_d = \text{Max}[X - S_d, 0]$
$P_d = \text{Max}[\$50 - \$47.50, 0] = \$2.50$

b. Replicating Portfolio

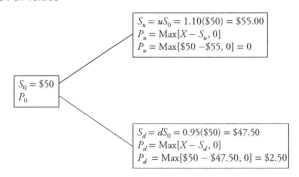

$V_u = H_0^P uS_0 + r_f I_0$
$V_u = (-0.3333)(\$55) + (1.025)(\$17.89)$
$V_u = 0$

$V_0 = H_0^P S_0 + I_0$
$P_0^* = V_0 = (-0.3333)(\$50) + (\$17.89)$
$P_0^* = V_0 = \$1.22$

$V_d = H_0^P uS_0 + r_f I_0$
$V_d = (-0.3333)(\$47.50) + (1.025)(\$17.89)$
$V_d = \$2.50$

security (Note: I_0 is the negative of borrowing B_0 dollars). The current value of this portfolio, V_0, is:

$$V_0 = H_0^P S_0 + I_0$$

and the portfolio's two possible values at expiration are:

$$V_u = H_0^P u S_0 + r_f I_0$$

$$V_d = H_0^P d S_0 + r_f I_0$$

For this portfolio to have possible values at expiration that match those of the put, H_0^P and I_0 must be such that:

$$H_0^P u S_0 + r_f I_0 = P_u$$

$$H_0^P d S_0 + r_f I_0 = P_d$$

Thus, solving the equation system simultaneously for H_0^{P*} and I_0^* we obtain:

$$H_0^{P*} = \frac{P_u - P_d}{u S_0 - d S_0}$$

$$I_0^* = \frac{-[P_u(d S_0) - P_d(u S_0)]}{r_f(u S_0 - d S_0)}$$

Note that since $P_d > P_u$, H_0^{P*} will be negative and I_0^* will be positive, except for the case in which $P_d = 0$. This implies that the replicating put portfolio is constructed with a short position in the stock (selling H_0^{P*} shares short) and a long position in the risk-free security (investing I_0^* dollars in a risk-free security). Thus, this strategy is just the opposite of the replicating call portfolio that is formed with a long position in the stock and borrowing funds.

In terms of out example:

$$H_0^{P*} = \frac{P_u - P_d}{u S_0 - d S_0} = \frac{0 - \$2.50}{\$55 - \$47.50} = -0.33333$$

$$I_0^* = \frac{-[P_u(d S_0) - P_d(u S_0)]}{r_f(u S_0 - d S_0)} = \frac{-[0(\$47.50) - (\$2.50)(\$55)]}{(1.025)(\$55 - \$47.50)} = \$17.89$$

At the end of the period, this portfolio would have possible values that match those of the put:

$$V_u = H_0^P u S_0 + r_f I_0 = (-0.33333)(\$55) + (1.025)(\$17.89) = 0$$

$$V_d = H_0^P d S_0 + r_f I_0 = (-0.33333)(\$47.50) + (1.025)(\$17.89) = \$2.50$$

Thus, by the law of one price, the equilibrium price of the put, P_0^*, would have to be equal to the value of the replicating put portfolio or arbitrage opportunities would exist. The equilibrium price of the put therefore is:

$$P_0^* = H_0^{P*} S_0 + I_0^*$$

And in terms of our example (see Exhibit 10.4b):

$$P_0^* = H_0^{P*} S_0 + I_0^*$$
$$P_0^* = (-0.33333)(\$50) + \$17.89 = \$1.22$$

Single-Period Arbitrage Strategy

If a put is not equal to its equilibrium value, then riskless profit can be earned from an arbitrage portfolio consisting of a position in the put and an opposite position in the replicating put portfolio. If the market price of the put, P_0^M is above P_0^*, then arbitrageurs would take a short position in the put and a long position in the replicating portfolio. For example, if the market price of the put in our above example were P_0^M = 2.22, then, as shown in Exhibit 10.5, an initial cash flow of $1.00 could be earned by selling the put, selling 0.33333 shares of the stock short, and investing $17.89 in a risk-free security. At expiration, the replicating portfolio would have possible values of

EXHIBIT 10.5 Overpriced Put Arbitrage Strategy, Single-Period Case

$S_0 = \$50$, $u = 1.1$, $d = .95$, $R_f = 0.025$, $X = \$50$, $P_0^* = \$1.22$, $H_0^{P*} = -0.33333$, $I_0^* = \$17.89$, $P_0^M = \$2.22$		
Initial Position	Cash Flow	Cash Flow
Sell Put	$P_0^M = \$2.22$	$2.22
Short H_0^{P*} Shares of Stock at $50	$H_0^{P*}(S_0) = (-0.3333)(\$50)$	$16.66
Invest I_0^* Dollars	$-I_0^* = \$17.89$	$-\$17.89
Initial Cash flow	$P_0^M - (H_0^{P*} S_0 + I_0^*) = \$2.22 - \$1.22$	$1.00
	Cash Flow at Expiration	
Closing Position	$S_u = \$55$	$S_d = \$47.50$
	$P_u = 0$	$P_d = \$2.50$
Put: IV	0	$-\$2.50
Stock: $(-0.3333) S_T$	$-\$18.33	$-\$15.83
Investment: $(\$17.89)(1.025)$	$18.33	$18.83
	0	0
Value of Initial Cash Flow $= \$1.00(1.025)$	$1.025	$1.025

EXHIBIT 10.6   Underpriced Put Arbitrage Strategy, Single-Period Case

$$S_0 = \$50, \ u = 1.1, \ d = .95, \ R_f = 0.025, \ X = \$50,$$
$$P_0^* = \$1.22, \ H_0^{P*} = -0.3333, \ I_0^* = \$17.89, \ P_0^M = \$0.22$$

Initial Position	Cash Flow	Cash Flow
Buy Put	$P_0^M = \$0.22$	−$0.22
Buy H_0^{P*} Shares of Stock at $100	$H_0^{P*}(S_0) = (-0.33333)(-\$100)$	−$16.66
Borrow I_0^* Dollars	$I_0^* = \$17.89$	$17.89
Initial Cash flow	$(H_0^{P*}S_0 + I_0^*) - P_0^M = \$1.22 - \$0.22$	$1.00

	Cash Flow at Expiration	
Closing Position	$S_u = \$55$	$S_d = \$47.50$
	$P_u = 0$	$P_d = 2.50$
Put: IV	0	$2.50
Stock: $(0.33333) \, S_T$	$18.33	$15.83
Debt: ($17.89)(1.025)	−$18.33	−$18.33
	0	0
Value of Initial Cash Flow = $1.00(1.025)	$1.025	$1.025

either 0 or $2.50 that would cover the possible put obligations, and the $1.00 initial cash flow would be worth $1.025. In contrast, if the put is below P_0^*, then an initial positive cash flow could be earned by going long in the put and short in the replicating put portfolio. For example, as shown in Exhibit 10.6, at $P_0^M = \$0.22$, a $1.00 profit is earned by implementing this underpriced arbitrage strategy.

Rewriting the Equilibrium Put Price Equation

The equation for equilibrium put value can be defined alternatively by substituting the equations for H_0^{P*} and I_0^* into equilibrium put equation and rearranging as follows:

$$P_0^* = H_0^{P*}S_0 + I_0^*$$

$$P_0^* = \left[\frac{P_u - P_d}{(uS_0 - dS_0)}\right]S_0 + \left[\frac{-[P_u(dS_0) + P_d(uS_0)]}{r_f(uS_0 - dS_0)}\right]$$

$$P_0^* = \frac{r_f S_0[P_u - P_d] - [P_u(d) - P_d(u)]S_0}{r_f S_0(u - d)}$$

$$P_0^* = \frac{1}{r_f} \left[\left(\frac{u - r_f}{u - d} \right) P_d + \left(\frac{r_f - d}{u - d} \right) P_u \right]$$

$$P_0^* = \frac{1}{r_f} [pP_u + (1 - p)C_d]$$

where

$$p = \frac{r_f - d}{u - d}$$

$$1 - p = \frac{u - d}{u - d} - \frac{r_f - d}{u - d} = \frac{u - r_f}{u - d}$$

In terms of our illustrated example:

$$P_0^* = \frac{1}{1.025} [(0.50)(0) + (0.50)(\$2.50)] = \$1.22$$

where

$$p = \frac{1.025 - 0.95}{1.10 - 0.95} = 0.50$$

Put-Call Parity Model

In Chapter 9, we delineated the put-call parity model. Recall that this model specifies the equilibrium relationship between the prices of call and put options on the same stock. In terms of the model, the equilibrium price of a European put is determined by the current value of a portfolio consisting of long positions in the call and riskless bond with a face value equal to the exercise price and a short position in the stock:

$$P_0^* = C_0^* + PV(X) - S_0$$

Using this model, we can determine the same equilibrium put price that we obtained using the binomial put model by substituting the equilibrium call price, as determined by the binomial call model. In terms of our examples, substituting the call value of $2.44, we obtain the same put values of $1.22 that we did using the binomial put model. That is:

$$P_0^* = C_0^* + PV(X) - S_0$$

$$P_0^* = \$2.44 + \frac{\$50}{1.025} - \$50 = \$1.22$$

Note on the Risk-Free Rate

In the BOPM, the risk-free rate used is the rate for the period. In calculating the risk-free rate, the rate on a Treasury or other risk-free security with a maturity equal to the option's expiration can be used. These rates are often quoted in terms of a simple annual rate (with no compounding). If a simple annual rate (R^A) is given, the period rate (R^P) needed for the BOPM is:

$$R^P = (1 + R^A)^{\Delta t} - 1$$

where Δt = Length of the binomial period as a proportion of a year

Thus, given a length of the binomial period of a quarter of a year, $\Delta t = 0.25$, and an annual risk-free rate of 3%, the periodic quarterly risk-free rate would be 0.7417% and r_f would be 1.007417:

$$R^P = (1.03)^{0.25} - 1 = 0.007417$$

$$r_f = (1 + R^P) = (1 + R^A)^{\Delta t}$$

$$r_f = (1 + 0.03)^{0.25} = 1.007417$$

Note, if we assume continuous compounding, the periodic rate is 0.7528% and r_f is 1.007528 for a binomial period of length 0.25 per year:

$$1 + R^P = r_f = e^{R^A \Delta t}$$

$$R^P = e^{R^A \Delta t} - 1$$

$$R^P = e^{(.03)(0.25)} - 1 = 0.007528$$

$$r_f = e^{R^A \Delta t}$$

Since most rates are quoted an annual basis, it is common to express the p term in the binomial equation in terms of the annualized risk-free rate:

$$p = \frac{r_f - d}{u - d} = \frac{e^{R^A \Delta t} - d}{u - d} \text{ or } p = \frac{(1 + R^A)^{\Delta t} - d}{u - d}$$

Pricing Options on Dividend-Paying Stocks—Single-Period BOPM

A future dividend payment affects the value of an option in two ways. First, on the ex-dividend date the price of the stock usually falls by an amount approximately equal to the dividend. This, in turn, leads to a decrease in the price of a call and an increase in the price of a put. Second, as we discussed in Chapter 9, a dividend payment may lead to an early exercise of a call just prior to the ex-dividend date and possibly a put on the ex-dividend date. If early exercise is advantageous, then an American option would be more valuable than a European one.

European Call Option

To see the implications dividends have on the BOPM, assume that in the illustrative example, the call is European and period starts on a non–ex-dividend date but expires on the stock's ex-dividend date where the stock falls by an amount equal to the value of the dividend on the ex-dividend date (D_1). If we let uS_0 and dS_0 be the possible stock prices at the end of the period, but just before the ex-dividend date, then the stock's possible prices on the ex-dividend date would be $S_u^x = uS_0 - D_1$ and $S_u^x = dS_0 - D_1$ (where x indicates ex-dividend date). Thus, if the stock in our single-period call example was expected to pay a dividend worth \$0.50 on the ex-dividend date, then the possible stock prices would be \$54.50 and \$47.00. Since exchange-traded call options are not dividend protected, the price of the call would, in turn, be less on an ex-dividend date (as compared to a non–ex-dividend date) if the call is in the money. In this example, the two possible call prices (equal to their *IV*s) at the ex-dividend expiration date would be \$4.50 and 0. See Exhibit 10.7a.

When the price of the underlying stock falls by an amount equal to the value of the dividend on the ex-dividend date, the dividend an arbitrageur with a replicating portfolio would earn (pay), $H_0 D_1$, from her long (short) position in the stock would be negated by the decrease in the price of the stock on the ex-dividend date. Thus, the arbitrageur's stock position in her replicating portfolio is determined by the stock prices just before the ex-dividend date (uS_0 and dS_0) and not the ex-dividend prices. See Exhibit 10.7b.

Given the possible call values and replicating portfolio values at expiration, the call's replicating portfolio is found by setting the two possible ex-dividend call prices equal to their respective replicating portfolio values and solving the two equations simultaneously for the H_0 and B_0:

$$H_0 uS_0 - r_f B_0 = C_u^x$$

$$H_0 dS_0 - r_f B_0 = C_d^x$$

$$H_0^* = \frac{C_u^x - C_d^x}{uS_0 - dS_0}$$

$$B_0^* = \frac{C_u^x(dS_0) - C_d^x(uS_0)}{r_f(uS_0 - dS_0)}$$

Thus, for the single-period BOPM, the only adjustment needed in forming the replicating portfolio is to subtract the value of the dividend from the two non–dividend-adjusted stock prices (uS_0 or dS_0) in computing both the call's possible intrinsic values (IV^x). In terms of our example, the H_0^* and B_0^* values needed to form

EXHIBIT 10.7 Single-Period Binomial Values of Stock, Call, and Replicating Portfolio When Stock Pays Dividend: $S_0 = \$50$, $u = 1.1$, $d = 0.95$, $D_1 = \$0.50$, $R_f = 0.025$

a. Stock and Call Value on Ex-Dividend Date, $D_1 = \$0.50$

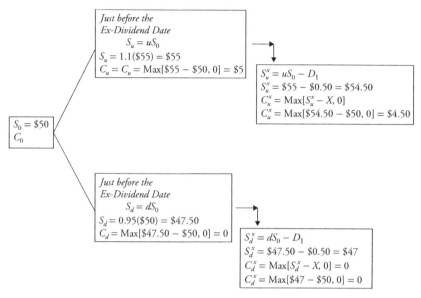

b. Replicating Portfolio

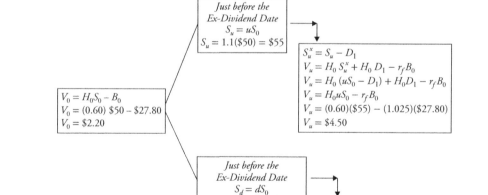

a replicating portfolio to match the possible call values of $C_u^x = Max[(\$55 - \$0.50) - \$50, 0] = \$4.50$ and $C_d^x = Max[(\$47.50 - \$0.50) - \$50, 0] = 0$ would be $\$0.60$ and $\$27.80$:

$$H_0^* = \frac{C_u^x - C_d^x}{uS_0 - dS_0} = \frac{\$4.50 - 0}{\$55 - \$47.50} = 0.60$$

$$B_0^* = \frac{C_u^x(dS_0) - C_d^x(uS_0)}{r_f((uS_0 - dS_0)} = \frac{(\$4.50)(\$47.50) - (0)(\$55)}{1.025[\$55 - \$47.50]} = \$27.80$$

The equilibrium call price therefore would be:

$$C_0^* = H_0^* S_0 - B_0^* = 0.6(\$50) - \$27.80 = \$2.20$$

$$C_0^* = \frac{1}{r_f}[pC_u^x + (1-p)C_d^x] = \frac{1}{1.025}[(0.50)(\$4.50) + (0.50)(0)] = \$2.20$$

Thus, when the ex-dividend date coincides with expiration, the BOPM is adjusted simply by subtracting the dividends from the possible stock prices just before the ex-dividend date in computing the intrinsic values of the call (see Exhibit 10.7b).

Note, if the market failed to incorporate the dividend in its call pricing, then an arbitrage opportunity would exist. For example, if the market priced the call with the BOPM, but failed to include the $0.50 dividend, then the market price of the call would be $2.44. At $C_0^M = \$2.44$, the call would be overpriced ($C_0^* = \$2.20$). To exploit this, arbitrageurs would go short in the call and long in the replicating portfolio: buy $H_0^* = 0.60$ shares of stock and borrow $B_0^* = \$27.80$. This strategy would yield arbitrageurs an initial cash flow of $0.24 with no liabilities at expiration. See Exhibit 10.8.

In the absence of arbitrage, the price of the European call would therefore be $2.20. Thus, by lowering the price of the stock on the ex-dividend date, dividends decrease the value of the call by approximately 10%. Moreover, the example highlights that a failure to incorporate dividend could lead to large pricing errors.

American Call Options

Suppose that in the preceding example the call was American and as a result could be exercised the instant before it traded ex-dividend. Given this early exercise opportunity, the call holder would find it advantageous at the upper node to exercise the call the instant before expiration when the exercise value is $5.00, instead of holding the option to expiration when the call value is only $4.50. No exercise advantage exists at the lower node when the stock price is at $47.50 just before expiration and $47 at expiration.

EXHIBIT 10.8 Arbitrage When the Market Price of the Call Excludes the Dividend—Single-Period Case

$$S_0 = \$50, \; u = 1.1, \; d = .95, \; R_f = 0.025, \; X = \$50, \; D_1 \; \$0.50,$$
$$C_0^* = \$2.20, \; H_0^* = 0.60, \; B_0^* = \$27.80, \; C_0^M = \$2.44$$

Initial Position	Cash Flow	Cash Flow
Sell Call	$C_0^M = \$2.44$	$2.44
Buy H_0^* Shares of Stock at $50	$-H_0^*(S_0) = -(0.60)(\$50)$	−$30
Borrow B_0^* Dollars	$B_0^* = \$27.80$	$27.80
Initial Cash Flow	$C_0^M - (H_0^* S_0 - B_0^*) = \$2.44 - \$2.20$	$0.24

	Cash Flow at Expiration	
Closing Position	$S_u^x = \$55 - \$0.50 = \$54.50$	$S_d^x = \$47.50 - \$0.50 = \$47$
	$C_u^x = \$4.50$	$C_d^x = 0$
Call ($C_T^M = IV$)	−$ 4.50	0
Stock ($H_0^* S_T = 0.6 \, S_T^x$)	$32.70	$28.20
Dividend ($H_0^* D = 0.6(\$0.50)$)	$0.30	0.30
Debt ($B_0^* r_f = \$27.80(1.025)$)	−$28.50	−$28.50
	0	0

Value of Initial Cash Flow = $0.24(1.025) = $0.246

The value of the American option in this case would be $2.44, compared to the $2.20 value for the European call that cannot be exercised until expiration:

$$C_0^{a*} = (0.6667)(\$50) - (\$30.89) = \$2.44$$

$$H_0^* = \frac{\text{Max}[IV_u, C_u^x] - \text{Max}[IV_d, C_d^x]}{uS_0 - dS_0} = \frac{\$5 - 0}{\$55 - \$47.50} = 0.6667$$

$$B_0^* = \frac{(\text{Max}[IV_u, C_u^x])(dS_0) - (\text{Max}[IV_d, C_d^x])(uS_0)}{r_f(uS_0 - dS_0)}$$

$$B_0^* = \frac{(\$5)(\$47.50) - (0)(\$55)}{1.025[\$55 - \$47.50]} = \$30.89$$

Or

$$C_0^{a*} = \frac{1}{r_f}[p(\text{Max}[IV_u, C_u^x]) + (1 - p)(\text{Max}[IV_d, C_d^x])]$$

$$C_0^{a*} = \frac{1}{1.025}[(0.50)(\$5) + (0.50)(0)] = \$2.44$$

Note: because of the early exercise advantage, the arbitrage position for the American option has a different replicating portfolio than the European call's replicating portfolio.

European Put Options

The dividend adjustments required for European put options are similar to those for calls. In the single-period case, if expiration is on the stock's ex-dividend date, the value of the dividend is subtracted from the stock price in determining the put's intrinsic value, and as with calls, no changes are necessary in the composition of the replicating put portfolio.

In terms of our illustrative example, the European put option on the stock would have possible intrinsic values at expiration of 0.00 and $3.00:

$$P_u^x = \text{Max}[X - (uS_0 - D_1),\ 0] = \text{Max}[\$50 - (\$55 - \$0.50),\ 0] = 0$$

$$P_d^x = \text{Max}[X - (dS_0 - D_1),\ 0] = \text{Max}[\$50 - (\$47.50 - \$0.50),\ 0] = \$3.00$$

and the equilibrium put price would be

$$P_0^* = H_0^{P*} S_0 + I_0^* = (-0.40)(\$50) + \$21.46 = \$1.46$$

$$P_0^* = \frac{1}{r_f}[pP_u + (1 - p)P_d] = \frac{1}{1.025}[(0.50)(0) + (0.50)(\$3)] = \$1.46$$

where

$$H_0^* = \frac{P_u^x - P_d^x}{uS_0 - dS_0} = \frac{0 - \$3.00}{\$55 - \$47.50} = -0.40$$

$$I_0^* = \frac{-[P_u^x(dS_0) - P_d^x(uS_0)]}{r_f(uS_0 - dS_0)} = \frac{-[(0)(\$47.50) - (\$3)(\$55)]}{1.025[\$55 - \$47.50]} = \$21.46$$

Note, if the market priced the put with the BOPM, but failed to include the dividend, then the market price of the put would be $1.22. At $P_0^M = \$1.22$, the put would be underpriced ($P_0^* = \$1.46$). To exploit this, arbitrageurs would go long in the put and short in the replicating put portfolio: buy 0.4 shares of stock and borrow $21.46. This strategy would yield arbitrageurs with an initial cash flow of $0.24 with no liabilities at expiration. See Exhibit 10.9.

In the absence of arbitrage, the price of the put on this dividend-paying stock is $1.46, approximately 20% greater than a comparable put on a non–dividend-paying stock. In general, by lowering the price of the stock on the ex-dividend date, a dividend increases the value of the put.

American Put Options

If the put option were American, then the exercise value just before the stock goes ex-dividend would be $2.50 at the stock's lower node (zero at the upper node), and an

EXHIBIT 10.9 Arbitrage When the Market Price of the Put Excludes the Dividend—
Single-Period Case

$$S_0 = \$50, \ u = 1.1, \ d = .95, \ R_f = 0.025, \ X = \$50, \ D_1 \ \$0.50,$$
$$P_0^* = \$1.46, \ H_0^{P*} = -0.40, \ I_0^* = \$21.46, \ P_0^M = \$1.22$$

Initial Position	Cash Flow	Cash Flow
Initial Cash flow	$-(H_0^{P*}S_0 - B_0^*) - P_0^M = \$1.46 - \$1.22$	$0.24
	Cash Flow at Expiration	
Buy Put	$P_0^M = \$1.22$	$-\$1.22$
Buy H_0^* Shares of Stock at $50	$H_0^*(S_0) = (0.40)(\$50) = \$20$	$-\$20.00$
Borrow I_0^* Dollars	$I_0^* = \$21.46$	$21.46
Closing Position	$S_u^x = \$55 - \$0.50 = 54.50$	$S_d^x = \$47.50 - \$0.50 = \$47$
	$P_u^x = 0$	$P_d^x = \$3$
Put ($C_T^x = IV$)	$0.00	$3.00
Stock ($H_0^{P*} \ S_T^x = 0.4 \ S_T$)	$21.80	$18.80
Dividend ($H_0^{P*}D = 0.4(\$0.50)$)	$0.20	0.20
Debt ($I_0^* r_f = \$21.46(1.025)$)	$-\$22.00$	$-\$22.00$
	0	0

Value of Initial Cash Flow = $0.24(1.025) = $0.246

instant later at expiration its intrinsic value would be $3.00. Thus, unlike an American call, the early exercise advantage for an American put does not occur just before the ex-dividend date. In this single-period example, the put would be equal to $3 at expiration when the stock is trading at its ex-dividend value of $47.00. If there were more periods to expiration, it is possible that the exercise value of $3.00 could exceed the binomial put value at the ex-dividend date. To reiterate, for an American put option on a dividend-paying stock, the early exercise advantage occurs on the ex-dividend dates, while for an American call option, the advantage occurs just before the ex-dividend date.

Put-Call Parity Model with Dividends

From Chapter 9, recall that when the underlying stock pays a dividend, the put-call parity model must be adjusted so that the value of a conversion ($\{+S_0, + P_0^e, - C_0^e\}$) will be equal to the present value of a portfolio consisting of a riskless pure discount bond with a face value equal to X plus the dividend value on the stock. That is:

$$P_0^e - C_0^e + S_0 = PV(X + D)$$

In our single-period dividend examples, the price of the European call was $2.20 and the price of the European put was $1.46, using the dividend-adjusted binomial option model. The same put (call) price can also be found using the above dividend-adjusted put-call parity model with the call (put) value determined from the binomial model. That is:

$$P_0^e - C_0^e + S_0 = PV(X + D)$$

$$P_0^e = C_0^e - S_0 + PV(X + D)$$

$$P_0^e = C_0^e - S_0 + \frac{X + D}{r_f}$$

$$P_0^e = \$2.20 - \$50 + \frac{\$50 + \$0.50}{1.025} = \$1.46$$

Multiple-Period BOPM

The Multiple-Period BOPM for Calls

In constructing the more realistic multiple-period BOPM, we divide the time to expiration into a number of subperiods of smaller length. As the length of the time period becomes smaller, the assumption that stock price changes follow a binomial process of either increasing or decreasing in each period then becomes more plausible, and, as the number of periods increases, the number of possible states at expiration is greater—again, adding more realism to the model. The mechanic for deriving a multiple-period model can be seen by examining a two-period model.

Two-Period BOPM

To illustrate option pricing in a two-period case, start with our preceding one-period case in which $S_0 = \$100$, $R_f = 0.025$, $u = 1.1$, and $d = 0.95$ and break the expiration period into two periods in which $u = 1.0488$, $d = 0.9747$, and $R_f = 0.0125$. With two periods, there are now three possible stock prices at expiration. As shown in Exhibit 10.10, the stock can either increase two consecutive periods to equal $S_{uu} = u^2 S_0 = (1.0488)^2 \$50 = \$55$, decrease two periods to equal $S_{dd} = d^2 S_0 = (0.9747)^2(\$100) = \$47.50$, or increase one period and decrease another to equal $S_{ud} = udS_0 = (1.0488)(0.9747)(\$50) = \$51.11$.

Follow this method for pricing a call option on a stock with two periods to expiration:

- Start at expiration, where we know the possible call values are equal to their intrinsic values.
- Next, move from expiration to period 1 and use the single-period BOPM to price the call at each possible stock price (S_u and S_d).
- Last, move to the present and price the call again using the single-period model.

As shown in Exhibit 10.11, the three possible call prices at expiration are: $C_{uu} = \text{Max}[\$55 - \$50, 0] = \$5$, $C_{ud} = \text{Max}[\$51.11 - \$50, 0] = \$1.11$, and $C_{dd} = \text{Max}[\$47.50 - \$50, 0] = 0$. Moving to period 1, the price of the call when the stock

EXHIBIT 10.10   Two-Period Binomial Values of Stock, $u = 1.0488$, $d = 0.9747$, and $n = 2$

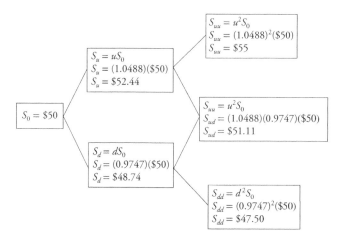

EXHIBIT 10.11   Two-Period Binomial Values of Stock, Call, and Replicating Portfolios: $S_0 = \$50$, $u = 1.0488$, $d = 0.9747$, $R_f = 0.0125$, $n = 2$

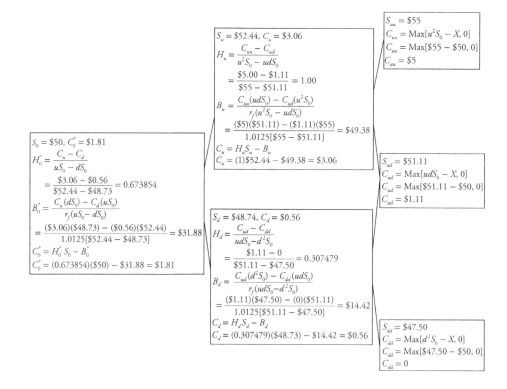

is $52.44 is $3.06, and the price when the stock is $48.75 is $0.56. That is, using the single-period BOPM, the call with one period to expiration would be priced at $C_u = \$3.06$ when the stock is at $S_u = \$52.44$:

$$C_u = \frac{1}{r_f}[pC_{uu} + (1-p)C_{ud}]$$

$$C_u = \frac{1}{1.0125}[(0.510121)(\$5.00) + (0.489879)(\$1.11)]$$

$$C_u = \$3.06$$

where

$$p = \frac{r_f - d}{u - d} = \frac{1.0125 - 0.9747}{1.0488 - 0.9747} = 0.510121$$

Or

$$C_u = H_u S_u - B_u$$

$$C_u = (1)\$52.44 - \$49.38$$

$$C_u = \$3.06$$

where

$$H_u = \frac{C_{uu} - C_{ud}}{u^2 S_0 - ud S_0} = \frac{\$5.00 - \$1.11}{\$55 - \$51.11} = 1.00$$

$$B_u = \frac{C_{uu}(ud S_0) - C_{ud}(u^2 S_0)}{r_f(u^2 S_0 - ud S_0)} = \frac{(\$5)(\$51.11) - (\$1.11)(\$55)}{1.0125[\$55 - \$51.11]} = \$49.38$$

If the call is not priced at $3.06, an arbitrage portfolio could be formed with a position in the call (long if the call is underpriced and short if it is overpriced) and an opposite position in a replicating portfolio with $H_u = 1$ and B_u of $49.38.

When the stock is priced at $48.73, the call would have to be priced at $C_d = \$0.56$ or an arbitrage profit could be obtained by taking opposite positions in the call and a replicating portfolio with $H_d = 0.307479$ and $B_d = \$14.42$:

$$C_d = \frac{1}{r_f}[pC_{ud} + (1-p)C_{dd}]$$

$$C_d = \frac{1}{1.0125}[0.510121(\$1.11) + (0.489879)(0)]$$

$$C_u = \$0.56$$

Or

$$C_d = H_d S_d - B_d$$

$$C_d = (0.307479)(\$48.73) - \$14.42$$

$$C_d = \$0.56$$

where

$$H_d = \frac{C_{ud} - C_{dd}}{udS_0 - d^2S_0} = \frac{\$1.11 - 0}{\$51.11 - \$47.50} = 0.307479$$

$$B_d = \frac{C_{ud}(d^2S_0) - C_{dd}(udS_0)}{r_f(udS_0 - d^2S_0)} = \frac{(\$1.11)(\$47.50) - (0)(\$51.11)}{1.0125[\$51.11 - \$47.50]} = \$14.42$$

Finally, given the possible stock prices S_u and S_d and call values C_u and C_d for period 1, we move to the present and again use the single-period BOPM to find the call's current value. In this example, the 50 call would be worth $C_0^* = \$1.81$:

$$C_0^* = \frac{1}{r_f}[pC_u + (1-p)C_d]$$

$$C_0^* = \frac{1}{1.0125}[(0.510121)(\$3.06) + (0.489879)(\$0.56)]$$

$$C_0^* = \$1.81$$

Or

$$C_0^* = H_0^* S_0 - B_0^*$$

$$C_0^* = (0.673854)(\$50) - \$31.88$$

$$C_0^* = \$1.81$$

where

$$H_0^* = \frac{C_u - C_d}{uS_0 - dS_0} = \frac{\$3.06 - \$0.56}{\$52.44 - \$48.73} = 0.673854$$

$$B_0^* = \frac{C_u(dS_0) - C_d(uS_0)}{r_f(uS_0 - dS_0)} = \frac{(\$3.06)(\$48.73) - (\$0.56)(\$52.44)}{1.0125[\$52.44 - \$48.73]} = \$31.88$$

If the call is not priced at $1.81, an arbitrage profit could be earned from an arbitrage portfolio with $H_0^* = 0.673854$ and $B_0^* = \$31.88$:

Equation for the Two-Period BOPM

Mathematically, the model for pricing a European call with two periods consists of three equations for C_d, C_u, and C_0. The model can be defined in terms of one equation, by substituting the equations for C_d and C_u into the equation for C_0 and rearranging so that:

$$C_0^* = \frac{1}{r_f}[pC_u + (1-p)C_d]$$

$$C_0^* = \frac{1}{r_f}\left[p\left[\frac{pC_{uu} + (1-p)C_{ud}}{r_f}\right] + \left[\frac{pC_{ud} + (1-p)C_{dd}}{r_f}\right]\right]$$

$$C_0^* = \frac{1}{r_f^2}[p^2 C_{uu} + 2p(1-p)C_{ud} + (1-p)^2 C_{dd}]$$

n-Period BOPM

If the time interval to expiration is subdivided into three subperiods ($n = 3$), the terminal stock prices can take one of four possibilities: $S_{uuu} = u^3 S_0$, $S_{uud} = u^2 d S_0$, $S_{udd} = ud^2 S_0$, and $S_{ddd} = d^3 S_0$. Using the binomial approach to value a call option, we again would start at expiration where we know the call's four possible intrinsic values, and then we would move to each preceding period, using the single-period BOPM to price the call at each possible stock price. In general, if the time interval is subdivided into n-subperiods, the terminal stock prices can take on one of $n + 1$ possible values at expiration. To obtain a general n-period equation for the equilibrium call price that is similar to two-period equation, we again move from expiration to each preceding period, substituting the single-period BOPM equations associated with each call value and stock price in each period. This process results in the following n-period BOPM equation

$$C_0^* = \frac{1}{r_f^n}\left[\sum_{j=0}^{n} \frac{n!}{(n-j)!j!} \; p^j \; (1-p)^{(n-j)} \; [\text{Max}[u^j d^{(n-j)} S_0 - X, 0)]\right]$$

where

j = the number of upward moves in the stock price in n periods
$u^j d^{(n-j)} S_0$ = possible stock prices at expiration
$\text{Max}[u^j d^{(n-j)} S_0 - X, 0]$ = possible intrinsic values
$n!$ (read as n factorial) is the product of all the numbers from n to 1, and also $0! = 1$
$n!/(n-j)!j!$ = the number of ways in which the stock can increase (j) in n-periods

In our preceding two-period example ($n = 2$), three possible intrinsic values exist:

$$j = 2 : \text{ Max}[u^2 d^0 S_0 - X, \, 0] = C_{uu}$$

$$j = 1 : \text{ Max}[u^1 d^1 S_0 - X, \, 0] = C_{ud}$$

$$j = 0 : \text{ Max}[u^0 d^2 S_0 - X, \, 0] = C_{dd}$$

We have $= n!/(n-j)!j!$ for:

$$j = 0 := \frac{2!}{2! \, 0!} = 1$$

$$j = 1 := \frac{2!}{1! \, 1!} = 2$$

$$j = 2 := \frac{2!}{0! \, 2!} = 1$$

Thus, summing over $j = 0$ to $n = 2$ yields our two-period model:

$$C_0^* = \frac{1}{r_f^2} \left[\begin{array}{c} 1 p^0 (1-p)^2 \text{Max}[u^0 d^2 S_0 - X, \, 0] + 2p(1-p) \text{Max}[ud S_0 - X, \, 0] \\ + p^2 (1-p)^0 \text{Max}[u^2 d^0 S_0 - X, 0] \end{array} \right]$$

$$C_0^* = \frac{1}{r_f^2} \left[(1-p)^2 C_{dd} + 2p(1-p) C_{ud} + p^2 C_{uu} \right]$$

Multiple-Period Arbitrage Strategy

As in the single-period case, arbitrage opportunities exist if the initial market price, C_0^M, does not equal the BOPM value, C_0^*. Except for the last period (when the call's value equals its intrinsic value), there are no guarantees that the call option will be valued correctly at the end of each period. However, if the arbitrage portfolio is correctly adjusted each period, then the initial position eventually will be profitable. The arbitrage strategy and mechanics required to adjust the position each period depend on whether the call is initially overpriced or underpriced.

Overpriced Arbitrage Strategy

If the call is initially overpriced ($C_0^M > C_0^* = H_0^* S_0 - B_0^*$), then the overpriced arbitrage strategy can be set up by taking a short position in the call $\{-C_0^M\}$ and a long position in the replicating portfolio $\{+(H_0^* S_0 - B_0^*)\}$: buying H_0^* shares of stock at price S_0 and borrowing B_0^* dollars. To both ensure that the initial profit of at least $C_0^M - C_0^*$ is kept and to avoid losses, this strategy must be adjusted at the end of each subsequent period t, if the option is overpriced for that period ($C_t^M > C_t^*$), by adjusting the replicating portfolio position for that period (H_t and B_t). This is done by buying or selling shares of stock necessary to obtain the hedge ratio (H_t) associated with that period and stock price (S_t). In adjusting, a *self-financing requirement* is needed to maintain the arbitrage position. This requirement prohibits any outside funds from being added or initial funds removed from the strategy. Thus, if additional shares are needed to obtain the new hedge (i.e., $H_t > H_{t-1}$), then to satisfy the self-financing requirement, funds equal to $(H_t - H_{t-1})S_t$ are borrowed at a rate R_f. If shares of stock need to be sold to move to the new hedge $(H_t < H_{t-1})$, then the proceeds from the sale $((H_t - H_{t-1})S_t)$ are used to pay off part of the debt. This adjustment of moving to a new hedge with a self-financing constraint will automatically move the debt level to its correct one: $B_t = (H_t - H_{t-1})S_t + r_f B_{t-1}$. Finally, readjustment needs to occur each period until that period is reached in which the option is underpriced or equal in value. Closing the position then will result in the optimal arbitrage return.

Underpriced Arbitrage Strategy

If the call option is initially underpriced, then the exact opposite strategy and adjustment rules to the overpriced strategy apply. Specifically, if $C_0^M < C_0^* = H_0^* S_0 - B_0^*$, then an underpriced arbitrage strategy should be formed by taking a long position in the call, $\{+C_0^M\}$, and a short position in the replicating portfolio, $\{-(H_0^* - B_0^*)\} = \{-H_0^* + B_0^*\}$: sell H_0^* shares short and invest B_0^* dollars in a risk-free security. To ensure a minimum arbitrage profit of $C_0^* - C_0^M$, this strategy must be adjusted each period t the call is underpriced $(C_t^M < C_t^*)$ and then closed when the call is overpriced or equal in value.

Pricing American Call Options on Non–Dividend-Paying Stock

In using a multiple-period BOPM to price an American call option, one needs to determine whether the right to exercise early adds value over and above the European value. The nodes in our two-period example where this may happen are at $t = 0$ and 1. At $S_u = \$52.44$ (Exhibit 10.11), if the call option were American and were exercised, the cash flow would only be $uS_0 - X = \$2.44$; whereas the BOPM price is $C_u = \$3.06$. Hence, early exercise is not optimal. At $S_d = \$48.74$, the call is out of the money. The implication here is that for a non–dividend-paying stock, the American call is worth the same as the European call in the BOPM framework: $C_0^{*a} = C_0^{*e}$. Alternatively stated, as long as there is some time until expiration and the interest rate is not zero, the European call will be worth more than the immediate exercise value.

The Multiple-Period BOPM for Puts

Two-Period Case

The multiple-period put model is similar to the multiple-period call model. For a European put with two periods to expiration, we start at expiration where the three possible put values are equal to their intrinsic value: $P_{uu} = \text{Max}[X - u^2 S_0, 0]$,

EXHIBIT 10.12 Two-Period Binomial Values of Stock, Put, and Replicating Portfolios: $S_0 = \$50$, $u = 1.0488$, $d = 0.9747$, $R_f = 0.0125$, $n = 2$

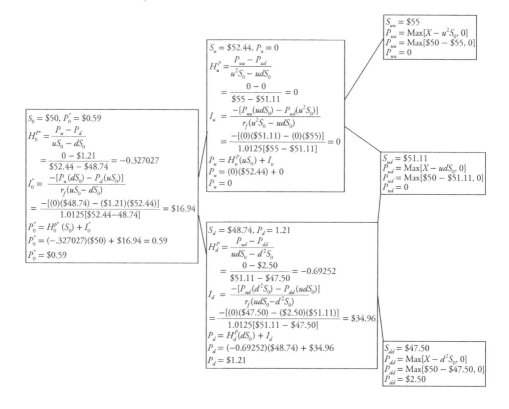

$P_{ud} = [X - udS_0, 0]$, and $P_{dd} = \text{Max}[X - d^2S_0, 0]$. We then move to period 1 and use the single-period binomial put model to determine the put values P_u and P_d when the stock is at uS_0 and dS_0, respectively. Finally, we move to the present to determine P_0^* given P_u and P_d. For example, to price a 50 European put on the stock in our two-period example where $u = 1.0488$, $d = 0.9747$, and $R_f = .0125$, there are, as shown in Exhibit 10.12, three possible put values at expiration: $P_{uu} = 0$, $P_{ud} = 0$, and $P_{dd} = \$2.50$. Moving to period 1, the put value is $P_u = 0$, when the price of the stock is $S_u = \$52.44$, and $P_d = \$1.21$ when $S_d = \$48.74$:

$$P_u = \frac{1}{r_f}[pP_{uu} + (1 - p)P_{ud}]$$

$$P_u = \frac{1}{1.0125}[(0.510121)(0) + (0.489879)(0)] = 0$$

$$P_u = H_u^P(uS_0) + I_u$$

$$P_u = (0)(\$52.44) + 0 = 0$$

where

$$p = \frac{r_f - d}{u - d} = \frac{1.0125 - 0.9747}{1.0488 - 0.9747} = 0.510121$$

$$H_u^P = \frac{P_{uu} - P_{ud}}{u^2 S_0 - ud S_0} = \frac{0 - 0}{\$55 - \$51.11} = 0$$

$$I_u = \frac{-[P_{uu}(ud S_0) - P_{ud}(u^2 S_0)]}{r_f(u^2 S_0 - ud S_0)} = \frac{-[(0)(\$51.11) - (0)(\$55)]}{1.0125[\$55 - \$51.11]} = 0$$

and

$$P_d = \frac{1}{r_f}[pP_{ud} + (1 - p)P_{dd}]$$

$$P_d = \frac{1}{1.0125}[(0.510121)(0) + (0.489879)(\$2.50)] = \$1.21$$

$$P_d = H_d^P(d S_0) + I_d$$

$$P_d = (-0.69252)(\$48.74) + \$34.96 = \$1.21$$

where

$$H_d^P = \frac{P_{ud} - P_{dd}}{ud S_0 - d^2 S_0} = \frac{0 - \$2.50}{\$51.11 - \$47.50} = -0.69252$$

$$I_d = \frac{-[P_{ud}(d^2 S_0) - P_{dd}(ud S_0)]}{r_f(ud S_0 - d^2 S_0)} = \frac{-[(0)(\$47.50) - (\$2.50)(\$51.11)]}{1.0125[\$51.11 - \$47.50]} = \$34.96$$

Finally, given $P_d = \$1.21$ and $P_u = 0$, the equilibrium price of the put using the single period put model is $P_0^* = \$0.59$:

$$P_0^* = H_0^{P*}(S_0) + I_0^*$$

$$P_0^* = (-.327027)(\$50) + \$16.94 = 0.59$$

$$P_0^* = \$0.59$$

$$P_0^* = \frac{1}{r_f}[pP_u + (1 - p)P_d]$$

$$P_0^* = \frac{1}{1.0125}[(0.510121)(0) + (0.489879)(\$1.21)] = 0.59$$

where

$$H_0^{P*} = \frac{P_u - P_d}{uS_0 - dS_0} = \frac{0 - \$1.21}{\$52.44 - \$48.74} = -0.327027$$

$$I_0^* = \frac{-[P_u(dS_0) - P_d(uS_0)]}{r_f(uS_0 - dS_0)} = \frac{-[(0)(\$48.74) - (\$1.21)(\$52.44)]}{1.0125\,[\$52.44 - 48.74]} = \$16.94$$

Equation for the Multiple-Period Put Model

The two-period put model can be expressed in terms of one equation by substituting equations for P_u and P_d into the equation P_0 and rearranging:

$$P_0^* = \frac{1}{r_f}[pP_u + (1-p)P_d]$$

$$P_0^* = \frac{1}{r_f}\left[p\left[\frac{pP_{uu} + (1-p)P_{ud}}{r_f}\right] + \left[\frac{pP_{ud} + (1-p)P_{dd}}{r_f}\right]\right]$$

$$P_0^* = \frac{1}{r_f^2}[p^2 P_{uu} + 2p(1-p)P_{ud} + (1-p)^2 P_{dd}]$$

This equation takes on the same form as the binomial equation for calls. Like calls, for n-periods, the equilibrium put price can be found by using the following n-period equation:

$$P_0^* = \frac{1}{r_f^n}\sum_{j=0}^{n}\frac{n!}{(n-j)!j!}\,(1-p)^j p^{n-j}\;\text{Max}[X - u^j d^{(n-j)}S_0) - X,\,0]$$

Multiple-Period Arbitrage Strategies for Puts

The same overpriced and underpriced arbitrage strategies defined earlier for the single-period case can be used to set up the multiple-period arbitrage strategies for puts. For multiple periods, though, the arbitrage position (like those for calls) must be adjusted each period until profitable conditions exist to close. For example, for the case of an initially overpriced put $(P_0^M > P_0^* = H_0^{P*}S_0 + I_0^*)$, the arbitrage portfolio consisting of a short position in the put $(\{-P_0^M\})$ and a long position in the replicating put portfolio $(\{+(H_0^{P*}S_0 + I_0^*)\})$ is readjusted each subsequent period t if the put is overpriced by moving the position to the H_t^p required for that period and stock price. The overpriced strategy is then closed when the put is underpriced or equal in value. Moreover, given a self-financing requirement, the adjustments needed to attain H_t^p will require either additional investments or borrowing, which will automatically result in the required I_t^* needed for the correct replicating portfolio for that period. The arbitrage strategy and adjustments for an initially underpriced put are just the opposite of the overpriced case.

Put-Call Parity Model: Multiple-Period Case

The same equilibrium put price also can be determined using the put-call parity model. In terms of our illustrative two-period example, the two-period binomial model's put value on the 50 put of $0.59 (allow for slight rounding) is obtained using the put-call parity model by substituting the two-period binomial call value of $1.81 into the model:

$$P_0^* = C_0^* + PV(X) - S_0$$

$$P_0^* = \$1.81 + \frac{\$50}{(1.0125)^2} - \$50$$

$$P_0^* = \$0.59$$

Pricing American Put Options

In examining Exhibit 10.12, note that with one period to expiration the value of the European put is $P_d = \$1.21$ when the stock is at $S_d = \$48.74$. If the put were American and priced at this European BOPM value, then a put holder would find it advantageous to exercise the put, since it would provide him with a return of $X - dS_0 = \$50 - \$48.74 = \$1.26$, compared to the put value of $1.21. Thus, the above multiple-period BOPM for puts is only applicable for European puts.

The BOPM can be adjusted to value American puts, P_0^{*a}, by constraining the put price at each node to be: $P^a = \text{Max}[P, \text{Max}[X - S, 0]]$, in which P is the binomial value of the put as determined by using the single-period model with the two possible put prices determined for the next period. In Exhibit 10.13, the two-period BOPM for pricing an American put is shown for our illustrative case. With the advantage of early exercise, the price of an American put, P_0^{*a}, is $0.61 in this example, which is greater than the BOPM's European put price of $0.59. This contrast with call options in which there is no early exercise advantage and therefore no difference between European and American call when the underlying stock pays no dividends. In the case of puts, an early exercise advantage can exist even when the underlying stock pays no dividends.

Pricing Options on Dividend-Paying Stocks — Multiple-Period Case

Suppose in our previous two-period example, the first period was an ex-dividend date with the value of the dividend being $0.50. The instant before the ex-dividend date the stock was $52.44 or $48.74 and on the ex-dividend date $51.94 or $48.24, respectively. In the next period, the stock will either rise or fall. Assuming the up and down parameters stay the same ($u = 1.0488$ and $d = 0.9747$ and the stock trades ex-dividend), if the stock were at $51.94, then it could either increase to $54.47 or decrease to $50.62; if the stock were at $48.24, then its two possible prices would be $50.59 or $47.02 (see Exhibit 10.14). Note that in this dividend case, the tree does not recombine. As a result, there are now four possible stock prices after two periods instead of three. Moreover, if there are multiple periods and multiple dividends, and there are

EXHIBIT 10.13 Two-Period Binomial Values of American Put: $S_0 = \$50$, $u = 1.0488$, $d = 0.9747$, $R_f = 0.0125$, $n = 2$

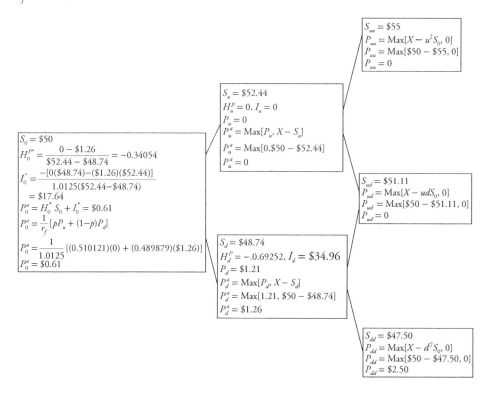

$S_0 = \$50$
$H_0^{p*} = \dfrac{0 - \$1.26}{\$52.44 - \$48.74} = -0.34054$
$I_0^{*} = \dfrac{-[0(\$48.74) - (\$1.26)(\$52.44)]}{1.0125(\$52.44 - \$48.74)}$
$\quad = \$17.64$
$P_0^{a} = H_0^{*}S_0 + I_0^{*} = \$0.61$
$P_0^{a} = \dfrac{1}{r_f}[pP_u + (1-p)P_d]$
$P_0^{a} = \dfrac{1}{1.0125}[(0.510121)(0) + (0.489879)(\$1.26)]$
$P_0^{a} = \$0.61$

$S_u = \$52.44$
$H_u^{p} = 0, I_u = 0$
$P_u = 0$
$P_u^{a} = \text{Max}[P_u, X - S_u]$
$P_u^{a} = \text{Max}[0, \$50 - \$52.44]$
$P_u^{a} = 0$

$S_d = \$48.74$
$H_d^{p} = -.69252, I_d = \$34.96$
$P_d = \$1.21$
$P_d^{a} = \text{Max}[P_d, X - S_d]$
$P_d^{a} = \text{Max}[1.21, \$50 - \$48.74]$
$P_d^{a} = \$1.26$

$S_{uu} = \$55$
$P_{uu} = \text{Max}[X - u^2 S_0, 0]$
$P_{uu} = \text{Max}[\$50 - \$55, 0]$
$P_{uu} = 0$

$S_{ud} = \$51.11$
$P_{ud} = \text{Max}[X - ud S_0, 0]$
$P_{ud} = \text{Max}[\$50 - \$51.11, 0]$
$P_{ud} = 0$

$S_{dd} = \$47.50$
$P_{dd} = \text{Max}[X - d^2 S_0, 0]$
$P_{dd} = \text{Max}[\$50 - \$47.50, 0]$
$P_{dd} = \$2.50$

EXHIBIT 10.14 Two-Period Binomial Values of Stock, when Stock Pays Dividend: $S_0 = \$50$, $u = 1.0488$, $d = 0.9747$, $D_1 = \$0.50$, and Ex-Dividend in Period 1, $R_f = 0.0125$

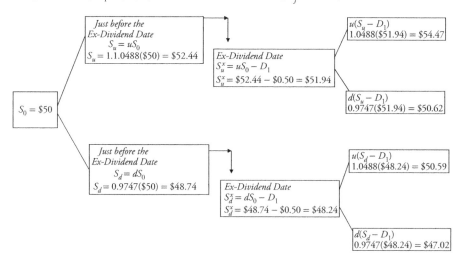

$S_0 = \$50$

Just before the
Ex-Dividend Date
$S_u = u S_0$
$S_u = 1.1.0488(\$50) = \$52.44$

Ex-Dividend Date
$S_u^{x} = u S_0 - D_1$
$S_u^{x} = \$52.44 - \$0.50 = \$51.94$

$u(S_u - D_1)$
$1.0488(\$51.94) = \$54.47$

$d(S_u - D_1)$
$0.9747(\$51.94) = \$50.62$

Just before the
Ex-Dividend Date
$S_d = d S_0$
$S_d = 0.9747(\$50) = \$48.74$

Ex-Dividend Date
$S_d^{x} = d S_0 - D_1$
$S_d^{x} = \$48.74 - \$0.50 = \$48.24$

$u(S_d - D_1)$
$1.0488(\$48.24) = \$50.59$

$d(S_d - D_1)$
$0.9747(\$48.24) = \$47.02$

some periods when the stock trades ex-dividend, some when it trades cum dividend, and finally some periods when the stock goes from ex-dividend to cum-dividend, then the number of possible nodes to evaluate can be quite large, making the binomial modeling of possible stock prices almost impossible.

To resolve this problem, there are two approaches to adjusting the binomial model for dividends. The first is the discrete dividend payment approach. This approach assumes that the stock price reflects a future dividend payment, which is known with certainty, and all other factors affecting the stock prices, which are uncertain. This approach is presented in Appendix 10B. The second approach is to assume the stock pays a continuous dividend yield over the life of the option. This latter approach is based on the dividend-adjusted model developed by Robert Merton for the Black-Scholes model and accordingly is referred to here as the Merton continuous dividend-yield approach. Since most stocks pay a fixed dollar dividend at specific dates, the Merton approach should be viewed as an approximation. The model treats dividends as if they were repayments of a portion of the share value of the stock. As such, dividends are thought of as a leakage of value of the stock, with the stock value dropping (as it does on the ex-dividend date) due to the leakage of the dividend. More formally, options on assets that generate a continuous dividend or interest payment, such as an index or currency option, are referred to as *continuous-leakage* options. If the underlying asset on the option engenders benefits only discretely, such as an option on a stock making one dividend payment during the period, then the option is referred to as a *discrete-leakage* option; if the option's underlying asset generates no benefits, then it is called a *zero-leakage* option.

Merton's Continuous Dividend Yield Approach

Merton's continuous dividend yield approach assumes the dividend is paid out at a continuous rate. As a result, instead of accounting for a stock decrease on the ex-dividend date, the Merton approach assumes that the underlying stock pays a dividend at a continuous rate. In the Merton Model, the dividend yield is treated as a negative interest rate in which the dividend yield represents a continuous leakage of value from the stock.

The binomial model can be adjusted for a continuous dividend payment by subtracting the annual dividend yield, ψ, from the annual risk-free rate, R^A, for the r_f term in the equation for p:

$$r_f = [(1 + R^A - \psi)]^{\Delta t}$$

or for continuous compounding:

$$r_f = e^{(R^A - \psi)\Delta t}$$

Thus:

$$p = \frac{e^{(R^A - \psi)\Delta t} - d}{u - d} \quad \text{or} \quad p = \frac{[1 + R^A - \psi)]^{\Delta t} - d}{u - d}$$

The Merton model is derived from the option valuation based on risk-neutral pricing. The derivation is presented in Appendix 10A, which presents the risk-neutral pricing approach.

Example

To see the application of the Merton dividend-adjusted approach, suppose $S_0 = \$50$, $u = 1.09356$ and $d = 0.9144$, call and put options with $X = \$50$, $n = 5$, binomial periods length $\Delta t = 0.20$, and $R^A = 2.5\%$, and the estimated annual dividend yield $= \psi = 3\%$. The dividend-adjusted p value is 0.47221:

$$p = \frac{e^{(R^A - \psi)\,\Delta t} - d}{u - d}$$

$$p = \frac{e^{(0.025 - 0.03)(0.20)} - 0.9144}{1.09356 - 0.9144} = 0.47221$$

Given the values for the p, u, and d parameters, the binomial option prices are determined using the normal recursive process of starting at expiration with the possible intrinsic values and then rolling the tree to the current period. Exhibit 10.15 shows the resulting binomial tree for American and European call and put prices. For this five-period case, the European call price is \$3.95 and the American price is \$4.00; the European put price is \$4.19 and the American is \$4.20. If the dividend is not included, the price of the European and American call would be \$4.77, overpricing the European call by approximately 21.7% and the American call by 19.25%. Without the dividend adjustment, the European put price would be \$3.54, underpricing the European put by 15.5%, and the American put would be \$3.65, underpricing the American put by 13%. Depending on the size of the dividend, considerable mispricing can result by failing to take into account the dividend.

Estimating the BOPM

To apply the BOPM to the pricing of option, the u and d parameters need to be estimated. One approach to estimating u and d is to solve mathematically for the u and d values that make the statistical characteristics (mean and variance) of the stock's logarithmic return equal to the characteristics' estimated values. As background to understanding this approach, let us first examine the probability distribution that characterizes a binomial process.

Probability Distribution Resulting from a Binomial Process

In the last section, we assumed a binomial approach where in each period the stock price would either increase to equal a proportion u times its initial value or decrease

EXHIBIT 10.15 Merton's Dividend-Adjusted Binomial Model $S_0 = \$20$, $u = 1.09356$, $d = 0.9144$, $\psi = 3\%$, $R^A = 2.5\%$, $n = 5$, $\Delta t = 0.20$

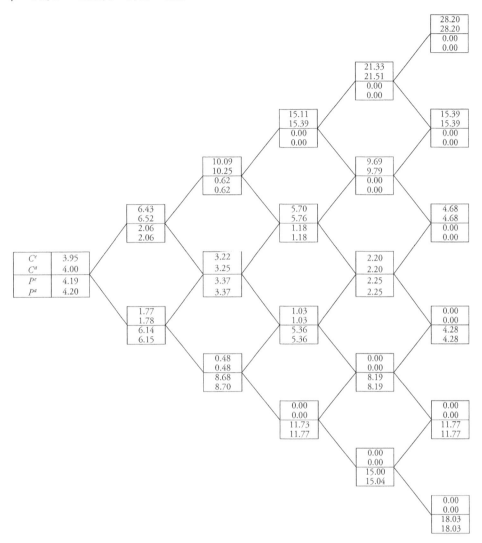

to equal a proportion d times the initial value. At the end of n periods, this binomial process yields a distribution of $n + 1$ possible stock prices (e.g., for $n = 3$, there are four possible prices: $S_{uuu} = u^3 S_0$, $S_{uud} = u^2 d S_0$, $S_{udd} = u d^2 S_0$, and $S_{ddd} = d^3 S_0$). Since stock prices cannot be negative, this distribution is not normally distributed. That is, the normal distribution extends from plus infinity to minus infinity. Since one tail of the distribution for stock prices is equal to zero (no negative prices), the distribution is not normal. However, the distribution of stock prices can be converted into a distribution of logarithmic returns, g_n, where: $g_n = \ln(S_n/S_0)$. This distribution can take on negative values and will be normally distributed if the probability of an increase in one period, q,

EXHIBIT 10.16   Binomial Process of Stock Prices and Logarithmic Returns

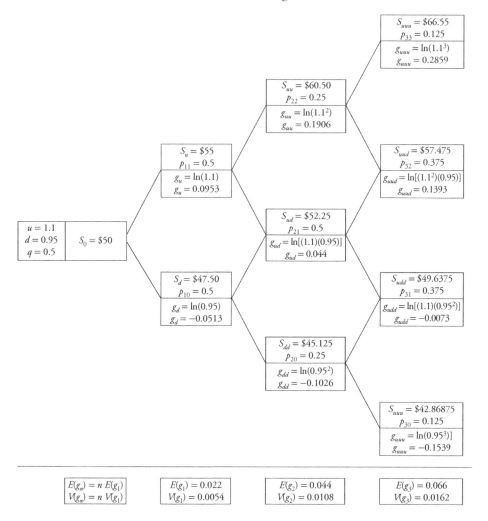

is equal to 0.5. Exhibit 10.16 shows the binomial distributions of stock prices for $n = 1$, 2, and 3 periods and their corresponding logarithmic returns for the case in which $S_0 = \$50$, $u = 1.1$, $d = 0.95$, and $q = 0.5$. As shown in the exhibit, when $n = 1$, there are two possible stock prices of \$55 and \$47.50, with respective logarithmic returns of 0.0953 and -0.0513:

$$g_u = \ln\left(\frac{uS_0}{S_0}\right) = \ln u = \ln 1.1 = 0.0953$$

$$g_d = \ln\left(\frac{dS_0}{S_0}\right) = \ln d = \ln 0.95 = -0.0513$$

When $n = 2$, there are three possible stock prices of $60.50, $52.25, and $54.125 with corresponding logarithmic returns of

$$g_{uu} = \ln\left(\frac{u^2 S_0}{S_0}\right) = \ln u^2 = \ln(1.1^2) = 0.1906$$

$$g_{ud} = \ln\left(\frac{ud S_0}{S_0}\right) = \ln ud = \ln[(1.1)(0.95)] = 0.044$$

$$g_{dd} = \ln\left(\frac{d^2 S_0}{S_0}\right) = \ln(d^2) = \ln(0.95^2) = -0.1026$$

When $n = 3$, there are four possible stock prices of $66.55, $57.475, $49.6375, and $42.86875, with corresponding logarithmic returns of 0.2859, 0.1393, −0.0073, and −0.1539 (see Exhibit 10.16).

The probability of attaining any one of these rates is equal to the probability of the stock price increasing j times in n periods, p_{nj}. That is, the probability of attaining stock price $52.25 in period 2 is equal to the probability of the stock price increasing one time ($j = 1$) in two periods ($n = 2$), p_{21}. In a binomial process, this probability can be found using the following formula:

$$p_{nj} = \frac{n!}{(n-j)!j!} q^j (1-q)^{n-j}$$

Thus after two periods, the probability of the stock price equaling $60.50 is $p_{22} = 0.25$, $52.25 is $p_{21} = 0.5$, and $45.125 is $p_{20} = 0.25$. Using these probabilities, the expected value and the variance of the distribution of logarithmic returns after two periods would be equal to $E(g_2) = 0.044$ and $V(g_2) = 0.0108$:

$$E(g_n) = \sum_{j=0}^{n} p_{nj} g_{nj}$$

$$E(g_2) = \sum_{j=0}^{2} p_{2j} g_{2j}$$

$$E(g_2) = 0.25(-0.1026) + 0.5(0.0440) + 0.25(0.1906)$$

$$E(g_2) = 0.044$$

$$V(g_n) = E[g_n - E(g_n)]^2 = \sum_{i=0}^{n} p_{nj}[g_{nj} - E(g_n)]^2$$

$$V(g_2) = \sum_{j=0}^{2} p_{2j}[g_{2j} - E(g_n)]^2$$

$$V(g_2) = 0.25\,[-0.1026 - 0.044]^2 + 0.5\,[0.044 - 0.044]^2$$
$$+\, 0.25[0.1906 - 0.044]^2$$

$$V(g_2) = 0.0108$$

The means and variances for the three distributions are shown at the bottom of Exhibit 10.16. In examining each distribution's mean and variance, note that as the number of periods increases, the expected value and variance increase by a multiplicative factor such that $E(g_n) = nE(g_1)$ and $V(g_n) = nV(g_1)$. Also, note that the expected value and the variance are also equal to

$$E(g_n) = nE(g_1) = n[q \ln u + (1-q) \ln d]$$
$$V(g_n) = nV(g_1) = nq(1-q)[\ln(u/d)]^2$$

Thus, for $n = 2$:

$$E(g_2) = 2\,[0.5\ \ln(1.1) + (1 - .05)\ \ln(0.95)] = 0.044$$
$$V(g_2) = 2(0.5)(0.5)[\ln(1.1/.95)]^2 = 0.0108$$

Solving for u and d

Given the features of a binomial distribution, the formulas for estimating u and d are found by mathematically solving for the u and d values that make the expected value and the variance of the binomial distribution of the logarithmic return of stock prices equal to their respective estimated parameter values under the assumption that $q = 0.5$ (or equivalently that the distribution is normal). If we let μ_e and V_e be the estimated mean and variance of the logarithmic return of the stock price for a period equal in length to the period comprising the n periods, then out objective is to solve for the u and d values that satisfy the following equations:

$$nE(g_1) = n[q \ln u + (1-q) \ln d] = \mu_e$$
$$nV(g_1) = nq(1-q)[\ln(u/d)]^2 = V_e$$

If $q = 0.5$, then the formula values for u and d that satisfy the two equations are

$$u = e^{\sqrt{V_e/n} + \mu_e/n}$$
$$d = e^{-\sqrt{V_e/n} + \mu_e/n}$$

The algebraic derivation of equation u and d formulas are presented in Box 10.1.

BOX 10.1: ALGEBRAIC DERIVATION OF u AND d FORMULAS

The u and d formulas are found by solving the following two equations simultaneously for the unknowns:

$$nE(g_1) = n[q \ln u + (1-q) \ln d] = \mu_e$$

$$nV(g_1) = nq(1-q)[\ln(u/d)]^2 = V_e$$

This equation system consists of two equations and three unknowns, u, d, and q, and cannot be solved without a third equation or information about one of the unknowns. If we assume, however, that the distribution of logarithmic returns is symmetrical, then we can set $q = 0.5$. Doing this yields the following two-equation system with two unknowns (u and d):

$$n[0.5 \ln u + (1-.05) \ln d] = \mu_e \qquad (1)$$

$$n(0.5)(1-0.5)[\ln(u/d)]^2 = V_e \qquad (2)$$

To solve Equations (1) and (2) simultaneously for u and d, first rewrite Equation (1) in terms of the $\ln d$:

$$n[0.5 \ln u + (1-0.5) \ln d] = \mu_e$$

$$0.5[\ln u + \ln d] = \frac{\mu_e}{n}$$

$$\ln d = 2\left(\frac{\mu_e}{n}\right) - \ln u \qquad (3)$$

Next we rewrite Equation (2) in terms of the $\ln u$:

$$n(0.5)(1-.05)[\ln(u/d)]^2 = V_e$$

$$0.5^2[\ln u - \ln d]^2 = \frac{V_e}{n}$$

$$\sqrt{0.5^2[\ln u - \ln d]^2} = \sqrt{\frac{V_e}{n}}$$

$$0.05[\ln u - \ln d] = \sqrt{\frac{V_e}{n}}$$

$$\ln u - \ln d = 2\sqrt{\frac{V_e}{n}}$$

$$\ln u = 2\sqrt{\frac{V_e}{n}} + Lnd \qquad (4)$$

Substituting Equation (3) for $\ln d$ in (4), we obtain:

$$\ln u = 2\sqrt{\frac{V_e}{n}} + 2\left(\frac{\mu_e}{V_e}\right) - \ln u$$

$$2\ \ln u = 2\sqrt{\frac{V_e}{n}} + 2\left(\frac{\mu_e}{V_e}\right)$$

$$\ln u = \sqrt{\frac{V_e}{n}} + \left(\frac{\mu_e}{V_e}\right) \qquad\qquad (5)$$

Similarly, substituting Equation (5) for $\ln u$ in Equation (3), we obtain:

$$\ln d = 2\left(\frac{\mu_e}{n}\right) - \sqrt{\frac{V_e}{n}} - \frac{\mu_e}{n}$$

$$\ln d = -\sqrt{\frac{V_e}{n}} + \frac{\mu_e}{n} \qquad\qquad (6)$$

Finally, expressing Equations (5) and (6) as exponents we obtain the u and d values that simultaneously satisfy Equations (1) and (2):

$$u = e^{\sqrt{V_e/n} + \mu_e/n}$$

$$d = e^{-\sqrt{V_e/n} + \mu_e/n}$$

In terms of our example, if the estimated expected value and variance of the logarithmic return were $\mu_e = 0.044$ and $V_e = 0.0108$ for a period equal in length to $n = 2$, then using u and d formulas, u would be 1.1 and d would be 0.95—the u and d values with which we started the example:

$$u = e^{\sqrt{0.0108/2} + 0.044/2} = 1.1$$

$$d = e^{-\sqrt{0.0108/2} + 0.044/2} = 0.95$$

Annualized Mean and Variance

In estimating u and d for a number of options on the same stock but with different expiration, it is helpful to use an annualized mean and variance (μ_e^A and V_e^A). Annualized parameters are obtained by simply multiplying the parameter value of a given length by the number of periods of that length that make up a year. Thus, if quarterly data are used to estimate the mean and variance (μ_e^q and V_e^q), then we simply multiply those estimated by four to obtain the annualized parameters ($\mu_e^A = 4\mu_e^q$ and $V_e^A = 4V_e^q$). If the quarterly mean and variance were 0.022 and 0.0054, then the annualized mean and variance would be 0.088 and 0.0216, respectively. Note: When the annualized mean and variance are used in the u and d formulas, then the annualized parameters must be multiplied by a proportion t, defined as the period being analyzed expressed as a proportion of a year:

$$u = e^{\sqrt{tV_e^A/n + (t\,\mu_e^A/n)}}$$

$$d = e^{-\sqrt{tV_e^A/n + (t\,\mu_e^A)/n}}$$

Typically, the period being analyzed is the option expiration. In turn, n is the number of subperiods of a specified length that we want to divide the tree. If we want the length of our binomial periods to be monthly for an option expiring in six months ($t = 0.5$), then we would subdivide the tree into $n = 6$ subperiods each of length one month. If we want the length of the period to be weekly, then we subdivided the tree into $n = 24$ subperiods of length of a week; if we want the length to be daily, then we would subdivide the tree into $n = 180$ subperiods. Note that t/n is the length of the binomial period expressed as a proportion of a year, which we defined earlier as Δt. As an example, suppose the annualized mean and variance of the logarithmic return of a stock were $\mu_e^A = 0.044$ and $V_e^A = 0.0108$, and we wanted to evaluate an option on the stock expiring in six months ($t = 0.5$). If we want a single-period model, then $n = 1$ and the length of period in the binomial process would be six months (length of binomial period: $\Delta t = t/1 = 0.5/1 = 0.5$ per year). In this case, u and d for a period of length six months would be 1.1 and 0.95:

$$u = e^{\sqrt{(0.5)(0.0108)/1 + (0.5)(0.044)/1}} = 1.1$$

$$d = e^{-\sqrt{(0.5)(0.0108)/1 + (0.5)(0.044)/1}} = 0.95$$

If we want to make the binomial tree a two-period one, then $n = 2$ and the length of the period binomial period is 0.25 per year (length of binomial period: $\Delta t = t/n = 0.5/2 = 0.25$ per year). In this case, u and d for a period of length 0.25 per year would be equal to 1.065 and 0.96:

$$u = e^{\sqrt{(0.5)(0.0108)/2 + (0.5)(0.044)/2}} = 1.065$$

$$d = e^{-\sqrt{(0.5)(0.0108)/2 + (0.5)(0.044)/2}} = 0.96$$

Finally, if we want to make the binomial tree daily, then $n = 90$ and the length of the period is 0.0055 per year (length of binomial period: $\Delta t = t/n = 0.5/90 = 0.0055$ per year). In this case, u and d for a period of length one day would be to 1.008022 and 0.992527:

$$u = e^{\sqrt{(0.5)(0.0108)/90 + (0.5)(0.044)/90}} = 1.008022$$

$$d = e^{-\sqrt{(0.5)(0.0108)/90 + (.5)(0.044)/90}} = 0.992527$$

It is common also to express the u and d equations in terms of the annualized standard deviation (σ^A) and Δt:

$$u = e^{\sqrt{tV_e^A/n}+(t\,\mu_e^A/n)}$$

$$u = e^{\sigma^A\sqrt{\Delta t}+\mu_e^A\,\Delta t}$$

$$d = e^{-\sqrt{tV_e^A/n}+(t\,\mu_e^A)/n}$$

$$d = e^{-\sigma^A\sqrt{\Delta t}+\mu_e^A\,\Delta t}$$

Note that the annualized standard deviation cannot be obtained simply by multiplying the standard deviation of a given length by the number of periods of that length in a year. Rather, one must first annualize the variance and then take the square root of the resulting annualized variance to obtain the annualized standard deviation.

u and d Formulas for Large n

In examining the u and d formulas, note that as the n term increases, the mean term in the exponent goes to zero quicker than the square root term.

$$u = e^{\sqrt{tV_e^A/n}+(t\,\mu_e^A/n)}$$

$$d = e^{-\sqrt{tV_e^A/n}+(t\,\mu_e^A)/n}$$

$$As\ n\uparrow \Rightarrow\ (t\,\mu_e^A/n)\rightarrow\ 0\ faster\ than\ \sqrt{tV_e^A/n}\ \rightarrow 0$$

As a result, for large n (e.g., $n = 40$), the mean term's impact on u and d is negligible. Thus for large n, u, and d can be estimated with just the variance:

$$u = e^{\sqrt{(tV_e^A)/n}} = e^{\sigma^A\sqrt{\Delta t}}$$

$$d = e^{-\sqrt{(tV_e^A)/n}} = e^{-\sigma^A\sqrt{\Delta t}} = 1/u$$

Thus, as n becomes large, or equivalently, as the length of the period becomes smaller, the impact of the mean on u and d becomes smaller, and u and d can be estimated by simply using the variance. Note that for cases where n is large or where $\mu_e = 0$, u and d are inversely proportional to each other. Note, also, that the case of μ_e being insignificant for large n only holds if the underlying distribution of the logarithmic return is symmetrical.

Estimating *u* and *d*

To estimate u and d requires estimating the mean and variance: μ_e and V_e. The two most common ways of estimating these parameters are to calculate the stock's average mean and variance from a historical sample of stock prices or to determine the stock's implied parameter values.

Historical Mean and Volatility

Historical quarterly closing prices of a non–dividend-paying stock over 13 quarters are shown in Exhibit 10.17. The 12 logarithmic returns are calculated by taking the natural log of the ratio of the stock price in one period to the price in the previous period (S_t/S_{t-1}). From these data, the historical quarterly mean return and variance are:

$$\mu_e^q = \frac{\sum_{t=1}^{12} g_t}{12} = \frac{0}{12} = 0$$

$$V_e^q = \frac{\sum_{t=1}^{12} [g_t - \mu_e]^2}{11} = \frac{0.046297}{11} = .004209$$

Multiplying the historical quarterly mean and variance by four, we obtain an annualized mean and variance of 0 and 0.016836, respectively. Given the estimated annualized mean and variance, u and d can be estimated using the formulas for u and d once we determine the number of periods to subdivide the expiration period. For example, for an option expiring in 180 days $(t = 0.5)$, if we want to make the length of the period quarterly, then we set n equal to 2 to obtain a u of 1.0670 and a d of 0.9372. If we want a weekly period, then we set $n = 26$ to obtain $u = 1.0182$ and $d = 0.9822$. Finally, if we want a daily period, then we make $n = 180$, and obtain u and d values of 1.0069 and 0.9932 (see lower panel of Exhibit 10.17).

Implied Volatility

The implied variance is the variance that equates the OPM's value to the market price. The implied variance can be found by trial and error by substituting different variance values into the BOPM until that variance is found that yields an OPM value equal to the market price. Using Taylor series expansion, the implied variance can also be approximated for an at-the-money option using the following formula:

$$\sigma^2 = \frac{0.5(C_0^M + P_0^M)\sqrt{2\pi/t}}{X(1+R)^t}$$

EXHIBIT 10.17 Estimating μ_e and V_e, with Historical Data, u and d Calculations, and Binomial Option Prices

Quarter	S_t	S_t/S_{t-1}	$g_t = \ln(S_t/S_{t-1})$	$(g_t - \mu_e)^2$
Y1.1	$53			
Y1.2	$50	0.9434	−0.0583	0.003395
Y1.3	$47	0.9400	−0.0619	0.003829
Y1.4	$44	0.9362	−0.0660	0.004350
Y2.1	$47	1.0682	0.0660	0.004350
Y2.2	$50	1.0638	0.0619	0.003829
Y2.3	$53	1.0600	0.0583	0.003395
Y2.4	$50	0.9434	−0.0583	0.003395
Y3.1	$47	0.9400	−0.0619	0.003829
Y3.2	$44	0.9362	−0.0660	0.004350
Y3.3	$47	1.0682	0.0660	0.004350
Y3.4	$50	1.0638	0.0619	0.003829
Y4.1	$53	1.0600	0.0583	0.003395

$\Sigma = 0.0000$ $\Sigma = 0.046297$

$\mu_e^q = 0.00$ $V_e^q = 0.004209$

$\mu_e^A = 0.00$ $V_e^A = 0.016836$

$$u = e^{\sqrt{V_e^A t/n}} = e^{\sqrt{(0.016836)(0.5)/n}} \qquad d = e^{-\sqrt{V_e^A t/n}} = e^{-\sqrt{(0.016836)(0.5)/n}}$$

n	Length of Binomial Period in Years $\Delta t = t/n = 0.5/n$	Length of Binomial Period Per Length	u	d	C^* & C^a	P^*	P^a
2	0.25	Quarter	1.0670	0.9372	$1.93	$1.32	$1.46
6	0.083333333	Month	1.0382	0.9632	$2.07	$1.45	$1.54
26	0.019230769	Week	1.0182	0.9822	$2.12	$1.52	$1.57
90	0.005555556	Two Days	1.0097	0.9904	$2.14	$1.52	$1.58
180	0.002777778	Day	1.0069	0.9932	$2.14	$1.52	$1.58

For example, if the risk-free rate is 2.5% and an ABC 50 call and 50 put expiring in six months are trading at $1.88 and $0.63, respectively, when ABC stock is trading at $50, the stock's implied variance would be approximately 0.09:

$$\sigma^2 = \frac{0.5(\$1.88 + \$0.63) \sqrt{2 \pi / 0.5}}{\$50 \, (1.025)^{0.5}} = 0.09$$

The implied variance is examined in more detail in Chapter 12.

Interest Rates

In estimating the risk-free rate for the BOPM, the rate on a Treasury bill, commercial paper, or short-term Treasury note, with a maturity equal to the option's expiration usually is used. These rates are typically quoted in terms of a simple annual rate (with no compounding). The rate needs to be converted to the periodic rates in the BOPM. For large number of subperiods, the BOPM is not very sensitive to interest rate changes. Thus, obtaining an exact interest rate is not critical to estimating the equilibrium value of an option using the BOPM as is good estimates of the volatility.

BOPM Computer Programs

To use the BOPM to estimate the equilibrium value of an option first requires that we estimate μ_e and V_e, determine the risk-free rate, and specify S_0, X, T, and n. Given these values, we can determine u, d, and r_f. Second, we calculate the possible intrinsic values of the option. Third, we use the recursive multiple-period model to obtain the option price. Finally, if the option is American, at each node we constrain the price of the option to be the maximum of its binomial value or its *IV*, (*Note:* For call options on non–dividend-paying stocks, there is no early exercise advantage, and thus, the European and American call values are equal.) This procedure for determining the price of an option is rather cumbersome, especially when a number of subperiods to expiration are used. The recursive procedure of the BOPM, though, easily lends itself to computer programming. Excel option programs that values American and European calls and puts are provided as part of the software that accompanies this book. Several end-of-the-chapter problems are included that make use of this software.

Example

The BOPM values for a $50 call, $50 European put, and a $50 American put all expiring in one quarter on a non–dividend-paying stock are shown for different n values in the lower panel of Exhibit 10.17. The call values were generated using the BOPM Excel program. The u and d values were calculated using the estimated annualized mean of zero and annualized variance of 0.016836; the current price on the underlying stock was assumed to be $50, and the annual risk-free rate was 2.5%. As shown in the exhibit, when the number of subperiods to expiration is $n = 6$, then $u = 1.0382$, $d = 0.9632$, and the equilibrium call price is $C_0^* = \$2.07$ (American and European are the same with dividends), the European put price is $P_0^e = \$1.45$, and the American put price is $P_0^a = \$1.54$. If the number of subperiods is divided into 26, then $u = 1.0182$, $d = 0.9822$, and the option prices are $C_0^* = \$2.12$, $P_0^e = \$1.52$, $P_0^a = \$1.57$. Exhibit 10.18, in turn, shows the binomial tree of option prices for the six-period case. If the number of subperiods is divided into 180, then $u = 1.0069$, $d = 0.9932$, and the option prices are $C_0^* = \$2.14$, $P_0^e = \$1.52$, $P_0^a = \$1.58$. *Note:* There is a small difference between the option values at $n = 26$ and $n = 180$ but no difference in values at $n = 90$ and

EXHIBIT 10.18   Binomial Prices of American and European Calls and Puts for $n = 6$

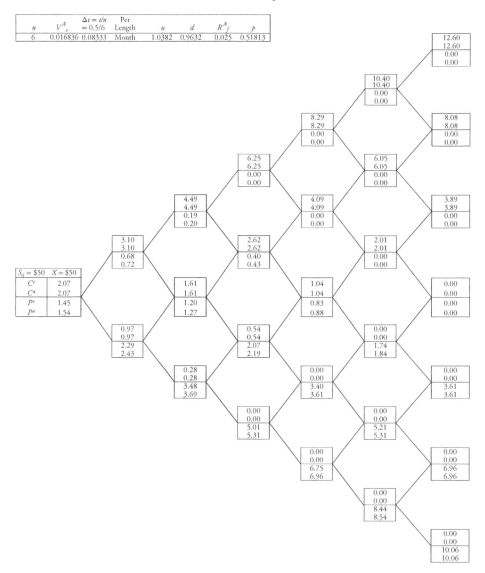

$n = 180$. In examining the American and European put values shown in Exhibit 10.18, note that there are early exercise advantages that make the American put value equal to its IV. The early exercise advantages, in turn, explain why the American put is valued greater than the European put. In the case of the call, however, there are no dividends and therefore no early exercise advantages, making the American and European call values the same.

Features of the BOPM

In the BOPM, the equilibrium call price depends on the underlying stock price, exercise price, time to expiration, risk-free rate, and the stock's volatility (and mean for the case of small n). Mathematically, the impacts that changes in these variables have on the equilibrium call price can be seen in terms of the simulation presented in Exhibit 10.19 (top panel). In the exhibit, combinations of the BOPM call values and stock prices are shown for different parameter values. The first column (1) shows the call values given the parameter values used in the preceding example: $X = \$50$, $t = 0.50$, $R_f = 2.5\%$, and annualized variance of 0.016836 ($\sigma^A = 0.12975$). For purposes of comparison, the other columns show the call and stock price relations generated with the same parameter values used in column 1, except for one variable: in column 2, $X = \$45$; in column 3, $t = 0.75$; and in column 4, $\sigma^A = 0.2595$.

In examining Exhibit 10.19, one should note several of the relationships that were explained either intuitively or with arbitrage arguments in Chapter 9. First, as shown in any of the columns, when the stock is relatively low and the call is deep out of the money, the BOPM yields a very low call price. As the price of the stock increases by equal increments, the BOPM call prices increase at increasing rates up to a point, with the values never being below the difference between the stock price and the present value of the exercise price. Thus, over a range of stock prices, the BOPM yields a call and stock price relation that is nonlinear and satisfies the minimum and maximum boundary conditions. The nonlinear relationship also can be seen in the figure in Exhibit 10.19 where the BOPM call values and stock prices from Column 1 are plotted. As shown, the slope of this BOPM option price curve increases as the stock price increases, the curve does not yield negative values, and it is above the *IV* line and the minimum boundary $S - PV(X)$ (not shown). The slope of the curve is referred to as the option's *delta*. Delta is equal to H^* in the BOPM. For a call, the delta ranges from 0 for deep-out-of-the-money calls to approximately 1 for deep-in-the-money ones. This can be seen in the figure that shows that the option curve is relatively flat for low stock prices and starts to become parallel to the minimum boundary line for high stock values. The nonlinear call and stock price relation also can be seen by the change in the slope of the BOPM option price curve as the stock price increases. In options literature, the change in slope (i.e., delta) per small change in the stock price defines the option's *gamma*.

Second, examining columns 1 and 2, observe that for each stock price, higher call prices are associated with the call with the lower exercise price. Thus, as the exercise price decreases, the BOPM call price increases. Third, comparing column 3

EXHIBIT 10.19 BOPM Call Price, Put Price, and Stock Price Relations for Different Parameter Values

	1	2	3	4
	$X = \$50$	$X = \$45$	$X = \$50$	$X = \$50$
	$t = 0.5$	$t = 0.5$	$t = 0.75$	$t = 0.5$
	$\sigma^A = 0.12975$	$\sigma^A = 0.12975$	$\sigma^A = 0.12975$	$\sigma^A = 0.2595$
	$R^A_f = 0.025$	$R^A_f = 0.025$	$R^A_f = 0.025$	$R^A_f = 0.025$
Stock Price	Call Price	Call Price	Call Price	Call Price
$35	$0.0001	$0.0051	$0.0016	$0.0878
$40	$0.0148	$0.2408	$0.0069	$0.5051
$45	$0.0351	$1.9250	$0.6650	$0.6885
$50	$2.1389	$5.7568	$2.7054	$3.9425
$55	$5.8952	$10.5676	$6.3926	$7.2621
$60	$10.6438	$15.5528	$11.0066	$11.3532
$65	$15.6155	$20.5522	$15.9301	$15.9199
Stock Price	Put Price*	Put Price*	Put Price*	Put Price*
$35	$14.0065	$9.5429	$14.0842	$14.4743
$40	$9.0031	$4.6880	$9.1494	$9.8915
$45	$4.7375	$1.3792	$4.7482	$6.0750
$50	$1.5254	$0.2044	$1.7879	$3.3290
$55	$0.2817	$0.0156	$0.4751	$1.6480
$60	$0.0303	$0.0006	$0.0892	$0.7397
$65	$0.0019	$0.0000	$0.0120	$0.3064

*European Put Prices

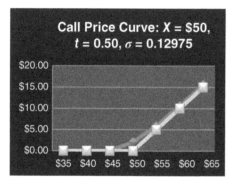

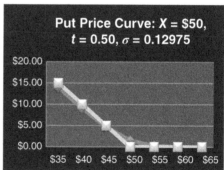

with column 1, observe that the BOPM call price increases, the greater the time to expiration. The change in an option's prices with respect to a small change in the time to expiration (with other factors held constant) is defined as the option's *theta*. Fourth, comparing columns 4 and 1, observe that the greater the stock's variability, the greater the call price. The change in the call price given a small change in the stock's variability is referred to as the option's *vega* (also called *kappa*).

Like the BOPM for calls, most of the relationships between the equilibrium price of a put and S, X, T, and σ that were examined both intuitively and with arbitrage arguments in Chapter 9 are captured in the BOPM put model. This can be seen in the lower panel of Exhibit 10.19 in which combinations of the BOPM European put prices and stock prices are shown for different parameters: X (column 2), t (column 3), and σ^A (column 4). It should be noted, however, that the European binomial put model is unconstrained. That is, the model does not constrain the European put value to being equal to at least its intrinsic value. Thus, for an in-the-money put, the premium can be less than its IV, as shown in column 1 when the stock is at \$45 or less. The possibility that $P^E < $ IV reflects the fact that the BOPM model is limited to determining the price of a European put, in which negative time value premiums are possible.

Conclusion

The BOPM is based on the law of one price in which the equilibrium price of an option is equal to the value of a replicating portfolio constructed so it has the same cash flow as the option. In this chapter, we have derived the binomial call and put models for the cases of single and multiple periods to expiration, and we have investigated the arbitrage arguments by examining the strategies one can use if the option is not priced in the market to equal its BOPM value. In the next chapter, we turn our attention to the Black-Scholes OPM. As we will see, this model is simpler to use (though more complicated to derive), and under certain assumptions, it yields the same values as the BOPM.

BLOOMBERG: SCREENS FOR APPLYING THE BOPM

VOLATILITY
OVDV displays Bloomberg's implied volatility surfaces for a selected equity or equity index. The "Dividend" tab shows forecasted discrete dividends on ex-dividend dates.

HVG, Historical Volatility Graph: The HVG screen plots the historical volatility of a security and implied volatility of a loaded security. Historical volatility is the annualized standard deviation of the logarithmic returns. The implied volatility is the annualized standard deviation that equates the market price of the option to the model price.

(Continued)

For a loaded stock or option: Enter HVG (see Exhibit 10.20).

EXHIBIT 10.20   HVG Screens

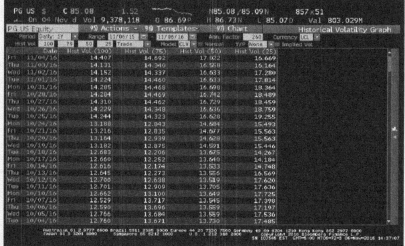

DIVIDENDS

DVD Shows historical dividends for a loaded stock or index.

   BDVD screen shows Bloomberg's forecasted dividends and dividend yield (see Exhibit 10.21).

EXHIBIT 10.21 BDVD Screen

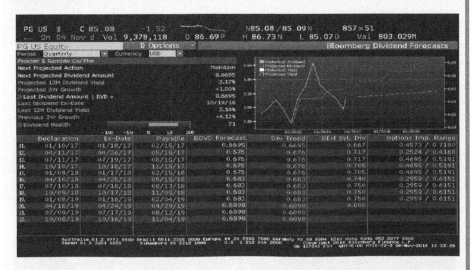

RISK-FREE RATE

The **FIT** screen displays current Treasury rates (see Exhibit 10.22).

EXHIBIT 10.22 FIT Screen

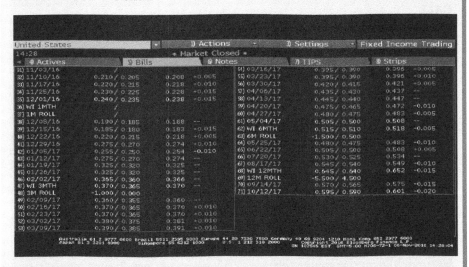

(Continued)

OPTION INFORMATION

Information for a specific option can be found on the option's DES, CALL, and OVDV screens. Option's Ticker <Equity>; DES and OVDV (see Exhibit 10.23).

P&G Call, *X* = $85, Expiration: 4/21/17:

Enter: PG 4/21/17 C85 <Equity>

EXHIBIT 10.23   DES, CALL, and OVDV Screens

DES

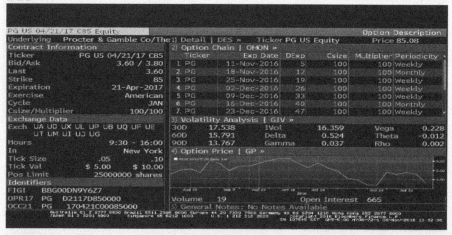

CALL

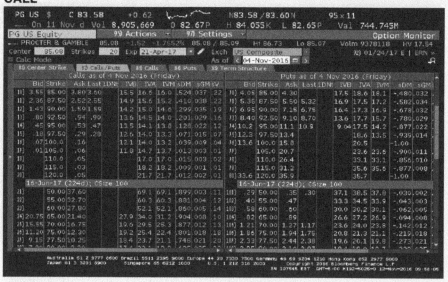

EXHIBIT 10.23 (*Continued*)

OVDV

Note: Given surface is more than 24hrs older than requested

PG US Equity	90) Asset	91) Actions	92) Views	93) Settings	Volatility Surface
PROCTER & GAMBLE	85.17 USD Bloomberg	Mid	As of 04-Nov-2016	15:45	

1) Vol Table 2) 3D Surface 3) Term 4) Skew 5) Dividends 6) Prices
Moneyness · Listed · 10) Edit Fwd Dates Strikes

Expiry	80.0%	90.0%	95.0%	97.5%	100.0%	102.5%	105.0%	110.0%	120.0%
	68.136	76.653	80.912	83.041	85.17	87.299	89.429	93.687	102.204
Nov-16	67.26	41.87	28.92	24.54	21.28	18.93	18.55	20.32	24.02
Nov-16	52.56	32.04	24.13	21.51	19.47	17.73	17.05	18.61	22.54
Nov-16	43.80	27.04	21.61	19.46	17.55	16.05	15.26	15.94	18.54
Dec-16	38.77	24.50	20.56	18.84	17.17	15.75	15.27	16.71	18.70
Dec-16	35.33	23.10	19.98	18.54	17.01	15.58	14.94	16.09	17.87
Dec-16	34.94	24.38	20.29	18.55	17.05	15.78	14.99	15.90	20.43
Dec-16	31.85	22.45	19.51	18.20	16.91	15.67	14.81	15.34	18.74
Jan-17	30.33	22.34	18.84	17.48	16.41	15.55	14.88	14.26	16.58
Apr-17	26.61	21.52	18.96	17.69	16.51	15.48	14.67	13.71	14.09
Jun-17	24.89	20.08	18.16	17.35	16.65	16.02	15.46	14.51	13.86
Jan-18	22.81	19.54	18.14	17.52	16.95	16.43	15.96	15.17	14.06
Jan-19	21.18	19.03	18.02	17.55	17.10	16.68	16.29	15.58	14.41
4Q-19	20.74	18.92	18.09	17.70	17.33	16.99	16.66	16.06	15.06

97) Option Pricing (OVME)   98) Legend   Zoom — 100%
99) Quick Pricer

Strike	85.17	Call	Vol	16.75%	Price	2.810	Dividend yield	3.109%
Expiry	04-Feb-2017	Buy	Spot	85.170	Delta	52.16%	Impl forward	84.686

Australia 61 2 9777 8600 Brazil 5511 2395 9000 Europe 44 20 7330 7500 Germany 49 69 9204 1210 Hong Kong 852 2977 6000
Japan 81 3 3201 8900   Singapore 65 6212 1000   U.S. 1 212 318 2000   Copyright 2016 Bloomberg Finance L.P.
SN 107545 EST   GMT-5:00 H706-72-1 06-Nov-2016 13:47:58

BINOMIAL PRICING OF P&G CALL ON 10/4/16

BOPM Excel Program

Input Information for BOPM

Stock price = $85.17 (OVDV)

X = $85 (DES)

Expiration: 4/21/17; Days to Expiration = 167 days (DES)

Annual Dividend Yield = 3.17% (BDVD)

Annualized Volatility = Historical Volatility (50-day average): $\sigma = 0.1770$ (HVG); Variance = 0.0313

Annualized Risk-Free Rate = 0.465% (FIT screen; T-bill rate maturing on 4/20/17) (See Exhibit 10.24.)

Call: BOPM for $n = 10$ Subperiods: Model Price = $3.65; Market Price = $3.60

(*Continued*)

EXHIBIT 10.24   BOPM Excel Program

⦿ Call	⦿ American	⦿ Spot	
◯ Put	◯ European	◯ Future	

Security Price	85.17		t	0.458
Exercise Price	85		q	0.5000
Number of Periods	10		Period u	1.03857
Days	167		Period d	0.9629
Time to Expiration (t)		Periodic Interest Rate		
Annualized Risk-Free	0.47%	Calculation	Period Rate	0.0212%
OR Period RF		◯ Continuous		
Annualized Mean	0	◉ Discrete	Risk-Neutral Prob, p	0.47420
Annualized Variance	0.0313			
OR u				
d				
Continuous Asset Yield	0.0317			

	0	1	2	3	4	5	6	7	8	9	10	11
0	39.3472	34.7295	30.2833	26.0021	21.8800	17.9109	14.0892	10.5552	7.6430	5.3617	3.6549	
1	30.2833	26.0021	21.8800	17.9109	14.0892	10.4178	7.3722	5.0196	3.3064	2.1171		
2	21.8800	17.9109	14.0892	10.4095	7.1108	4.6284	2.9000	1.7627	1.0454			
3	14.0892	10.4095	6.8664	4.1387	2.3915	1.3424	0.7377	0.3989				
4	6.8664	3.4548	1.6803	0.8167	0.3967	0.1926	0.0935					
5	0.1700	0.0806	0.0382	0.0181	0.0086	0.0041						
6	0.0000	0.0000	0.0000	0.0000	0.0000							
7	0.0000	0.0000	0.0000	0.0000								
8	0.0000	0.0000	0.0000									
9	0.0000	0.0000										
10	0.0000											

Selected References

Arditti, F., and K. John. "Spanning the State Space with Options." *Journal of Financial and Quantitative Analysis* 15 (March 1980): 1–9.

Arrow, K. "The Role of Securities in the Optimal Allocation of Risks Bearing." *Review of Economic Studies* (1964): 91–96.

Baily, W., and R. Stulz. "The Pricing of Stock Index Options in a General Equilibrium Model." *Journal of Financial and Quantitative Analysis* 24 (March 1989): 1–12.

Black, Fischer, and M. Scholes. "The Pricing of Options and Corporate Liabilities." *Journal of Political Economy* 81 (May–June 1973): 637–659.

Boyle, P. "A Lattice Framework for Option Pricing with Two State Variables." *Journal of Financial and Quantitative Analysis* 23 (March 1988): 1–12.

Brennan, M. "The Pricing of Contingent Claims in Discrete Time Models." *Journal of Finance* 34 (March 1979): 53–68.

Cox, John C., and S. Ross. "The Valuation of Options for Alternative Stochastic Processes." *Journal of Financial Economics* 3 (January–March 1976): 145–166.

Cox, John C., S. Ross, and M. Rubinstein. "Option Pricing: A Simplified Approach." *Journal of Financial Economics* 7 (September 1979): 229–263.

Cox, John C., and M. Rubinstein. *Option Markets*. Upper Saddle River, NJ: Prentice-Hall, 1985, Chapter 5.

Hsia, Chi-Cheng. "On Binomial Option Pricing." *The Journal of Financial Research* 6 (Spring 1983): 41–50.

Jarrow, Robert, and A. Rudd. *Option Pricing*. Homewood, IL: Irwin, 1983, Chapters 7–13.

Johnson, R. S. *Introduction to Derivatives: Options, Futures, and Swaps*. New York: Oxford University Press, 2009, Chapter 5.

Kolb, Robert. *Futures, Options, and Swaps*. Malden, MA: Blackwell Publishing, 2003, Chapter 16.

Rendleman, R., and B. Bartter. "Two-State Option Pricing." *Journal of Finance* 34 (December 1979): 1093–1110.

Ritchken, Peter. *Options: Theory, Strategy, and Applications*. Glenview, IL: Scott Foresman, 1987, Chapters 8–10.

Rubinstein, M. "The Valuation of Uncertain Income Streams and the Pricing of Options." *Bell Journal of Economics* 7 (Autumn 1976): 407–424.

Smith, Clifford W. Jr., "Option Pricing: A Review." *Journal of Financial Economics* 3 (January–March 1976): 3–51.

Problems and Questions

1. Consider a one-period, two-state case in which ABC stock is trading at $S_0 = \$100$, has u of 1.10 and d of 0.95, and the period risk-free rate is 5%.

   a. Using the BOPM, determine the equilibrium price of an ABC 100 European call option expiring at the end of the period.

   b. Explain what an arbitrageur would do if the ABC European call were priced at $5.35. Show what the arbitrageur's cash flow would be at expiration when she closed. Show the cash flows at both possible stock prices at expiration.

   c. Explain what an arbitrageur would do if the ABC European call were priced at $7.35. Show at both possible stock prices what the arbitrageur's cash flow would be at expiration when she closed.

   d. Using the BOPM, determine the equilibrium price of an ABC 100 European put option expiring at the end of the period.

   e. Explain what an arbitrageur would do if the ABC 100 European put were priced at $1.18. Show what the arbitrageur's cash flow would be at both possible stock prices at expiration when she closed.

   f. Explain what an arbitrageur would do if the ABC 100 European put were priced at $2.00. Show what the arbitrageur's cash flow would be at both possible stock prices at expiration when she closed.

2. Using the put-call parity model, determine the equilibrium price of the put in Question 1, given the equilibrium call value as determined by the binomial model. Comment on the consistency of the binomial call and put models and the put-call parity model.

3. Assume two periods to expiration, $u = 1.05$, $d = 1/1.05$, $r_f = 1.02$, $S_0 = \$100$, no dividends, and $X = \$100$ on a European call expiring at the end of the second period. Find: C_{uu}, C_{ud}, C_{dd}, C_d, C_u, C_0^*, H_u, H_d, H_0^*, B_u, B_d, and B_0^*.

4. Assume two periods to expiration, $u = 1.05$, $d = 1/1.05$, $r_f = 1.02$, $S_0 = \$100$, no dividends, and $X = \$100$ on a European put expiring at the end of the second period.

   a. Find: P_{uu}, P_{ud}, P_{dd}, P_d, P_u, P_0^*, $H^p{}_u$, H^p_d, H^{P*}_0, I_u, I_d, and I_0^*.

   b. Determine the equilibrium price of a comparable call on the stock using the put-call parity model. Is the call price consistent with the binomial call price you determined in Question 3?

   c. If the put is American, what would its equilibrium price be?

5. Assume ABC stock price follows a binomial process, is trading at $S_0 = \$100$, has $u = 1.10$, $d = 0.95$, and probability of its price increasing in one period is 0.5 ($q = 0.5$).

   a. Show with a binomial tree ABC's possible stock prices, logarithmic returns, and probabilities after one period, two periods, and three periods.

   b. What are the stock's expected logarithmic return and variance for each period?

   c. Define the properties of a binomial distribution.

   d. Verify that the u and d formulas yield the u and d values of 1.10 and 0.95, given the logarithmic return's mean and variance after three periods:

$$u = e^{\sqrt{V_e/n} + \mu_e/n}$$

$$d = e^{-\sqrt{V_e/n} + \mu_e/n}$$

6. Describe the methodology used to derive the formulas for estimating u and d.

7. Suppose ABC stock has the following prices over the past 13 quarters:

Quarter	S_t (in $)
Y1.1	106
Y1.2	100
Y1.3	94
Y1.4	88
Y2.1	94
Y2.2	100
Y2.3	106
Y2.4	100
Y3.1	94
Y3.2	88
Y3.3	94
Y3.4	100
Y4.1	106

   a. Calculate the stock's average logarithmic return and variance.

   b. What is the stock's annualized mean and variance?

   c. Calculate the stock's up and down parameters (u and d) for periods with the following lengths:

      i. One quarter

      ii. One month

      iii. One week (assume 12 weeks in a quarter)

      iv. One day (assume 90 days in a quarter)

   d. Using the BOPM Excel Program determine the equilibrium price for an ABC 100 call expiring in three months for binomial periods of length one quarter, one month, and one day. Assume the stock is currently priced at $100 and the annual risk-free rate is 6%.

   e. Using the BOPM Excel Program determine the equilibrium price for an ABC 100 European put on the stock expiring in three months for binomial periods of length one quarter, one month, and one day. Assume the stock is currently priced at $100 and the annual risk-free rate is 6%. Are the binomial put prices consistent with put-call parity?

   f. Suppose the 100 put were American. Using the BOPM Excel Program determine the equilibrium prices for the American put for periods of lengths one month ($n = 3$) and one day ($n = 90$). Assume the stock price is $100, the put expires in three months, and the annual risk-free rate is 6%. Do the binomial put prices for the American put differ from the European values you calculate? If so, why?

8. Assume a binomial, risk-neutral world where $n = 1$, $S_0 = \$100$, $R_f = 0.05$, $u = 1.10$, and $d = 0.95$.

   a. What are the risk-neutral probabilities of the stock increasing in one period and decreasing in one period?

   b. Solve for the probabilities using the equation: $S_0 = PV(E(S_T))$.

   c. Using risk-neutral pricing, determine the equilibrium price of a call on a stock with an exercise price of $100 and expiration at the end of the period.

   d. Using risk-neutral pricing, determine the equilibrium price of a put on the stock with an exercise price of $100 and expiration at the end of the period.

   e. Are your answers in c and d consistent with the BOPM's replicating approach (Question 1)?

9. Explain what is meant by risk-neutral pricing. What is the reason for pricing options using a risk-neutral pricing approach?

10. Consider a one-period, two-state case in which ABC stock is trading at $S_0 = \$100$, $u = 1.1$, and $d = 0.95$, the period risk-free rate is 5%, and the stock is expected to go ex-dividend at the end of the period with a dividend worth $1.00 at the ex-dividend date.

   a. Using the BOPM, determine the equilibrium price of an ABC 100 European call option.

   b. Using the BOPM, determine the equilibrium price of an ABC 100 European put option.

    c. Using the put-call parity model, show that the put price is equal to BOPM's put value.

    d. What is the equilibrium price of the call option if it was American and therefore could be exercised just before the expiration date?

11. Explain what an arbitrageur would do if the market priced the ABC European 100 call in Question 10 were equal to the BOPM's value without the $1.00 dividend. Show what the arbitrageur's cash flow would be at expiration when she closed at the ex-dividend stock prices. Does the arbitrage strategy also apply if the call were American?

12. Explain what an arbitrageur would do if the market priced the ABC 100 European put in Question 10 were equal to the BOPM's value without the $1.00 dividend. Show what the arbitrageur's cash flow would be at expiration when she closed at the ex-dividend stock prices.

13. ABC stock is trading at $100, its annualized standard deviation is $\sigma^A = 0.3$, its mean is zero, and its continuous annual dividend yield is 2.5%. The annual risk-free rate is 2.5%. Determine the equilibrium prices of ABC American and European 100 call and put options expiring in 180 days using the BOPM Excel program. Also determine the prices of the options for the following number of subperiods: $n = 5, 10, 20,$ and 100.

Bloomberg Exercises

1. Using Bloomberg information, estimate the equilibrium price on a call and put option on a selected stock using the BOPM Excel program. Bloomberg option input information:

    a. Stock price: DES or GP screen.

    b. Option exercise price: Option's DES, OMON, or Call screen or OSA.

    c. Option exercise price and expiration: Option's DES, OMON, or Call screen or OSA. Input days to expiration.

    d. Risk-free rate: FIT screen; "Treasury" tab. Select Treasury with maturity closest to the option's expiration.

    e. Volatility: HVG screen. Select historical volatility or implied volatility.

    f. Annual dividend yield: BDVD screen.

    Use the BOPM Excel program and evaluate the option price for $n = 30$ subperiods. The Excel program can be downloaded from the text's website.

    How close does the model's option price come to the market price? Experiment with different volatilities until you find one that gives you a binomial option value that is close to the market price.

2. Using the BOPM Excel program, evaluate the prices of the call and put options you analyzed in Exercise 1 for different stock prices.

3. For one of the options that you evaluated in Exercise 1, evaluate the sensitivity of its binomial option values to different volatilities. Use the HVG screen to help you

select the volatilities (e.g., a past volatility or one calculated with different moving averages).

4. Download Bloomberg stock price data from a selected stock's GP screen (right-click your mouse in the graph area; click "Send Data to Clipboard" to download data to Excel). In Excel:

   a. Calculate columns for stock price relatives (S_t/S_{t-1}) and logarithmic returns $(\ln(S_t/S_{t-1}))$.

   b. Use Excel Average and Variance functions to calculate the historical mean and variance.

   c. Annualize the historical mean and variance.

   d. Determine the annualized standard deviation.

   Compare your historical annualized standard deviation to those calculated in HVG.

5. Using the historical volatility and mean you calculated in Exercise 4, select an option on the stock and determine its equilibrium price using the BOPM Excel program. See Exercise 1 for finding input information from Bloomberg screens.

Appendix 10A: Risk-Neutral Pricing

Risk-Neutral Probability Pricing—Single-Period Case

A risk-neutral market is defined as one in which investors will accept the same expected return $(E(k))$ from a risky investment as they would from a risk-free one. That is: $E(k) = R_f$; or equivalently the risk premium is zero: $RP = E(k) - R_f = 0$.

The values of the call, put, and stock are equal to the present value of their expected cash flow. In our one-period, two-state example ($u = 1.1, d = 0.95, S_0 = \$50$, $X = \$50$, and $R_f = 1.025$),

$$S_0 = \frac{E(S_T)}{(1+k)} = \frac{q(uS_0) + (1-q)(dS_0)}{1+k} = \frac{q(\$55) + (1-q)(\$47.50)}{1+k}$$

$$C_0 = \frac{E(C_T)}{(1+k)} = \frac{q(C_u) + (1-q)(C_d)}{1+k} = \frac{q(\$5.00) + (1-q)(0)}{1+k}$$

$$P_0 = \frac{E(P_T)}{(1+k)} = \frac{q(P_u) + (1-q)(P_d)}{1+k} = \frac{q(0) + (1-q)(\$2.50)}{1+k}$$

where q is the objective probability of the stock increasing in one period, and $(1-q)$ is the probability of it decreasing.

We would normally expect that most investors would want a higher expected rate of return from the risky investment. Such a market is referred to as risk-averse. Suppose, though, we assume that we have a risk-neutral market in which investors will accept the same expected rate of return from a risky investment as they would from a risk-free one. In a risk-neutral market, the prices of all assets (risky and risk-free) are priced without regard to risk and determined by discounting the expected future payouts at the risk-free rate. In our option pricing example, if we assume a risk-neutral market, then the price of our stock, call, and put would be:

$$S_0 = \frac{E(S_T)}{(1+k)} = \frac{q(uS_0) + (1-q)(dS_0)}{r_f} = \frac{q(\$55) + (1-q)(\$47.50)}{1.025}$$

$$C_0 = \frac{E(C_T)}{(1+k)} = \frac{q(C_u) + (1-q)(C_d)}{r_f} = \frac{q(\$5.00) + (1-q)(0)}{1.025}$$

$$P_0 = \frac{E(P_T)}{(1+k)} = \frac{q(P_u) + (1-q)(P_d)}{r_f} = \frac{q(0) + (1-q)(\$2.50)}{1.025}$$

Given the current price of the stock ($S_0 = \$50$) and the period rate on the risk-free security ($R_f = 2.5\%$), we can solve mathematically for the probabilities: q and $1 - q$ (that is, in a risk-neutral market, the market price of the stock determines the market's estimates of the probabilities of the stock increasing and decreasing). Solving the equation for q we obtain:

$$\$50 = \frac{q(\$55) + (1-q)(\$47.50)}{1.0125}$$

$$q = 0.5$$

Or in parameter terms:

$$S_0 = \frac{q(uS_0) + (1-q)(dS_0)}{r_f}$$

$$q = \frac{r_f - d}{u - d}$$

Note, q is the same as the p term in the BOPM call and put equations, q and $1 - q$ are, in turn, referred to as *risk-neutral probabilities*. Substituting the risk-neutral probabilities into the one-period call and put equations, we obtain:

$$C_o^* = \frac{1}{r_f}\,[q\,C_u + (1-q)C_u] = \frac{1}{1.025}\,[0.50(\$5.00) + (0.50)\,(0)] = \$2.44$$

$$P_0^* = \frac{1}{r_f}\,[q\,P_u + (1-q)P_d] = \frac{1}{1.025}\,[0.50(0) + (0.50)\,(\$2.50)] = \$1.22.$$

The present value of the expected stock price is also equal to its current value using the risk-neutral probabilities:

$$S_0 = PV(E(S_t)) = \frac{E(S_T)}{r_f}$$

$$S_0 = \frac{1}{r_f}[quS_0 + (1-q)dS_0]$$

$$S_0 = \frac{1}{1.025}[(0.50)(\$55) + (0.50)(\$47.50)] = \$50$$

Risk-Neutral Probability Pricing—Multiple-Period Case

In a multiple-period case, the expected terminal value of a call ($E(C_T)$) or put ($E(P_T)$) after n periods can be obtained once we know the probabilities of the option's intrinsic values. In a binomial process, the probabilities of an option equaling one of its possible intrinsic values is given by the probability of j upward moves in n period, p_{nj}. The risk-neutral probability, p_{nj}, in turn, can be found using the following equation:

$$p_{nj} = \frac{n!}{(n-j)!j!}q^j(1-q)^{n-j}$$

where p is the risk-neutral probability of the stock increasing in one period, and as we showed in the single-period case, is equal to $[r_f-d]/[u-d]$.

In our two-period example in $u = 1.0488$, $d = .9747$, $r_f = 1.0125$, $S_0 = \$50$, and $X = \$50$, the risk-neutral probability of the stock increasing in one period is

$$p = \frac{r_f - d}{u - d} = \frac{1.0125 - 0.9747}{1.0488 - 0.9747} = 0.510121$$

Thus, the probabilities of the number of upward moves in n periods being $j = 2$, 1, or 0 in our example, are:

$$j = 2 : \quad p_{22} = \left[\frac{2!}{0!\,2!}\right](0.510102)^2 = 0.26022$$

$$j = 1 : \quad p_{21} = \left[\frac{2!}{1!\,1!}\right](0.510121)(1 - 0.510121) = 0.499795$$

$$j = 0 := p_{20} = \left[\frac{2!}{2!\,0!}\right](1 - 0.510121)^2 = 0.23998$$

With the period risk-free rate of 1.25%, the value of the 50 European call and 50 European put are $1.81 and $0.59:

$$j = 2 : \quad C_{uu} = \text{Max}[u^2 d^0 S_0 - X, \ 0] = \text{Max}[\$55 - \$50, 0] = \$5$$

$$j = 1 : \quad C_{ud} = \text{Max}[u^1 d^1 S_0 - X, \ 0] = \text{Max}[\$51.11 - \$50, 0] = \$1.11$$

$$j = 0 : \quad C_{dd} = \text{Max}[u^0 d^2 S_0 - X, \ 0] = \text{Max}[\$47.50 - \$50, 0] = 0$$

$$C_0^* = \frac{E(C_T)}{r_f^n} = \frac{p_{22} C_{uu} + p_{21} C_{ud} + p_{20} C_{dd}}{r_f^2}$$

$$C_0^* = \frac{p_{22} C_{uu} + p_{21} C_{ud} + p_{20} C_{dd}}{r_f^2}$$

$$C_0^* = \frac{(0.26022)(\$5.00) + (0.499795)(\$1.11) + (0.239988)(0)}{(1.0125)^2} = \$1.81$$

$$j = 2 : \quad P_{uu} = \text{Max}[X - u^2 d^0 S_0, \ 0] = \text{Max}[\$50 - \$55, 0] = 0$$

$$j = 1 : \quad P_{ud} = \text{Max}[X - u^1 d^1 S_0, \ 0] = \text{Max}[\$50 - \$51.11, 0] = 0$$

$$j = 0 : \quad P_{dd} = \text{Max}[X - u^0 d^2 S_0, \ 0] = \text{Max}[\$50 - \$47.50, 0] = \$2.50$$

$$P_0^* = \frac{p_{22} P_{uu} + p_{21} P_{ud} + p_{20} P_{dd}}{r_f^2}$$

$$C_0^* = \frac{(0.26022)(0) + (0.499795)(0) + (0.239988)(2.50)}{(1.0125)^2} = \$0.59$$

These values are the same as those we obtained using the replicating approach.

Derivation of Merton's Continuous Dividend Yield Model

Merton's continuous dividend yield approach assumes the dividend is paid out at a continuous rate. To apply the binomial model to a stock paying a continuous dividend requires treating the stock as having a continuous leakage of value resulting from its continuous dividend payments. The binomial model can be adjusted for a continuous dividend payment by substituting the following continuous dividend-adjusted stock price for the current stock price in the binomial model:

$$S_0^D = S_0 \, e^{-\psi t}$$

where

$\quad \psi =$ annual dividend yield = annual dividend/stock price

The most direct way to incorporate the dividend-adjusted stock price into the binomial model is to make use of risk-neutral pricing approach. Substituting the dividend-adjusted stock price for the current price, we obtain:

$$S_0 = \frac{1}{r_f}[puS_0 + (1-p)dS_0]$$

$$S_0 e^{-\psi \, \Delta t} = \frac{1}{e^{R^A \Delta t}}[puS_0 + (1-p)dS_0]$$

$$S_0 e^{-\psi \, \Delta t} = e^{-R^A \Delta t}[puS_0 + (1-p)S_0]$$

$$S_0 e^{(R^A-\psi) \, \Delta t} = [puS_0 + (1-p)dS_0]$$

Solving the above equation for p, yields a dividend-adjusted risk-neutral probability reflecting a continuous dividend yield:

$$S_0 e^{(R^A-\psi) \, \Delta t} = [puS_0 + (1-p)dS_0]$$

$$e^{(R^A-\psi) \, \Delta t} = pu + (1-p)d$$

$$e^{(R^A-\psi) \, \Delta t} = p(u-d) + d$$

$$p = \frac{e^{(R^A-\psi) \, \Delta t} - d}{u-d}$$

This equation can be used to determine p in the equilibrium equations for call and put options:

$$C_0 = \frac{1}{e^{R^A\Delta t}}[pC_u + (1-p)C_d]$$

$$P_0 = \frac{1}{e^{R^A\Delta t}}[pP_u + (1-p)P_d]$$

The equation also shows that the dividend-adjusted risk-neutrality probability treats the dividend yield as a negative interest rate in which the dividend yield represents a continuous leakage of value from the stock.

Appendix 10B: Discrete Dividend-Payment Approach

The discrete dividend-payment approach consists of the following steps:

1. Calculate the current present value of all dividends to be paid during the life of the option: $PV(D)$.
2. Subtract the present value of all dividends from the current price of the stock to obtain a dividend-adjusted stock price: $S_0^D = S_0 - PV(D)$.
3. Apply the up and down parameters to the dividend-adjusted stock price, S_0^D, to generate a binomial tree of stock prices.

4. After generating the tree, add to the stock prices at each node the present value of all future dividends to generate a dividend-adjusted binomial stock tree.
5. Given the dividend-adjusted binomial tree of stock prices, compute the option value by starting at expirations and applying the normal recursive method.
6. If the option is American, start one period before expiration and place a constraint that the American option price is the maximum of the binomial value or exercise value, and then roll the tree forward applying the same constraint.

The first three steps yield a binomial tree of stock prices that reflect the stock's approximate value after it pays a dividend. The fourth step of adding the value of the dividend back to the stock price, allows the option's exercise values to be evaluated at different nodes to determine if early exercise is beneficial.

Example

Suppose XYZ stock is trading at $50, its annualized standard deviation is $\sigma^A = 0.4$, its mean is zero, and the stock will go ex-dividend in 100 days, with the value of the dividend worth $2 at that date. Suppose, also, that there are American call and put options on XYZ stock, both with exercise prices of $50 and expirations of 120 days, and that the annual risk-free rate is $R^A = 6\%$. For a three-period binomial tree, the following steps would be used to price the options using the discrete dividend-payment approach.

1. The first step in valuing the options is to subtract the present value of the dividend from the current stock price to obtain the dividend-adjusted stock price. With continuous compounding, the present value of the dividend is $1.97, and the dividend-adjusted stock price is $48.03:

$$PV(D) = D e^{-Rt^*}$$

$$PV(D) = \$2 \, e^{-(0.06)(100/365)} = \$1.97$$

$$S_0^D = S_0 - PV(D)$$

$$S_0^D = \$50 - \$1.97 = \$48.03$$

2. The second step is to generate a three-period binomial tree starting with the dividend-adjusted stock price. In this case, $u = 1.141584$, $d = 1/u = 0.875976$, and $p = .491781$:

$$u = e^{\sigma^A \sqrt{t/n}} = e^{0.4\sqrt{(120/365)/3}} = 1.141584$$

$$d = e^{-\sigma^A \sqrt{t/n}} = e^{-0.4\sqrt{(120/365)/3}} = 0.875976 = 1/u$$

$$p = \frac{r_f - d}{u - d} = \frac{e^{R^A(t/n)} - d}{u - d} = \frac{e^{(0.06)((120/365)/3)} - 0.875976}{1.141584 - 0.875976} = 0.491781$$

The top number at each node in Exhibit 10B.1 shows the stock prices for the three-period tree obtained from applying Step 2.

3. The third step is to add to the stock price at each node the present value of the dividend associated with that period. With the option expiring in 120 days, the length of each period in this example is $120/3 = 40$ days. Thus, 40 days will expire at the end of period 1 and 80 days at the end of period 2. With the ex-dividend date in 100 days, possible stock prices therefore have to be adjusted for periods 1 and 2 but not 3. At period 1, there are 60 days to the ex-dividend date $(100 - 40)$, and at period 2, there are 20 days $(100 - 80)$. The present values of the $2.00 dividend value at the end of periods 1 and 2 are $1.98 and $1.99:

$$n = 1 : \quad PV(D_1) = De^{-Rt_1^*} = \$2\,e^{-(0.06)(60/365)} = \$1.98$$

$$n = 2 : \quad PV(D_2) = De^{-Rt_1^*} = \$2\,e^{-(0.06)(20/365)} = \$1.99$$

The second number at each node in Exhibit 10B.1 shows the stock prices adjusted by adding the present value of the dividend to the non–dividend-adjusted stock prices.

4. Given the binomial tree of dividend-adjusted stock prices, the fourth step is to calculate the call and put prices using the normal recursive method: Start at expiration where the option values are equal to their intrinsic values and then roll the tree forward using the single period model. For American options, this step requires constraining the option price in each period to be the maximum of its exercise value or binomial value. The third row in each node in Exhibit 10B.1 shows the binomial call values, and the last row shows the binomial put values.

As shown in the exhibit, the price of the American call is $4.65, while the price of the European is $4.25. The price difference reflects an early exercise advantage for the call in period 2 at the upper node. There is no early exercise advantage, however, for the put in this discrete three-period case with dividends. The price of the American put and European put are therefore both equal to $5.24. If the stock had not paid a dividend during the option period, then the value of the American and European calls would be equal to $5.40, and the price of the American put would be $4.51 and the European put would be $4.43. Thus, as we would expect, in the discrete dividend-adjusted model, dividends have an inverse impact on the price of a call option, and in cases where early exercise is beneficial, the dividend-adjusted model values an American call more than a European one. In the case of a put, if there were no dividends paid during the option period, then the price of the American put would be $4.51, while the European value would be $4.43. Thus, without dividends, an early exercise advantage exists with puts.

The discrete dividend-payment approach for pricing options on stocks paying dividends is more accurate when we subdivide the tree into more periods (at least up to $n = 30$ subperiods). An Excel option program that values American and European calls and puts using the discrete-dividend payment approach can be accessed from the text's website. Using the "Discrete Dividend-Payment Binomial Model" Excel program, the equilibrium prices for the call and put options for 100 subperiods are $C^a = \$4.52$, $C^e = 3.95$, $P^a = \$5.00$, and $P^e = \$4.94$ (see lower panel of Exhibit 10B.1).

EXHIBIT 10B.1   Discrete Dividend-Payment Approach

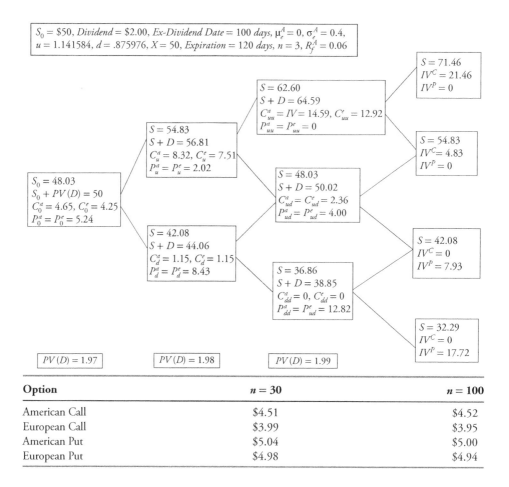

Option	$n = 30$	$n = 100$
American Call	$4.51	$4.52
European Call	$3.99	$3.95
American Put	$5.04	$5.00
European Put	$4.98	$4.94

CHAPTER 11

The Black-Scholes Option Pricing Model

As we subdivide the expiration period in applying the BOPM, or equivalently make the length of each period smaller, the number of possible stock prices at expiration increases and the assumption of only two states in one period is more plausible. Thus, for the pricing of most options, the binomial model for large n is more realistic. As n becomes large, the BOPM becomes the equation for the Black-Scholes (B-S) OPM. Thus, for large n the equilibrium values of an option derived by the BOPM are approximately the same as those obtained by the OPM developed by Black and Scholes. In this chapter, we examine the B-S OPM and it application.

The Black-Scholes Call Model

Like the binomial, the B-S model determines the equilibrium value as the call price that is equal to the value of a replicating portfolio. The mathematics used in deriving the B-S OPM (stochastic calculus and a heat exchange equation) are complex; if fact, part of the contribution of the BOPM is that it is simpler to derive, yet still yields the same solution as the B-S OPM for the case of large n. The B-S model, though, is relatively easy to use (the mathematical foundation and the derivation of the B-S OPM are presented in several derivative texts).

B-S OPM Formula

The B-S formula for determining the equilibrium call price is:

$$C_0^* = S_0 N(d_1) - \left[\frac{X}{e^{Rt}}\right] N(d_2)$$

$$d_1 = \frac{\ln(S_0/X) + (R + 0.5\,\sigma^2)t}{\sigma\sqrt{t}}$$

$$d_2 = d_1 - \sigma\sqrt{t}$$

where

$$
\begin{aligned}
t &= \text{time to expiration expressed as a proportion of the year} \\
R &= \text{continuously compounded annual risk-free rate of return} \\
\sigma &= \text{annualized standard deviation of the logarithmic return} \\
N(d_1), N(d_2) &= \text{cumulative normal probabilities}
\end{aligned}
$$

In the B-S equation, X/e^{Rt} is the present value of the exercise price $(PV(X))$ with continuously compounding. R in the equation is the continuously compounded annual risk-free rate. This rate can be found by taking the natural logarithm of one plus the simple annual rate on a risk-free security with a maturity equal to the call's expiration date. Thus, if 0.025 is the simple annual, then the continuous compounded rate is $\ln(1 + 0.025) = 0.0247$. σ^2 is the annualized variance of the logarithmic return we defined in Chapter 10. The cumulative normal probabilities, $N(d_1)$ and $N(d_2)$, are the probabilities that deviations of less than d_1 and d_2 will occur in a standard normal distribution with a zero mean and a standard deviation of one. The following power function can be used to compute $N(d_1)$ and $N(d_2)$:

$$
\begin{aligned}
n(d) = 1 - 0.5[1 &+ 0.196854\,(|d|) + 0.115194\,(|d|)^2 \\
&+ 0.00344\,(|d|)^3 + 0.019527\,(|d|)^4]^{-4}
\end{aligned}
$$

where

$|d| = $ absolute value of d.

If d is negative, then the $N(d)$ value obtained from the power function is subtracted from 1; if d is positive then the $N(d)$ obtained from the function is used:

$$N(d) = 1 - n(d), \text{ for } d < 0$$

$$N(d) = n(d), \text{ for } d > 0$$

Example

To see how to use the B-S OPM formula, consider the case of an XYZ 50 call that expires in six months ($t = 0.50$), in which XYZ stock is trading at $50 and has an estimated annualized variance of 0.09 ($\sigma = 0.30$) and in which the continuously compounded annual risk-free rate is 2.5%. To determine the equilibrium price of the XYZ call, we first calculate the values for d_1 and d_2:

$$d_1 = \frac{\ln(\$50/\$50) + [0.025 + 0.5(0.30)^2] \,(0.50)}{0.3\sqrt{0.50}} = 0.164992$$

$$d_2 = 0.164992 - 0.30\sqrt{0.5} = -0.04714$$

Next, we use the power function to find the corresponding values of $N(d_1)$ and $N(d_2)$:

$$N(d_1) = N(0.164992)$$

$$= 1 - 0.5[1 + 0.196854(0.164992) + 0.115194(0.164992^2)$$

$$+ 0.000344(0.164992^3) + 0.019527(0.164992^4)]^{-4}$$

$$N(d_1) = N(0.164992) = 0.56534$$

$$N(d_2) = N(-0.04714)$$

$$= 1 - \{1 - 0.5[1 + 0.196854(0.04714) + 0.115194(0.04714^2)$$

$$+ 0.000344(0.04714^3) + 0.019527(0.04714^4)]^{-4}\}$$

$$N(d_2) = N(-0.04714) = 0.481374$$

Last, we use the B-S equation to obtain the equilibrium call price:

$$C_0^* = S_0\,N(d_1) - \left[\frac{X}{e^{Rt}}\right] N(d_2)$$

$$C_0^* = (\$50)(0.56534) - \left[\frac{\$50}{e^{(0.025)(0.50)}}\right] (0.481374) = \$4.50$$

As we noted previously, the B-S price differs from the BOPM prices for small n, but is approximately the same for large. This can be seen in Exhibit 11.1 in which the B-S price of $4.50 is compared with the prices obtained using the binomial model for different values of n. As shown in the table, at $n = 10$, the binomial price is $0.09 less than the B-S price; at $n = 20$, the difference is $0.04, at $n = 40$, the difference is only $0.01, and at $n = 60$ and greater, the binomial price exactly equals the B-S price of $4.50. Thus, the example illustrates our earlier point that as n increases, the BOPM yields equilibrium call values approximately equal to the B-S OPM.

Features

Like the BOPM call price, the B-S model's equilibrium call price is positively related to underlying security price, time to expiration, risk-free rate, and the security's volatility and negatively related to the exercise price. Exhibit 11.2 shows combinations of the

EXHIBIT 11.1   BOPM Values for Different n

$S_0 = \$50$, $X = \$50$, $t = 0.50$, $R = 0.025^+$, $\sigma = 0.30$

n	BOPM C*
10	$4.41
20	$4.46
40	$4.49
60	$4.50
100	$4.50

B-S OPM Price = $4.50

+ R is the continuously compounded annual rate used in the B-S model.
In the BOPM, the periodic rate obtained from the simple annual rate (R^A)
is used:

$R^A = $ simple annual rate $= e^R - 1 = e^{0.025} - 1 = 0.02531$

B-S OPM values and stock prices for different parameter values. The first column shows the call values given the parameter values used in the preceding example: $X = \$50$, $t = 0.5$, $R = 0.025$, and $\sigma = 0.30$. The other columns show the call and stock price relations generated with the same parameter values used in column 1, except for one variable: in column 2, $X = 45$; in column 3, $t = 0.75$; in column 4, $\sigma = 0.40$; and in column 5, $R = 0.04$.

Also like the BOPM, over a range of stock prices, the B-S OPM yields a call and stock price relation that is nonlinear and satisfies the minimum and maximum boundary conditions. The relationship is shown in the figure in Exhibit 11.2, where the B-S option call values and stock prices from column 1 are plotted. The slope of the call price curve is referred to as the option's *delta*. Delta is equal to H^* in the BOPM and to $N(d_1)$ in the B-S model. For a call, the delta ranges from 0 for deep-out-of-the-money calls to approximately 1.00 for deep-in-the-money ones. This can be seen in Exhibit 11.2's graph that shows that the option curve is relatively flat for low stock prices and starts to become parallel to the minimum boundary line for high stock values. The nonlinear call and stock price relation also can be seen by the change in the slope of the B-S option price curve as the stock price increases. In option literature, the change in slope (i.e., delta) per small change in the stock price defines the option's *gamma* (it is the second-order partial derivative of the call price with respect to changes in the stock price).

Mathematically, the impacts that changes in these variables have on the equilibrium call price can be found by taking the partial derivatives of the B-S OPM equation with respect to S, X, t, R, and σ. The change in an option's prices with respect to a small change in the time to expiration (with other factors held constant) is defined as the option's *theta*. The change in the call price given a small change in the stock's variability is referred to as the option's *vega* (also called *kappa*). The change in the call price given a small change in R is called the call's *rho*.

EXHIBIT 11.2 B-S OPM Option Price and Stock Price Relation Given Different Parameter Values

	1	2	3	4	5
	$X = \$50$	$X = \$45$	$X = \$50$	$X = \$50$	$X = \$50$
	$t = 0.5$	$t = 0.5$	$t = 0.75$	$t = 0.5$	$t = 0.5$
	$\sigma^A = 0.30$	$\sigma^A = 0.30$	$\sigma^A = 0.30$	$\sigma^A = 0.40$	$\sigma^A = 0.30$
	$R = 0.025$	$R = 0.025$	$R = 0.025$	$R = 0.025$	$R = 0.04$
Stock Price	Call Price	Call Price	Call Price	Call Price	Call Price
$35	0.20	0.54	0.49	0.65	0.22
$40	0.79	1.77	1.40	1.64	0.84
$45	2.18	4.05	3.11	3.42	2.29
$50	4.50	7.36	5.58	5.89	4.69
$55	7.77	11.42	8.86	9.11	8.01
$60	11.73	15.96	12.68	12.83	12.02
$65	16.18	20.73	16.96	17.01	16.51
Stock Price	Put Price	Put Price	Put Price	Put Price	Put Price
$35	14.58	9.98	14.57	15.02	14.23
$40	10.17	6.22	10.47	11.02	9.85
$45	6.56	3.49	7.18	7.80	6.30
$50	3.88	1.80	4.65	5.26	3.70
$55	2.15	0.86	2.93	3.49	2.02
$60	1.11	0.40	1.75	2.21	1.03
$65	0.56	0.17	1.04	1.39	0.52

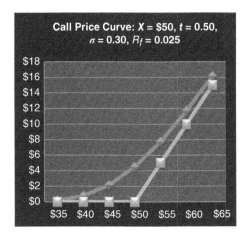

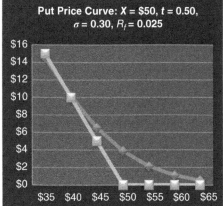

Black-Scholes Arbitrage Portfolio

Like the BOPM, the B-S OPM's equation is equal to the value of the replicating call portfolio. That is:

$$C_0^* = H_0^* S_0 - B_0^*$$

where from the B-S model:

$$H_0^* = N(d_1)$$

$$B_0^* = \left[\frac{X}{e^{Rt}}\right] N(d_2)$$

Thus, the OPM call value of \$4.50 in our previous example is equal to the value of a replicating portfolio consisting of 0.56534 shares of stock, partially financed by borrowing \$23.767:

$$C_0^* = H_0^* S_0 - B_0^* = 0.56534(\$50) - \$23.767 = \$4.50$$

where

$$H_0^* = N(d_1) = 0.56534$$

$$B_0^* = \left[\frac{X}{e^{Rt}}\right] N(d_2) = \left[\frac{\$50}{e^{(0.025)(0.5)}}\right](0.48134) = \$23.767$$

If the market price of the call does not equal the B-S value, then arbitrage opportunities will exist by taking a position in the call and an opposite position in the replicating portfolio. Moreover, in the continuous-time B-S model, the hedge ratio is changing continuously with the passage of time, as well as with stock price changes; thus, to keep the portfolio riskless, arbitrageurs would need to readjust frequently and close as soon as profit opportunities appear.

Dividend Adjustments for the Black-Scholes Call Model

As examined in Chapters 9 and 10, dividends cause the price of a call to decrease on the ex-dividend date and can lead to an early exercise of the call if it is American. Since the B-S OPM values a European call without dividends, it needs to be adjusted for dividends and for American calls given the early exercise possibility when dividends are expected. Two dividend adjustment models that use the B-S OPM are Fisher Black's pseudo-American call model, applicable to American and European calls when there are dividends, and Merton's continuous dividend yield approach applicable for European calls. Black's pseudo model is analogous to the discrete dividend payment approach examined in Appendix 10B, and Merton's continuous dividend payment model is simply an extension of Merton's constant dividend yield approach for the discrete BOPM to the continuous B-S model.

Black's Pseudo-American Call Model

In applying the Black's pseudo-American call model to an American call option, we use a dividend-adjusted stock price (S_0^D) in the OPM instead of the current stock price.

When there is one dividend payment (D), the adjusted stock price is:

$$S_0^D = S_0 - PV(D)$$

$$S_0^D = S_0 - \frac{D}{e^{Rt^x}}$$

where

t^x = time to the ex-dividend date expressed as a proportion of the year.

If more than one dividend payment is made during the option period, then the present value of each dividend is subtracted from the current stock price.

In the pseudo-American model, the call value computed with the dividend-adjusted stock price $C^*(S_0^D, T, X)$, is compared to the estimated call value obtained by assuming the call is exercised just prior to the ex-dividend date. This early exercise call price (C^{ex}) is found using the time to the ex-dividend date (t^x) instead of expiration (t), the dividend-adjusted stock price (S_0^D) instead of S_0, and a dividend-adjusted exercise price $(X - D)$ instead of X; that is, $C^{ex}(S_0^D, t^x, X - D)$. The dividend-adjusted exercise price is used instead of X to account for the advantage of early exercise that occurs just before the ex-dividend date. Finally, given the two estimated call prices, the larger of the two is selected as the estimate for the equilibrium call price:

$$C_0^a = \text{Max}[\, C(S_0^D, t, X), \; C^{ex}(S_0^D, t^x, X - D)\,]$$

To illustrate the pseudo-American call model, consider again the B-S call pricing example in which the B-S price of the call was $4.50, given: $S_0 = \$50$, $X = \$50$, $t = 0.5$, $\sigma = 0.3$ and $R = 0.025$. In this example also assume that XYZ stock is expected to go ex-dividend three months from the present $(t^x = 3/12 = 0.25)$ with the value of the dividend equal to $1.00. Using the pseudo-American model to estimate the value of the XYZ 50 call, we first compute the adjusted stock price:

$$S_0^D = S_0 - \frac{D}{e^{Rt*}}$$

$$S_0^D = \$50 - \frac{\$1.00}{e^{(0.025)(0.25)}} = \$49.01$$

Using $S_0^D = \$49.01$ in the B-S model instead of $S_0 = \$50$, we obtain a dividend-adjusted call price of $3.95, which is less than the B-S price of $4.50 obtained without the adjustment.

Next, we estimate the call price, with the assumption that it is exercised just prior to the ex-dividend date. In this example, the early exercise call price is $4.41. This value is obtained by using $S_0^D = \$49.01$, $X - D = \$50 - \$1 = \$49$, and $t^x = 3/12 = 0.25$, for S_0, X, and t, respectively, in the B-S formula.

Finally, given the two prices, we select the larger of the two. Thus, in this example the estimated call price is $4.41:

$$C_0^a = \text{Max}[C_0^*(S_0^D, t, X), \; C_0^{ex}(S_0^D, t^x, X - D)]$$

$$C_0^a = \text{Max}[C_0^*(\$49.01,\ 0.5,\ \$50),\ C_0^{ex}(\$49.01,\ 0.25,\ \$49)]$$

$$C_0^a = \text{Max}[\$3.95,\ \$4.41]$$

$$C_0^a = \$4.41$$

Note, if the call option were European, then only the call value using the time to expiration is used ($3.95).

Merton's Continuous Dividend Adjustment Call Model

The other dividend-adjustment procedure is to use Merton's continuous dividend adjustment model that we examined in Chapter 10. In this model, we substitute the dividend-adjusted stock price for the current stock price in the B-S formula:

$$S_0^D = S_0\,e^{-\psi t}$$

where

ψ = annual dividend yield = annual dividend/stock price

The B-S model with a continuous dividend yield is:

$$C_0^* = S_0 e^{-\psi t}\,N(d_1) - X e^{-Rt}\,N(d_2)$$

$$d_1 = \frac{\ln(S_0^D/X) + (R + 0.5\,\sigma^2)t}{\sigma\sqrt{t}} = \frac{\ln(S_0/X) + (R - \psi + 0.5\,\sigma^2)t}{\sigma\sqrt{t}}$$

$$d_2 = d_1 - \sigma\sqrt{t}$$

In terms of the above example, if the underlying stock is expected to generate an annual dividend yield of $\psi = 0.08$ (for example, a $4 annual dividend per a stock price of $50), then the dividend-adjusted stock price is $S_0^D = \$448.04$:

$$S_0^D = S_0\,e^{-\psi t}$$

$$S_0^D = \$50 e^{-(0.08)(0.5)} = \$48.04$$

and the continuous B-S dividend-adjusted call price is $3.48.

In Chapter 10, we used the Merton dividend-adjusted binomial model to price American and European call options. Applying the Merton BOPM to price the XYZ call ($S_0 = \$50$, $\sigma^A = 0.30$, $\mu^A = 0$, $X = \$50$, $t = 0.5$, $R^A = 2.531\%$ (simple annual rate), and $\psi = 8\%$), we obtain the same call price of $3.48 for the case of $n = 200$ subperiods. The Merton BOPM also prices the American call at $3.62. Note that the Merton B-S model does not price American options. Thus, one of the advantages of the discrete binomial model over the continuous B-S model is that one can stop at each node to determine if there is an early exercise advantage, which is not the case with Merton's continuous-dividend B-S model. In this example, the differences in prices using the American and European binomial models equate to a $0.14 early exercise value for the American call option. With Black's pseudo model, one is also able to stop at the ex-dividend date to determine if there is an early exercise advantage—the only time such an advantage would exist for a call.

Black-Scholes Excel option programs that value calls (and puts) using the B-S OPM, the Merton model, and Black's pseudo American model can be accessed from the text's website.

The Black-Scholes Put Model

B-S Put Formula

The B-S OPM model for puts can be derived using the same methodology used to determine the B-S call value. It also can be derived from the binomial model by letting n approach infinity. A simpler approach is to solve for it from the put-call parity model. Specifically, assuming European options, the equilibrium put price in terms of the put-call parity model is

$$P_0^* = C_0^* - S_0 + PV(X)$$

$$P_0^* = C_0^* - S_0 + \frac{X}{e^{Rt}}$$

where

C_0^* = call price determined by the B-S OPM.

By substituting the B-S call price equation for C_0^*, the equilibrium B-S put price is

$$P_0^* = -S_0\left(1 - N(d_1)\right) + \left[\frac{X}{e^{RT}}\right](1 - N(d_2))$$

Extending our illustrative example to determining the equilibrium price of a put, the B-S put price for an XYZ European 50 put expiring in six months is $3.88:

$$P_0^* = -S_0\left(1 - N(d_1)\right) + \left[\frac{X}{e^{Rt}}\right](1 - N(d_2))$$

$$P_0^* = -\$50\,(0.43457) + \left[\frac{\$50}{e^{(0.025)(0.5)}}\right](0.518626)$$

$$P_0^* = \$3.88$$

where

$$1 - N(d_1) = N(-d_1) = 1 - 0.56543 = 0.43457$$

$$1 - N(d_2) = N(-d_2) = 1 - 0.481374 = 0.518626$$

Features

Like the B-S OPM for calls, most of the a priori relationships between the equilibrium price of a put and S, T, σ, X, and R are captured in the B-S put model. These relationships can be seen in the lower panel in Exhibit 11.2 in which combinations of the B-S put prices and stock prices are shown for different parameters: X (Column 2), t (Column 3), σ (Column 4), and R (Column 5). In examining any of the columns in the table, one first should observe the negative, nonlinear relationship between the B-S put price and the stock price (i.e., the put has a negative delta and nonzero gamma). It should be noted that the model is unconstrained. That is, the B-S put model, like the BOPM, does not constrain the put value to being equal to at least its intrinsic value.

B-S Arbitrage Put Portfolio

The B-S put equation is equal to the value of the replicating put portfolio. That is:

$$P_0^* = H_0^{P*} S_0 + I_0^*$$

where from the B-S model:

$$H_0^{P*} = -(1 - N(d_1))$$

$$I_0^* = \left[\frac{X}{e^{RT}}\right](1 - N(d_2))$$

Thus, the put value of $3.88 in our previous example is equivalent to the value of a portfolio formed by selling 0.43457 shares of stock short at $50 per share and investing $25.61 in a risk-free security:

$$P_0^* = -(0.43457)(\$50) + \$25.61 = \$3.88$$

where

$$H_0^{P*} = -(1 - N(d_1)) = -0.43457$$

$$I_0^* = \left[\frac{X}{e^{Rt}}\right](1 - N(d_2)) = \left[\frac{\$50}{e^{(0.025)(0.5)}}\right](0.518626) = \$25.61$$

If the market price of the put exceeds the B-S put value, then an arbitrage opportunity exists by taking a short position in the put and a long position in the replicating put portfolio. If the market price is below the equilibrium value, then an arbitrage portfolio can be constructed by going long in the put and short in the replicating portfolio. The overpriced and underpriced arbitrage put portfolios would need to be readjusted continuously (very frequently) until it is profitable to close. The same readjustment rules defined for BOPM's multiple-period arbitrage strategies apply to the continuous B-S arbitrage case.

Dividend Adjustments for the B-S Put Model

If a stock pays a dividend with the ex-dividend date occurring during the option period, then the price of the put would increase on the ex-dividend date as the price of the stock decreases by an amount approximately equal to the dividend. The values of American and European puts can be estimated using the dividend-adjusted pseudo-American model and a European put can be estimated using Merton's continuous dividend-adjusted stock price model.

Black's Pseudo-American Put Model

When an ex-dividend date occurs during the option period, Black's pseudo-American option model, defined previously for call options, can be extended to estimate the value of an American put. Applied to puts, the pseudo-American put model selects the greater of either the European B-S put value, $P(S_0^D, t, X)$, or the early exercise put value obtained by assuming the put is exercised at the ex-dividend date. As we did earlier for calls, in computing the early exercise put price, the time to the ex-dividend date (t^x) is used instead of t and the dividend-adjusted stock price (S_0^D) is used instead of S_0. However, for puts the exercise price is used instead of the dividend-adjusted exercise price $(X - D)$ that was used for calls. This is done to account for the fact that the early exercise advantage for puts occurs on the ex-dividend date when the stock decreases, not just before as in the case of calls; thus, $P^{ex}(S_0^D, t^x, X)$. If XYZ stock in our illustrative example had an ex-dividend date in three months with the value of the dividend on that date equal to $1.00, then the dividend-adjusted stock price for a discrete dividend payment is $49.01 and the dividend-adjusted put price is $4.32:

$$P_0^a = \text{Max}[P_0^*(S_0^D, t, X),\ P_0^{ex}(S_0^D, t^x, X)]$$

$$P_0^a = \text{Max}[P_0^*(\$49.01,\ 0.5,\ \$50),\ P_0^{ex}(\$49.01,\ 0.25,\ \$50)]$$

$$P_0^a = \text{Max}[\$4.32,\ \$3.30]$$

$$P_0^a = \$4.32$$

Note that if the put option were European, then only the put value using the time to expiration is used, which in this case is $4.32. Thus, in this example the European and American prices are the same, implying there is no early exercise advantage at the ex-dividend date.

The Value of an American Put without Dividends

The pseudo-American model estimates the value of an American put given an ex-dividend date. When dividends are not paid, we do not have a specific reference date to apply the pseudo-American model. As a result, determining the value of an American put becomes quite difficult. This is not a problem when applying the B-S call model for stock options, since the advantage of early exercise occurs only when an ex-dividend date exists. In such a case, a reference point for an early exercise is known and therefore the pseudo-American call model can be applied to determine the value of an American call. In the case of put options, if the price of the stock is such that the put is deep in the money, then it is possible for the price of the European put to be less than its intrinsic value. If the put were American, then at that stock price, it would have to be priced to equal at least its IV, or an arbitrage opportunity would exist by exercising the put early. Thus, the right of early exercise makes the price of an American put greater than a European, even if no dividends are paid during the life of the put.

Merton's Continuous Dividend Adjustment Model

Like Merton's dividend-adjusted call model, Merton's adjusted put model uses the dividend-adjusted stock price for the current stock price in the B-S formula. The B-S put model with continuous dividend yield is:

$$P_0^* = -S_0 e^{-\psi t} \left(1 - N(d_1)\right) + Xe^{-Rt} \left(1 - N(d_2)\right)$$

$$d_1 = \frac{\ln(S_0^D/X) + (R + 0.5\,\sigma^2)t}{\sigma\sqrt{t}} = \frac{\ln(S_0/X) + (R - \psi + 0.5\,\sigma^2)t}{\sigma\sqrt{t}}$$

$$d_2 = d_1 - \sigma\sqrt{t}$$

In our previous Merton example, the underlying stock was expected to generate an annual dividend yield of $\psi = 0.08$. This yields a dividend-adjusted stock price equal to $S_0^D = \$48.04$, and using the Merton model, a put price equal to \$4.82. Note that the same put price is obtained using put-call parity with the continuous dividend-adjusted Merton model call price of \$3.48:

$$P_0^* = C_0^* - S_0^D + \frac{X}{e^{Rt}}$$

$$P_0^* = \$3.48 - \$48.04 + \frac{\$50}{e^{(0.025)(0.5)}}$$

$$P_0^* = \$4.82$$

Pricing American Put Options with the BOPM

Note that one of the advantages of the Merton discrete BOPM over the Merton continuous OPM is that the binomial model can price American options. In this example, Merton's dividend-adjusted BOPM prices an American put the same as the European at \$4.82, indicating that there is no early exercise advantage. This is because the dividend yield relative to the risk-free rate is large.

In the BOPM, the equilibrium prices of an American put or call are determined by constraining at each possible stock price the put or call value to be the maximum of either its binomial value or its IV. In the discrete BOPM in which limits can be placed on the number of possible stock prices (which still can be quite large, given that calculations are done by a computer), this approach is feasible. However, in the B-S model in which time is continuous, the BOPM approach of constraining each possible put or call price does not apply.

Estimating the B-S OPM

Like the BOPM, the B-S OPM is defined totally in terms of the stock price, exercise price, time to expiration, interest rate, and volatility. The first three variables are observable. The interest rate needs to be defined and the stock's volatility needs to be estimated.

Interest Rates

Like the BOPM, the rates on a Treasury bill, commercial paper, or shorter-term Treasury note with a maturity equal to the option's expiration are typically used as estimates of the risk-free rate. These rates are typically quoted in terms of a simple annual rate (with no compounding). The rate used in the B-S OPM, though, is the continuous compounded annual rate. As we noted earlier in this chapter, the natural logarithm of one plus the simple annual rate, R^A, gives us the continuous compounded rate: $R = \ln(1 + R^A)$.

Volatility

As we noted in Chapter 10, there are two approaches to estimating the variance of the logarithmic return: calculating the stock's historical variance and solving for the stock's implied variance.

The implied variance is that variance that equates the OPM's value to the market price. As discussed in Chapter 10, the implied variance can be found iteratively, by substituting different variance values into the B-S until that variance is found that yields an OPM value equal to the market price. Using Taylor series expansion, the implied variance can also be approximated for an at-the-money option using the following formula:

$$\sigma^2 = \frac{0.05(C_0^M + P_0^M)\ \sqrt{2\,\pi/t}}{X(1 + R)^t}$$

Ideally, the implied variance for different options on the same stock should be the same. In practice, this does not occur. One way to select an implied variance is to use the arithmetic average for the different implied variances on the stock. With arithmetic averaging, however, equal weight is given to all the options. If the implied variance represents the market's consensus, then perhaps options with relatively low demands, such as deep in- and out-of-the-money ones, should not be given the same weight as other options. A third approach is to select the one implied variance that has the minimum pricing error. The Newton-Raphson approach is a commonly used one that selects volatility that minimizes errors.

Newton-Raphson Implied Volatility Program

Newton-Raphson implied volatility search technique was first suggested by Manaster and Koehler. The algorithm inputs are: security price (S), annual security yield, exercise price (X), annual continuously compounded risk-free rate (R), time to expiration (t), and market price of the call (C^M). Given the inputs, the program's first standard deviation estimate is

$$\sigma_1 = \sqrt{\left| \ln\left(\frac{S}{X}\right) + Rt \right| \left(\frac{2}{t}\right)}$$

Given σ_1, the program then calculates the Black-Scholes-Merton call value, $C(\sigma_1)$. If this call price is not close to the market call price, C^M, then the next standard deviation estimate is

$$\sigma_2 = \sigma_1 - \frac{[C(\sigma_1) - C^M]e^{d_1^2/2}\sqrt{2\pi}}{S\sqrt{t}}$$

where d_1 is computed based on σ_1. Given σ_2, the program then calculates the Black-Scholes-Merton call value, $C(\sigma_2)$. If this call price is not close to the market call price, C^M, then the procedure is repeated with the next estimate:

$$\sigma_3 = \sigma_2 - \frac{[C(\sigma_2) - C^M]e^{d_1^2/2}\sqrt{2\pi}}{S\sqrt{t}}$$

The process is repeated until the model price is sufficiently close to the market price.

The Newton-Raphson implied variance Excel program is available on the text website. For a call option with $X = \$50$, $S = \$50$, $t = 0.50$, $R_f = 0.025$, annual dividend yield of 8%, and call price of $3.48 (which equals the B-S Merton price in our previous example), the program calculates an implied variance of $\sigma = 0.30$, which equals the volatility used in our B-S Merton OPM example.

Volatility Smiles and Term Structure

A common approach among option traders is to select the volatility based on the option's *volatility smile* and its *volatility term structure*. A volatility smile is a plot of the implied volatilities given different exercise prices. The volatility term structure, in turn, refers to the relation between an option's implied volatility and the option's time to expiration. Exhibit 11.3 shows a volatility smile for P&G on 11/11/16. The smile shows that the stock's volatility decreases the higher the exercise price. Thus, the volatility used to price a lower exercise-priced option (deep-in-the-money call or a deep-out-of-the-money put) is greater than the volatility used to price a higher exercised-priced option (deep-out-of-the money call or a deep-in-the-money put). The negatively sloped smile shown in Exhibit 11.3 is typical for many stock options. An implied probability distribution for the underlying stock's price or logarithmic return

EXHIBIT 11.3   Volatility Smile

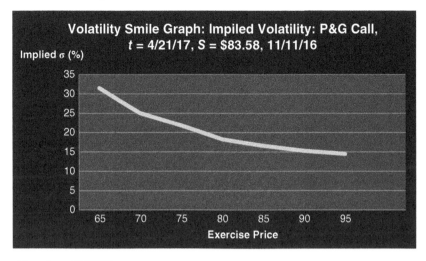

Source: Bloomberg, SKEW Screen

can be generated from a volatility smile. When a smile is relatively flat, then the implied distribution of the logarithmic returns approaches a normal distribution (or equivalently stated, the distribution of stock prices is lognormal). In this case, the smile is consistent with the Black-Scholes models' standard assumption of normality. When the smile is negatively slope, though, the implied probability distribution of logarithmic returns tends to be skewed to the left. Accordingly, a negatively sloped smile is called a *volatility skew*.

Volatility term structure shows the relation between a stock's implied volatility and the time to the option's expiration. Based on their smile, when volatilities are relatively low, volatility tends to increase, the greater the option's maturity. In contrast, when volatilities are relatively high, it tends to decrease, the greater the option's maturity. Exhibit 11.4 shows the volatility term structure of P&G on 11/11/16. Combining a stock's volatility smile with an estimate of its volatility term structure in a table generates what is referred to as a *volatility surface*. Exhibit 11.5 shows the volatility surface for P&G. Option traders use volatility surfaces to help them determine the appropriate volatilities to use when pricing an option with either the B-S OPM or the binomial model.

Applications of the OPM

Option Positions with Different Holding Periods

In Chapter 7, we examined a number of option strategies in terms of their profit and stock price relations. These strategies, though, were evaluated at expiration in terms of the option's intrinsic value. With the OPM, one can examine these strategies in terms of their profit and stock price relations prior to expiration. Exhibit 11.6 shows the stock price and profit relations for the long and short call and put positions. The relations

EXHIBIT 11.4   Volatility Term Structures

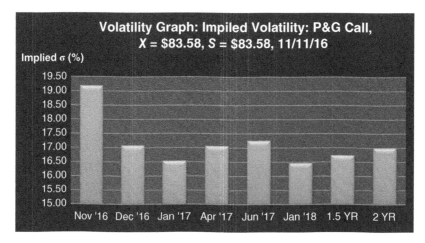

Source: Bloomberg, SKEW Screen

EXHIBIT 11.5   Volatility Surface, P&G, 11/11/16

Term	Expiration	85%	90%	95%	100%	105%	110%	115%
1 MO	12/11/2016	27.39	25.51	20.27	17.09	15.55	15.58	16.73
2 MO	01/10/2017	25.45	22.53	19.06	16.66	15.25	14.71	15.83
3 MO	02/09/2017	25.47	21.85	18.87	16.76	15.43	15.17	15.69
6 MO	05/10/2017	23.15	20.73	18.85	17.14	15.70	15.12	14.52
1 YR	11/06/2017	21.16	19.27	18.14	16.62	15.73	15.16	14.51
1.5 YR	05/05/2018	20.13	18.68	17.87	16.74	16.05	15.45	14.94
2 YR	11/01/2018	19.44	18.37	17.77	17.00	16.36	15.69	15.34

Source: Bloomberg, SKEW Screen

are defined for two points in time—t_1 and t. t is the time to expiration and t_1 is a time to a date prior to expiration. In determining the profits at t_1, the B-S OPM is used to estimate the price of the call and put for each stock price, with the times to expiration being $t - t_1$ when the positions are closed.

In examining the call and put purchase strategies, one should note that the profit is greater at each stock price the shorter the holding period. This relationship reflects the fact that the earlier a call or put is sold, the greater its time value premium. One should be careful in concluding that the call and put positions are more dominant the shorter the horizon period. That is, although a shorter holding period does provide a greater time premium than a longer one, the shorter period also means that the range in possible stock prices is more limited than the price range for a longer period. That is, with a shorter holding period, there is less time available for the stock to move to a profitable position. In contrast, a naked call and put write positions yield greater profits per stock price the longer the holding period. This is because the option's time value premium is smaller the closer the option is to expiration. As a result, the cost of closing the short position is less per stock price.

EXHIBIT 11.6 Option Profit Graphs at Expiration and Prior to Expiration: Stock Price = $50, X = $50, σ = 0.30, R_f = 0.025, t = 0.5, t_1 = 0.25

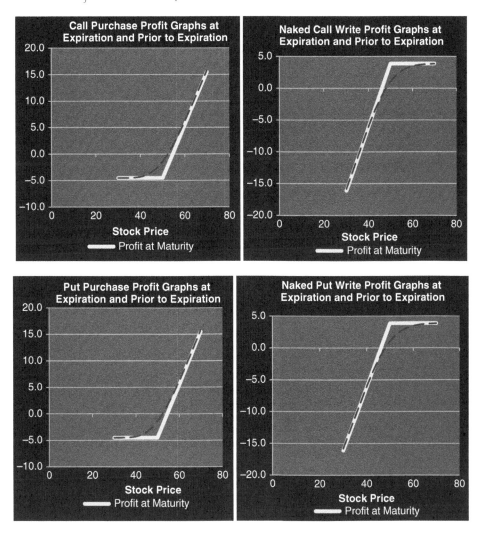

Option Return-Risk Characteristics

Investors often evaluate and select stocks and portfolios in terms of their expected return and risk characteristics. The BOPM or B-S OPM can be used to derive the equations for an option's expected rate of return and risk.

The replicating call portfolio consists of the purchase of H_0^* shares of stock, partially financed by borrowing B_0^* dollars. The expected rate of return on the call, $E(R^C)$, is equal to the expected rate of return on the replicating call portfolio, $E(R^{RP})$:

$$E(R^C) = E(R^{RP}) = w_S E(R^S) + w_R R_f$$

where

$$w_S = \text{proportion of investment allocated to stock}$$

$$w_R = \text{proportion of investment allocated to risk-free security}$$

$$E(R^S) = \text{stock expected return}$$

$$w_R + w_S = 1$$

The total investment in the replicating call portfolios is $H_0^* S_0 - B_0^*$, which in equilibrium is equal to the call value (C_0^*); the investment in the stock is $H_0^* S_0$; and the risk-free investment is $-B_0^*$ (i.e., negative investment or borrowing). Thus, $E(R^C)$ equation can be written as

$$E(R^C) = E(R^{RP}) = w_S E(R^S) + w_R R_f$$

$$E(R^C) = E(R^{RP}) = \left[\frac{H_0^* S_0}{C_0^*}\right] E(R^S) + \left[-\frac{B_0^*}{C_0^*}\right] R_f$$

The risk of a portfolio consisting of risky and risk-free securities can be defined in terms of the portfolio's standard deviation or beta. The standard deviation and beta for the call or, equivalently, the replicating portfolio are:

$$\sigma(R^C) = \sigma(R^{RP}) = w_S \sigma(R^S) = \left[\frac{H_0^* S_0}{C_0^*}\right] \sigma(R^S)$$

$$\beta^C = \beta^{RP} = w_S \beta^S = \left[\frac{H_0^* S_0}{C_0^*}\right] \beta^S$$

in which β^S = beta of the stock. In the B-S OPM H_0^* is equal to $N(d_1)$ and B_0^* is equal to $[X/e^{(Rt)}]N(d_2)$.

For a put, the equilibrium expected rate of return ($E(R^P)$) is equal to the expected rate of return of a replicating put portfolio formed by selling H_0^{P*} shares of stock short and investing I_0^* in a risk-free security. The total investment in the replicating put portfolio is $H_0^{P*} S_0 + I_0^*$ (with $H_0^{P*} < 0$), which, in equilibrium, is equal to P_0^*. Thus, a put's expected rate of return, standard deviation, and beta can be defined as:

$$E(R^P) = E(R^{RP}) = \left[\frac{H_0^{P*}}{P_0^*}\right] E(R^S) + \left[\frac{I_0^*}{P_0^*}\right] R_f$$

$$\sigma(R^P) = \sigma(R^{RP}) = \sqrt{w_S^2 \sigma(R^S)^2} = \sqrt{\left[\frac{H_0^{P*}}{P_0^*}\right]^2 \sigma(R^S)^2}$$

$$\beta^P = \beta^{RP} = w_S \beta^S = \left[\frac{H_0^{P*}}{P_0^*}\right] \beta^S$$

In the B-S put model, $H_0^{P*} = -(1 - N(d_1))$ and $I_0^* = [X/e^{(\text{RT})}](1 - N(d_2))$. It should be noted that with $H_0^{P*} < 0$, the put has a negative beta. The negative sign reflects the inverse relationship between the put's rate of return and the market's rate of return.

Consider our illustrative example of the 50 call and put with $t = 0.5$ per year. Using the B-S model, the call's price, hedge ratio, and B_0^* were $C^* = \$4.50$, $H_0^* = N(d_1) = 0.56534$, and $B_0^* = \$23.767$, given $S_0 = \$50$ and $R = 0.025$. Similarly, the price, hedge ratio, and I_0^* for the put were found to be $P_0^* = \$3.88$, $H_0^{P*} = -(1 - N(d_1)) = -0.43457$, and $I_0^* = \$25.61$. If the underlying stock has an expected rate of return of $E(R^S) = 0.10$, standard deviation of $\sigma(R^S) = 0.5$, and a beta of $\beta = 1.0$, then for the call: $E(R^C) = 0.4962$, $\sigma(R^C) = 1.8846$, and $\beta^C = 6.282$ (see Box 11.1); for the put: $E(R^P) = -0.3945$, $\sigma(R^P) = 1.68004$, and $\beta^P = -5.6001$ (see Box 11.2).

Compared to the stock, the call and put positions yield significantly higher expected returns and risks, with the put's negative expected return implying that the price of the stock must decline for a long position in the put to be profitable. The higher return-risk characteristics should not be surprising given that a call is equivalent to a leveraged stock position and a put is equivalent to a leveraged short sale. It is important to note that the above measures for an option's return and risk hold only for a small period and for small stock price changes. The equations for the expected return and risk using the B-S OPM are measures of the *instantaneous* expected rates of return, standard deviations, and betas.

BOX 11.1: CALL EXPECTED RETURN, σ AND β, STOCK PRICE $= \$50$,
$X = \$50$, $\sigma = 0.30$, $R_F = 0.025$, $T = 0.5$, $E(R^S) = 0.10$, $\sigma(R^S) = 0.30$, $\beta^S = 1.00$

$$E(R^C) = \left[\frac{H_0^* S_0}{C_0^*}\right] E(R^S) + \left[-\frac{B_0^*}{C_0^*}\right] R_f$$

$$E(R^C) = \left[\frac{N(d_1) S_0}{C_0^*}\right] E(R^S) + \left[-\frac{(X/e^{\text{Rt}})N(d_2)}{C_0^*}\right] R_f$$

$$E(R^C) = \left[\frac{(0.56543)(\$50)}{\$4.50}\right] E(R^S) + \left[-\frac{(\$50/(e^{(0.025)(0.50)}))(0.481374)}{\$4.50}\right] R_f$$

$$E(R^C) = 6.282\, E(R^S) - 5.281\, R_f$$

$$E(R^C) = 6.282\,(0.10) - 5.281\,(0.025) = 0.4962$$

$$\sigma(R^C) = \left[\frac{H_0^* S_0}{C_0^*}\right] \sigma(R^S)$$

$$\sigma(R^C) = \left[\frac{(0.56543)(\$50)}{\$4.50}\right] \sigma(R^S)$$

$$\sigma(R^C) = 6.282\,(0.30) = 1.8846$$

$$\beta^C = \left[\frac{H_0^* S_0}{C_0^*} \right] \beta^S$$

$$\beta^C = \left[\frac{(0.56543)(\$50)}{\$4.50} \right] \beta^S$$

$$\beta^C = 6.282(1.0) = 6.282$$

BOX 11.2: PUT EXPECTED RETURN, σ AND β, STOCK PRICE = \$50,
$X = \$50$, $\sigma = 0.30$, $R_F = 0.025$, $T = 0.5$, $E(R^S) = 0.10$, $\sigma(R^S) = 0.30$, $\beta^S = 1.00$

$$E(R^P) = \left[\frac{H_0^{P*} S_0}{P_0^*} \right] E(R^S) + \left[\frac{I_0^*}{P_0^*} \right] R_f$$

$$E(R^P) = \left[\frac{-(1 - N(d_1))(S_0)}{P_0^*} \right] E(R^S) + \left[\frac{(X/e^{R_t})(1 - N(d_2))}{P_0^*} \right] R_f$$

$$E(R^P) = \left[\frac{-(0.43457)(\$50)}{\$3.88} \right] E(R^S) + \left[\frac{\$25.61}{\$3.88} \right] R_f$$

$$E(R^P) = -5.6001 \, E(R^S) + 6.6005 \, R_f$$

$$E(R^P) = -5.6001 \, (0.10) + 6.6005 \, (0.025) = -0.3945$$

$$\sigma(R^P) = \sqrt{ \left[\frac{H_0^{P*} S_0}{P_0^*} \right]^2 \sigma(R^S)^2 }$$

$$\sigma(R^P) = \sqrt{ \left[\frac{-(0.43457)(\$50)}{\$3.88} \right]^2 (0.30)^2 }$$

$$\sigma(R^P) = 1.68004$$

$$\beta^P = \left[\frac{H_0^{P*} S_0}{P_0^*} \right] \beta^S$$

$$\beta^P = \left[\frac{-(0.43457)(\$50)}{\$3.88} \right] (1.00)$$

$$\beta^P = -5.6001$$

Delta, Gamma, and Theta

The OPM also can be used to measure the delta (Δ), gamma (Γ), theta (θ), vega (Λ), and rho values for call and put options defined earlier. The equations for the Greeks are

EXHIBIT 11.7 Greek Formulas: Derivatives of the B-S Model for European Call and Put Options

	Call on Stock Paying No Dividends	Call on Stock Paying Annual Dividend Yield of ψ
Delta	$\Delta = \dfrac{\partial C}{\partial S} = N(d_1)$	$\Delta = e^{-\Psi t}\, N(d_1)$
Gamma	$\Gamma = \dfrac{\partial \Delta}{\partial S} = \dfrac{N'(d_1)}{S_0\, \sigma\, \sqrt{t}}$	$\Gamma = \dfrac{N'(d_1)e^{-\psi t}}{S_0\, \sigma\, \sqrt{t}}$
Theta	$\theta = -\dfrac{\partial C}{\partial t} = -\dfrac{S_0\, N'(d_1)\, \sigma}{2\sqrt{t}} + RXe^{-Rt}\, N(d_2)$	$\theta = -\dfrac{S_0\, N'(d_1)\, \sigma\, e^{-\Psi t}}{2\sqrt{t}} - \Psi\, S_0\, N(-d_1)e^{-\Psi t} + RXe^{-Rt}\, N(-d_2)$
Vega (Kappa)	$\Lambda = \dfrac{\partial C}{\partial \sigma} = S_0\sqrt{t}\ N'(d_1)$	$\Lambda = S_0\sqrt{t}\ N'(d_1)e^{-\Psi t}$
Rho	$\dfrac{\partial C}{\partial R} = Xt\, N(d_2)\, e^{-Rt}$	$\dfrac{\partial C}{\partial R} = Xt\, N(d_2)\, e^{-Rt}$
	$N'(d) = \dfrac{1}{\sqrt{2\pi}}\ e^{-d^2/2}$	

	Put on Stock Paying No Dividends	Put on Stock Paying Annual Dividend Yield of ψ
Delta	$\Delta = \dfrac{\partial P}{\partial S} = N(d_1) - 1$	$\Delta = e^{-\Psi T}\, [N(d_1) - 1]$
Gamma	$\Gamma = \dfrac{\partial \Delta}{\partial S} = \dfrac{N'(d_1)}{S_0\, \sigma\, \sqrt{t}}$	$\Gamma = \dfrac{N'(d_1)e^{-\psi t}}{S_0\, \sigma\, \sqrt{t}}$
Theta	$\theta = -\dfrac{\partial P}{\partial t} = -\dfrac{S_0\, N'(d_1)\, \sigma}{2\sqrt{t}} + RXe^{-Rt}\, N(-d_2)$	$\theta = -\dfrac{S_0\, N'(d_1)\, \sigma\, e^{-\Psi t}}{2\sqrt{t}} - \Psi\, S_0\, N(-d_1)e^{-\Psi t} + RXe^{-RT}\, N(-d_2)$
Vega (Kappa)	$\Lambda = \dfrac{\partial P}{\partial \sigma} = S_0\sqrt{t}\ N'(d_1)$	$\Lambda = S_0\sqrt{t}\ N'(d_1)e^{-\Psi t}$
Rho	$\dfrac{\partial P}{\partial R} = X\, t\, N(-d_2)\, e^{-Rt}$	$\dfrac{\partial P}{\partial R} = X\, t\, N(-d_2)\, e^{-Rt}$
	$N'(d) = \dfrac{1}{\sqrt{2\pi}}\ e^{-d^2/2}$	

shown in Exhibit 11.7. These parameter values can be calculated using the B-S OPM Excel program available on the text's website.

Delta

Delta is used to measure an option's price sensitivity to a small change in the price of the underlying stock. The delta (Δ) for a European call on a non–dividend-paying stock is $N(d_1)$, and for a European put is $N(d_1) - 1$. The delta for a call is positive, ranging in value from approximately zero for deep-out-of-the-money calls to approximately 1.00 for deep-in-the-money ones. In contrast, the delta for a put is negative, ranging from approximately zero to −1.00. Deltas change in response to not only stock price changes, but also the time to expiration. As the time to expiration decreases the delta of an in-the-money call or put increases, while an out-of-the-money call or put tends to decrease.

In addition to measuring a derivative security's price sensitivity to a change in the stock price, an option's delta also can be used to measure the probability that the option will be in the money at expiration. Thus, the call with a $\Delta = N(d_1) = 0.56534$, has an approximate 56.534% chance of its stock price exceeding the option's exercise price at expiration.

Theta

Theta (θ) is the change in the price of an option with respect to changes in its time to expiration, with all other factors constant. It is a measure of the option's time decay. Since theta measures the time decay of an option, it is usually defined as the negative of the change in the option's price with respect to expiration. The thetas on options are negative.

Using our illustrative call and put examples in which $S_0 = \$50$, $X = \$50$, $t = 0.5$, $\sigma = 0.30$, $R = 0.025$, $N(d_1) = N(0.164992) = 0.56543$, $N(d_2) = 0.481347$, $N(-d_2) = 0.518626$, and $= N'(d_1) = (1/\sqrt{2\pi})\ e^{(-0.164992)^2/2} = 0.393549$, the call has a theta of −3.48 and the put has a theta of −3.54:

Call:

$$\theta = -\frac{S_0\ N'(d_1)\ \sigma}{2\sqrt{t}} + RXe^{-Rt}\ N(d_2)$$

$$\theta = -\frac{(\$50)(0.393549)\ (0.30)}{2\sqrt{0.50}} + (0.025)(\$50)e^{-(0.025)(0.50)}\ (0.481347)$$

$$\theta = -3.58$$

Put:

$$\theta = -\frac{S_0\ N'(d_1)\ \sigma}{2\sqrt{t}} + RXe^{-Rt}\ N(-d_2)$$

$$\theta = -\frac{(\$50)(0.393540)\ (0.30)}{2\sqrt{0.50}} + (0.025)(\$50)e^{-(0.025)(0.50)}\ (0.518626)$$

$$\theta = -3.54$$

Thus, if the option is held 1% of a year (approximately 2.5 trading days) and there were no changes in the stock's price, the call would decline in value by $0.0358 and the put would decrease by $0.0354. Like delta, theta changes in response to changes in the stock price and time to expiration.

Gamma

Gamma (Γ) measures the change in an option's delta for a small change in the stock price. It is the second derivative of the option price with respect to the stock price. In our illustrative example, the gamma for the call or put is 0.0371:

$$\Gamma = \frac{N'(d_1)}{S_0 \, \sigma \, \sqrt{t}} = \frac{0.393459}{(50)(0.30) \, \sqrt{0.5}} = 0.0371$$

Thus, a $1 increase in the stock price would increase the delta of the call or put by approximately 0.0371. The gamma for calls and puts change with respect to the stock price and time to expiration.

Vega

Vega (Λ) measures the change in the option price for a small change in the volatility (σ). In our illustrative example, the vega for the call and put is 13.91:

$$\Lambda = S_0 \sqrt{t} \;\; N'(d_1)$$

$$\Lambda = \$50\sqrt{0.50} \;\; (0.393549)$$

$$\Lambda = 13.91$$

Position Delta, Gamma, and Theta Values

Option positions or portfolios can be described in terms of their Greek characteristics. For example, consider an investor who purchases n_1 calls at a price of C_1 per call and n_2 calls on another option on the same stock at a price of C_2 per call. The value of this portfolio (V) is:

$$V = n_1 C_1 + n_2 C_2$$

The call prices are functions of S, T, σ, and R. The position's delta is

$$\Delta_p = n_1 \Delta_1 + n_2 \Delta_2$$

where

$$\Delta_1 = H_1^* = N(d_1)_1$$

$$\Delta_2 = H_2^* = N(d_1)_2$$

The position delta measures the change in the position's value in response to a small change in the stock price, with other factors being constant.

The position gamma (Γ_p) defines the change in the position's delta for a small change in the stock price, with other factors being constant. The gamma of the above call portfolio is

$$\Gamma_p = n_1 \Gamma_1 + n_2 \Gamma_2$$

Finally, the position theta (θ_p) measures the position value with respect to change in t:

$$\theta_p = n_1\theta_1 + n_2\theta_2$$

Neutral Delta Position

For arbitrageurs, a common delta position is a neutral position delta position. The position is constructed by determining the allocations of a portfolio of options on the same stock such that the position value is invariant to small changes in the stock price. Consider, for example, a position formed with two call options on the same stock but with different exercise prices. A neutral position is formed by setting the position delta, Δ_p equal to zero and solving for n_1 in terms of n_2:

$$\Delta_p = n_1\Delta_1 + n_2\Delta_2$$

$$0 = n_1\Delta_1 + n_2\Delta_2$$

$$n_1 = -\left[\frac{\Delta_2}{\Delta_1}\right]n_2$$

$$n_1 = -\left[\frac{N(d_1)_2}{N(d_1)_1}\right]n_2$$

The neutral position can be constructed by purchasing (selling) $n_2 = 1$ of one of the calls and selling (purchasing) $n_1 = -N(d_1)_2/N(d_1)_1$ of the other call or a multiple of this strategy (the negative sign in the equation indicates opposite positions). For example, from our illustrative example, the hedge ratio for the 50 call is $N(d_1)_1 = 0.5654$ and the hedge ratio for a 45 call on the same stock is $N(d_1)_2 = 0.7460$. The ratio spread (also referred to as a delta spread) needed to form a riskless position would be:

$$-\left[\frac{N(d_1)_2}{N(d_1)_1}\right] = -\frac{0.7460}{0.5654} = -1.3194$$

A riskless ratio spread therefore could be constructed by purchasing one 45 call and selling 1.3194 July 50 calls. If the stock increased by $1.00, the value of the long position in the 45 call would increase by $0.7460. This, however, would be offset by the decrease of $0.7460 = (1.3194)(0.5654) in the value of the short position in the 50 call. Thus, a small change in the price of the stock would not change the value of this ratio spread.

For a neutral delta, positions are often examined in terms of their gamma. If the gamma is positive, the neutral delta portfolio declines in value if there is little or no change in the stock price, and increases in value if there is a large positive or negative change in the stock price. On the other hand, if the delta-neutral portfolio has a negative gamma, the portfolio value will increase if there is little or no change in the stock price and decrease in value if there is a positive or negative change in the stock

EXHIBIT 11.8 Neutral Delta Position with Positive Gamma

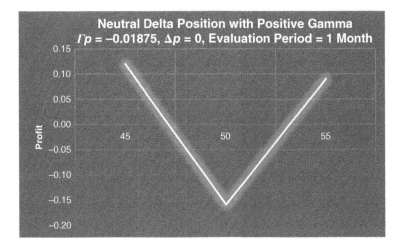

price. In terms of our example, the 50 call's gamma is 0.0371 and the 45 call's gamma is 0.0302, and the gamma for the neutral delta position is 0.01875:

$$\Gamma_P = n_1 \Gamma_1 + n_2 \Gamma_2$$

$$\Gamma_P = (1.3194)(0.0371) + (-1.00)(0.0302)$$

$$\Gamma_P = 0.01875$$

As shown in Exhibit 11.8, this position realizes a profit after one month of $0.12 if stock is at $45, a profit of $0.09 if the stock is at $55, and a loss of $0.16 if stock stays at $50 with the 50 call and 45 call closed at their B-S OPM values.

Neutral Delta Position and Arbitrage Strategies

The riskless ratio spread can be used with the OPM to define arbitrage strategies. For example, a neutral ratio spread is formed by buying an underpriced call and selling an overpriced or equal-in-value call on the same stock. In terms of our illustrative example, the B-S OPM value on the 50 European call is $4.4973 and its delta is 0.5653, and the B-S OPM value on a 45 European call is $7.3612 and its delta is 0.7460. The neutral delta position formed by selling one 45 call and buying 1.3194 50 calls generates an initial cash flow of $1.427 if calls are priced equal to their B-S OPM values:

$$CF_0 = n_{50} C_0^*(50) - n_{45} C_0^*(45)$$

$$CF_0 = (-1.3194)(\$4.4973) + (1.00)(\$7.3612)$$

$$CF_0 = \$1.427$$

The neutral delta strategy is set up to yield a net cash flow of zero when it is closed if the call prices are equal to their OPM values or, equivalently, the call prices change by exactly $N(d_1)$ as the stock prices changes. For example, if the stock increased by $1.00, the 50 call would increase by approximately $N(d_1) = \$0.5653$ to $C(50) = \$4.4973 + 0.5653 = \$5.0626$ and the 45 call would increase by approximately $N(d_1) = \$0.7460$ to $C(45) = \$7.3612 + \$0.7460 = \$8.1072$. The cash flow from closing the position at these prices would be $-\$1.427$, yielding a net cash flow of zero:

$$CF_T = n_{50}\, C_0^*(50) - n_{45}\, C_0^*(45)$$

$$CF_T = (1.3194)(\$5.0626) - (1.00)(\$8.1072)$$

$$CF_T = -\$1.427$$

$$Net\ CF = CF_0 - CF_T = \$1.427 - \$1.427 = 0$$

Similarly, if the stock decreases by $1, the 50 call would decrease by approximately $N(d_1) = \$0.5653$ to $C(50) = \$4.4973 - 0.5653 = \$3.932$ and the 45 call would decrease by approximately $N(d_1) = \$0.7460$ to $C(45) = \$7.3612 - \$0.7460 = 6.6152$. The cash flow from closing would again be approximately $1.427, yielding a net flow of zero.

$$CF_T = n_{50}\, C_0^*(50) - n_{45}\, C_0^*(45)$$

$$CF_T = (1.3194)(\$3.932) - (1.00)(\$6.6152)$$

$$CF_T = -\$1.427$$

$$Net\ CF = CF_0 - CF_T = \$1.427 - \$1.427 = 0$$

The neutral delta position can be used like the replicating portfolio to construct arbitrage position when the option is mispriced. For example, suppose the price of the 45 call were equal to its B-S OPM value, but the 50 call was underpriced at $4.40. With the 50 call underpriced, one could profit by forming a neutral delta strategy by going long in 1.3194 50 calls priced at $4.40 and short in one 45 call priced at $7.3612. This would yield an initial cash inflow of $1.557 and a closing cost of only $1.427 when the position is closed a short time later at the OPM values. For example, if shortly after the stock increased to $51, then the OPM values for the calls would be approximately $C_t(50) = \$5.11$ and $C_t(45) = \$8.12$, and the cost of closing would be $1.427 as shown above, leaving a profit of $0.13. On the other hand, if the stock decreased to $49, then the OPM values would be approximately $C_t(50) = \$3.95$ and $C_t(45) = \$6.64$, and the cost of closing would again be $1.427, leaving a profit of $0.13.

If the 50 call were overpriced at say $4.55 and 45 call were equal to its OPM value of $7.3612, then one could profit by reversing the neutral delta strategy: go short in 1.3194 50 calls priced at $4.55 and long in one 45 call. This would yield an initial cash outflow of $1.356 and an inflow of $1.427 when the position is closed shortly after at either $S_t = \$51$ or $49, $C_t(50) = \$1.55$, leaving a profit of $0.07.

$$\text{Initial cash flow} = (1.3194)(\$4.55) - \$7.3612 = -\$1.356$$

At $S_t = \$51$:

$$\text{Closing cash flow} = -(1.3194)(\$5.0626) + \$8.1072 = \$1.427$$

$$\text{Net} = \$1.427 - \$1.356 = \$0.07$$

At $S_t = \$49$:

$$\text{Closing cash flow} = -(1.3194)(\$3.932) + \$6.6152 = \$1.427$$

$$\text{Net} = \$1.427 - \$1.356 = \$0.07$$

Like the arbitrage strategy constructed with opposite positions in an option and the replicating portfolio, the neutral delta arbitrage strategy for overpriced (underpriced) options requires readjustment each period (frequently) until the option price is underpriced (overpriced) or equal to the OPM value. That is, given that $N(d_1)$ changes as the stock price and time change, this ratio spread strategy would need to be readjusted each period to keep the spread riskless until it is profitable to close. The riskless ratio spread can be thought of as an alternative arbitrage strategy to the arbitrage portfolio defining the B-S OPM; in fact, with the latter strategy often involving short sales and margin requirements, the ratio spread may in some cases be a better strategy to implement.

It should be noted that the call prices at $S_t = \$51$ and $\$49$ are: $C_t^* = C_0^* + N(d_1)$ ΔS. These values are slightly different from the B-S values. This is because $N(d_1)$ and $N(d_2)$ are defined for very small changes in the stock price. For a discrete change, such as $\$1$, the new equilibrium call prices will be different than the preceding values. That is, at $S_t = \$51$, the B-S OPM prices are $C(50) = \$5.11$ and $C(45) = \$8.12$, not $\$5.0626$ and $\$8.1072$, and at $S_t = \$49$, the prices are $C(50) = \$3.95$ and $C(45) = \$6.64$, not $\$3.932$ and $\$6.6152$.

Empirical Studies

A number of empirical studies have tested the validity of the OPM. A general conclusion from many of these studies is that the B-S OPM is relatively good at pricing options when there is some time to expiration and the option is near the money.

Early Empirical Studies

One of the first empirical studies of the OPM was by Black and Scholes (1972). Using option price data from the over-the-counter (OTC) market, they simulated trading strategies using their model on approximately 550 options. In their simulation, if the market price of a call were below its B-S OPM value, Black and Scholes assumed the call was purchased and hedged by selling $N(d_1)$ shares of stock short. On the other hand, if the call were overpriced relative to the B-S's values, then they assumed the call was sold and hedged by purchasing $N(d_1)$ shares. Black and Scholes also posited that the initial positions were adjusted daily by buying and selling shares necessary to maintain $N(d_1)$. From the simulations, they found opportunities for abnormal returns existed on a before-commission cost basis. However, when transaction costs were included, they found the abnormal returns disappeared. Thus, the results of their study suggested that the differences in observed and model values were significant statistically, but not economically.

Galai in a 1977 study found results similar to Black's and Scholes'. In his study, he replicated the Black-Scholes simulation tests using data on options traded on the CBOE. Galai, in turn, found excess returns from the hedging strategies on a before-transaction cost basis, but found they disappeared once such costs were included. Hence, the Galai study, like the Black and Scholes, suggested that applying arbitrage trading strategies based on the B-S model would not generate excess returns for nonmembers.

In a 1979 study, MacBeth and Merville compared the B-S prices, computed using implied variances, with daily closing prices. They found that the B-S model tended to underprice in-the-money calls and overprice out-of-the money calls, with the degree of mispricing being greater the shorter the option's time to expiration. MacBeth and Merville did find, though, that the B-S model was good at pricing in-the-money calls with some time to expiration.

Stochastic Errors

Stochastic errors result from the exclusion of important explanatory variables and/or an incorrect mathematical specification of the model. In the Galai studies, one omission was the treatment of dividends. Not surprisingly, Whaley (1982) and Sterk (1982) found less measurement error associated with the B-S OPM with dividend adjustments than without such corrections. Thus, for the Galai study, the nontreatment of dividends on options on dividend-paying stocks probably did lead to errors.

Stochastic errors resulting from model misspecifications were examined in a study by Bhattacharya (1980). Bhattacharya calculated the rates of return resulting from theoretical hedged portfolios formed using the B-S OPM that were closed using the B-S OPM prices instead of market prices. Bhattacharya found that, with the exception of near-the-money calls with short periods to expiration, no significant mispricing by the B-S OPM existed, thus supporting the theoretical soundness of the B-S OPM.

Stochastic errors can also result from the variance not being constant. MacBeth and Merville (1980) provided evidence showing that the variance tends to change as the stock price changes. If this is the case, then an option pricing model such as Merton's diffusion-jump model or Cox's and Ross's constant elasticity of substitution model yield better results than the B-S OPM. Similarly, stochastic errors can also be the result of the model's assumption that the option's underlying security's logarithmic return is normally distributed. Several empirical studies have provided evidence that the distributions of stock and stock index returns exhibit persistent skewness (e.g., Kon (1990), Aggarwal and Rao (1990), and Turner and Weigel (1992)). Studies by Stein and Stein (1991), Wiggins (1987), and Hestin (1993) have demonstrated that when skewness exists, the B-S model consistently misprices options. To address the pricing bias resulting from the assumption of normality, Jarrow and Rudd (1982) and Corrado and Tie Su (1996) have extended the B-S model to account for cases in which there is skewness in the underlying security's return distribution, and Johnson, Pawlukiewicz, and Mehta have extended the binomial option pricing model to include skewness.

Conclusion

The empirical studies provide general support for the B-S model as a valid pricing model, especially for near-the-money options. The overall consensus is that the B-S OPM is a useful pricing model. In fact, aside from empirical studies (many of which are biased by errors), the strongest endorsement of the B-S OPM comes from its ubiquitous use. Today, the OPM may be the most widely accepted model in the field of finance.

BLOOMBERG OPTION VALUATION SCREEN, OVME

Equity Option Valuation, OVME, determines OPM prices for exchange-traded, over-the-counter, and inputted derivative contracts for equity. OVME uses interpolated market-implied volatilities when the underlying security has an active market of listed options, allowing you to replicate the market conditions at the time of the trade.

Features:

- OVME provides dividend adjustment for discrete dividend payments (B-S Discrete) or with a continuous dividend yield (B-S continuous).

- The B-S continuous model uses a continuous dividend yield pulled from Bloomberg's BDVD screen, and the B-S Discrete model uses discrete dividends pulled from Bloomberg's BDVD screen. American options for the continuous B-S uses a Trinomial adjusted B-S model to identify times for early exercise.

- Different dividend payments and models can be used by going to the red "Settings" tab (see Exhibit 11.9).

- OVME also pulls implied volatilities from a volatility surface and historical volatility. You can access the volatility from the "Volatility" Tab (see Exhibit 11.10).

- Option prices and the Greek values can be plotted against different underlying security prices, time, and other parameter values from the "Scenario" tab (see Exhibit 11.11).

- On the "Backtest" tab, you can analyze a strategy or multiple strategies (see Exhibit 11.12).

- OVME allows you to input your own option information.

- From the "Deal" tabs you can construct multiple deals simultaneously and then analyze them from the "Scenario" tab.

(Continued)

EXHIBIT 11.9   OVME for P&G Call: 11/29/2016: $X = 82.50$, Expiration = 2/17/17

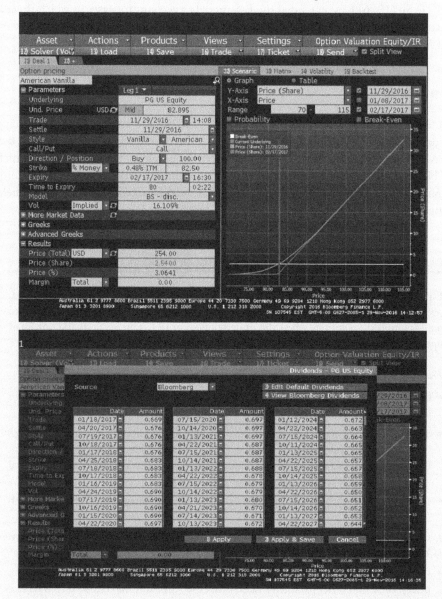

EXHIBIT 11.10   Volatility Tab

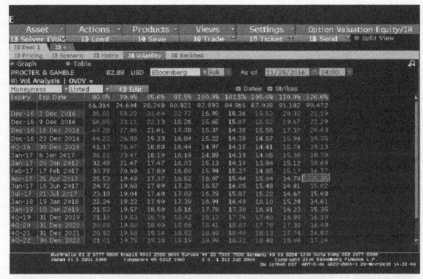

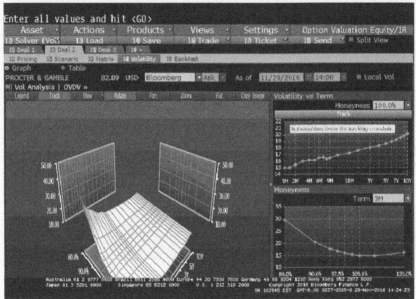

(Continued)

EXHIBIT 11.11   Scenario Tab

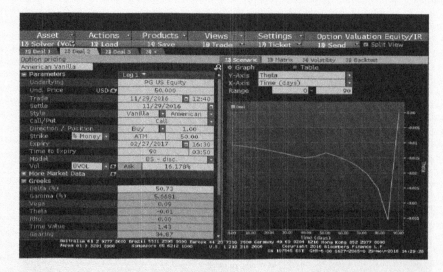

EXHIBIT 11.12   Backtest Tab

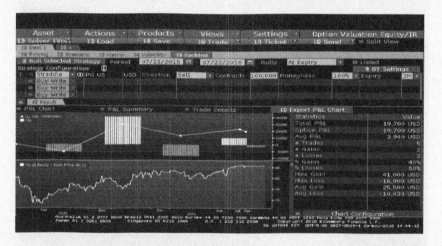

Example: OVME screen for Neutral Delta strategy: $S = \$50$, $\sigma = 30\%$, $R = 2.5\%$, $t = 0.5$ (182 days); Position: Sell 1.32 calls with $X = \$50$; purchase 1 call with $X = \$45$. The OVME using the B-S continuous model prices the 50 call at \$4.51 (close to our example) and the 45 call at \$7.35. For a neutral strategy with short 1.32 50 calls and long one 45 call, the position generates an initial cash flow of \$1.40, a position delta of zero, and position gamma of -0.7088% (see Exhibit 11.13).

EXHIBIT 11.13 Exhibit OVME Setting Tab

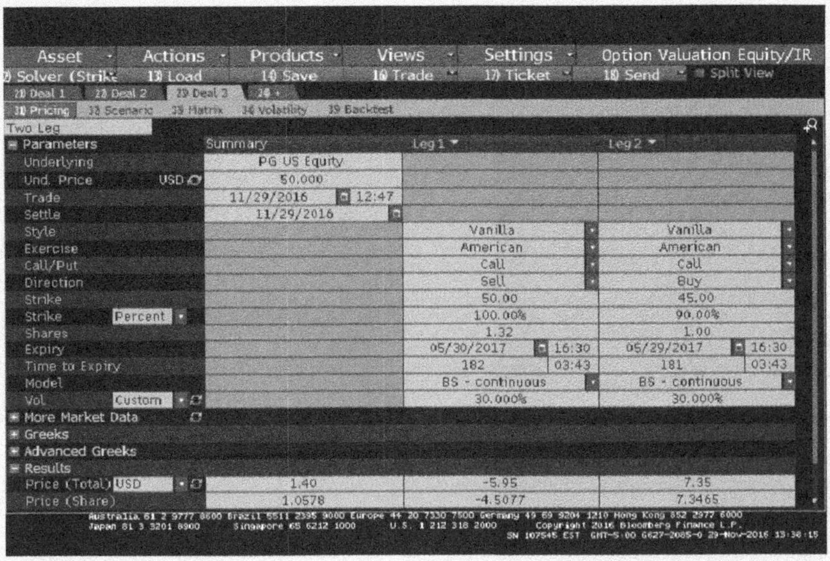

VOLATILITY

OVDV displays Bloomberg implied volatility surfaces for a selected equity or equity index. The "Dividend" tab shows forecasted discrete dividends on ex-dividend dates.

HVG, Historical Volatility Graph, screen plots the historical volatility of a security and implied volatility of a loaded security. Historical volatility is the annualized standard deviation of the logarithmic returns. The implied volatility is the annualized standard deviation that equates the market price of the options to market price.

B-S OPM Pricing of P&G Call on 11/30/16

B-S Excel Program

Input Information for B-S OPM

- Stock price = $82.75 (OVDV)
- X = $85 (OVDV)
- Expiration: 4/21/17; Days to expiration = 141 days (DES); $t = 141/365 = 0.3863$
- Annual dividend yield = 3.17% (BDVD)
- Annualized volatility = Implied volatility: $\sigma = 0.1589$ (OVDV); Variance = 0.02525
- Annualized risk-free rate = 0.992% (FIT screen; T-bill rare maturing on 4/20/17)

See Exhibit 11.14.

(Continued)

EXHIBIT 11.14   Call: B-S OPM: Model Price = $2.03; Market Price = Bid = $1.80;
Ask = $2.02

BS OPM	
Data input	
Exercise Price	85.0000
Risk-Free Rate	0.0099
Time to Expiration	0.3863
Variance	0.0253
Security Yield	0.0317

Input		Call			
Security Price	Yield-Adjust. Sec. Price	C*	IV	H	B
$82.75	$81.74	$2.03	$-	0.3792	28.9670
$75.00	$74.09	$0.32	$-	0.0964	6.8156
$77.50	$76.56	$0.63	$-	0.1660	12.0721
$80.00	$79.03	$1.15	$-	0.2578	19.2293
$82.50	$81.50	$1.93	$-	0.3675	28.0184
$85.00	$83.97	$2.97	$-	0.4859	37.8238
$87.50	$86.44	$4.34	$2.50	0.6017	47.6675
$90.00	$88.90	$5.94	$5.00	0.7066	56.8816
$92.50	$91.37	$7.79	$7.50	0.7939	64.7571
$95.00	$93.84	$9.84	$10.00	0.8620	71.0499
$97.50	$96.31	$12.05	$12.50	0.9120	75.7876
$100.00	$98.78	$14.35	$15.00	0.9464	79.1448

Selected References

Ball, C., and W. Torous. "On Jumps in Common Stock Prices and Their Impact on Call Pricing." *Journal of Finance* 40 (1985): 155–173.

Barone-Adesi, G., and R. Whaley. "Efficient Analytic Approximation of American Option Values." *The Journal of Finance* 42 (June 1987): 301–320.

Beckers, S. "Standard Deviations Implied in Option Prices as Predictors of Future Stock Price Variability." *Journal of Banking and Finance* 5 (September 1981): 363–382.

Bhattacharya, M. "Empirical Properties of the Black-Scholes Formula Under Ideal Conditions." *Journal of Financial and Quantitative Analysis* 15 (December 1980): 1081–1095.

Bhattacharya, M. "Transaction Data Tests of Efficiency of the Chicago Board Options Exchange." *Journal of Financial Economics* 12 (1983): 161–185.

Black, F. "Fact and Fantasy in the Use of Options." *Financial Analysis Journal* 31 (July–August 1975): 36–41, 61–72.

Black, F., and M. Scholes. "The Pricing of Options and Corporate Liabilities." *Journal of Political Economy* 81 (May–June 1973): 637–659.

Boyle, P., and A. Ananthanarayanan. "The Impact of Variance Estimation in Option Valuation Models." *Journal of Financial Economics* 5 (December 1977): 375–388.

Corrado, C. J., and Su Tie. "Skewness and Kurtosis in S&P 500 Index Returns Implied by Option Prices." *The Journal of Financial Research* 19 (1996): 175–192.

Copeland, T. E., and J. F. Weston. *Financial Theory and Corporate Policy.* Reading, MA: Addison-Wesley, 1984, 230–275.

Cox, J., and S. Ross. "The Valuation of Options for Alternative Stochastic Processes." *Journal of Financial Economics* 3 (January–March 1976): 145–166.

Cox, J., and M. Rubinstein. "A Survey of Alternative Option Pricing Models." In *Option Pricing*, edited by Menachem Brenner. Lexington, MA: D. C. Heath, 1983.

Cox, J., S. Ross, and M. Rubinstein. "Option Pricing: A Simplified Approach." *Journal of Financial Economics* (September 1979): 229–263.

Galai, D. "A Survey of Empirical Tests of Option Pricing Models." In *Option Pricing*, edited by M. Brenner. Lexington, MA: D. C. Heath, 1983, 45–80.

Galai, D. "A Convexity Test for Traded Options." *Quarterly Review of Economics and Business* 19 (Summer 1979): 83–90.

Galai, D. "Empirical Tests of Boundary Conditions for CBOE Options." *Journal of Financial Economics* 6 (June–September 1978): 187–211.

Galai, D. "Tests of Market Efficiency of the Chicago Board Options Exchange." *Journal of Business* 50 (April 1977): 167–197.

Geske, R., and R. Roll. "On Valuing American Call Options with the Black-Scholes Formula." *Journal of Finance* 39 (June 1984): 443–455.

Geske, R. "A Note on an Analytic Formula for Unprotected American Call Options on Stocks with Known Dividends." *Journal of Financial Economics* 7 (December 1979): 375–380.

Geske, R. "Pricing of Options with Stochastic Dividend Yield." *Journal of Finance* 33 (May 1978): 618–625.

Geske, R., and H. Johnson. "The American Put Option Valued Analytically." *The Journal of Finance* 39 (December 1984): 1511–1524.

Geske, R., and R. Roll. "On Valuing American Call Options with the Black-Scholes Formula." *Journal of Finance* 39 (June 1984): 443–455.

Hull, J. C. *Options, Futures, and Other Derivatives.* Upper Saddle River, NJ: Prentice Hall, 2006, Chapter 16.

Hull, J. C., and A. White. "Value at Risk when Daily Changes in Market Variables Are Not Normally Distributed." *Journal of Derivatives* 5 (Spring 1998): 9–19.

Itô, K. "On Stochastic Differential Equations." Memoire, *American Mathematical Society* 4 (December 1951): 1–51.

Jackwerth, J. C., and M. Rubinstein. "Recovering Probability Distributions from Option Prices." *Journal of Finance* 51 (December 1996): 1611–1631.

Jarrow, R. and A. Rudd. "Approximate Option Valuation for Arbitrary Stochastic Processes." *Journal of Financial Economics* 10 (1982): 347–369.

Johnson, R. S., J. E. Pawlukiewicz, and J. Mehta. "Binomial Option Pricing with Skewed Asset Returns." *Review of Quantitative Finance and Accounting* 9 (1997): 89–101.

Klemkosky, R., and B. Resnick. "An *Ex Ante* Analysis of Put-Call Parity." *Journal of Financial Economics* 8 (1980): 363–378.

Lantane, H., and R. Rendleman Jr., "Standard Deviations of Stock Price Ratios Implied in Option Prices." *Journal of Finance* 31 (May 1976): 369–382.

MacBeth, J., and L. Merville. "An Empirical Examination of the Black-Scholes Call Option Pricing Model." *Journal of Finance* 34 (December 1979): 1173–1186.

MacBeth, J., and L. Merville. "Tests of the Black-Scholes and Cox Call Option Valuation Models." *Journal of Finance* (May 1980): 285–300.

Manaster, S., and R. Rendleman Jr., "Option Prices as Predictors of Equilibrium Stock Prices." *Journal of Finance* 37 (September 1982): 1043–1058.

Manaster, S., and G. Koehler. "The Calculation of Implied Variances from the Black-Scholes Option Model: A Note." *The Journal of Finance* 37 (March 1982): 227–230.

Merton, R. "Option Pricing When Underlying Stock Returns Are Discontinuous." *Journal of Financial Economics* 3 (January–February 1976): 125–144.

Rogalski, R. "Variances of Option Prices in Theory and Evidence." *Journal of Portfolio Management* 4 (Winter 1978): 43–51.

Roll, R. "An Analytic Valuation Formula for Unprotected American Call Options on Stocks with Known Dividends." *Journal of Financial Economics* 5 (November 1977): 251–258.

Rubinstein, M. "Implied Binomial Trees." *Journal of Finance* 49 (July 1994): 771–818.

Rubinstein, M. "Nonparametric Tests of Alternative Option Pricing Models Using All Reported Trades and Quotes on the 30 Most Active CBOE Option Classes from August 23, 1976, through August 31, 1978." *Journal of Finance* 40 (June 1985): 455–480.

Schmalensee, R., and R. Trippi. "Common Stock Volatility Expectations Implied by Option Premia." *Journal of Finance* 33 (March 1978): 129–147.

Singleton, J. C., and J. Wingender. "Skewness Persistence in Common Stock Returns." *Journal of Financial and Quantitative Analysis* 21 (1986): 335–341.

Stapleton, R. C., and M. G. Subrahmanyam. "The Valuation of Options When Asset Returns Are Generated by a Binomial Process." *Journal of Finance* 39 (1984): 1525–1539.

Stein, E. M., and J. C. Stein. "Stock Price Distributions with Stochastic Volatility: An Analytical Approach." *Review of Financial Studies* 4 (1991): 727–752.

Sterk, W. "Comparative Performance of the Black-Scholes and Roll-Geske-Whaley Option Pricing Models." *Journal of Financial and Quantitative Analysis* 18 (September 1983): 345–354.

Turner, A. L., and E. J. Weigel. "Daily Stock Return Volatility: 1928–1989." *Management Science* 38 (1992): 1586–1609.

Whaley, R. "Valuation of American Call Options on Dividend Paying Stocks: Empirical Tests." *Journal of Financial Economics* 10 (March 1982): 29–58.

Whaley, R. "On the Valuation of American Call Options on Stocks with Known Dividends." *Journal of Financial Economics* 9 (June 1981): 207–212.

Problems and Questions

Note: Many of these problems can be done using the B-S OPM Excel program found on the text's website.

1. Suppose XYZ stock currently is trading at $100 per share, has an annualized standard deviation of 0.50, will not pay any dividends over the next three months, and the continuously compounded annual risk-free rate is 3%.

   a. Using the Black-Scholes OPM, calculate the equilibrium price for a three-month XYX 100 European call option.

   b. Using the Black-Scholes OPM, calculate the equilibrium price for a three-month XYZ 100 European put option.

   c. Show the Black-Scholes put price is the same price obtained using the put-call parity model.

   d. Describe the arbitrage strategy one would pursue if the XYZ 100 call was overpriced and if it was underpriced.

   e. Describe the arbitrage strategy one would pursue if the XYZ 100 put was overpriced and if it was underpriced.

2. Suppose the XYZ stock described in Problem 1 is expected to go ex-dividend in exactly one month with the value of the dividend on that date expected to be $2.00. Using the pseudo-American option model, calculate the equilibrium prices of the call and put options described in Problem 1.

3. Using the continuous-dividend-adjusted option model, calculate the dividend-adjusted stock price, dividend-adjusted call price, and dividend-adjusted put price for the XYZ stock and options described in Problem 1. In your calculations, assume an annual dividend yield of 8%.

4. Discuss the applicability of the pseudo-American model for pricing American call options.

5. Using the B-S OPM Excel program calculate the call option price for each stock price shown below. Assume $R = 3\%$, $\sigma = 0.50$, $t = 0.25$ per year, $X = \$100$, and no dividends.

$$S_0 = 80,\ 85,\ 90,\ 46,\ 95,\ 100,\ 105,\ 110,\ 115,\ \text{and}\ 120.$$

Comment on the ability of the B-S OPM to capture the features of the call and stock price relations described in Chapter 11.

6. Using the B-S OPM Excel program, calculate the put option price for each stock price shown below. Assume $R = 3\%$, $\sigma = 0.50$, $t = 0.25$ per year, $X = \$100$, and no dividends.

$$S_0 = 80,\ 85,\ 90,\ 46,\ 95,\ 100,\ 105,\ 110,\ 115,\ \text{and}\ 120.$$

Comment on the ability of the B-S OPM to capture the feature that the put price is less than its IV.

7. Using the B-S OPM Excel program, calculate the call option price for each annualized standard deviation shown below. Assume $R = 3\%$, $S_0 = \$100$, $t = 0.25$, $X = \$100$, and no dividends.

$$\sigma = 0.50,\ 0.60,\ 0.70,\ \text{and}\ 0.80.$$

Comment on the relationship.

8. Given the following information on the XYZ stock: $S_0 = \$50$, $\sigma = 0.175$, $R = 3\%$, and $\beta^S = 0.35$, determine the following characteristics of an XYZ 50 European call with an expiration of $t = 0.25$:

a. Equilibrium OPM call price
b. Expected rate of return of the call
c. Standard deviation of the call
d. Beta of the call

Comment on relative sizes of the expected returns, standard deviations, and β of the XYZ call and stock.

9. Given the information on the XYZ stock: $S_0 = \$50$, $\sigma = 0.175$, $R = 3\%$, $\beta^S = 0.35$, and $E(R_s) = -0.10$, determine the following characteristics of an XYZ 50 European put with an expiration of $t = 0.25$:

a. Equilibrium OPM put price
b. Expected rate of return of the put
c. Standard deviation of the put
d. Beta of the put

10. Suppose XYZ stock is trading at $50, its annualized standard deviation is 0.175, and the continuously compounded risk-free rate is 6% (annual).

   a. Calculate the B-S equilibrium call prices for an XYZ 50 European call expiring in 90 days ($t = 0.25$) and an XYZ 48 European call expiring in 90 days.
   b. Determine the delta, theta, and gamma for the 50 call and 48 call.
   c. Construct a neutral ratio spread with the 50 and 48 calls. What would your initial cash flow be if the calls were priced equal to their OPM values?
   d. What is your neutral delta position theta and gamma?
   e. What would happen to your neutral ratio hedge if the stock immediately increased by $1 and you closed your positions at call prices equal to their OPM values? What would happen if you closed your position after the stock decreased by $1?
   f. Define the arbitrage strategy using the neutral delta strategy you could employ if the price of the XYZ 48 call were equal to its equilibrium value, but the 50 call were underpriced at $2.05. Show the initial cash flow from closing the position shortly afterward at $S_t = \$51$ and $S_t = \$49$ and with the call values equal to the equilibrium values you used in 10a.
   g. Describe the arbitrage strategy one could use if the 50 call were overpriced at $2.25.

11. Explain the methodology and findings of the following empirical studies, examining the B-S OPM:

   a. Black-Scholes (1972)
   b. Galai (1977)
   c. MacBeth and Merville (1979)

Bloomberg Exercises

1. Using Bloomberg's OVME screen, estimate the equilibrium price on a selected call and put option. Guide:

   - Select the options from the selected stock's OMON or CALL screen.
   - Load the option: Option Ticker <Equity>
   - Enter OVME
   - On OVME screen, determine the B-S price using the continuous dividend yield (select Black-Scholes Continuous). Select dividend yield provided or input your own estimate (click "More Market Data" and keep the Bloomberg default dividend yield or input you own). Select Bloomberg's implied volatility, historical, or provide your own volatility estimate.
   - On OVME screen, determine the B-S price using the discrete dividend (select Black-Scholes Discrete or Trinomial). Select dividend payments provided or input your own estimates by going to "Settings." Select Bloomberg's implied volatility, historical, or provide your own volatility estimate.

Compare your option values to the market prices (bid, ask, and last). Current option prices can be found on OMON, CALL, and the option's GP and DES screens.

2. Using the OVME screen for the call and put options you evaluated in Exercise 1, evaluate the prices of the call and put options for different stock prices. Click the "Scenario" tab and set the axis for option prices and underlying stock prices.

3. Using the OVME screen for the call and put option you evaluated in Exercise 1, evaluate the Greeks for different stock prices and time to expiration by clicking the "Scenario" tab and setting the axis.

4. Create a portfolio of at least two options on the same stock and evaluate the position in terms of the position's OPM value, delta, gamma, and theta. On the OVME screen, click the + icon next to "Deals" to add a new deal, and then click "Add Legs" from the gray "Leg" dropdown. Input information for each option in the input box (different exercise price, expiration, and call or put, and buy or sell). Click "Scenario" tab to view your position's value and profit-loss relation for different stock prices.

5. Using OVME, analyze the profit and stock price relation for different times prior to expiration and expiration for the following option strategies:

   a. Straddle Purchase
   b. Straddle Sale
   c. Bull Call Spread
   d. Bear Call Spread
   e. Bull Put Spread
   f. Bear Put Spread
   g. Calendar Spread

   On the OVME screen, click the + icon next to "Deals" to add a new deal, and then click "Add Legs" from the gray "Leg" dropdown. Input information for each option in the input box (different exercise price, expiration, and call or put, and buy or sell). Click "Scenario" tab to view your position's value and profit-loss relation for different stock prices.

6. Create a neutral delta portfolio with two options on the same stock and evaluate the position in terms of the position's OPM value and gamma. On the OVME screen, click the + icon next to "Deals" to add a new deal, and then click "Add Legs" from the gray "Leg" dropdown. Input information for each option in the input box (different exercise price and expirations). Given each option's delta, solve for the number of options needed to create a neutral delta position. Click the white "Greeks" + icon row to see the Greek display. Click the "Scenario" tab to view your position's value and profit-loss relation for different stock prices.

CHAPTER 12

Pricing Non-Stock Options and Futures Options

In this chapter, we continue our analysis of the B-S OPM and the BOPM by showing how those models are adjusted to price options on stock indexes, currency, futures contracts, and convertible securities. In Chapter 13, we will complete our analysis on option pricing by examining the pricing of interest rate and bond options.

Pricing of Spot Index and Currency Options

Proxy Portfolio

As we discussed in Chapter 6, an index can be defined in terms of proxy portfolios that are highly correlated with the spot index or with a highly diversified index fund. Whether it is an index fund, ETF, or a highly correlated portfolio, the proxy portfolio can be viewed as a position in the index. For example, suppose the spot S&P 500 were at 2,000. A highly diversified portfolio valued at $5 million and with annual dividends of $250,000 and beta of one could be viewed as equivalent to a hypothetical S&P 500 spot portfolio consisting of $N_0 = 2,500$ hypothetical shares of the index, with each share priced at $S_0 = \$2,000$, and with a dividend per share of $100 ($D_T = \$250,000/2,500$):

$$V_0^P = N_0 S_0$$

$$V_0^P = (2,500)(\$2,000) = \$5,000,000$$

$$D_T = \frac{\text{Total expected annual dividends}}{N_0} = \frac{\$250{,}000}{2{,}500} = \$100$$

A proxy portfolio, in turn, can be used to determine the price of an index option using the replication approach. In terms of the single-period BOPM, the equilibrium price of the index call is equal to the value of a replicating portfolio consisting of H_0^* hypothetical shares of the spot index, partially financed by borrowing B_0^* dollars. Suppose $u = 1.1$, $d = 0.95$, $R_f = 0.025$, and the current spot S&P 500 index is $S_0 = 2{,}000$. For a one-period binomial model, the equilibrium price of a 2,000 S&P 500 call option would be 97.65. In this case, the replicating portfolio would consist of $H_0^* = 0.666667$ hypothetical shares of the index, partially financed by borrowing $B_0^* = \$1{,}235.77$:

$$C_u = \text{Max}[uS_0 - X,\, 0] = \text{Max}[(1.1)(2{,}000) - 2{,}000,\, 0] = 200$$

$$C_d = \text{Max}[dS_0 - X,\, 0] = \text{Max}[0.95(2{,}000) - 2{,}000, 0] = 0$$

$$H_0^* = \frac{C_u - C_d}{uS_0 - dS_0} = \frac{200 - 0}{2{,}200 - 1{,}900} = 0.666667$$

$$B_0^* = \frac{C_u(dS_0) - C_d(uS_0)}{r_f(uS_0 - dS_0)} = \frac{200(1{,}900) - (0)(2{,}200)}{1.025(2{,}200 - 1{,}900)} = 1{,}235.77$$

$$C_0^* = H_0^* S_0 - B_0^* = 0.666667(2{,}000) - 1{,}235.77 = 97.56$$

$$p = \frac{r_f - d}{u - d} = \frac{1.025 - 0.95}{1.1 - 0.95} = 0.50$$

$$C_0^* = \frac{1}{r_f}[pC_u + (1 - p)C_d] = \frac{1}{1.025}[(0.50)(200) + (1 - 0.50)(0)] = 97.56$$

If the market price of the index call did not equal 97.56, an arbitrage portfolio could be formed by taking a position in the call and an opposite position in the replicating portfolio. In terms of a proxy portfolio, the 0.666667 index shares priced at $S_0 = 2{,}000$ would be equivalent to buying \$1,333.33 (= (0.666667)(2,000)) worth of a proxy index portfolio. Thus, the replicating portfolio consists of an investment of \$1,333.33 in a proxy portfolio finance in part by borrowing $B_0^* = \$1{,}235.77$.

Dividend Adjustments

Suppose the stocks making up the proxy portfolio all went ex-dividend at the end of the period. Like the single-period stock case, dividends will cause the stock index and proxy portfolio to fall on the ex-dividend date by the amount of the dividend. Suppose the proxy portfolio had quarterly dividends expected to be worth \$62,500 on an ex-dividend occurring at the end of the period of length one quarter. For the index, the dividend would therefore be equal to $D_1 = \$25$ per index share.

$$D_T = \frac{\text{Total expected dividends}}{N_0} = \frac{\$62{,}500}{2{,}500} = \$25$$

At expiration, the two possible call values would be $C_u^x = \text{Max}[(2,200 - 25) - 2,000, 0] = 175$ and $C_d^x = \text{Max}[1,900 - 100 - 2,000, 0] = 0$. The only adjustment needed in forming the replicating portfolio for dividends is to subtract the value of the dividend from the two non-dividend-adjusted index prices (uS_0 or dS_0) in computing both the call's possible intrinsic values (C_u^x and C_d^x) and the H_0^* and B_0^* values for the replicating portfolio. In terms of our example, the H_0^* and B_0^* values needed to form a replicating portfolio to match the possible call values of $C_u^x = 175$ and $C_d^x = 0$ would be 0.583333 and \$1,081.30:

$$H_0^* = \frac{C_u^x - C_d^x}{uS_0 - dS_0} = \frac{175 - 0}{2,200 - 1,900} = 0.583333$$

$$B_0^* = \frac{C_u^x(dS_0) - C_d^x(uS_0)}{r_f(uS_0 - dS_0)} = \frac{(175)(1,900) - (0)(2,000)}{1.025[2,200 - 1,900]} = 1,081.30$$

Using the replication approach, the equilibrium call price therefore would be 85.37:

$$C_0^* = H_0^* S_0 - B_0^* = 0.583333(2,000) - 1,081.30 = 85.37$$

$$C_0^* = \frac{1}{r_f}[pC_u^x + (1 - p)C_d^x] = \frac{1}{1.025}[(0.50)(175) + (1 - 0.50)(0)] = 85.37$$

If the market price of the index option did not equal 85.37, then an arbitrage opportunity would exist by taking a position in the option and an opposite position in the replicating portfolio. In this case, a long position in the replicating portfolio would be equivalent to investing $\$1,166.67 = (H_0^* S_0^* = (0.58333)(2,000))$ in a proxy index portfolio and borrowing $B_0^* = \$1,081.30$, with the proxy portfolio consisting of stocks expected to go ex-dividend at the end of the quarter, with the value of those dividends expected to be \$14.58 (= (0.583333)(\$25)).

In the absence of arbitrage, the price of the call would therefore be 85.37. Thus, by lowering the price of the stocks that comprise the index portfolio on their ex-dividend dates, dividends decrease the value of the index call. Just the opposite applies to put options. It should be noted that if there are futures contracts on the index, the price of a spot index option can alternatively be defined in terms of a replicating portfolio formed with the index futures.

Merton's BOPM Approach

The single-period binomial case helps to illustrate how arbitrage strategies using an option and a proxy portfolio determine the price of an index option. The practical application of the binomial model to pricing index option, however, requires a multiple-period model. As we noted in the case of stock options, in a multiple-period binomial model, the binomial tree fails to recombine when discrete dividend payments are included. This, in turn, causes the number of nodes to increase dramatically as the number of subperiods increase. Both the discrete dividend payment approach and the

Merton continuous dividend yield approach examined in Chapter 10, however, can be extended to the pricing of index options.

To see the application of the Merton model, suppose we want to price an S&P 500 index call and put options each with $X = 2,500$ and 180 days to expiration, using a five-period binomial model. In pricing the options, suppose the following:

- The current S&P 500 is at $S_0 = 2,500$.
- The index's estimated volatility and mean are $\sigma^A = 0.3$ and $\mu^A = 0$.
- The annual continuous dividend yield generated from the stocks comprising the index portfolio is $\psi = 0.04$.
- $R^A = 0.06$.

Using the Merton model, the dividend-adjusted risk-neutral probability, p, would be 0.48693:

$$p = \frac{e^{(R^A - \psi)\,\Delta t} - d}{u - d}$$

$$p = \frac{e^{(0.06 - 0.04)(.09863)} - 0.910086}{1.098797 - 0.910086} = 0.48693$$

where

$$u = e^{0.3\sqrt{0.09863}} = 1.0988$$

$$d = 1/u = 0.9101$$

$$\Delta t = t/n = (180/365)/5 = 0.09863$$

Exhibit 12.1 shows the resulting five-period binomial tree for the American and European calls and American and European puts. For this five-period case, the Merton model prices the American and European calls equally at 227.18. In contrast, the model prices the American put at 206.34 and the European put at 203.13. Unlike the call options, there are early exercise advantages with the put that occur at the two lower nodes in period 4. Using the Merton BOPM Excel program, the prices of the American and European index calls are 215.20 for $n = 30$ subperiods and 216.39 for $n = 100$; for the American index put, the prices are 194.52 for $n = 30$ and 195.36 for $n = 100$; for the European index put, the prices are 191.12 for $n = 30$ and 192.31 for $n = 100$.

Note, in this example the dividend yield is less than the risk-free rate and there is an early exercise advantage with the put, but not the call. This is often the case if the dividend yield is less than the risk-free rate. In general, for the early exercise of an index call to be profitable, the dividend yield has to be relatively large (exceeding at least the risk-free rate). In contrast to index calls, the early exercise of an American put is advantageous if the dividend yield is less than the risk-free rate and the put is deep in the money. Thus, in periods in which dividend yields on stock indexes are considerably less than the rates on risk-free securities, there is a greater chance that

EXHIBIT 12.1 Merton's Dividend-Adjusted Binomial Model $S_0 = \$2,500$, $\sigma = 0.30$, $\mu = 0.00$, $\psi = 4\%$, $R^A = 6\%$, $n = 5$, $t = 180/365$, $\Delta t = t/n = 0.09863$, $X = 2,500$, $u = 1.09880$, $d = 0.9101$, $p = 0.48693$

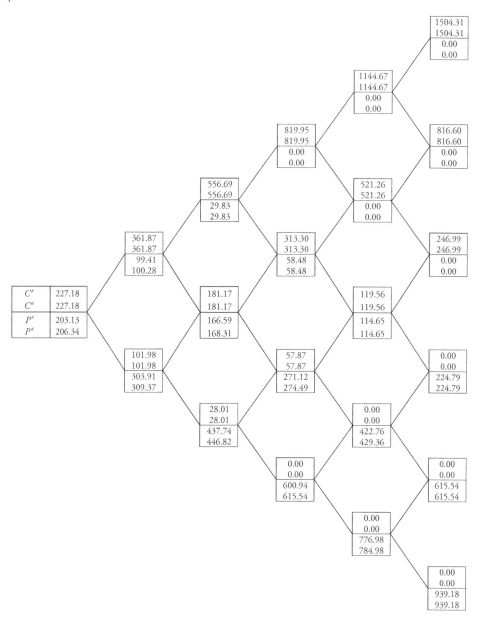

an American index put could be exercised early and an American index call would not. On the hand, in periods when dividend yields are greater than interest rates, the chance of early exercise is greater for American index calls than puts.

Even though stock indexes such as the S&P 500 have many dividend-paying stocks, the dividend payments from those stocks often are paid discretely. As a result, the known dividend payment approach may be more applicable to adjusting the index options for dividends than the Merton approach. This approach is explained in Appendix 10A.

Merton's Continuous Dividend-Adjusted Black-Scholes Model

Merton's continuous dividend-adjusted B-S model can alternatively be used to determine the equilibrium price of a European index option. Using Merton's dividend-adjusted B-S model, the equilibrium price of the S&P 500 call in the above example is 215.90, which is only 0.23% less than the binomial price ($n = 100$), and the price of the put is 191.85, which is only 0.38% less than the binomial put value.

For American stock options, the pseudo-American OPM can be used to price American call options on dividend-paying stocks. For index options this would require identifying ex-dividend dates for the stocks comprising the index. Using the pseudo model would be comparable to using the known dividend payment binomial model. The other alternative for pricing American index options is to use Merton's continuous dividend adjusted BOPM constrained to price American options. In terms of the above example, the Merton-adjusted BOPM for an American call option prices the American index option at 216.39 (the same as the European in this example), and it prices the American put at 194.52—$3.40 more than the binomial European value. For American put options on stock and indexes with dividends, the Merton BOPM should be used instead of the Merton continuous dividend-adjusted B-S model.

Pricing Foreign Currency Spot Options

Since foreign currency can be invested in interest-bearing securities, the option pricing model for currency options needs to include the foreign interest rate. One way to adjust the binomial model for foreign interest rates is to use the Merton model. In applying the Merton model to currency options, the interest rate paid on the foreign currency (R_F) is treated as the continuous asset yield (ψ). For example, consider call and put options on the British pound (BP), each with $X = \$1.50/BP$ and expiration of 180 days, spot $/BP exchange rate of $1.50/BP, estimated volatility and mean of $\sigma^A = 0.3$ and $\mu^A = 0$, annual risk-free rate paid on dollars of $R_f = 0.02$, and annual risk-free rate paid on British pounds of $R_{BP} = \psi = 0.04$. Using the Merton BOPM Excel program, the prices of the American BP call are $0.1175 for $n = 30$ subperiods and $0.1180 for $n = 100$, and for the European call, the prices are $0.1185 for $n = 30$ and $0.1165 for $n = 100$; for the American and European BP puts, the prices are $0.1304 for $n = 30$ and $0.1311 for $n = 100$.

The Merton dividend-adjusted B-S model can also be used to price European currency option. This use was first proposed by Garman and Kohlhagen (G-K). Using Merton/G-K-adjusted B-S model, the equilibrium price of the European BP call is $0.1162, which is only slightly less than the binomial price, and the price of the European put is $0.1308, which is slightly more than the binomial put value.

Binomial Pricing of Futures Options

Single-Period BOPM for Futures Options

The equilibrium price of a European call or put option on a futures contract is equal to the value of a replicating portfolio consisting of the underlying futures contract and debt (or investment) positions. To see this, assume a single period to expiration in which the possible values are $f_u = uf_0$ and $f_d = df_0$. The relationship between the futures and spot price, as defined by the carrying-cost model, is

$$f_0 = S_0 \, r_f^{n_f} + K n_f + TRC \ - D_T$$

where

$\qquad n_f \;=\;$ number of periods to expiration on the futures contract
$\qquad r_f \;=\;$ 1 + periodic risk-free rate
$\qquad K \;=\;$ storage costs per period for holding the underlying asset
$\qquad TRC \;=\;$ transportation cost of transporting the underlying asset from the storage facility to the destination point on the futures contract or vice versa at expiration
$\qquad D_T \;=\;$ value of benefits (e.g., dividends) on the underlying asset assumed to be realized at expiration

In the case of an index or currency option in which the stock index or currency is adjusted to reflect a continuous dividend yield or a continues compounded foreign risk-free rate, the futures prices is

$$f_0 = S_0 e^{(R^A - \psi)n_f \Delta t}$$

where

$\qquad \psi \;=\;$ annual continuously compounded dividend yield or foreign risk-free rate
$\qquad R^A \;=\;$ annualized continuously compounded risk-free rate (domestic (US) rate for currency option)
$\qquad \Delta t \;=\;$ length of binomial steps as a proportion of a year
$\qquad n_f \;=\;$ number of periods to expiration

The equilibrium price on a European call (put) option on the futures contract is found by constructing a replicating portfolio with cash flows that match the futures call (put) option's possible values of $C_u = \text{Max}[f_u - X, 0]$ and $C_d = \text{Max}[f_d - X, 0]$ ($P_u = \text{Max}[X - f_u, 0]$ and $P_d = \text{Max}[X - f_d, 0]$). The replicating futures call portfolio (RP_C) is formed by taking a position in H_0^f futures contracts at f_0 and borrowing or investing B_0 dollars. The two possible values of the call replicating position are:

$$H_0^f \, (f_u - f_0) - B_0 \, r_f$$
$$H_0^f \, (f_d - f_0) - B_0 \, r_f$$

Similarly, the replicating futures put portfolio (RP_P) is formed by taking a position in H_0^f futures contracts at f_0 and investing I_0 dollars. The possible values of the portfolio are:

$$H_0^f\,(f_u - f_0) + I_0\,r_f$$

$$H_0^f\,(f_d - f_0) + I_0\,r_f$$

For the futures call, the equilibrium price is obtained by solving first for the H_0^{f*} and B_0^* that make the two possible replicating portfolio values at expiration equal to the possible call values and then setting the price of the call equal to value of the replicating portfolio defined in terms of H_0^{f*} and B_0^*:

$$H_0^f\,(f_u - f_0) - B_0\,r_f = C_u$$

$$H_0^f\,(f_d - f_0) - B_0\,r_f = C_d$$

$$H_0^{f*} = \frac{C_u - C_d}{f_u - f_d}$$

$$B_0^* = \frac{C_u(f_d - f_0) - C_d(f_u - f_0)}{r_f(f_u - f_d)}$$

$$C_0^* = H_0^{f*}V_0^f - B_0^*$$

$$C_0^* = H_0^{f*}(0) - B_0^*$$

$$C_0^* = -B_0^*$$

$$C_0^* = -B_0^* = -\frac{C_u(f_d - f_0) - C_d(f_u - f_0)}{r_f(f_u - f_d)}$$

Note, the futures contract has no initial value ($V_0^f = 0$).

Given $f_d < f_0 < f_u$, the bracket expression in the equation for C_0^* is negative, making B_0^*, and therefore C_0^*, positive and H_0^{f*} positive. This implies that if the futures call is overpriced the arbitrage portfolio would require an investment of B_0^* dollars in a risk-free security and a long position in H_0^{f*} futures contract.

For the futures put, the equilibrium price is obtained in a similar way by solving for the H_0^{f*} and I_0^* that make two possible replicating portfolio values at expiration equal to their possible put values and then setting the price of the put equal to the value of the replicating portfolio defined in terms of H_0^{f*} and I_0^*:

$$H_0^f\,(f_u - f_0) + I_0\,r_f = P_u$$

$$H_0^f\,(f_d - f_0) + I_0\,r_f = P_d$$

$$H_0^{f*} = \frac{P_u - P_d}{f_u - f_d}$$

$$I_0^* = -\frac{[P_u(f_d - f_0) - P_d(f_u - f_0)]}{r_f(f_u - f_d)}$$

$$P_0^* = H_0^{f\,*} V_0^f + I_0^*$$

$$P_0^* = H_0^{f\,*}(0) + I_0^*$$

$$P_0^* = I_0^*$$

$$P_0^* = I_0^* = -\frac{P_u(f_d - f_0) - P_d(f_u - f_0)}{r_f(f_u - f_d)}$$

Given $f_d < f_0 < f_u$, $H_0^{f\,*}$ is negative and I_0^* is positive, the arbitrage portfolio for an overpriced put requires a short position in the futures contract and an investment in the risk-free security.

The equations for the equilibrium call price and the equilibrium put price can alternatively be expressed in terms of risk-neutral probabilities (p) by rewriting the equations for C_0^* and P_0^*:

$$C_0^* = \frac{1}{r_f}[pC_u + (1 - p)C_d]$$

$$P_0^* = \frac{1}{r_f}[pP_u + (1 - p)P_d]$$

where

$$p = \frac{1 - d}{u - d}$$

Note that p for the futures option is similar to p for spot options except it excludes r_f.

The formulas for estimating the up and down parameters as defined in terms of futures price (u^f and d^f) are:

$$u = e^{\sigma_f^A \sqrt{\Delta t} + \mu_f^A \Delta t}$$

$$d = e^{-\sigma_f^A \sqrt{\Delta t} + \mu_f^A \Delta t}$$

where

σ_f^A and μ_f^A = annualized volatility and mean on the futures price's logarithmic return

σ_S^A and μ_S^A = annualized volatility and mean on the spot price's logarithmic return

The relationship between the volatility and mean on the futures price's logarithmic return and the spot's volatility, σ_S, and mean, μ_S, in turn, is

$$\sigma_f^A = \sigma_S^A$$

$$\mu_f^A = \mu_S^A - (R^A - \psi)$$

EXHIBIT 12.2 Algebraic Derivation of the Relation between Spot and Futures Upward and Downward Parameters and Volatility and Mean

u = futures upward parameter, d = futures downward parameter,

u^S = spot upward parameter, and d^S = spot downward parameter

σ_f^A = futures volatility, μ_f^A = futures mean, σ_S^A = spot volatility, μ_S^A = spot mean

$$u = \frac{f_u}{f_0} = \frac{u^S S_0 e^{(R^A - \psi)(n_f - 1)\Delta t}}{S_0 e^{(R^A - \psi)n_f \Delta t}} = \frac{u^S}{e^{(R^A - \psi)\Delta t}} \qquad d = \frac{f_d}{f_0} = \frac{d^S S_0 e^{(R^A - \psi)(n_f - 1)\Delta t}}{S_0 e^{(R^A - \psi)n_f \Delta t}} = \frac{d^S}{e^{(R^A - \psi)\Delta t}}$$

$$u^S = u e^{(R^A - \psi)\Delta t} \qquad\qquad d^S = d e^{(R^A - \psi)\Delta t}$$

$$u = \frac{u^S}{e^{(R^A - \psi)\Delta t}} \qquad\qquad d = \frac{d^S}{e^{(R^A - \psi)\Delta t}}$$

$$e^{\sigma_f^A \sqrt{\Delta t} + \mu_f^A \Delta t} = \frac{e^{\sigma_S^A \sqrt{\Delta t} + \mu_S^A \Delta t}}{e^{(R^A - \psi)\Delta t}} \qquad e^{-\sigma_f^A \sqrt{\Delta t} + \mu_f^A \Delta t} = \frac{e^{-\sigma_S^A \sqrt{\Delta t} + \mu_S^A \Delta t}}{e^{(R^A - \psi)\Delta t}}$$

$$\ln(e^{\sigma_f^A \sqrt{\Delta t} + \mu_f^A \Delta t}) = \ln\left(\frac{e^{\sigma_S^A \sqrt{\Delta t} + \mu_s^A}}{e^{(R^A - \psi)\Delta t}}\right) \qquad \ln(e^{-\sigma_f^A \sqrt{\Delta t} + \mu_f^A \Delta t}) = \ln\left(\frac{e^{-\sigma_S^A \sqrt{\Delta t} + \mu_s^A}}{e^{(R^A - \psi)\Delta t}}\right)$$

$$\sigma_f^A \sqrt{\Delta t} + \mu_f^A \Delta t = \sigma_S^A \sqrt{\Delta t} + \mu_S^A \Delta t \qquad -\sigma_f^A \sqrt{\Delta t} + \mu_f^A \Delta t = -\sigma_S^A \sqrt{\Delta t} + \mu_S^A \Delta t$$

$$- (R^A - \psi)\Delta t \qquad\qquad - (R^A - \psi)\Delta t$$

$$\sigma_f^A = \frac{\sigma_S^A \sqrt{\Delta t} + \mu_S^A \Delta t - (R^A - \psi)\Delta t - \mu_f^A \Delta t}{\sqrt{\Delta t}} \quad (1) \qquad \sigma_f^A = \frac{\sigma_S^A \sqrt{\Delta t} - \mu_S^A \Delta t + (R^A - \psi)\Delta t + \mu_f^A \Delta t}{\sqrt{\Delta t}} \quad (2)$$

Solving Equations (1) and (2) simultaneously for σ_S^A and μ_S^A:

Equation (1):

$$\sigma_f^A \sqrt{\Delta t} = \sigma_S^A \sqrt{\Delta t} + \mu_S^A \Delta t - (R^A - \psi)\Delta t - \mu_f^A \Delta t \tag{3}$$

Equation (2) expressed in terms of $\mu_f^A \Delta t$:

$$\mu_f^A \Delta t = -\sigma_S^A \sqrt{\Delta t} + \mu_S^A \Delta t - (R^A - \psi)\Delta t + \sigma_f^A \sqrt{\Delta t} \tag{4}$$

Substituting (4) into (3) and solving for σ_f^A:

$$\sigma_f^A \sqrt{\Delta t} = \sigma_S^A \sqrt{\Delta t} + \mu_S^A \Delta t - (R^A - \psi)\Delta t + \sigma_f^A \sqrt{\Delta t} - \mu_S^A \Delta t + (R^A - \psi)\Delta t - \sigma_f^A \sqrt{\Delta t}$$

$$\sigma_f^A = \sigma_S^A \tag{5}$$

Substituting σ_S^A for σ_f^A in Equation (4) and solving in terms of μ_f^A:

$$\mu_f^A \Delta t = -\sigma_S^A \sqrt{\Delta t} + \mu_S^A \Delta t - (R^A - \psi)\Delta t + \sigma_S^A \sqrt{\Delta t}$$

$$\mu_f^A = \mu_S^A - (R^A - \psi) \tag{6}$$

The algebraic proof of the relation is presented in Exhibit 12.2. Recall, for a multiple-period model that is defined by a large number of subperiods, the impact of μ_f^A on u and d values is negligible. Thus, for the case of large n, the only input that needs to be estimated to determine the price of an option is the underlying spot variability, σ_S.

In general, for financial futures the single-period binomial equations defining the equilibrium prices for call and put options on a futures contract are similar in form to the BOPM for the spot securities except for the C_u and C_d and P_u and P_d, which are defined in terms of the contract prices on the futures instead of the spot prices. If the futures contract and the futures option expire at the same time, then the possible prices on the futures contract at expiration will be equal to the possible spot prices ($f_u = S_u$ and $f_d = S_d$); in this case, C_u and C_d and P_u and P_d will be the same for the spot option and the futures option. Thus, if the futures contract and the option have the same expiration, the carrying-cost model holds, and the futures and spot options are both European, then futures and spot options will be equivalent.

Multiple-Period BOPM for Futures Options

The single-period binomial cases help to illustrate how arbitrage strategies using option and futures contracts determine the price of a futures option. The practical application of the binomial model to pricing futures option, though, requires a multiple-period model.

Pricing S&P 500 Index Futures Call and Put Options

To illustrate the application of the multiple-period binomial model to the pricing of futures options, consider the pricing of European and American call and put options on an S&P 500 index futures, each with $X = 2,500$ and expiration of 90 days, using a three-period binomial model. In pricing the options, suppose the following:

- The current S&P 500 is at $S_0 = 2,500$.
- The spot index's estimated volatility and mean are $\sigma_S^A = 0.3$ and $\mu_S^A = 0$.
- The annual continuous dividend yield generated from the stocks comprising the index portfolio is $\psi = 0.04$.
- $R^A = 0.06$.
- The futures index's estimated volatility and mean are $\sigma_f^A = 0.30$ and $\mu_f^A = -0.02$:

$$\sigma_f^A = \sigma_S^A = 0.3$$

$$\mu_f^A = \mu_S^A - (R^A - \psi)$$

$$\mu_f^A = 0.00 - (0.06 - 0.04) = -0.02$$

- The S&P 500 futures contract expires in 120 days and is priced at its carrying-cost value of 2,516.49:

$$f_0 = S_0 e^{(R^A - \psi)n_f \Delta t}$$

$$f_0 = 2,500 \, e^{(0.06 - 0.04)(120/365)}$$

$$f_0 = 2,516.49$$

- The length of the binomial period in years is $t/n = \Delta t = (90/365)/3 = 0.082192$, with the call and put option expiring in $n_{\text{Option}} \Delta t = (3)(0.082192) = 0.246575$ years, and the futures expiring in $n_f \Delta t = (4)(0.082192) = 0.328767$ years. Using the up and down parameters on the futures contract, the risk-neutral probability is $p = 0.48806$:

$$u = e^{\sigma_f^A \sqrt{\Delta t} + \mu_f^A \Delta t} = e^{0.3\sqrt{.082192} + (-0.02)(.082192)} = 1.088024$$

$$d = e^{-\sigma_f^A \sqrt{\Delta t} + \mu_f^A \Delta t} = e^{-0.3\sqrt{.082192} + (-0.02)(.082192)} = 0.91608$$

$$p = \frac{1-d}{u-d} = \frac{1 - 0.91608}{1.088024 - 0.91608} = 0.488064$$

- The up and down parameters on the spot index are $u^S = 1.089144$ and $d^S = 0.09175874$, respectively, and the risk-neutral probability is $p = 0.489945$:

$$u^S = e^{\sigma_S^A \sqrt{\Delta t} + \mu_S^A \Delta t} = e^{0.3\sqrt{.082192} + (0)(0.082192)} = 1.0898144$$

$$d^S = e^{-\sigma_S^A \sqrt{\Delta t} + \mu_S^A \Delta t} = e^{-0.3\sqrt{.082192} + (0)(.082192)} = 0.9175874$$

$$p = \frac{e^{(R_f - \psi)\Delta t} - d}{u-d} = \frac{e^{(0.06-0.04)(0.082192)} - 0.9175874}{1.0898144 - 0.9175874} = 0.488064$$

Exhibit 12.3 shows the resulting binomial tree for the underlying S&P 500 index, index futures, European and American futures call, and European and American futures put. For this three-period option case, the binomial model prices the European call at 167.46 and the European put at 151.22. There is an early exercise advantage for the American call at the upper node in period 2, and an early exercise advantage for the American futures put at the lower node in period 2. As a result, both the American futures put and call options are priced slightly higher than their European counterparts.

Using the Merton BOPM Excel program for futures options, the prices of the European and American S&P 500 futures calls are 154.79 and 155.20, respectively, for $n = 100$ subperiods. For the European and American futures puts, the prices are 138.54 and 138.91 for $n = 100$ (see table at the bottom of Exhibit 12.3).

Exhibit 12.4 shows the binomial tree for an S&P 500 index futures expiring at the same time as the futures options (90 days), along with the prices of the S&P spot index, European and American futures call and put options, and European and American spot index call and put options. The carrying-cost price of the S&P 500 futures contract expiring in 90 days is 2,512.36:

$$f_0 = S_0 e^{(R^A - \psi)n_f \Delta t}$$

$$f_0 = 2,500\, e^{(0.06-0.04)(90/365)}$$

$$f_0 = 2,512.36$$

EXHIBIT 12.3   Multiple-Period Binomial Pricing of Index Futures Call and Put Options

$S_0 = 2,500, \mu_S^A = 0, \sigma_S^A = 0.3, \psi = .04, R^A = .06,$ *Spot:* $u^S = 1.089814, d^S = 0.91758,$
Futures: $f_0 = 2,500e^{(0.06-0.04)(120/365)} = 2,516.08, u = 1.088024, d = 0.91608, p = 0.488064,$
$\Delta t = 0.082192, n_f = 4, n_{option} = 3, X = 2,500$

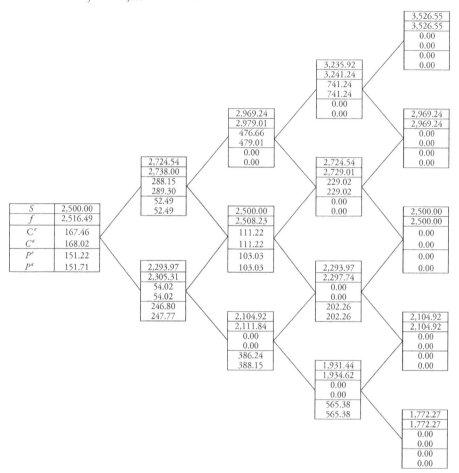

n	European Call	American Call	European Put	American Put
3	167.46	168.02	151.22	151.77
100	154.79	155.20	138.54	138.91

The spot S&P 500 index options have the same exercise price of 2,500 and expiration of 90 days as do the futures options. The table at the bottom of Exhibit 12.5 shows the binomial prices of the spot and futures options for 100 subperiods.

As expected, in the case of European options, the futures and spot option prices are identical. This, in turn, confirms an earlier point that if the futures and the spot and futures options expire at the same time and the options are European, then the futures

EXHIBIT 12.4 Multiple-Period Binomial Pricing of Index Spot and Futures Call and Put Options with the Same Expirations

$S_0 = 2,500$, $\mu_S^A = 0$, $\sigma_S^A = 0.3$, $\psi = .04$, $R^A = .06$, *Spot*: $u = 1.089814$, $d = 0.91758$,
Futures: $f_0 = 2,500e^{(0.06-0.04)(90/365)} = 2,512.36$, $u = 1.088024$, $d = 0.91608$, $p = 0.488064$,
$\Delta t = 0.082192$, $n_f = 3$, $n_{option} = 3$, $X = 2,500$

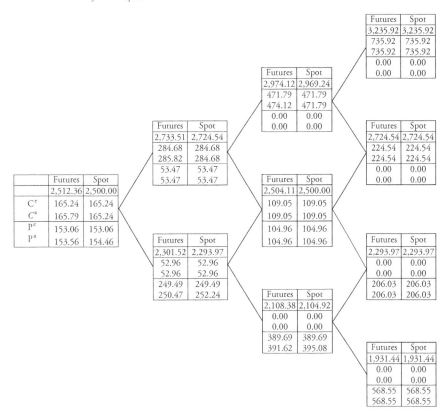

n	European Futures Call	American Futures Call	European Futures Put	American Futures Put
3	165.24	165.79	153.03	153.56
100	152.42	152.82	140.24	140.59

n	European Spot Call	American Spot Call	European Spot Put	American Spot Put
3	165.24	165.24	153.03	154.46
100	152.42	152.42	140.24	141.49

and spot options are identical. As such, the price on the futures option is equal to price on spot option. Price differences can be observed, however, between the American futures and American spot options. In the three-period case of the call options, the price of the American futures call is 165.79, while the price of the European spot call is slightly less at 165.24. The price difference between the American futures and spot

EXHIBIT 12.5   Multiple-Period Binomial Pricing of Currency Futures Call and Put Options

$E_0 = \$1.50/BP$, $\mu_S^A = 0$, $\sigma_S^A = 0.3$, $R_{BP} = 0.04$, $R_\$ = 0.02$, $u^S = 1.089814$,
$d^S = 0.91758$, $f_0 = \$1.50e^{(0.02-0.04)(120/365)} = 1.490169$, $u = 1.09160937$, $d = 0.91909701$,
$p = 0.4689746$, $\Delta t = 0.082192$, $n_f = 4$, $n_{option} = 3$, $X = \$1.50/BP$

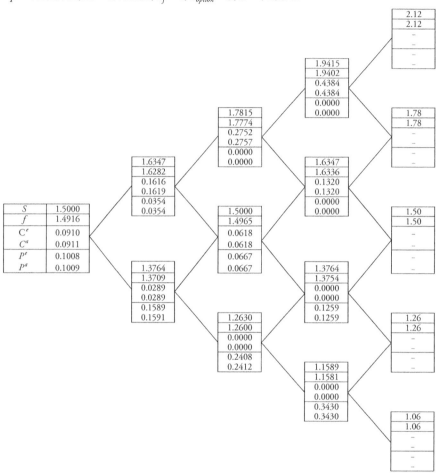

n	European Call	American Call	European Put	American Put
100	0.0799	0.0805	0.0970	0.0970

call options can be explained by the fact that the futures prices are higher than the spot prices prior to maturity and also the presence of an early exercise advantage on the futures option that occurs at the upper node in period 2. Similarly, an early exercise advantage also exists (lower node in period 2) for the American futures put, but not the American spot put. The American futures put price, though, is still less than the American spot because of the futures prices exceeding the spot prices prior to maturity. As a result, the price on the American futures put is less than the price on the American spot put in this example.

In general, if futures markets are normal with futures prices greater than spot prices prior to maturity, then the futures prices will be consistently greater than the corresponding spot prices. As a result, an American futures call will, in turn, be worth more than its corresponding American spot call. Conversely, for a normal market an American futures put will be priced less than its corresponding American spot put. As noted, this is the case in our example. Specially, with the risk-free rate of 6% exceeding the dividend yield of 4%, the futures market for the index is normal with the S&P 500 futures prices exceeding the corresponding spot prices at all nodes prior to maturity. Accordingly, the binomial model prices the American futures call (152.82 in 100-period example) slightly more than the American spot call (152.42), and American futures put price (140.59) less than the American spot put (141.49). If the futures market were inverted, with the futures price consistently less than the spot price prior to maturity, then the opposite will occur: The American futures call will be less than the American spot call and the American futures put will be priced more than the American spot put.

Pricing Foreign Currency Futures Call and Put Options

As a second example of pricing futures option with a multiple-period binomial model, consider the pricing of call and put options on a British pound futures contract each with $X = \$1.50/BP$ and expiration of 90 days, using a three-period binomial model. In pricing the options, suppose the following:

- The spot $/BP exchange rate is at $E_0 = \$1.50/BP$.
- The annual continuously compounded risk-free rate paid on dollars is $R_\$ = 0.02$.
- The annual continuously compounded risk-free rate paid on BP is $R_{BP} = \psi = 0.04$.
- The estimated spot exchange rate's volatility and mean are $\sigma^A = 0.3$ and $\mu^A = 0$.
- The futures index's estimated volatility and mean are $\sigma_f^A = 0.3$ and $\mu_f^A = 0.02$.

$$\sigma_f^A = \sigma_S^A = 0.3$$

$$\mu_f^A = \mu_S^A - (R^A - \psi)$$

$$\mu_f^A = 0.00 - (0.02 - 0.04) = 0.02$$

- Carrying-cost model holds.
- Options on BP futures option expire in 90 days.
- Futures contract on the BP expires in 120 days and is priced at its carrying-cost value of $1.490169/BP:

$$f_0 = E_0 e^{(R_\$ - R_{BP})n_f \Delta t}$$

$$f_0 = \$1.50 \, e^{(0.02 - 0.04)(120/365)}$$

$$f_0 = \$1.490169$$

- The length of the binomial period in years is $t/n = \Delta t = 90/365 = (90/365)/3 = 0.082192$, with the call and put option expiring in $n_{\text{Option}}\Delta t = (3)(0.082192) = 0.246575$ years, and the BP futures expiring in $n_f \Delta t = (4)(0.082192) = 0.328767$ years. The up and down parameters on the futures contract are $u = 1.09160739$ and $d = 0.91909701$, and the risk-neutral probability is $p = 0.4689746$:

$$u = e^{\sigma_f^A \sqrt{\Delta t} + \mu_f^A \Delta t} = e^{0.3\sqrt{.082192} + (0.02)(.082192)} = 1.09160739$$

$$d = e^{-\sigma_f^A \sqrt{\Delta t} + \mu_f^A \Delta t} = e^{-0.3\sqrt{.082192} + (0.02)(.082192)} = 0.91909701$$

$$p = \frac{1 - d}{u - d} = \frac{1 - 0.91909701}{1.09160739 - 0.91909701} = 0.4689746$$

- The up and down parameters on the spot index are $u^S = 1.089144$ and $d^S = 0.9175874$, respectively, and the risk-neutral probability is $p = 0.468974727$:

$$u^S = e^{\sigma_S^A \sqrt{\Delta t} + \mu_S^A \Delta t} = e^{0.3\sqrt{.082192} + (0)(0.082192)} = 1.0898144$$

$$d^S = e^{-\sigma_S^A \sqrt{\Delta t} + \mu_S^A \Delta t} = e^{-0.3\sqrt{.082192} + (0)(.082192)} = 0.9175874$$

$$p = \frac{e^{(R_\$ - R_{BP})\Delta t} - d}{u - d} = \frac{e^{(0.02 - 0.04)(0.082192)} - 0.9175874}{1.0898144 - 0.9175874} = 0.468974727$$

The binomial tree for the underlying spot $/BP exchange rate, BP futures contract, European and American futures call, and European and American futures put are shown in Exhibit 12.5; the table at the bottom of the exhibit shows the binomial prices on the futures options for 100 subperiods. In the three-period option case, the binomial model prices the European call at $0.0910 and the American call at $0.0911, and the European put at $0.1008 and the American put at $0.1009. There is an a very slight early exercise advantage for the American call at the upper node in period 2, and an early exercise advantage for the American futures put at the lower node in period 2. As a result, both the American futures put and call options are price slightly higher than their European counterparts. Using the Merton BOPM Excel program for futures option, for $n = 100$ subperiods, the prices of the European and American futures call are $0.08 and the prices of the European and American BP futures are both $0.097 (there are slight rounding differences between the American and European).

Black Model for Pricing Futures Options

In 1976, Fisher Black extended the B-S OPM for spot options to the pricing of futures options. The Black futures model is:

$$C_0^* = [f_0 N(d_1) - X N(d_2)] e^{-R_f T}$$

$$P_0^* = [X(1 - N(d_2)) - f_0(1 - N(d_1))] e^{-R_f T}$$

$$d_1 = \frac{\ln(f_0/X) + (\sigma_f^2/2)T}{\sigma_f \sqrt{T}}$$

$$d_2 = d_1 - \sigma_f \sqrt{T}$$

where

σ_f^2 = variance of the logarithmic return of futures prices = $V(\ln(f_n/f_0))$

σ_f^2 = σ_S^2 (volatility of spot prices)

The Black futures model differs from the B-S OPM for spot securities with the exclusion of the risk-free rate in the equations for d_1 and d_2. The exclusion of the risk-free rate was also the case for the binomial model where $p = (1 - d)/(u - d)$. Like the BOPM for futures options, if the carrying-cost model holds and the underlying futures contract and the futures option expire at the same time, then the B-S OPM for European spot options and the Black model for European futures options will be the same. This can be proved by substituting the carrying-cost price of the futures (e.g., $S_0 e^{-RT}$) for f_0 in the Black futures OPM to obtain the B-S OPM for the spot asset. It should also be noted that the Black model, like the B-S OPM, only prices European futures options.

Example: Pricing S&P 500 Futures Options

To illustrate the application of the Black model, consider the previous multiple-period binomial example in which we priced European call and put options on the S&P 500 index futures with $X = 2,500$ and expiration of 90 days. In that example, the current S&P 500 was at $S_0 = 2,500$, the spot index's estimated volatility was $\sigma^A = 0.3$, the annual continuous dividend yield generated from the stocks comprising the index portfolio was $\psi = 0.04$, $R_f = 6\%$, the S&P 500 futures contract expired in 120 days, and the price on the futures was equal to its carrying-cost value:

$$f_0 = S_0 e^{(R^A - \psi)t}$$

$$f_0 = 2,500 \, e^{(.06 - .04)(120/365)}$$

$$f_0 = 2,516.49$$

Using the Black futures option model, the price of the call option is 154.12 and the price of the put is 137.88:

$$C_0^* = [f_0 N(d_1) - X N(d_2)] e^{-R_f t}$$

$$C_0^* = [2,516.49 \, (0.546981) - 2,500 \, (0.48802)] \, e^{-(0.06)(90/365)} = 154.12$$

$$P_0^* = [X(1 - N(d_2)) - f_0(1 - N(d_1))] e^{-R_f t}$$

$$P_0^* = [2,500 \, (1 - 0.48801) - 2,516.49 \, (1 - 0.546981)] e^{-(0.06)(90/365)} = 137.87$$

$$d_1 = \frac{\ln(f_0/X) + (\sigma_f^2/2)t}{\sigma_f \sqrt{t}} = \frac{\ln(2{,}516.49/2{,}500) + (0.09/2)(90/365)}{0.3 \sqrt{90/365}}$$

$$= 0.118617$$

$$d_2 = d_1 - \sigma_f \sqrt{t} = .118617 - 0.3\sqrt{90/365} = -0.030352$$

$$N(d_1) = N(0.118617) = 0.546981$$

$$N(d_2) = N(-0.030352) = 0.48802$$

The Black OPM call price of 154.12 is $0.67 less than the 100-period binomial value of 154.79 and the Black put value of 137.87 is 0.67 less than the 100-period binomial value of 138.54. As noted in examining the binomial model, there was an early exercise advantage, making the American options more valuable, with the binomial model pricing the American call at 155.20 and the American put at 138.91. It should be noted that the call and put prices are also consistent with put-call futures parity:

$$P_0^* - C_0^* = PV(X - f_0)$$

$$P_0^* = (X - f_0)e^{-R_f t} + C_0^*$$

$$P_0^* = (2{,}500 - 2{,}516.49)e^{-(0.06)(90/365)} + 154.12$$

$$P_0^* = 137.87$$

Example: Pricing British Pound Futures Options

We previously priced call and put options on a British pound (BP) futures contract using the binomial model. In that example, we assumed $X = \$1.50/BP$, $E_0 = \$1.50/BP$, $\sigma^A = 0.3$, $R_{US} = 0.02$, $R_{BP} = 0.04$, expiration on BP futures = 120 days, and expiration on BP futures option = 90 days. The carrying-cost price on the BP futures was $1.490169. Using the Black futures option model, the price of a European BP futures call option is $0.083 and the price of the European put is $0.0928:

$$C_0^* = [f_0 N(d_1) - X N(d_2)]e^{-R_s t}$$

$$C_0^* = [(\$1.490169)(0.511976) - (\$1.50)(0.453016]e^{-(0.02)(90/365)} = \$0.083$$

$$P_0^* = [X(1 - N(d_2)) - f_0(1 - N(d_1))]e^{-R_s T}$$

$$P_0^* = [(\$1.50)(1 - 0.453016) - (\$1.490169)(1 - 0.511976)]e^{-(0.02)(90/365)}$$

$$= \$0.0928$$

$$d_1 = \frac{\ln(f_0/X) + (\sigma_f^2/2)t}{\sigma_f \sqrt{t}} = \frac{\ln(\$1.490169/\$1.50) + (0.09/2)(90/365)}{0.3 \sqrt{90/365}}$$

$$= 0.030344$$

$$d_2 = d_1 - \sigma_f \sqrt{t} = 0.030344 - 0.3\sqrt{90/365} = -0.11863$$

$$N(d_1) = N(0.030344) = 0.511976$$

$$N(d_2) = N(-0.11863) = 0.453016$$

The Black OPM call price of $0.083 is $0.003 greater than the 100-period bino-mial value of $0.08 and the Black put value of $0.0928 is $0.0042 less than the binomial value. These call and put prices are consistent with put-call futures parity:

$$P_0^* - C_0^* = PV(X - f_0)$$

$$P_0^* = (X - f_0)e^{-R_f T} + C_0^*$$

$$P_0^* = (\$1.50 - \$1.490169)e^{-(0.02)(90/365)} + \$0.083$$

$$P_0^* = \$0.0928$$

Example: Pricing Corn Futures Options

As a final example, consider European call and put options on corn futures options. Recall, the carrying-cost model for a commodity futures contract is:

$$f_0 = S_0(1 + R_f)^t + (K)(t) + TRC$$

where

$$K = \text{storage costs per unit of the commodity per period}$$
$$TRC = \text{transportation costs}$$
$$t = \text{time to delivery as a proportion of a year}$$

Suppose the following:

- The time to expiration on the futures contract is 90 days.
- The spot price of a bushel of corn is $3.66.
- The annual storage cost is $0.35 per/bushel.
- The risk-free rate is 2%.
- The costs of hauling corn from the destination point specified on the futures contract to a local grain elevator, or vice versa, is $0.035/bu.
- The price of the futures is equal to its cost of carry of $3.81/bu.
- $f_0^* = \$3.66(1.03)^{(90/365)} + (\$0.35/\text{bu.})(90/365) + \$0.035/\text{bu.} = \$3.81$.
- Call and put options on the corn futures contract with expiration of 90 days, exercise prices of $3.81.
- $\sigma^A = 0.30$.

Using the Black model, both the European call and put prices are $0.223:

$$C_0^* = [f_0 N(d_1) - X N(d_2)]e^{-R_f t}$$

$$C_0^* = [(\$3.81)(0.52946) - (\$3.81)(0.470531)]e^{-(0.02)(90/365)} = \$0.223$$

$$P_0^* = [X(1 - N(d_2)) - f_0(1 - N(d_1))] e^{-R_f t}$$

$$P_0^* = [(\$3.81)(1 - 0.470531) - (\$3.81)(1 - 0.52946)]e^{-(0.02)(90/365)} = \$0.223$$

where

$$d_1 = \frac{\ln(f_0/X) + (\sigma^2/2)T}{\sigma_f \sqrt{T}} = \frac{\ln(\$3.81/\$3.81) + (0.30^2/2)(90/365)}{0.3 \sqrt{90/365}}$$

$$= 0.074485$$

$$d_2 = d_1 - \sigma_f \sqrt{T} = 0.074485 - 0.30\sqrt{90/365} = -0.074485$$

$$N(d_1) = N(0.074485) = 0.470531$$

$$N(d_2) = N(-0.074485) = 0.470531$$

Pricing Equity Convertibles with the B-S OPM

In Chapter 6, we examined convertibles securities. The equity convertibles included warrants and rights. We also examined how the equity of a leveraged company can be viewed as call options. As options, these convertibles can also be priced using the option pricing models.

Valuing Warrants

Warrants are call options written by the corporation. As noted in Chapter 6, the fundamental difference between a call on a stock and a warrant on the same stock is that the writer of the warrant is the corporation, while the writer of a call option is an individual investor. This difference implies that when a warrant holder exercises, the corporation must issue new shares of stock. When the company, in turn, sells the shares on the warrant contract, it will receive cash from the warrant holders, which it can use to finance its assets; however, the company also will have its stock diluted. Formally, as we showed in Chapter 6, the intrinsic value of a warrant (IV_w) is equal to the intrinsic value of a call option (IV_C) on the same underlying stock times the dilution factor:

$$IV_W = \left[\frac{n_0}{n_0 + n_w}\right] IV_C$$

where n_0 = number of existing shares, n_w is number of new shares created from exercising, and the term $n_0/(n_0 + n_w)$ is the dilution factor. Since warrants and call options on the same stock are perfectly correlated (they both derive their values from the same asset), the current warrant price (W_0), in turn, should be equal to the current call value times the dilution factor:

$$W_0 = \left[\frac{n_0}{n_0 + n_w}\right] C_0$$

Accordingly, to price a warrant we can use the OPM to value the warrant as a call, then multiply that value by the dilution factor to determine the value of the warrant.

Valuing Rights

A right is similar to a warrant. Technically, it is a call option issued by the corporation, giving the holder the right to buy new shares at a specified price (subscription price) on or before a specific date. Like warrants, when a right is exercised, new shares are created and the company has additional capital. Also, like warrants, rights can be sold in a secondary market. Rights differ from warrants in that their expiration periods are shorter (e.g., one to three months compared to three to five years for a warrant), and their exercise prices usually are set below their stock prices, while warrants usually have exercise prices above. To price a subscription right, we can use the OPM to value the right as a call, then multiply that value by the dilution factor to determine the value of the right.

Valuing Equity as a Call Option

The limited liability feature of common stock enables the stockholders of a leveraged corporation to view their equity position as a call option on the assets of the corporation, with the corporation's creditors viewed as the writers of the call option and the owners of the firm. Consider a company with debt consisting only of a zero-coupon bond with a face value of F and maturing at time T. The stockholders of the company can view their equity position as a call option in which they can buy the company from the bondholders at an exercise price equal to the face value of the debt, with an expiration date equal to the bond's maturity. As shown in Exhibit 6.23 in Chapter 6, if the value of the firm's assets (V^A) exceeds F at maturity, $V_T^A > F$, the shareholders of the company would exercise their option and purchase the company from the bondholders at the exercise price of F. If $V_T^A < F$ at maturity, then the shareholders would not (or could not) exercise. Thus, at expiration, the total value of equity of the company (V_T^E) would be:

$$V_T^E = \text{Max}[V_T^A - F, 0]$$

Prior to maturity, the value of the stock (V_t^E) would be equal to its intrinsic value plus a time value premium, and the value of the debt would be equal to the value of the firm minus the equity value (see Exhibit 6.24). The current value of equity can be estimated using the B-S OPM. Specifically:

$$V_0^E = V_0^A \, N(d_1) - \left[\frac{F}{e^{RT}} \right] N(d_2)$$

$$d_1 = \frac{\ln (V_0^A / F) + (R + 0.5 \, \sigma^2)t}{\sigma \sqrt{t}}$$

$$d_2 = d_1 - \sigma \sqrt{t}$$

As an example, suppose the ABC Company currently is worth $15 million, has a debt obligation consisting of a zero-coupon bond maturing in two years with a face value of $10 million, and has an asset variability of $\sigma = 0.5$. If the annual risk-free rate is 6%, the value of ABC stock, using the B-S OPM, would be $7,170,113 and the value of its debt would be $7,829,887:

$$d_1 = \frac{\ln(\$15,000,000/\$10,000,000) + [0.06 + 0.5(0.5)^2](2)}{0.5\sqrt{2}} = 1.09667$$

$$d_2 = 1.09667 - 0.5\sqrt{2} = 0.38957$$

$$N(1.09667) = 0.86338$$

$$N(0.38957) = 0.65175$$

$$V_0^E = (\$15,000,000)(0.86338) - \left[\frac{\$10,000,000}{e^{(0.06)(2)}}\right](0.65175) = \$7,170,113$$

$$V_0^B = V_0^A - V_0^E = \$15,000,000 - \$7,170,111 = \$7,829,887$$

Note that the value of the stock is an increasing function of the variability of the firm's assets when we value equity as an option. This direct relation reflects the fact that equity provides an unlimited profit potential and limited loss (or limited liability) characteristic. Given the direct relationship between equity value and variability, it follows that if the objective of the company's managers is to maximize the wealth of its shareholders, then with other factors constant, managers in selecting among mutually exclusive investment projects should select the riskier one. If the market, in turn, values stock as a call option, then managers can augment the equity values of their company by selecting riskier investments (and finding creditors to help finance them).

Greeks

As discussed in Chapter 11, the OPM can be used to examine option strategies in terms of their profit and stock price relations prior to expiration, and also to measure the delta, gamma, vega, and rho values. The formulas for the Greeks for spot indexes and futures options are similar to the ones presented in Chapter 11.

Conclusion

In this chapter, we have examined the pricing of non-stock options—spot index, spot currency, futures, and equity convertibles. With equity indexes and currency having dividend-like features, the dividend-adjusted B-S and BOPM are applicable for pricing these contracts. For futures options, the same replication approach to pricing stock options is also applied, except that the replicating portfolio is defined by a position in the futures contract that derives its value from the underlying spot asset. In the next chapter, we complete our analysis of option pricing by examining the option models for the pricing of bond and interest rate spot and futures options. As we will see, these options derive their values from the underlying interest rates. As such, the binomial pricing of options on bonds, interest rate and bond futures contracts, caplets, floorlets, and convertibles starts with the derivation of a binomial model for spot interest rates.

BLOOMBERG OPTION VALUATION SCREENS FOR INDEXES AND FUTURES OPTIONS, OVME

OVME
OVME determines OPM prices for index and futures options. For a loaded index of futures: OVME <Enter>.

Features:

- OVME provides dividend adjustment for discrete dividend payments (B-S Discrete) or with a continuous dividend yield (B-S Continuous).

- The B-S Continuous model uses a continuous dividend yield pulled from Bloomberg's BDVD screen, and the B-S Discrete model uses discrete dividends pulled from Bloomberg's BDVD screen.

- American options for the continuous B-S use a Trinomial adjusted B-S model to identify times for early exercise.

- Different dividend payments and models can be used by going to the red "Settings" tab.

- OVME pulls implied volatilities from a volatility surface and historical volatility. You can access the volatility from the "Volatility" Tab.

- Option prices and the Greek values can be plotted against different underlying security prices, time, and other parameters from the "Scenario" tab.

- On the "Backtest" tab, you can analyze a strategy or multiple strategies.

- OVME allows you to input your own option information.

- From the "Deal" tabs you can construct multiple deals simultaneously and then analyze them from the "Scenario" tab. See Chapter 11, "Bloomberg Option Valuation Screen, OVME."

VOLATILITY
OVDV displays Bloomberg implied volatility surfaces for a selected equity index. The "Dividend" tab shows forecasted discrete dividends on ex-dividend dates.

    HVG, Historical Volatility Graph, screen plots the historical volatility of a security and implied volatility of a loaded index. Historical volatility is the annualized standard deviation of the logarithmic returns. The implied volatility is the annualized standard deviation that equates the market price of the options to market price.

(Continued)

Futures Option Valuation, OVME determines OPM prices for futures options using the Black futures OPM. For a loaded futures options, enter OVME (see Exhibits 12.6 and 12.7).

OVME for Index Futures

EXHIBIT 12.6   OVME for S&P 500 Spot Index: 12/14/16, $S_0 = 2{,}269.27$, $X = 2{,}270$, Expiration = 3/17/17 (SPX C2270 3/17/17 <Index>, OVME)

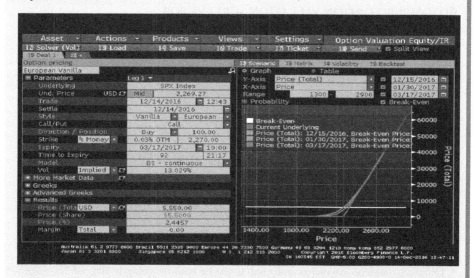

EXHIBIT 12.7   OVME for March S&P 500 Futures Contract: 12/14/16, $f_0 = 2{,}265$, $X = 2{,}265$, Expiration = 3/17/17, European (SPH7 <Comdty>, OVME).

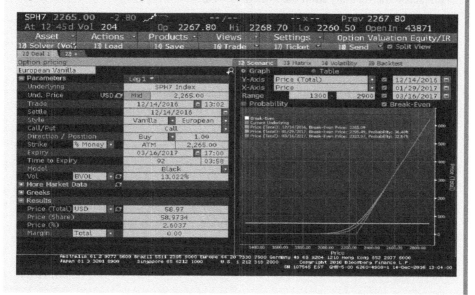

OV, Option Valuation for Futures

The OV screen values loaded futures options (see Exhibits 12.8 and 12.9).

EXHIBIT 12.8 OV for March 2017 British Pound Futures Contract: 12/14/16, f_0 = $1.2698/BP, X = $1.27, Expiration = 3/17/17, American (BPH7 <Curncy>, OV)

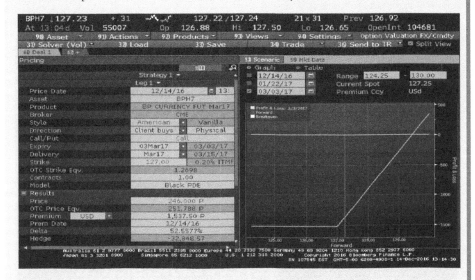

EXHIBIT 12.9 OV for March 2017 Crude Oil Futures Contract: 12/14/16, f_0 = $53.75, X = $53, Expiration = 3/17/17, American (CLH7C 53 <Comdty>, OV)

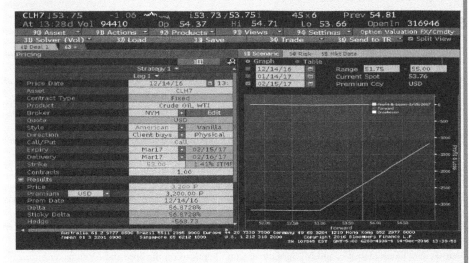

(Continued)

OVME, Warrants

To search for warrants, go to the SECF screen. On the screen, click "Equity" from the "Category" dropdown, click the "Warrants" tab, and select the type of warrants from the "Type" download. For a loaded warrant, OVME calculates the OPM value of the warrant (see Exhibit 12.10).

EXHIBIT 12.10   OVME, Warrants

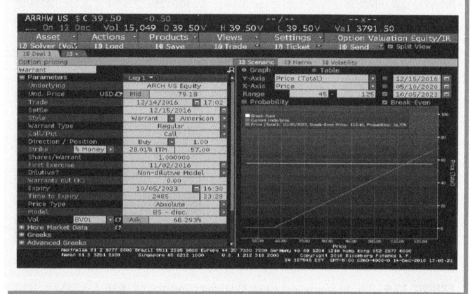

Selected References

Baily, W., and R. Stulz. "The Pricing of Stock Index Options in a General Equilibrium Model." *Journal of Financial and Quantitative Analysis* 24 (March 1989): 1–12.

Baumol, W., Malkiel, B., and R. Quandt. "The Valuation of Convertible Securities." *Quarterly Journal of Economics* (1966).

Biger, N., and J. Hull. "The Valuation of Currency Options." *Financial Management* (Spring 1983): 24–29.

Black, F., and M. Scholes. "The Pricing of Options and Corporate Liabilities." *Journal of Political Economy* 81 (1973): 637–659.

Bodurtha, J., and G. Courtadon. "Efficiency Tests of the Foreign Currency Options Market." *Journal of Finance* 41 (March 1986): 151–162.

Bodurtha, J., and G. Courtadon. "Tests of an American Option Pricing Model on the Foreign Currency Options Market." *Journal of Financial and Quantitative Analysis* 22 (June 1987): 153–167.

Breeden, D. T., and R. H. Litzenberger. "Prices of State-Contingent Claims in Option Prices," *Journal of Business*, 51 (1978): 621–651.

Brenner, M., Courtadon, G., and M. Subrahmanyam. "Options on the Spot and Options on Futures." *The Journal of Finance* 40 (December 1985): 1303–1317.

Brigham, E. "An Analysis of Convertible Debentures: Theory and Some Empirical Evidence." *Journal of Finance* (December 1985).

Chance, D. "Empirical Tests of the Pricing of Index Call Options." *Advances in Futures and Options Research* 1 (1986): 141–166.

Constantinides, G. "Warrant Exercise and Bond Conversion in Competitive Markets." *Journal of Financial Economics* 13 (September 1984): 371–397.

Corrado, C. J., and Tie Su. "Skewness and Kurtosis in S&P 500 Index Returns Implied by Option Prices." *The Journal of Financial Research* 19 (1996): 175–192.

Courtadon, G., and J. J. Merrick. "The Option Pricing Model and the Valuation of Corporate Securities." *Midland Corporate Finance Journal* (Fall 1983).

Ervine, J., and A. Rudd. "Index Options: The Early Evidence." *Journal of Finance* 40 (July 1985): 743–756.

Followill, R. "Relative Call Futures Option Pricing: An Examination of Market Efficiency." *The Review of Futures Markets* 6 (1987): 354–381.

Galai, D., and M. Schneller. "Pricing Warrants and the Value of the Firm." *Journal of Finance* 33 (December 1978): 1333–1342.

Garman, M., and W. Kohlhagen. "Foreign Currency Option Values." *Journal of International Money and Finance* 2 (December 1983); 231–237.

Geske, R. "The Valuation of Compound Options." *Journal of Financial Economics* (March 1979).

Hsia, C. "Optimal Debt of a Firm: An Option Pricing Approach." *Journal of Financial Research* 4 (Fall 1981): 221–231.

Ingersoll, J. "A Contingent-Claims Valuation of Convertible Securities." *Journal of Financial Economics* (May 1977).

Ramaswamy, K., and S. Sundaresan. "The Valuation of Options on Futures Contracts." *Journal of Finance* 60 (December 1985): 1319–1340.

Schwartz, E. "The Valuation of Warrants: Implementing a New Approach." *Journal of Financial Economics* (January 1977).

Shastri, K., and K. Tandon. "Options on Futures Contracts: A Comparison of European and American Pricing Models." *The Journal of Futures Markets* 6 (Winter 1986): 593–618.

Thorp, E. "Options on Commodity Forward Contracts." *Management Science* 29 (October 1985): 1232–1242.

Whaley, R. "Valuation of American Futures Options: Theory and Tests." *The Journal of Finance* 41 (March 1986): 127–150.

Wolf, A., and Pohlman, L. "Tests of the Black and Whaley Models for Gold and Silver Futures Options." *The Review of Futures Markets* 6 (1987): 328–347.

Problems and Questions

Note: Many of these problems can be done using the B-S and Binomial OPM Excel program found on the text's website.

1. Assume: Current spot S&P 500 index is at 2,500, annual risk-free rate = 4%, zero dividends, logarithmic return's annualized mean = $\mu^A = 0.10$, and logarithmic return's annualized standard deviation = $\sigma^A = 0.25$.

   a. Using the single-period BOPM, determine the price of a European S&P 500 index call with an exercise price of 2,500 and expiring in 30 days.

   b. Define the index call's replicating portfolio in terms of a proxy portfolio.

   c. Show with a binomial tree the values of the spot index, proxy portfolio, and replicating portfolio.

   d. Explain what an arbitrageur would do if the market priced the index call at 85. Show what the arbitrageur's cash flow at expiration would be at the two possible index prices at expirations.

   e. Explain what an arbitrageur would do if the market priced the index call at 100. Show what the arbitrageur's cash flow would be at expiration when she closed.

    f. Use the single-period BOPM to determine the price of a European S&P 500 index put with an exercise price of 2,500 and expiring in 30 days.

    g. Show with a binomial tree the values of the spot index, proxy portfolio, and replicating portfolio. Include with your tree the values of the index and proxy portfolio.

    h. Explain what an arbitrageur would do if the index put were priced at 80.

2. Suppose the following:

- Spot S&P 500 is currently at 3,000
- Continuous annual dividend yield of $\psi = 5\%$
- Annualized standard deviation is $\sigma^A = 0.25$
- Annual risk-free rate is $R = 4\%$.
- European call and put options on the S&P 500 each with an exercise price of 3,000 and expiration of 180 days

    a. Determine the equilibrium prices of the call and put options using Merton's dividend adjusted B-S OPM. Use the B-S Excel program.

    b. Determine both the American and European options prices using Merton's dividend adjusted binomial model for $n = 100$ subperiods. Use the Excel program.

    c. Compare the price for Merton's European binomial with Merton's B-S model.

    d. Compare the prices for Merton's American binomial with the European binomial value. Is there any early exercise advantage?

3. Given the following:

- The S&P 500 futures option expiring at the end of 60 days.
- The S&P 500 futures contract expiring at the end of 120 days.
- The current spot index is at $S_0 = 3,000$.
- The estimated annualized volatility and mean of the spot index's logarithmic return are $\sigma^A = 0.25$ and $\mu^A = 0$.
- The annual risk-free rate is $R_f = 3\%$.
- The futures price is determined by the carrying-cost model: $f_0 = S_0 e^{(R_f - \psi)n_f \Delta t}$
- Ψ = continuous annual dividend yield = 5%.

Determine the following:

    a. Show the spot index and futures prices at each node for a two-period binomial tree with a length of each step equal to 60 days ($\Delta t = 60/365 = 0.164384$). In generating the tree, use the up and down parameters defining the spot index and those defining the futures.

    b. Explain the relationship between the spot and futures prices that you obtained in 3a.

    c. Using the BOPM, determine the equilibrium price for the 3,000 index futures call expiring in 60 days ($n = 1$).

    d. Explain the arbitrage strategy you would employ if the price of the 3,000 index futures call were priced at 135.

    e. Using the BOPM, determine the equilibrium price for the 3,000 index futures put expiring in 60 days ($n = 1$).

 f. Explain the arbitrage strategy you would employ if the price of the 3,000 index futures put were priced at 155.

4. Given the futures and spot information in Question 3, determine the following option prices using a 30-period binomial tree and the BOPM Excel programs:

 a. American futures call
 b. European futures call
 c. American spot call
 d. European spot call
 e. American futures put
 f. European futures put
 g. American spot put
 h. European spot put

  Based on your findings, comment on the relations between futures options and spot options.

5. Given the futures and spot information in Question 3, determine the price of European futures call with $X = 3,000$ using the Black futures option model (Excel model). Show in a table and with a graph the Black futures option model's option prices and intrinsic values for different futures prices for the European futures call. Generate your table and graph using spot index values of 2,700, 2,800, 2,900, 3,000, 3,100, 3,200, and 3,300.

6. Given the futures and spot information in Question 3, determine the price of European futures put with $X = 3,000$ using the Black futures option model (Excel model). Show in a table and with a graph the Black futures option model's option prices and intrinsic values for different futures prices for the European futures put. Generate your table and graph using spot index values of 2,700, 2,800, 2,900, 3,000, 3,100, 3,200, and 3,300.

7. Given the following futures and spot information:

 • The S&P 500 futures option expiring at the end of 60 days.
 • The S&P 500 futures contract expiring at the end of 60 days.
 • The current spot index is at $S_0 = 3,000$.
 • The estimated annualized volatility and mean of the spot index's logarithmic return are $\sigma^A = 0.25$ and $\mu^A = 0$.
 • The annual risk-free rate is $R_f = 3\%$.
 • The futures price is determined by the carrying-cost model: $f_0 = S_0 e^{(R_f - \psi)n_f \Delta t}$.
 • Ψ = continuous annual dividend yield = 5%.

  Determine the following option prices for a 30-period binomial option model using the BOPM Excel program:

 a. American futures call
 b. European futures call
 c. American spot call
 d. European spot call
 e. American futures put
 f. European futures put

g. American spot put

h. European spot put

Based on your findings, comment on the relations between American and European futures options and spot options.

8. Assume the following:

- Annual risk-free rate on US dollars = 4%.
- Annual risk-free rate on British pounds = 2%.
- $/BP spot exchange rate = $1.30/BP.
- Mean annualized logarithmic return (for $/BP exchange rate) = $\mu^A = 0$.
- Annualized logarithmic return's standard deviation = $\sigma^A = 0.25$.
- BP futures contract expiring in 120 days.
- The BP futures price is determined by the interest-rate-parity condition:

$$f_0 = E_0 e^{(R_\$ - R_{BP})n_f \Delta t}$$

Determine the following:

a. The price of a European BP futures call option with an exercise price of $1.30 and expiration of 60 days using the Black futures option model.

b. The price of a European BP futures call with an exercise price of $1.30 and expiration of 60 days using the binomial Excel program for the case of $n = 30$ subperiods of length $\Delta t = 2/365$.

c. The price of a European BP futures put with an exercise price of $1.30 and expiration of 60 days using the Black futures option model.

d. The price of an European BP futures put with an exercise price of $1.30 and expiration of 60 days using the binomial Excel program for the case of $n = 30$ subperiods of length $\Delta t = 2/365$.

9. Given the following information:

- $\sigma^A = 0.25$
- $R_f = 4\%$
- Price on crude oil futures expiring in 120 days = $50
- European call and put options on crude oil futures, each with exercise price of $50 and expiration of 120 days

Using the Black OPM Excel program, determine the equilibrium futures call and put prices.

10. Mailin Developers is a real estate development company with a project in the Midwest currently valued at $20 million. The company financed the project by borrowing from Commerce Bank. The loan calls for a principal payment of $10 million at the end of four years (no-coupon interest).

a. Use the B-S OPM to determine the equity value of Mailin Developers' Midwest project. Assume $R = 6\%$ and the volatility of the project's value is $\sigma = 0.3$.

b. What is the value of the creditors' position?

c. Use the B-S OPM to determine the equity value of Mailin Developers' Midwest project and its debt value if the volatility was $\sigma = 0.5$.

d. Using an option perspective, comment on the relation between stock value and variability.

Bloomberg Exercises

1. Using Bloomberg's OVME screen, estimate the equilibrium price on a selected call and put spot index option. For information on how to find options from the SECF and how to upload and index options, see section: "Bloomberg: Options Screens," Chapter 6.

   • For options on spot equity indexes: SECF <Enter>; select "Equities" from the "Category" dropdown and click the "Index Options" tab.
   • Select the options from the selected indexes' OMON or CALL screens.
   • Load the option: Option Ticker <Index>.
   • Enter OVME.
   • On the OVME screen, determine the B-S price using the continual dividend yield (select Black-Scholes Continuous). Select dividend yield provided or input your own estimate (click "More Market Data" and either keep the Bloomberg default dividend yield or input you own). Select Bloomberg's implied volatility or select historical or provide your own volatility estimate.
   • On the OVME screen, determine the B-S price using the discrete dividend (select Black-Scholes Discrete or Trinomial). Select dividend payments provided or input your own estimates by going to "Settings." Select Bloomberg's implied volatility or select historical or provide your own volatility estimate.

   Compare your option values to the market prices (bid, ask, and last). Current option prices can be found on OMON, CALL, and the option's GP and DES screens.

2. Using the OVME screen for the options you evaluated in Exercise 1, evaluate the prices of the options for different index prices. Click the "Scenario" tab and set the axis for option prices and underlying index prices.

3. Using the OVME screen for the option you evaluated in Exercise 1, evaluate the Greeks for different index prices and time to expiration by clicking the "Scenario" tab and setting the axis.

4. Using Bloomberg's OVME screen, estimate the equilibrium price on a selected call and put futures index. For information on how to find options from the SECF and CTM screens and how to upload the futures options, see section: "Bloomberg: Options Screens," Chapter 6.

   • To find futures indexes on SECF, click "Index/Stat" from the "Category" dropdown and then click "futr" tab or click "opts." Use OMON on the futures screen to find the futures options.
   • Select the options from the selected stock's OMON or CALL screen.

- Load the option: Option Ticker <Comdty>.
- Enter OVME.
- On the OVME screen, determine the Black OPM price using the continuous dividend yield (select Black). Select Bloomberg's implied volatility, historical, or provide your own volatility estimate.

   Compare your option values to the market prices (bid, ask, and last). Current option prices are found on OMON, CALL, and the option's GP and DES screens.

5. Using the OVME screen for the call and put options you evaluated in Exercise 4, evaluate the prices of the call and put options for different futures prices. Click the "Scenario" tab and set the axis for option prices and underlying futures prices.

6. Using the OVME screen for the call and put option you evaluated in Exercise 4, evaluate the Greeks for different futures prices and time to expiration by clicking the "Scenario" tab and setting the axis.

7. Create a portfolio of at least two options on the same futures and evaluate the position in terms of the position's OPM value, delta, gamma, and theta. On the OVME screen, click the + icon next to "Deals" to add a new deal, and then click "Add Legs" from the gray "Leg" dropdown. Input information for each option in the input box (different exercise prices, expirations, call and/or put, and long and short positions). Click "Scenario" tab to view your position's value and profit-loss relation for different futures prices.

8. Create a neutral delta portfolio with two options on the same index or futures index you evaluated in Exercise 1 or Exercise 4 and evaluate the position in terms of the position's OPM value and gamma. On the OVME screen, click the + icon next to "Deals" to add a new deal, and then click "Add Legs" from the gray "Leg" dropdown. Input information for each option in the input box (different exercise prices and/or expirations). Given each option's delta, solve for the number of options needed to create a neutral delta position. Click the white "Greeks" + icon row to see the Greek display. Click the "Scenario" tab to view your position's value and profit-loss relation for different stock prices.

9. Using Bloomberg's OV screen, estimate the equilibrium price on a selected call and put currency futures. For information on how to find options from the SECF and CTM screens and how to upload the futures options, see section: "Bloomberg: Options Screens," Chapter 6.

- To find currency futures on SECF, click "Currencies" from the "Category" dropdown and then select "Active Futures" from the "futr" tab. Use OMON on the currency futures screen (Currency Futures Ticker <Curncy>) to find the currency futures options.
- Load the option: Option Ticker <Curncy>.
- Enter OV.
- On OV screen, determine the Black OPM price. Select Bloomberg's implied volatility, historical, or provide your own volatility estimate.

10. Using Bloomberg's OV screen, estimate the equilibrium price on a selected call and put commodity futures. For information on how to find options from the SECF and CTM screens and how to upload the futures options, see section: "Bloomberg: Options Screens," Chapter 6.

    • To find commodity options on SECF, click "Commodities" from the "Category" dropdown and then click the "Opt" tab.
    • Load the option: Option Ticker <Comdty>.
    • Enter OV.
    • On OV screen, determine the Black OPM price. Select Bloomberg's implied volatility, historical, or provide your own volatility estimate.

11. Determine the equilibrium price on an equity warrant. To search for warrants, go to the SECF screen. On the screen, click "Equities" from the "Category" dropdown, click the "Warrants" tab, and select type of warrants from the "Type" download. Determine the OPM value of the warrant using the OVME screen.

CHAPTER 13

Pricing Bond and Interest Rate Options

Determining the value of a bond or interest rate option requires identifying the possible random paths that interest rates follow over time. One model that can be used to price bonds over time, as well as determine the values of derivative on the bond, is the *binomial interest rate tree*. Patterned after the binomial option pricing model this model assumes that spot interest rates follow a binomial process. In this chapter, we examine the pricing of bond and interest rate options using the binomial interest rate model, as well as the B-S and Black futures options models.

The Binomial Interest Rate Model

Binomial Interest Rate Trees

The equilibrium price of a bond is the value obtained by discounting the bond's cash flows, *CF*s, by appropriate spot rates, S_t (rates on zero-coupon bonds). If the market does not price a bond with spot rates, arbitrageurs would be able to realize a risk-free return by buying the bond and stripping it into a number of zero-coupon bonds, or by buying strip bonds and bundling them into a coupon bond to sell. Thus, in the absence of arbitrage, the *equilibrium price* of a bond is determined by discounting each of its *CF*s by their appropriate spot rates.

A binomial model of interest rates assumes a spot rate of a given maturity follows a binomial process where in each period it has either a higher or lower rate. To illustrate,

EXHIBIT 13.1 Binomial Tree of Spot Rates: $u = 1.1$, $d = 0.95$, $S_0 = 5\%$

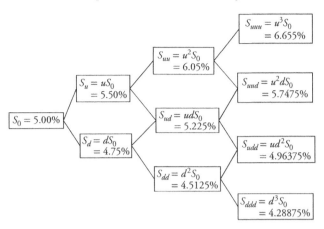

suppose the current one-period spot rate (S) is 5%, the upward parameter u is 1.1 and the downward parameter d is 0.95. As shown in Exhibit 13.1, the two possible one-period rates after one period are 5.5% and 4.75%, the three possible one-period rates after two periods are 6.05%, 5.225%, and 4.5125%, and the four possible rates are three periods are 6.665%, 5.7475%, 4.96375%, and 4.28875%.

Valuing a Bond with a Binomial Interest Rate Tree

Given the possible one-period spot rates, suppose we wanted to value a bond that matures in three periods. Assume that there is no default risk or embedded options on the three-period bond and that it pays a 5.00% coupon each period and a $100 principal at maturity. Since there is no default or option risk, the only risk an investor assumes in buying this bond is interest rate risk (changes in interest rates that change the value of the bond). In this case, interest-rate risk exists in two periods: Period 2, where there are three possible spot rates, and period 1, where there are two possible rates. To value the bond, we first determine the three possible values of the bond in period 2, given the three possible spot rates and the bond's cash flow next period (maturity) of 105. As shown in Exhibit 13.2, the three possible values in period 2 are $B_{uu} = 105/1.0605 = 99.0099$, $B_{ud} = 105/1.05225 = 99.7862$, and $B_{dd} = 105/1.045125 = 100.46645$. Given these values, we next roll the tree to the first period and determine the two possible values there. Note, in this period the values are equal to the present values of the expected cash flows in period 2. If we assume there is an equal probability of the spot rate increasing or decreasing in one period $(q = 0.5)$, then the two possible values in period 1 would be 98.9555 and 100.35926:

$$B_u = \frac{0.5(99.0099 + 5) + 0.5(99.7862 + 5)}{(1.055)} = 98.9555$$

$$B_d = \frac{0.5(99.7862 + 5) + 0.5(100.46645 + 5)}{(1.0475)} = 100.35926$$

EXHIBIT 13.2 Binomial Value of Bond Maturing in Three Periods: Coupon = 5%, Face Value = 100, Maturity = Three Periods, $u = 1.1$, $d = 0.95$, $S_0 = 5\%$

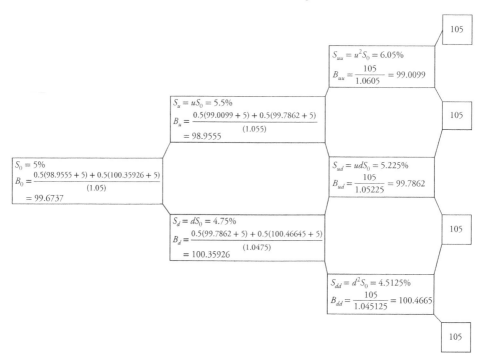

Finally, using the bond values in period 1, we roll the tree to the current period where we determine the value of the bond to be 99.6737:

$$B_0 = \frac{0.5(98.9555 + 5) + 0.5(100.35926 + 5)}{(1.05)} = 99.6737$$

Valuing Options on a Bond with a Binomial Interest Rate Tree

A T-bond underlying an OTC T-bond option is often a specified bond. As a result, the first step in valuing such an option is to determine the values of the specified bond at the various nodes on the binomial tree as we just did in the above case. As an example, consider OTC European call and put options on the three-period 5% coupon bond with exercise prices of 100 and expirations at the end of second period.

Given the three-period, 5% bond's values in terms of the tree, the values of call and put options on the bond can be determined using the normal recursive process in which we start at expiration where the options are equal to their IVs, and then roll the tree to the present. At the option's expiration, the underlying bond

EXHIBIT 13.3 Binomial Value of Call Option on a Bond: Coupon = 5%, Face Value = 100, Maturity = 3 Periods, Call Option: $X = 100$, Expiration = 2 Periods, $u = 1.1$, $d = 0.95$, $S_0 = 5\%$

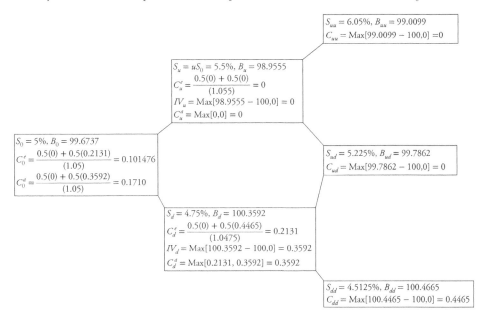

would have three possible values: 99.0099, 99.7862, and 100.46645. The 100 T-bond call's respective IVs are therefore 0.00, 0,00, and 0.4665 (see Exhibit 13.3). Given these values, the call's possible values in period 1 are 0.00 and 0.2131 (= (0.5(0) + 0.5(0.4665))/1.0475). Rolling these values to the current period, we obtain the price on the European call of 0.101476 (= (0.5(0) + 0.5(0.2131))/1.05). If the call option were American, then its value at each node would be the greater of the value of holding the call or the value from exercising. This valuation requires constraining the American price to be the maximum of the binomial value or the IV. In this example, if the call option contract were American, then in period 1 the option's price would be equal to its IV of 0.3592 at the lower rate. Rolling this price and the upper rate's price of 0.00 to the current period yields a price of 0.1710.

The same recursive process can also be used to value the American and European put options (see Exhibit 13.4). In this case, given the bond's possible prices at expiration of 99.0099, 99.7862, and 100.46645, the corresponding IVs of the put would be 0.9901, 0.2138, and 0.00. In period 1, the put's two possible values would be 0.5706 (= (0.5(0.9901) + 0.5(0.2138))/1.055) and 0.10205 (= (0.5(0.2138) + 0.5(0))/1.0475). Rolling these values to the current period yields a price on the European put of 0.3203 (= (0.5(0.5706) + 0.5(0.10205))/1.05). Note, that if the put were American, then its possible prices in period 1 would be 1.0445 and 0.10205, and its current price would be 0.5460 (= (0.5(1.0445) + 0.5(0.10205))/1.05).

EXHIBIT 13.4 Binomial Value of Put Option on a Bond: Coupon = 5%, Face Value = 100, Maturity = Three Periods, Put Option: $X = 100$, Expiration = 2 Periods, $u = 1.1$, $d = 0.95$, $S_0 = 5\%$

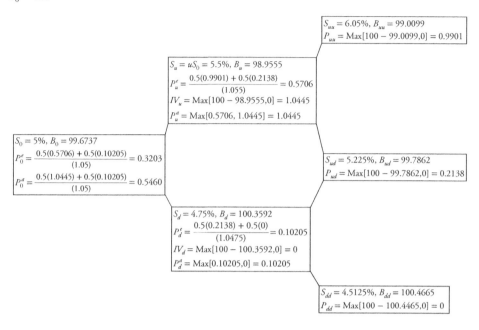

Valuing Bond and Interest Rate Futures Options with a Binomial Interest Rate Tree

Valuing Bond Futures Call and Put Options with a Binomial Interest Rate Tree

A T-bond or T-note underlying a T-bond or T-note futures is a specified bond from an eligible group of bonds that are the most likely to be delivered. Because of the specified bond clause on a futures contract, the first step in valuing futures, and in turn the futures option, is to determine the values of the specified T-bond (or bond most likely to be delivered) at the various nodes on the binomial tree.

As an example, suppose the spot interest rate is currently at 10%, the yield curve is flat at 10%, the spot rates upward and downward parameters are $u = 1.10$, $d = 1/u = 0.9091$, and $q = 0.5$. Exhibit 13.5a shows the binomial valuations of the bond and call and put options on the bond with $X = 100$ and expiration at the end of period two. The bond's value of $B_0 = 99.9197$ was obtained by using the recursive approach described above:

1. Determine the bond's three possible values in period 2, given the three possible spot rates.
2. Roll these three values to period 1, where the two possible values in that period are attained by calculating the present values of their expected cash flows.
3. Roll these two values to the current period, where the current value is found by again determining the present value of the two expected cash flows.

As shown in the exhibit, the price of the European call is $0.334 and the price of American call is 0.7128. The price of European put value is 0.3835 and the price of American is 0.793.

Exhibit 13.5b shows the prices at each binomial tree node of a futures contract on the bond with the futures expiring at the end of period 2. The futures prices are determined by the carrying-cost model (see Chapter 4):

$$f_0 = [B_0 - PV(C)](1 + y_{n_f})^{n_f}$$

where

$PV(C)$ = present value of coupons paid on the bond during the life of the futures contract

n_f = number of periods to the expiration on the futures contract

y_{nf} = *n*-period risk-free rate for the expiration period on the futures contract

The assumption of a flat yield curve at 10% implies that implied forward rates are equal to the spot rate of 10%. A flat yield curve at 10% is also consistent with the implied yield curve generated from $u = 1.10$, $d = 1/1.10 = 0.9091$, and $q = 0.5$ (see Exhibit 13.6). (Note: If u and d parameter value are not inversely proportional and q is not equal to 0.5, then the implied yield curve from the binomial tree will not necessarily be flat.)

Given the 10% rates and the current bond price on the underlying bond of 99.9197, the current carrying-cost futures price is 99.9028:

$$f_0 = [B_0 - PV(C)](1 + y_{n_f})^{n_f}$$

$$f_0 = \left[\left[99.9197 - \frac{10}{1.10} - \frac{10}{(1.10)^2}\right](1.10)^2\right] = 99.9028$$

This equilibrium futures prices ensure that no cash-and-carry arbitrage opportunities exist or, equivalently, that the yield implied on the futures contract is equal to the implied forward rate.

Exhibit 13.5b also shows the binomial tree values for call and put options on the futures contract with $X = 100$ and expiration at the end of two periods. The European futures option prices are obtained like the spot options values by determining the futures option's intrinsic value at expirations and then rolling the tree to the present where the option price at each node is equal to the present value of the expected option values for the next period. The price of the American option is found by constraining the price at each node to be the maximum of its intrinsic value or the binomial value. The option prices shown in the exhibit can also be obtained using the replication approach.

Comparing the futures option shown in Exhibit 13.5b with the spot option values shown in 13.5a, observe that that the prices on the European futures options are equal to the prices on the European spot options. This is consistent given the futures and spot options are European, expire at the same time, and the carrying-cost model holds. The American futures and spot option values, however, are not equal. This is because futures and spot prices are not equal except at expiration.

EXHIBIT 13.5   Binomial Tree Valuation of Bond, Spot Options, Futures, and Futures Options

a. Binomial Bond and Spot Option Values

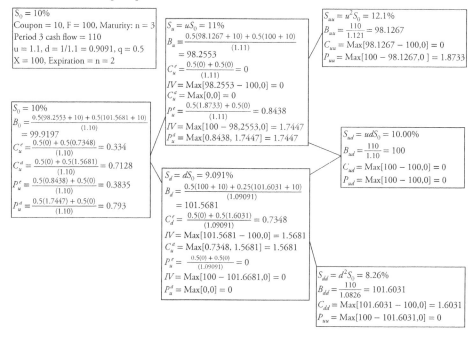

b. Binomial Bond, Futures, and Futures Option Values

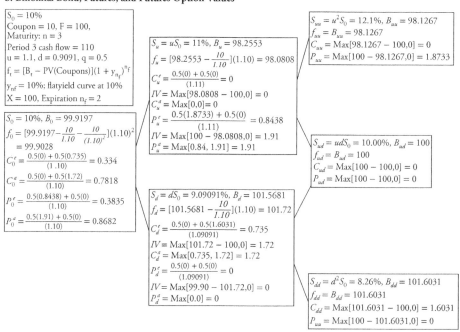

EXHIBIT 13.6 Binomial Trees for Zero Coupon Bonds, Implied Spot Rates for the Case: u and d Inversely Proportional and $q = 0.5$, $u = 1.10$, $d = 1/u = 0.9091$, $q = 0.5$

	Maturity Years	Binomial Price	Spot Yield (y)	Implied Forward Rates One Year	Two Years
Binomial prices and yields (y) on zero-coupon bonds with $F = \$100$ and maturities of $n = 1, 2,$ and 3 periods	1	90.91	0.10	0.10	0.10
	2	82.62	0.10	0.10	
	3	75.06	0.10		

```
100.00  90.91        y₁ = [$100/$90.91] − 1 = 0.10
   100.00
```
$$y_1 = [\$100/\$90.91] - 1 = 0.10$$

```
100.00  90.09  82.62        y₂ = [$100/$82.62]^{1/2} − 1 = 0.10
   100.00  91.67
      100.00
```
$$y_2 = [\$100/\$82.62]^{1/2} - 1 = 0.10$$

```
100.00  89.21  81.13  75.06        y₃ = [$100/$75.06]^{1/3} − 1 = 0.10
   100.00  90.91  84.00
      100.00  92.37
         100.00
```
$$y_3 = [\$100/\$75.06]^{1/3} - 1 = 0.10$$

Valuing a T-Bill Futures Option with a Binomial Interest Rate Tree

Exhibit 13.7 shows a two-period binomial tree of annualized spot rates and prices on a futures contract and futures options contract on a T-bill with a maturity of 0.25 years and with expirations of one year (at the end of period 2) on the futures and futures options and with an 98.75 exercise price on the options. The length of each binomial period is six months (six-month steps; $\Delta t = 0.5$ years), the upward parameter on the spot rate is 1.1, and the downward parameter is $1/1.1 = 0.9091$, the probability of spot rate increasing in each period is $q = 0.5$, and the yield curve is assumed flat at 5%. As shown in the exhibit, given an initial spot rate of 5% (annual), the two possible spot rates after one period (six months) are 5.5% and 4.54545%, and the three possible rates after two periods (one year) are 6.05%, 5.00%, and 4.13223%.

The futures prices are equal to their carrying-cost values:

$$f_0 = B_0 (1 + S_0)^T$$

where

> f_0 = contract price on the T-bill futures contract
>
> T = time to expiration on the futures contract $= n\Delta t = (2)(0.5 \text{ years}) = 1$
>
> B_0 = $B_0(T + 0.25)$ current spot price on a T-bill identical to the T-bill underlying the futures ($M = 0.25$ and $F = \$100$) except it has a maturity of $T + M = 1 + 0.25 = 1.25$
>
> S = risk-free spot rate

EXHIBIT 13.7   Binomial Tree Valuation of T-Bill Futures and Futures Options

a. Binomial Interest Rates, Spot Rate, T-Bill, and T-Bill Futures

S = Annualized Spot Rate; flat yield curve
u = 1.1, d = 1/1.1 = 0.9091, n = 2, length of period = Δt = 0.5 years
T-bill futures: Contract on T-bill with maturity of 0.25 years, F = $100
Futures expiration = n(0.5 years)
B = price of T-Bill with F = $100, maturity of n(0.5 years) + 0.25 years
Carrying-cost futures price: $f = B(1 + R)^{n(.5)}$

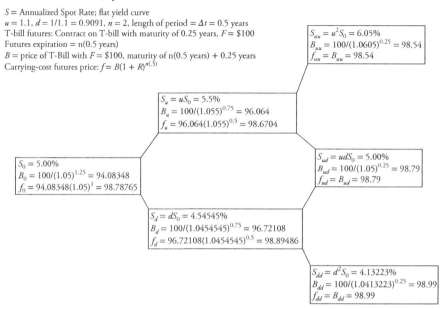

$S_{uu} = u^2 S_0 = 6.05\%$
$B_{uu} = 100/(1.0605)^{0.25} = 98.54$
$f_{uu} = B_{uu} = 98.54$

$S_u = uS_0 = 5.5\%$
$B_u = 100/(1.055)^{0.75} = 96.064$
$f_u = 96.064(1.055)^{0.5} = 98.6704$

$S_0 = 5.00\%$
$B_0 = 100/(1.05)^{1.25} = 94.08348$
$f_0 = 94.08348(1.05)^{1} = 98.78765$

$S_{ud} = udS_0 = 5.00\%$
$B_{ud} = 100/(1.05)^{0.25} = 98.79$
$f_{ud} = B_{ud} = 98.79$

$S_d = dS_0 = 4.54545\%$
$B_d = 100/(1.0454545)^{0.75} = 96.72108$
$f_d = 96.72108(1.0454545)^{0.5} = 98.89486$

$S_{dd} = d^2 S_0 = 4.13223\%$
$B_{dd} = 100/(1.0413223)^{0.25} = 98.99$
$f_{dd} = B_{dd} = 98.99$

b. Binomial T-Bill Futures Option Values

S = Annualized Spot Rate; flat yield curve
u = 1.1, d = 1/1.1 = .9091, n = 2, length of period = .5 years
f = price of T-Bill future, expiration: n = 2
P = price on put option on futures T-Bill, X = 98.75, expiration: n = 2
C = price on call option on futures T-Bill, X = 98.75, expiration: n = 2

$S_{uu} = 6.05\%$
$f_{uu} = B_{uu} = 98.54$
$C_{uu} = \text{Max}[98.54 - 98.75, 0] = 0$
$P_{uu} = \text{Max}[98.75 - 98.54, 0] = 0.21$

$S_u = 5.5\%, f_u = 98.6704$
$C_u^e = \dfrac{0.5(0) + 0.5(0.04)}{(1.055)^{0.5}} = 0.0195$
$IV_u^C = \text{Max}[98.6704 - 98.75, 0] = 0$
$C_u^a = \text{Max}[0.0195, 0] = 0.0195$
$P_u^e = \dfrac{0.5(0.21) + 0.5(0)}{(1.055)^{0.5}} = 0.1022$
$IV_u^P = \text{Max}[98.75 - 98.6704, 0] = 0.0796$
$P_u^a = \text{Max}[0.1022, 0.0796] = 0.1022$

$S_0 = 5\%, f_0 = 98.78765$
$C_0^e = \dfrac{0.5(0.0195) + 0.5(0.1369)}{(1.05)^{0.5}} = 0.07631$
$C_0^a = \dfrac{0.5(0.0195) + 0.5(0.14846)}{(1.05)^{0.5}} = 0.08196$
$P_0^e = P_0^a = \dfrac{0.5(0.1022) + 0.5(0)}{(1.05)^{0.5}} = 0.05048$

$S_{ud} = 5.00\%$
$B_{ud} = f_{ud} = 98.79$
$C_{ud} = \text{Max}[98.79 - 98.75, 0] = 0.04$
$P_{ud} = \text{Max}[98.75 - 98.79, 0] = 0$

$S_d = 4.454545\%, f_d 98.89846$
$C_d^e = \dfrac{0.5(0.04) + 0.5(0.24)}{(1.0454545)^{0.5}} = 0.1369$
$IV_d^C = \text{Max}[98.89846 - 98.75, 0] = 0.14846$
$C_d^a = \text{Max}[0.1369, 0.14846] = 0.14846$
$P_d^e = \dfrac{0.5(0) + 0.5(0)}{(1.0454545)^{0.5}} = 0$
$IV_d^P = \text{Max}[98.75 - 98.89846, 0] = 0$
$P_d^a = \text{Max}[0, 0] = 0$

$S_{dd} = 4.13223\%$
$B_{dd} = f_{dd} = 98.99$
$C_{dd} = \text{Max}[98.99 - 98.75, 0] = 0.24$
$P_{dd} = \text{Max}[09.75 - 98.99, 0] = 0$

At expiration, the prices on the expiring futures are equal to the price on the underlying T-bill ($=100/(1 + S)^{0.25}$). If the yield curve is flat, then the price of the futures simplifies to

$$f_0 = B_0 (1 + S_0)^T$$

$$f_0 = \frac{100}{(1 + S_0)^{T+0.25}}(1 + S_0)^T$$

$$f_0 = \frac{100}{(1 + S_0)^{0.25}}$$

Exhibit 13.7 shows both European and American call and put option prices on the T-bill futures contract. The European futures option prices are obtained by determining the futures option's possible intrinsic values at expirations and then rolling the tree to the present where the option price at each node is equal to present value of the expected option values for the next period. The price of the American option is obtained by constraining the price at each node to be the maximum of its intrinsic value or the binomial value. The price of the European call is 0.07631 and the price of the American call is 0.08196; the prices of the European and American puts are both 0.05048.

Valuing Caplets and Floorlets with a Binomial Interest Rate Tree

The price of a caplet or floorlet can also be valued using a binomial tree of the option's reference rate. Exhibit 13.8 shows our previous illustrative two-period binomial tree for an annualized risk-free spot rate (S) defining an interest rate call and put. The length of each period is six months (six-month steps; $\Delta t = 0.5$ years), $u = 1.1$ and $d = 1/1.1 = 0.9091$, the probability of spot rate increasing in each period is $q = 0.5$, and the yield curve is assumed flat. As shown in the exhibit, given an initial spot rate of 5% (annual), the two possible spot rates after one period (six months) are 5.5% and 4.54545%, and the three possible rates after two periods (one year) are 6.05%, 5%, and 4.13223%.

Consider a caplet on the spot rate defined by our binomial tree, with an exercise rate of 5%, a period applied to the payoff of $\phi = 0.25$, and notional principal of $NP = 100$. As shown in Exhibit 13.8, the interest rate call is in the money at expiration only at the spot rate of 6.05%. At that rate, the caplet's payoff is 0.2625 ($= (0.0605 - 0.05)(0.25)(100)$). In period 1, the value of the caplet is 0.1278 ($= [0.5(0.2625) + 0.5(0)]/(1.055)^{0.5}$) at spot rate 5.5% and 0 at spot rate 4.54545%. Rolling theses values to the current period, in turn, yields a price on the caplet of 0.06236 ($= [0.5 (0.1278) + 0.5(0)]/(1.05)^{0.5}$). In contrast, a floorlet with similar features would be in the money at expiration at the spot rate of 4.13223%, with a payoff of 0.2169 ($= (0.05 - 0.0413223)(0.25)(100)$) and out of the money at spot rates 5% and 6.05%. In period 1, the floorlet's values would be 0.1061 ($= [0.5(0) + 0.5(0.2169)]/(1.0454545)^{0.5}$) at spot rate 4.454545% and 0 at spot rate 6.05%.

EXHIBIT 13.8   Binomial Tree: Caplet and Floorlet

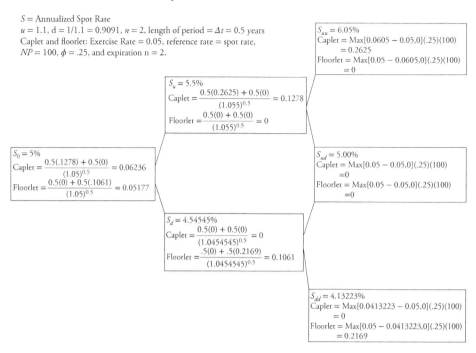

Rolling these values to the present period, we obtain a price on the floorlet of 0.05177 $(= [0.5(0) + 0.5 (0.1061)]/(1.05)^{0.5})$.

Since a cap is a series of caplets, its price is simply equal to the sum of the values of the individual caplets making up the cap. To price a cap, we can use a binomial tree to price each caplet and then aggregate the caplet values to obtain the value of the cap. The value of a floor can similarly be found by summing the values of the floorlets comprising the floor.

Valuing Callable and Putable Bonds with a Binomial Interest Rate Tree

When an investor buys a callable bond, she is in effect selling a call option to the issuer, giving the issuer the right to buy the bond from the bondholder before maturity at a specified price. The price of a callable bond is equal to the value of an identical option-free bond minus the value of the call feature. The inclusion of option features in a bond contract also makes the evaluation of such bonds more difficult. A 10-year, 10% callable bond issued when interest rate are relatively high may be more like a three-year bond given that a likely interest rate decrease would lead the issuer to buy the bond back. Determining the value of such a bond requires taking into account not only the value of the bond's cash flow, but also the value of the call option embedded in the bond. The binomial interest rate tree can be used to determine the value of a callable bond.

Valuing a Three-Period Callable Bond with a Binomial Tree

We previously valued a three-period, 5% option-free bond at 99.6737 using a two-period binomial interest rate tree with a current spot rate of $S_0 = 5\%$, $u = 1.1$, and $d = 0.95$ (Exhibit 13.2). Now suppose that the bond has a call feature that allows the issuer to buy back the bond at a call price (CP) of 100. Using the binomial tree approach, this call option can be incorporated into the valuation of the bond by determining at each node whether or not the issuer would exercise his right to call. The issuer will find it profitable to exercise whenever the call price is less than the bond price (assuming no transaction or holding costs). Thus, the value of the callable bond in each period is the minimum of its call price or its binomial value:

$$B_t^C = \text{Min}[B_t, CP]$$

To incorporate this constraint into the tree, we first compare each of the non-callable bond values with the call price in period 2 (one period from maturity) and take the minimum of the two as the callable bond value. We next roll the callable bond values from period 2 to period 1 where we determine the two bond values at each node as the present value of the expected cash flows, and then for each case we select the minimum of the value we calculated or the call price. Finally, we roll those two callable bond values to the current period and determine the callable bond's price as the present value of period 1's expected cash flows. Exhibit 13.9a shows the binomial tree value of the three-period, 5% bond given a call feature with a $CP = 100$. Note, at the lower node in period 2, the bond would be called at 100 and therefore the callable bond price would be 100; at the top two nodes, the binomial bond price would be the minimum. Rolling these prices to period 1, the present values of the expected cash flows are 98.955 at the 5.5% spot rate and 100.1366 at the 4.75% rate. At 4.75% the CP of 100 would be the minimum and thus the callable bond value at that node. Rolling these two values to the current period, we obtain a value of 99.50 for the three-period callable bond. As we should expect, the bond's embedded call option lowers the value of the bond from 99.6737 to 99.50.

Instead of using a price constraint at each node, the price of the callable bond can alternatively be found by determining the value of the call option at each node, C_t, and then subtracting that value from the noncallable bond value ($B_t^C = B_t^{NC} - C_t$). When there are three periods or more, we need to take into account that prior to maturity the bond issuer has an American call options in which the issuer can either exercise the option or hold it for another period. The exercising value, IV, is

$$IV = \text{Max}[B_t^{NC} - CP, 0]$$

while the value of holding, V_H, is the present value of the expected call value, C, next period:

$$V_H = \frac{qC_u + (1-q)C_d}{1+S}$$

If V_H exceeds IV, the issuer will hold the option another period and the value of the call in this case will be the holding value. In contrast, if IV is greater than V_H,

EXHIBIT 13.9 Binomial Value of Callable Bond: Coupon = 5%, Face Value = 100, Maturity = 3 Periods, Call Price = CP = 100, u = 1.1, d = 0.95, S_0 = 5%

a. Price Constraint Approach

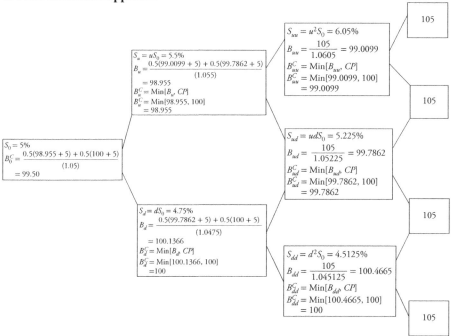

b. Call Valuation Approach

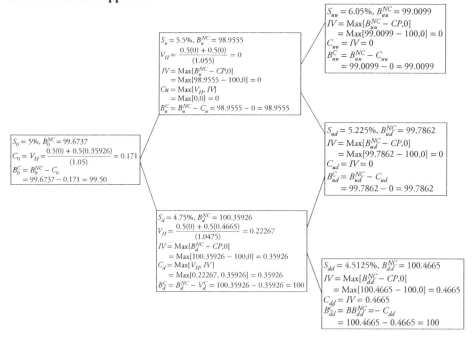

then the issuer will exercise the call immediately and the value of the option will be *IV*. Thus, the value of the call option is equal to the maximum of *IV* or V_H:

$$C_t = \text{Max}[IV, \ V_H]$$

Exhibit 13.9b shows this valuation approach applied to the three-period callable bond. Note, in period 2 the value of holding is zero at all three nodes since the next period is maturity where it is too late to call. When rates are 6.05% and 5.225% the bond price is less than the call price and there is no value for the issuer to exercise. The issuer, however, would find it profitable to exercise at spot rate 4.5125% when the bond price is 100.4665. The three call values in period 2 are 0.00, 0.00, and 0.4665:

$$C_{uu} = IV = \text{Max}[B_{uu}^{NC} - CP, \ 0] = \text{Max}[99.0099 - 100, \ 0] = 0$$

$$C_{ud} = IV = \text{Max}[B_{ud}^{NC} - CP, \ 0] = \text{Max}[99.7862 - 100, \ 0] = 0$$

$$C_{dd} = IV = \text{Max}[B_{dd}^{NC} - CP, \ 0] = \text{Max}[100.4665 - 100, \ 0] = 0.4665$$

In period 1, the noncallable bond price is greater than the call price at the lower node. In this case, the *IV* is $100.35926 - 100 = 0.35926$. The value of holding the call is 0.22267:

$$V_H = \frac{0.5(0) + 0.5(0.4665)}{(1.0475)} = 0.22267$$

Thus, the issuer would find it more valuable to exercise than to defer the exercise one period. As a result, the value of the call option is $\text{Max}[IV, \ V_H] = \text{Max}[0.35926, 0.22267] = 0.35926$ and the value of the callable bond is 100 (the same value we obtained using the price constraint approach):

$$B_d^C = B_d^{NC} - C_d = 100.35926 - 0.35926 = 100$$

At the upper node in period 1 where the price of the noncallable is 98.9555, the exercise value and value of holding are zero. The value of the call option in this case is equal to zero and the value of the callable bond is equal to the noncallable value. Finally, rolling the two possible option values of 0.35926 and 0 in period 1 to the current period, we obtain the current value of the option of 0.171 and the same callable bond value of 99.50 that we obtained using the first approach:

$$C_0 = V_H = \frac{0.5(0) + 0.5(0.35926)}{(1.05)} = 0.171$$

$$B_0^C = B_0^{NC} - C_0 = 99.6737 - 0.171 = 99.50$$

Note that the value of the embedded call option on the bond of 0.171 is the same value we obtained earlier when we valued a 100 American call option on the three-period 5% bond (see Exhibit 13.3).

Valuing a Three-Period Putable Bond with a Binomial Tree

A putable bond gives the holder the right to sell the bond back to the issuer at a specified exercise price (or put price), PP. In contrast to callable bonds, putable bonds benefit the holder. If the price of the bond decreases below the exercise price, then the bondholder can sell the bond back to the issuer at the exercise price. Given that the bondholder has the right to exercise, the price of a putable bond will be equal to the price of an option-free bond plus the value of the put option (P_0):

$$B_0^{\text{P}} = B_0^{\text{NP}} + P_0$$

Since the bondholder will find it profitable to exercise whenever the put price exceeds the bond price, the value of a putable bond can be found using the binomial approach by comparing bond prices at each node with the put price and selecting the maximum of the two, $\text{Max}[B_t, PP]$. To illustrate, suppose the three-period, 5% bond in our first example has a put option giving the bondholder the right to sell the bond back to the issuer at an exercise price of $PP = 100$ in periods 1 or 2. Using the two-period tree of one-period spot rates, we start at period 2. At rates 6.05% and 5.225%, the exercise price exceeds the bond price; thus, the price of the bond would be equal to the 100 put price (see Exhibit 13.10a). When the spot rate is 4.5125%, there is no exercise advantage with the bond price of 100.4665 exceeding the put price; thus, the putable bond price is equal to their option-free value. Rolling these prices to period 1, the present values of the expected cash flows are 99.526 at the 5.5% spot rate and 100.4613 at the 4.75% rate. At 5.5%, the PP of 100 would be the maximum and thus the putable bond value at that node. At 4.75%, the binomial bond price of 100.4613 would be the maximum and thus the putable bond value at that node. Rolling these two values to the current period, we obtain a value of 100.2197 for the three-period putable bond. As we should expect, the bond's embedded put option increases the value of the bond from its option-free value of 99.6737 to 100.2197.

The same binomial value can also be found by determining the value of the put option at each node and then pricing the putable bond as the value of an option-free bond plus the value of the put option. In using the second approach, the value of the put option will be the maximum of either its intrinsic value (or exercising value), $IV = \text{Max}[PP - B_t, 0]$, or its holding value (the present value of the expected put value next period). Exhibit 13.10b shows this valuation approach applied to the three-period putable bond. As shown in the exhibit, the value of the embedded put option on the bond is 0.5460 and the value of the putable bond is 100.2197. Note that the 0.5460 embedded put value is the same value we obtained earlier when we valued a 100 American put option on the three-period 5% bond (see Exhibit 13.4).

Valuing a Convertible Bond with a Binomial Tree

Consider a three-period, 10% convertible bond with a face value of $1,000 that can be converted to 10 shares of the underlying company's stock (conversion ratio = $CR = 10$). Suppose spot rates are constant and the convertible bond's underlying stock

EXHIBIT 13.10 Binomial Value of Putable Bond: Coupon = 5%, Face Value = 100, Maturity = 3 Periods, Put Price = PP = 100, u = 1.1, d = 0.95, S_0 = 5%

a. Price Constraint Approach

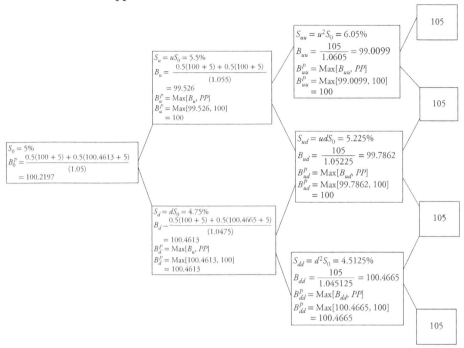

b. Put Valuation Approach

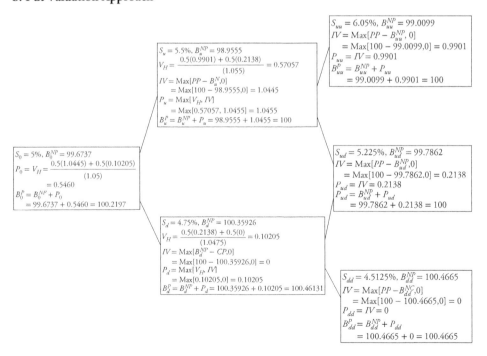

price follows a binomial process where in each period it has an equal chance it can either increase to equal u times its initial value or decrease to equal d times the initial value, where $u = 1.1$, $d = 1/1.1 = 0.9091$, and the current stock price is \$92. The possible stock prices resulting from this binomial process are shown in Exhibit 13.11a, along with the convertible bond's conversion values.

Since spot rates are constant, the value of the convertible bond will only depend on the stock price. To value the convertible bond, we start at the maturity date of the bond. At that date, the bondholder will have a coupon worth 100 and will either convert the bond to stock or receive the principal of \$1,000. At the top stock price of \$122.45, the convertible bondholder would exercise her option, converting the bond to 10 shares of stock. The value of the convertible bond, B^{CB}, at the top node in period 3 would therefore be equal to its conversion value of \$1,224.50 plus the \$100 coupon:

$$B^{CB}_{uuu} = \text{Max}[CV_t,\ F] + C$$
$$B^{CB}_{uuu} = \text{Max}[1{,}224.50,\ 1{,}000] + 100$$
$$B^{CB}_{uuu} = 1{,}324.50$$

Similarly, at the next stock price of \$101.20, the bondholder would also find it profitable to convert; thus, the value of the convertible in this case would be its conversion value of \$1,012 plus the \$100 coupon. At the lower two stock prices in period 3 of \$83.64 and \$69.12, the conversion is worthless; thus, the value of the convertible bond is equal to the principal plus the coupon: \$1,100.

In period 2, at each node the value of the convertible bond is equal to the maximum of either the present value of the bond's expected value at maturity or its conversion value. At all three stock prices, the present values of the bond's expected values next period are greater than the bond's conversion values, including at the highest stock price; that is, at $P^S_{uu} = \$111.32$, the CV is \$1,113.20 compared to the convertible bond value of \$1,160.24; thus the value of the convertible bond is \$1,160.24:

$$B_{uu} = \frac{0.5[1,324.50] + 0.5[1,112]}{1.05} = 1{,}160.24$$
$$B^{CB}_{uu} = \text{Max}[B_{uu},\ CV] = [1,160.24,\ 1,113.20] = 1{,}160.24$$

Thus, in all three cases, the values of holding the convertible bond are greater than the conversion values. Similarly, the two possible bond values in period 1 (generated by rolling the three convertible bond values in period 2 to period 1) also exceed their conversion values. Rolling the tree to the current period, we obtain a convertible bond value of \$1,164.29. As we would expect, this value exceeds both the convertible bond's current conversion value of \$920 and its straight debt value, SDV, of \$1,136.16 (assuming a 5% discount rate):

$$SDV = \frac{\$100}{(1.05)} + \frac{\$100}{(1.05)^2} + \frac{\$1{,}100}{(1.05)^3} = \$1{,}136.16$$

EXHIBIT 13.11   Binomial Value of a Convertible Bond

Convertible Bond without Call Options

Stock Price = $P_0^S = 92$, $u = 1.10$
$d = 0.9091$, Spot Rate = 5%,
Convertible: Coupon = 100, $F = 1,000$,
Conversion Ratio = 10

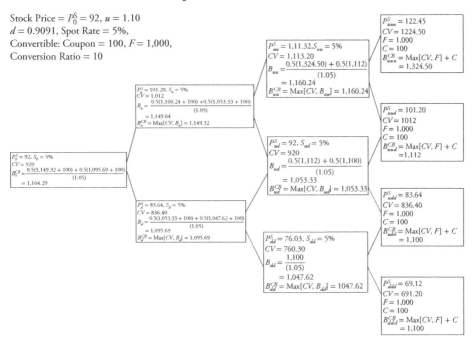

Convertible Bond with Call Option

Stock Price = $P_0^S = 92$, $u = 1.10$
$d = 0.9091$, Spot Rate = 5%,
Convertible: Coupon = 100, $F = 1,000$,
Conversion Ratio = 10, Callable at $CP = 1,100$

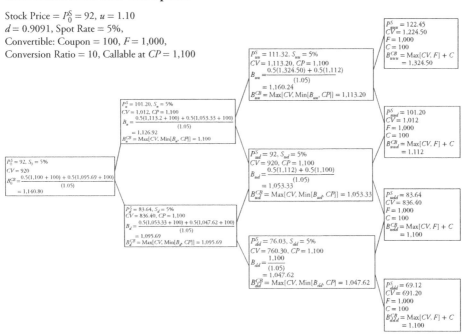

The valuation of a convertible becomes more complex when the bond is callable. With callable convertible bonds, the issuer will find it profitable to call the convertible prior to maturity whenever the price of the convertible is greater than the call price. However, when the convertible bondholder is faced with a call, she usually has the choice of either tendering the bond at the call price or converting it to stock. Since the issuer will call whenever the call price is less than the convertible bond price, he is in effect forcing the holder to convert. By doing this, the issuer takes away the bondholder's value of holding the convertible, forcing the convertible bond price to equal its conversion value.

To see this, suppose the convertible bond is callable in periods 1 and 2 at a $CP = \$1,100$. At the top stock price of $111.32 in period 2, the conversion value is $1,113.20 (see Exhibit 13.11b). In this case, the issuer can force the bondholder to convert by calling the bond. That is, when the bond is at $1,160.24, the issuer would call the bond given the call price of $1,100. However, if the bond price were equal to the call price of $1,100, the bondholder would convert the bond to stock valued at $1,113.20. The call option therefore reduces the value of the convertible from $1,160.24 to $1,113.20. At the other nodes in period 2, neither conversion by the bondholders or calling by the issuer is economical; thus the bond values would prevail. In period 1, at the upper node the call price of $1,100 is below the bond value ($1,126.92), but above the conversion value ($1,012). In this case, the issuer would call the bond and the holder would take the call instead of converting. The value of the callable convertible bond in this case would be the call price of $1,100. At the lower node, calling and converting are not economical and thus the bond value of $1,095.69 prevails. Rolling period 1's upper and lower convertible bond values to the current period, we obtain a value for the callable convertible bond of $1,140.80, which is less than the noncallable convertible bond value of $1,164.29 and greater than the straight debt value of a noncallable bond of $1,136.16.

In the above two cases, we assumed for simplicity that the yield curve remained constant at 5% for the period. Another complexity of valuing convertibles is taking into account the uncertainty of two variables—stock prices and interest rates. A simple way to model such behavior is to use correlation or regression analysis to first estimate the relationship between a stock's price and the spot rate, and then either with a binomial model of spot rates identify the corresponding stock prices or with a binomial model of stock prices identify the corresponding spot rates.

Estimating the Binomial Interest Rate Tree

Estimating the Upward and Downward Parameters

There are two general approaches to estimating binomial interest rate trees. The first (models derived by Rendleman and Bartter (1980) and Cox, Ingersoll, and Ross (1979)) is to estimate the u and d parameters based on estimates of the spot rate's mean and variability. Similar to estimating the u and d values for stock, indexes, and currency, the estimating formula for u and d are obtained by solving for the u and d

values that make the expected value and the variance of the binomial distribution of the logarithmic return of spot rates equal to their respective estimated parameter values:

$$u = e^{\sqrt{V_e/n} + \mu_e/n}$$
$$d = e^{-\sqrt{V_e/n} + \mu_e/n}$$

where μ_e and V_e are the estimated mean and variance of the logarithmic return of spot rates for a period equal in length to n periods.

If the annualized mean and variance are used, then the estimating formulas are

$$u = e^{\sqrt{hV_e^A + h\mu_e^A}}$$
$$d = e^{-\sqrt{hV_e^A + h\mu_e^A}}$$

where h = length of the binomial period as a proportion of a year

For a three-year bond (maturity: $M = 3$ years) with six-month periods ($h = 0.5$), if the annualized mean and variance of the logarithmic return of one-year spot rates were 0.044 and 0.0108, then u and d would be 1.1 and 0.95:

$$u = e^{\sqrt{(0.5)(0.0108)} + (0.5)(0.044)} = 1.1$$
$$d = e^{-\sqrt{(0.5)(0.0108)} + (0.5)(0.044)} = 0.95$$

Suppose the three-period bond in our illustrative example were a three-year, 5% bond. Instead of using a three-period binomial tree, where the length of each period is a year, suppose we evaluate the bond using a 36-period tree with the length of each period being one month. If we do this, we would need to divide the one-year spot rates and the annual coupon (or accrued interest) by 12, adjust the u and d parameters to reflect changes over a one-month period instead of one year, and define the binomial tree of spot rates for 35 periods, each with a length of one month. For example, if the annualized mean and variance of the logarithmic return of one-year spot rates were 0.044 and 0.0108, then h = length of period in years = 1/12 and u and d would be equal to 1.03424 and 0.9740:

$$u = e^{\sqrt{(1/12)(0.0108)} + (1/12)(0.044)} = 1.03424$$
$$d = e^{-\sqrt{(1/12)(0.0108)} + (1/12)(0.044)} = 0.9740$$

The monthly coupon of accrued interest would be $0.41667 ($5.00/12), and the monthly spot rate would be the annual spot rate divided by 12. Excel programs for generating multiple-period binomial interest rate trees and valuing callable and putable bonds (Binomial Bond Valuation Excel program) can be downloaded from the text's website. Using these programs to value the three-year 5% bond, for this 36-period case and with an annualized mean and variance of 0.044 and 0.0108, we obtain an option-free bond price of 98.99, a callable bond price of 98.83 ($CP = 100$), and a putable bond price of 100.20 ($PP = 100$).

Valuation of Options on a Bond Futures Contract: n = 30 Periods

Exhibit 13.12 shows the last eight periods of a 30-period binomial tree of spot rates. The spot rates reflect the case in which the current annual spot rate is 10%, the quarterly spot rate is 2.5%, the annualized mean for the spot rate's logarithmic return is zero, and the annualized standard deviation is 0.039604 (annualized variance is 0.00156853). The length on the binomial tree is $h = 0.25$ years and the u and d values are $u = 1.02$ and $d = 1/u = 0.980392$:

$$u = e^{\sqrt{(0.25)(0.00156853)}+(0.25)(0)} = 1.02$$

$$d = e^{-\sqrt{(0.25)(0.00156853)}+(0.25)(0)} = 0.980392 = 1/1.02$$

EXHIBIT 13.12   Binomial Value of Bond, Futures, and Futures Options for $n = 30$-Period Case

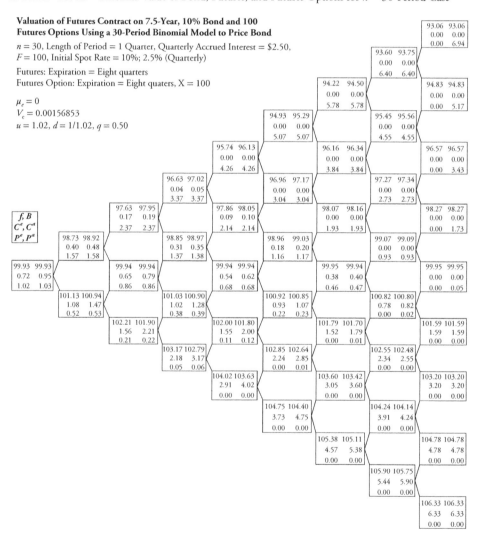

With u and d inversely proportional and $q = 0.5$, the implied yield curve using the tree is 10% and the implied forward rates are 10%.

The exhibit also shows the possible binomial prices for the last eight periods of a bond with a maturity of 7.5 years and a 10% coupon. The bond is valued with a 30-period tree, with the length of the period being a quarter and with the bond yielding a quarterly accrued interest of $2.50.

Lastly, the tree shows binomial futures prices on the bonds with the futures expiring in two years, and the prices on call and put options on the futures contract, with the options expiring in two years and with exercise prices of $100. The futures contract's price is equal to its carrying-cost value. With a yield flat at 10 and implied forward rates equal to 10%, the binomial futures price and spot bond price are both equal to 99.93. The price of the European call, in turn, is 0.72, the price of the American call is 0.95, and the prices of the European and American puts are 1.02 and 1.03, respectively.

Note: Using the Binomial Bond Valuation Excel program, the price of 7.5-year, 10% callable bond with a call price of 100 is 98.89, which is approximately equal to the option-free bond price of 99.93 minus the American call futures price of 0.95. Similarly, the price of a putable bond with a put price of 100 is 101.50, which is approximately equal to the option-free bond price of 99.93 plus the American put futures price of 1.03.

Valuation of T-Bill Futures Options: n = 8 Subperiods

Exhibit 13.13 shows the binomial valuation of call and put option contracts on a T-bill futures contract. The futures contract is on a T-bill with $100 face value and maturity of 0.25 years. The expiration on the futures is in two years. The options have an exercise price of 98.75 and expiration of two years. The exhibit shows an eight-period binomial tree of spot rates, futures prices, and futures options prices. The length of binomial tree is $h = 0.25$ years, the current spot rate is 5%, the yield curve is flat, the annualized variance of the spot rate's logarithmic return is 0.016836 and its mean is zero, and the corresponding u and d values for a binomial period of 0.25 years are $u = 1.067028$ and $d = 1/u = 0.937183$:

$$u = e^{\sqrt{(0.25)(0.016836)}+(0.25)(0)} = 1.067028$$

$$d = e^{-\sqrt{(0.25)(0.016836)}+(0.25)(0)} = 1/1.067028 = 0.937183$$

With a flat yield curve the carrying-cost prices on the T-bill futures are equal to $f_t = 100/(1 + S_t)^{0.25}$. As shown earlier with the two-period case, the European futures option prices are obtained by determining the futures option's intrinsic value at expirations and then rolling the tree to the present where the option price at each node is equal to the present value of the expected option values for the next period. The price of the American option is calculated by constraining the price at each node to be the maximum of its intrinsic value or the binomial value. The price of the European call is 0.1368 and the price of the American call is 0.1465; the prices of the European and American puts are both 0.0757.

EXHIBIT 13.13   Binomial Values of T-Bill Futures and Futures Options: $n = 8$ Periods

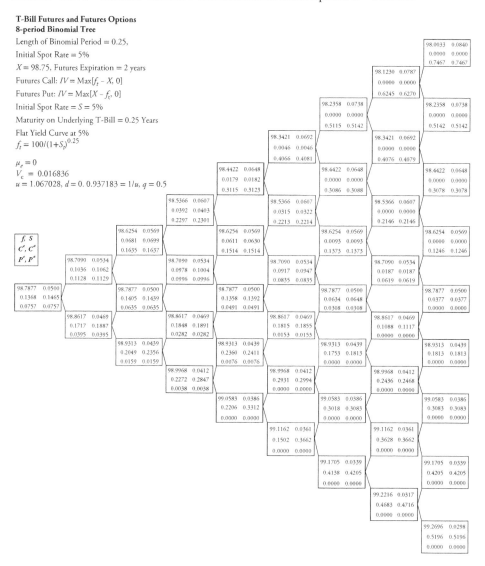

T-Bill Futures and Futures Options
8-period Binomial Tree
Length of Binomial Period = 0.25,
Initial Spot Rate = 5%
$X = 98.75$, Futures Expiration = 2 years
Futures Call: $IV = \text{Max}[f_t - X, 0]$
Futures Put: $IV = \text{Max}[X - f_t, 0]$
Initial Spot Rate = S = 5%
Maturity on Underlying T-Bill = 0.25 Years
Flat Yield Curve at 5%
$f_t = 100/(1+S_t)^{0.25}$

$\mu_e = 0$
$V_e = 0.016836$
$u = 1.067028, d = 0.\ 0.937183 = 1/u, q = 0.5$

Valuation of Caplet and Floorlet: n = 8 Subperiods

Exhibit 13.14 shows the valuation of a caplet and floorlet. The interest rate options
have an exercise rate of 5%, a period applied to the payoff of $\phi = 0.25$, expiration
of two years, and notional principal of $10 million. The reference rate is the spot
rate. The exhibit shows an eight-period binomial tree of spot rates. The length
of binomial tree is $h = 0.25$ years, the current spot rate is 5%, the annualized
variance of spot rate's logarithmic return is 0.016836 and its mean is zero, and the

EXHIBIT 13.14   Binomial Values of a Floorlet and Caplet: $n = 8$ Periods

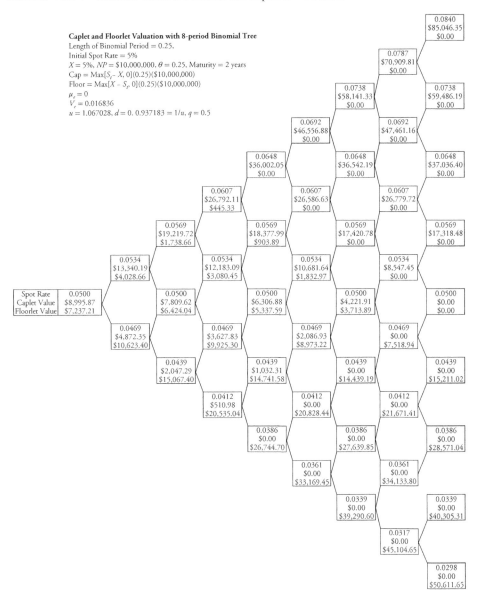

corresponding u and d values for a binomial period of 0.25 years are $u = 1.067028$ and $d = 1/u = 0.937183$:

$$u = e^{\sqrt{(0.25)(0.016836)}+(0.25)(0)} = 1.067028$$

$$d = e^{-\sqrt{(0.25)(0.016836)}+(0.25)(0)} = 1/1.067028 = 0.937183$$

As shown in the exhibit, the interest rate call is in the money in four of the nine spot rate possibilities at expiration, while the interest rate put is in the money in five cases. At the spot rate of 8.40%, where the spot rate increases in each period $((u^n)S_0 = (1.067028^8)(0.05) = 0.0840188)$, the caplet payoff is \$85,046 $(= Max[0.0840188 - 0.05, 0] (0.25)(\$10,000,000))$. At the spot rate of 2.98%, where the spot rate decreases in each period $((d^n)S_0 = (0.937183^8)(0.05) = 0.0975537)$, the floorlet payoff is \$50,611 $(= Max[0.05 - 0.02975536, 0] (0.25)(\$10,000,000))$. Rolling these expiration value to the present period, we obtain a price on the caplet of \$8.995.87 and on the floorlet of \$7,237.21. Note if we subdivide the tree into 30 subperiods, the length of each binomial period would be 0.06667 years, and the price of the caplet is \$9,172.41 and the price of the floorlet is \$7,430.72.

Calibration Model

Recall, the equilibrium price of a bond is the price that discounts each future cash flow by their respective spot rates. That is, if the bond is underpriced, an arbitrageur could strip the bond into zero-coupon bonds, and sell them at the equilibrium price; if it is overpriced, the arbitrageur could buy zero-coupon bonds, bundle them, and sell a coupon bond at the market price. Arbitrageurs exploiting such opportunities would, in turn, drive the bond price it its equilibrium value. A binomial interest rates tree generated using the u and d estimation approach is constrained to have an end-of-the-period distribution with a mean and variance that matches the analyst's estimated mean and variance. The tree is not constrained, however, to yield an option-free bond price that matches its equilibrium price. As a result, analysts using such models would need to make additional assumptions about the risk premium in order to explain the bond's equilibrium price, otherwise the model would be flawed. The second approach to generating a binomial interest-rate tree (models derived by Black, Derman, and Toy (1990), Ho and Lee (1986), and Heath, Jarrow, and Morton (1992)) is to calibrate the binomial tree to the current spot yield curve. This *calibration model*, in turn, generates a binomial tree of spot rates that will price option-free bonds equal to their equilibrium values, and therefore is arbitrage free.

Black-Derman-Toy Calibration Model

The Black-Derman-Toy calibration model generates a binomial tree by first finding spot rates that satisfy a variability condition between the upper and lower rates. Given the variability relation, the model then solves for the lower spot rate that satisfies a price condition in which the bond value obtained from the tree is consistent with the equilibrium bond price given current spot rates.

Variability Condition
The variability condition defines the relationship between the upper and lower spot rates. The condition is

$$S_u = S_d \, e^{2\sqrt{V_e/n}}$$

This variability condition follows directly from the estimating formulas for u and d. That is, from the binomial process we know

$$S_u = uS_0$$
$$S_d = dS_0$$

Therefore:

$$\frac{S_u}{u} = S_0 = \frac{S_d}{d}$$
$$S_u = S_d\frac{u}{d}$$

Substituting the equations for u and d, we obtain:

$$S_u = S_d\frac{e^{\sqrt{V_e/n}+\mu_e/n}}{e^{-\sqrt{V_e/n}+\mu_e/n}} = S_d e^{2\sqrt{V_e/n}}$$

or in terms of the annualized variance:

$$S_u = S_d e^{2\sqrt{hV_e^A}}$$

Thus, given a lower rate of 4.75% and an annualized variance of 0.0054, the upper rate for a one-period binomial tree of length one year ($h = 1$) would be 11%:

$$S_u = 4.75\%e^{2\sqrt{0.0054}} = 5.5\%$$

If the current one-year spot rate were 5%, then these upper and lower rates would be consistent with the upward and downward parameters of $u = 1.1$ and $d = 0.95$. This variability condition would therefore result in a binomial tree for one period that is identical to the one shown in Exhibit 13.1.

Price Condition
In addition to the variability relation between upper and lower spot rates, the calibration model also requires that the binomial tree be consistent with the current spot yield curve. To calibrate the tree to the current spot yield curve requires solving for the lower spot rates at each node such that the resulting tree yields option-free bond prices that are equal to the equilibrium bond prices. To see this, suppose the current market yield curve of spot rate has one-, two-, and three-year spot rates of $S^m_1 = 5\%$, $S^m_2 = 5.06184\%$, and $S^m_3 = 5.124\%$, respectively, and that the estimated annualized variance is 0.0054. To satisfy the price condition, let us first generate a one-period binomial interest rate tree that will price a two-year zero-coupon bond with a face value of $100 equal to its equilibrium price of $B^M_0 = 90.5962$:

$$B^M_0 = \frac{100}{(1 + S^m_2)^2} = \frac{100}{(1.0506184)^2} = 90.5962$$

Using a trial and error approach, we find that at a lower rate of $S_d = 4.75\%$, $S_u = 5.5\%$ and the binomial bond value is equal to the equilibrium price of the two-year bond of 90.5962 (see Exhibit 13.15a). Thus, at $S_d = 4.75\%$, we have a binomial tree of one-year spot rates of $S_d = 4.75\%$ and $S_u = 5.5\%$ that simultaneously satisfy our variability and price conditions.

Given the one-year spot rates after one period of 4.75% and 5.5%, we next move to the second period and determine the tree's three possible spot rates using a similar methodology. The variability condition follows the same form as the one period:

$$S_{ud} = S_{dd}e^{2\sqrt{hV_e^A}}$$

$$S_{uu} = S_{ud}e^{2\sqrt{hV_e^A}} = S_{dd}e^{4\sqrt{hV_e^A}}$$

Similarly, the price condition requires that the binomial value of a three-year zero coupon bond be equal to the equilibrium price. Analogous to the one-period case, this condition is found by solving for the lower rate S_{dd} that, along with the above variability conditions and the rates for S_u and S_d obtained previously, yields a value for a three-year zero coupon bond that is equal to the price on a three-year zero coupon bond yielding 5.124%. Using again an iterative approach, we find that a lower rate of $S_{dd} = 4.5125\%$ yields a binomial value that is equal to the equilibrium price of the three-year bond of 80.078 (see Exhibit 13.15b):

$$B_0^M = \frac{100}{(1 + S_3^m)^3} = \frac{100}{(1.05124)^3} = 80.078$$

Note: The lower rates of 4.75% and 4.5125% represent decreases from the preceding period, which is what we tend to expect in a binomial process. This is because we have calibrated the binomial tree to a relatively flat yield curve. If we had calibrated the tree to a positively sloped yield curve, then it is possible that both rates next period could be greater than the current rate; if we had calibrated the tree to a negatively sloped yield curve, then it is possible that both rates next period could be less than the current rate.

The two-period binomial tree shown in the exhibit combines the upper and lower rates found for the first period with the three rates found for the second period (see Exhibit 13.5c). This yields a tree that is consistent with the estimated variability condition and with the current term structure of spot rates. To grow the tree, we continue with this same process. For example, to obtain the four rates in period 3, we solve for the S_{ddd} that along with the spot rates found previously for periods one and two and the variability relations, yields a value for a four-year zero-coupon bond that is equal to the equilibrium price.

Note that one of the features of using a calibrated tree to determine bond values is that the tree will yield prices that are equal to the bond's equilibrium price; that is, the price obtained by discounting cash flows by spot rates. For example, the value of a three-year, 5% option-free bond using the tree we just derived is 99.67 (this is the illustrative example shown in Exhibit 13.2). This value is also equal to the equilibrium

EXHIBIT 13.15 Calibration Model

a. Calibration of Binomial Tree to Two-Period Zero-Coupon Bond

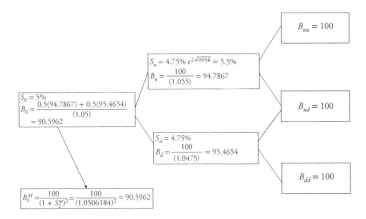

b. Calibration of Binomial Tree to Three-Period Zero-Coupon Bond

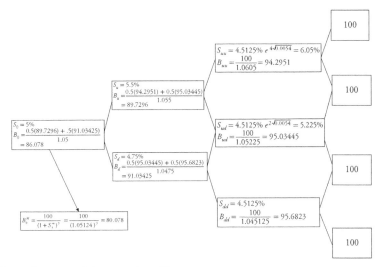

c. Calibrated Binomial Interest Rate Tree

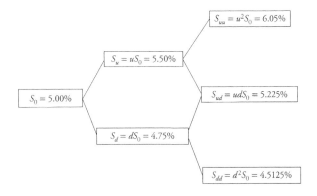

bond price obtained by discounting the bond's periodic cash flows at the spot rates of 5%, 5.06184% and 5.124%:

$$B_3^M = \frac{5}{1.05} + \frac{5}{(1.0506184)^2} + \frac{105}{(1.05124)^3} = 99.67$$

This feature should not be too surprising since we derived the tree by calibrating it to current spot rates. Nevertheless, one of the features of the calibrated tree is that it yields values on option-free bonds that are equal to the bond's equilibrium price. Recall, a bond's equilibrium price is an arbitrage-free price. That is, if the market does not price the bond at its equilibrium value, then arbitrageurs would be able to realize a riskless return either by buying the bond, stripping it into a number of zero discount bonds, and selling them, or by buying a portfolio of zero discount bonds, bundling them into a coupon bond, and selling it. Thus, one of the important features of the calibration model is that it yields prices on option-free bonds that are arbitrage free. Given this feature, the calibration model is a practical model for generating a binomial tree of spot rates for determining the value of options on bonds and bonds with embedded options.

Calibration Model — 30-Period Case

Exhibit 13.16 shows the first eight periods of a 30-period binomial tree of spot rates (*S*) calibrated to the spot yield curve shown at the bottom of the exhibit. The length of the binomial periods is quarterly. The annualized variance of the logarithmic return for the spot rate is $V_e = 0.005012997$ and the variability condition governing the upper and lower rate is

$$S_u = S_d e^{2\sqrt{\frac{V_e}{n}}} \quad S_d = S_d e^{2\sqrt{\frac{0.005012997}{30}}} = 1.02619052\,S_d$$

The yield curve is positively sloped. For the first period, the S_d value that equates the binomial-generated price of a two-quarter zero coupon bond ($F = \$100$) to the equilibrium price ($100/1.0251564^2 = 95.1524$) is 2.4999%, with the upper rate satisfying the variability condition being $S_u = (1.02619052)(2.4999\%) = 2.56\%$. For the tree's second period, the S_{dd} value that equates the binomial price of a three-quarter zero to its equilibrium price ($100/1.02531^3 = 92.7745$) is 2.497%, with the successive upper rates satisfying the variability conditions being $S_{ud} = 2.56\%$ and $S_{uu} = 2.63\%$.

The tree also shows the first eight periods of 30-period binomial bond prices (*B*) for a 7.5-year, 10% option-free bond. The 30-period binomial tree reflected a binomial length of one quarter with the bond paying a quarterly accrued interest of $2.50. As shown in Exhibit 13.16, the calibrated 30-period interest rate model prices the 30-period, 2.5% quarterly coupon bond at 91.39.

EXHIBIT 13.16   Calibration Model: 30-Period Case

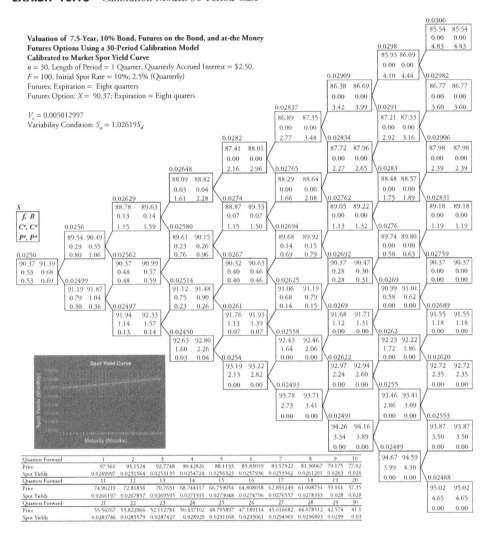

Quarters Forward	1	2	3	4	5	6	7	8	9	10
Price	97.561	95.1524	92.7748	90.42826	88.1133	85.83019	83.57922	81.36067	79.175	77.02
Spot Yields	0.0249997	0.0251564	0.0253135	0.0254724	0.0256323	0.0257936	0.0259562	0.0261201	0.0263	0.026
Quarters Forward	11	12	13	14	15	16	17	18	19	20
Price	74.90219	72.81856	70.7631	68.744117	66.759054	64.808058	62.891249	61.008731	59.161	57.35
Spot Yields	0.0266197	0.0267857	0.0269595	0.0271315	0.0273048	0.0274796	0.0276557	0.0278333	0.028	0.028
Quarters Forward	21	22	23	24	25	26	27	28	29	30
Price	55.56767	53.822966	52.112781	50.437102	48.795897	47.189114	45.616682	44.078512	42.574	41.1
Spot Yields	0.0283746	0.0285579	0.0287427	0.028929	0.0291168	0.0293061	0.0294969	0.0296893	0.0299	0.03

Finally, the exhibit shows the futures prices (f) and at-the-money futures option prices. The futures contract is a contract on the 7.5-year, 10% bond with an expiration of two years (eight quarters). The binomial futures prices are equal to their carrying-cost values. The carrying-cost prices ensure that the total return implied on the futures contracts, TR^f, is equal to the implied forward rate. The current futures price is 90.37 on the contract and the implied total return is 3.152%, which matches the implied forward rate for a 22-quarter bond, eight periods forward, $y^f_{22,8}$. The call and put options on the futures contract have an exercise price of 90.37 and the same expiration as the futures contract. As shown, the binomial European and American futures call prices are 0.53 and 0.68, and European and American futures put prices are 0.53 and 0.69.

Pricing Bond and Interest Rate Options with the B-S and Black OPMs

Pricing Bond Spot Options with the B-S OPM

The value of a spot option on a bond can also be estimated using the B-S OPM. The B-S formula for determining the equilibrium price of a call or put option on a bond is:

$$C_0^* = B_0 N(d_1) - X\, N(d_2)\, e^{-R_f t}$$

$$P_0^* = X(1 - N(d_2))\, e^{-R_f t} - B_0(1 - N(d_1))$$

$$d_1 = \frac{\ln(B_0/X) + (R_f + 0.5\sigma^2)t}{\sigma\sqrt{t}}$$

$$d_2 = d_1 - \sigma\sqrt{t}$$

where

σ^2 = variance of the logarithmic return of bond prices = $V(\ln(B_n/B_0))$

As an example, suppose there is a three-year bond with a 10% annual coupon selling at par ($F = 100$), and call and put options on the bond each with an exercise price of 100 and expiration of one year. Assuming the risk-free rate is 6% and the variability on the underlying bond's logarithmic return is $\sigma = 0.10$, the call and put prices using the Black-Scholes model are 7.45 and 1.63, respectively.

$$C_0^* = B_0 N(d_1) - X\, N(d_2)\, e^{-R_f t}$$

$$C_0^* = 100(0.7423) - 100(0.7091)\, e^{-(.06)(1)} = 7.45$$

$$P_0^* = X(1 - N(d_2))\, e^{-R_f t} - B_0(1 - N(d_1))$$

$$P_0^* = 100(1 - .7091)e^{-(.06)(1)} - 100(1 - .7423) = 1.63$$

$$d_1 = \frac{\ln(100/100) + (0.06 + 0.5(0.10^2)1}{0.10\sqrt{1}} = 0.6500$$

$$d_2 = 0.6500 - 0.10\sqrt{1} = 0.5500$$

$$N(d_1) = N(0.6500) = 0.7423$$

$$N(d_2) = N(0.5500) = 0.7091$$

There are several problems using the standard OPM to price bond options. First, recall the B-S OPM assumes a constant variance. In the case of bond prices, however, variability tends to decrease as a bond's maturity becomes shorter. Second, the OPM assumes that the interest rate is constant. For debt options, an inherent inverse relationship between interest rates and the price of the underlying bond exists. Finally, in the case of options on specific bonds such as a spot T-bond option, the underlying bond changes maturity and value over time. Because of these problems, mispricing can result in determining the equilibrium price of a debt option with the B-S OPM. Thus, the use of the B-S OPM to value the call and put option on a bond should be viewed only as an approximation. The binomial interest rate tree, in turn, is a more accurate approach to pricing bond options than the B-S model.

Using the B-S OPM to Price Embedded Call and Put Options

In examining binomial interest rate models and their use in valuing bonds with embedded options, it should be noted that an approximate value of the embedded option features of a bond can also be estimated using the B-S OPM. The B-S formula for determining the equilibrium price of an embedded call or put option is:

$$V_0^C = B_0 N(d_1) - X N(d_2) e^{-R_f t}$$

$$V_0^P = X(1 - N(d_2)) e^{-R_f t} - B_0(1 - N(d_1))$$

$$d_1 = \frac{\ln(B_0/X) + (R_f + 0.5\sigma^2)t}{\sigma \sqrt{t}}$$

$$d_2 = d_1 - \sigma\sqrt{t}$$

where

X = call price (CP) or put price (PP)
σ^2 = variance of the logarithmic return of bond prices = $V(\ln(B_n/B_0))$
t = maturity of the bond expressed as a proportion of a year

For example, suppose a three-year, option-free bond with a 10% annual coupon is selling at par ($F = 100$). A callable bond that is identical in all respects except for its call feature should sell at 100 minus the call price. In this case, suppose the call feature gives the issuer the right to buy the bond back at any time during the bond's life at an exercise price of 115. Assuming a risk-free rate of 6% and a variability of $\sigma = 0.10$ on the option-free bond's logarithmic return, the call price using the Black-Scholes model would be 8.95:

$$V_0^C = B_0 N(d_1) - X N(d_2) e^{-R_f t}$$

$$V_0^C = 100(0.62519) - 115(0.55772) e^{-(0.06)(3)} = 8.95$$

$$d_1 = \frac{\ln(100/115) + (0.06 + 0.5(0.10^2)3}{0.10 \sqrt{3}} = .31892$$

$$d_2 = 0.31892 - 0.10\sqrt{3} = 0.14571$$

$$N(d_1) = N(0.31892) = 0.62519$$

$$N(d_2) = N(0.14571) = 0.55772$$

Thus, the price of the callable bond is 91.05:

Price of callable bond = Price of noncallable Bond − Call premium

Price of callable bond = 100 − 8.95 = 91.05

As we noted, the B-S OPM assumes interest rates are constant. For bonds, though, the change in their value is due to interest rate changes. Thus, the use of the B-S OPM to value the call or a put option embedded in a bond should also be viewed only as an approximation.

Black Model for Pricing Futures Options

In Chapter 12, we defined the Fisher Black's futures option model for pricing futures options on index, currency, and commodity futures contracts:

$$C_0^* = [f_0 N(d_1) - X N(d_2)] e^{-R_f t}$$

$$P_0^* = [X(1 - N(d_2)) - f_0(1 - N(d_1))] e^{-R_f t}$$

$$d_1 = \frac{\ln(f_0/X) + (\sigma_f^2/2)t}{\sigma_f \sqrt{t}}$$

$$d_2 = d_1 - \sigma_f \sqrt{t}$$

where

σ_f^2 = variance of the logarithmic return of futures prices = $V(\ln(f_n/f_0))$

σ_f^2 = σ_S^2 (volatility of spot prices), given dividend yield and cost of carrying are functions of time

As noted in Chapter 12, the Black futures model differs from the B-S OPM for spot securities by the exclusion of the risk-free rate in the equations for d_1 and d_2. The exclusion of the risk-free rate was also the case for the binomial model with a large number of subperiods. Like the BOPM for futures options, if the carrying-cost model holds and the underlying futures contract and the futures option expire at the same time, then the B-S OPM for European spot options and the Black model for European futures options will be the same. It should also be noted that the Black model, like the B-S OPM, only prices European futures options. If the futures option is American, then an early exercise advantage may exist for both calls and puts. In such cases, the American binomial model presented in the last section can be used to estimate the option price.

Example: T-Bond Futures

As an example, consider one-year put and call options on a T-bond futures contract, with each option having an exercise price of $100,000. Suppose the current futures price is $96,115, the futures volatility is $\sigma(\ln(f_n/f_0)) = 0.10$, and the continuously compound risk-free rate is 0.065. Using the Black futures option model, the price of the call option would be $2,137 and the price of the put would be $5,777:

$$C_0^* = [\$96,115\,(0.36447) - \$100,000\,(0.327485)]\,e^{-(.065)(1)} = \$2,137$$

$$P_0^* = [\$100,000(1 - 0.327485) - \$96,115(1 - 0.36447)]\,e^{-(.065)(1)} = \$5,777$$

where

$$d_1 = \frac{\ln(96,115/100,000) + (0.01/2)(1)}{0.10\,\sqrt{1}} = -0.34625$$

$$d_2 = -0.34625 - 0.10\sqrt{1} = -0.44625$$

$$N(-0.34625) = 0.36447$$

$$N(-0.44625) = 0.327485$$

Pricing Caplets and Floorlets with the Back Futures Option Model

The Black futures option model also can be extended to pricing caplets and floorlets:

1. Substitute t^* for t in the equation for C^* (for a caplet) or P^* (for a floorlet), where t^* is the time to expiration on the option plus the time period applied to the interest rate payoff time period, ϕ: $t^* = t + \phi$.
2. Use an annual continuous compounded risk-free rate for period t^* instead of t.
3. Multiply the Black adjusted-futures option model by the notional principal times the time period: $(NP)\,\phi$.

$$C_0^* = \phi(NP)[RN(d_1) - R_X N(d_2)]\,e^{-R_f t^*}$$

$$P_0^* = \phi(NP)[R_X(1 - N(d_2)) - R(1 - N(d_1))]\,e^{-R_f t^*}$$

$$d_1 = \frac{\ln(R/R_X) + (\sigma^2/2)t}{\sigma - \sigma\,\sqrt{t}}$$

$$d_2 = d_1 - \sigma\sqrt{t}$$

Example: Pricing a Caplet

Consider a caplet with an exercise rate of $X = 7\%$, $NP = \$100,000$, $\phi = 0.25$, expiration $= t = 0.25$ year, and reference rate = LIBOR. If the current LIBOR were $R = 6\%$, the estimated annualized standard deviation of the LIBOR's logarithmic return were 0.2, and the continuously compounded risk-free rate were 5.8629%, then using the Black model, the price of the caplet would be 4.34.

$$C_0^* = 0.25(\$100,000)\,[0.06(0.067845) - 0.07\,(0.055596)]\,e^{-(0.058629)(0.5)} = 4.34$$

where

$$d_1 = \frac{\ln(0.06/0.07) + (0.04/2)(0.25)}{0.2\,\sqrt{.25}} = -1.49151$$

$$d_2 = d_1 - 0.2\sqrt{0.25} = -1.59151$$

$$N(-1.49151) = 0.067845$$

$$N(-1.59151) = 0.055596$$

Example: Pricing a Cap

Suppose the caplet represented part of a contract that caps a two-year floating-rate loan of $100,000 at 7% for a three-month period. The cap consist of seven caplets, with expirations of $t = 0.25$ years, 0.5, 0.75, 1.00, 1.25, 1.50, and 1.75. The value of the cap is equal to the sum of the values of the caplets comprising the cap. If we assume a flat yield curve such that the continuous rate of 5.8629% applies, and we use the same volatility of 0.2 for each caplet, then the value of the cap would be $254.53 (see Exhibit 13.17).

EXHIBIT 13.17   Pricing a Cap

Expiration	Price of Caplet
0.25	4.34
0.50	15.29
0.75	26.74
1.00	37.63
1.25	47.73
1.50	57.04
1.75	65.61
	254.38

In practice, different volatilities for each caplet are used in valuing a cap or floor. The different volatilities are referred to as spot volatilities and are often estimated by calculating the implied volatility on comparable Eurodollar futures options.

Conclusion

In this chapter, we examined the option models for the pricing of bond and interest rate spot and futures options. We began our analysis by deriving the binomial interest rate model. This model values bonds, their derivatives, embedded options, and interest rate option by identifying the possible random paths that interest rates follow over time. We then examined two approaches to estimating binomial interest rate trees—estimating u and d and the calibration model. We concluded by examining how the B-S OPM and Black futures model are used to estimate bond options. This completes our analysis of option pricing. In the next chapter, we begin our analysis of another popular derivative used extensively in managing interest rate, currency, and equity positions—swaps.

BLOOMBERG OPTION VALUATION SCREENS FOR BOND AND INTEREST RATE OPTIONS, OVME

Bond and Interest Rate Option Valuation, OVME determines OPM prices for spot and options contracts. For a loaded futures: OVME <Enter>

Features:

- OVME pulls implied volatilities from a volatility surface and historical volatility. You can access the volatility from the "Volatility" tab.
- Option prices and the Greek values can be plotted against different underlying security prices, time and other parameters from the "Scenario" tab.
- On the "Backtest" tab, you can analyze multiple strategies.
- OVME allows you to input your own option information.
- From the "Deal" tabs, you can construct multiple deals simultaneously and then analyze them from the "Scenario" tab. See Chapters 11 and 12, "Bloomberg Option Valuation Screen."

OVME FOR OTC SPOT BOND
For a loaded bond, OVME calculates the value of an option on the bond.

OVME FOR BOND AND INTEREST RATE FUTURES
For a loaded futures, OVME calculates the value of an option on the contract (see Exhibits 13.18 and 13.19).

(Continued)

EXHIBIT 13.18 OVME for Call Option on Five-Year T-Note Futures Contract: 1/23/17; Futures: $f_0 = 117$ -24, Expiration = March; Call Option: $X = 117$ - 24, Expiration = 3/31/17, Volatility = 3.694%, American, and Black OPM Value = 0.6183.

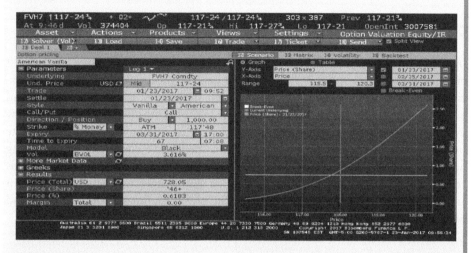

EXHIBIT 13.19 OVME for Call Option on Eurodollar Futures Contract: 1/23/17; Futures: $f_0 = 98.752$, Expiration = 6/19/17; Call Option: $X = 98.752$, Expiration = 6/19/2017, Volatility = 0.309%, American, and Black OPM Value = 0.0784.

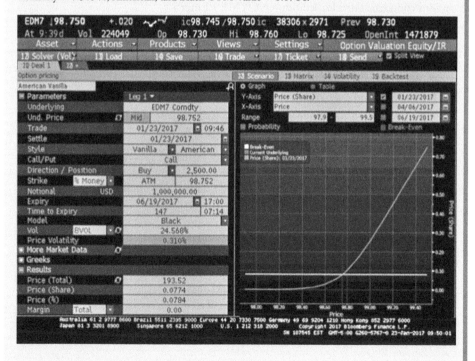

BVAL: CONVERTIBLE BOND

- Convertible bonds can be found using **SECF**. To find if a specific company has a convertible, you can bring up the company's bond menu (Ticker <Corp> <Enter>) and then select "Convertible" from the "Mty type."
- **SRCH:** The bond search screen, SRCH, can also be used to find convertibles. On the SRCH screen type in "Convertible" in the amber box. You may also want to narrow the search by also entering Country and Ratings. Click "Results" to see your search. To bring up the convertible's menu screen, enter: Convertible's ticker <Corp>.
- **CSCH: Convertible Bond Search:** You can use the CSCH screen to search for convertibles. You may want to screen by "Trading Activity" (e.g., Active), by Country, and by "Maturity Type" (e.g., convertible/callable or Convertible/callable/putable). Click "Results" to see your search. To bring up the convertible's menu screen, enter the convertible's ticker <Corp>.
- OVCV: Convertible valuation.
- BVAL: For a loaded convertible, values the bond (see Exhibit 13.20).

SWPM: VALUING CAPS AND FLOORS

SWPM: Bloomberg Swaps and Interest Rate Derivatives screen: The Caps/Floors screen in SWPM can be used to create caps and floors and value them. To access the screen: go to the "Products" tab, click "Cap" under the "Options" dropdown. This will bring up the main screen that can be used to create the cap. You can then change the settings on the main screen. For a floor, click "Floor" from the "Products" tab (see Exhibit 13.21).

1. **Options:** Notional Principal, Payment Frequency, Cap Strike Rate, Spread (the amount of basis points to add or subtract from the floating rate, LIBOR).
2. **Forward Graph Options:** SWPM determines future cash flows at each reset date based on the forward rate at that date. The user can select which yield curve the forward rates are to be determined. On the "Curve" screen ("Curve" tab), one can view the forward graph and make shift adjustment.
3. **Discount Rate Option:** SWPM also discounts cash flows to determine the market value (shown at the bottom of main screen; the user can also select which yield curve to be used for discounting).

Tab Screens

1. "Details" tab shows the detail of the swap.
2. "Resets" tab shows the reset rate at each effective date (forward LIBOR plus basis point you added to spread). One can change the rates from this tab.
3. "Cashflow" tab shows cash flows.
4. "Scenario" tab allows one to make scenario changes.
5. The cap is valued by using a forward rate curve and the Black futures option model; each caplet is valued in the cash flow table.

(Continued)

EXHIBIT 13.20 BVAL Screen: Intel Convertible Bond

EXHIBIT 13.21 SWPM: Cap Valuation

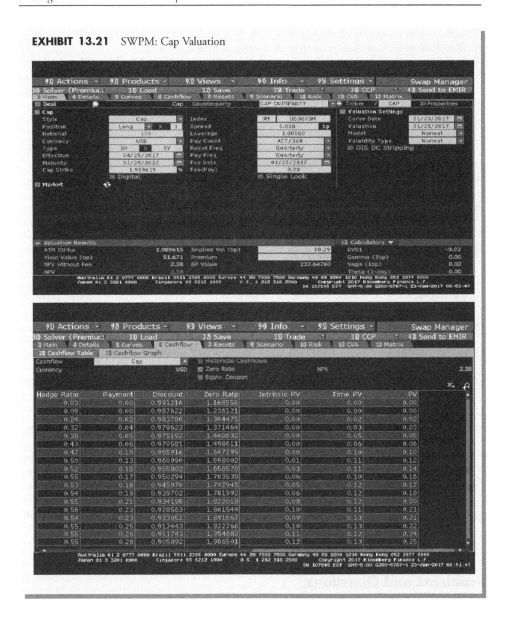

Selected References

Abken, P. "Interest Rate Caps, Collars, and Floors." *Federal Reserve Bank of Atlanta Economic Review* 74, no. 6 (1989): 2–24.

Abken, Peter A. "Chapter 25: Introduction to Over-the-Counter (OTC) Options." *The Handbook of Interest Rate Risk Management*. Edited by Jack Clark Francis and Avner Simon Wolf. New York: Irwin Professional Publishing, 1994.

Andersen, L. "A Simple Approach to the Pricing of Bermudan Swaption in the Multi-Factor LIBOR Market Model." *Applied Mathematical Finance* 7, no. 1 (2000): 1–32.

Bhattacharya, Anand K. "Interest-Rate Caps and Floors and Compound Options." *The Handbook of Fixed Income Securities*, 6th edition. Editor, Frank Fabozzi. New York: McGraw-Hill, 2001.

Black, F., E. Derman, and W. Toy. "A One-Factor Model of Interest Rates and Its Application to Treasury Bond Options." *Financial Analysts Journal* (January/February 1990): 33–39.

Black, Fisher, Emanuel Derman, William Toy, and Jack C. Francis. "Using a One-Factor Model to Value Interest Rate-Sensitive Securities: With an Application to Treasury Bond Options." *The Handbook of Interest Rate Risk Management*. Edited by Jack Clark Francis and Avner Simon Wolf. New York: Irwin Professional Publishing, 1994.

Black, Fisher, and Piotr Karasinski. "Bond and Option Pricing when Short Rates are Lognormal." *Financial Analysts Journal* 47, no. 4 (1991): 52–59.

Dehnad, Kosrow. "Characteristics of OTC Options." *The Handbook of Interest Rate Risk Management*. Edited by Jack Clark Francis and Avner Simon Wolf. New York: Irwin Professional Publishing, 1994.

Goldman, B., H. Sosin, and M. A. Gatto. "Path Dependent Options: Buy at the Low, Sell at the High." *Journal of Finance* 34 (December 1979): 1111–1127.

Heath, D., R. Jarrow, and A. Morton. "Bond Pricing and the Term Structure of Interest Rates: A Discrete Time Approximation." *Journal of Financial and Quantitative Analysis* 25, no. 4 (December 1990): 419–440.

Heath, D., R. Jarrow, and A. Morton. "Bond Pricing and the Term Structure of the Interest Rates: A New Methodology." *Econometrica* 60, no. 1 (1992): 77–105.

Ho, T. S., R. S. Stapleton, and M. G. Subrahmanyam. "The Valuation of American Options with Stochastic Interest Rates: A Generalization of the Geske-Johnson Technique." *Journal of Finance* 52, no. 2 (June 1997): 827–840.

Ho, T. S. Y., and S. B. Lee. "Term Structure Movements and Pricing Interest Rate Contingent Claims." *Journal of Finance* 41 (December 1986): 1011–1029.

Hull, J., and A. White. "The Pricing of Options on Interest Rate Caps and Floors Using the Hull-White Model." *Journal of Financial Engineering* 2, no. 3 (1993): 287–296.

Hull, J., and A. White. "Using Hull-White Interest Rate Trees." *Journal of Derivatives* (Spring 1996): 26–36.

Jamshidian, F. "An Exact Bond Option Pricing Formula." *Journal of Finance* 44 (March 1989): 205–209.

Johnson, R. Stafford, *Bond Evaluation, Selection, and Management*. 2nd Edition, John Wiley & Sons, 2010, Chapters 14 and 15.

Johnson, R. Stafford, Richard Zuber, and John Gandar, "Binomial Pricing of Fixed-Income Securities for Increasing and Decreasing Interest Rate Cases." *Applied Financial Economics*, 2006, 16, 1029–1046.

Johnson, R. Stafford, Richard Zuber, and John Gandar, "Binomial Interest Rate Tree: A Synopsis of Uses and Estimation Approaches." *Journal of Financial Education* 27 (2001): 53–75.

Taggart, R. A., *Quantitative Analysis for Investment Management*. Upper Saddle River, NJ: Prentice Hall, 1996, 118–160.

Problems and Questions

1. Assume: binomial process; current annualized spot rate on risk-free bond with maturity of one year of $S_0 = 5\%$; up and down parameters for period equal in length to one year of $u = 1.1$ and $d = 1/1.1$; length of binomial period equal to one year; probability of the spot rate increasing in one period of $q = 0.5$.

   a. Generate a two-period binomial tree of spot rates.

   b. Using the binomial tree, calculate the values at each node of a risk-free bond with a $100 face value, 5% annual coupon, and maturity of three years.

   c. Using the binomial tree, determine the value of a European call option with an exercise price of 100 and expiration of two years.

   d. Using the binomial tree, determine the value of an American call option with an exercise price of 100 and expiration of two years.

    e. Using the binomial tree, determine the value of a European put option with an exercise price of 100 and expiration of two years.

    f. Using the binomial tree, determine the value of an American put option with an exercise price of 100 and expiration of two years.

2. Assume the following: binomial process; current annualized spot rate on risk-free bond with maturity of 0.25 years of $S_0 = 4\%$; up and down parameters for period equal in length to 0.5 years of $u = 1.1$, $d = 1/1.1$; length of binomial period 0.5 years (six-month steps); probability of the spot rate increase in one period of $q = 0.5$.

    a. Generate a three-period binomial interest-rate tree of spot rates.

    b. Using the binomial tree, calculate the values at each node of a T-bill with a $100 face value and maturity of 0.25 years.

    c. Assuming a flat yield curve, calculate the values at each node of a futures contract on the above T-bill with the expiration on the futures being at the end of the third period (1.5 years).

3. Using the binomial tree from Question 2, determine the values of the following futures options on the T-bill futures described in Question 2:

    a. European call option with an exercise price of 99 and expiration of 1.5 years (the end of three periods).

    b. American call option with an exercise price of 99 and expiration of 1.5 years (the end of three periods).

    c. European put option with an exercise price of 99 and expiration of 1.5 years (the end of three periods).

    d. American put option with an exercise price of 99 and expiration of 1.5 years (the end of three periods).

4. Assume:

- Binomial process
- Current annualized spot rate on risk-free bond with maturity of 0.25 years of $S_0 = 4\%$
- Up and down parameters for period equal in length to 0.5 years of $u = 1.1$, $d = 1/1.1$
- Length of binomial period 0.5 years (six-month steps)
- Probability of the spot rate increase in one period of $q = 0.5$

    Generate a three-period binomial tree of spot rates. Using the binomial tree, determine the values of an interest rate call option and interest rate put options, each with exercise rates of 4%, spot rates as reference rates, times periods of 0.25 years, and notional principal of 100.

5. Given a current one-period spot rate of $S_0 = 10\%$, upward and downward parameters of $u = 1.1$ and $d = 0.9091$, and probability of the spot rate increasing in one period of $q = 0.5$:

    a. Generate a two-period binomial tree of spot rates.

    b. Using the binomial interest rate tree from Question 5.a, determine the value of a two-period, option-free 9% coupon bond with $F = 100$.

c. Using the binomial interest rate tree from Question 5.a, determine the value of the 9% bond assuming it is callable at a call price of $CP = 99$. Use the minimum constraint approach.

d. Using the binomial interest rate tree, show at each node the call option values of the callable bond ($CP = 99$). Given your call option values, determine the values at each node of the callable bond as the difference between the option-free values found in Question 5.b and the call option values. Do your callable bond values match the ones you found in Question 5.c.

e. Comment on values of your call options being equal to the present value of the interest savings the issuer realizes from refunding the bond at lower rates.

f. Using the binomial interest rate tree, determine the value of the bond assuming it is putable in periods one and two at a put price of $PP = 99$. Use the maximum constraint approach.

g. Using the binomial interest rate tree, show at each node the put option values of the putable bond ($PP = 99$). Given your put option values, determine the values at each node of the putable bond as the sum of the option-free bond values found in Question 1.b and the put option values. Do your putable bond values match the ones you found in Question 5.f?

6. Given an ABC convertible bond with $F = \$1,000$, maturity of three periods, Conversion Ratio $= 10$, current stock price of $\$100$, and $u = 1.1$, $d = 0.95$, and $q = 0.5$ on the stock:

a. Calculate the value of the bond using a binomial tree of stock prices. Assume no call on the bond and a flat yield curve at 10% that is not expected to change.

b. Calculate the value of the bond using a binomial tree of stock prices. Assume the bond is callable at $CP = \$1,200$ and a flat yield curve at 10% that is not expected to change.

7. Suppose a spot rate has the following prices over the past 13 quarters:

Quarter	Annualized Spot Rate (%)
y 1.1	5.5
y 1.2	5.0
y 1.3	4.7
y 1.4	4.4
y 2.1	4.7
y 2.2	5.0
y 2.3	5.4
y 2.4	5.0
y 3.1	4.7
y 3.2	4.4
y 3.3	4.7
y 3.4	5.0
y 4.1	5.5

   a. Calculate the spot rate's average logarithmic return and variance.

   b. What is the rate's annualized mean and variance?

   c. Calculate the spot rate's up and down parameters for periods with the following lengths:

     i. One quarter (h = length in years = 1/4)

     ii. One month (h = 1/12)

     iii. One week (h = 1/52)

     iv. One day (h = 1/360)

    Excel Problems: Problems 8 and 9 can be done using the Excel program: "Binominal Bond Valuation—Callable and Putable.xls." The program can be downloaded from the text's website.

8. Suppose the current spot rate in Question 7 is currently at 5%. Using the estimated spot rate's mean and variance calculated in Question 7.c determine the value of a five-year, 5% option-free bond (F = 100) using a binomial tree with monthly steps (h = 1/12). Determine the value of the bond given it is callable with a call price of 100.

9. Given the following:

   • Current spot = 0.08

   • Annualized mean for the spot rate's logarithmic return of 0.022

   • Annualized variance for the spot rate's logarithmic return of 0.0054

   • Binomial interest rate tree with monthly steps

   Determine the values of the following:

   a. Five-year, 8% option-free bond, with F = 100

   b. Five-year, 8% callable bond (F = 100) with call price = 100

   c. Five-year, 8% putable bond (F = 100) with put price = 100

10. Comment on the arbitrage-free features of valuing a bond using a binomial interest rate tree generated by estimating u and d in terms of mean and variance.

11. Explain the methodology for estimating a binomial tree using the calibration model. Comment on the arbitrage-free features of this approach.

12. Given a variability of $\sigma = \sqrt{hV_e^A} = 0.10$ and current one- and two-period spot rates of $S^m{}_1 = 0.07$ and $S^m{}_2 = 0.0804$:

   a. Generate a one-period binomial interest rate tree using the calibration model. (Hint: Try $S_d = 0.08148$.)

   b. Using the calibrated tree, determine the equilibrium price of a two-period, option-free, 10.5% coupon bond (F = 100).

   c. Does the binomial tree price the 10.5% option-free bond equal to the bond's equilibrium price? Comment on this feature of the calibration model.

13. Suppose a T-bond futures expiring in six months is priced at f_0 = 95,000 and has an annualized standard deviation of 0.10, and that the continuously compounded annual risk-free rate is 5%.

   a. Using the Black futures option model, calculate the equilibrium price for a six-month T-bond futures call option with an exercise price of $100,000.

   b. Using the Black futures option model, calculate the equilibrium price for a six-month T-bond futures put option with an exercise price of $100,000.

1. Using Bloomberg's OVME screen, determine the equilibrium price on a selected call and put options on a futures contract on a T-Note or T-bond. For information on how to find options from the SECF and CTM screens and how to upload the futures options, see section: "Bloomberg: Options Screens," Chapter 6. For information on how to value options on bond futures, see section: "Bloomberg Option Valuation Screens for Bond and Interest Rate Options, OVME" in Chapter 13. Guide:

   • To find futures on T-Note or T-Bond on SECF, click "Fixed Income" from the "Category" dropdown and then click "futr" tab or click "opts." Use OMON on the futures screen to find the futures options.
   • Select the options from the selected futures' OMON or CALL screen.
   • Load the option: Option Ticker <Comdty>.
   • Enter OVME.

   a. On OVME screen, determine the Black OPM price (select Black). Select Bloomberg's implied volatility, historical, or provide your own volatility estimate.
   b. Using the OVME screen for the call and put options contracts, evaluate the prices of the call and put options for different futures prices. Click the "Scenario" tab and set the axis for option prices and underlying futures prices.
   c. Using the OVME screen for the call and put options contracts, evaluate the Greeks for different futures prices and time to expiration by clicking the "Scenario" tab and setting the axis.

2. Create a portfolio of at least two options on the same futures you selected in Exercise 1 and evaluate the position in terms of the position's OPM value, delta, gamma, and theta. On the OVME screen, click the + icon next to "Deals" to add a new deal, and then click "Add Legs" from the grey "Leg" dropdown. Input information for each option in the input box (different exercise prices, expirations, call and/or put, and long and short positions). Click "Scenario" tab to view your position's value and profit-loss relation for different futures prices.

3. Using Bloomberg's OVME screen, determine the equilibrium price on a selected call and put option on a Eurodollar futures contract. For information on how to find options from the SECF and CTM screens and how to upload the futures options, see section: "Bloomberg: Options Screens," Chapter 6. For information on how to value options on bond futures, see section: "Bloomberg Option Valuation Screens for Bond and Interest Rate Options, OVME" in Chapter 13. Guide:

   • To find futures indexes on SECF, click "Fixed Income" from the "Category" dropdown and then click "futr" tab or click "opts." Use OMON on the futures screen to find the futures options.
   • Select the options from the selected futures' OMON or CALL screen.
   • Load the option: Option Ticker <Comdty>.
   • Enter OVME.

a. On the OVME screen, determine the Black OPM price (select Black). Select Bloomberg's implied volatility, historical, or provide your own volatility estimate.

b. Using the OVME screen for the call and put options contracts, evaluate the prices of the call and put options for different futures prices. Click the "Scenario" tab and set the axis for option prices and underlying futures prices.

4. Find descriptions, recent prices, and other information on a convertible bond. Use SECF, SRCH, or CSCH to search for convertible bonds. Upload the convertible's menu screen (convertible's Ticker <Corp>). Examine the price of the convertible and its option value using BVAL: BVAL <Enter>.

5. Use the Bloomberg SWPM screen to create and analyze a cap. Tabs to include in your analysis: Details, Resets, Cashflows, and Curves.

6. Use the Bloomberg SWPM screen to create and analyze a floor. Tabs to include in your analysis: Details, Resets, Cashflows, and Curves.

PART 4

Financial Swaps

CHAPTER 14

Interest Rate Swaps

A swap, by definition, is a legal arrangement between two parties to exchange specific payments. There are three types of financial swaps:

1. **Interest rate swaps:** The exchange of fixed-rate payments for floating-rate payments
2. **Credit default swaps:** the exchange of premium payments for default protection
3. **Currency swaps:** The exchange of liabilities in different currencies

In this chapter, we examine the markets, uses, and pricing of standard interest rate swaps and two interest rate swap derivatives—forward swaps and swaptions. In Chapter 15, we examine the markets, uses, and pricing of credit default swaps and currency swaps.

Generic Interest Rate Swaps

The simplest type of interest rate swap is the *plain vanilla swap* or *generic swap*. In this agreement, one party provides fixed-rate interest payments to another party who provides floating-rate payments. The parties to the agreement are *counterparties*. The party who pays fixed interest and receives floating is the *fixed-rate payer*; the other party (who pays floating and receives fixed) is the *floating-rate payer*.

On a generic swap, principal payments are not exchanged. As a result, the interest payments are based on a notional principal (*NP*).

The interest rate paid by the fixed payer often is specified in terms of the yield to maturity (*YTM*) on a T-note plus basis points; the rate paid by the floating payer on a generic swap is the LIBOR. Swap payments on a generic swap are semiannual and the maturities typically range from 3 to 10 years. In the swap contract, a trade date, effective date, settlement date, and maturity date are specified. The *trade date* is the date the parties agree to commit to the swap; the *effective date* is the date when interest begins to accrue; the *settlement* or *payment date* is when interest payments are made (interest is paid in arrears six months after the effective date); and the *maturity date* is the last payment date. On the payment date, only the interest differential between the counterparties is paid. That is, generic swap payments are based on a *net settlement basis*: The counterparty owing the greater amount pays the difference between what is owed and what is received. Thus, if a fixed-rate payer owes $3 million and a floating-rate payer owes $2.5 million, then only a $0.5 million payment by the fixed payer to the floating payer is made. All of the terms of the swap are specified in a legal agreement signed by both parties called the *confirmation*. The drafting of the confirmation often follows document forms suggested by the *International Swap and Derivative Association* (ISDA) in New York. This organization provides a number of master agreements delineating the terminology used in many swap agreements (e.g., what happens in the case of default, the business day convention, and the like).

Interest Rate Swap: Example

Consider an interest rate swap with a maturity of three years, first effective date of 3/15/Y1 and a maturity date of 3/15/Y3. In this swap agreement, assume the fixed-rate payer agrees to pay the current YTM on a three-year T-note of 4% plus 50 basis points and the floating-rate payer agrees to pay the six-month LIBOR as determined on the effective dates with no basis points. Also, assume the semiannual interest rates are determined by dividing the annual rates (LIBOR and 4.5%) by two. Finally, assume the notional principal on the swap is $10 million.

Exhibit 14.1 shows the interest payments on each settlement date based on assumed LIBORs on the effective dates. In examining the table, several points should be noted. First, the payments are determined by the LIBOR prevailing six months prior to the payment date; thus, payers on swaps would know their obligations in advance of the payment date. Second, when the LIBOR is below the fixed 4.5% rate, the fixed-rate payer pays the interest differential to the floating-rate payer; when it is above 4.5%, the fixed-rate payer receives the interest differential from the floating-rate payer. The net interest received by the fixed-rate payer is shown in Column 5 of the table, and the net interest received by the floating-rate payer is shown in Column 6.

The fixed-rate payer's position is very similar to a short position in a series of Eurodollar futures contracts, with the futures price determined by the fixed rate. The fixed payer's cash flows also can be replicated by the fixed payer shorting (issuing) a $10 million, 4.5% fixed-rate bond at par and buying a $10 million, three-year, floating-rate note (FRN) paying the LIBOR.

The floating-rate payer's position, on the other hand, is similar to a long position in a Eurodollar strip, and it can be replicated by shorting (issuing) a three-year,

EXHIBIT 14.1   Interest Rate Swap: 4.5%/LIBOR Swap with NP = $10 million

1	2	3	4	5	6
Effective Dates	LIBOR	Floating-Rate Payer's Payment*	Fixed-Rate Payer's Payment**	Net Interest Received by Fixed-Rate Payer Column 3 − Column 4	Net Interest Received by Floating-Rate Payer Column 4 − Column 3
3/15/Y1	0.035				
9/15/Y1	0.040	$175,000	$225,000	−$50,000	$50,000
3/15/Y2	0.045	$200,000	$225,000	−$25,000	$25,000
9/15/Y2	0.050	$225,000	$225,000	$0	$0
3/15/Y3	0.055	$250,000	$225,000	$25,000	−$25,000
9/15/y3	0.060	$275,000	$225,000	$50,000	−$50,000
3/15/Y3		$300,000	$225,000	$75,000	−$75,000

*(LIBOR/2)($10,000,000)
**(0.045/2)*($10,000,000)

$10 million FRN paying the LIBOR and purchasing a three-year, $10 million, 4.5% fixed-rate bond at par.

Synthetic Loans

One of the important uses of swaps is in creating a synthetic fixed-rate or floating-rate liability or changing a conventional fixed-rate loan (or floating) to a floating-rate (fixed-rate) one. To illustrate, suppose a corporation with an AAA credit rating wants a three-year, $10 million fixed-rate loan starting on 3/15/Y1. Suppose one possibility available to the company is to borrow $10 million from a bank at a fixed rate of 5% (assume semiannual payments) with a loan maturity of three years. Suppose, however, that the bank also is willing to provide the company with a three-year floating-rate loan, with the rate set equal to the LIBOR on March 15 and September 15 each year for three years. If a swap agreement identical to the one described above were available, then instead of a direct fixed-rate loan, the company alternatively could attain a fixed-rate loan by borrowing $10 million on the floating-rate loan, then fix the interest rate by taking a fixed-rate payer's position on the swap:

Conventional floating-rate loan	Pay floating rate
Swap: fixed-rate payer position	Pay fixed rate
Swap: fixed-rate payer position	Receive floating rate
Synthetic fixed rate	Pay fixed rate

As shown in Exhibit 14.2, if the floating-rate loan is combined with a swap, any change in the LIBOR would be offset by an opposite change in the net receipts on the swap position. In this example, the company (as shown in the exhibit) would end up paying a constant $225,000 every sixth month, which equates to an

EXHIBIT 14.2 Synthetic Fixed-Rate Loan: Floating-Rate Loan set at LIBOR and Fixed-Payer
Position on 4.5%/LIBOR Swap

1	2	3	4	5	6	7	8
Effective Dates	LIBOR	Swap Floating-Rate Payer's Payment*	Swap Fixed-Rate Payer's Payment**	Swap Net Interest Received by Fixed-Rate Payer Column 3 − Column 4	Loan Interest Paid on Floating-Rate Loan*	Synthetic Loan Payment on Swap and Loan Column 6 − Column 5	Synthetic Loan Effective Annualized Rate***
3/15/Y1	0.0350						
9/15/Y1	0.0400	$175,000	$225,000	−$50,000	$175,000	$225,000	0.045
3/15/Y2	0.0450	$200,000	$225,000	−$25,000	$200,000	$225,000	0.045
9/15/Y2	0.0500	$225,000	$225,000	$0	$225,000	$225,000	0.045
3/15/Y23	0.0550	$250,000	$225,000	$25,000	$250,000	$225,000	0.045
9/15/Y3	0.0600	$275,000	$225,000	$50,000	$275,000	$225,000	0.045
3/15/Y4		$300,000	$225,000	$75,000	$300,000	$225,000	0.045

*(LIBOR/2)($10,000,000)
**(0.045/2)*($10,000,000)
***2 (Payment on Swap and Loan)/$10,000,000

annualized borrowing rate of 4.5%: $R = 2(\$225,000)/\$10,000,000 = 0.045$. Thus,
the corporation would be better off combining the swap position as a fixed-rate payer
with the floating-rate loan to create a synthetic fixed-rate loan than simply taking the
straight 5% fixed-rate loan.

In contrast, a synthetic floating-rate loan is formed by combining a floating-rate
payer's position with a fixed-rate loan. This loan then can be used as an alternative to
a floating-rate loan:

Conventional fixed-rate loan	Pay fixed rate
Swap: Floating-rate payer position	Pay floating rate
Swap: Floating-rate payer position	Receive fixed rate
Synthetic floating rate	Pay floating rate

An example of a synthetic floating-rate loan is shown in Exhibit 14.3. The synthetic loan is formed with a 4% fixed-rate loan (semiannual payments) and the
floating-rate payer's position on our illustrate swap. As shown in the exhibit, the synthetic floating-rate loan yields a 0.5% lower interest rate each period (annualized rate)
than a floating-rate loan tied to the LIBOR.

Note, in both of the above examples, the borrower is able to attain a better borrowing rate with a synthetic loan using swaps than with a direct loan. When differences between the rates on actual and synthetic loans do exist, then swaps provide an
apparent arbitrage use in which borrowers and investors can obtain better rates with
synthetic positions formed with swap positions than they can from conventional loans.

EXHIBIT 14.3 Synthetic Floating-Rate Loan: 4.00% Fixed-Rate Loan and Floating-Payer Position on 4.5%/LIBOR Swap

1	2	3	4	5	6	7	8
Effective Dates	LIBOR	Swap Floating-Rate Payer's Payment*	Swap Fixed-Rate Payer's Payment**	Swap Net Interest Received by Floating-Rate Payer Column 4 − Column 3	Loan Interest Paid on 5% Fixed-Rate Loan	Synthetic Loan Payment on Swap and Loan Column 6 − Column 5	Synthetic Loan Effective Annualized Rate***
3/15/Y1	0.0350						
9/15/Y1	0.0400	$175,000	$225,000	$50,000	$200,000	$150,000	0.030
3/15/Y2	0.0450	$200,000	$225,000	$25,000	$200,000	$175,000	0.035
9/15/Y2	0.0500	$225,000	$225,000	$0	$200,000	$200,000	0.040
3/15/Y3	0.0550	$250,000	$225,000	−$25,000	$200,000	$225,000	0.045
9/15/Y3	0.0600	$275,000	$225,000	−$50,000	$200,000	$250,000	0.050
3/15/Y4		$300,000	$225,000	−$75,000	$200,000	$275,000	0.055

*(LIBOR/2)($10,000,000)
**(0.045/2)*($10,000,000)
***2 (Payment on Swap and Loan)/$10,000,000

Similarities between Swaps and Bond Positions and Eurodollar Futures Strips

Bond Positions

Swap positions can be replicated with opposite positions in a fixed-rate bond and floating-rate note (FRN). As noted, a fixed-rate payer position is equivalent to buying a FRN paying the LIBOR and shorting (issuing) a fixed-rate bond at the swap's fixed rate. From the previous example, the purchase of $10 million worth of three-year FRNs with the rate reset every six months at the LIBOR and the sale of $10 million worth of three-year, 4.5% fixed-rate bonds at par would yield the same cash flow as the fixed-rate payer's swap. On the other hand, a floating-rate payer's position is equivalent to shorting (or issuing) a FRN at the LIBOR and buying a fixed-rate bond at the swap's fixed rate. Thus, the purchase of $10 million worth of three-year 4.5% fixed-rate bonds at par and the sale of $10 million worth of FRNs paying the LIBOR would yield the same cash flow as the floating-rate payer's swap in the above example.

Eurodollar Futures Strip

A swap can also be replicated with a position in Eurodollar strip. For example, the fixed-rate payer position on our illustrative swap can be replicated with a short position on Eurodollar strip consisting of six forward contracts with face values of $10 million, maturities of six months, and each priced at 95.5 (CME index) or discount yield of $R_D = 4.5\%$. Exhibit 14.4 shows the cash flows at the expiration dates from closing the short Eurodollar contracts at the same assumed LIBOR used in the above swap

EXHIBIT 14.4 Short and Long Positions in Eurodollar Futures

1	2	3	4	5
Closing Dates	LIBOR	f_T	Cash Flow from Short Position $[f_0 - f_T]$	Cash Flow from Long Position $[f_T - f_0]$
3/15/Y1	0.035	$9,825,000	−$50,000	$50,000
9/15/Y1	0.040	$9,800,000	−$25,000	$25,000
3/15/Y2	0.045	$9,775,000	$0	$0
9/15/Y2	0.050	$9,750,000	$25,000	−$25,000
3/15/Y3	0.055	$9,725,000	$50,000	−$50,000
9/15/Y3	0.060	$9,700,000	$75,000	−$75,000

$f_0 = 9,775,000$

$$f_T = \left[\frac{100 - (LIBOR)(180/360)}{100} \right] (\$10,000,000)$$

example, with the Eurodollar settlement Index being 100 − LIBOR. Comparing the fixed-rate payer's net receipts shown in Column 5 of Exhibit 14.1 with the cash flows from the short positions on the Eurodollar strip shown in Exhibit 14.4, one can see that the two positions yield the same numbers. However, one difference to note between the Eurodollar strip and the swap is the six-month differential between the swap payment and the futures payments. This time differential is a result of the interest payments on the swap being determined by the LIBOR at the beginning of the period, whereas the futures position's profit is based on the LIBOR at the end of the period.

Swap Markets

Structure

Swap banks consist primarily of commercial banks and investment bankers who act as brokers and dealers. As brokers swap banks match parties with opposite needs (see Exhibit 14.5). Many of the first interest rate swaps were customized brokered deals between counterparties, with the parties often negotiating and transacting directly between themselves. With a *brokered swap*, the swap bank's role in the contract is to bring the parties together and provide information. Once the swap agreement is closed, the swap broker usually has only a minor continuing role. With some brokered swaps, the swap bank guarantees one or both sides of the transaction. With many, however, the counterparties assume the credit risk and make their own assessment of the other party's default potential.

One of the problems with a brokered swap is that it requires each party to have knowledge of the other party's risk profile. This problem led to swap banks taking more positions as dealers instead of as brokers. With *dealer swaps*, the swap dealer makes commitments to enter a swap as a counterparty before the other party has been located. Each of the counterparties contract separately with the swap bank, which acts as a counterparty to each. The counterparties, in turn, assume the credit risk of the financial institution instead of that of the other party, whereas the swap dealer assumes the credit risk of both of the end parties.

In acting as dealers, swap banks often match a swap agreement with multiple end parties. For example, as illustrated in Exhibit 14.5, a $30 million fixed-for-floating swap between a swap dealer and Party A is matched with two $15 million floating-for-fixed swaps. Ideally, a swap bank tries to maintain a perfect hedge. In practice, though, swap banks are prepared to enter a swap agreement without an opposite counterparty. This practice is referred to as *warehousing*. In warehousing, swap banks will hedge their swap positions with opposite positions in T-notes and FRNs or Eurodollar futures contracts. For example, a swap bank could hedge a $10 million, two-year floating-rate position by shorting $10 million worth of two-year T-notes, and then use the proceeds to buy FRNs tied to the LIBOR. In general, most of the commitments a swap bank assumes are hedged through a portfolio of alternative positions—opposite swap positions, spot positions in T-notes and FRNs, or futures positions. This type of portfolio management by swap banks is referred to as *running a dynamic book*.

Swap Market Price Quotes

On a generic swap, the floating rate on a swap is quoted flat without basis points, and the fixed rate is quoted in terms of the yield to maturity (*YTM*) on an on-the-run (recently issued) T-bond or T-note. In a dealer swap, the swap dealer's compensation comes from the bid-ask spread extended to the counterparties. The quotes are stated in terms of the bid rate the dealer will pay as a fixed payer in return for the LIBOR, and the ask rate the dealer will receive as a floating payer in return for paying the LIBOR. For example, a 70/75 swap spread implies the dealer will buy (take fixed-payer position)

EXHIBIT 14.5 Swap Market Structure

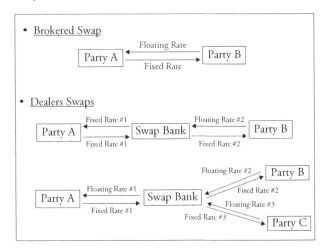

at 70 basis points over the T-note yield and sell (take floating-payer position) at 75 basis points over the T-note yield. The average of the bid and ask rates is known as the *swap rate*.

Opening Swap Positions

Suppose the treasurer of a corporation wants to fix the rate on a five-year, $50 million floating-rate debt of the company by taking a fixed-rate payer's position on a five-year swap with a *NP* of $50 million. After assessing the corporation's credit risk, suppose a swap dealer gives the treasurer a swap quote of 50 basis points (bp) over the current five-year T-note yield, and the corporate treasurer, in turn, accepts. Thus, the treasurer would agree to take the fixed payer's position on the swap at 50 bp above the current five-year T-note. After agreeing to the terms, the actual rate paid by the fixed payer would typically be set once the swap banker hedges her swap position by taking, for example, a position on an on-the-run T-note. After confirming a quote on a five-year T-note from her bond trader, the swap banker would then instruct the trader to sell (or short) $50 million of five-year T-notes with the proceeds invested in a five-year FRN paying LIBOR. The yield on the T-note purchased plus the 50 bp would determine the actual rate on the swap. The swap banker would most likely close the bond positions used to hedge the swap later as she finds a floating-rate swap position to take on one or more swaps with similar terms.

Note, since swap banks can hedge an opening swap position with positions in an on-the-run T-note and FRN, the rates they, in turn, set on a swap contract is determined by the current T-note yields (with basis points added to reflect credit risk). Thus, the rates on generic swap contracts are tied to T-note yields.

Closing Swap Positions

Prior to maturity, swap positions can be closed by selling the swap to a swap dealer or another party. If the swap is closed in this way, the new counterparty either pays or receives an upfront fee to or from the existing counterparty in exchange for receiving the original counterparty's position. Alternatively, the swap holder could also hedge his position by taking an opposite position in a current swap or possibly by hedging the position for the remainder of the maturity period with a futures position. A fixed-rate payer that wants to close his position could do so by selling the swap to a dealer, taking a floating-rate payer's position in a new swap contract, or by going long in an appropriate futures contract.

If the fixed-payer swap holder decides to hedge his position by taking an opposite position on a new swap, the new swap position would require a payment of the LIBOR that would cancel out the receipt of the LIBOR on the first swap. The difference in the positions would therefore be equal to the difference in the fixed interest that is paid on the first swap and the fixed interest rate received on the offsetting swap. For example, suppose in our first illustrative swap example (Exhibit 14.1), a decline in interest rates occurs one year after the initiation of the swap, causing the fixed-rate payer on the 4.5% for LIBOR swap to want to close his position. To this end, suppose the fixed-rate payer offsets his position by entering a new two-year swap as a floating-rate payer in which he agrees to pay the LIBOR for a 4% fixed rate. The two positions would result in a fixed payment of $25,000 semiannually for two years ((.005/2) NP). If interest rates decline over the next year, this offsetting position would turn out to be the correct strategy.

Offsetting Swap Positions		
Original swap: Fixed payer's position	Pay 4.5%	−4.5%
Original swap: Fixed payer's position	Receive LIBOR	+LIBOR
Offsetting swap: Floating payer's position	Pay LIBOR	−LIBOR
Offsetting swap: Floating payer's position	Receive 4.0%	+4%
Annual	Pay 0.5%	−0.5%
Semiannual	Pay 0.25%	−0.25%

Instead of hedging the position, the fixed-rate payer is more likely to close his position by simply selling it to a swap dealer. In acquiring a fixed position at 4.5%, the swap dealer would have to take a floating-payer's position to hedge the acquired fixed position. If the fixed rate on a new two-year swap were at 4%, the dealer would likewise lose $25,000 semiannually for two years on the two swap positions, given a *NP* of $10 million. Thus, the price the swap bank would charge the fixed payer for buying his swap would be at least equal to the present value of $25,000 for the next four semiannual periods. Given an annual discount rate of 4%, the swap bank would charge the fixed payer a minimum of $95,193 for buying his swap:

$$SV_0^{\text{Fix}} = \sum_{t=1}^{4} \frac{-\$25,000}{(1 + (0.04/2))^t} = -\$95,193$$

In contrast, if rates had increased, the fixed payer would be able to sell the swap to a dealer at a premium. For example, if the fixed rate on a new swap were 5%, a swap dealer would realize a semiannual return of $25,000 for the next two years by buying the 4.5%/LIBOR swap and hedging it with a floating position on a two-year, 5%/LIBOR swap. Given a 5% discount rate, the dealer would pay the fixed payer a maximum of $94,049 for his 5.5%/LIBOR swap:

$$SV_0^{\text{Fix}} = \sum_{t=1}^{4} \frac{\$25,000}{(1 + (0.05/2))^t} = \$94,049$$

Swap Valuation

At origination, most plain vanilla swaps have an economic value of zero. This means that the counterparties are not required to pay each other in the agreement. An economic value of zero requires that the swap's underlying bond positions trade at par—*par value swap*. If this were not the case, then one of the counterparties would need to compensate the other. In this case, the economic value of the swap is not zero. Such a swap is referred to as an *off-market swap*.

Although most plain vanilla swaps are originally par value swaps with economic values of zero, as the above example illustrated, the economic values of existing swaps change over time as rates change; that is, existing swaps become off-market swaps as rates change. In our previous example, the fixed-payer's position on the 4.5%/LIBOR swap had a value of −$95,193 one year later when the fixed-rate on new two-year par value swaps was 4%; that is, the holder of the fixed position would have to pay the swap bank at least $95,193 to assume the swap. On the other hand, the fixed-payer's position on the 4.5%/LIBOR swap had a value of $94,049 when the fixed rate on new two-year par value swaps was 5%; that is, the holder of the fixed position would receive $94,049 from the swap bank.

Just the opposite values apply to the floating position. Continuing with our illustrative example, if the fixed rate on new two-year par value swaps were at 4%, then a swap bank who assumed a floating position on a 4.5%/LIBOR swap and then hedged it with a fixed position on a current two-year 4%/LIBOR swap would gain $25,000 semiannually over the next two years. As a result, the swap bank would be willing to pay $95,193 for the floating position. Thus, the floating position on the 4.5% swap would have a value of $95,193:

Offsetting Swap Positions		
Original swap: Floating payer's position	Pay LIBOR	−LIBOR
Original swap: Floating payer's position	Receive 4.5%	+4.5%
Offsetting swap: Fixed payer's position	Pay 4%	−4%
Offsetting swap: Fixed payer's position	Receive LIBOR	+LIBOR
$SV_0^{FL} = \sum_{t=1}^{4} \dfrac{\$25{,}000}{(1 + (0.04/2))^t} = \$95{,}193$	Receive 0.5% (annual) Receive 0.25% (semiannual)	+0.5% (annual) +0.25 (semiannual)

If the fixed rate on new two-year par value swaps were at 5%, then a swap bank assuming the floating position on a 4.5%/LIBOR swap and hedging it with a fixed position on a current two-year 5%/LIBOR swap would lose $25,000 semiannually over the next year. As a result, the swap bank would charge $94,049 for assuming the floating position. Thus, the floating position on the 4.5% swap would have a negative value of $94,049:

Offsetting Swap Positions		
Original swap: Floating payer's position	Pay LIBOR	−LIBOR
Original swap: Floating payer's position	Receive 5.5%	+5.5%
Offsetting swap: Fixed payer's position	Pay 6%	−5%
Offsetting swap: Fixed payer's position	Receive LIBOR	+LIBOR
$SV_0^{FL} = \sum_{t=1}^{4} \dfrac{-\$25{,}000}{(1 + (0.05/2))^t} = -\$94{,}049$	Pay 0.5% (annual) Pay 0.25 (semiannual)	−0.5% (annual) −0.25% (semiannual)

Note that the swap values were obtained by discounting the net cash flows at the current YTM. This approach to valuing off-market swaps is referred to as the *YTM approach*. However, recall that the equilibrium price of a bond is obtained by discounting all of the bond's cash flows by their appropriate spot rates. Similar to bond valuation, the equilibrium value of a swap is obtained by discounting each of the swap's cash flows by their appropriate spot rates. The valuation of swaps using spot rates is referred to as the *zero-coupon approach*. A corollary to the zero-coupon approach to valuation is that in the absence of arbitrage, the fixed rate on the swap (the swap rate) is that rate that makes the present value of the swap's fixed-rate payments equal to the present value of the swap's floating payments, with implied forward rates being used to estimate the future floating payments. This valuation approach is presented in Appendix 14A.

Comparative Advantage

Suppose the Sun Chemical Company wants to raise $500 million with a five-year loan to finance an expansion of one of its production plants. Based on its moderate credit ratings, suppose Sun can borrow five-year funds at a 5.5% fixed rate or at a floating rate equal to LIBOR + 150 bp. Given the choice of financing, Sun prefers the fixed-rate loan. Suppose the treasurer of the Sun Company contacts her investment banker for suggestions on how to finance the acquisition. The investment banker knows that Boeing is also looking for five-year funding to finance its proposed $500 million plant expansion. Given its high credit rating, suppose Boeing can borrow the funds for five years at a fixed rate of 4.5% or at a floating rate equal to the LIBOR + 100 bp. Given the choice, Boeing prefers a floating-rate loan. In summary, Sun and Boeing have the following fixed and floating rate loan opportunities:

Company	Fixed Rate	Floating Rate	Preference	Comparative Advantage
Sun Company	5.5%	LIBOR + 150 bp	Fixed	Floating
Boeing Company	4.5%	LIBOR + 100 bp	Floating	Fixed
Credit Spread	100 bp	50 bp		

In this case, Boeing has an absolute advantage in both the fixed and floating markets because of its higher quality rating. However, after looking at the credit spreads of the borrowers in each market, the investment banker realizes that there is a *comparative advantage* for Boeing in the fixed market and a comparative advantage for Sun in the floating market. That is, Boing has a relative advantage in the fixed market where it gets 100 basis points less than Sun. Sun, in turn, has a relative advantage (or relatively less disadvantage) in the floating-rate market where it only pays 50 basis points more than Boeing. Thus, lenders in the fixed-rate market apparently assess the difference between the two creditors to be worth 100 basis points, whereas lenders in the floating-rate market assess the difference to be only 50 basis points. Whenever a comparative advantage exists, opportunities can be realized by each firm borrowing in the market where it has a comparative advantage and then swapping loans or having a swap bank set up a swap.

For the swap to work, the two companies cannot just pass on their respective costs. Typically, the companies divide the differences in credit spreads, with the most creditworthy company taking the most savings. In this case, suppose the investment banker arranges a five-year, 3.75%/LIBOR generic swap with a NP of $500 million in which Sun takes the fixed-rate payer position and Boeing takes the floating-rate payer position.

The Sun Company would then issue a $500 million FRN paying LIBOR + 150 bp. This loan, combined with the fixed-rate position on the 3.75%/LIBOR swap would give Sun a synthetic fixed-rate loan paying 5.25%, which is 25 basis points less than its direct fixed-rate loan:

Sun Company's Synthetic Fixed-Rate Loan		
Issue FRN	Pay LIBOR + 150bp	−LIBOR − 1.50%
Swap: Fixed-rate payer's position	Pay 3.75%	−3.75%
Swap: Fixed-rate payer's position	Receive LIBOR	+LIBOR
Synthetic fixed rate	Pay 3.75% + 1.50%	−5.25%
Direct fixed rate	Pay 5.5%	−5.5%

Boeing, on the other hand, would issue a $500 million, 4.5% fixed-rate bond that, when combined with its floating-rate position on the 3.75%/LIBOR swap, would give Boeing a synthetic floating-rate loan paying LIBOR plus 75 bp, which is 25 basis points less than the rates paid on the direct floating-rate loan of LIBOR plus 100 bp:

Boeing's Synthetic Floating-Rate Loan		
Issue 4.5% fixed-rate bond	Pay 4.5%	−4.5%
Swap: Floating-rate payer's position	Pay LIBOR	−LIBOR
Swap: Floating-rate payer's position	Receive 3.75%	+3.75%
Synthetic floating rate	Pay LIBOR + 0.75%	−LIBOR − 0.75%
Direct floating rate	Pay LIBOR + 100bp	−LIBOR − 1.00%

Thus, the swap makes it possible for both companies to create synthetic loans with better rates than direct ones.

As a rule, for a swap to provide gains, at least one of the counterparties must have a comparative advantage in one market. The total gain available to each party depends on whether one party has an absolute advantage in both markets or each has an absolute advantage in one market. If one party has an absolute advantage in both markets (as in this case), then the arbitrage gain is the difference in the comparative advantages in each market: 50 bp = 100 bp − 50 bp. In this case, Sun and Boeing split the difference in the 50 bp gain. In contrast, if each party has an absolute advantage in one market, then the arbitrage gain is equal to the sum of the comparative advantages.

Hidden Option

The comparative advantage argument is one explanation for the dramatic growth in the swap market. Some scholars (Smith, Smithson, and Wakeman) argue that the credit spreads that exist in the fixed and floating market are due to the nature of the contracts available to firms in fixed and floating markets. In the floating market, the lender usually has the opportunity to review the floating rate each period and increase the spread over the LIBOR if the borrower's creditworthiness has deteriorated. This hidden option, though, does not usually exist in the fixed market.

In the preceding example, the Sun Company is able to get a synthetic fixed rate at 5.25% (0.25% less than the direct loan). However, using the hidden option argument, this 5.25% rate is only realized if Sun can maintain its creditworthiness and continue to borrow at a floating rate that is 150 basis points above LIBOR. If its credit ratings were to subsequently decline and it had to pay 200 basis points above the LIBOR, then its synthetic fixed rate would increase to reflect the deterioration in its credit ratings.

Swap Applications

Arbitrage Applications — Synthetic Positions

In general, the presence of comparative advantage or a hidden option makes it possible to create not only synthetic loans with lower rates than direct, but also synthetic investments with rates exceeding those from direct investments. To illustrate this, four cases showing how swaps are used to create synthetic fixed-rate and floating-rate loans and investments are presented below.

Synthetic Fixed-Rate Loan

Suppose a company is planning on borrowing $50 million for five years at a fixed-rate. Given a swap market, suppose its alternatives are to issue a five-year, 5%, fixed-rate bond or create a synthetic fixed-rate bond by issuing a five-year floating-rate notes paying LIBOR plus 100 bp and taking a fixed-rate payer's position on a swap with a *NP* of $50 million. The synthetic fixed-rate note will be equivalent to the direct fixed-rate loan if it is formed with a swap that has a fixed rate equal to 4%:

Synthetic Fixed-Rate Loan		
Issue FRN	Pay LIBOR + 1%	−LIBOR − 1%
Swap: Fixed-rate payer's position	Pay 4% fixed rate	−4%
Swap: Fixed-rate payer's position	Receive LIBOR	+LIBOR
Synthetic rate	Pay 4% + 1%	−5%
Direct loan rate	Pay 5%	−5%

If the company can obtain a fixed rate on a swap that is less than 4%, then the company would find it cheaper to finance with the synthetic fixed-rate note than the direct. For example, if the company could obtain a 3.75%/LIBOR swap, then the company would be able to create a synthetic 4.75% fixed-rate loan by issuing a floating-rate FRN at LIBOR plus 100 basis points and taking the fixed payer's position on the 3.75%/LIBOR swap:

Synthetic Fixed-Rate Loan		
Issue floating-rate note	Pay LIBOR + 1%	−LIBOR − 1%
Swap: Fixed-rate payer's position	Pay 3.75% fixed rate	−3.75%
Swap: Fixed-rate payer's position	Receive LIBOR	+LIBOR
Synthetic rate	Pay 3.75% + 1%	−4.75%
Direct loan rate	Pay 5%	−5%

Synthetic Floating-Rate Loan

Suppose a bank has just made a five-year, $30 million floating-rate loan that is reset every six months at the LIBOR plus 100BP. The bank could finance this floating-rate asset by either selling CDs every six months at the LIBOR or by creating a synthetic floating-rate loan by selling a five-year fixed-rate note at 4.5% and taking a floating-rate payer's position on a five-year swap with a NP of $30 million. The synthetic floating-rate loan will be equivalent to the direct floating-rate loan paying LIBOR if the swap has a fixed rate that is equal to the 4.5% fixed rate on the note:

Synthetic Floating-Rate Loan		
Issue 4.5% fixed-rate note	Pay 4.5% fixed rate	−4.5%
Swap: Floating-rate payer's position	Pay LIBOR	−LIBOR
Swap: Floating-rate payer's position	Receive 4.5% fixed rate	+4.5%
Synthetic rate	Pay LIBOR	−LIBOR
Direct loan rate	Pay LIBOR	−LIBOR

Thus, if the bank can obtain a fixed rate on the swap that is greater than 4.5%, say 5.0%, then it would find it cheaper to finance its floating-rate loan asset by issuing fixed-rate notes at 4.5% and taking the floating-rate payer's position on the swap. By doing this, the bank's effective interest payments are 50 basis points less than LIBOR with a synthetic floating-rate loan formed by selling the 4.5% fixed rate note and taking a floating-rate payer's position on a five-year, 5.0%/LIBOR swap with NP of $30 million:

Synthetic Floating-Rate Loan		
Issue 4.5% fixed-rate note	Pay 4.5% fixed rate	−4.5%
Swap: Floating-rate payer's position	Pay LIBOR	−LIBOR
Swap: Floating-rate payer's position	Receive 5.0% fixed rate	+5.0%
Synthetic rate	Pay LIBOR − 0.5%	−(LIBOR − 0.5%)
Direct loan rate	Pay LIBOR	−LIBOR

Synthetic Fixed-Rate Investment

In the early days of the swap market, swaps were primarily used as a liability management tool. In the late 1980s, investors began to use swaps to try to increase the yield on their investments. A swap used with an asset is sometimes referred to as an *asset-based interest rate swap* or simply an asset swap. In terms of synthetic positions, asset-based swaps can be used to create either fixed-rate or floating-rate investment positions.

Consider the case of an investment fund that plans to invest $50 million in five-year, investment-grade, option-free, fixed-rate bonds. If the *YTM* on such bonds is 6%, then the investment company could invest $50 million in the 6% coupon bonds at par. Alternatively, it could try to earn a higher return by creating a synthetic fixed-rate bond by buying five-year, investment-grade FRNs currently paying the LIBOR plus 100 basis points and taking a floating-rate payer's position on a five-year swap with a *NP* of $50 million. If the fixed rate on the swap is equal to 5%, then the synthetic fixed-rate investment will yield the same return as the 6% fixed-rate bonds:

Synthetic Fixed-Rate Investment		
Purchase FRN	Receive LIBOR + 1%	+LIBOR + 1%
Swap: Floating-rate payer's position	Pay LIBOR	−LIBOR
Swap: Floating-rate payer's position	Receive 5% fixed rate	+5%
Synthetic rate	Receive 5% + 1%	+6%
Direct investment rate	Receive 6%	+6%

If the fixed rate on the swap is greater than 5%, then the synthetic fixed-rate investment will yield a higher return than the 6% bonds. For example, if the investment company took a floating-payer's position on a 5.50%/LIBOR swap with maturity of five years, *NP* of 50 million, and effective dates coinciding with the FRNs' dates, then the investment company would earn a fixed rate of 6.50%:

Synthetic Fixed-Rate Investment		
Purchase FRN	Receive LIBOR + 1%	+LIBOR + 1%
Swap: Floating-rate payer's position	Pay LIBOR	−LIBOR
Swap: Floating-rate payer's position	Receive 5.50% fixed rate	+5.50%
Synthetic rate	Receive 6.50%	+6.50%
Direct investment rate	Receive 6%	+6%

Synthetic Floating-Rate Investment

This time consider an investment fund that is looking to invest $50 million for three years in a FRN. Suppose the fund can either invest directly in a high quality, five-year FRN paying LIBOR plus 50 basis points, or it can create a synthetic floating-rate investment by investing in a five-year, 7% fixed-rate note selling at par and taking a fixed-rate payer's position. If the fixed rate on the swap is equal to 6.5%, then the synthetic floating-rate investment will yield the same return as the FRN:

Synthetic Floating-Rate Investment		
Purchase fixed-rate note	Receive 7%	+7%
Swap: Fixed-rate payer's position	Pay 6.5% fixed rate	−6.5%
Swap: Fixed-rate payer's position	Receive LIBOR	+LIBOR
Synthetic rate	Receive LIBOR + 0.5%	+ LIBOR + 0.5%
Floating investment rate	Receive LIBOR + 0.5%	+LIBOR + 0.5%

If the fixed rate on the swap is less than 6.5%, then the synthetic floating-rate investment will yield a higher return than the FRN.

For example, the fund could obtain a yield of LIBOR plus 100 basis points from a synthetic floating-rate investment formed with an investment in the five-year, 7% fixed-rate note and fixed-rate payer's position on a 6%/LIBOR swap:

Synthetic Floating-Rate Investment		
Purchase fixed-rate note	Receive 7%	+7%
Swap: Fixed-rate payer's position	Pay 6% fixed rate	−6%
Swap: Fixed-rate payer's position	Receive LIBOR	+LIBOR
Synthetic rate	Receive LIBOR + 1%	+LIBOR + 1%
Floating investment rate	Receive LIBOR + 0.5%	+LIBOR + 0.5%

Hedging

Hedging with swaps is done to minimize the market risk of positions currently exposed to interest rate changes. For example, suppose a company had previously financed its capital projects with intermediate-term FRNs tied to the LIBOR. Furthermore, suppose the company was expecting higher interest rates and wanted to fix the rate on its floating-rate debt. To this end, one alternative would be for the company to refund its floating-rate debt with fixed-rate obligations. This, though, would require the cost of issuing new debt (underwriting, registration, etc.), as well as the cost of calling the current FRNs or buying the notes in the market if they were not callable. Thus, refunding would be a relatively costly alternative. Another possibility would be for the company to hedge its floating-rate debt with a strip of short Eurodollar futures contracts. This alternative is relatively inexpensive, but there may be hedging risk. The third alternative would be to combine the company's FRNs with a fixed-rate payer's position on a swap, thereby creating a synthetic fixed-rate debt position. This alternative of hedging FRNs with swaps, in turn, is less expensive and more efficient than the first alternative of refinancing.

An opposite scenario to the above case would be a company that has intermediate to long-term fixed-rate debt that it wants to make floating either because of a change in its economic structure or because it expects rates will be decreasing. Given the costs of refunding fixed-rate debt with floating-rate debt and the hedging risk problems with futures, the most efficient way for the company to meet this objective would be to create synthetic floating-rate debt by combining its fixed-rate debt with a floating-rate payer's position on a swap.

Speculation

Interest rate swaps can be used to speculate on interest rate movements. For example, speculators who expect short-term rates to increase in the future could take a fixed-rate payer's position; in contrast, speculators who expect short-term rates to decrease could take a floating-rate payer's position.

For financial and nonfinancial corporations, speculative positions often take the form of the company changing the exposure of its balance sheet to interest rate changes. For example, suppose a fixed-income bond fund with a portfolio managed against a bond index wanted to increase the duration of its portfolio relative to the index's duration based on an expectation of lower interest rate across all maturities. The fund could do this by selling its short-term Treasuries and buying longer-term ones or by taking long positions in Treasury futures. With swaps, the fund could also change its portfolio's duration by taking a floating-rate payer's position on a swap. If the company did this and rates were to decrease as expected, then not only would the value of the fund's bond portfolio increase, but the fund would also profit from the swaps. On the other hand, if rates were to increase, then the company would see decreases in the value of its bond portfolio, as well as losses from its swap positions. By adding swaps, though, the fund has effectively increased its interest rate exposure by increasing its duration.

Instead of increasing its portfolio's duration, suppose the fund wanted to reduce or minimize the bond portfolio's interest rate exposure based on an expectation of higher interest rates. In this case, the fund could effectively shorten the duration of its bond fund by taking a fixed-rate payer's position on a swap. If rates were to later increase, then the decline in the value of the company's bond portfolio would be cushioned by the gains realized from the fixed-payer's position on the swap.

Forward Swaps

A forward swap is an agreement to enter into a swap that starts at a future date at an interest rate agreed upon today. Like futures contracts on debt securities, forward swaps provide borrowers and investors with a tool for locking in a future interest rate. As such, they can be used to manage interest rate risk for debt and fixed-income positions.

Hedging a Future Loan with a Forward Swap

Suppose a company wanted to lock in a fixed rate on a seven-year, $100 million loan to start two years from today. To do so, suppose the company enters a two-year forward swap agreement with a swap bank to pay the fixed rate on a seven-year 6%/LIBOR swap. At the expiration date on the forward swap, the company could then issue floating-rate debt at, say, LIBOR that, when combined with the fixed position on the swap, would provide the company with a synthetic fixed rate loan paying 6% on the floating debt.

At the expiration date on the forward swap:

Instrument	Action	
Issue flexible rate note	Pay	−LIBOR
Swap: Fixed-rate payer's position	Pay fixed rate	−6%
Swap: Fixed-rate payer's position	Receive LIBOR	+LIBOR
Synthetic fixed rate	Net payment	6%

Alternatively, at the forward swaps' expiration date, the company is more likely to sell the seven-year 6%/LIBOR swap underlying the forward swap contract and issue seven-year fixed rate debt. Suppose the rate on seven-year fixed rate bonds were higher than 6%, for example, at 8%. The company would then be able to offset the higher interest on its fixed-rate loan by selling its fixed position on the 6%/LIBOR swap to a swap dealer at a price equal to the present value of a seven-year annuity equal to 2% (difference in rates: 8% − 6%) times the *NP*. For example, at 8% the value of the underlying 6%/LIBOR swap would be $10,563,123 using the YTM swap valuation approach:

$$SV^{fix} = \left[\sum_{t=1}^{14} \frac{(0.08/2) - (06/2)}{(1 + (0.08/2))^t} \right] \$100,000,000 = \$10,563,123$$

With the proceeds of $10,563,123 from closing its swap, the company would only need to raise $89,436,877 (= $100,000,000 − $10,563,123). The company, though, would have to issue $89,436,877 worth of seven-year fixed-rate bonds at the higher 8% rate.

In contrast, if the rate on seven-year fixed-rate loans were lower than 6%, say 4%, then the company would benefit from the lower fixed-rate loan, but would lose an amount equal to the present value of a seven-year annuity equal to 2% (difference in rates: 4% − 6%) times the *NP* when it closed the fixed position. Specifically, at 4%, the value of the underlying 6%/LIBOR swap is −$12,106,249 using the YTM approach:

$$SV^{fix} = \left[\sum_{t=1}^{14} \frac{(0.04/2) - (06/2)}{(1 + (0.04/2))^t} \right] \$100,000,000 = -\$12,106,249$$

The company would therefore have to pay the swap bank $12,106,249 for assuming its fixed-payers position. With a payment of $12,106,249, the company would need to raise a total of $112,106,249 from its bond issue. The company, though, would be able to issue $112,106,249 worth of seven-year fixed-rate bonds at the lower rate of 4% rate.

Hedging a Future Investment

Forward swaps can also be used on the asset side to fix the rate on a future investment. Consider the case of an institutional investor planning to invest an expected $10 million cash inflow one year from now in a three-year, high-quality fixed-rate bond. The investor could lock in the future rate by entering a one-year forward swap agreement to receive the fixed rate and pay the floating rate on a three-year, 6%/LIBOR swap with a *NP* of $10 million. At the expiration date on the forward swap, the investor could invest the $10 million cash inflow in a three-year FRN at LIBOR that, when combined with the floating position on the swap, would provide the investor with a synthetic fixed rate investment paying 6%:

Instrument	Action	
Buy flexible rate note	Receive	LIBOR
Swap: Floating-rate payer's position	Pay LIBOR	−LIBOR
Swap: Floating-rate payer's position	Receive fixed rate	+6%
Synthetic fixed rate investment	Net receipt	6%

Instead of a synthetic fixed investment position, the investor is more likely to sell the three-year 3%/LIBOR swap underlying the forward swap contract and invest in a three-year fixed-rate note. If the rate on the three-year fixed-rate note were lower than the 6% swap rate, then the investor would be able to sell his floating position at a value equal to the present value of an annuity equal to the $10 million *NP* times the difference between 6% and the rate on three-year fixed-rate bonds. This gain would offset the lower return on the fixed-rate bond. On the other hand, if the rate on three-year fixed-rate securities were higher than 6%, the investment company would benefit from the higher investment rate, but would lose when it closed its swap position.

Other Uses of Forward Swaps

The examples illustrate that forward swaps are like futures on debt securities. As such, they are used in many of the same ways as futures: locking in future interest rates, speculating on future interest rate changes, and altering a balance sheet's exposure to interest rate changes. Different from futures, though, forward swaps can be customized to fit a particular investment or borrowing need and can be applied to not only short-run but also long-run positions.

Valuation of Forward Swaps

As with many nongeneric swaps, there can be an up-front fee for a forward swap. Similar to bond valuation, the equilibrium value of a forward swap is obtained by discounting each of the swap's expected cash flows by their appropriate spot rates, with the cash flows being estimated with implied forward rates. Like generic swaps, a corollary to the zero-coupon approach to valuation is the break-even rate. The break-even rate on a forward swap is that rate that equates the present value of the fixed-rate flows to the present value of floating-rate flows corresponding to the period of the underlying swap. Break-even forward rates and the valuation of forward swaps are presented in Appendix 14A.

Swaptions

As the name suggests, a *swaption* is an option on a swap. The purchaser of a swaption buys the right to start an interest rate swap with a specific fixed rate (exercise rate) and with a maturity at or during a specific period in the future. If the holder exercises, she takes the swap position, with the swap seller obligated to take the opposite counter-party position. For swaptions, the underlying instrument is a forward swap and the option premium is the up-front fee.

A swaption can be either a right to be a payer or the right to be receiver of the fixed rate. A *payer swaption* gives the holder the right to enter a particular swap as the fixed-rate payer (and floating-rate receiver), whereas a *receiver swaption* gives the holder the right to enter a particular swap agreement as the fixed-rate receiver (and floating-rate payer). Swaptions are similar to interest rate options or options on debt securities. They can range from options to begin a one-year swap in three months to options to begin an eight-year option in 10 years (sometimes referred to as a 10 × 8 swaption). Like interest rate and debt options, swaptions are used for speculating on interest rates, hedging debt and asset positions against market risk, and managing a balance sheet's exposure to interest rate changes. In addition, like swaps they also can be used in combination with other securities to create synthetic positions.

Speculation

Suppose a speculator expects the rates on high quality, five-year fixed rate bonds to increase from their current 5% level. As an alternative to a short T-note futures or an interest rate call position, the speculator could buy a payer swaption. Suppose she elects to buy a one-year European payer swaption on a five-year, 5%/LIBOR swap with a *NP* of $10 million for 50 basis points times the NP:

- 1 × 5 payer swaption
- Exercise date = one year
- Exercise rate = 5%
- Underlying swap = five-year, 5%/LIBOR with *NP* = $10 million
- Swap position = fixed payer
- Option premium = 50 bp times *NP*

On the exercise date, if the fixed rate on a five-year swap were greater than the exercise rate of 5%, then the speculator would exercise her swaption at 5%. To profit, she could take her 5% fixed-rate payer's swap position obtained from exercising and sell it to a swap bank. For example, if current five-year par value swaps were trading at 6% and swaps were valued by the YTM approach, then she would be able to sell her 5% swap for $426,510:

$$\text{Value of swap} = \left[\sum_{t=1}^{10} \frac{(0.06/2) - (0.05/2)}{(1 + (0.06/2))^t} \right] (\$10,000,000) = \$426,510$$

If the swap rate at the expiration date were less than 5%, then the payer swaption would have no value and the speculator would simply let it expire, losing the premium she paid.

More formally, the intrinsic value or expiration value of the payer swaption is

$$\text{Value of payer swaption} = \left[\sum_{t=1}^{10} \frac{\text{Max}[(R/2) - (0.05/2), \, 0]}{(1 + (R/2))^t} \right] (\$10,000,000)$$

For rates, R, on par value five-year swaps exceeding the exercise rate of 5%, the value of the payer swaption will be equal to the present value of the interest differential times the notional principal on the swap and for rates equal or less than 5%, the swap is worthless. Exhibit 14.6 shows the values and profits at expiration obtained from closing the payer swaption on the five-year 5%/LIBOR swap given different rates at expiration.

Instead of higher rates, suppose the speculator expects rates on five-year high quality bonds to be lower one year from now. In this case, her strategy would be to buy a receiver swaption. Suppose she bought a receiver swaption similar in terms to the above payer swaption (a one-year option on a five-year, 5%/LIBOR swap for $50,000). If the swap rate on a five-year swap were less than 5% on the exercise date, then she would realize a gain from exercising and then selling the floating-payer position. For example, if the fixed rate on a five-year par value swap were 4%, the investor would exercise her receiver swaption by taking the 5% floating-rate payer's swap and then sell the position to a swap bank or another party. With the current swap rate at 4%, she would be able to sell the 5% floating-payer's position for $449,129:

$$\text{Value of swap} = \left[\sum_{t=1}^{10} \frac{(0.05/2) - (0.04/2)}{(1 + (0.04/2))^t} \right] (\$10,000,000) = \$449,129$$

If the swap rate were equal or higher than 5% on the exercise date, then the investor would allow the receiver swaption to expire, losing, in turn, her premium of $50,000.

Formally, the value of the 5%/LIBOR receiver swaption at expiration is

$$\text{Value of receiver swaption} = \left[\sum_{t=1}^{10} \frac{\text{Max}[(0.05/2) - (R/2), \, 0]}{(1 + (R/2))^t} \right] (\$10,000,000)$$

EXHIBIT 14.6 Value and Profit at Expiration from 5%/LIBOR Payer Swaption

Rates on 5-year Par Value Swaps at Expiration R	Payer Swaption's Interest Differential Max$((R - 0.05)/2,0)$	Value of 5%/LIBOR Payer Swaption at Expiation PV(Max$[(R - 0.05)/2, 0]$($10m))	Payer Swaption Cost	Profit from Payer Swaption
0.030	0.0000	$0	$50,000	−$50,000
0.035	0.0000	$0	$50,000	−$50,000
0.040	0.0000	$0	$50,000	−$50,000
0.045	0.0000	$0	$50,000	−$50,000
0.050	0.0000	$0	$50,000	−$50,000
0.055	0.0025	$216,002	$50,000	$166,002
0.060	0.0050	$426,510	$50,000	$376,510
0.065	0.0075	$631,680	$50,000	$581,680
0.070	0.0100	$831,661	$50,000	$781,661
0.075	0.0125	$1,026,598	$50,000	$976,598

$$\text{Value of Payer Swaption} = \left[\sum_{t=1}^{10} \frac{\text{Max}[(R/2) - (0.05/2), \, 0]}{(1 + (R/2))^t} \right] (\$10,000,000)$$

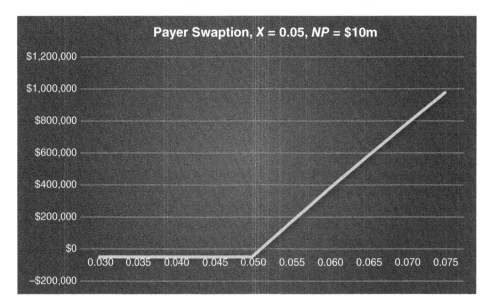

For rates, R, on par value five-year swaps less than the exercise rate of 5%, the value of the receiver swaption will be equal to the present value of the interest differential times the notional principal on the swap and for rates greater than or equal to 5%, the swap is worthless. Exhibit 14.7 shows graphically and in a table the values and profits at expiration obtained from closing the receiver swaption on the five-year 5%/LIBOR swap given different rates at expiration.

EXHIBIT 14.7   Value and Profit at Expiration from 5%/LIBOR Receiver Swaption

Rates on 5-year Par Value Swaps at Expiration R	Receiver Swaption's Interest Differential Max$((0.05 - R)/2,0)$	Value of 5%/LIBOR Receiver Swaption at Expiation PV(Max$[(0.05 - R)/2, 0]$($10m))	Receiver Swaption Cost	Profit from Receiver Swaption
0.030	0.0100	$922,218	$50,000	$872,218
0.035	0.0075	$682,592	$50,000	$632,592
0.040	0.0050	$449,129	$50,000	$399,129
0.045	0.0025	$221,655	$50,000	$171,655
0.050	0.0000	$0	$50,000	−$50,000
0.055	0.0000	$0	$50,000	−$50,000
0.060	0.0000	$0	$50,000	−$50,000
0.065	0.0000	$0	$50,000	−$50,000
0.070	0.0000	$0	$50,000	−$50,000

$$\text{Value of Receiver Swaption} = \left[\sum_{t=1}^{10} \frac{\text{Max}[(0.05/2) - (R/2), 0]}{(1 + (R/2))^t} \right] (\$10,000,000)$$

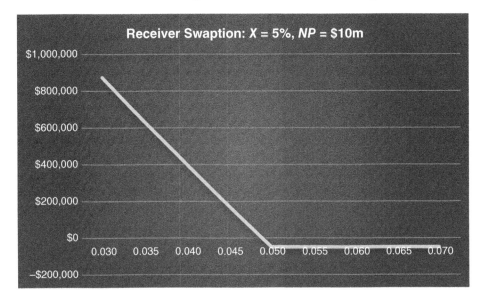

Hedging

Caps and Floors on Future Debt and Investment Positions

Like other option hedging tools, swaptions give investors and borrowers protection against adverse price or interest rate movements, while allowing them to benefit if prices or rates move in their favor. Since receiver swaptions increase in value as rates decrease below the exercise rate, they can be used to establish floors on the rates of return obtained from future fixed-income investments. In contrast, since payer swaptions increase in value as rates increase above the exercise rate, they can be used for capping the rates paid on debt positions.

To illustrate how receiver swaptions are used for establishing a floor, consider the case of an investment fund that has an investment-grade fixed-rate portfolio worth $30 million in par value that is scheduled to mature in two years. Suppose the fund plans to reinvest the $30 million in principal for another three years in investment-grade bonds that are currently trading to yield 6%, but is worried that interest rate could be lower in two years. To establish a floor on its investment, suppose the fund purchases a two-year receiver swaption on a three-year 6%/LIBOR generic swap with a notional principal of $30 million from First Bank for $100,000. Two years later, the swaption's value will be greater if interest rates are less than 6%; this in turn, would offset the lower yields the fund would obtain from investing in lower yielding securities. On the other hand, for rates equal or greater than 6%, the swaption is worthless, but the fund is able to invest in higher yield securities. Thus, for the cost of $100,000, the receiver swaption provides the fund a floor.

In contrast to the use of swaptions to establish a floor on a future investment, suppose a firm had a future debt obligation and it wanted to cap the rate. In this case, the firm could purchase a payer swaption. For example, suppose a company has a $60 million, 6% fixed-rate bond obligation maturing in three years that it plans to refinance at that time by issuing new five-year fixed-rate bonds. Suppose the company is worried that interest rates could increase in three years and as a result wants to establish a cap on the rate it would pay on its future five-year bond issue. To cap the rate, suppose the company purchases a three-year payer swaption on a five-year 6%/LIBOR generic swap with notional principal of $60 million from First Bank for $200,000. Two years later, the swaption's value will be greater if interest rates are higher than 6%; this, in turn, would offset the higher borrowing rates the firm would have when it issues its new fixed-rate bonds. On the other hand, for rates equal or less than 6%, the swaption is worthless, but the firm benefits with lower rate on new debt issues. Thus, for the cost of $200,000, the payer swaption provides the fund a cap on it future debt.

Investor Hedging the Risk of an Embedded Call Option

The cap and floor hedging examples illustrate that swaptions are a particularly useful tool in hedging future investment and debt position against adverse interest rate changes. Swaptions can also be used to hedge against the impacts that unfavorable interest rate changes have on investment and debt positions with embedded options. Consider the case of a fixed-income manager holding $10 million worth of 10-year, high quality, 8% fixed-rate bonds that are callable in two years at a call price equal to par. Suppose the manager expects a decrease in rates over the next two years, increasing the likelihood that his bonds will be called and she will be forced to reinvest in a market with lower rates. To minimize her exposure to this call risk, suppose the manager buys a two-year receiver swaption on an eight-year, 8%/LIBOR swap with a *NP* of $10 million. If two years later, rates were to increase, then the bonds would not be called and the swaption would have no value. In this case, the fixed-income manager would lose the premium she paid for the receiver swaption. However, if two years later, rates on eight-year bonds were lower at, say, 6%, and the bonds were called at a call price equal to par, then the manager would be able to offset the loss from reinvesting the call proceeds at lower interest rates by the profits from exercising the receiver swaption.

Black Futures Option Model

As with other options, the value of a swaption can be broken down into its intrinsic value, *IV*, and time value premium, *TVP*. In determining a swaption's *IV*, the asset underlying the swaption is a forward contract. That is, a three-year payer swaption on a two-year 5%/LIBOR swap is an option to take a fixed-payer's position on a two-year swap three years forward. The asset underlying this payer swaption is therefore the fixed-payer's position on a three-year forward contract with a forward swap rate of 5%. Thus, the first step in calculating a swaption's *IV* is to determine the break-even rate on the underlying forward contract. Appendix 14A describes how break-even rate is used to determine the *IV* of a swaption.

Swaptions can be valued using a binomial interest rate framework similar to the one presented in Chapter 13. They can also be valued using the Black futures option model described in Chapter 12.

Non-Generic Swaps

Today, there are a number of non-generic interest rate swaps used by financial and nonfinancial corporations to manage their varied cash flow and return-risk positions. Non-generic swaps usually differ from generic swaps in terms of their rates, principal, or effective dates. For example, instead of defining swaps in terms of the LIBOR, some swaps use the T-bill rate, prime lending rate, or the Federal Reserve's Commercial Paper Rate Index with different maturities. Similarly, the principals defining a swap can vary. An *amortizing swap*, for example, is a swap in which the *NP* is reduced over time based on a schedule, whereas a *set-up swap* (sometimes called an *accreting swap*) has its *NP* increasing over time. A variation of the amortizing swap is the *index-amortizing swap* (also called *index-principal swap*). In this swap, the *NP* is dependent on interest rates; for example, the lower the interest rate the greater the reduction in principal. There is a *zero-coupon swap* in which the parties do not exchange payments until the maturity on the swap. There are also a number of *non-US dollar interest rate swaps*. Finally, there are cancelable and extendable swaps. A *cancelable swap* is a swap in which one of the counterparties has the option to terminate one or more payments. Cancelable swaps can be callable or putable. A *callable cancelable swap* is one in which the fixed payer has the right to early termination. Thus, if rates decrease, the fixed-rate payer on the swap with this embedded call option to early termination can exercise her right to cancel the swap. A *putable cancelable swap*, on the other hand, is one in which the floating payer has the right to early cancellation. A floating-rate payer with this option may find it advantageous to exercise his early termination right when rates increase. An *extendable swap* is just the opposite of a cancelable swap. It is a swap that has an option to lengthen the terms of the original swap. The swap allows the holder to take advantage of current rates and extend the maturity of the swap. Box 14.1 summarizes some of the common non-generic swaps.

BOX 14.1: NON-GENERIC SWAPS

1. **Non-LIBOR Swap:** Swaps with floating rates different than LIBOR. Example: T-bill rate, CP rate, or prime lending rate.
2. **Delayed-Rate Set Swap:** allows the fixed payer to wait before locking in a fixed swap rate—the opposite of a forward swap.
3. **Zero Coupon Swap:** Swap in which one or both parties do not exchange payments until maturity on the swap.
4. **Prepaid Swap:** Swap in which the future payments due are discounted to the present and paid at the start.
5. **Delayed-Reset Swap:** The effective date and payment date are the same. The cash flows at time t are determined by the floating rate at time t rather than the rate at time $t - 1$.
6. **Amortizing Swaps:** Swaps in which the NP decreases over time based on a set schedule.
7. **Set-Up Swap or Accreting Swap:** Swaps in which the NP increases over time based on a set schedule.
8. **Index Amortizing Swap:** Swap in which the NP is dependent on interest rates.
9. **Equity Swap:** Swap in which one party pays the return on a stock index and the other pays a fixed or floating rate.
10. **Basis Swap:** Swaps in which both rates are floating; each party exchanges different floating payments: One party might exchange payments based on LIBOR and the other based on the Federal Reserve Commercial Paper Index.
11. **Total Return Swap:** Returns from one asset are swapped for the returns on another asset.
12. **Non-US Dollar Interest Rate Swap:** Interest-rate swap in a currency different that US dollar with a floating rate often different that the LIBOR: Frankfort rate (FIBOR), Vienna (VIBOR), and the like.

Conclusion

In this chapter, we have examined the market, uses, and valuations of generic interest rate swaps and swap derivatives. Like interest rate options and futures, swaps provide investors and borrowers with a tool for hedging asset and liability positions against interest rate risk, speculating on interest rate movements, and improving the returns received on fixed-income investments or paid on debt positions. Swaps, in turn, have become a basic financial engineering tool. In Chapter 15, we continue our analysis of swaps by examining currency and credit default swaps.

BLOOMBERG SCREENS FOR SWAPS

SWPM SCREEN FOR ANALYZING GENERIC FIXED-/FLOATING-RATE SWAPS

Fixed-/Floating-Rate Swap: To create a fixed-/floating-rate swap on SWPM, go to the "Products" tab and click "Fixed — Float Swap." This will bring up the main screen for a generic swap. The swap shown on the Main screen defaults to a five-year swap. You can then change the settings on the Main screen.

1. Options on Swaps: On the dropdown "Pay Fixed" or "Receive Fixed" (this will automatically adjust for the other leg (counterparty), Notional Principal, Currency, Payment Frequency, Coupon (this is the fixed rate), Spread (the amount of basis points to add or subtract from the floating rate, LIBOR).
2. Forward Graph Options: SWPM determines future cash flows at each reset date based on the forward rate at that date. The user can select which yield curve the forward rates are to be determined. On the "Curve" screen (gray "Curve" tab), one can view the forward graph and make shift adjustments.
3. Discount Rate Option: SWPM also discounts cash flows to determine the market value (shown at the bottom of main screen); the user can also select which yield curve to be used for discounting.

Tab Screens:

1. "Details" tab shows the details of the swap.
2. "Resets" tab shows the reset rate at each effective date.
3. "Cashflow" tab shows cash flows for each counterparty (leg).
4. "Chart" tab show graphically the payments, receipts, and net payments. This tab screen can be adjusted to show each counterparty (pay fix or receive fix), cash flow, and market values.
5. "Scenario" tab allows one to make scenario changes for different time and determine the change in value.

Example: Fixed/Floating swap (leg 1 is fixed-rate payer); $NP = \$10$ million; fixed rate (coupon) = 2%; floating rate = 6-month LIBOR; frequency = semiannual; maturity = 5 years; forward curve = US swaps (#51) (see Exhibit 14.8).

BLOOMBERG SWPM SCREEN FOR ANALYZING SWAPTION: SWPM <ENTER>

On the SWPM screen, you create, value, and analyze swaptions. To create a swaption on SWPM, go to the "Products" tab and click "Swaption" in the Options dropdown. This will bring up the Main screen for a swaption. The default on swaption shown is for a one-year, five-year swaption (1 × 5). You can then change the settings on the main screen.

- Positions: Long Payer, Long Receiver, Short Payer, Short Receiver, and Long Payer; Principal; Payment Frequency; Exercise Rate; and Currency.
- Reset: Reset rate at each effective date.

(Continued)

EXHIBIT 14.8   Fixed/Floating Swap

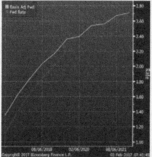

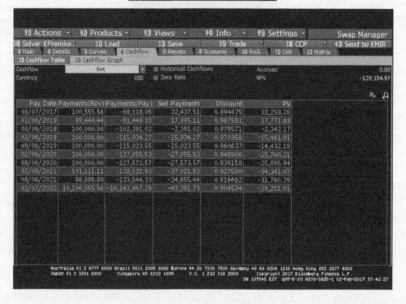

- "Cashflow" tab shows cash flows for each counterparty (leg).
- Swaption valuation: The Black-Scholes model is used to price the swaption. The user can change the model and the volatility.

Example: 1×5 payer swaption; $NP = \$10$ million; fixed rate (coupon) = Exercise Rate = 2.280104%; floating rate = 6-month LIBOR = semiannual; swap maturity = 5 years; swaption expiration = 1 years; forward curve = US swaps (#23) (see Exhibit 14.9).

EXHIBIT 14.9 Payer Swaption

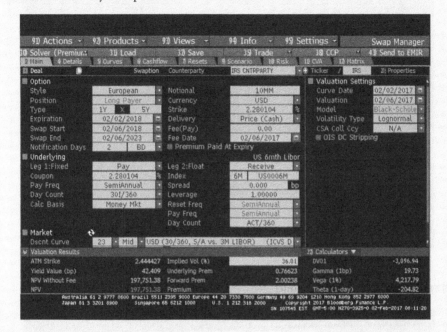

ANALYZING A FIXED-INCOME BOND PORTFOLIO WITH SWAP AND SWAPTIONS POSITION USING MARS

Saving and Loading a Swap to a Portfolio

To save and load a swap position or swaption created in SWPM, go to the "Action" tab and click "Save." This will bring up an input box. In the box, name the swap position (Custom ID), click "Add to MARS Portfolio" in the lower part of the input box, and click "Save."

To add the swap or swaption created in SWPM to a portfolio created in PRTU, click "Add to Portfolio" from the "Action" tab. In the input box, name the swap (Custom ID), then select portfolio from the "Portfolio Name" dropdown, and then click the "Add" tab. On SWPM Action dropdown, click MARS. This will bring up MARS with your bond portfolio and swap.

On the MARS screen, you can evaluate the portfolio with and without the swap from the "Scenario" tab.

Example: $\$11.467$ million Xavier Bond Fund and 2%/LIBOR fixed payer swap with $NP = \$10$ million and maturity of five years (see Exhibits 14.10 to 14.14).

(Continued)

EXHIBIT 14.10 Fixed-Rate Payer Swap

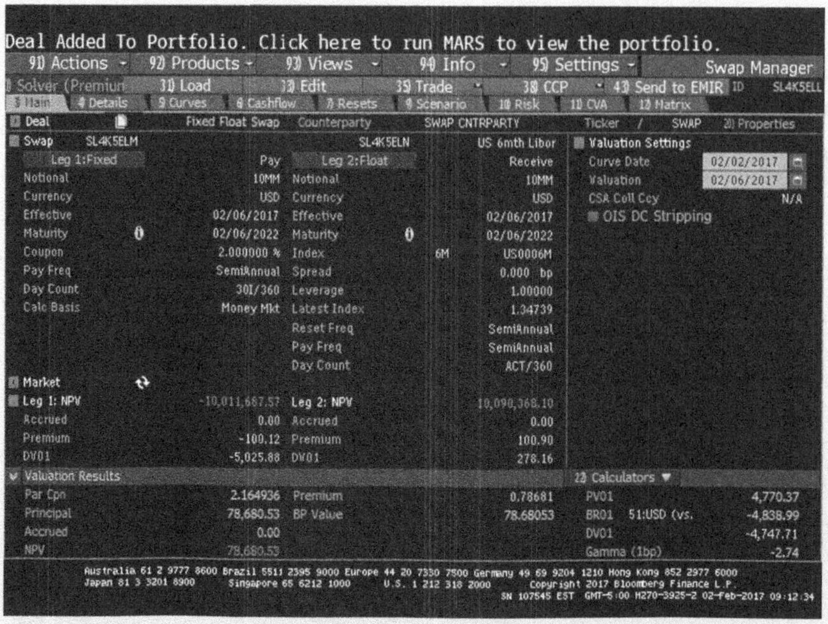

EXHIBIT 14.11 MARS Scenario Analysis without Swap

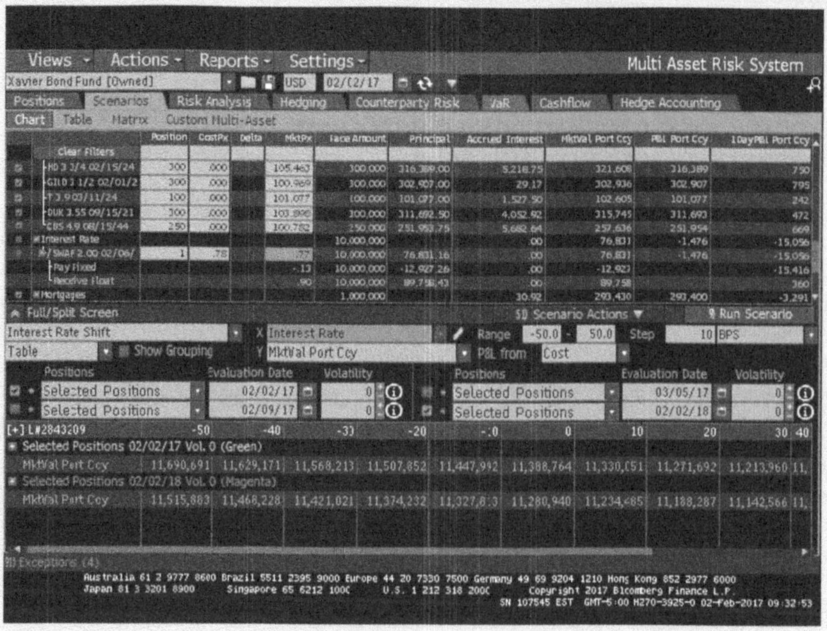

EXHIBIT 14.12 MARS Scenario Analysis with Fixed-Payer Swap

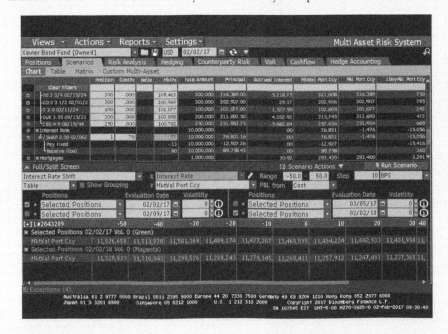

EXHIBIT 14.13 Payer Swaption

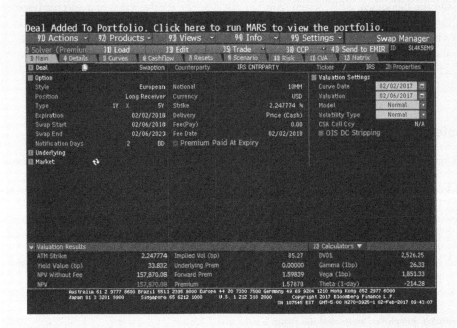

(Continued)

EXHIBIT 14.14   MARS Scenario Analysis with Payer Swaption

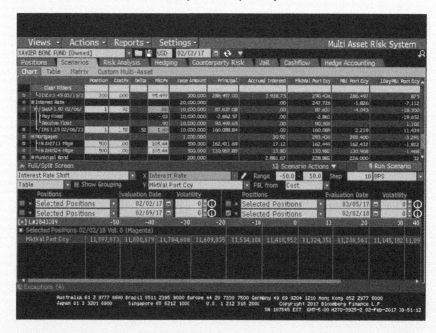

Bloomberg ASW Screen

On the Bloomberg ASW screen, you can calculate the relative value of a selected bond through the interest rate swap market. For example, you could use ASW to determine if it is better to enter into an asset swap versus purchasing a floating-rate instrument. You can also use ASW to determine how much money you could save in interest costs by issuing a fixed-rate bond and swapping the fixed payments for floating payments.

Selected References

Bhattacharya, Anand K., and Frank J. Fabozzi. "Interest-Rate Swaps." *The Handbook of Fixed Income Securities*, 6th edition. Editor, Frank Fabozzi. New York: McGraw-Hill, 2001.

Bicksler, J., and A. H. Chen. "An Economic Analysis of Interest Rate Swaps." *Journal of Finance* 41 (1986): 645–655.

Brown, Keith C., and Donald J. Smith. "Plain Vanilla Swaps: Market Structures, Applications, and Credit Risk." *Interest Rate Swaps*. Edited by Carl R. Beidleman. Homewood, IL: Business One Irwin, 1991.

Cucchissi, Paul G., and Reto M. Tuffli. "Swaptions Applications." *Interest Rate Swaps*. Edited by Carl R. Beidleman. Homewood, IL: Business One Irwin, 1991.

Goodman, Laurie S. "Capital Market Applications of Interest Rate Swaps." *Interest Rate Swaps*. Edited by Carl R. Beidleman. Homewood, IL: Business One Irwin, 1991.

Haubrich, Joseph G. "Swaps and the Swaps Yield Curve." *Economic Commentary*, Federal Reserve Bank of Cleveland (December 2001): 1–4.

Hull, John C. Option, *Futures, and Other Derivatives*, 6th ed., Upper Saddle River, NJ: Prentice Hall, 2005, Chapters 20–21.

Iben, Benjamin. "Chapter 12: Interest Rate Swap Evaluation." *Interest Rate Swaps*. Edited by Carl R. Beidleman. Homewood, IL: Business One Irwin, 1991.

Johnson, R. Stafford, *Introduction to Derivatives: Options, Futures, and Swaps*. Oxford University Press, 2009, Chapters 17–19.

Kawaller, Ira B. "A Swap Alternative: Eurodollar Strips." *Interest Rate Swaps*. Edited by Carl R. Beidleman. Homewood, IL: Business One Irwin, 1991.

Litzenberger, R. H., "Swaps: Plain and Fanciful." *Journal of Finance* 47, no. 3 (1992): 831–850.

Marshall, J. F., and K. R. Kapner. *Understanding Swaps*. New York: John Wiley & Sons, 1993.

Pergam, Albert S. "Swaps: A Legal Perspective." *The Handbook of Interest Rate Risk Management*. Edited by Jack Clark Francis and Avner Simon Wolf. New York: Irwin Professional Publishing, 1994.

Smith, D. J. "Aggressive Corporate Finance: A Close Look at the Procter and Gamble-Bankers Trust Leveraged Swap." *Journal of Derivatives* 4, no. 4 (Summer 1997): 67–79.

Smith, C. W., C. W. Smithson, and L. M. Wakeman. "The Evolving Market for Swaps." *Midland Corporate Finance Journal* 3 (1986): 20–32.

Smith, C. W., C. W. Smithson, and L. M. Wakeman. "The Market for Interest Rate Swaps." *Financial Management* 17 (1988): 34–44.

Sun, T., S. Sundaresan, and C. Wang. "Interest Rate Swaps: An Empirical Investigation." *Journal of Financial Economics* 36 (1993): 77–99.

Titman, S. "Interest Rate Swaps and Corporate Financing Choices." *Journal of Finance* 47, no. 4 (1992): 1503–1016.

Turnbull, S. M. "Swaps: A Zero Sum Game." *Financial Management* 16, no. 1 (Spring 1987): 15–21.

Wall, L. D., and J. J. Pringle. "Alternative Explanations of Interest Rate Swaps: A Theoretical and Empirical Analysis." *Financial Management* 18, no. 2 (Summer 1989): 59–73.

Problems and Questions

1. Given the following interest-rate swap:
   - Fixed-rate payer pays half of the YTM on a T-note of 3.0%
   - Floating-rate payer pays the LIBOR
   - Notional principal is $10 million
   - Effective dates are 3/23 and 9/23 for the next three years

   Questions:

   a. Determine the net receipts of the fixed-rate payer given the following LIBORs:
      - 3/23/y1 .020
      - 9/23/y1 .025
      - 3/23/y2 .030
      - 9/23/y2 .035
      - 3/23/y3 .040
      - 9/23/y3 .045

   b. Show in a table how a company with a three-year, $10 million floating-rate loan, with the rate set by the LIBOR on the dates coinciding with the swap, could make the loan a fixed-rate one by taking a position in the swap. What would be the fixed rate?

   c. Show in a table how a company with a two-year, $10 million fixed-rate loan at 3.0%, could make the loan a floating-rate one by taking a position in the swap.

2. Explain how the fixed-payer and floating-payer positions in Question 1 can be replicated with positions in fixed-rate and floating-rate bonds.

3. Using a table showing payments and receipts, prove that the following positions are equivalent:

   a. Floating-rate loan plus fixed-rate payer's position is equivalent to a fixed-rate loan.

   b. Fixed-rate loan plus floating-rate payer's position is equivalent to a floating-rate loan.

   c. Floating-rate note investment plus floating-rate payer's position is equivalent to a fixed-rate investment.

   d. Fixed-rate bond investment plus fixed-rate payer's position is equivalent to a floating-rate investment.

4. Explain the alternative ways a swap holder could hedge her swap position instead of selling it to a swap bank.

5. If the fixed rate on a new par value two-year swap were at 3%, how much would a swap dealer pay or charge to assume an existing fixed-payer's position on a 3.5%/LIBOR generic swap with two years left to maturity and notional principal of $20 million? How much would the dealer pay or charge if the fixed rate on a new par value two-year swap were at 4%?

6. If the fixed rate on a new par value two-year swap were at 5%, how much would a swap dealer pay or charge for assuming an existing 5.5%/LIBOR floating-rate position on a generic swap with two years left to maturity and notional principal of $20 million? How much would the dealer pay or charge if the fixed rate on a new par value two-year swap were at 6%?

7. Given a generic five-year par value swap with a fixed rate of 6%, determine the values of the following off-market swap positions using the YTM approach:

   a. Fixed-rate position on a five-year, 5%/LIBOR generic swap with $NP =$ $50 million.

   b. Floating-rate position on a five-year 5%/LIBOR generic swap with $NP =$ $50 million.

   c. Fixed-rate position on a five-year 7%/LIBOR generic swap with $NP =$ $50 million.

   d. Floating-rate position on a five-year 7%/LIBOR generic swap with $NP =$ $50 million.

8. The Beta Chemical Company wants to finance an expansion of one of its production plants by borrowing $150 million for five years. Based on its moderate credit ratings, Beta can borrow five-year funds at a 10.5% fixed rate or at a floating rate equal to LIBOR + 75 bp. Given the choice of financing, Beta prefers the fixed-rate loan. The Alpha Development Company is also looking for five-year funding to finance its proposed $150 million office park development. Given its high credit rating, suppose Alpha can borrow the funds for five years at a fixed rate of 9.5% or at a floating rate equal to the LIBOR + 25 bp. Given the choice, Alpha prefers

a floating-rate loan. In summary, Beta and Alphas have the following fixed- and floating-rate loan alternatives:

Company	Fixed Rate	Floating Rate	Preference
Beta Company	10.5%	LIBOR + 75 BP	Fixed-rate loan
Alpha Company	9.5%	LIBOR + 25 BP	Floating-rate loan

Questions:

a. Describe Alpha's absolute advantage and each company's comparative advantage?

b. What is the total possible interest rate reduction gain for both parties if both parties were to create synthetic positions with a swap?

c. Explain how a swap bank could arrange a five-year, 9.5%/LIBOR swap that would benefit both the Alpha and Beta companies. What is the total interest rate reduction gain and how is it split?

9. Explain the idea of hidden options in terms of Question 8.

10. Suppose a company wants to borrow $100 million for five years at a fixed-rate. Suppose the company can issue both a five-year, 6%, fixed-rate bond paying coupons on a semiannual basis and a five-year FRN paying LIBOR plus 100 BP.

a. Explain how the company could create a synthetic five-year fixed-rate loan with a swap.

b. What would the fixed rate on the swap have to be for the synthetic position to be equivalent to the direct loan position?

c. Define the company's criterion for selecting the synthetic loan.

11. Suppose a financial institution wants to finance its three-year $100 million floating-rate loans by selling three-year floating-rate notes. Suppose the institution can issue a three-year, 7%, fixed-rate note paying coupons on a semiannual basis and also a three-year FRN paying LIBOR plus 100 bp.

a. Explain how the institution could create a synthetic three-year floating rate note with a swap.

b. What would the fixed rate on the swap have to be for the synthetic position to be equivalent to the floating-rate note?

c. Define the institution's criterion for selecting the synthetic loan.

12. Suppose a financial institution wants to invest $100 million in a three-year fixed-rate note. Suppose the institution can invest in a three-year, 7%, fixed-rate note paying coupons on a semiannual basis and selling at par and also in a three-year FRN paying LIBOR plus 100 bp.

a. Explain how the institution could create a synthetic three-year fixed-rate note with a swap.

b. What would the fixed rate on the swap have to be for the synthetic position to be equivalent to the fixed-rate note? Show the synthetic position in a table.

c. Define the institution's criterion for selecting the synthetic investment.

13. Suppose a financial institution wants to invest $100 million in a three-year floating-rate note. Suppose the institution can invest in a three-year, 7%, fixed-rate note paying coupons on a semiannual basis and selling at par and also in a three-year FRN paying LIBOR plus 100 bp.

   a. Explain how the institution could create a synthetic three-year floating-rate note with a swap.

   b. What would the fixed rate on the swap have to be for the synthetic position to be equivalent to the floating-rate note? Show the synthetic position in a table.

   c. Define the institution's criterion for selecting the synthetic investment.

14. Short-Answer Questions

   a. Who generally assumes the credit risk in a brokered swap?

   b. Who assumes the credit risk in a dealer's swap?

   c. What is one of the problems with brokered swaps that contributed to the growth in the dealer-swap market?

   d. What does the term warehousing mean?

   e. What does the term running a dynamic book mean?

   f. How do dealers typically quote the fixed-rate and floating-rate on swap agreement they offer?

   g. Describe the comparative advantage argument that is often advanced as the reason for the growth in the swap market.

   h. If one borrower has a comparative advantage in the fixed-rate market and another borrower has a comparative advantage in the floating-rate market, what is the total possible interest rate reduction gain for both borrowers from creating synthetic debt positions using swaps given that one of the borrowers has an absolute advantage in both the fixed-rate and floating-rate credit markets?

   i. If one borrower has a comparative advantage in the fixed-rate market and another borrower has a comparative advantage in the floating-rate market, what is the total possible interest rate reduction gain for both borrowers from creating synthetic debt positions using swaps given that each party has an absolute advantage in one market?

   j. What is the hidden option, and does it relate to a difference in credit spreads in the fixed and floating credit markets?

   k. Explain how a company could take a swap position to replace its current floating-rate debt with a fixed-rate debt obligation.

15. Explain how a company planning to issue four-year, fixed-rate bonds in two years could use a forward swap to lock in the fix rate it will pay on the bonds. Explain how the hedge works at the expiration of the forward contract.

16. Suppose a speculative hedge fund anticipating higher rates in several years purchased a two-year payer swaption on a three-year 6%/LIBOR generic swap with semiannual payments and a notional principal of $20 million for a price equal to 50 basis points times the *NP*. Show graphically and in a table the values

and profits/losses at expiration that the fund would obtain from closing its payer swaption. Evaluate at fixed rates on three-year par value swap at expiration of 4%, 4.5%, 5%, 5.5%, 6%, 6.5%, 7%, 7.5%, and 8%.

17. Suppose the speculative hedge fund in Question 16 was anticipating lower rates in several years and purchased a two-year receiver swaption on a three-year 6%/LIBOR generic swap with semiannual payments and notional principal of $20 million for a price equal to 60 basis times the *NP*. Show graphically and in a table the values and profits/losses at expiration that the hedge fund would obtain from closing its receiver swaption. Evaluate at fixed rates on three-year par value swaps at expiration of 4%, 4.5%, 5%, 5.5%, 6%, 6.5%, 7%, 7.5%, and 8%.

Bloomberg Exercises

1. Use the Bloomberg SWPM screen to create and analyze a fixed-/floating-rate swap. Tabs to include in your analysis: Main, Resets, Curve, Cashflow, and Scenario.

2. Use the Bloomberg SWPM screen to create and analyze a swaption on a fixed-/floating-rate swap similar to the one you created in Exercise 1. To create a swaption on SWPM, go to the "Products" tabs and click "Swaption" in Options dropdown. This will bring up the main screen for a swaption. Tabs to include in your analysis: Main, Resets, Curve, Cashflow, and Scenario.

3. Construct a bond portfolio using PRTU or select a bond portfolio you have already constructed.

   a. On your MARS screen, create a fixed-payer position on a generic swap. Add your swap to a portfolio you have created. From the red "Add Positions" tab, click "Add to Portfolio" and then select the portfolio. Analyze the interest rate exposure of the portfolio with and without the swap using the MARS screen. On the MARS "Scenario Chart" tab, set scenario periods, interest rate shifts (e.g., −50 basis points to 50 basis points) and *y*-axis market value. Comment on the relation between the market value and interest rate relation.

   b. On your MARS screen, create a floating-payer position on a generic swap. Add your swap to a portfolio you have created. From the red "Add Positions" tab, click "Add to Portfolio" and then select the portfolio. Analyze the interest rate exposure of the portfolio with and without the swap using the MARS screen. On the MARS "Scenario Chart" tab, set scenario periods, interest rate shifts (e.g., −50 basis points to 50 basis points) and *y*-axis market value. Analyze your portfolio with and without the swap. Comment on the relation between the market value and interest rate relation.

   c. On your MARS screen, create a payer swaption. Add your swaption to a portfolio you have created. From the red "Add Positions" tab, click "Add to Portfolio" and then select the portfolio. Analyze the interest rate exposure of the portfolio with and without the swaption using the MARS screen. On the MARS "Scenario Chart" tab, set scenario periods, interest rate shifts (e.g., −50 basis points to 50 basis points), and *y*-axis market value. Analyze your portfolio with and without the swap. Comment on the relation between the market value and interest rate relation.

d. On your MARS screen, create a receiver swaption. Add your swaption to a portfolio you have created. From the red "Add Positions" tab, click "Add to Portfolio" and then select the portfolio. Analyze the interest rate exposure of the portfolio with and without the swaption using the MARS screen. On the MARS "Scenario Chart" tab, set scenario periods, interest rate shifts (e.g., −50 basis points to 50 basis points), and *y*-axis market value. Analyze your portfolio with and without the swap. Comment on the relation between the market value and interest rate relation.

4. The Bloomberg ASW screen allows you to calculate the relative value of a selected bond through the interest rate swap market. Select a dollar-denominated, fixed-income, intermediate-term Treasury or investment-grade bond and use ASW to determine how much money you could save in interest costs by issuing the bond and swapping the fixed payments for floating payments on the swap created in ASW. To access: load bond: Bond Ticker <Govt> or <Corp>; type ASW. "ASW tab screens to consider are:" Swap Detail tab (upper right)), deal details ("Deal Summary" tab), and cash flows ("Cashflow" tab).

Appendix 14A: Valuation of Forward Swaps and Swaptions

Equilibrium Value of a Swap — Zero-Coupon Approach

The equilibrium price of a bond is obtained by discounting each of the bond's cash flows by their appropriate spot rates—the rate on a zero discount bond. Pricing bonds by using spot rates instead of a common *YTM* ensures that there are no arbitrage opportunities from buying bonds and stripping them or buying zero discount bonds and bundling them. The argument for pricing bonds in terms of spot rates also applies to the valuation of off-market swaps. Similar to bond valuation, the equilibrium value of a swap is obtained by discounting the swap's cash flows by their appropriate spot swap rates. The valuation of swaps using spot swap rates is referred to as the *zero-coupon approach*. The approach, in turn, requires generating a spot yield curve for swaps.

Zero-Coupon Swap Yield Curve — Bootstrapping

Since there is not an active market for zero discount swaps, implied zero-coupon swap rates need to be determined. One approach used to estimate spot rates is a sequential process commonly referred to as *bootstrapping*. This approach requires having at least one zero-coupon bond. Given this bond's rate, a coupon bond with the next highest maturity is used to obtain an implied spot rate; then another coupon bond with the next highest maturity is used to find the next spot rates, and so on. For swaps, bootstrapping uses a series of current generic swaps. For a yield curve defined by annual periods, the first step is to calculate the one-year zero-coupon rate, $Z(1)$. Since current generic swaps are priced at par, the one-year zero-coupon rate for a swap would be equal to the annual coupon rate on a one-year generic swap, $C(1)$ (assume annual payment frequency instead of the normal semiannual). For a par value of $1:

$$1 = \frac{1 + C(1)}{1 + Z(1)}$$

$$Z(1) = C(1)$$

The two-year swap, with an annual coupon rate of $C(2)$ and the one-year zero-coupon rate of $Z(1)$ can be used to calculated the two-year zero discount rate, $Z(2)$:

$$1 = \frac{C(2)}{1 + Z(1)} + \frac{1 + C(2)}{(1 + Z(2))^2}$$

$$Z(2) = \left[\frac{1 + C(2)}{1 - [C(2)/(1 + Z(1))]} \right]^{1/2} - 1$$

The three-year zero-coupon rate is found using the three-year swap and the one-year and two-year zero-coupon rates. Other rates are determined in a similar manner. Using this recursive method, a zero-coupon (or spot) yield curve for swaps can be generated from a series of generic swaps. These zero-coupon rates can then be used to discount the cash flows on a swap to determine its value.

Exhibit 14A.1 shows a yield curve of zero-coupon rates generated from a series of current generic swap rates. The swap rates shown in Column 4 are the annual fixed rates paid on the swaps. Each rate is equal to the yield on a corresponding T-note plus the swap spread. The swap spread reflects the credit risk of the swap party and the maturity of the swap. The zero-coupon swap rates shown in Column 5 are generated from these swap rates using the bootstrapping approach.

Note that since swaps involve semiannual cash flows, the annualized zero spot rates at 0.5 intervals are usually interpolated. Thus, the rate at 1.5 years is (0.05 + 0.055138)/2 = 0.05269; the rate at 2.5 years is (0.055138 + 0.060395)/2 = 0.0577664; the rate at 3.5 years is 0.05925; the rate at 4.5 years is 0.06385.

Valuation

Given the zero-coupon rates, suppose there is a 6.5%/LIBOR off-market swap with a maturity of two years and NP of $10 million. Given the two-year par value swap (Exhibit 14A.1) has a swap rate of 5.5%, the value of the fixed-payer's position on the 6.5% off-market swap using the zero-coupon approach would be −$187,473 and the value of the floating-position would be $187,473:

$$SV^{fix} = \begin{bmatrix} \dfrac{(0.055/2) - (0.065/2)}{(1 + (.05/2))^1} + \dfrac{(0.055/2) - (0.065/2)}{(1 + (.05/2))^2} \\ + \dfrac{(0.055/2) - (0.065/2)}{(1 + (0.052569/2))^3} + \dfrac{(0.055/2) - (0.065/2)}{(1 + (0.055138/2))^4} \end{bmatrix} \$10,000,000$$

$$= -\$187,473$$

EXHIBIT 14A.1 Generic Swap Yield Curve for Zero-Coupon Rates

1	2	3	4	5	6
Maturity in Years	Yield on T-Note	Swap Spread bp	Swap Rate	Zero-Coupon Rate Z	Implied 1-Year Forward Rate
1	0.040	100	0.050	0.050000	$RI_{10} = 0.05$
2	0.045	100	0.055	0.055138	$RI_{11} = 0.0603$
3	0.050	100	0.060	0.060395	$RI_{12} = 0.07099$
4	0.055	100	0.065		$RI_{13} = 0.082402$

Zero-coupon rates from bootstrapping
$Z(1) = .05$

$$Z(2): 1 = \frac{.055}{1+.05} + \frac{1.055}{(1+Z(2))^2}$$

$$Z(2) = \left[\frac{1.055}{1-.052381}\right]^{1/2} - 1 = .05513$$

$$Z(3): 1 = \frac{.06}{1.05} + \frac{.06}{(1.055138)^2} + \frac{1.06}{(1+Z(3))^3}$$

$$Z(3) = \left[\frac{1.06}{1-.111}\right]^{1/3} - 1 = .060395$$

One-year implied forward rates, RI_{1t}
$RI_{10} = Z(1) = .05$

$$RI_{11}: Z(2) = [(1+Z(1))(1+RI_{11})]^{1/2} - 1$$

$$RI_{11} = \frac{(1+Z(2))^2}{(1+Z(1))} - 1 = \frac{(1.055138)^2}{1.05} - 1 = .0603$$

$$RI_{12}: Z(3) = [(1+Z(1))(1+RI_{11})(1+RI_{12})]^{1/3} - 1$$

$$RI_{12} = \frac{(1+Z(3))^3}{(1+Z(1))(1+f_{11})} - 1 = \frac{(1.060395)^3}{(1.05)(1.0603)} - 1 = .07099$$

$$RI_{13}: Z(4) = [(1+Z(1))(1+RI_{11})(1+RI_{12})(1+RI_{13})]^{1/4} - 1$$

$$RI_{13} = \frac{(1+Z(4))^4}{(1+Z(1))(1+f_{11})(1+f_{12})} - 1 = \frac{(1.0658547)^4}{(1.05)(1.0603)(1.07099)} - 1 = .082402$$

$$SV^{fl} = \begin{bmatrix} \dfrac{(0.065/2)-(0.055/2)}{(1+(0.05/2))^1} + \dfrac{(0.065/2)-(0.055/2)}{(1+(0.05/2))^2} \\[2ex] + \dfrac{(0.065/2)-(0.055/2)}{(1+(0.052569/2))^3} + \dfrac{(0.065/2)-(0.055/2)}{(1+(0.055138/2))^4} \end{bmatrix} \$10,000,000$$

$$= \$187,473$$

Note that with the current *YTM* on the two-year bonds at 5.5%, the value of the 6.5%/LIBOR swap positions using the YTM approach would be −$186,971 (fixed), and $186.971 (floating):

$$SV^{fix} = \begin{bmatrix} \dfrac{(0.055/2)-(0.065/2)}{(1+(.055/2))^1} + \dfrac{(0.055/2)-(0.065/2)}{(1+(.055/2))^2} \\[2ex] + \dfrac{(0.055/2)-(0.065/2)}{(1+(0.055/2))^3} + \dfrac{(0.055/2)-(0.065/2)}{(1+(0.055/2))^4} \end{bmatrix} \$10,000,000$$

$$= -\$186,971$$

$$SV^{fl} = \begin{bmatrix} \dfrac{(0.065/2)-(0.055/2)}{(1.+(0.055/2))^1} + \dfrac{(0.065/2)-(0.055/2)}{(1+(.055/2))^2} \\[2ex] + \dfrac{(0.065/2)-(.055/2)}{(1+(.055/2))^3} + \dfrac{(0.065/2)-(.055/2)}{(1+(.055/2))^4} \end{bmatrix} \$10,000,000$$

$$= \$186,971$$

Thus, if the fixed position were valued by the YTM approach at $186,971, then a swap dealer could realize an arbitrage by buying the two-year swap at $186,971, and then selling (i.e., taking floating positions) four off-market 6.5%/LIBOR swaps with maturities of one to four years priced to yield their zero-coupon rates for a total of $187,473. As swap dealers try to exploit this arbitrage, they would drive the price of the swap to the $187,473. Thus, like bonds, the equilibrium price of a swap is obtained by discounting each of the net cash flows from an existing and current swap by their appropriate spot rates.

Implied Forward Swap Rates

Just as implied forward interest rates can be generated from current spot rates, implied forward rates on swaps can also be determined from current zero-coupon swap rates. Column 6 in Exhibit 14A.1 shows the one-year implied forward rates obtained from the zero-coupon rates (Column 5). The one-year implied forward swap rate (RI_{11}) of 6.03% is obtained given the one-year and two-year zero-coupon swap rates:

$$(1+Z_2)^2 = (1+Z(1))(1+RI_{11})$$

$$Z(2) = [(1+Z(1)(1+RI_{11})]^{1/2} - 1$$

$$RI_{11} = \frac{(1 + Z(2))^2}{(1 + Z(1))} - 1$$

$$RI_{11} = \frac{(1.055138)^2}{1.05} - 1 = 0.0603$$

Similarly, the implied one-year forward rate two years from the present (RI_{12}) of 7.099% is calculated from the current three-year zero-coupon swap rate, one-year zero-coupon swap rates, and the implied forward swap rate RI_{11}:

$$(1 + Z(3))^3 = (1 + Z(1))(1 + RI_{11})(1 + RI_{12})$$

$$Z(3) = [(1 + Z(1))(1 + RI_{11})(1 + RI_{12})]^{1/3} - 1$$

$$RI_{12} = \frac{(1 + Z(3))^3}{(1 + Z(1))(1 + RI_{11})} - 1$$

$$RI_{12} = \frac{(1.060395)^3}{(1.05)(1.0603)} - 1 = 0.07099$$

Finally, the implied one-year forward swap rate three years from the present (RI_{13}) of 8.2402% is calculated from the current four-year and one-year zero-coupon swap rates and the implied forward rates RI_{11} and RI_{12}:

$$(1 + Z(4))^4 = (1 + Z(1))(1 + RI_{11})(1 + RI_{12})(1 + RI_{13})$$

$$Z(4) = [(1 + Z(1))(1 + RI_{11})(1 + RI_{12})(1 + RI_{13})]^{1/4} - 1$$

$$RI_{13} = \frac{(1 + Z(4))^4}{(1 + Z(1))(1 + RI_{11})(1 + RI_{12})} - 1$$

$$RI_{13} = \frac{(1.0658547)^4}{(1.05)(1.0603)(1.07099)} - 1 = 0.082402$$

Break-Even Swap Rate

A corollary to the zero-coupon approach to valuation is that in the absence of arbitrage, the fixed rate on the swap (the swap rate) is that the rate, C^*, that makes the present value of the swap's fixed-rate payments equal to the present value of the swap's floating payments, with implied forward rates being used to estimate the future floating payments. The rate C^* is referred to as the *break-even swap rate*. For an N-year swap with a NP of $1, this condition states that in equilibrium:

$$\frac{C^*}{(1 + Z(1))} + \frac{C^*}{(1 + Z(2))^2} + \cdots + \frac{C^*}{(1 + Z(N))^N}$$

$$= \frac{Z(1)}{(1 + Z(1))} + \frac{RI_{11}}{(1 + Z(2))^2} + \cdots + \frac{RI_{1,N-1}}{(1 + Z(N))^N}$$

$$C^* = \frac{\dfrac{Z(1)}{(1+Z(1))} + \dfrac{RI_{11}}{(1+Z(2))^2} + \cdots + \dfrac{RI_{1,N-1}}{(1+Z(N))^N}}{\dfrac{1}{(1+Z(1))} + \dfrac{1}{(1+Z(2))^2} + \cdots + \dfrac{1}{(1+Z(N))^N}}$$

In terms of our example in Exhibit 14A.1, by substituting the one-year implied forward rates (Column 6) into the above equation, we can obtain the break-even swap rates of 5% for the one-year swap, 5.5% for the two-year, and 6% for the three-year swap. These break-even rates along with their calculations are shown in Exhibit 14A.2.

The break-even swap rate swap rate C^* is sometimes referred to as *market rate*. Accordingly, if swap dealers were to set swap rates equal to the break-even rates, then there would be no arbitrage from forming opposite positions in fixed-rate and floating-rate bonds priced at their equilibrium values nor any arbitrage from taking opposite positions in a swap and a strip of swaps. The break-even swap rates that we just calculated in turn matches the swap rates on the current swaps, implying that all three are par value swaps with no arbitrage opportunities. Break-even rates are used by swap dealers to help them determine the rates on new par value swaps, as well as the compensation to receive or pay on new off-market swaps in which the swap rates are set different than the break-even rates.

Break-Even Forward Swap Rates and the Valuation of Forward Swap

Like the break-even rate on a generic swap, the break-even rate on a forward swap, C_f^*, is that rate that equates the present value of the fixed-rate flows to the present value of floating-rate flows corresponding to the period of the underlying swap.

To illustrate, consider a two-year 6%/LIBOR swap, one year forward, in which the applicable zero swap yield curve and corresponding implied forward rates are the ones shown in Exhibit 14A.1. The break-even forward rate for this two-year 6%/LIBOR swap, one year forward, is found by solving for that coupon rate, C_f^*, that equates the present value of the forward swap's future fixed-rate payments of C_f^* in years 2 and 3 to the present value of the implied one-year forward rates one year and two years from the present of $RI_{11} = 0.0603$ and $RI_{12} = 0.07099$ (assume that the first effective date on the underlying swap starts at the expiration date of the forward swap). That is, C_f^* where:

$$\frac{C_f^*}{(1 + Z(2))^2} + \frac{C_f^*}{(1 + Z(3))^3} = \frac{RI_{11}}{(1 + Z(2))^2} + \frac{RI_{12}}{(1 + Z(3))^3}$$

$$C_f^* = \frac{\dfrac{RI_{11}}{(1+Z(2))^2} + \dfrac{RI_{12}}{(1+Z(3))^3}}{\dfrac{1}{(1+Z(2))^2} + \dfrac{1}{(1+Z(3))^3}}$$

Substituting the implied forward rates and zero-coupon rates into the above equation, we obtain a 6.546% break-even forward rate for the two-year 6%/LIBOR

EXHIBIT 14A.2 Break-Even Rates Generated from Information in Exhibit 14A.1

1	2		3	4	5
Maturity in Years	Zero-Coupon Rate Z	Implied 1-Year Forward Rate	Current Break-Even Rates C^*	Break-Even Forward Rates One Year Forward	Break-Even Forward Rates Two Years Forward
1	0.05	0.05	0.05		
2	0.055138	0.0603	0.055	0.0603	
3	0.060395	0.07099	0.06	0.06546	0.07099
4		0.082402			

1-year $C^* = Z(1) = 0.05$

2-year
$$C^* = \frac{\frac{Z(1)}{(1+Z(1))} + \frac{RI_{11}}{(1+Z(2))^2}}{\frac{1}{(1+Z(1))} + \frac{1}{(1+Z(2))^2}} = \frac{\frac{.05}{(1.05)} + \frac{.0603}{(1.055138)^2}}{\frac{1}{(1.05)} + \frac{1}{(1.055138)^2}} = 0.055$$

3-year
$$C^* = \frac{\frac{Z(1)}{(1+Z(1))} + \frac{RI_{11}}{(1+Z(2))^2} + \frac{RI_{12}}{(1+Z(3))^3}}{\frac{1}{(1+Z(1))} + \frac{1}{(1+Z(2))^2} + \frac{1}{(1+Z(3))^3}} = \frac{\frac{.05}{(1.05)} + \frac{.0603}{(1.055138)^2} + \frac{.07099}{(1.060395)^3}}{\frac{1}{(1.05)} + \frac{1}{(1.055138)^2} + \frac{1}{(1.060395)^3}} = 0.06$$

1-year swap, one year forward
$$\frac{C_f^*}{(1+Z(2))^2} = \frac{RI_{11}}{(1+Z(2))^2}$$
$$C_f^* = RI_{11} = 0.0603$$

2-year swap, one year forward
$$\frac{C_f^*}{(1+Z(2))^2} + \frac{C_f^*}{(1+Z(3))^3} = \frac{RI_{11}}{(1+Z(2))^2} + \frac{RI_{12}}{(1+Z(3))^3}$$
$$C_f^* = \frac{\frac{RI_{11}}{(1+Z(2))^2} + \frac{RI_{12}}{(1+Z(3))^3}}{\frac{1}{(1+Z(2))^2} + \frac{1}{(1+Z(3))^3}} = \frac{\frac{.0603}{(1.055138)^2} + \frac{.07099}{(1.060395)^3}}{\frac{1}{(1.055138)^2} + \frac{1}{(1.060395)^3}} = 0.06546$$

1-year swap, two years forward
$$\frac{C_f^*}{(1+Z(3))^3} = \frac{RI_{12}}{(1+Z(3))^3}$$
$$C_f^* = RI_{12} = 0.07099$$

swap, one year forward:

$$C_f^* = \frac{\dfrac{RI_{11}}{(1+Z(2))^2} + \dfrac{RI_{12}}{(1+Z(3))^3}}{\dfrac{1}{(1+Z(2))^2} + \dfrac{1}{(1+Z(3))^3}} = \frac{\dfrac{0.0603}{(1.055138)^2} + \dfrac{0.07099}{(1.060395)^3}}{\dfrac{1}{(1.055138)^2} + \dfrac{1}{(1.060395)^3}} = 0.06546$$

The value of a forward swap depends on whether the rate on the forward contract's underlying swap is different than its break-even forward swap rate. Given the specified fixed rate on the forward swap is at 6% and not at its break-even rate of 6.546%, the fixed payer's position on the underlying swap would have a value beginning in year one equal to the annual rate differential of 0.546% times the swap's NP for two years: $(0.00546)(\$10,000,000) = \$54,600$. The present value of this cash flow is equal to $94,835. Thus, the current value of the two-year 6%/LIBOR swap, one year forward, is \$94,835:

$$\text{Present value} = \frac{\$54,600}{(1.055138)^2} + \frac{\$54,600}{(1.060395)^3} = \$94,835$$

where

$$\text{Forward swap rate} = 6\% \text{ per year}$$

$$\text{Break-even swap rate} = 6.546\% \text{ per year}$$

$$\text{Fixed payer's cash flow} = (0.06546 - 0.06)\$10,000,000$$

$$= \$54,600 \text{ for years 2 and 3}$$

The floating-payer's position on the forward swap would be −$94,835, implying the forward position holder would require compensation. Note: If the forward swap rate had been set equal to the 6.546% break-even rate, then the economic value of the forward swap would be zero.

The Valuation of a Swaption

As with other options, the value of a swaption can be broken down into its intrinsic value, IV, and time value premium, TVP. In determining a swaption's IV, the asset underlying the option is a forward contract. That is, a three-year payer swaption on a two-year 7%/LIBOR swap is an option to take a fixed-payer's position on a two-year swap three years forward. The asset underlying this payer swaption is therefore the fixed-payer's position on a three-year forward contract with a forward swap rate of 7%. Thus, the first step in calculating a swaption's IV is to determine the break-even rate on the underlying forward contract, C_f^*. For example, in our above case, we found the break-even forward rate for a two-year swap, one year forward to be equal to $C_f^* = 6.546\%$.

Consider a one-year payer swaption on a two-year 6%/LIBOR swap. The buyer of this swaption would be purchasing a one-year option on a two-year swap to pay the fixed rate of 6% and receive the LIBOR. With the break-even forward rate equal to 6.546% and a strike rate of 6%, the payer swaption's intrinsic value is the 0.546% interest rate differential on the NP for two years beginning one years from the present. Using the zero-coupon swap rates from Exhibit 14A.1, the IV of this payer swaption is $94,835:

$$IV_p = \text{Max}[C_f^* - C^X, 0] \left[\sum_{t=1}^{M} \frac{1}{(1 + Z(T + t))^t} \right] NP$$

$$IV_p = \text{Max}[0.06546 - .06, 0] \left[\frac{1}{(1.055138)^2} + \frac{1}{(1.060395)^3} \right] (\$10,000,000)$$

$$IV_p = \$94,835$$

where

$\qquad T =$ expiration on the swaption
$\qquad M =$ Maturity on the underlying swap
$\qquad C_f^* =$ Break-even forward swap rate $= 6.546\%$
$\qquad C^X =$ Exercise rate
$\qquad NP = \$10,000,000$

Note, the IV of the payer swaption is directly related to the underlying break-even rate. That is, for break-even rates above the exercise rate, C^X (6%), the IV increases as the break-even rate increases, and for rates below C^X (6%), it is zero.

Just the opposite relations hold for receiver swaptions. The receiver swaption's IV is

$$IV_C = \text{Max}[C^X - C_f^*, 0] \left[\sum_{t=1}^{M} \frac{1}{(1 + Z(T + t))^t} \right] NP$$

Thus, the IV on a one-year receiver swaption on a two-year swap with an exercise rate of 7% (the right to receive 7% and pay LIBOR) with NP of $10 million would be $78,855.

$$IV_C = \text{Max}[0.07 - 0.06546, 0] \left[\frac{1}{(1.055138)^2} + \frac{1}{(1.060395)^3} \right] (\$10,000,000)$$

$$= \$78,855$$

Given that there is some time to expiration, a swaption will trade at a value above its IVs. Like other options, the swaption's TVP depends primarily on the volatility of the underlying forward rate, with the greater the volatility, the greater the swaption's TVP and value. The volatility of forward rates is often estimated using current swap rates or spot Treasury rates as a proxy for the implied futures rates.

CHAPTER 15

Credit Default and Currency Swaps

Historically, a bond portfolio manager with speculative-grade bonds or a financial institution with a portfolio of loans managed their portfolio's exposure to credit risk by the selection and allocation of credits (bonds or loans) in their portfolio. With the development of the credit default swap market, however, a bond manager or lender could alternatively change her credit risk by simply buying or selling swaps to change the credit risk profile on either an individual bond or loan or on a bond or loan portfolio. Similarly, a multinational company with earnings exposed to exchange rate changes could reduce their exchange-rate exposure by swapping their dollar-denominated debt for debt denominated in another currency. In this chapter, we continue our analysis of swaps by examining currency and credit default swaps.

Generic Credit Default Swap

Credit default swaps and other related credit derivatives are contracts in which the payoffs depend on the credit quality of a company. In a standard *credit default swap* (CDS), a counterparty buys protection against default by a particular company or economic entity from another counterparty (seller). The company or entity is known as the reference entity and a default is known as a credit event. The buyer of the CDS makes periodic payments or a premium to the seller until the end of the life of the CDS or until the credit event occurs. The payments on a CDS are quoted as an annual percentage of the notional principal (NP). The payment is referred to as the *CDS spread.* If the credit event occurs, then the buyer has the right to sell a particular bond (or loan) issued by the company for its par value (physical delivery). Alternatively, if the event occurs, some contracts allow the buyer to receive a cash settlement based on the difference between the par value and the defaulted bond's market price times a notional principal equal to the bond's total par value. In the standard CDS, payments are made in arrears either on a quarterly, semiannual, or annual basis. The par value of the bond or debt is the notional principal used for determining the payments of the buyer. In many CDS contracts, a number of bonds or credits can be delivered in the case of a default. In the event of a default, the payoff from the CDS is equal to the face value of the bond (or *NP*) minus the value of the bond just after the default. The value of the bond just after the default expressed as a percentage of the bond's face value is the *recovery rate* (*RR*). Thus, the payoff from the CDS is

$$\text{CDS payoff} = (1 - RR)NP - \text{Accrued payment}$$

If the value on the $100 million CDS were $30 per $100 face value, then the recovery rate would be 30% and the payoff to the CDS buyer would be $70 million (= (1 − 0.30)$100 million) minus any accrued payment.

Z-Spread, CDS Spread, and Credit Spread

Suppose a five-year BBB corporate bond was trading at a 3% credit spread over a five-year risk-free bond that was yielding 5% (assume no option or liquidity risk). If the spread on a five-year CDS on a BBB-quality bond, in turn, were 3%, then an investor could obtain a five-year risk-free investment yielding 5% by either buying a five-year Treasury or by buying the five-year BBB corporate yielding 8% and purchasing the CDS on the underlying credit at a 3% spread.

If the spread on a CDS were not equal to the credit spread on the underlying bond, then an arbitrage opportunity would exist by taking positions in the bond, risk-free security, and the CDS.

For example, suppose a swap bank were offering the above CDS for 2% instead of 3%. In this case, an investor looking for a five-year risk-free investment would find it advantageous to create the synthetic risk-free investment with the BBB bond and the CDS. That is, the investor could earn 1% more than the yield on the Treasury by buying the five-year BBB corporate yielding 8% and purchasing the CDS on the underlying credit at 2%. In addition to the investor gaining, an arbitrageur could also realize a free lunch equivalent to a five-year cash flow of 1% of the par value of the bond by shorting the Treasury at 5% and then using the proceeds to buy the BBB corporate and the CDS. These actions by investors and arbitrageurs, in turn, would have the impact of pushing the spread on the CDS towards 3%—the underlying bond's credit risk spread.

The strategy of selling a higher-quality bond (e.g., AAA bonds), buying lower-quality bonds (e.g., BBB), and buying CDS was the basis of many synthetic collateralized debt obligation (CDO) structures formed prior to 2008. That is, the manager or sponsor of a CDO would issue AAA-quality CDOs, buy CDS, and purchase speculative-grade bonds.

On the other hand, suppose a swap bank were offering the CDS at a 4% spread instead of 3%. In this case, an investor looking to invest in the higher yielding five-year BBB bonds could earn 1% more than the 8% on the BBB bond by creating a synthetic five-year BBB bond by purchasing the five-year Treasury at 5% and selling the CDS at 4%. Similarly, a bond portfolio manager holding five-year BBB bonds yielding 8% could pick up an additional 1% yield with the same credit risk exposure by selling the bonds along with the CDS at 4% and then using the proceeds from the bond sale to buy the five-year Treasuries yielding 5%. In addition, an arbitrageur could realize a free lunch equivalent to a five-year cash flow of 1% of the par value on the bond by shorting the BBB bond, selling the CDS, and then using proceeds to purchase five-year Treasuries. With these positions, the arbitrageur for each of the next five years would receive 5% from her Treasury investment and 4% from her CDS, while paying only 8% on her short BBB bond position. Furthermore, her holdings of Treasury securities would enable her to cover her obligation on the CDS if there was a default. Finally, a manager or sponsor of a collateralized debt obligation could issue BBB-quality CDOs, sell CDS, and purchase investment-grade bonds. Theses actions of arbitrageurs would cause the spread on a credit default swap to equal the credit spread on the bond.

To reiterate, the collective actions of investors, bond portfolio managers, CDO managers, and arbitrageur would have the effect of pushing the spread on CDS toward the spread on the underlying bond. This equilibrium arbitrage-free spread is referred to as the *Z-spread*.

Z-Spread, CDS Spread, and Probability of the Loss of Principal

In an efficient market, the credit spread on bonds and the equilibrium spreads on CDSs represent the market's implied expectation of the expected loss from the principal from default. To see this, consider a portfolio of five-year BBB bonds trading at a 3% credit spread. The 3% premium that investors receive from the bond portfolio represents their compensation for an implied expected loss of 3% per year of the principal from the defaulted bonds. If the spread were 5% instead of 3% and bond investors believed that the expected loss from default on such bonds would be only 3% per year of the principal, then the bond investors would want more BBB bonds, driving the price up and the yield down until the premium reflected a 3% spread. Similarly, if the spread were 1% instead of 3% and bond investors believed the default loss on a portfolio of BBB bonds would be 3% per year, then the demand and price for such bonds would decrease, increasing the yield to reflect a credit spread of 3%. Thus, in an efficient market, the credit spread on bonds and the equilibrium spreads on CDS represent the market's implied expectation of the expected loss per year from the principal from default. In the case of a CDS, the equilibrium spread can therefore be defined as the implied probability of default loss of the principal on the contract.

CDS Valuation

The total value of a CDS's payments is equal to the sum of the present values of the periodic CDS spread (Z) times the NP over the life of the CDs, discounted at the risk-free rate (R):

$$PV(\text{CDS payments}) = \sum_{t=1}^{M} \frac{Z\,NP}{(1 + R)^t}$$

The present value of the payment on a five-year CDS with an equilibrium spread of 2% and a NP of \$100 would be \$8.42 (assuming annual compounding):

$$PV(\text{CDS payments}) = \sum_{t=1}^{5} \frac{(0.02)(\$100)}{(1.06)^t} = \$8.42$$

The buyer (seller) of this five-year CDS would therefore be willing to make (receive) payments over five years that have a present value of \$8.42 per \$100 of NP.

The value of the CDS payments is also equal to the expected default protection the buyer (seller) receives (pays). The value of the CDS protection, in turn, is equal to the present value of the expected payout in the case of default:

$$PV(\text{Expected payout}) = \sum_{t=1}^{M} \frac{p_t\, NP(1 - RR)}{(1 + R)^t}$$

where

p_t = probability of default in period t conditional on no earlier default
RR = recovery rate (as a proportion of the face value) on the bond at the time of default
NP = notional principal equal to the par value of the bond

Note that the probability of default, p_t, is the conditional probability of no prior defaults. Thus, the conditional probability of default in year 3 is based on the probability that the bond will survive until year 3. Conditional default probabilities are referred to as *default intensities*.

Instead of defining a CDS's expected payout in terms periodic probability density, p_t, the CDS's expected payout can alternatively be defined by the average conditional default loss probability, $\bar{p}$:

$$PV(\text{Expected payout}) = \sum_{t=1}^{M} \frac{\bar{p}\, NP(1 - RR)}{(1 + R)^t} = \bar{p}NP(1 - RR) \sum_{t=1}^{M} \frac{1}{(1 + R)^t}$$

Given an equilibrium spread of 0.02 and a recovery rate of 30%, the implied probability density for our illustrative CDS would be 0.02857. This implied probability is obtained by solving for $\bar{p}$ that makes the present value of the expected payout equal to present value of the payments of $8.42:

$$PV(\text{Expected payout}) = PV(\text{Payments})$$

$$\sum_{t=1}^{M} \frac{\bar{p}\, NP(1 - RR)}{(1 + R)^t} = \sum_{t=1}^{M} \frac{Z\, NP}{(1 + R)^t}$$

$$\bar{p} = \frac{Z}{(1 - RR)}$$

$$\bar{p} = \frac{0.02}{(1 - 0.30)} = 0.02857$$

Note that if there were no recovery ($RR = 0$), then the implied probability would be equal to the spread Z, which as we noted earlier can be thought of as the probability of default of principal. The probability density implied by the market is referred to as the risk-neutral probability since it is based on an equilibrium spread that is arbitrage free.

Alternative CDS Valuation Approach

Suppose in our preceding example, the estimated default intensity, sometimes referred to as the *real-world probability*, on the five-year BBB bond were 0.02 and not the implied probability of 0.02857. In this case, the present value of the CDS expected payout would be $5.897 instead of $8.42:

$$PV(\text{Expected payout}) = \sum_{t=1}^{5} \frac{(0.02)(\$100)(1 - 0.30)}{(1.06)^t} = \$5.897$$

Given the spread on the CDS is at 2% and the present value of the payments are $8.42, buyers of the CDS would have to pay more on the CDS than the value they receive on the expected payoff ($5.897). If the real-world probability density is 0.02 is accurate, then buyers of the CDS would eventually push the spread down until it is equal to the value of the protection. For the payment on the CDS to match the expected protection, the spread would have to equal 0.014. This implied spread is found by solving for the Z that equates the present value of the payments to the present value of the expected payout given the real-world probability of $\bar{p} = 0.02$ and the estimated recovery rate of $RR = 0.30$. That is:

$$PV(\text{Payments}) = PV(\text{Expected payout})$$

$$\sum_{t=1}^{M} \frac{Z\, NP}{(1 + R)^t} = \sum_{t=1}^{M} \frac{\bar{p}\, NP(1 - RR)}{(1 + R)^t}$$

$$Z = \bar{p}(1 - RR)$$

$$Z = (0.02)(1 - 0.30) = 0.014$$

We now have two alternative methods for pricing a CDS. On the one hand, we can value the CDS swap given the credit spread in the market and then determine the present value of the payments. Thus, in terms of our example, we would use the market spread of 2% and value the swap at $8.42 with the implied probability density (or risk-neutral probability) being 0.02857. On the other hand, we can value the swap given the estimated probabilities of default and then determine the present value of the expected payout. In terms of our example, we would use the estimated real-world probability of 0.02 and value the CDS at $5.897 with the implied credit spread being 0.014.

The argument for pricing CDS using real-world probabilities ultimately depends on the ability of practitioners to estimated default probabilities. There are several approaches for estimating conditional probabilities. The simplest and most direct one is to estimate the probabilities based on historical default rates. Exhibit 15.1 shows the cumulative default rates, unconditional probability rates, and conditional probability rates (probability intensities) for corporate bonds with quality ratings of Aaa, Baa, B, and Caa. The probabilities shown in the table are the average historical cumulative default rates as compiled by Moody's. The unconditional probabilities are the probabilities of default in a given year as viewed from time zero. The unconditional probability of a bond defaulting during year t is the difference in the cumulative probability in year t minus the cumulative probability of default in year $t-1$. As shown in the table, the probability of a Caa bond default during year 4 is equal to 7.18% (= 46.90% − 39.72%). Finally, the conditional probability is the probability of default in a given year conditional on no prior defaults. This probability is equal to unconditional probability of default in time t as a proportion of the bond's probability of survival at the beginning of the period. The probability of survival is equal to 100 minus the cumulative probability. For example, the probability that a Caa bond will survive until the end of year 3 is 60.28% (100 minus its cumulative probability of 39.72%), and the probability that the Caa bond will default during year 4 conditional on no prior defaults is 11.91% (= 7.18%/60.28%). As noted earlier, conditional probabilities of default are known as default intensities. These probabilities, in turn, can be used to determine the expected payoff on a swap.

Using the conditional probabilities generated from the historical cumulative default rates, the values and spreads for four CDS with quality ratings of Aaa, Baa, B, and Caa are also shown in Exhibit 15.1. Each swap has a maturity of five years, annual payments, NP of $100, and recovery rate of 30%. The values are obtained by calculating the present values of the expected payoff. The spreads on the CDS are the spreads that equate the present value of the payments to the present value of the

EXHIBIT 15.1 Cumulative Default Rates, Probability Intensities, and CDS Values and Spreads

Average Cumulative Default Rates 1970-2006 (Moody's) in %

Year	1	2	3	4	5	PV(Expected Payoff) NP = $100 and RR = .3	CDS Z-Spread
Aaa							
Cumulative Probability (%)	0.00000	0.00000	0.00000	0.03000	0.10000		
Unconditional Probability (%)	0.00000	0.00000	0.00000	0.03000	0.07000		
Conditional Probability p (%)	0.00000	0.00000	0.00000	0.03000	0.07002		
Present Value of p at 6%	0	0	0	0.0237628	0.052324	0.053260605	0.00013
Baa							
Cumulative Probability (%)	0.18000	0.51000	0.93000	1.43000	1.94000		
Unconditional Probability (%)	0.18000	0.33000	0.42000	0.50000	0.51000		
Conditional Probability p (%)	0.18000	0.33060	0.42215	0.50469	0.51740		
Present Value of p at 6%	0.169811321	0.294228	0.354448	0.3997646	0.38663	1.123417867	0.002666953
B							
Cumulative Probability (%)	5.24000	11.30000	17.04000	22.05000	26.79000		
Unconditional Probability (%)	5.24000	6.06000	5.74000	5.01000	4.74000		
Conditional Probability p (%)	5.24000	6.39510	6.47125	6.03905	6.08082		
Present Value of p at 6%	4.943396226	5.691619	5.433387	4.7834972	4.543943	17.77709035	0.04220217
Caa							
Cumulative Probability (%)	19.48000	30.49000	39.72000	46.90000	52.62000		
Unconditional Probability (%)	19.48000	11.01000	9.23000	7.18000	5.72000		
Conditional Probability p (%)	19.48000	13.67362	13.27866	11.91108	10.77213		
Present Value of p at 6%	18.37735849	12.16947	11.14902	9.4346923	8.049561	41.42607634	0.098344009

$$PV(\text{Expected Payoff}) = \sum_{t=1}^{M} \frac{p_t \, NP(1 - RR)}{(1+R)^t} \qquad Z = \frac{\displaystyle\sum_{t=1}^{M} \frac{p_t(1 - RR)}{(1+R)^t}}{\displaystyle\sum_{t=1}^{M} \frac{1}{(1+R)^t}}$$

expected payoff. For example, the present value of the expected payoff for the CDS with a B-quality rating is 17.78:

$$PV(\text{Expected payoff}) = \sum_{t=1}^{M} \frac{p_t NP(1 - RR)}{(1 + R)^t}$$

$$PV(\text{Expected payoff}) = (\$100)(1 - 0.3)$$

$$\left[\frac{0.0524}{(1.06)} + \frac{0.06395}{(1.06)^2} + \frac{0.0647125}{(1.06)^3} + \frac{0.0603905}{(1.06)^4} + \frac{0.0608082}{(1.06)^5} \right]$$

$$PV(\text{Expected payoff}) = 17.78$$

The spread on the B-quality CDS that equates the present value of its payments to the expected payoff of $17.78 is 0.0422:

$$\sum_{t=1}^{M} \frac{Z\,NP}{(1 + R)^t} = \sum_{t=1}^{M} \frac{p_t\,NP(1 - RR)}{(1 + R)^t}$$

$$Z \sum_{t=1}^{5} \frac{\$100}{(1.06)^t} = \$17.78$$

$$Z = \frac{\$17.78}{\displaystyle\sum_{t=1}^{5} \frac{\$100}{(1.06)^t}} = \frac{\$17.78}{\$421.2364} = 0.0422$$

As shown in the exhibit, the present value of the expected payoffs on the Caa-quality CDS is greater ($41.43) than the B-quality CDS quality. As expected, the CDS values and spreads are greater, the greater the default risk.

The Value of an Off-Market CDS Swap

Similar to a generic par value interest rate swap, a swap rate on a new CDS is generally set so that there is not an initial exchange of money. Over time and as economic conditions change, though, the value of an existing CDS will change. For example, suppose a bond fund manager bought the illustrative five-year CDS on BBB bond at the 2% spread, and one year later the economy became weaker, causing credit spreads on four-year BBB bonds and new CDS spreads to increase to 2.5% (assume for this discussion that CDS spreads are determined by bond credit spreads in the market). Suppose the bond fund manager sold her 2% CDS to a swap bank who hedged the CDS by selling a new 2.5% CDS on the four-year BBB bond. With a buyer's position on the assumed 2% CDS and seller's position on the 2.5% CDS, the swap bank, in turn, would gain 0.5% of the NP for the next four years. Given a discount rate of 6%, the present value of this gain would be $1.73 per $100 *NP*. The swap banks would therefore pay the bond manager a maximum of $1.73 for assuming the swap.

Offsetting Swap Positions

Buyer of 2% CDS swap	Pay 2% of NP	Receive default protection
Seller of 2.5% CDS swap	Receive 2.5%	Pay default protection
	Receive 0.5% per year	

$$SV = \sum_{t=1}^{4} \frac{(\text{Current spread} - \text{Existing Spread})(NP)}{(1 + R)^t} = \sum_{t=1}^{4} \frac{0.005\,(\$100)}{(1.06)^t} = \$1.73$$

With four years left on the current swap, the increase in credit spreads in the market has increased the value of the buyer's position on the CDS swap by $1.73 from $6.93 to 8.66:

$$\text{Existing CDS: PV(CDS payments)} = \sum_{t=1}^{4} \frac{(0.02)(\$100)}{(1.06)^t} = \$6.93$$

$$\text{Current PV(CDS payments)} = \sum_{t=1}^{4} \frac{(.025)(\$100)}{(1.06)^t} = \$8.66$$

Change in value = $1.73

The increase in value on the buyer's position of the exiting swap reflects the fact that with poorer economic conditions, the 2% swap payments now provide greater default protection (i.e., the present value of the expect payout is greater).

For the seller of the CDS, the increase in credit spreads causes a decrease in the value of the seller's positions. For example, suppose that an insurance company was the one who sold the five-year CDS on the BBB bond at the 2% spread to the bond portfolio manager (via a swap bank) and that one year later the credit spread on new four-year CDS on BBB bonds was again at 2.5%. If the insurance company were to sell its seller's position to a swap bank, the swap bank could hedge the assumed position by taking a buyer's position on a new four-year, 2.5% CDS on the BBB bond. With the offsetting positions, the swap bank would lose 0.5% of the NP for the next four years. Given a discount rate of 6%, the present value of this loss would be $1.73 per $100 *NP*. The swap banks would therefore charge the insurance company at least $1.73 for assuming the seller's position on the swap:

To summarize, an increase in the credit spread will increase the value of the buyer's position on an existing CDS and decrease the seller's position. Just the opposite occurs if economic conditions improve and credit spreads decrease.

Other Credit Derivatives

The market for CDS has grown dramatically over the last decade. With growth, there has also been an increase in the creation of other credit derivatives. The most noteworthy of these other credit derivative are the binary swap, credit swap basket, CDS forward contracts, CDS option contracts, contingent swaps, and total return swaps (see Box 15.1).

BOX 15.1: OTHER CDSs AND CREDIT DERIVATIVES

1. ***Binary CDS:*** A binary CDS is identical to the generic CDS except that the payoff in the case of a default is a specified dollar amount. Often the fixed payoff is the principal on the underlying credit. When this is the case, then the only difference between the generic and binary swap is that the generic CDS adjusts the payoff by subtracting the recovery value, whereas the binary CDS does not. Without the recovery value, the value of a binary CDS is more sensitive to changes in credit spreads or default probabilities.
2. ***Basket CDS:*** In a basket credit default swap, there is a group of reference entities or credits instead of one, and there is usually a specified payoff whenever one of the reference entities defaults. Basket CDS can vary by the type of agreement governing the payout. For example, an *add-up basket CDS* provides a payout when any reference credit in the basket defaults; a *first-to-default CDS* provides a payout only when the first entry defaults; a *second-to-default CDS* provides a payout when the second default occurs; an *nth-to-default CDS* provides a payout when the *n*th credit entry defaults. Typically, after the relevant entry defaults, the swap is terminated.
3. ***CDS Forward Contracts:*** A CDS forward contract is a contract to take a buyer's position or a seller's position on a particular CDS at a specified spread at some future date. CDS forward contract provide a tool for locking in the credit spread on future credit position.
4. ***CDS Option Contracts:*** A CDS option is an option to buy or sell a particular CDS at specified swap rate at a specified future time. For example, a one-year option to buy a five-year CDS on GE for 300 basis points. At expiration, the holder of this option would exercise her right to take the buyer's position at 300 basis points if current five-year CDSs on GE were greater than 300 basis points; in contrast, she would allow the option to expire and take the current CDS on GE if it is offered at 300 basis points or less.
5. ***Contingent CDS:*** A contingent CDS provides a payout that is contingent on two or more events occurring. For example, the payoff might require both a credit default of the reference entity and an additional event such as a credit event with another entity or a change in a market variable.
6. ***Total Return Swaps:*** In a total return swap, there is an agreement to exchange the return on an asset (such as a bond, bond portfolio, stock, or stock portfolio) for some benchmark rate such as LIBOR plus basis points. In the case of an exchange of the return on a bond or bond portfolio for LIBOR and basis points, the return on the bond includes coupons and gains and losses on the bond. Such a swap allows parties to trade different risk, including credit risk.

7. **Equity Swap:** In an equity swap, one party agrees to pay the return on an equity index, such as the S&P 500, and the other party agrees to pay a floating rate (LIBOR) or fixed rate. For example, on an S&P 500/LIBOR swap, the equity-payer would agree to pay the six-month rate of change on the S&P 500 (e.g., proportional change in the index between effective dates) times a *NP* in return for LIBOR times *NP*, and the debt payer would agree to pay the LIBOR in return for the S&P 500 return. Equity swaps are useful to fund managers who want to increase or decrease the equity or bond exposure of their portfolios as part of their overall asset allocation strategy.

8. **CAT Bond:** A CAT bond pays the buyer a higher-than-normal interest rate. In return for the additional interest, the CAT bondholder agrees to provide protection for losses from a specified event up to a specified amount or when the losses exceed a specified amount. For example, an insurance company could issue a CAT bond with a principal of $200 million against a hurricane cost exceeding $300 million. The CAT bondholders would then lose some or possibly all principal if the event occurs and the cost exceeds $300 million.

Currency Swaps

In its simplest form, a currency swap involves a loan exchange of principal and interest in one currency for the interest and principal in another. For example, a US company swaps a 6% loan in dollars to a British company for their 4.5% loan in sterling. The market for currency swaps consists of corporations and other economic entities that can borrow in one currency at relatively favorable terms but need to borrow in another. For example, a US multinational corporation that can obtain favorable borrowing terms for a dollar loan made in the United States, but really needs a loan in sterling to finance its operations in London, might use a currency swap. To meet such a need, the company would go to a swap dealer who would try to match its needs with another party wanting the opposite position. For example, the dealer might match the US multinational with a British multinational corporation with operations in the US that it is financing with a sterling-denominated loan, but would prefer instead a dollar-denominated loan. If the loans are approximately equivalent, then the dealer could arrange a swap agreement in which the companies simply exchange their principal and interest payments. If the loans are not equivalent, the swap dealer may have to bring in other parties who are looking to swap, or the dealer could take the opposite position and then hedge it with positions in dollar-denominated and sterling-denominated bonds or by using the forward exchange market.

Example

As an example, suppose a British company plans to issue five-year bonds worth £100 million at 4.5% interest, but actually needs an equivalent amount in dollars, $150 million (current $/£ rate is $1.50/£), to finance its new manufacturing facility in the United States. Also, suppose there is a US company that plans to issue $150 million in bonds at 6%, with a maturity of five years that really needs £100 million to set up its distribution center in London. To meet each other's needs, suppose that both companies go to a swap bank that sets up the following swap agreement.

1. The British company will issue five-year £100 million bonds paying 4.5% interest. It will then deliver the £100 million to the swap bank that will pass it on to the US company to finance its British operation.

    The US company will issue five-year $150 million bonds. The US company will then pass the $150 million to the swap bank that will pass it on to the British company who will use the funds to finance the construction of its US manufacturing facility (see Exhibit 15.2a).

EXHIBIT 15.2 Currency Swap

(a) Initial Cash Flow

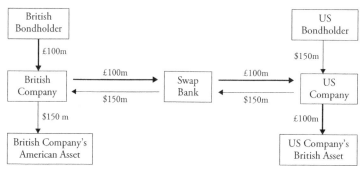

(b) Annual Interest Cash flow

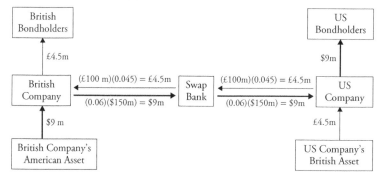

(c) Principal Payment at Maturity

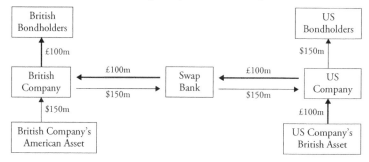

2. The British company will pay the 6% interest on $150 million ($9 million) to the swap bank who will pass it on to the US company so it can pay its US bondholders.

   The US company will pay the 4.5% interest on £100 million ((0.045) (£100 million) = £4.5 million), to the swap bank who will pass it on to the British company so it can pay its British bondholders (see Exhibit 15.2b).

3. At maturity, the British company will pay $150 million to the swap bank who will pass it on to the US company so it can pay its US bondholders.

   At maturity, the US company will pay £100 million to the swap bank, which will pass it on to the British company so it can pay its British bondholders (see Exhibit 15.2c).

Comparative Advantage

The currency swap in the above example represents an exchange of equivalent loans. Most currency swaps, however, are the result of financial and nonfinancial corporations exploiting a comparative advantage resulting from different rates in different currencies for different borrowers.

To see the implications of comparative advantage with currency swaps, suppose the US and British companies in the preceding example both have access to each country's lending markets and that the US company is more creditworthy, and as such, can obtain lower rates than the British company in both the US and British markets. For example, suppose the US company can obtain 6% US dollar-denominated loans in the US market and 4.25% sterling-denominated loans in the British market, while the best the British company can obtain is 7% in the US dollar market and 4.5% in the British pound market.

Loan Rates for US and British Companies in Dollars and Pounds

Spot: $E_0 = \$1.50/BP$

	US Dollar Market (rate on $)	British Pound Market (rate on BP)
US Company	6.00%	4.25%
British Company	7.00%	4.50%

With these rates, the US company has a comparative advantage in the US dollar market. It pays 1% less than the British company in the US dollar market, compared to only 0.25% less in the British pound market. On the other hand, the British company has a comparative advantage in the British market. It pays 0.25% more than the US company in the Britain pound market, compared to 1% more in the US dollar market. When such a comparative advantage exists, a swap bank is in a position to arrange a swap to benefit one or both companies. For example, suppose in this case a swap bank sets up the following swap arrangement:

1. The US company borrows $150 million at 6% and agrees to swap it for £100 million loan at 4%.
2. The British company borrows £100 million at 4.5% and agrees to swap it for $100 million loan at 6.75%.

Exhibit 15.3 shows the cash flow of interest for the agreement (the initial cash flows at the outset and principal payment at maturity are the same as in previous example shown in Exhibit 15.2a and 15.2c). In this swap arrangement, the American company benefits by paying 0.25% less than it could obtain by borrowing British pounds directly in the British pound market, and the British company gains by paying 0.25% less than it could obtain directly from the US dollar market.

EXHIBIT 15.3 Currency Swap Comparative Advantage

Annual Interest Cash flow

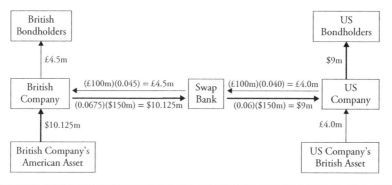

Swap Bank's $ Position			Swap Bank's £ Position		
Receives:(0.0675)($150m)	=	$10.125m	Receives: (0.04)(£100m)	=	£4m
Pays: (0.06)($ 150m)	=	−$9m	Pays: (0.045)(£100m)	=	−£4.5m
Net $ Receipt:		$1.125m	Net £ Payment:		−£0.5m

1	2	3	4	5	6
Year	$ Cash Flow	£ Cash Flow	Forward Exchange: $/£	$ Cost of Sterling Column (4) X Column (3)	Net $ Revenue Column (2) − Column (5)
1	$1,125,000	£500,000	$1.529126	−$764,563	$360,437
2	$1,125,000	£500,000	$1.558818	−$779,409	$345,591
3	$1,125,000	£500,000	$1.589086	−$794,543	$330,457
4	$1,125,000	£500,000	$1.619942	−$809,971	$315,029
5	$1,125,000	£500,000	$1.651398	−$825,699	$299,301
					$1,650,815

Note that the swap bank in this case will receive $10.125 million each year from the British company, while only having to pay $9 million to the US company, for a net dollar receipt of $1.125 million. On the other hand, the swap bank will receive only £4 million from the US company, while having to pay £4.5 million to the British company, for a net sterling payment of £0.25 million (see table in Exhibit 15.3).

The swap bank has a position equivalent to a series of long currency forward contracts in which it agrees to buy £0.5 million for $1.125 million each year. The swap bank's implied forward rate on each of these contracts is $2.25/£:

$$E_f = \frac{\$1.125\text{m}}{£0.5\,\text{m}} = \frac{\$2.25}{£}$$

The swap bank can, in turn, hedge its position with currency forward contracts. If the forward rate is less than $2.25/£, then the bank would gain from hedging the swap agreement with forward contracts to buy £0.5 million each year for the next five years. For example, suppose the yield curves applicable for the swap bank is flat at 5.0% in US dollars and flat at 3.0% in British pounds. Using the interest rate parity relation, the one-, two-, three-, four-, and five-year forward exchange rates would be:

$$E_f = E_0 \left(\frac{1 + R_{\text{US}}}{1 + R_{\text{GB}}} \right)^T$$

$$T = 1 : \quad E_f = (\$1.50/£)\left(\frac{1.05}{1.03} \right)^1 = \$1.529126/£$$

$$T = 2 : \quad E_f = (\$1.50/£)\left(\frac{1.05}{1.03} \right)^2 = \$1.558818/£$$

$$T = 3 : \quad E_f = (\$1.50/£)\left(\frac{1.05}{1.03} \right)^3 = \$1.589086/£$$

$$T = 4 : \quad E_f = (\$1.50/£)\left(\frac{1.05}{1.03} \right)^4 = \$1.619942/£$$

$$T = 5 : \quad E_f = (\$1.50/£)\left(\frac{1.05}{1.03} \right)^5 = \$1.651398/£$$

The swap bank could enter into forward contracts to buy £0.5M each year for the next five years at these forward rates. With all of the forward rates less than implied forward swap rate of $2.25/£, the bank's dollar costs of buying £0.5M each year would be less than its $1.125 million annual inflow from the swap. By combining its swap position with forward contracts, the bank would be able to earn a total profit from the deal of $1,650,815 (see table in Exhibit 15.3). (Note: Instead of forward contracts, the swap bank also could hedge its swap positions by using a money market position; see Chapter 2.)

In summary, the presence of comparative advantage creates a currency swap market in which swap banks look at the borrowing rates offered in different currencies to different borrowers and at the forward exchange rates and money market rates that they can obtain for hedging. Based on these different rates, they will arrange swaps that provide each borrower with rates better than the ones they can directly obtain and a profit for them that will compensate them for facilitating the deal and assuming the credit risk of each counterparty.

Changing Earnings Exposure to Exchange Rate Changes Using Swaps

In addition to comparative advantage, another important use of currency swaps is reducing a multinational company's earnings or balance sheet to exchange-rate exposure. Consider a US-owned company that operates an oil refinery in Great Britain and sells its oil in BP to the British market. Specifically, the company buys 320,000 barrels per year at $50/brl. (cost in dollars = ($50/brl.)(320,000 barrels) = $16,000,000), refines the oil in Britain, incurring an operating cost of £2 million, and then sells the oil to a pipeline at £62.50 (Revenue = (£62.50/brl.)(320,000 barrels) = £20 million). The company's effective tax rate is 40%, it has no depreciation or depletion allowances, and it regularly remits it earnings in dollars (converts its net revenue from BPs to dollars). The company also has $100 million in debt (used to finance the construction of the British refinery) in which it pays an annual 8% interest ($8 million annual interest payment). The first panel in Exhibit 15.4 shows the US company's income statement in US dollars for the case in which the $/£ exchange rate is $2.00/£. In this case, the US company's earnings after taxes (EAT) in dollars are $7.2 million.

As shown in Exhibit 15.4, if the exchange rate were to decrease by 25% to $1.50/£, the US company's EAT would decrease 75% to $1.8 million. By contrast, if the exchange rate were to increase by 25% to $2.50/£, the company's EAT would increase 75% to $12.6 million. The US firm's revenue is exposed to exchange-rate changes. However, by operating in Great Britain it does reduce its operating exposure to exchange-rate risk. That is, it has a British pound cost to offset its British pound revenue. This is known as an *operational hedge*. An operational hedge is considered a natural hedge—hedging without derivatives. However, with the British pound operating cost relatively small, its operational hedge is very small as well. As shown in the exhibit, the company's percentage change in EAT to percentage change in the exchange rate is 3.00.

One of the firm's expenses is its $8 million interest payment on its debt (= (0.08)($100 million). If that debt were instead in British pounds, then the company would have an interest payment expense in British pounds. Such an expense would serve to reduce the US company's exchange-rate exposure. To do this, the company could refinance its $100 million debt by borrowing the equivalent amount in British pounds. Alternatively, it could simply swap it current debt for British pound debt in the swap market. The second panel shows the company's income statement for the case in which it swapped its $100 million 8% debt for £50 million 8% debt (current exchange rate is $2.00/£). In this case, if the exchange rate were to decrease by 25%

EXHIBIT 15.4 Reducing Earnings Exposure to Exchange-Rates Changes with Currency Swaps

Revenue	$40,000,000	($2.00/BP)(20mBP) = $40m	$30,000,000	($1.50/BP)(20mBP) = $30m	$50,000,000	($2.50/BP)(20mBP) = $50m
− Operating Cost	$4,000,000	($2.00/BP)(2mBP) = $4m	$3,000,000	($1.50/BP)(2mBP) = $3m	$5,000,000	($2.50/BP)(2mBP) = $5m
− Oil Cost	$16,000,000		$16,000,000		$16,000,000	
equals EBIT	$20,000,000		$11,000,000		$29,000,000	
− Interest	$8,000,000		$8,000,000		$8,000,000	
equals EBT	$12,000,000		$3,000,000		$21,000,000	
− Tax	$4,800,000		$1,200,000		$8,400,000	
equals EAT	$7,200,000		$1,800,000		$12,600,000	
		Proportional Δ in Exchange Rate		($1.50/$2.00) − 1 = −0.25		($2.50/$2.00) − 1 = 0.25
		Proportional Δ in Earnings		($1.8m/$7.2m) − 1 = −0.75		($12.6m/$7.2m) − 1 = 0.75
		Elasticity: $\varepsilon = \%\Delta EAT/\%\Delta F_0$		$\varepsilon = -75\%/-25\% = 3$		$\varepsilon = 75\%/25\% = 3$

Swap of $100m 8% debt for BP 50m 8% debt

Revenue	$40,000,000	($2.00/BP)(20mBP) = $40m	$30,000,000	($1.50/BP)(20mBP) = $30m	$50,000,000	($2.50/BP)(20mBP) = $50m
− Operating Cost	$4,000,000	($2.00/BP)(2mBP) = $4m	$3,000,000	($1.50/BP)(2mBP) =$3m	$5,000,000	($2.50/BP)(2mBP) = $5m
− Oil Cost	$16,000,000		$16,000,000		$16,000,000	
equals EBIT	$20,000,000		$11,000,000		$29,000,000	
− Interest	$8,000,000	($2.00/BP)(0.08)(50mBP)	$6,000,000	($1.50/BP)(0.08)(50mBP)	$10,000,000	($2.50/BP)(0.08)(50mBP)
equals EBT	$12,000,000		$5,000,000		$19,000,000	
− tax	$4,800,000		$2,000,000		$7,600,000	
equals EAT	$7,200,000		$3,000,000		$11,400,000	
		Proportional Δ in Exchange Rate		($1.50/$2.00) − 1 = −0.25		($2.50/$2.00) − 1 = 0.25
		Proportional Δ in Earnings		($3.0m/$7.2m) − 1 = −0.5833		($11.4/$7.2m) − 1 = 0.5833
		Elasticity: $\varepsilon = \%\Delta EAT/\%\Delta F_0$		$\varepsilon = -58.33\%/-25\% = 2.33$		$\varepsilon = 58.33\%/25\% = 2.33$

to $1.50/£, the firm's EAT would decrease only 58.33% to $3 million, instead of 75% without the swap. In this case, the reduction in revenue in dollars if partially offset by the lower dollar cost of $6 million (compared to $8 million without the swap) that was used to purchase £4 million to pay the interest on the British pound debt. On the other hand, if the exchange rate were to increase by 25% to $2.50/£, the company's EAT would increase only 58.33% (compared to 75% without the swap). Here, the company's greater dollar revenue is offset by a higher dollar cost to cover the British pound interest payments. By swapping its dollar-denominated debt for British pound-denominated debt, the company has improved its operational hedge—stabilized its earnings exposure to exchange rate changes. Specifically, its percentage change in EAT to percentage change in the exchange rate has decreased from 3.00 to 2.33.

Currency Swap Valuation

Equivalent Bond Positions

In our illustrative swap agreement, the US company agreed to pay £4.0 million each year for five years and £100 million at maturity, and in return receive $9 million each year for five years and a principal of $150 million at maturity. To the US company, this swap agreement is the equivalent to a position in two bonds: A long position in a dollar-denominated, five-year, 6% annual coupon bond with a principal of $150 million and trading at par and a short position in a sterling-denominated, five-year, 4.0% annual coupon bond with a principal of £100 million and trading at par. The dollar value of the US company's swap position in which it will receive dollars and pay sterling is:

$$SV = B_\$ - E_0\, B_£$$

where

$B_\$$ = Dollar-denominated bond value
$B_£$ = Sterling-denominated bond value
E_0 = Spot exchange rate = $/£

The dollar value of the swap to the US company in terms of equivalent bond positions is zero:

$$SV = \$150 \text{ million} - (\$1.50/£)(£100 \text{ million}) = 0$$

The British company's swap position in which it will receive sterling and pay dollars is just the opposite of the American's position. It is equivalent to a long position in a sterling-denominated bond and short position in a dollar denominated bond. It likewise has a value of zero:

$$SV = E_0\, B_£ - B_\$$$

$$SV = (\$1.50/£)(£100 \text{ million}) - \$100 \text{ million} = 0$$

Similar to interest rate swaps, the currency swap's economic value of zero means that neither counterparty is required to pay the other. The zero value also implies that the underlying bond positions trade at par. Thus, the currency swap in this example is a par value swap. Note that the swap dealer in this example has a perfect hedge given his two opposite positions. If the dealer, though, had been warehousing swaps and provided a swap to just the US company, then the swap bank would issue (or short) a five-year, 4%, £100 million loan, swap it for a five-year, 6%, $150 million loan from the US company, and then purchase a five-year, 6%, $150 million bond (see Exhibit 15.5).

The economic values of the swap positions will change with changes in US dollar rates, $R_\$$, British rates, $R_\pounds$, and the spot exchange rate:

$$SV = f(R_\$, R_\pounds, E_0)$$

For example, suppose in our example that a year later, British pound rates and the exchange rate were the same, but rates in the United States were higher with the *YTM* on the US dollar-denominated bond at 6.5%. In this case, the value of a four-year,

EXHIBIT 15.5 Swap Bank Hedge: Swap Bank Issues Five-Year, 4%, £100 Million Loan, Swaps It for Five-Year, 6%, $150 Million Loan from US Company, and Purchases Five-Year, 6%, $150 Million Bond

Initial Cash Flow

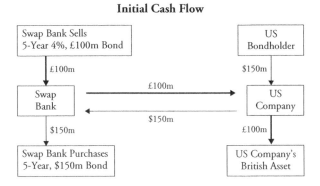

Interest Payment Flow

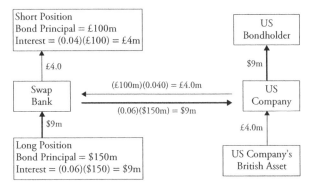

6% dollar-denominated bond would be $147,430,651 and the value of the $9 million interest received/£4 million paid swap would be −$2,569,349:

$$SV = \$147{,}430{,}651 - (\$1.50/\pounds)(\pounds\,100{,}000{,}000) = -\$2{,}569{,}349$$

where

$$B_\$ = \sum_{t=1}^{4} \frac{\$9{,}000{,}000}{(1.065)^t} + \frac{\$150{,}000{,}000}{(1.065)^4} = \$147{,}430{,}651$$

$$B_{\text{BP}} = \sum_{t=1}^{4} \frac{\pounds 4{,}000{,}000}{(1.04)^t} + \frac{\pounds 100{,}000{,}000}{(1.04)^4} = \pounds 100{,}000{,}000$$

If the US company wanted to close its swap position by selling its $9 million interest received/£4 million paid swap to a dealer, that dealer would require compensation of at least $2,569,349. The dealer's fee of $2,569,349 would in turn defray the net hedging cost of selling a four-year, 6% dollar-denominated bond trading at 6.5% and receiving a four-year, 4% sterling-denominated swap.

In general, the value of a dollar received/foreign currency paid swap is inversely related to US interest rates and the exchange rate and directly related to the foreign rate. In contrast, the value of a foreign currency received/dollar paid swap, valued in dollars, is directly related to US rates and the exchange rate and inversely related to the foreign rate.

Equivalent Forward Exchange-Rate Positions

Instead of viewing its swap as a bond position, the US company could alternatively view its swap agreements to pay £4 million each year for $9 million and pay £100 million at maturity for $150 million as a series of short currency forward contracts. In contrast, the British company could view its swap position as a series of long currency forward contracts in which it agrees to pay $10.125 million for £4.5 million each year for five years and agree to pay $150 million for £100 million at maturity. Exhibit 15.6 shows the annual cash flow exchanges for the two companies, with each of the exchanges representing a forward exchange contract.

In the absence of arbitrage, the value of the US company's swap of dollar's received/British pounds paid should be equal to:

1. The sum the present values of $9 million received each year from the swap minus the dollar payment of £4.0 million at the forward exchange rate
2. The present value of the $150 million received at year five minus the dollar cost of paying £100 million at the five-year forward exchange rate.

The lower panel of Exhibit 15.6 shows the forward rates using the carrying-cost model and the value of the US company's swap of dollars received/British pounds paid. The forward rates are equal to the carrying-cost rate given a flat yield curve on

EXHIBIT 15.6 Swap Cash Flows and Swap Value

US Company: Swap 5-Year, 6%, $150 Loan for 5-Year, 4%, £100m Loan

Year	$ CF (Million)	£ CF
0	−$150,000,000	£100,000,000
1	$9,000,000	−£4,000,000
2	$9,000,000	−£4,000,000
3	$9,000,000	−£4,000,000
4	$9,000,000	−£4,000,000
5	$150,000,000	−£100,000,000

British Company: Swap 5-Year, 4.5% £100m Loan for 5-Year, 6.75%, $150m Loan

Year	$ CF (Million)	£ CF
0	$150,000,000	−£100,000,000
1	−$10,125,100	£4,500,000
2	−$10,125,100	£4,500,000
3	−$10,125,100	£4,500,000
4	−$10,125,100	£4,500,000
5	−$150,000,000	£100,000,000

Forward rates given a flat yield curve on dollars of 6% and British pounds of 4%.

$$E_f = E_0 \left(\frac{1 + R_\$}{1 + R_£} \right)^T$$

$T = 1$: $E_f = (\$1.50/£)\left(\dfrac{1.06}{1.04}\right)^1$
$\quad = \$1.528846154/£$

$T = 2$: $E_f = (\$1.50/£)\left(\dfrac{1.06}{1.04}\right)^2$
$\quad = \$1.558247041/£$

$T = 3$: $E_f = (\$1.50/£)\left(\dfrac{1.06}{1.04}\right)^3$
$\quad = \$1.588213331/£$

$T = 4$: $E_f = (\$1.50/£)\left(\dfrac{1.06}{1.004}\right)^4$
$\quad = \$1.618755895/£$

$T = 5$: $E_f = (\$1.50/£)\left(\dfrac{1.06}{1.04}\right)^5$
$\quad = \$1.649885816/£$

Swap value for the US Company's swap of dollars received/British pounds paid:

$$SV = 0$$

$$SV = \sum_{t=1}^{M} \frac{(\$ \text{ Received}) - E_{ft}(\text{FC Paid})}{(1 + R_{US})^t}$$

$$SV = \frac{\$9,000,000 - (\$1.528846154/£)(£4,000,000)}{(1.06)^1}$$

$$+ \frac{\$9,000,000 - (\$1.558247041/£)(£4,000,000)}{(1.06)^2}$$

$$+ \frac{\$9,000,000 - (\$1.588213331/£)(£4,000,000)}{(1.06)^3}$$

$$+ \frac{\$9,000,000 - (\$1.618755895/£)(£4,000,000)}{(1.06)^4}$$

$$+ \frac{\$9,000,000 - (\$1.649885816/£)(£4,000,000)}{(1.06)^5}$$

$$+ \frac{\$150,000,000 - (\$1.649885816/£)(£100,000,000)}{(1.06)^5}$$

$$SV = 0$$

dollars of 6% and flat yield curve on British pounds of 4%. As shown, the swap is a par value swap with a swap value of zero.

Similarly, in the absence of arbitrage, the dollar value of the British company's swap of sterling received/dollars paid using forward exchange rate positions is equal to

1. The sum of present values from receiving £4.5 million each year and converting it to dollars at the forward exchange rate minus the $10.125 million payments.
2. The present value of the £100 million principal received times the five-year forward exchange minus the $150 million paid.

Like the US company, given flat yield curves at 6.75% and 4.5%, the value of the British company's swap is also zero.

In general, the value of a dollar received/foreign currency paid swap as series of forward contracts is

$$SV = \sum_{t=1}^{M} \frac{(\$\,\text{Received}) - E_{fi}(FC\,\text{Paid})}{(1 + R_{US})^t}$$

and the dollar value of a FC received/$paid swap is:

$$SV = \sum_{t=1}^{M} \frac{E_{fi}(FC\,\text{Paid}) - (\$\,\text{Received})}{(1 + R_{US})^t}$$

Note that in the absence of arbitrage, the values of the swap positions as forward contracts are equal to their values as bond positions:

$$SV = \sum_{t=1}^{M} \frac{(\$\,\text{Received}) - E_{fi}(FC\,\text{Paid})}{(1 + R_{US})^t} = B_\$ - E_0 B_{FC}$$

For example, if rates on dollars were 6.5% one year later, then the value of the US dollar received/British pound paid swap position as forward contracts would be −$2,569,349—the same value we obtained using the bond valuation approach (see Exhibit 15.7).

Non-Generic Currency Swaps

In addition to the generic currency swap, there are a number of non-generic swaps. Of particular note is the *cross-currency swap* that is a combination of the currency swap and interest rate swap. This swap calls for an exchange of floating-rate payments in one currency for fixed-rate payments in another. There are also currency swaps with amortizing principals, cancelable and extendable currency swaps, forward currency swaps, and options on currency swaps.

EXHIBIT 15.7 Swap Value: Four-Year Swap with Rate on Dollars at 6.5%

Forward rates given a flat yield curve on dollars of 6.5% and British pounds of 4%.	Swap value for the US company's swap of dollars received/British pounds paid:

$$E_f = E_0 \left(\frac{1 + R_\$}{1 + R_£} \right)^T$$

$SV = 0$

$$SV = \sum_{t=1}^{M} \frac{(\$ \, Received) - E_{ft}(FC \, Paid)}{(1 + R_{US})^t}$$

$T = 1$: $E_f = (\$1.50/£) \left(\dfrac{1.065}{1.04} \right)^1$
$= \$1.536057692/£$

$$SV = \frac{\$9,000,000 - (\$1.536057692/£)(£4,000,000)}{(1.065)^1}$$

$$+ \frac{\$9,000,000 - (\$1.572982156/£)(£4,000,000)}{(1.065)^2}$$

$T = 2$: $E_f = (\$1.50/£) \left(\dfrac{1.065}{1.04} \right)^2$
$= \$1.572982156/£$

$$+ \frac{\$9,000,000 - (\$1.610794227/£)(£4,000,000)}{(1.065)^3}$$

$T = 3$: $E_f = (\$1.50/£) \left(\dfrac{1.065}{1.04} \right)^3$
$= \$1.610794227/£$

$$+ \frac{\$9,000,000 - (\$1.649515242/£)(£4,000,000)}{(1.065)^4}$$

$$+ \frac{\$150,000,000 - (\$1.649515242/£)(£100,000,000)}{(1.065)^5}$$

$T = 4$: $E_f = (\$1.50/£) \left(\dfrac{1.065}{1.004} \right)^4$
$= \$1.649515242/£$

$SV = -2,569,349$

Swap value as long position in four-year, 6%, $150 million bond priced at $147,430,651 to yield 6.5% and the dollar value of a short position in four-year, 4%, £4,000,000 priced at par.

$$SV = \$147,430,651 - (\$1.50/£)(£ \, 100,000,000) = -\$2,569,349$$

where

$$B_\$ = \sum_{t=1}^{4} \frac{\$9,000,000}{(1.065)^t} + \frac{\$150,000,000}{(1.065)^4} = \$147,430,651$$

$$B_{BP} = \sum_{t=1}^{4} \frac{£4,000,000}{(1.04)^t} + \frac{£100,000,000}{(1.04)^4} = £100,000,000$$

Conclusion

In this and the previous chapter, we have examined the markets, uses, and valuations of generic interest rate swaps, swap derivatives, CDS, and currency swaps. Like options and futures, swaps provide investors and borrowers with a tool for hedging asset and liability positions against interest rate, credit, and exchange-rate risks, speculating on interest rate, credit, and exchange rate movements, and improving the returns received on fixed income investments or paid on debt positions. Like options and futures, swaps, in turn, have become a basic financial engineering tool to apply to a variety of financial positions.

We have examined in this book a wide-ranging market for derivatives. However, we have not exhausted all of the derivative securities. For example, there are *exotic options*, which are non-generic products often created by financial engineers to meet specific hedging needs and return-risk objectives. In contrast to the exchange-traded generic derivatives, exotic options have more-diverse properties. For example, a number of exotics exhibit path dependency in which the price of the option depends on previous or future prices of the underlying asset. In addition to path-dependent options, there are exotic options characterized by different types of payoffs, such as the entire asset or an exchange of one asset for another. There are options on options, options to choose either a call or a put, and options on a basket of assets. Exotic options have been referred to as the second generation of options. In this book, we have from time to time identified some of these non-generic options—the average caps and barrier options, the CDS basket, and the callable bond as an option on an option. Several derivative texts examine these derivatives in detail, including exotic options pricing.

Although we have not exhausted all derivatives, my hope is that we have developed a foundation for the understanding of derivative products and their important applications in financial and investment management. To that extent, I also hope our journey into the world of derivatives has established a foundation and methodology for understanding the markets and uses of derivatives.

BLOOMBERG CDS AND CURRENCY SWAP SCREENS

CDS SCREENS—CORPORATIONS

- To access the CDS list on a specified company: Ticker CDS <Corp>
- To access the menu for a specific CDS: CDS Ticker BB ID <CORP>
- Example: Macy's: M CDS <CORP>
- Example: Macy's five-year CDS: FD CDS USD SR 5Y D14 <CORP>
- Screens to access on the menu:
  - DES
  - AllQ (Composite Quotes)
  - GP
  - CDSW (Valuation)

See Exhibit 15.8.

EXHIBIT 15.8 CDSW: Macy's

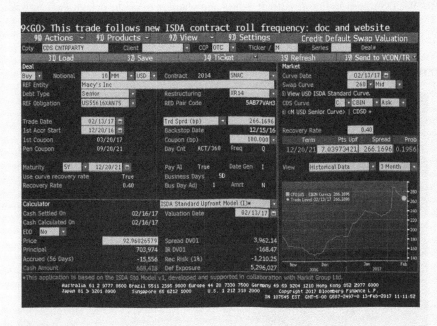

SECF

To find CDS from the SECF screen (SECF <Enter>), click "Fixed Income" in the "Category" dropdown, and the "CDS" tab (see Exhibit 15.9).

EXHIBIT 15.9 SECF Screen

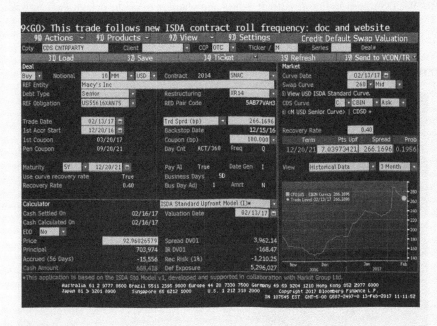

(Continued)

WCDS

The WCDS screen monitors current values and changes to credit default swap spreads (see Exhibit 15.10).

EXHIBIT 15.10 WCDS Screen

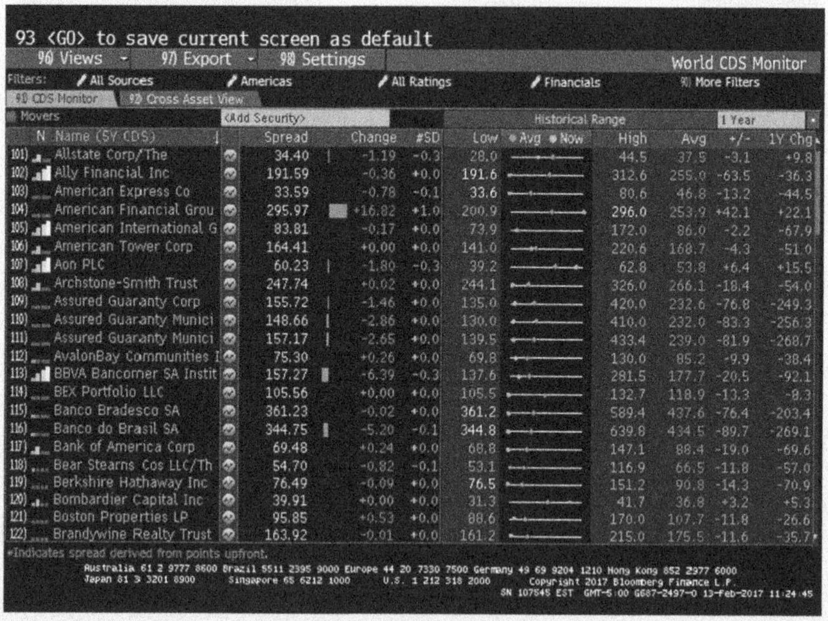

N	Name (5Y CDS)	Spread	Change	#SD	Low	High	Avg	+/-	1Y Chg
101)	Allstate Corp/The	34.40	-1.19	-0.3	28.0	44.5	37.5	-3.1	+9.8
102)	Ally Financial Inc	191.59	-0.36	+0.0	191.6	312.6	255.0	-63.5	-36.3
103)	American Express Co	33.59	-0.78	-0.1	33.6	80.6	46.8	-13.2	-44.5
104)	American Financial Grou	295.97	+16.82	+1.0	200.9	296.0	253.9	+42.1	+22.1
105)	American International G	83.81	-0.17	+0.0	73.9	172.0	86.0	-2.2	-67.9
106)	American Tower Corp	164.41	+0.00	+0.0	141.0	220.6	168.7	-4.3	-51.0
107)	Aon PLC	60.23	-1.80	-0.3	39.2	62.8	53.8	+6.4	+15.5
108)	Archstone-Smith Trust	247.74	+0.02	+0.0	244.1	326.0	266.1	-18.4	-54.0
109)	Assured Guaranty Corp	155.72	-1.46	+0.0	135.0	420.0	232.6	-76.8	-249.3
110)	Assured Guaranty Munici	148.66	-2.86	+0.0	130.0	410.0	232.0	-83.3	-256.3
111)	Assured Guaranty Munici	157.17	-2.65	+0.0	139.5	433.4	239.0	-81.9	-268.7
112)	AvalonBay Communities I	75.30	+0.26	+0.0	69.8	130.0	85.2	-9.9	-38.4
113)	BBVA Bancomer SA Instit	157.27	-6.39	-0.3	137.6	281.5	177.7	-20.5	-92.1
114)	BEX Portfolio LLC	105.56	+0.00	+0.0	105.5	132.7	118.9	-13.3	-8.3
115)	Banco Bradesco SA	361.23	-0.02	+0.0	361.2	589.4	437.6	-76.4	-203.4
116)	Banco do Brasil SA	344.75	-5.20	-0.1	344.8	639.8	434.5	-89.7	-269.1
117)	Bank of America Corp	69.48	+0.24	+0.0	68.8	147.1	88.4	-19.0	-69.6
118)	Bear Stearns Cos LLC/Th	54.70	-0.82	-0.1	53.1	116.9	66.5	-11.8	-57.0
119)	Berkshire Hathaway Inc	76.49	-0.09	+0.0	76.5	151.2	90.8	-14.3	-70.9
120)	Bombardier Capital Inc	39.91	+0.00	+0.0	31.3	41.7	36.8	+3.2	+5.3
121)	Boston Properties LP	95.85	+0.53	+0.0	88.6	170.0	107.7	-11.8	-26.6
122)	Brandywine Realty Trust	163.92	-0.01	+0.0	161.2	215.0	175.5	-11.6	-35.7

*Indicates spread derived from points upfront.

Australia 61 2 9777 8600 Brazil 5511 2395 9000 Europe 44 20 7330 7500 Germany 49 69 9204 1210 Hong Kong 852 2977 6000
Japan 81 3 3201 8900 Singapore 65 6212 1000 U.S. 1 212 318 2000 Copyright 2017 Bloomberg Finance L.P.
SN 107545 EST GMT-5:00 G687-2497-0 13-Feb-2017 11:24:45

SWPM SCREEN

On the SWPM screen, you can create, evaluate, and value a number of different swap and interest rate derivative positions, including currency, cross currency, cancelable, and total return swaps. On SWPM, click "Cross Currency Swap (Fixed-Fixed)" from the "Products" tab. On the "Main" screen, select currency and rates (see Exhibit 15.11).

EXHIBIT 15.11 SWPM Screen

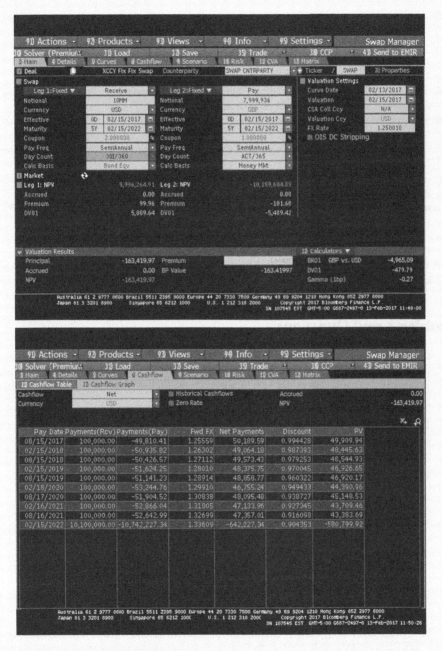

Selected References

Cooper, I., and A. S. Mello. "The Default Risk of Swaps." *Journal of Finance* 48 (1991): 597–620.

Hull, J., M. Predescu, and A. White. 56 "Relationship between Credit Default Swap Spreads, Bond Yields, and Credit Rating Announcements." *Journal of Banking and Finance* 28 (November 2004): 2789–2811.

Hull, J. C., and A. White. "Valuing Credit Default Swaps I: No Counterparty Default Risk." *Journal of Derivatives* 8, no. 1 (Fall 2000): 29–40.

Hull, J. C., and A. White. "Valuing Credit Default Swaps II: Modeling Default Correlations." *Journal of Derivatives* 8, no. 3 (Spring 2001): 12–22.

Johnson, R. Stafford. *Introduction to Derivatives: Options, Futures, and Swaps.* Oxford University Press. 2009, Chapter 17–19.

Johnson, R. Stafford. *Bond Evaluation, Selection, and Management.* Malden, MA: Blackwell Publishing, 2004, Chapter 17.

Titman, S. "Interest Rate Swaps and Corporate Financing Choices." *Journal of Finance* 47, no. 4 (1992): 1503–1516.

Turnbull, S. M. "Swaps: A Zero Sum Game." *Financial Management* 16, no. 1 (Spring 1987): 15–21.

Wall, L. D., and J. J. Pringle. "Alternative Explanations of Interest Rate Swaps: A Theoretical and Empirical Analysis." *Financial Management* 18, no. 2 (Summer 1989): 59–73.

Problems and Questions

1. Given a discount rate of 5%, determine the present value of the payments on a five-year CDS with a spread of 3% and a *NP* of $100. If the recovery rate on the underlying credit is 30%, what is the probability intensity implied by the spread?

2. Given an estimated five-year average probability intensity of 0.0375 on a five-year, BB-rated CDS, a recovery rate of 30%, and discount rate of 5%, determine the value and spread on the CDS. Assume *NP* = $100.

3. The table below shows the historical cumulative probabilities for corporate bonds with quality ratings of B:

Cumulative Probabilities

Year	1	2	3	4	5
	6%	13%	20%	28%	36%

a. Determine the conditional default probabilities from the cumulative probabilities shown in the table.

b. Given your probability calculations, determine the values and spreads on a five-year CDS with a B-quality rating. Assume each swap has an *NP* of $100 and a recovery rate of 30% and that the appropriate discount rate is 6%.

4. How much would a swap bank pay or require as compensation for assuming the buyer's position on a four-year BBB-rated CDS with a spread of 2.5% if current four-year BBB-rated CDS are trading at a spread of 2%. Assume the appropriate discount rate is 6%, NP is $100, and the recovery rate is 30%. Explain why the value of the swap position changes.

5. How much would a swap bank pay or require as compensation for assuming the seller's position on a four-year BBB-rated CDS with a spread of 2.5% if current four-year BBB-rated CDS were trading at a spread of 2%. Assume the appropriate discount rate is 6%, *NP* is $100, and the recovery rate is 30%. Explain why the value of the swap position changes.

6. The table shows the annual loan rates that American and British multinational companies can each obtain on a five-year, $150 million loan in dollars and an equivalent five-year, £100 million loan in the pounds.

Loan Rates for American and British Companies in Dollars and Pounds

Spot: $E_0 = \$/£ = \$1.50/£$

	Dollar Market (rate on $)	Pound Market (rate on £)
American Company	10%	7.25%
British Company	11%	7.5%

a. Suppose the American multinational wants to borrow £100 million for five years to finance its British operations, whereas the British company wants to borrow $150 million for five years to finance its US operations. Explain how a swap bank could arrange a currency swap that would benefit the American company by lowering the rate on its British pound loan by 0.25% and would benefit the British company by lowering its dollar loan by 0.4%.

b. Show the swap arrangement's dollar and pound interest payments and receipts in a diagram.

c. Describe the swap bank's dollar and British pound positions. What is the swap bank's implied forward exchange rate on the contracts?

d. Assume that forward rates are determined by the interest rate parity theorem, that the swap bank can borrow and lend dollars at 9.5% and British pounds at 7%, and that the yield curves for rates in both currencies are flat? Explain how the bank could hedge its swap position using currency forward contracts. What would be the swap bank's profit from it swap and forward positions?

7. Currency swap valuation questions:

   a. What is the bond equivalent of a currency swap position in which the counterparty agrees to swap a three-year, 10% loan of $15 million for a three-year, 7% loan of £10 million?

   b. What is the bond equivalent of a currency swap position in which the counterparty agrees to swap a three-year, 7% loan of £10 million for a three-year, 10% loan of $15 million?

   c. What is the forward exchange rate equivalent of a currency swap position in which the counterparty agrees to swap a three-year, 10% loan of $15 million for a three-year, 7% loan of £10 million?

   d. What is the forward exchange rate equivalent of a currency swap position in which the counterparty agrees to swap a three-year, 7% loan of £10 million for a three-year, 10% loan of $15 million?

   e. What is the value of an existing currency swap position in which the counterparty agrees to swap a two-year, 10% loan of $15 million for a two-year, 7% loan of £10 million if the current dollar rate is 9%, sterling rate is 7.5%, and spot $/£ exchange rate is $1.45/£?

8. Explain with an example an operational exchange rate hedge or natural hedge. In your example, assume a US-owned company with its operation and sales in the United Kingdom, material expenditures in US dollars, and with the following annual cash flows:

   • Revenue = £40 million
   • Operating cost = £4 million
   • Crude oil expenditures = $32 million
   • Interest expense on $100 million debt = (0.08)($100,000,000) = $8 million
   • Effective tax rate = 0.4

   Evaluate the company's foreign currency exposure by evaluating the company's EAT to a change in the exchange rate from $1.50/£ to $1.25/£. Explain what would happen to the company's foreign currency exposure if it swapped its $100 million 8% debt for £66.67 million debt at 8% (BP interests = (0.08)(£66.67 million BP) = £5.33333 million).

Bloomberg Exercises

1. Select a CDS on a company of interest with investment-grade bonds (Ticker CDS <Corp>), CDS Ticker <Corp>) and analyze it using the following screens: DES, AllQ (Composite Quotes), GP, and CDSW (Valuation).

2. Select a CDS on a company of interest with non-investment-grade bonds (Ticker CDS <Corp>, CDS Ticker <Corp>) and analyze it using the following screens: DES, AllQ (Composite Quotes), GP, and CDSW (Valuation).

3. Select a CDS from the WCDS screen (Ticker CDS <Corp>, CDS Ticker <Corp>) and analyze it using the following screens: DES, AllQ (Composite Quotes), GP, and CDSW (Valuation).

4. Select a CDS on a sovereign country's CDS. From the SECF screen (SECF <Enter>), click "Fixed Income" in the "Category" dropdown, click the "CDS" tab, and type in the name of the country (e.g., Greece) in the amber CDS Ticker box. Analyze the CDS (CDS Ticker <Corp>) using the following screens: DES, AllQ (Composite Quotes), GP, and CDSW (Valuation).

5. On the SWPM screen, create and then evaluate a currency swap. On SWPM screen, click "Cross Currency Swap (Fixed-Fixed)" from the "Products" tab. On the "Main" screen, select currency and interest rates. Evaluate your swap's cash flow ("Cashflow" tab).

PART 5

Supplemental Appendixes

Appendix A
Overview and Guide to the Bloomberg System

Bloomberg is a computer information and retrieval system providing access to financial and economic data, news, and analytics. Bloomberg terminals are common in most trading floors and are becoming more common in universities where they are used for research, teaching, and managing student investment funds. The Bloomberg system provides 24-hour, instant access to information on most US and foreign securities: stocks, bonds, asset-backed securities, swaps, and derivatives; economic information by country; current and historical news and information on corporations and countries; and analytical packages for evaluating bonds, stocks, indexes, derivatives, and portfolios.

In this appendix, we present an overview and introductory guide to the Bloomberg system: how the systems works, its functionality, and some of the information that can be accessed from its monitors, screens, and search tools. Many of the Bloomberg descriptive and analytical screens can be used in the study of investments. The appendix serves as a foundation for understanding how one can access such information and tools with a Bloomberg terminal, as well as a "show-and-tell" presentation of the Bloomberg screens.

Bloomberg System—Bloomberg Keyboard

The Bloomberg keyboard allows one to access information within the "Bloomberg system." The keyboard consists of several specialized, color-coded function keys and yellow functional buttons:

- **Green action keys** send a specific request to the system with the system in turn responding:

- **Enter:** Press <Enter> for entering commands.
- **NEWS:** Press <News> for accessing 24-hour, online global news service.
- **HELP:** Press <Help> for terminology, formulas, and defaults. For specific information, type a name, and then press <Help>; for help from a Bloomberg representative, press <Help> twice.
- **MENU:** Press <Menu> to back up to the previous screen or menu.
- **PRINT:** To send a document to the printer.
- **PAGE FWD.**
- **PAGE BACK.**

- **Yellow functional buttons** take the user to information and analytical functions for specific markets:
  - **GOVT:** Domestic and foreign securities.
  - **EQUITY:** Equity news, company information, company financial information, historical prices, mutual fund information, equity derivatives (a company's option, futures, warrants, convertibles, and swaps), and equity analytical functions.
  - **CMDTY:** Commodities by sector, futures, options, and OTC pricing contributors.
  - **CORP:** Corporate bonds and bond analytical functions.
  - **INDEX:** Indices for markets and countries, index composition, index derivatives, and other information and analytics.
  - **CRNCY:** Foreign exchange spot rates, forward rates, and cross rates, currency monitors, and currency indexes.
  - **M-MKT:** Money market rates and indexes (e.g., London Interbank Offered Rate [LIBOR], commercial paper rates, and federal funds rates).
  - **MRTG:** Mortgage securities, agency pool reports, and prepayment statistics.
  - **MUNI:** Municipal bonds and municipal information.
  - **PFD:** Preferred stocks and related information.

Note: One can also type "Main" and hit <Enter> to bring up the Bloomberg "Main" menu where you can access specific market screens.

The yellow functional buttons are a good way for one to get started on Bloomberg. One can simply enter the yellow key to bring up a menu screen providing access to information and analytical functions related to the category. For example, to access information on a company and its securities, you press the "Equity" button, <Equity>, and then press the "Enter" button, <Enter>. A menu will appear that will identify where a function or information is located. You can then move your cursor to the subscreen of interest and click it, or you can type the screen's name (e.g., DES) or its number in the top left corner of the screen and hit <Enter>. For example, to find a company's stock ticker symbol from the Equity menu screen, you would:

Press <Equity> and hit <Enter>.

Click "Security Finder" to bring up the "SECF" screen, or just type SECF in the left corner and hit <Enter>.

On the SECF screen, click the type of security from the "Category" dropdown (e.g., "Equities" for equity) and then type the name of the company in the amber "company Name" box.

The SECF screen can be used to find tickers or identifiers (CUSIPS or ISN number) for bonds, corporate securities, countries, commodities, currencies, and indexes. Note, if you know the ticker symbol or identifier, then you can access the menu screen for the stock, bond, index, or currency directly by typing the ticker/identifier and then pressing the relevant key; for example, to access IBM, enter: IBM <Equity> <Enter>. You can also find most securities and information by simply typing the name. This will bring a dropdown list of names, allowing you to just click the name to bring up the menu.

Uploading Information on a Stock, Bond, Currency, or Index

In general, to upload a corporation's security (e.g., stock or bond), index, currency, or commodity in Bloomberg: (1) type in the ticker or identifier, (2) press the yellow key that represents the type of asset (e.g., <Equity> or <Corp>), and (3) hit <Enter>. Examples:

- To pull up IBM's stock screen: IBM <Equity> <Enter>.
- To pull up the screen for the IBM's 6.5% coupon bond maturing in 01/15/28: IBM 6.5 01/15/28 <Corp> <Enter> or CUSIP <Corp> <Enter>.
- To pull up the S&P 500 index screen: SPX <Index> <Enter>.
- To pull up the British Pound screen: GBP <Curncy> <Enter>.
- To pull up the screen for crude oil futures contracts traded on the New York Mercantile Exchange: Enter CLa <Comdty> <Enter>.
- To pull up the screen for the US Treasury note paying a 2% coupon and maturing 01/31/16: T 2 11/15/26 <Govt> <Enter>.

It should be noted that when one begins typing the name of the security a dropdown will appear on the screen listing securities corresponding with the information being typed; clicking the security from the dropdown will bring up its menu. Once a security or index has been loaded, you are taken to a "homepage" menu that categorizes all the functions on the selected security and submenu screens. The functions can be accessed by either clicking the name on the menu option page or typing the name of the function in the left corner of the screen. Additional menu screens can be found on the homepage menu by clicking the white topic heading (e.g., "Company Overview").

There are two main types of screens in Bloomberg: descriptive and analytical. Descriptive screens provide information about the underlying security, such as trade information, expiration, and risk information. Descriptive screens pull data from Bloomberg and present it in an orderly fashion; they usually do not perform calculations. Analytical screens, on the other hand, determine prices, returns, variability, and other statistical and mathematical calculations based on customized inputs. In Bloomberg, many of the functions that are used for evaluating securities are common and as a result have a common command. For instance, the GP function is a price graph that can be used for each security type. Derivatives, indexes, interest rates, currencies, commodities, and bond futures often use many of the same functions. If you know the name of the function (e.g., DES for description) and the security is already loaded, then you can access the function's screen directly by simply typing the name of the function (e.g., DES) in the top left corner. If the security is not loaded, then you can type the ticker, hit the yellow key, and type the function (e.g., IBM <Equity>; DES <Enter>). Also, note that once you have accessed the function screen, you can always press the "?" tab in the upper right corner to bring up a screen with information, defaults, and instructions related to that function or to access a message box to send questions to the Bloomberg helpdesk.

Accessing Security Information

Bloomberg Menu for a Stock: Ticker <Equity> <Enter>

The Bloomberg menu for a stock (e.g., Amazon: AMZN <Equity> <Enter>) provides information on the stock and company: company information, historical prices, financials, derivatives, and news (see Exhibit A.1). Some of the functions and information on a stock's equity menu include:

- **DES:** Provides details about the company. The Description screen usually has a number of pages summarizing products, management, stock information, board members, financial summaries, and geographical distribution.
- **EVT:** List past and current events, such as earning announcements, stockholders' meetings, security issues, and the like.
- **CF:** Corporate filings and SEC filings (EDGAR [Electronic Data Gathering, Analysis, and Retrieval system]), 10-K reports, 10-Q reports, and other filings.
- **GP:** Price and volume graph.
- **SPLC**: Supply chain.
- **OMON**: Option monitor.
- **OSA**: Option scenario analysis.

Bloomberg Corporate Bond Information and Functions: Ticker <Corp> <Enter>

To find a corporate bond for a company (e.g., Amazon), you first access the screen for all of the company's bonds (e.g., AMZN <Corp> <Enter>). From this screen, you can bring up a menu screen for a specific bond by clicking the bond of interest (see Exhibit A.2). Some of functions and information on that menu include:

- **DES:** Description
- **HDS:** Shows the holders of the bond

EXHIBIT A.1 Bloomberg Description (DES) and Price Graph (GP)

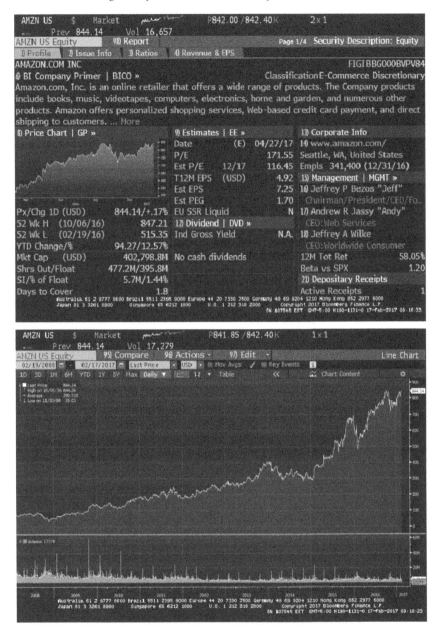

- **CSHF:** Shows the cash flows promised on the bond: semiannual interest and principal
- **QR:** Trade recap: Tick-by-tick prices reported from TRACE
- **GP:** graphs historical closing prices
- **YAS:** Yield analysis
- **TRA:** Total return analysis

EXHIBIT A.2　Bloomberg Menu and Description (DES) for a Bond

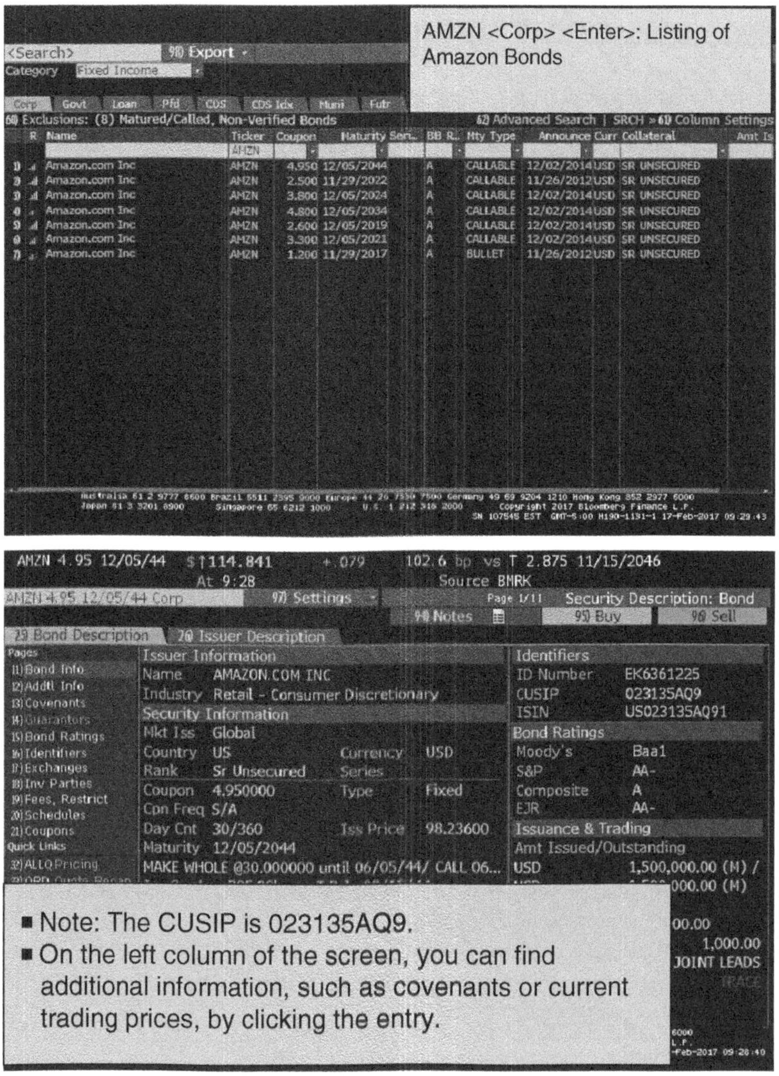

Bloomberg Government Bond Information and Functions: Ticker GOVT <Enter>

To access a specific government bond, you first need to find a government bond's ticker. As noted, you can find a ticker by using SECF: SECF <Enter>, Click "Fixed Income" from the "Category" dropdown, click the "Govt" tab, and screen by typing or using the dropdowns from the tabs for Name (e.g., United States), ticker, coupon, and Currency. You can also find a ticker by entering <GOVT> TK <Enter>. This will bring up a Country screen that allows you to click the country (e.g., U.S.A.) and then select the bond group of interest (e.g., T for "U.S. Treasury Notes and Bonds" or CT for "Current U.S. Treasury Notes and Bonds"; see Exhibit A.3). Finally, you can click the bond of interest to bring up its menu and then click DES to bring up the note's description page (Exhibit A.4).

EXHIBIT A.3 Bloomberg Government Bond Ticker Symbols: <GOVT> TK <Enter>

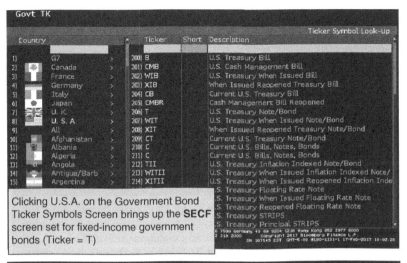

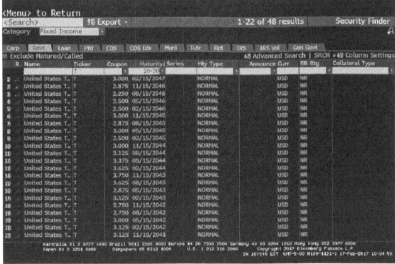

On the description page, you will find the bond's CUSIP number, which, as noted, can also be used to bring up the bond's menu screen: CUSIP <Govt> <Enter> (912810QA9 <Govt> <Enter>.) As noted, you can also bring up the menu page for a specific bond by starting to type the bond's coupon interest and maturity: T 3.5 2/15/39 (for Treasury, coupon, and maturity). This will bring up a dropdown list of bonds; clicking the bond of interest will bring up that bond's menu screen. Some of the information screens found on a specific government or corporate bond's menu include:

- **DES:** Issue and issuer information, access to the TRACE, prospectus, and other screens
- **HDS:** Bondholders
- **CSHF:** Shows the cash flows promised on the bond

EXHIBIT A.4   Bloomberg Government Bond Description Slide

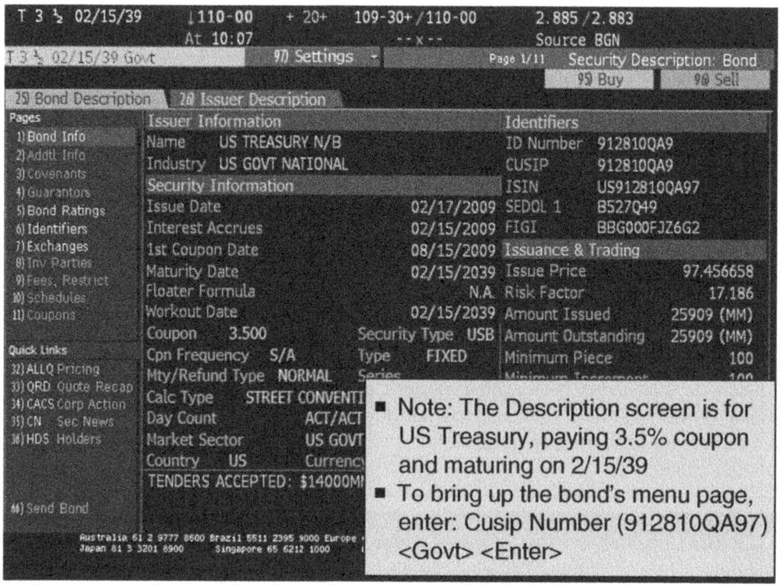

- **QR:** Trade recap: Tick-by-tick prices reported from TRACE
- **GP:** Historical price graph
- **YAS:** Yield analysis screen
- **TRA:** Total return analysis

Finding Other Security Types

As noted, you can use SECF to find a government bond ticker or you can enter <Govt> TK <Enter>. These approaches can also be used to quickly search for other securities: foreign government securities, agencies, municipals, money market securities, preferred securities, and currency.

Foreign Government Bonds

- SECF <Enter>, Click "Fixed Income" from the "Category" dropdown, click "Govt" tab, and screen by typing Name (e.g., United Kingdom), Ticker (e.g., UKT), Coupon, Maturity (e.g., 10-30), and Currency (e.g., GBP).
- Or enter: <Govt> TK <Enter>, and click country of choice (e.g., United Kingdom).
- Click bond of interest to bring up its menu screen or CUSIP <Govt> <Enter>.

Municipal Bonds

- SECF <Enter>, Click "Fixed Income" from the "Category" dropdown, click "Muni" tab, and screen by typing Name (e.g., Georgia), Ticker (e.g., GA), Coupon, Maturity (e.g., 10–30), and Tax Status (e.g., Tax-Exempt).
- Or enter: <Muni> TK <Enter> and enter State.

Preferred Stocks

- SECF <Enter>, Click "Fixed Income" from the "Category" dropdown, click "Pfd" tab, and screen by typing Name (e.g., General Electric), Ticker (e.g., GE), Dividend (e.g., fixed), Maturity, and Mty type.
- Or enter: <Pfd> TK <Enter>.

Currency

- SECF <Enter>, Click "Currencies" from the "Category" dropdown, click "Spots" tab, and screen by typing Name (e.g., Euro), Ticker (e.g., USDEUR), CCYI (e.g., USD), and CCY2 (e.g., Eur).
- Or enter: <Curncy)> TK <Enter>.

Indexes

The menu page for indexes provides information on different indexes by category, such as equity, world indexes, bonds, real estate, and municipals. You can use SECF to find the ticker for a specific index: SECF <Enter>; click "Index/Stats" from the "Category" dropdown; type the general name of the index (e.g., S&P, Russell, or Dow); or click the tab for type (e.g., "Eqty") and then select the index group from the dropdown "Source" (e.g., Russell). See Exhibit A.5.

Two well-known indexes are the S&P 500 and the Russell 3,000. Entering their tickers (SPX and RAY), pressing <Index> and hitting <Enter> brings up their menu screens showing descriptive and analytical functions: description (DES), holdings (in Description), index weighting (MEMB), price graph (GP), and stock movers in the index (MOV) (see Exhibit A.6).

EXHIBIT A.5   Bloomberg Index Search (SECF)

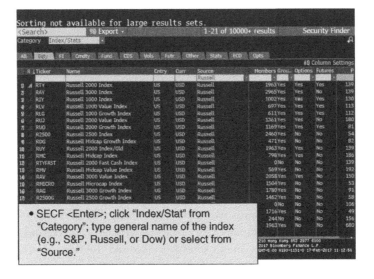

EXHIBIT A.6   Bloomberg DES and MEMB Screens for Russell 3,000

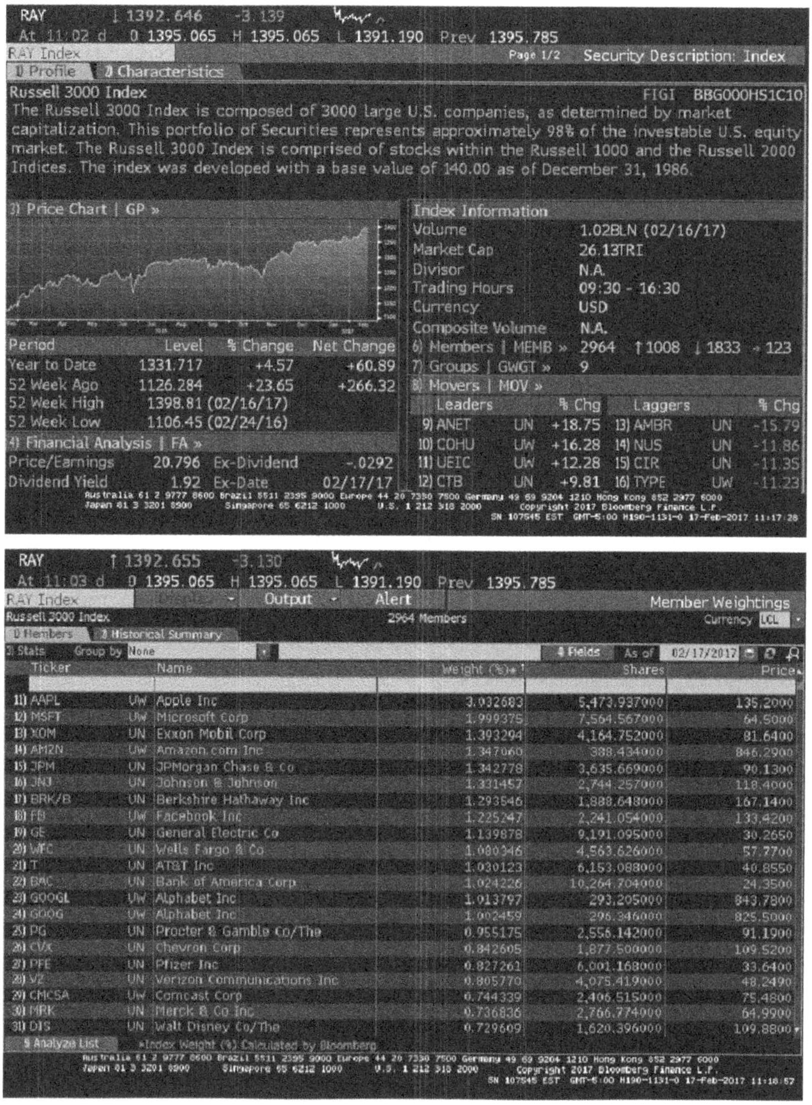

Functionality

Many Bloomberg screens provide functions and links that facilitate one's analysis of a company, security, market, fund, portfolio, or a country. For example, the relative valuation (RV), financial analysis (FA), and fundamental graphs (GF) functions for companies, indexes, portfolios, governments, and municipals give you access to key financial information for a company, index, or municipality (FA and GF) or for a group of peers (RV). For a company (e.g., Macy's (M)), its FA, RV, and GF screens can be accessed from its equity menu screen or accessed directly: M <Equity> RV <Enter>; M <Equity> FA <Enter>; M <Equity> GF <Enter>).

Financial Analysis: FA

The FA screen displays financial history for a specific company, equity index, or municipality (Exhibit A.7). Using the FA screen, you can either select from a list of standard templates (e.g., income statements, ratio analysis, or detailed financial statements) or customize your own template. The data can be seen on a quarterly, semiannual, annual, or trailing 12-month basis. On the FA screen, the template information can be viewed on the left panel and can be changed to chart form by clicking the chart icon in the left

EXHIBIT A.7   Bloomberg's Financial Analysis (FA) Screen, Macy's

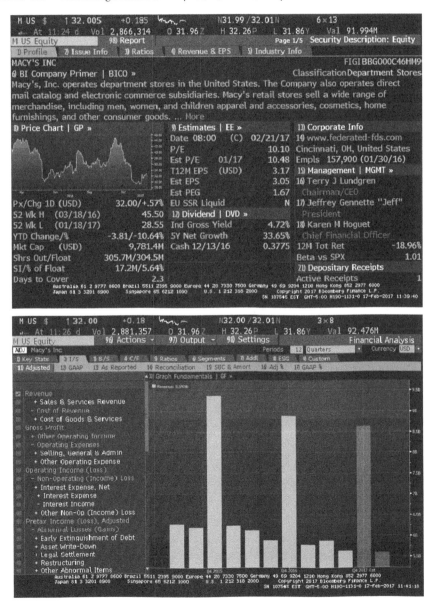

corner. Using the dropdown "Output" tab, you can create a PDF report of the table and graph, as well as send the data to Excel. The graphs on an FA screen and most of the other Bloomberg graphs can be exported to a clipboard: hover over the graph and then right click to bring up a dropdown list of graph functions for editing, as well as copying and exporting the data or image to a clipboard.

Relative Valuation: RV

The RV screen shows financial and market information of a company relative to its peers (Exhibit A.8). On the screen, you can change the peer grouping by selecting a different peer group from the dropdown "Comp Source" menu tab. From the peers menu, you can then select a larger sector or subsector. In addition, you can also bring up a portfolio that you constructed or a group of stocks identified from an equity screen/search that you have conducted and saved (portfolio construction and security searches are discussed later in this appendix). In addition to changing peers, the RV menu also allows you to change the template (gray tabs: Overview, Comp Sheets, Markets, EPS Preview, and Credit).

The gray "Custom" tab on the right side of the RV screen allows you to customize the table. You can customize the screen by setting your cursor in the column heading area and holding the right clicker down on the mouse to access a menu. From the dropdown menu, you can bring up a description of the measure and how it is calculated, add a row displaying minimum, maximums, averages, and standard deviation, delete the column, insert a new entry (Edit Column), and change the order for one of the measures (sort by ascending or descending). New columns with new measures can also

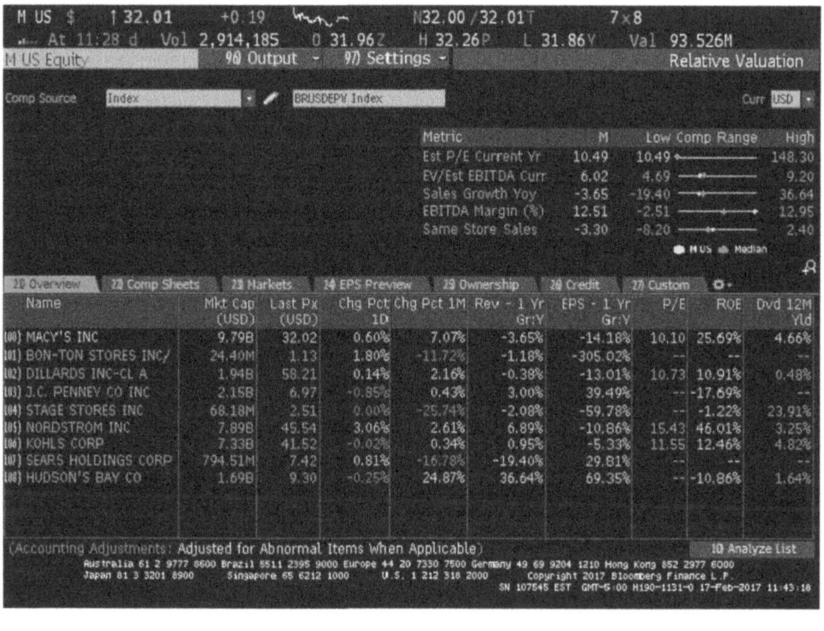

EXHIBIT A.8   Bloomberg's Relative Valuation (RV) Screen, Macy's

be added by clicking the gray button on the far right of the screen to bring up a menu and clicking "Add Column" from the menu to bring up an "Add Column" ribbon box area in the middle of the screen (this can also be done in the custom mode). In the box, you can type the name of the measure (e.g., market cap) and then hit <enter> to activate. Doing this, the new entry will appear in the right column. Information on each of the companies can also be accessed by right clicking the company's name. This will bring up a menu that will allow you to access the company's description page (DES), its financials (FA), and other information. Finally, from the "Output" tab, you can send the screen data and information to Excel.

Fundamental Graphs: GF

The GF function (graphical financial analysis) allows you to graphically compare company fundamentals and ratios against other companies and indexes (see Exhibit A.9). On the screen, you select a fundamental measure or measures from a field (e.g., the price-to-earnings ratio and earnings-per-share) and panels to display the measure over time, as well as other companies and indexes (e.g., S&P 500) for comparisons. Using the functions found in the tabs at the top of the GF screen, you can create a report (Actions) and save the settings (Templates) for future access. Similarly, the data or the graph images can be exported to a clipboard by clicking the function from the gray dropdown "Chart" tab in the graph panel.

Note that there are GF, RV, and FA screens for indexes. The RV screen for an index consists of the stocks making up the index. Like the stock RV screen, these screens also have considerable functionality. The screens can be accessed from the index's menu screen: Index ticker <Index> <Enter>.

EXHIBIT A.9 Bloomberg's Graphical Financial Analysis (GF) Screen, Macy's

Economic, Industry, Law, and Municipal Information Screens

Many screens in Bloomberg can be accessed directly by typing in the name of the screen and hitting <Enter>. For example, typing EPR brings up a page showing the listing of exchanges with information on each exchange and its website; PRTU takes you to a screen for constructing portfolios; CIXB brings up a screen for inputting securities, indexes, or a portfolio in which historical prices and returns are calculated. This data can be later used in other functions to analyze the portfolio. Some useful screens for investments include those for economic, industry, municipal, and legal analysis.

Economic Information Screens: ECST, ECO, and EIM

ECST

Country economic data on employment, business conditions, housing, balance of payments, prices, and other macroeconomic data can be accessed from the ECST screen (Exhibit A.10). Clicking an entry (e.g., nominal GDP) on the ECST menu screen brings up a table and graph showing an economic measure and a listing of related measures. The graph of the economic measure can be accessed by clicking the graph icon next to the entry's ticker. You can copy the data or image to a clipboard. You can also find data for another country by typing the name of the country in the amber box in the left corner. Finally, using the ticker for the economic series, you can upload a menu of screens for the series on the index screen: Ticker <Index> <Enter>.

EXHIBIT A.10   Bloomberg's ECST Screen

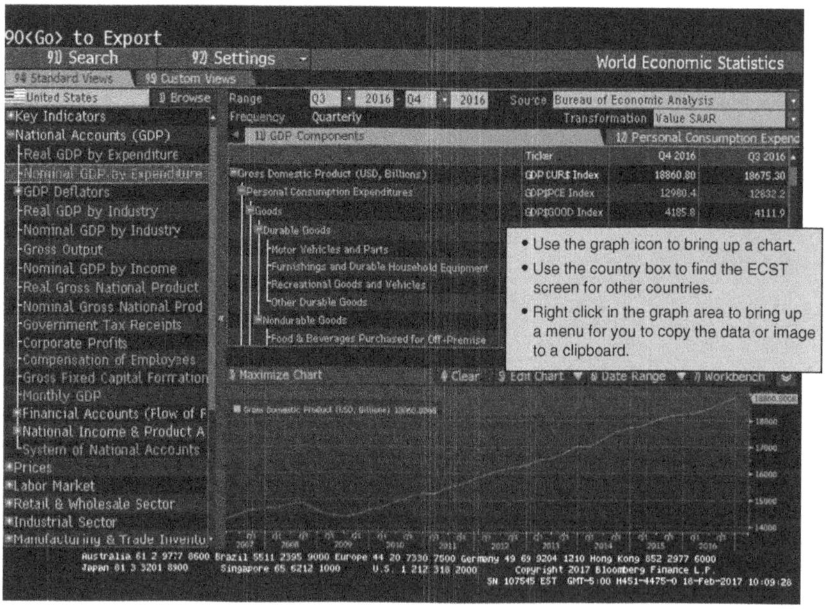

ECO

The ECO screen displays current, historical, and upcoming economic releases and events by region, country, and event type. Clicking an entry (e.g., Industrial Production) brings up a screen showing a graph of the economic measure or indictor and a listing of news stories and commentaries related to the release or event. Using the dropdown tabs on the ECO screen, you can bring up ECO screens for different releases and events by countries. Also, you can access a menu of additional functions (e.g., description or graphs) by moving your cursor to an entry and right clicking. On the ECO graphs, you can copy the data or image to a clipboard or bring up its menu screen: Ticker <Index> <Enter> (see Exhibit A.11).

EXHIBIT A.11   Bloomberg's ECO Screen

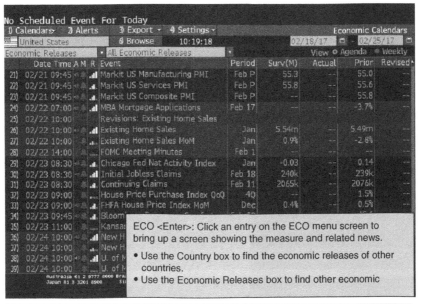

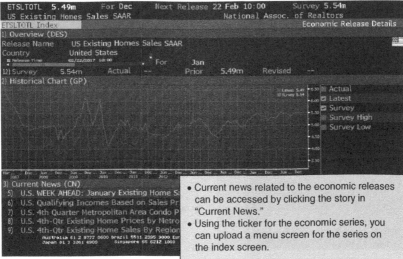

ECOF, ECOW, and ECMX

The ECOF, ECOW, and ECMX screens display current and historical economic statistics by country (Exhibit A.12). The screens provide functions for changing the country and economic measure, converting the data to graphs, changing the period, and exporting the information to Excel.

Sector and Industry Information: BI and BIE

The BI platform (BI <Enter>) is Bloomberg's proprietary industry research portal (Exhibit A.13). Information on the BI screen includes data, research, and analysts'

EXHIBIT A.12   Bloomberg's ECOF

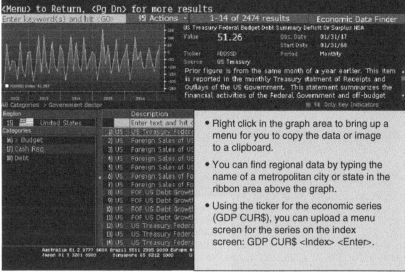

EXHIBIT A.13   Bloomberg's Sector and Industry Information (BI) and Economics (BIE) Screens

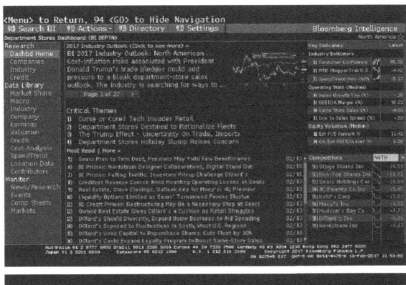

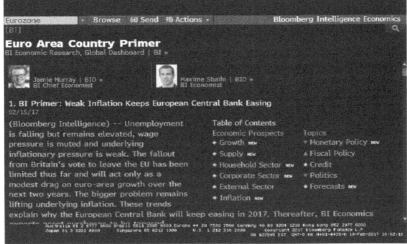

insights about industries and companies in an industry, topics, and special reports. On the BI screen, one can click an industry (e.g., Consumer Discretionary) to bring up its screen. On a selected industry's screen (e.g., Department Stores), you can then click entries for events, markets, comp sheets, and credit ratings. Historical financial data and information for the industry and the companies comprising it can be found by accessing the "Data Library" tab, and industry insights and analysis by sector analysis experts is found by accessing the "Dashbd Home" tab.

The BIE platform (BIE <Enter>) is Bloomberg's proprietary Business Intelligence Economics portal (Exhibit A.13). Information on the BIE screen includes in depth analysis of countries and links.

Municipal Screens

The municipal MIFA screen can be used to access financial information on state governments (MIFA <Enter>). The screen allows you to select a state and then access information on the state from a dropdown. On the dropdown, the state's identification number is also shown (e.g., Georgia: STOGA1 US). Using the identification number, you can access the state's menu directly: STOGA1 US <Index> <Enter> or STOGA1 <Equity> <Enter>. Information on the dropdown or state screen that can be accessed includes description (DES), financials (FA), relative evaluations (RV), demographics, (DEMS), employment (BLS), and a municipal search (SMUN). The municipal FA and RV screens displays income statements, balance sheets, and other information useful for evaluating the government's financial strength. On the FA and RV screens, you can also change the fund category from general to pension to view the municipality's pension position. Information on municipal securities of the state or municipalities in the state can be accessed from the municipal screener screen (SMUN <Enter>). Finally, municipals can be found using the SECF screen: SECF <Enter>, click "Fixed Income" from the "Categories" dropdown tab and "Muni" tab, and type the name of the municipality (e.g., California) in the "Issuer Name" box.

Legal Information: BLAW and BBLS

The BLAW is Bloomberg's Law website. The site provides legal, regulatory, and compliance information and functions. The menu is useful for not only accessing laws as they relate to certain industries and regions, but also identifying judgments, rulings, and pending cases. The BBLS screen can be used to look for laws, codes, filings, decisions, and other information.

Monitor and Portal Screens

There are a number of screens that monitor current prices and events occurring in the various markets, as well as economic and financial events in different countries.

Bond Monitors: FIT, WB, RATC, RATT, and CSDR

Using the FIT screen, you can access US Treasuries and other sovereign securities directly. For the United States, on the FIT screen, you can select the types of Treasuries based on their maturities (bills, notes, bonds, TIPs, and strips) or those most recently issued and more actively traded (Actives). To access the menu screen for a particular bond, you place your cursor on the bond of interest, right click to access the description (DES) screen to obtain a CUSIP or ISN number, and then enter: CUSIP <Govt> <Enter>. Like the FIT screen, the WB monitor (WB <Enter>) displays and compares bonds by different global areas. From the monitor, you can compare bonds of different countries in terms of yields and spreads. From the screen's icon, you can also bring up historical yields and current yield curves.

Four other bond monitors to note are RATC, RATT, and CSDR. RATC displays and searches for credit rating changes, RATT shows trends in quality ratings, and CSDR shows sovereign debt ratings.

Stock Monitors: IMAP, WEI, MMAP, and MOST

IMAP

The IMAP screen displays intraday price movements and news across industries, regions, and the companies (see Exhibit A.14). It includes a heat map showing the performances of stocks and sectors. Using the "Source" dropdown menu, you can select all securities, different indexes, constructed portfolios, and saved searches. On the table menu listing stocks or areas, you can select sectors or regions, and on the table menu for stocks and areas, you can access both price information and news information.

WEI

The World Equity Indices (WEI) screen (WEI <Enter>) monitors world equity indexes. On the WEI screen, you can also select different information about the indexes, such as futures prices, movers (advance and declines), ratios (e.g., P/E ratio), and currency. On the screen, you can click the country area to bring up more indexes for that geographical area.

EXHIBIT A.14   Bloomberg IMAP Screen

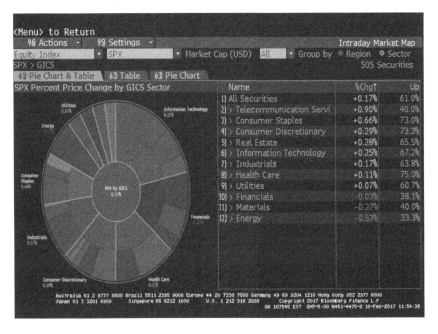

MMAP

MMAP displays global market segments, and the companies that operate within those segments. The user can select investment parameters, (e.g., growth in earnings) for different global areas and sectors to do a comparative evaluation of stocks in a sector or a region.

MOST

MOST displays the day's most active stocks by volume, the leading advancers and decliners by percentage or net gain/loss, stocks with the most value traded on an exchange, and stocks with the largest volume increase for the day. On the screen, you can change to different indexes, sectors, and periods, as well as access portfolios and searches you created.

New Bond and Equity Offerings: NIM and IPO

The NIM screen monitors news headlines and security data for new stock and bond issues. Clicking a category on the NIM screen (e.g., U.S. Bond Market) brings up a screen showing new or pending bond issues; clicking an issue brings up a description screen with details about the issue. New equity issues can be accessed from the IPO screen: IPO <Enter>. On the IPO screen, you can search for issues in different stages of the issuance process.

Country Information Indicators: COUN and BTMM

Selecting a country on the COUN screen (Exhibit A.15) takes you to that country's screen where there is summary information on the country's security markets, debt ratings, events, and most active stocks. On the country screen, you can also click summary areas to bring up screens with more detail information and other links. The BTMM screen (BTMM <Enter>) provides interest rate and security price information by country.

Calendar Screens

Bloomberg has several event calendar screens that allow you to monitor events, securities, and corporate actions. Two screens of note are EVTS and CACT.

EVTS

The EVTS calendar screen displays a calendar of corporate events and corresponding details, including transcripts and audio recordings (Exhibit A.16). You can opt to

EXHIBIT A.15 Bloomberg Country Information and Indicators, COUN

EXHIBIT A.16 Bloomberg's EVTS Screen

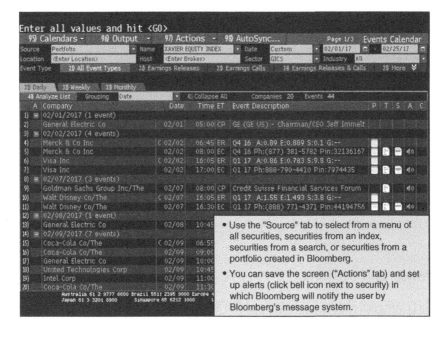

display historical or upcoming events on a daily, weekly, or monthly basis. You can also select from the dropdown "Source" tab all securities, securities from an index, securities from a search, or securities from a portfolio created in Bloomberg. You can also save the screen and set up alerts ("Actions" tab) in which Bloomberg will notify you by Bloomberg's message system.

CACT—Class Action and Corporate Action Filings

The CACT monitor screen displays a calendar of class actions and corporate action filings of corporations, such as stock buybacks, capital changes, and mergers and acquisitions. At the top of the CACT screen, you can select a period, geographical area, and types of actions (e.g., merger and acquisition or stock splits). You can also customize the actions.

Other Monitors and Portals

> MNSA Today's announced merger and acquisition deals
>
> PREL Pipeline of announced bonds
>
> DIS Distressed bonds
>
> BNKF Bankruptcy filings
>
> PE Private equity
>
> TACT Trade activity
>
> BRIEF Daily Economic Newsletter
>
> EIU Economist Intelligence Unit
>
> IECO Global Comparison of Economic Statistics
>
> FXIP Foreign Exchange Information Portal
>
> CENB Central Bank Menu: Use to access platforms of central banks
>
> FED Federal Reserve Bank portal
>
> ECB European Central Bank portal
>
> LTOP Top News
>
> FICM Fixed-Income Credit Monitor
>
> PGM Money Market Lookup by Program Type

Portfolios and Baskets

Portfolio Construction and Analysis: PRTU and PMEN

You can set up a stock or fixed-income portfolio on Bloomberg using PRTU and, once loaded, analyze and monitor the portfolio using screens on the PMEN screen.

Steps for Creating Portfolios in PRTU

1. PRTU <Enter>.
2. On the PRTU screen, click the "Create" button. This will bring up a two-page screen for inputting information:
   a. Settings Page: Name of your portfolio, asset class (equity, fixed income, balanced), and benchmark (e.g., S&P 500).
   b. Portfolio Display Page: Screen for inputting securities by their identifiers.
3. Securities can be inputted by:
   a. Entering tickers or identifiers (e.g., CUSIP for bonds) in the security boxes.
   b. Importing securities from searches, indexes, or other portfolios that have been saved in Bloomberg. To import, you click the "Actions" tab on the PRTU screen, click "Import," and then identify the specific portfolio, search, or index from a dropdown.
   c. Drag and drop securities from another screen (e.g., RV or a member holding screen of a fund (MHD)). The entire portfolio can be dropped by dragging the green arrow icon appearing in the right corner.
4. Once the portfolio is loaded, hit "Save." The name given to the portfolio will then be displayed on the PRTU screen. See Exhibit A.17.

Historical Portfolio Returns

To analyze the past return performances of portfolio, a history of portfolio rates of return needs to be created in PRTU. With history, you can analyze the historical performance of the portfolio using the PORT screen.

Steps for Creating Historical Data for Portfolios in PRTU

1. Bring up the PRTU screen for your portfolio.
2. On the screen, change the date in the amber "Date" box (e.g., Month/Day/Year). You should see the stocks disappear from the screen.
3. Click "Actions" tab. From the "Actions" dropdown, select "Import Securities" to bring up the import box. On the import box, select "Portfolio" from the "Source" dropdown, the name of your portfolio from the "Name" dropdown, change the date (e.g., back to the current period), hit the "Import" tab, and then click "Save." You should now have a portfolio with historical data.

PMEN and PORT

With the portfolio loaded, type PMEN to access a menu of functions to apply to the portfolio. Many of the screens found on the PMEN menu provide in depth portfolio analysis (see Exhibit A.18). The Portfolio Risk & Analytics screen (PORT), for example, allows you to evaluate a portfolio in terms of its features and performance. By accessing the screen tabs (e.g., "Holdings," "Characteristics," "Performance," and

EXHIBIT A.17   Creating a Portfolio: PRTU Screen

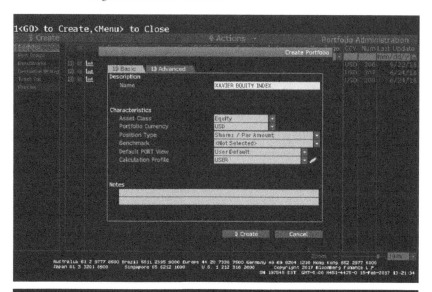

"Attributions"), you can evaluate the features, drivers, and historical performances of the portfolio, securities in the portfolio, and the portfolio's index. Other screens of note on the PMEN menu screen include Portfolio News (NPH), Events Calendar (EVTS), and Expected Cash Flow (PCF). Many of these screens have tabs for accessing different information, sending information to Excel, and downloading information to PDF and Excel reports.

Once a portfolio is created, you can export it to other screens or import it from other screens. For example, if you want to analyze a portfolio created in PRTU using

EXHIBIT A.18   Portfolio Analysis Screen: PORT, Characteristics Tab

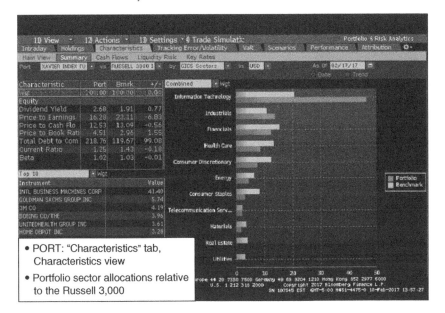

relative valuation, select a stock in the portfolio, access the stock's menu, and then bring up the stock's RV menu. On the RV menu of the stock, you can then import the portfolio by selecting "Portfolio" from the dropdown "Comp Source" tab and the name of the portfolio from the dropdown "Name" menu. Similarly, you can also import the portfolio from other screens, such as the CACT, MOST, IMAP, EVTS, and MMAP screens and from Excel using the Bloomberg Excel Add-In.

Creating Baskets: CIXB

Portfolios created in PRTU and securities found from searches (discussed in the next section) can be imported into CIXB. In CIXB, the portfolio's historical return data, in turn, can be created and stored in a CIXB basket, where it can be evaluated as an index using the screens on the Basket's index menu: Description (DES), Price Graph (GP), Comparative Total Return (COMP), Historical Regression (HRA), and other screens (see Exhibit A.19).

Steps for Creating and Analyzing a CIXB Index Basket

1. CIXB <Enter>.
2. On the CIXB screen, name the ticker and the portfolio in the ".Ticker" and "Name" yellow box and hit <Enter> to update (.XINDEX for ticker and Xavier Index for Name.
3. Click "Import" from the Actions dropdown tab.
4. On the "Import to CIXB" box, click "import from list" tab at bottom to bring up "Import from List" tab.

EXHIBIT A.19   GP and HRA Screen for CIXB-Created Portfolio

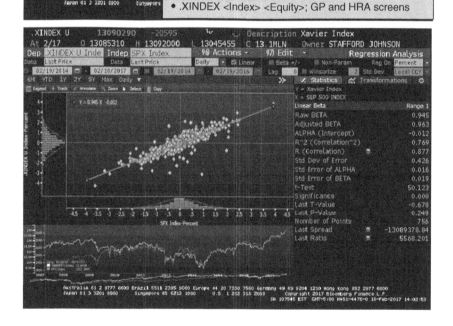

5. On "Import from List" tab: Select Portfolio (or EQS search or index) from the "Source" dropdown and the name of the portfolio (search, or index) from the "Name" dropdown, and then click the "Import" tab. These steps will import the portfolio's stocks, shares, and price to the CIXB screen.

6. On CIXB screen, click the "Create" tab to bring up a time period box for selecting the time period for price and return data. After selected the time period, hit "Save." This will activate a Bloomberg program for calculating the portfolio's daily historical returns.

7. The data will be sent to a report, RPT. To access this report, type "RPT" and hit<enter>.
8. To analyze a CIXB-generated portfolio as an index enter Ticker Name (remember the period) <Index> <Enter> (e.g., .XINDEX <Index> <Enter>) and then pull up screens from the index menu.

Screening and Search Functions

Equity Screener Analysis: EQS

Equity Screener Analysis, EQS, searches for equity securities. Using this screen, you can screen by general categories, such as countries, exchanges, indexes, security types, and security attributes, by security lists, and by data categories, such as fundamentals, estimates, financial and price ratios, and technical fields. You can also save the screening criteria so that the identified securities can be analyzed using other functions or inputted to form a portfolio in PRTU.

EQS Search Example Steps

- Bring up EQS screen: EQS <Enter>.
- Select a category such as "Indices."
- Scroll down the list of indexes and identify a specific index (e.g., S&P 500 Composite index).
- In the amber ribbon box, type in screening features, such as market cap greater than $15 billion, price-to-earnings ratio greater than 10, debt to total capital greater than 20% and less than 50%.
- Save the search by clicking "Save As" from the "Action" tab dropdown and then name the search (e.g., Equity SP 500 Style). Note: By clicking the "My Search" tab at the bottom of the ESQ screen, you can find the stocks found from the search. Also, you can import the stocks from your search to other Bloomberg screens such as Relative Valuation Analysis (RV).
- Click the "Results" tab at the bottom right corner to see the stocks found from the search.
- On the Results screen, you can export the screen information to Excel by clicking Excel from the "Output" tab.
- On the Results screen, you can click a stock on the output screen to access information on the stock (e.g., DES) or its menu.

Other Searches

Fund Searches: FSRC

From the FSRC screen, you can search and screen investment funds by general investment criteria, such as asset class (stock, bonds, balance, type (open, closed, unit investment trust, or exchange-traded product), by country, by asset holding criteria (industry, market cap, maturity, ratings), and by adding fields. You can save the screen menus of any of the funds listed from the search by clicking the name of the fund.

Bond Searches: SRCH and MSRC

From the SRCH screen, you can search for bonds that fit specified criteria based on coupon, maturity, country, currency, and structure type for government, corporate, structured notes, and private securities. Using the MSRC screen, you can search and screen the universe of municipal bonds. Information on municipal securities and other information of a state or municipality in the state can also be accessed from the municipal screener (SMUN): SMUN <Enter>.

News Searches: NI and N <Enter>

The menu screens for each stocks, bond, government security, and commodity provide a news function in which news and information on a selected company, country, or commodity can be accessed. The Bloomberg system also has news platforms that you can use to select areas for news or to conduct new searches. TNI can be used to conduct advanced news searches. Using TNI, the selected news search criteria can be saved and a corresponding custom news alert can be set so that you can receive messages from Bloomberg. Other new search menus can be found by entering N <Enter>.

Other Bloomberg Searches and Screeners

     MA Merger and acquisition searches

     RATC Search for credit rating changes

     PSCH Preferred stock search

     MSCH Money market search

     CTM Search commodities exchanges

     RES Research search

     AV Bloomberg's media links

     LIVE Bloomberg's live links

     BBLS Search for legal documents

     ETF Exchange-traded products

     BMAP World Energy and Commodity Map and Platform

The Bloomberg Excel Add-In: Importing Bloomberg into Excel

In Bloomberg, many screens showing information can be exported to Excel by clicking Excel from the "Action" or "Output" dropdown tab. The data behind many graphs also can be sent to a clipboard where it can be moved to Excel. Instead of exporting Bloomberg data, you can alternatively import Bloomberg information from Excel using the Bloomberg Excel Add-In. Using Excel to import Bloomberg data and information enables you to develop customized programs for analyzing securities and portfolios. On the Bloomberg Add-In, there are a number of templates, data wizards, screeners, and other functions. The DAPI screen in Bloomberg lists a number of Bloomberg Add-In functions and how to use them. From the list, the "Import Data Wizard," "Fundamental Analysis Wizard," and "Template Library" are good ways to get started using the Bloomberg Add-In functions.

Import Data Wizard

Using the Import Data Wizard, you can import Bloomberg data into Excel spreadsheets where you can customize it using a variety of functions and formulas. The Import Data Wizard generates tables for times-series and cross-sectional data for companies, stocks, bonds, and indexes. The wizards move sequentially. It starts with a window where you can select securities, portfolios, searches, and indexes. It next takes you to a field window where you can select data from an extensive list of financial, economics, and market information. The wizard then goes to a time period window for selecting the number of periods (for historical wizard) and finally to a window for selecting the Excel table layout.

Fundamental Analysis Wizard

Using the Fundamentals Analysis Wizard (accessed from the "Financial/Estimates" tab on the Bloomberg Excel Add-in), you can import customized data such as income statements, balance sheets, and cash flow statements on a company, index, or portfolio of stocks. You can view the information for selected single or multiple periods.

Template Library

The Template Library enables you to locate and download a pre-constructed Bloomberg spreadsheet from an extensive list of available spreadsheets. You can then save the spreadsheet to use as a template for future analysis. You can access the templates directly from the Bloomberg Add-In in Excel or by clicking "Excel Template Library" from the DAPI screen in Bloomberg, selecting the template, and then clicking "Open" to open the customized workshop in Excel.

Launchpad

Given the myriad of Bloomberg screens, using Bloomberg's Launchpad function you can customize a Window-esque interface, allowing you to easily access the information you need to conduct a specific type of analysis.

Steps for Creating a Launchpad Window

> **Step 1: BLP <Enter>:** Brings up the Bloomberg toolbar.
> **Step 2: Toolbar:** Click "Options" to bring up the toolbar showing the tabs with Views, Pages, Settings, and Tools.

Step 3: Load Screens: On the Launchpad toolbar, load Bloomberg screens.

- To find a screen, you type in a key word (e.g, FX to find and load the Foreign Exchange Information platform, WB for the World Bond Monitor, MOST for the most active stocks monitor, or IMAP for stock index heat maps).
- In the "Views" dropdown tab on the toolbar, save the screen by clicking "Save As" and then name the screen. To create new screens or access previously created screens, use the "New" and "Open" tabs in the "Views" tab.
- On the Launchpad toolbar, the "Views," "Pages," "Settings," and "Tools" tabs can be used to manage and customize screens:
  - In the "Pages" dropdown, you can create, delete, share, and send pages in the view.
  - In the "Settings" tab, you can set the default option for your Launchpad View.
  - The "Tools" tab allows you to create groups of functions.

Step 4: Load Screens from Browser:

- One quick and efficient way to load screens is to click the "Browser" tab. The "Browser" option tab lists common categories to load or you can type in a name in the amber search field box (e.g., MOST) to find and load a screen.
- Example: To load securities, currencies, or portfolios, a frequently used panel is the "Monitor" panel. Clicking "Monitor" and the "Launch Component" brings up a stock monitor screen similar to PRTU. From that screen, you can load securities by entering their tickers in the "Ticker" boxes. If you want to import a portfolio that you have created in PRTU or from a search or if you want to load an index, you can click the "Monitor" tab and then "Import Securities." This will bring up a box where you can select from a source type: portfolios (PRTU), equity searches (EQS), equity indexes, fund screens (FSCR), Bloomberg peers, and other sources. After selecting the type, you then select the portfolio, index, or search, and then click "Import".
- The loaded monitor screen can be further customized using tab functions on the screen: Monitor, View, Alerts, News, and Link:
  - Using the "View" tab, you can change the view to show securities grouped by industries or sectors (Group by), different panels (Panel), size (Zoom), and add or delete columns (Manage Columns).
  - Using the "Alert" tab, you can set alerts, such as security prices changing by a specified percentage or volume changes.
  - Using the "News Alerts," you can enable the "News Alert" to create a column to click on news for each security.
  - Using the "Link to" tab, you can bring up the portfolio or index's heat map.

Step 5: Loading Other Screens: Going back to the Launchpad toolbar, you can use the Browser option to find other screens to load or use the amber keyword box to search for other items. For example, type in ECO to find the ECO screen or "Live" to bring up the menu showing live news events to monitor.

Step 6: Saving Screen: Once the screens are loaded on the View screen, the view can be saved by clicking "Save As" in the "View" tab of the toolbar.

Step 7: Creating Additional Pages: Additional pages in the saved view can be created by clicking the + icon next to the "Pages" tab. For example, pages for each sector in the portfolio and stocks in each sector, other funds, and stock index and economic calendars. Pages in a view can be deleted by going to the "Pages" tab.

Step 8: Creating New Views: New views focusing on different topics can also be created by clicking the "View" tab and then "New."

Step 9: Exiting Bloomberg: You can exit Launchpad and return to a general Bloomberg screen by clicking "x" on the Launchpad toolbar (or by clicking "Exit Launchpad" from the "Views" tab). To access Launchpad again, you type in BLP and hit <Enter>.

Conclusion

A directory listing of many of the Bloomberg screens by functions is in Appendix B. A cursory look at those screens shows the breadth and depth of the Bloomberg system and its value in the study of financial markets and investments. For detailed applications of the system, you should view the Bloomberg video tutorials and training documents. The tutorials training documents (with topical cheat sheets) can be accessed directly from the Bloomberg system by typing BU to bring up the Bloomberg information menu.

Bloomberg Exercises

1. Select a stock of interest and study it by going to its equity menu and accessing the following screens:
   a. DES Description
   b. CF Corporate filings (view or download the company's 10-K)
   c. SPLC Supply Chain
   d. RELS Related securities (e.g., debt, preferred stocks)
   e. HDS Major holders of the stocks
   f. CN Company news
   g. GP Stock price graph (vary time period and activate events and volume)
   h. GIP Intraday price graph

2. Study some of the market trends by using MOST: MOST <Enter>. Using the MOST screen examine the S&P 500 stocks by selecting "Equity Indexes" and

"SPX" from the dropdowns. Use the bottom tabs to identify the high stocks, low stocks, stocks with the greatest volume, and so on.

3. Using the SECF screen, identify a broad-based index such as the S&P 500 and a sector index. Access the following information about the indexes from their menus (Index ticker <Index> <Enter>):

   a. DES Description of index
   b. MOV Index movers
   c. MRR Member returns
   d. IMAP Industry market heat map
   e. GP Price graph (vary time period and activate events and volume)

4. Using the index's FA screen, examine the index's summary statement and then select a stock that is a member of the index to compare its financials with the index: type stock's ticker and hit <Equity> in "Compare" box.

5. Select a corporation of interest and examine one of its bonds: Ticker <Corp> <Enter> and then select a bond. Possible screens to examine the selected bond:

   a. DES Description of the bond (see prospectus)
   b. HDS Bondholders
   c. AGGD Largest creditors
   d. DDIS Debt distribution
   e. GP Price graph
   f. GRBI Guarantors of the bond
   g. CRPR Credit rating
   h. CSHF Bond payment schedule
   i. QR Trade recap

6. Select and examine a U.S. Treasury note. <Govt> TK <Enter> and then select U.S.A. and T or CT (or use the SECF screen to find the issue). Possible screens to examine:

   a. DES Description of the bond
   b. HDS Bondholders
   c. DDIS Debt distribution
   d. GP Price graph
   e. GIP Intraday
   f. CSHF Bond payment schedule
   g. QR Trade recap

7. Explore different sources of economic information using the some of the following screens:

   a. Examine the economic statistics of the United States and other countries by going to ECST:
      i.   National Accounts
      ii. Consumer Prices
      iii. Business Conditions
      iv. Demographics
      v.   Labor Market

   vi.   Leading Indicators
   vii. Housing and Real Estate
   viii. Government Sector
   ix.   Monetary Sector
   x.   Financial Sector
   xi.   International Trade

b. Get an economic snapshot of several countries by going to ECOW (ECOW <Enter>) and clicking country of interest from the country dropdown.

c. Review some recent economic releases for the United States by going to ECO: ECO <Enter>.

d. Review some recent economic releases for a country or area by going to WECO: WECO <Enter>.

e. Study economic trends and analysis by going to BRIEF and downloading the "Economics" PDF.

f. Study the economy or a market by going to AV. On the AV screen, select a topic from AV Categories dropdown. To connect to a live broadcast, click "Live" tab; to connect to Bloomberg's radio and TV broadcast, click the "TV/Radio" tab.

g. Go to EIU to access news information and analysis from the *Economist* by topical areas (suggestion: economic information on countries can be found in "Economic Structure" and "Economic Indicators").

h. Go to research search (RES) to access research on a country: (1) RES <Enter>; (2) Search by country and Economics."

8. Using the BI screen, select an industry sector (e.g., Health Care and Biotech) and evaluate the sector using the following screens:

   a. Dashbd Home
   b. Data Library
   c. Monitor

9. Using the BI screen, read recent events covering the following topics:

   a. Economics
   b. Government
   c. Litigation
   d. Special Reports

10. Using the BIE screen, select a country and study its economic outlook.

11. Analyze an industry by examining the sector's index on the Index menu. The index ticker can be found from the SECF. Possible screens to examine:

   a. DES Description
   b. IMAP Heat map
   c. GP Price graph (vary time period and activate events and volume)
   d. FA Financials
   e. GF Fundamental graphs

12. Select research, news stories, and videos on a sector using the following screens:

   a. N News Search
   b. TNI Advanced News Search (click "Industries")

    c. RES Research search (click "Industry Overview Search")

    d. AV Videos

13. Conduct a screen and stock search using EQS. Suggestion: Limit search to S&P 500 stocks (search for the S&P 500 stocks using the "Index" dropdown or typing in S&P 500 in ribbon box) and with a market cap greater than $20 billion (in the ribbon box, type in "Market Cap" to bring down dropdown and follow input instructions). Be sure to save your search (go to "Actions" tab to find "Save As").

14. Select one of the stocks from the search you did in Exercise 13 and bring up its RV screen and then import your search to the RV screen: Company ticker <Equity> <Enter>; click RV; in "Comp Source" dropdown tab, click "Equity Screen" (EQS), and in "Name" tab, click the name of your search and hit <Enter> to activate. On the RV screen, evaluate your stocks by selecting different templates (gray tabs).

15. Create a basket consisting of the stocks from your search in Exercise 13 using the CIXB screen. After creating the basket, evaluate your portfolio of stocks from the search using the index menu (Basket ticker name [e.g., .Name] <Index> <Enter>). Possible screens to consider on the index screen:

    a. DES Description

    b. GP Price graph

    c. HRA Historical Regression

    d. COMP Comparative Return

16. Create a portfolio of the stocks of interest or a portfolio from stocks created in your EQS search done in Exercise 13.

17. Using the PMEN screen, analyze the portfolio you created in Exercise 16. Possible screens to consider on the PMEN screen:

    a. PORT Portfolio Risk and Analytics (select some of the gray tabs)

    b. PDSP Portfolio Display

    c. NPH Portfolio News

18. Select one of the stocks from the portfolio you created in Exercise 16 and bring up its RV screen and then import your portfolio to the RV screen: Company ticker <Equity> <Enter>; click RV; in the "Comp Source" dropdown tab, click "Portfolio," and in the "Name" tab, click the name of your portfolio, and hit <Enter> to activate. On the RV screen, evaluate your portfolio by selecting different tabs.

19. Using the EVTS screen, load the portfolio you created in Exercise 16 on that screen: EVTS <Enter>, on the "Source" dropdown tab click "Portfolio," and on the "Name" dropdown tab click the name of your portfolio. Once your portfolio is loaded, click the news announcement you want to monitor (e.g., All Event Types, Earnings Releases, etc.). Next, create alerts from the "Actions" tab (this will send Bloomberg messages to you).

20. Explore the following Wizards in Bloomberg's Excel Add-Ins:

    • Click "Real Time/Historical" and "Market, Reference, Analytical, and Data Sets."

    • Click "Real Time/Historical" and "Historical End of the Day."

    • Click Financial/Estimates and "Fundamental Data."

21. Explore the Template Library found in the Bloomberg Excel Add-In from Excel or by going to the DAPI screen: DAPI <Enter> and click "Excel Template Library."
22. Learn about the NYSE Euronext and other exchanges in the United States and throughout the world by going to their website. To find general information about exchanges and their website, go to Bloomberg's EPR screen.
23. Conduct a research and advanced news search to find stories related to a financial crisis (e.g., sovereign debt crisis): TNI <Enter>.
24. Create a Launchpad view with pages. Some possible views:

    a. Stock portfolio monitor of the portfolio or search you created
    b. Economic monitor that includes screens such as ECO

Appendix B
Directory Listing
of Bloomberg Screens
by Menu and Function

Functions to Get Started

    BU Bloomberg training resources

    DAPI Overview of how to import Bloomberg data to Excel

    BLP Bloomberg Launchpad for setting up interactive workstation

News

    N News menu screen; N <Enter>

    NI News search by category

    TOP Top news stories

    TOP NW Top news stories worldwide

    TOPD Top stock news

    TOP BON Top bond information

    NI FED Federal Reserve information

Monitors, Searches, and Screeners

    SECF Security finder screen searches

    EQS Equity screeners stock searches

    SRCH Custom bond search

    FSRC Fund search

MSRC Municipal bond search

SMUN Municipal bond search

CSCH Convertible bond search

MA Merger and acquisition searches

MARB Merger and arbitrage differentials

MADL Merger and acquisition deal list (for loaded security)

RATC Search for credit rating changes

PSCH Preferred stock search

MSCH Money market search

CTM Search commodities exchanges

RES Research search

AV Bloomberg's media links

LIVE Bloomberg's live links

BBLS Search for legal documents

ETF Exchange-traded products

PGM Money market securities by programs

MBSS Mortgage-back security search and screener monitors

FIT Bond monitor screen

WB Global bonds

RATT Show trends in bond quality ratings

RATC Displays and searches for bond credit rating changes

CSDR Sovereign debt ratings

BTMM Bond monitor

WEI Monitors world equity indexes

IMAP Monitors equity prices across regions, sectors, and stocks

MMAP Displays global markets segments and stocks in that segment

MOST Displays most active stocks

NIM Monitors news and security information for new security issues

IPO Monitors new stock issues

EVTS Monitors corporate events

MNSA Today's announced merger and acquisition deals

PREL Pipeline of announced bonds

DIS Distressed bonds

BNKF Bankruptcy filings

TACT Trade activity

BRIEF Daily economic newsletter

EIU Economist Intelligence Unit

ECST Key economic statistics by country

ECOF Macroeconomic information (employment, economic indicators, housing prices) by country and region

ECO Calendar of economic releases

IECO Global comparison of economic statistics

FXIP Foreign exchange information portal

CENB Central bank menu: Use to access platforms of central banks

FED Federal Reserve Bank portal

ECB European Central Bank portal

PE Private equity

RATD Displays links to Moody's, Standard and Poor's, Fitch, and other agency portals

DRAM Screen analyzes a group of securities or portfolios in terms of their default risk, CDS spread, and a Bloomberg credit risk score

GOVI Displays a matrix of yield spread information for sovereign debt of a selected tenor

IYC Menu for yield curves screens

CDSW Shows the terms of the selected bond's issuer's CDS and the implied probability of default

SOVR Displays CDS for countries in tables and graphs

FICM Fixed-income monitor

CPPR Direct CP issuers

HOIN Housing and construction

LEAG Underwriter rankings

DMMV Developed markets monitor

MOSB Most active exchange-traded bonds

PGM Money market lookup

EPR Exchange information

EIS Displays exchange products and menus

MMTK Displays a list of market makers and their corresponding codes

REIT Real Estate Investment Trust menu

RMEN Real estate indices of the world economic and financial market information

COUN Country information

WECO World economic calendar and economic indicators

FOMC Information on policy changes of the FOMC

GC Yield curve

YCRV Yield curves

G Custom chart

CHART Chart homepage

ALRT The ALRT screen monitors up to 3,000 security alerts on prices, earnings, economic events, and the like

BTST Screen back tests a number of different technical studies and compares them to a naïve buy-and-hold strategy

Bank Security Information

MMR Money market rates monitor

PGM Money market lookup program

MSCH Money market search

LSRC Search for loans, including leveraged loans

LOAN Screen provides search and analysis of syndicated loans

PREL Loan pipeline

BBAM Information on LIBOR and other rates

BTMM Money market rates

Investment Fund Screens

FMAP Fund map

FUND Funds and holding menu

FL Fund lookup

NI FND Fund news

FSRC Fund searches

HFND Hedged funds menu page

HFR Hedge fund research

HEDN Hedge fund news

FLNG Aggregated 13F filings

WHF Best hedge fund player snapshot

REIT REIT menu screen

NI REIT REIT news

Bloomberg Credit Screens

SBPR Subprime news

STNI Rumors and speculation

LEAD Economic activity trends

HSST US housing and construction statistics

DQRP Ranks deals by collateral performance

DQSP Delinquent loan data by servicer

DELQ Credit card delinquency rate

BBMD Mortgage delinquency monitor

REDQ Commercial real estate delinquencies

DQLO Delinquency rates by loan originators

TARP TARP recipients

NI TARP TARP news

Industrial Sectors

BI Industry research portal

BIE Bloomberg Intelligence Economics

Sample of Law Functions on BLAW: <Law>

BLAW Law website

BBLS Search for legal documents

Sample of Functions and Information on the Equity Menu Screen: <Equity> <Enter>

SECF Security finder

TK Ticker lookup

MMAP Market heat map

QRM Bid/ask quotes

MOV Equity index movers

MOST The most active stocks

HILO Stocks, mutual funds, ABS, and REITS that have 52-week high or low

HALT List of suspended or halted stocks by exchange

TOP STK Top Bloomberg news headlines related to stocks

CACT Displays calendar of corporate actions

FMAP Fund heat map

FLNG Filings

FSRC Fund search

IPO New issues

MBTR Monitors institutional trades

WPE World equity index ratios

CORR Correlation matrix

MRA Multiple regression

MRR Average returns for index or portfolio stocks for different periods

RVC Displays scatter data for a security (stock or fund) and its peer group (for loaded security)

MBTR Monitors block trades for stocks comprising an index or portfolio

GIMB Block money flowchart

Sample of Functions for a Loaded Stock on the Equity Menu Screen:
Ticker <Equity> <Enter>

GP Price and volume graph

GIP Intraday graph

PFP Point-and-figure chart

COMP Compares the returns of security with benchmark index

BETA Beta calculations

HRA Historical regression

HS Historical spreads

HVG Volatility graph

ECCG Credit company graph

SPLC Supply chain

OMON Options

WMON Warrants

FA Financials

RV Relative value of company's fundamentals with peer group

GF Fundamentals graphs

DDM Dividend discount model

ANR Analyst recommendation

RSI Relative strength index

IOIA Interest in stock

MACD Moving averages

GOC Overview chart

BOLL Bollinger bands

GM Money flow

CNDL Bullish and bearish trends

OWN Stock ownership

DDIS Debt distribution

ISSD Issuer description

HDS Equity holders

AGGD Debt holders

CACS Corporate action calendar

RELS Related securities

BRC Company research

EE Earnings and estimates

SI Short interest

EQRP Equity risk premium screen

WACC Calculates the WACC

EA Earnings analysis

EEO Earning, sales, margins, EPS, and DPS forecast

EEB Shows projections of earnings, sales, and other income statement items from a consensus of Bloomberg contributors

ERN Earnings history

EM Earnings trends

EE SURP Earnings surprises

EE Z Zach's earnings estimates

VAT Volume at time

VAT Prices along with trading volume, a moving average of volume, and the difference between volume and the average

OBV On-balance volume

VBAR Volume bar distribution screen: Shows volume at price over time.

VWAP Volume-weighted average price

GPO MA Moving average screen for simple moving average

GPMA Moving average price graph screen

GPO MAENV Moving-average envelopes

GPO ERPCR Erlanger put/call ratio

ROC Screen shows the rate of change from N-period back

GPO KAOS Hurst screen

Sample of Functions on Index Menu Screen: <Index> <Enter>

WEI Global indexes

MOV Index movers

SPG S&P global indexes

EMEQ Emerging markets

RMEN Real estate indexes

HOIN Housing/construction indexes

Sample of Functions on Index Menu for an Index: Index Ticker <Index> <Enter>

DES Description

MEMB Index weightings

GWGT Group sub-indexes and weighting

MRR Member returns

RV Relative value

IMAP Intraday market map

GP Price graph

GIP Intraday graph

FA Financial analysis

GF Fundamentals graphs

HRA Regression

COMP Total returns

HVG Volatility graph

OMON Index options

RSI Relative strength index

MACD Moving averages

GOC Overview chart

SIA Short interest for market indexes and exchange

BOLL Bollinger bands

GPO ADL Advances minus declines line

MCCL McClellan Oscillator screen shows a smooth line of the difference between advances and declines

TICK TICK index is equal to the number of NYSE securities trading on uptick minus the number trading on a downtick (TICK <Index>)

TIKX TIKX Index is equal to the number of S&P 500 stocks trading on an uptick minus the number trading on a downtick (TIKX <Index>)

TIKI TIKI index is equal to the number of Dow Jones stocks trading on an uptick minus the number trading on a downtick (TIKI <Index>)

TICKUSE TICKUSE index is equal to the number of all US stocks trading on an uptick minus the number trading on a downtick (TICKUSE <Index>)

PCUSEQTR CBOE put/call ratio (PCUSEQTR <Index>)

Sample of Functions for a Corporate Bond on the Bond Corp Menu: Bond Identifier (CUSIP) <Corp> <Enter> or <Corp> <Enter>

ISSD Quick overview of a company's key ratios

DDIS Company's outstanding debt

NIM Monitoring new bonds using Bloomberg's

SRCH Finds corporate bonds using Bloomberg's search function

SECF Security finder

DES To obtain information on the bond's coupons, day-count convention, maturity, and other features

YAS Bonds price, YTM, and yield to worst

RATC Evaluates a corporation's current and historical credit ratings

CRPR Evaluates a corporation's current credit ratings

RVM Evaluates a bond's spread

COMB Comparative bond search

TRA Total return analysis

OAS1 OAS analysis

SP Strip valuation

FISA Fixed income scenario analysis

DRSK Analyzes credit risk of a company

RATT Displays current and historical numbers of upgrades and downgrades

RATD Displays links to Moody's, Standard and Poor's, Fitch, and other agency portals

DRAM Screen analyzes a group of securities or portfolios in terms of their default risk, CDS spread, and a Bloomberg credit risk score

CDSW Shows the terms of the selected bond's issuer's CDS and the implied probability of default

SOVR Displays CDS for countries in tables and graphs

FIHZ Calculates the total return on a selected bond for a selected horizon period, discount yield at the HD, and the reinvestment rate

CRPR Displays direct CP issuer

Sample of Functions on Treasury Securities from Govt Menu: Country Ticker <Govt> or Treasury Tk <Govt> <Enter>

DES Information on the bond's coupons, day-count convention, maturity, and other features

YAS Screen determines the bond's price, YTM, and yield to worst

OAS1 OAS analysis

SP Strip valuation

SRCH Searches for government bonds using different criterion

SECF Security finder

BTMM Finds major rates and security information

GGR Finds global summary of government bill and bond rates for countries

FMC Finds yields across maturities of multiple corporate and government bonds

TRA Determines a bond's total return

FIHZ Calculates the total return on a selected bond for a selected horizon period, discount yield at the HD, and the reinvestment rate

FISA Fixed income scenario analysis

FIT Monitors and compares prices of government security dealers

GC Yield curves

YCRV Yield curves

AUCR Auction results

ECO20 Select government auction/Purchase from dropdown

Agency Securities

FHLMC Federal Home Loan Mortgage Corporation (FHLMC <Corp>)

FNMA Federal National Mortgage Association (FNMA <Corp>)

FHLB Federal Home Loan Bank System (FHLB <Corp>)

FAMCA Federal Agriculture Mortgage Association (FAMCA <Corp>)

FFCB Federal Farm Credit Bank (FFCB <Corp>)

TVA Tennessee Valley Authority (TVA <Corp>)

IBRD International Bank for Reconstruction and Development (TVA <Corp>)

SLMA Student Loan Marketing Association (SLMA <Corp>)

EXI Bonds with export-import bank guarantee (EXI <Corp>)

PXAM Active agencies

Sample of Functions for Municipal Bonds on Muni Menu Screen: Ticker <Muni> <Enter> or <Muni> <Enter>

PICK Finds the latest municipal offering

SECF Security finder

MSRC Finds municipals using Bloomberg's customized search

SMUN Issuer search

MIFA Municipal screen

DES Description

RCHG Ratings history

TDH Trade report

YAS Yield analysis

TRA Total return analysis

HP Historical analysis

CF Municipal filings

ISSD Issuer description

IMGR Recently Issued

Sample of Functions for Currency on Currency Menu Screen: Ticker <Curncy> <Enter> or <Curncy> <Enter>

WCR World currency rates

FRD Forward rates

ALLQ Currency quotes

FXIP Currency market overview

FXC Currency rate matrix

GP Price graph

GIP Intraday graph

Sample of Functions on Mortgage and Asset-Backed Securities Menu: Security Ticker <Mtge> or <Mtge> <Enter>

SECF Security finder

TK Ticker lookup (<Mtge> TK)

CMBS Commercial MBS monitor

MOAS MBS monitors

MCAL New issue calendar

MP Mortgage payments

DES Description

BBMD Mortgage delinquency

HSST Housing and construction

HOIN Global housing

MBSS Mortgage back search and screener

CFT Cash flow table can be used to analyze the mortgage collateral

CLP Shows the historical performance of the collateral underlying a MBS issue

VAC Views all classes of MBS created from the collateral

SPA Shows structural pay down of all classes of a MBS

YAS Yield analysis

TRA Total return analysis

MTCL Collateral analysis

CLC Collateral composition

MTST Structure analysis

CLASS Listings, descriptions, and terms for different MBS and ABS securities

VBPM Prepayment vector graph

LLKU Commercial MBS screener

Yield Curve Information

GC Yield curves

YCRV Yield curves

IYC Yield curves menu

FWCV Projects implied forward rates

Investment Funds

ETF Exchange-traded funds

FSRC Investment fund search

FMAP Fund heat map

SECF Search screen

Sample of Portfolio Functions—PRTU

PRTU Create portfolio

PMEN Portfolio menu

BPRA Portfolio risk overview

RPT Reports menu

BBU Portfolio uploads from Excel

MARS Multi-Asset Risk System—Analyzes portfolio and derivative positions

Portfolio Reporting and Analytics

PORT Portfolio risk analytics

PDSP Portfolio display

NPH Portfolio news

FSTA Fund style

PDVD Dividend

PCF Cash flows

EVTS Events calendar

CACT Corporate actions

DRAM Default risk monitor

Portfolio Basket

CIXB calculate historical returns of inputted stocks, bonds, commodities, or portfolio, and allows the security or portfolio to be treated as an index to be analyzed on the Index menu.

Futures, Options, and Swaps

SECF Security finder

CTM Contract Table Menu for derivatives

IRDD Interest rate derivatives list

SWPM Bloomberg swaps and interest rate derivatives screen

FIHR Bloomberg hedging screen (use for loaded bond)

PDH1 Calculates the duration and determines hedge ratios (use for loaded bond)

EDA Eurodollar futures contracts screen; EDA <Comdty>

EDS Eurodollar futures analysis

OMON Option monitor

OMST Finds the most actively traded options on a particular stock

OSA Option strategy functions: Generates profit tables and graphs

OVME Values options using the Black-Scholes, binomial, and other option pricing models

SKEW Volatility smiles and surfaces

HVG Historical volatility function

HIVG Historical implied volatilities

MARS Multi-Asset Risk System: Analyzes portfolio and derivative positions

WCDS Credit default rate monitor

FVD Finds the fair value and carrying cost value—Menu

DLV Cheapest-to-deliver bond

CALL Finds a security's call values, implied volatilities, and Greeks

PUT Finds a security's put values, implied volatilities, and Greeks

CDSW Credit default swap valuation calculator

FXFR Forward and spot quotes

FXDV Foreign exchange derivative menu

EXS Futures expirations schedule

OVCV Convertible bond valuation

ASW Calculate the relative value of a selected bond with the interest rate swap market

IRSB Generic interest rate swaps menu

CSCH Convertible search

IRDL Interest rate derivative list created by user

WCDS World credit default spread monitor

Ticker CDS <Corp> Credit default swap menu list for a specified issuer

CDS BB ID <Equity> Menu for a specific issuer's credit default spread

VCDS Values a single bond based on its credit default spread

Appendix C
Uses of Exponents and Logarithms

Exponential Functions

An exponential function is one whose independent variable is an exponent. For example:

$$y = b^t$$

where

y = dependent variable
t = independent variable
b = base $(b > 1)$

In calculus, many exponential functions use as their base the irrational number 2.71828, denoted by the symbol e:

$$e = 2.71828$$

An exponential function that uses e as its base is defined as a natural exponential function. For example:

$$y = e^2$$

$$y = Ae^{Rt}$$

These functions also can be expressed as:

$$y = \exp(t)$$

$$y = A \exp(Rt)$$

In calculus, natural exponential functions have the useful property of being their own derivative. In addition to this mathematical property, e also has a finance meaning. Specifically, e is equal to the future value (FV) of \$1 compounded continuously for one period at a nominal interest rate (R) of 100 percent.

To see e as a future value, consider the future value of an investment of A dollars invested at an annual nominal rate of R for t years, and compounded m times per year. That is:

$$FV = A\left(1 + \frac{R}{m}\right)^{mt} \tag{C.1}$$

If we let $A = \$1$, $t =$ one year, and $R = 100\%$, then the FV would be:

$$FV = \$1\left(1 + \frac{1}{m}\right)^{m} \tag{C.2}$$

If the investment is compounded one time ($m = 1$), then the value of the \$1 at end of the year will be \$2; if it is compounded twice ($m = 2$), the end-of-year value will be \$2.25; if it is compounded 100 times ($m = 100$), then the value will be 2.7048138.

$$m = 1: \qquad FV = \$1\left(1 + \frac{1}{1}\right)^{1} = \$2.00$$

$$m = 2: \qquad FV = \$1\left(1 + \frac{1}{2}\right)^{2} = \$2.25$$

$$m = 100: \qquad FV = \$1\left(1 + \frac{1}{100}\right)^{100} = \$2.7048138$$

$$m = 1,000: \qquad FV = \$1\left(1 + \frac{1}{1000}\right)^{1,000} = \$2.716924$$

As m becomes large, the FV approaches the value of \$2.71828. Thus, in the limit:

$$FV = \lim_{m \to \infty}\left(1 + \frac{1}{m}\right)^{m} = 2.71828 \tag{C.3}$$

If A dollars are invested instead of \$1, and the investment is made for t years instead of one year, then given a 100 percent interest rate, the future value after t years would be:

$$FV = Ae^{t} \tag{C.4}$$

Finally, if the nominal interest rate is different than 100%, then the FV is:

$$FV = Ae^{Rt} \tag{C.5}$$

To prove Equation (C.5), rewrite Equation (C.1) as follows:

$$FV = A\left(1 + \frac{R}{m}\right)^{mt}$$

$$FV = A\left[\left(1 + \frac{R}{m}\right)^{m/R}\right]^{Rt}$$ (C.6)

If we invert R/m in the inner term, we get:

$$FV = A\left[\left(1 + \frac{1}{m/R}\right)^{m/R}\right]^{Rt}$$ (C.7)

The inner term takes the same form as Equation (C.2). This term, in turn, approaches e as m approaches infinity. Thus, for continuous compounding the *FV* is:

$$FV = Ae^{Rt}$$

Thus, a two-year investment of $100 at a 10 percent annual nominal rate with continuous compounding would be worth $122.14 at the end of year 2:

$$FV = \$100e^{(0.10)(2)} = \$122.14$$

Logarithms

A logarithm (or log) is the power to which a base must be raised to equal a particular number. For example, given:

$$5^2 = 25,$$

the power (or log) to which the base 5 must be raised to equal 25 is 2. Thus, the log of 25 to the base 5 is 2:

$$\log_5 25 = 2$$

In general:

$$y = b^t \iff \log_b y = t$$

Two numbers that are frequently used as the base are 10 and the number e. If 10 is used as the base, the logarithm is known as the common log. Some of the familiar common logs are:

$$\log_{10} 1000 = 3 \qquad (10^3 = 1000)$$

$$\log_{10} 100 = 2 \qquad (10^2 = 100)$$

$$\log_{10} 10 = 1 \qquad (10^1 = 10)$$

$$\log_{10} 1 = 0 \qquad (10^0 = 1)$$

$$\log_{10} 0.1 = -1 \qquad \left(10^{-1} = \frac{1}{10^1} = 0.10\right)$$

$$\log_{10} 0.01 = -2 \qquad \left(10^{-2} = \frac{1}{10^2} = \frac{1}{100} = 0.01\right)$$

When e is the base, the log is defined as the natural logarithm (denoted $\log_e$ or $\ln$). For the natural log we have:

$$y = e^t \iff \log_e y = \ln y = t$$
$$\ln e^t = t$$

Thus given an expression such as $y = e^t$, the exponent t is automatically the natural log.

Rules of Logarithms

Like exponents, logarithms have a number of useful algebraic properties. The properties are stated below in terms of natural logs; the properties, though, do apply to any log regardless of its base:

- Equality: If $X = Y$, then $\ln X = \ln Y$
- Product rule: $\ln(XY) = \ln X + \ln Y$
- Quotient rule: $\ln(X/Y) = \ln X - \ln Y$
- Power rule: $\ln(X^a) = a \ln X$

Uses of Logarithm

The above properties of logarithms make logarithms useful in solving a number of algebraic problems.

Solving for R

In finance, logs can be used to solve for R when there is continuous compounding. That is, from Equation (B.5):

$$FV = Ae^{Rt}$$

Using the above log properties, R can be found as follows:

$$Ae^{Rt} = FV$$
$$e^{Rt} = \frac{FV}{A}$$
$$\ln(e^{Rt}) = \ln\left(\frac{FV}{A}\right)$$
$$Rt = \ln\left(\frac{FV}{A}\right)$$
$$R = \frac{\ln(FV/A)}{t}$$

Thus, a $100 investment that pays $120 at the end of two years would yield a nominal annual rate of 9.12%, given continuous compounding: $R = \ln(\$120/\$100)/2 = 0.0912$. Similarly, a zero discount bond selling for $980 and paying $1,000 at the end of 91 days would yield a nominal annual rate of 8.10% given continuous compounding:

$$R = \frac{\ln(\$1{,}000/\$980)}{91/365} = 0.0810$$

Logarithmic Return

The expression for the rate of return on a security currently priced at S_0 and expected to be S_T at the end of one period ($t = 1$) can be found using Equation (C.5). That is:

$$S_T = S_0 e^{Rt}$$

$$R = \ln\left(\frac{S_T}{S_0}\right)$$

When the rate of return on a security is expressed as the natural log of S_T/S_0, it is referred to as the security's logarithmic return. Thus, a security currently priced at $100 and expected to be $110 at the end of the period would have an expected logarithmic return of 9.53%: $R = \ln(\$110/100) = 0.0953$.

Time

Using logarithms, one can solve for t in either the discrete or continuous compounding cases. That is:

Discrete:

$$FV = A(1 + R)^t$$

$$A(1 + R)^t = FV$$

$$\ln[(1 + R)^t] = \ln\left(\frac{FV}{A}\right)$$

$$t \ln[1 + R] = \ln\left(\frac{FV}{A}\right)$$

$$t = \frac{\ln(FV/A)}{\ln(1 + R)}$$

Continuous:

$$Ae^{Rt} = FV$$

$$e^{Rt} = \frac{FV}{A}$$

$$\ln(e^{Rt}) = \ln\left(\frac{FV}{A}\right)$$

$$Rt = \ln\left(\frac{FV}{A}\right)$$

$$t = \frac{\ln(FV/A)}{R}$$

The equations can be used in problems in which one knows the interest or growth rate and wants to know how long it will take for an investment to grow to equal a certain terminal value. For example, given an annual interest rate of 10%, an investment of $800 would take 2.34 years to grow to $1,000:

$$t = \frac{\ln(\$1{,}000/\$800)}{\ln(1.10)} = 2.34 \text{ years}$$

Selected Reference

Chiang, A. C. and K. Wainwright. *Fundamental Methods of mathematical economics*. New York: McGraw-Hill, 2005, 256–290.

Index

Printed and bound by CPI Group (UK) Ltd, Croydon, CR0 4YY

23/04/2025

14660909-0005